P9-ECM-262

Municipal Management Series

Management Policies in Local Government Finance

The International City Management Association is the professional and educational organization for chief appointed management executives in local government. The purposes of ICMA are to enhance the quality of local government and to nurture and assist professional local government administrators in the U.S. and other countries. In furtherance of its mission, ICMA develops and disseminates new approaches to management through training programs, information services, and publications.

Managers, carrying a wide range of titles, serve cities, towns, counties, and councils of governments in all parts of the United States and Canada. These managers serve at the direction of elected councils and governing boards. ICMA serves these managers and local governments through many programs that aim at improving the manager's professional competence and strengthening the quality of all local governments.

The International City Management Association was founded in 1914; adopted its City Management Code of Ethics in 1924; and established its Institute for Training in Municipal Administration in 1934. The Institute, in turn, provided the basis for the Municipal Management Series, generally termed the "ICMA Green Books." ICMA's interests and activities include public management education; standards of ethics for members; *The Municipal Year Book* and other data services; local government research; and newsletters, *Public Management* magazine, and other publications. ICMA's efforts for the improvement of local government management—as represented by this book—are offered for all local governments and educational institutions.

Contributors

J. Richard Aronson
David S. Arnold
Roy Bahl
Marvin R. Brams
Thomas J. DiLorenzo
Paul B. Downing
Philip J. Fischer
James A. Hall
William W. Holder
George G. Kaufman
Julius Margolis
Wallace E. Oates
John E. Petersen
Arnold H. Raphaelson
James D. Rodgers
Leonard I. Ruchelman
Larry D. Schroeder
Eli Schwartz
Paul L. Solano
Robert J. Thornton

Municipal Management Series

Management Policies in Local Government Finance

Third Edition

Editors

Published for the
ICMA Training
Institute

J. Richard Aronson
Lehigh University

By the
International
City
Management
Association

Eli Schwartz
Lehigh University

Municipal Management Series

Management Policies in Local Government Finance

Developing the Municipal Organization

Effective Communication: Getting the Message Across

The Effective Local Government Manager

Effective Supervisory Practices

Housing and Local Government

Local Government Police Management

Management of Local Planning

Management of Local Public Works

Managing Fire Services

Managing Human Services

Managing Municipal Leisure Services

The Practice of Local Government Planning

The Practice of State and Regional Planning

Small Cities and Counties: A Guide to Managing Services

Library of Congress Cataloging-in-Publication Data

Management policies in local government finance.
(Municipal management series)
Bibliography: p.
Includes index.
1. Local finance. 2. Municipal finance.
I. Aronson, J. Richard (Jay Richard), 1937–
II. Schwartz, Eli. III. ICMA Training Institute.
IV. Series.
HJ9105.M3 1987 352.1 87–2658
ISBN 0–87326–075–9

Printed in the United States of America.

93929190898887
54321

Foreword

As *Management Policies in Local Government Finance* goes into its third edition, its coverage reflects dramatic changes in the local government financial environment during the late 1980s.

When the second edition was published in 1981, the local financial climate was under the influence of inflation, the New York City debt crisis, and Proposition 13. Of the three, the tax and expenditure limitation movement probably had the greatest continuing effect on local finance, combining in subsequent years with new pressures to cut costs and reduce services.

The rampant inflation—and the high interest rates—of the early 1980s subsided. The effects of these changes are most evident in the coverage of such areas as debt management, cash management, and pension fund management.

Intergovernmental assistance continued its decline, forcing local government financial managers to become increasingly creative and entrepreneurial, to search for new sources of revenue, new self-sustaining enterprises, and new ways of controlling expenditures.

As the book was being written, the Tax Reform Act of 1986 was taking shape, and its effects on local jurisdictions were impossible to predict. After passage of the legislation, it was clear that local governments would need to reexamine the mix and level of property, income, and sales taxes.

In addition to reflecting these influences of the political and economic environment, the coverage of this book has been expanded with new material on computer applications, risk and insurance management, and procurement practices—fields that have become increasingly sophisticated and central to efficient management.

This book replaces the 1981 and 1975 editions of *Management Policies in Local Government Finance,* which in turn replaced *Municipal Finance Administration,* first published in 1937. With its distinguished lineage, this book has served for more than fifty years as a basic reference source for city and county finance officers, managers, budget officers, and planners and for teachers and students in public administration and local government finance.

Like its earlier editions, this book is designed to provide a better understanding of the economic environment for decision making. Because local governments must live and operate in a national economy, it emphasizes economic policy as it affects management decisions. The focus, however, remains on management. The contributors to the book are recognized authorities in their respective fields. Occasionally they express controversial and even contradictory points of view, but no attempt has been made editorially to interfere with the views expressed.

This book, like others in the Municipal Management Series, has been prepared for ICMA's Training Institute. The institute offers in-service training specifically designed for local government officials whose jobs are to plan, direct, and coordinate the work of others. ICMA has sponsored the institute since 1934.

ICMA is grateful to the editors, J. Richard Aronson and Eli Schwartz, for undertaking this revision and to the chapter authors for their fine work. Biographical information on all contributors is found at the end of the book.

We also appreciate the efforts of other individuals who reviewed portions of the book in manuscript and offered suggestions on coverage. They are Stephen B. Gordon, formerly Director, Professional Development and Procurement Research, National Institute of Governmental Purchasing; John Lawton, Director of Finance and Administrative Services, Billings, Montana; James A. Swanke, Jr., Consultant, Risk Management Services, The Wyatt Company; and Natalie Wasserman, Executive Director, Public Risk and Insurance Management Association.

ICMA staff members who contributed to the project included Barbara H. Moore, Director, Book Division, who oversaw the project; David S. Arnold, former editor, Municipal Management Series, who worked with Drs. Aronson and Schwartz at the outset of the project; Devorah Leibtag Mittelman, who edited the manuscript; Dawn Leland, Rebecca Geanaros, and Susan Gubisch, who supervised art and production; Alice R. Markham, who assisted in the final stages of production; and Mary W. Blair, publications secretary.

William H. Hansell, Jr.
Executive Director

International City
Management Association

Washington, D.C.

Contents

Tables

Figures

Part one: The local government setting

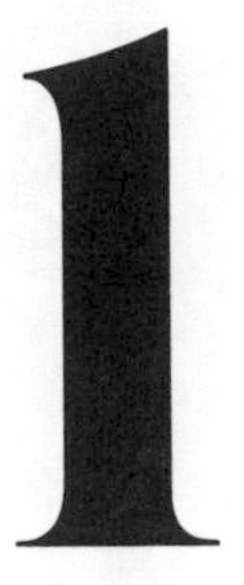

The finance function in local government

Financial administration in local government is set on a complex stage. Communities themselves vary in population, fiscal health, and governmental structure. They vary also in the values and expectations of their citizens and in the political context of financial decision making.

This opening chapter describes in detail major factors affecting the finance function in local government—community size and growth, social and economic environment, and governing structure. After World War II, when big city populations began to decline, these demographic, economic, and political factors gained in significance.

Currently, there are over 82,000 governments in the United States. Of these, all but 51 are local governments—i.e., counties, municipalities, townships, school districts, and special districts. Table 1–1 shows that the number of local governments has increased substantially over the past decade and that municipalities and special districts are the most rapidly expanding types of local government.

Table 1–2 takes a closer look at municipalities with populations of 2,500 and over. (Included here also are 404 municipalities under 2,500 that provide for a position of overall general management.) The mayor-council form of government tends to be the dominant form among the largest and smallest municipalities, and the council-manager form tends to be dominant among middle-sized municipalities. Regarding metro status (i.e., the relationship of a municipality to the larger region), the largest cities, with populations of 50,000 and over, tend to be central cities comprising the regional core, while the middle-sized communities comprise the cities of outlying suburban areas. The table also shows that the nation's largest cities are no longer confined primarily to the Northeast and North Central regions of the country as used to be the case. Rather, many are now located in the South and the West, which are the most rapidly developing regions of the country.

Population decreases in most cities of 100,000 or more people have continued from the 1970s into the 1980s, resulting in serious fiscal problems. The near

Table 1–1 Number of governments in the United States.

Type of government	1982	1977	1972
Total	82,341	79,913	78,269
U.S. government	1	1	1
State governments	50	50	50
Local governments	82,290	79,862	78,218
County	3,041	3,042	3,044
Municipal	19,076	18,862	18,517
Township	16,734	16,822	16,991
School district	14,851	15,174	15,781
Special district	28,588	25,962	23,885

Source: Bureau of the Census, *1982 Census of Governments*, vol. 1, no. 1: *Government Units in 1982*, GC 82(1) (Washington, D.C.: GPO, 1982), Table A.

Table 1–2 Cumulative distribution of U.S. municipalities.

Classification	All cities	Cities 2,500 & over	Cities 5,000 & over	Cities 10,000 & over	Cities 25,000 & over	Cities 50,000 & over	Cities 100,000 & over	Cities 250,000 & over	Cities 500,000 & over	Cities over 1,000,000
Total, all cities	7,043	6,639	4,355	2,611	1,066	450	170	57	23	6
Population group										
Over 1,000,000	6	6	6	6	6	6	6	6	6	6
500,000–1,000,000	17	17	17	17	17	17	17	17	17	
250,000– 499,999	34	34	34	34	34	34	34	34		
100,000– 249,999	113	113	113	113	113	113	113			
50,000– 99,999	280	280	280	280	280	280				
25,000– 49,999	616	616	616	616	616					
10,000– 24,999	1,545	1,545	1,545	1,545						
5,000– 9,999	1,744	1,744	1,744							
2,500– 4,999	2,284	2,284								
Under 2,500[a]	404									
Geographic region										
Northeast	1,961	1,842	1,292	757	264	100	23	6	3	2
North Central	2,035	1,941	1,240	751	291	112	39	14	6	2
South	2,064	1,943	1,169	655	252	115	61	23	8	1
West	983	913	654	448	259	123	47	14	6	1
Metro status										
Central	508	508	508	508	475	300	151	57	23	6
Suburban	3,761	3,649	2,543	1,519	479	150	19			
Independent	2,774	2,482	1,304	584	112					
Form of government										
Mayor-council	3,816	3,705	2,088	1,111	406	180	76	35	18	6
Council-manager	2,550	2,308	1,855	1,255	589	249	87	20	5	
Commission	177	175	135	100	46	16	7	2		
Town meeting	419	370	219	100	6	1				
Rep. town meeting	81	81	58	45	19	4				

Source: *The Municipal Year Book 1986* (Washington, D.C.: International City Management Association, 1986), p. xv.

[a] Limited to municipalities recognized by the International City Management Association as providing for the council-manager plan or providing for a position of overall general management.

bankruptcy of New York City in 1975 and the subsequent default by Cleveland in 1978 signaled a fiscal squeeze that compelled other cities to reduce service levels and capital plant maintenance.[1] Older central cities are struggling, their plight becoming more serious as thousands of middle-class and affluent residents move to the suburbs in search of better living conditions. High concentrations of poor households are left behind, increasing the need for social services while decreasing the capacity to pay for them.

Communities can be distinguished from one another by the degree of stress they experience.[2] Useful data include unemployment rate, number of poverty households, age of housing stock, and crime rate. As seen in Table 1–3, the troubled communities are mostly the big cities (250,000+) located in the Northeast and North Central regions of the United States. Cities listed as most healthy are predominantly middle-sized. In addition, data from various studies show an ever-widening gap between the fiscal health of central city areas and that of suburban areas.[3]

While significant differences in the degree of fiscal stress do exist, almost all communities, regardless of size or location, have had problems in managing their finances. Operating deficits, for example, are a common problem. Since

Table 1–3 Most troubled cities and most healthy cities (approx. 100,000+).

Most troubled cities	Pop. (1,000)	% change '70 to '80	Most healthy cities	Pop. (1,000)	% change '70 to '80
Atlanta, Ga.	425	−14.1	Virginia Beach, Va.	262	52.3
Boston, Mass.	563	−12.2	Livonia, Mich.	105	−4.8
Hartford, Conn.	136	−13.7	Parma, Ohio	93	−7.7
Newark, N.J.	329	−13.8	Torrance, Calif.	130	−3.8
Camden, N.J.	85	−17.2	Fremont, Calif.	132	30.8
Cleveland, Ohio	574	−23.6	Glendale, Calif.	139	4.8
Dayton, Ohio	203	−16.2	Hampton, Va.	123	1.5
Paterson, N.J.	138	−4.7	Independence, Mo.	112	.2
Trenton, N.J.	92	−12.1	Lincoln, Neb.	172	15.0
Buffalo, N.Y.	358	−22.7	Lubbock, Tex.	174	16.7
Detroit, Mich.	1,203	−20.5	Omaha, Neb.	314	−9.4
Miami, Fla.	347	3.6	Wichita, Kan.	279	1.0
Oakland, Calif.	339	−6.1			
Philadelphia, Pa.	1,688	−13.4			

Sources: Katherine L. Bradbury, Anthony Downs, and Kenneth A. Small, *Urban Decline and the Future of American Cities* (Washington, D.C.: The Brookings Institution, 1982), p. 9; U.S. Bureau of the Census, *Census of Population: 1970*, vol. 1, Chapters A and B (Washington, D.C.: GPO, 1970); and *1980 Census of Population*, vol. 1, Chapters A and B (Washington, D.C.: GPO, 1980).

many states require their cities to balance their budgets, a deficit usually portends either higher taxes or poorer services.

Reductions in federal aid such as consolidated and reduced federal grant programs to local governments, as well as growing citizen resistance to increases in local taxes, also contribute to the financial difficulties of cities. During the 1970s, actions aimed at limiting the growth of government expenditures or revenues began to spring up in various places around the country, the most radical being California's Proposition 13. Approved by the voters on June 6, 1978, Proposition 13 decreed that taxes on a home or other real property could not exceed 1 percent of its assessed value in 1975, and that this value could not be adjusted upward each year by more than 2 percent. As a result, California cities, counties, and school systems have been unable to increase their income significantly through the property tax levy. Between 1978 and 1982, 14 states followed California's example and adopted similar tax and expenditure limitations, thereby effecting major changes in the financial management policies of local governments. Tax-cutting initiatives have been voted down in some states, but the fiscal limitations movement nevertheless continues to pose significant constraints on localities throughout the country.[4] Indeed, mounting pressure for cutting costs and reducing services only magnifies the need for sound financial management.

Adding to the complexity of meeting this challenge is increased urbanization, which has generated a substantial array of specialized needs ranging from transportation to water supply. The subsequent spillover of local problems on neighboring jurisdictions has spawned even more intricate arrangements among government agencies for the provision of services.

Thus, another important factor influencing financial management is the blend of institutional arrangements that make up the formal administrative structure. Such arrangements determine where the financial function is located, who shares in it, and the degree of coordination of different jurisdictional components. A basic concern is how well the institutional framework, including intergovernmental relations, facilitates financial decision making for the efficient use of resources. Moreover, in a democratic society, the institutional framework must also ensure equity and accountability.

It is important to recognize that there is no universal model applicable to all communities for all time. Rather, as this chapter will demonstrate, individual communities tend to adopt a variety of governmental and organizational arrangements to accommodate different social, economic, and political conditions in the environment. With political reform and changing conditions, these arrangements also tend to change.

Finance managers play a major role in meeting the challenges of the modern urban environment. In the course of their work, they confront and respond to the internal dynamics of local finance management—budgeting, taxing, accounting, debt management, and related matters. Their tasks become especially difficult where there is fiscal stress: paying bills requires a careful balancing of creditors' demands and cash flow; labor-management relations involves greater conflict on questions of employee salaries and benefits; and budgeting becomes more politicized in the course of processing the funding requests of different agencies. A first step for local public managers is understanding the setting in which fiscal responsibilities are carried out. This chapter aims to guide the finance manager by providing an introductory overview of the following four topics: patterns of urban development, governmental response to changing community needs, organizational structure of financial administration, and financial decision making.

Patterns of urban development

A brief overview of urban development in the United States provides a useful perspective on the changing roles of American communities.

From urban concentration to deconcentration

Historically, the United States transformed itself from a predominantly rural and agricultural nation into a predominantly urban and industrial one within a relatively short period of time. With the exception of such East Coast cities as Boston, Philadelphia, Baltimore, and New York, few U.S. cities were highly developed before the mid-nineteenth century. In addition, cities such as Chicago, Detroit, Pittsburgh, Cleveland, and St. Louis faced the difficult tasks of rapidly assimilating large numbers of culturally disparate newcomers and of building complex social systems virtually from scratch.

Lacking cultural traditions as an integrating force, and being remarkably polyglot in nature, most U.S. cities were put together hastily, without clear physical or social goals. Most eastern and midwestern cities functioned primarily to coordinate the country's developing productive and commercial forces. In the West and Southwest, the economies of cities were oriented initially toward the development of natural resources in mining and agriculture.

Technological advances in long-distance transportation and communication, as represented by the railroad and telegraph systems, gradually linked small towns and large cities together in integrated systems. As cities became more accessible, more people and firms found it beneficial to settle in the city to live and to do business. Such concentrations, however, soon made accessibility within cities more difficult to achieve than accessibility among cities.

After the Second World War, significant changes took place in the way communities developed. Automobiles and expressways gave people and businesses more choices of location. Because technology had made the city and its amenities more accessible to the outlying areas, people could adopt an essentially urban life-style without having to reside in the city. Consequently, more and more households made the decision to leave the central city for the hinterland to take advantage of lower densities.

Census data show that the deconcentration of people and jobs has continued unabated into the 1980s with important social and economic implications. Between 1970 and 1982, central cities lost nearly 3.5 million white residents while accumulating large concentrations of poverty-level minorities. By 1982, only 23 percent of the white population lived in central cities while 43 percent lived outside central cities and 34 percent lived in nonmetropolitan areas. In 1970, the proportions were 28 percent, 40 percent, and 32 percent respectively. These figures compare with 55 percent of blacks and 49 percent of Hispanics who resided in central cities as of 1982 (see Figure 1–1). At the same time, substantial residential and commercial disinvestment has occurred in almost all of the older, larger central cities, and it far exceeds reinvestment. Although there has been some growth of central business district office employment during the 1970s and 1980s, this has not nearly compensated for the losses in blue-collar industrial jobs and retail and wholesale employment.[5]

Consequently, many cities are experiencing difficulties in performing their traditional functions. Historically, cities have provided such public services as water supply, public works, police, fire control, and education. Cities have also provided an economic environment for a variety of housing as well as a central market for goods and services. But as social needs have escalated, public service costs have spiraled beyond revenue capacity. Because of tight budgets, public works projects have in many instances been postponed and the physical plant ignored. Consequently, streets, bridges, sewers, water lines, parks, schools, firehouses, and police stations are wearing out faster than they are being replaced.[6] Furthermore, increased dispersion of population and low-density suburban development have contributed rising energy costs to all communities.

The assimilating function of cities has also waned. Whereas in the early 1900s, immigrants used urban opportunities to rise economically and socially, in the 1970s and 1980s, blacks and Hispanics have found this route blocked. Discrimination has restricted access to channels of social and economic mobility, while other routes of economic opportunity have been dispersed outside the central cities. In addition, the city's economy appears to have lost much of its capacity to generate the kinds of jobs that can be filled by unskilled and poor residents.

Regional cities

Population dispersion and low-density development have focused attention on the metropolitan area as a geographic unit of analysis. First introduced in the 1950 census, the Standard Metropolitan Statistical Area (SMSA) has been widely used by government agencies for data gathering and the publication of statistics. As characterized by the U.S. Bureau of the Census, an SMSA is a

Figure 1–1 Distribution of the white, black, and Spanish-origin populations, by metropolitan-nonmetropolitan residence: 1982.

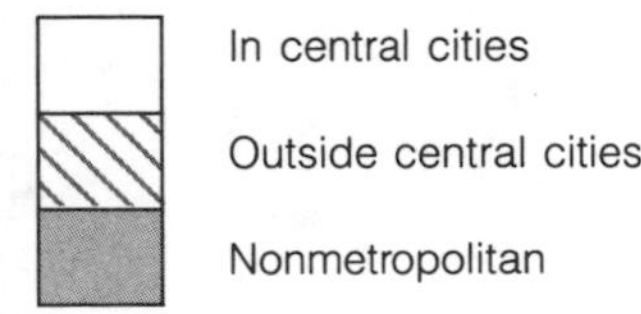

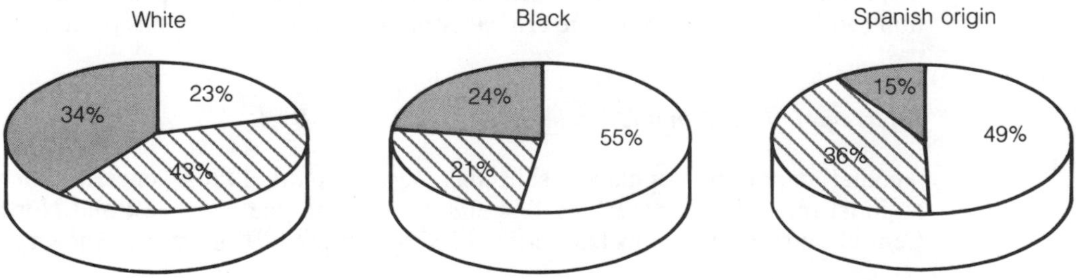

cluster of heavily settled communities that are geographically, socially, and economically related to one another and to a central urban core. A core consists of at least one central city having at least 50,000 inhabitants or "twin cities" with a combined population of at least 50,000. When SMSAs themselves are "socially and economically closely related," these areas are combined into a supermetropolitan category by the Census Bureau. Such an area is called a Standard Consolidated Statistical Area (SCSA). Each SCSA must have a population of at least 1 million, and at least 75 percent of the population of each SMSA must be classified as urban. In 1983, the Bureau of the Census changed the terms to Metropolitan Statistical Area (MSA) and Consolidated Metropolitan Statistical Area (CMSA).

In 1980 there were 329 MSAs in the United States including 86 new ones since the 1970 census. From 1950 to 1980, the population of metropolitan areas doubled, from 84.9 million to 171.7 million, and it rose from 56 percent to 75 percent of the national total. Perhaps more important, almost 45 percent of the nation's population now live in non–central city portions of MSAs—that is the suburbs—as compared with 32 percent who live in central cities. Indeed, the transformation of the United States from an urban to a metropolitan or suburban nation took place in only 50 years (1920 to 1970), more rapidly than did the rural-to-urban shift.

As metropolitan areas continue to expand, many of them eventually become linked into a new type of region: "Megalopolis." French geographer Jean Gottmann first discerned this vast urbanized complex in the 1950s as it was just beginning to crystallize along the northeastern seaboard of the United States from Boston to northern Virginia:

> In this area . . . we must abandon the idea of the city as a tightly settled and organized unit in which people, activities, and riches are crowded into a very small area clearly separated from its nonurban surroundings. Every city in this region spreads out far and wide around its original nucleus; it grows amidst an irregularly colloidal mixture of rural and suburban landscapes; it melts on broad fronts with other mixtures, of somewhat similar though different texture, belonging to the suburban neighborhoods of other cities.[7]

Popularly referred to as "Boswash," the area described by Gottmann contains about one fifth of the nation's population and such major cities as Boston, New York, Philadelphia, Baltimore, and Washington, which have come to serve as more specialized economic subcenters. Business travelers regularly fly from one city within the region to another and back in the course of a day. Regarding the future, prospects for continued growth in Boswash are mixed.The large cities will probably continue to lose population while the less densely settled areas will experience some growth. Table 1–4 shows only a 0.2 percent increase in population for Boswash from 1970 to 1980. This compares with other regional configurations such as the Phoenix, Arizona, area or the Florida Peninsula that have been growing dramatically. Because they function as integrated systems, linking communities into networks of interdependent relationships, we call them "regional cities."[8]

Such huge geographical clusters constitute an emerging spatial profile of urban development in America that will increase the scale and complexity of problems confronting local governments. With the need to match local government boundaries and human settlement patterns, intergovernmental fiscal relations will become an even more critical issue in the future than it has been in the past.

Interregional movements: from Snow Belt to Sun Belt

Another important population shift that began in the 1950s concerns interregional migrations. As Tables 1–4 and 1–5 reveal, the Northeast and North Central Snow Belt regions have either been losing population or have shown no

Table 1–4 Where growth occurs fastest and slowest among regional cities.

Area	1970 Pop.	1980 Pop.	% change 1970–80
Phoenix	863,357	1,409,279	63.2
Florida Peninsula	5,730,764	8,290,959	44.7
Texas Gulf Coast	2,744,131	3,769,719	37.4
Salt Lake Valley	821,689	1,128,328	37.3
Eastern Slope (Denver)	1,653,442	2,200,507	33.1
Centex (Austin/San Antonio)	1,555,989	1,994,053	28.2
Willamette Valley (Portland)	1,234,001	1,547,821	25.4
Dalworth (Dallas/Fort Worth)	2,434,793	3,020,312	24.0
Carolina Coastal Plain	1,145,097	1,406,371	22.8
Soonerland (Tulsa/Oklahoma City)	1,267,128	1,550,123	22.3
Nashville	818,216	1,000,725	22.3
Piedmont	5,280,515	6,359,479	20.4
Central Gulf Coast	2,868,144	3,447,126	20.2
Puget Sound	2,149,939	2,535,367	17.9
Southern California	10,887,954	12,647,607	16.2
Northern California	6,225,084	7,221,281	16.0
Central Alabama	1,358,439	1,547,604	13.9
Southern Virginia	2,255,466	2,526,187	12.0
Bluegrass (Louisville)	1,207,934	1,316,215	9.0
Twin Cities (St. Paul/Minneapolis)	2,235,444	2,431,154	8.8
Central Indiana	1,888,648	1,977,019	4.7
Missouri-Kansas Valley	1,685,260	1,758,957	4.4
Southern Ohio	3,227,179	3,363,971	4.2
Lower Great Lakes	20,265,576	20,827,980	2.8
Boswash	41,716,435	41,786,061	0.2
Upstate New York	4,689,370	4,617,434	−1.5
St. Louis	2,429,376	2,376,998	−2.2
Cleveburgh	8,370,354	8,141,391	−2.7

Source: Reprinted from *U.S. News & World Report*, issue of 3 October 1983, 56. Copyright, 1983, *U.S. News & World Report*.

Note: Area definitions by Economic Unit of *USN&WR*. *USN&WR*—Basic data: U.S. Dept. of Commerce.

significant gains, while the Sun Belt regions in the South and West have been making strong gains. Even more indicative are population shifts in the central cities. The 1980 Census showed absolute population declines of significant proportions in New York, Chicago, Milwaukee, Cleveland, Detroit, Washington, and other older cities of the East and Midwest. In contrast, the 1980 Census showed large population gains in Houston, San Diego, Dallas, San Antonio, San Jose, and other younger cities of the South and West.

Attraction to warm sunny climates certainly contributed to the population shift, but the interaction of job opportunities, economic development, corporate business decisions, and federal government policies played even greater roles. After World War II, large industries moved to the Deep South, Texas, southern California, and elsewhere in the Sun Belt. Most prominent among these industries were oil and gas extraction, computers, agribusiness, aerospace, and defense-related manufacturing. To support the newly established defense industries, the federal government spent billions of dollars to provide infrastructure such as highways and irrigation projects.

As previously noted in Table 1–3, Snow Belt cities are among the most fiscally distressed cities in the nation. Along with New York, these municipalities are subject to the highest perceived investment risks and highest interest rate premiums on loans. Thanks to special government guarantees, New York managed to avoid defaulting on its debts in the mid-1970s, but Cleveland did go into default in December 1978—the first city to do so since the Depression.

Table 1–5 Population change in cities from 1970 to 1980.

Classification	All cities (A)	Gain of more than 100% No.	% of (A)	Gain of 76%–100% No.	% of (A)	Gain of 51%–75% No.	% of (A)	Gain of 26%–50% No.	% of (A)	Gain of 11%–25% No.	% of (A)	Gain of 0%–10% No.	% of (A)	Loss of 1%–10% No.	% of (A)	Loss of more than 10% No.	% of (A)
Total, all cities	2,567	111	4.3	56	2.2	101	3.9	286	11.1	429	16.7	556	21.7	708	27.6	320	12.5
Population group																	
Over 1,000,000	6	0	0.0	0	0.0	0	0.0	1	16.7	0	0.0	1	16.7	2	33.3	2	33.3
500,000–1,000,000	16	0	0.0	0	0.0	0	0.0	3	18.7	2	12.5	2	12.5	4	25.0	5	31.3
250,000– 499,999	33	0	0.0	0	0.0	1	3.0	4	12.1	2	6.1	5	15.1	9	27.3	12	36.4
100,000– 249,999	112	2	1.8	2	1.8	6	5.4	14	12.5	20	17.9	22	19.6	32	28.6	14	12.5
50,000– 99,999	275	11	4.0	2	0.7	9	3.3	24	8.7	40	14.5	65	23.6	85	30.9	39	14.2
25,000– 49,999	607	31	5.1	21	3.5	29	4.8	49	8.1	113	18.6	128	21.1	169	27.8	67	11.0
10,000– 24,999	1,518	67	4.4	31	2.0	56	3.7	191	12.6	252	16.6	333	21.9	407	26.8	181	11.9
Geographic division																	
New England	310	1	0.3	4	1.3	8	2.6	27	8.7	56	18.1	98	31.6	100	32.3	16	5.2
Mid-Atlantic	432	2	0.5	3	0.7	11	2.5	21	4.9	42	9.7	56	13.0	183	42.4	114	26.4
East North Central	532	19	3.6	13	2.4	5	0.9	46	8.6	61	11.5	88	16.5	188	35.3	112	21.1
West North Central	209	9	4.3	4	1.9	6	2.9	15	7.2	38	18.2	57	27.3	52	24.9	28	13.4
South Atlantic	269	29	10.8	5	1.9	11	4.1	28	10.4	45	16.7	66	24.5	66	24.5	19	7.0
East South Central	133	3	2.3	2	1.5	5	3.8	17	12.8	30	22.6	41	30.8	29	21.8	6	4.5
West South Central	247	15	6.1	7	2.8	13	5.3	39	15.8	68	27.5	66	26.7	28	11.3	11	4.4
Mountain	111	14	12.6	4	3.6	12	10.8	25	22.5	32	28.8	17	15.3	7	6.3	0	0.0
Pacific Coast	324	19	5.9	14	4.3	30	9.3	68	21.0	57	17.6	67	20.7	55	17.0	14	4.3

Source: *The Municipal Year Book 1984* (Washington, D.C.: International City Management Association, 1984), p. 4.

The resurgence of small towns

For the first time since 1820, rural areas and small towns are growing faster than the nation's metropolitan areas. Between 1970 and 1980, when the national population increased by 11.4 percent to 226 million people, nonmetropolitan areas grew by 15 percent. Metropolitan areas (cities and suburbs) grew by only 10.2 percent. Earlier, in the 1960s, when people were still migrating in great numbers from the farms and towns to the cities, metropolitan areas grew by 16.6 percent, but nonmetropolitan areas grew by only 6.8 percent.[9]

Three major factors underlie the resurgence of small towns and rural living: (1) new technology has permitted industry to move from urban centers into the hinterland, and to establish highly sophisticated manufacturing plants in small communities where costs tend to be lower; (2) interstate highways and paved rural roads have enabled persons who wish to reside in small towns to work in metropolitan areas; and (3) the proliferation of recreational retirement developments and the opening of new resources in outlying areas have encouraged rural migration.

In addition, people are attracted to the natural environment and open spaces that are so much a part of small-town living. A study that attempted to discern reasons why employees would decide to move from the San Francisco Bay area to rural Oregon when their company opened a plant there found that economic bonds (such as concern for a career) and perceptions of the natural and cultural environment, not social bonds (involvement with family and friends), were the important considerations in the decision to move or stay.[10] Perceived urban disadvantages such as crowding, traffic, noise, pollution, and lack of personal safety encouraged movement away from the metropolis. Those who did choose to move to Oregon thought that such intangibles as a higher quality of life and peace of mind would be easier to find in the rural countryside than in the metropolitan area.

Whether these desires can be realized becomes problematic as more and more people decide to move to rural areas. Already, small communities are experiencing rising crime rates and rising tourism, which increase demands for new and expanded local government services and facilities. Expenditures have risen fastest for police service, parks, and recreation.[11] In fact, capital expenditures for roads, sewerage, and sanitation have been increasing at a greater rate in small municipalities than in cities as a whole. Such trends pose new and significant challenges for those who manage small communities in the United States.

The governmental response

In addition to studying the effects wrought by urbanization and new human settlement patterns, the fiscal manager must consider the organizational and administrative forms of government that respond to community's emerging needs. The following section of this chapter focuses on the principle of home rule, the intergovernmental system, and the structure of contemporary municipal governments. Within the context of these local government institutions, the process of organizing for financial decision making takes place.

The principle of home rule

According to the Constitution of the United States, the federal government and the states share sovereign power. This basic document, however, contains no provisions defining the status of local government; municipalities, therefore, possess no sovereignty and come into existence only at the will of the states. Accordingly, they have only those powers granted by the states. In this context, home rule may be defined as the achievement of statutory and constitutional provisions allowing municipalities to exercise powers of local self-government.

Local governmental units are legally established through a process of incorporation. Just as a business becomes incorporated so that its organizers may carry on certain legal and financial transactions in a state on a basis other than that of individual responsibility, so a city, town, borough, or village is given legal status as a "corporate body" through an appropriate municipal charter of incorporation. Nevertheless, charters granted to private business corporations differ in some important respects from those granted to municipal corporations.

Private and municipal charters A private charter is essentially a contract between two parties: a business corporation and a state. It can only be created, altered, or terminated with the consent of both parties. In the case of a municipal charter, however, a state has full authority over the municipality or municipalities concerned, unless the state has imposed limitations on itself through an amendment to its constitution. Many state governments are therefore empowered to alter the major features of a municipal corporation whenever they wish to do so. In such cases the state government can change the municipal corporation's powers, officers, jurisdiction, and requirements for carrying out such vital activities as borrowing money.

The second major difference between private and municipal charters is that a private business can do just about anything that is not illegal or does not violate the rights of others. A municipality, on the other hand, can carry on only those activities that are expressly authorized by state law. If no state law expressly allows the holding of a lottery, for example, then a community cannot authorize such a lottery.

Dillon's Rule Whenever there has been doubt about what a municipality can or cannot do, the courts have usually given a very strict interpretation of municipal powers. In the late nineteenth century, Judge John F. Dillon gave a succinct summary of the approach taken by the courts. His characterization, known as Dillon's Rule, is still applicable to the home rule principle. Dillon wrote:

> It is a general and undisputed proposition of law that a municipal corporation possesses and can exercise the following powers and no others: First, those granted in express words; second, those necessarily or fairly implied in or incident to the powers expressly granted; third, those essential to the accomplishment of the declared objects and purposes of the corporation—not simply convenient, but indispensable. Any fair, reasonable, substantive doubt concerning the existence of power is resolved by the courts against the corporation, and the power denied.[12]

Even though most states have adopted home rule guarantees enabling municipalities to exercise all powers of local self-government, the local community thus formed is still subject to the constitution and general laws of the state. While home rule has permitted municipalities greater discretion in routine matters of an essentially local character, such as recreation and zoning, the scope of municipal activity has not been enlarged significantly. For the most part, state legislatures and administrative bodies across the nation have continued to exercise the broad supervisory authority expressed in Dillon's Rule. The limited development of municipal power is in marked contrast to the broad interpretations of the Constitution made by the Supreme Court regarding the expansion of federal authority at the expense of that of the states.

Overseeing municipal finance The role of the states in overseeing municipal finance provides yet another gauge of the limits placed on localities. Generally, the states limit local financial powers by determining how localities may tax, how much they may tax, how much indebtedness they may incur, and how they should manage their finances. Two explanations have been advanced for this tight form of state control. One theory notes that state officials share a pervasive skepticism about the ability of cities to manage their resources successfully. The second explanation points out that states may not want cities to rely heavily on those tax sources that the states themselves wish to preserve for their own revenues.

State supervision of local government finance comprises the following:

1. Defining standards for performance of local government finance functions such as budgeting, accounting, and auditing
2. Limiting localities with respect to debt, taxes, expenditures, and so on
3. Coordinating state and local units to avoid unnecessary duplication and ensure cooperation in carrying out various functions (e.g., collection of state taxes by local officials)
4. Taking over the fiscal management function during periods of local fiscal emergency
5. Ensuring that local governments comply with contracts entered into with state agencies.

Most recently, as an outgrowth of the tax limitation movement, there has been a renewed emphasis on limiting the taxing and spending powers of local government. A survey by the United States Advisory Commission on Intergovernmental Relations (ACIR) shows that, as of October 1985, states had placed limits on local government taxing and spending in 96 instances. As can be seen in Table 1–6, 12 states have an overall property tax rate limit, 31 have a specific property tax rate limit, and 21 have a property tax levy limit. Many of these limits were approved by voters through citizen initiatives and legislative referenda in the late seventies and early eighties. However, with the defeat of tax-cutting initiatives in four states—California, Michigan, Oregon, and Nevada—there was indication that tax revolt fever had at least slowed.

The intergovernmental system

Federal funds are channeled to local communities either directly, through local governments, or indirectly, through the states. As Figure 1–2 shows, federal aid flowing directly to municipalities increased substantially during the 1960s and 1970s as the condition of cities worsened. City residents, including the poor, have used federal funds for such services as housing, education, social services, and mass transportation. Over the long run, virtually every function of local government, from police to community arts, has come to be supported by a counterpart federal aid program.

Overall, federal grant programs increased from 50 in 1960 at a cost of $7 billion dollars, to over 500 in 1980 at a cost of $83 billion dollars.[13] By the

Table 1–6 Restrictions on local government tax and expenditure powers.

Type of limit	Number of states
Overall property tax rate limit[a]	12
Specific property tax rate limit[b]	31
Property tax levy limit	21
General revenue limit	6
General expenditure limit	6
Limits on assessment increases	7
Full disclosure	13

Source: U.S. Advisory Commission on Intergovernmental Relations, *Significant Features of Fiscal Federalism: 1985–86 Edition* (Washington, D.C.; 1986), p. 146.

[a]Overall limits refer to limits on the aggregate tax rate of all local governments.

[b]Specific rate limits refer to limits on individual types of local governments or limits on narrowly defined services.

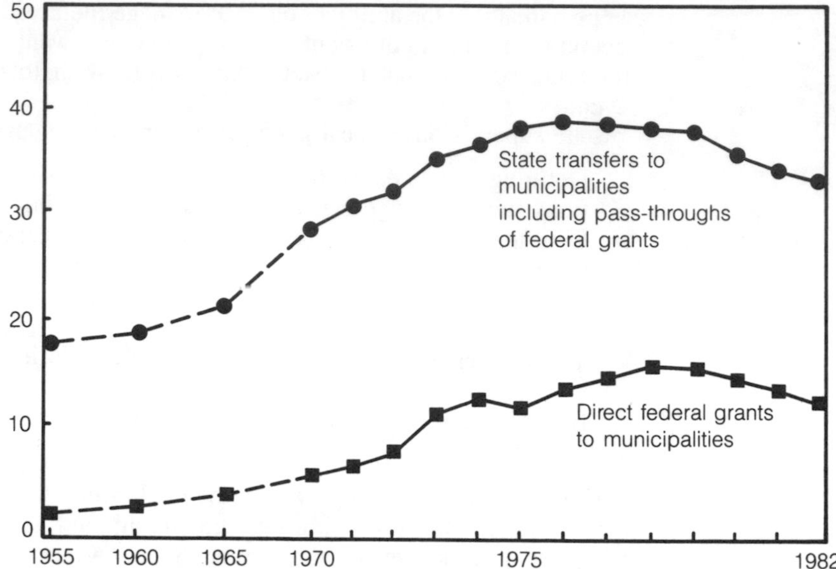

Figure 1–2 Intergovernmental transfers as a percentage of municipal revenues.

beginning of the 1980s, however, the trend toward federal expansion encountered growing resistance from taxpayers as well as from various interests to the left and the right of the political spectrum. When President Reagan entered the White House, he made reform of the federal system one of the highest priorities of his presidency. Not only was he concerned about the rising cost of federal aid, but he was also critical of the growing complexity of intergovernmental relations. The President agreed with an ACIR study[14] concluding that the federal government had become more pervasive, more unmanageable, more ineffective and costly, and above all more unaccountable. Thus, he insisted, it was time for a "new federalism" to decentralize governmental activities by transferring many federally established and administered programs to the states and localities.

To achieve this goal, the President proposed reducing federal funding to states and local governments, thereby forcing them to rely to a greater extent on their own revenue sources. Where the federal government would continue to play a role in the funding of state and local programs, he proposed diminishing the detail by which the federal government regulated these programs. Finally, he planned to reduce federal intervention in state and local program execution.

Figure 1–3 shows the President's success in achieving these goals: federal grants as a percentage of all state and local expenditures dropped from a peak of 26 percent in 1978 to 21 percent in 1982. It is estimated that 25 percent of such federal aid goes directly to local governments, 20 percent goes to local governments indirectly—after passing through state governments first—and the remainder goes to the states.

In 1981, the Reagan administration also succeeded in persuading Congress to combine 77 categorical grant-in-aid programs, each with regulations written in Washington, into nine block grants, with the rule-writing and oversight handled by state governments. These were in such fields as health, education, social services, and community development. Subsequently, the total number of grant-in-aid programs for state and local governments was reduced to 392, as of January 1984, from 534 counted three years previously.[15]

Clearly, by the mid-1980s, power was beginning to shift to the states from the cities and other local governments. The latter could no longer maintain a direct relationship with Washington via grants that bypassed the states. The shift in power has resulted in a redistribution of funds away from the larger cities to

Figure 1–3 Federal grants as a percentage of state and local expenditures: 1929–1982.

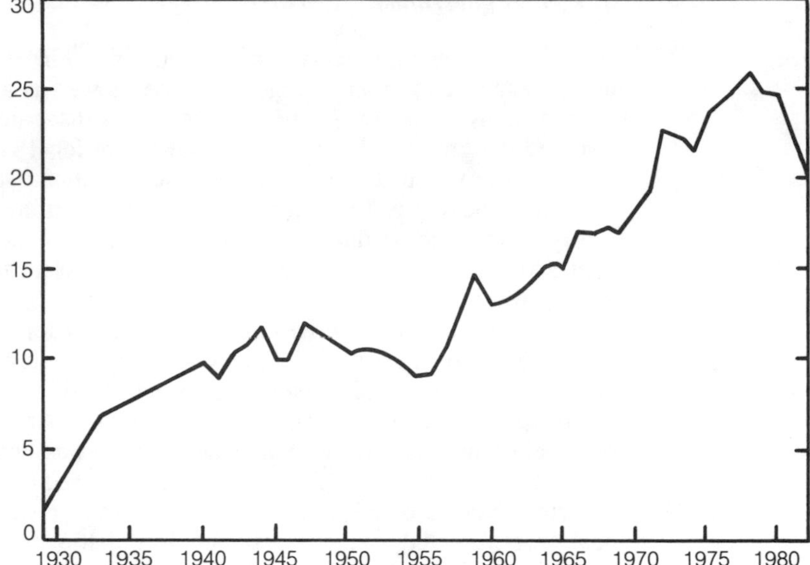

smaller communities where most of the voters live. Another serious effect of the shift in power shows up in Figure 1–2, where the states appear either unable or unwilling to make up for lower federal contributions to municipalities. Where replacement of federal cuts by state and local governments has occurred, it has been economically well-off and politically popular health and social services areas. There is also evidence of replacement funding through capital grants for transportation and wastewater treatment projects.

Regarding the future, federal grants to municipalities are likely to continue to decline regardless of which party controls the presidency and Congress. Consequently, local governments will need to rely more heavily on state governments as well as on their own resources. Recognizing this, many states have already assumed more responsibility for providing financial assistance to local jurisdictions. Table 1–7 shows that 42 states had state-local general revenue-sharing programs as of 1985, and 50 states had assumed, in part or in whole, the costs of local public welfare programs. In addition, 12 states reimbursed local governments for state-mandated programs, and 42 states had taken measures to improve local government access to credit markets. It is expected that such forms of assistance will increase over time.

Table 1–7 Number of states with selected direct and indirect aid programs to local governments: 1985.

Program	Number of states
State-local general revenue sharing	42
Education finance	50
Assumption of local public welfare	50
Reimbursement of state-mandated programs	12
Improving local government access to credit markets	42
Tax increment financing	31
Local income/sales taxes	34
Local discretionary authority	50
Local redevelopment authorities	49

Source: Advisory Commission on Intergovernmental Relations, *The States and Distressed Communities: The Final Report,* A–101 (Washington, D.C.: GPO, November 1985), pp. 218–19.

Municipal government structure

The way government is actually organized—the third vital aspect of the governmental response to urban change—may be viewed as a product of the evolving value systems of society. Herbert Kaufman has discerned three basic values that have had the greatest effect on the evolution of local government in the United States: (1) representativeness; (2) technical, nonpartisan competence; and (3) executive leadership.[16] Kaufman shows that at different periods in American history, each of these three values has had a significant effect on the arrangement and organization of government. It is also clear that all three continue to affect government practice.

What Kaufman characterizes as "the pursuit of representativeness" grew out of the Revolutionary period of American history. Rising antagonism between the colonies and the English monarch (represented by the colonial governors) generated deep-seated distrust of executive power. After 1776, executive rule—an unhappy reminder of the king's authority—was denigrated virtually everywhere. Citizens of the fledgling democracy deferred to their legislatures instead, believing them to be more representative of their respective interests.[17] On the local level, elected councils assumed leadership responsibilities and mayors were often reduced to little more than ceremonial figures.

The period following the inauguration of President Jackson in 1829 gave new meaning to values of representativeness in national life. The anti-aristocratic feelings of the common citizen were highlighted in what came to be termed Jacksonian Democracy. At that time it was widely held that "any man was as good as any other man"; the idea that a candidate for office should possess special qualifications to hold that office was frowned upon. During this time, too, the number of elected officers began to increase as the franchise was extended and elections became the primary mechanism for elevating candidates to office.

After the Civil War, representativeness began to erode as the country grew in size and complexity. The Industrial Revolution generated complicated problems of governmental management, problems that were often beyond the capabilities of part-time, amateur councilmen. The demonstrable corruption of many elected officials and the role of the urban party "boss" in dispensing patronage also played a major role in reassessing the values of representativeness in the late nineteenth century.

Consequently, values of technical, nonpartisan competence began to take on greater weight. By the beginning of the twentieth century, reformers devised new governing procedures intended to serve as antidotes to the perceived excesses of the existing system. Civil service systems, for example, were introduced in some of the larger cities in an attempt to ensure expertise, and multimember boards and commissions were created for the purpose of "taking politics out of government." The reformers believed that where a number of commissioners held long, overlapping terms of office, both special interests and party organizations would be denied effective influence. What reformers did not expect, however, was that proliferation of both elective offices (from the Jacksonian era) and of new boards and commissions would produce immense difficulties for government coordination. Far from being impeded, the opportunity for special interest groups and parties to sway decision making was encouraged, and the public became increasingly confused by the complexity of these governmental arrangements.

Consequently, during the 1920s and 1930s, reformers began to urge acceptance of a new set of doctrines to achieve integration and coordination in municipal government. Under the leadership of a strong executive, the number of independent administrative offices and agencies could be reduced. The reformers now believed that by establishing clear lines of command under a mayor, waste and inefficiency would be reduced while responsibility would be improved. Under these conditions, the reformers argued, it was the mayor who could be held accountable to the electorate for the administration of the government. This shift in beliefs and values gave mayors new powers of appointment and removal. In many jurisdictions they were given the veto for the first time. Gradually, in the twentieth century, mayoral staffs were increased, terms of office lengthened, and, in the larger cities, mayors were given authority to formulate and execute municipal budgets. In short, the values of executive leadership took on greater significance in response to the changing conditions of the larger community.

The values of government—representativeness; technical, nonpartisan competence; and executive leadership—have played a major part in shaping governmental structures at different periods in American history. They have also shaped the three formal models of municipal government that currently exist: mayor-council government, commission government, and council-manager government.

Mayor-council government Two types of mayor-council government exist—the weak mayor type and the strong mayor type—with many cities representing variations that fall between these two modes of government structure. The weak mayor form, with its roots in early United States history, reflects values of representativeness. This system features a mayor whose power in administrative matters is very weak when compared with the power of the council. The mayor, for example, has limited authority in the areas of appointment, removal, and budget making and may well be chief executive in name only. The weak mayor form persists in many mayor-council municipalities, particularly in smaller communities where the values of representativeness continue to exert a strong influence.

The strong mayor system, on the other hand, reduces the relative importance of the council while centralizing administrative powers in the hands of the executive. Historically, the strong mayor form may be traced to the first model city charter drafted by the National Municipal League in 1897. In addition to strengthening the role of the mayor, the charter recommended that ballots be shortened and that legislative powers be centralized in a unicameral city council as a way of reducing institutional complexity and making government more accountable to the citizenry. Through the influence of the National Municipal League, the strong mayor form of government began to take hold in the first decades of the twentieth century.

Responding to the growing administrative complexity of urban government, large cities such as New York, Chicago, Philadelphia, and New Orleans have assisted their mayors by providing them with chief administrative officers (CAOs). Subject to the will of the mayor, the CAO is expected to look after the many details of interagency communication, budget preparation, personnel administration, and other management areas, thereby freeing the mayor to concentrate on policy matters.

The strong mayor, then, is an elected chief executive who prepares the budget, appoints and removes department heads and other principal officers, and is responsible for both the political and administrative functioning of the city government. Proponents of the strong mayor form point to the political as well as the administrative advantages of this form of government. The strong mayor has a constituency that looks to him or her for leadership. At the same time, the mayor is held responsible and accountable to the constituency. Furthermore, the strong mayor may be in a better position to use political power in those very large cities where competition and conflict between interest groups tend to be more intense.

By the 1980s, the mayor-council form of government was the most popular form of municipal governmental structure, existing in 3,705 of those cities with a population of 2,500 or more (see Table 1–2). It was particularly popular in the very large cities; of 23 cities 500,000 and over in population, 18 had the mayor-council form. All 6 cities of over 1 million population had mayor-council governments.

Commission and town meeting governments The commission form of government, on the other hand, was of only limited importance by the 1980s. It was the prevailing system in only 177 municipalities, and was, in fact, less popular than the town meeting form of government, which was the preferred system in 419 municipalities.

The commission form originated with the appointment of five businessmen authorized by the governor of Texas to administer the city of Galveston following the catastrophic hurricane of 1900. It stems from the values of representativeness and nonpartisan, technical competence. This system of government allows a small number of commissioners, between five and seven, to be elected on a nonpartisan ticket. As a group they are responsible for policy formation and legislation. Each commissioner also serves as the head of an administrative department; thus, in contrast with the mayor-council form, commission government places both administrative and legislative authority in the hands of the same officers.

Proponents of the commission plan point to the advantage derived from the short ballot, which makes it easier for the electorate to exercise choice among the candidates for office. Critics, on the other hand, point to the dangers inherent in a government run by amateurs and subject to administrative fragmentation. However, since the commission form has long since passed the peak of popularity enjoyed in the early decades of the twentieth century, such discussion becomes increasingly academic.

The town meeting is another form of government, largely associated with the New England region. The roots of this form reach back into the colonial period, when it played a major role in reinforcing the democratic consciousness that led to the Revolution. Although it illustrates the community values of representativeness, the town meeting is of minor significance in the overall national structure of municipal government.

The council-manager form The council-manager form of government exhibits the influence of all three core values that have been discussed: representativeness as effected through an elected council serving as the policymaking body; nonpartisan, technical competence as implemented through nonpartisan elections in most cities and through a professional manager who directs administration; and executive leadership as effected by a reduction in the number of independent agencies and their integration in a chain-of-command structure headed by the manager.

In the council-manager plan the council performs the legislative function. It appoints a manager, who, in turn, selects appropriate department heads and directs their activities. Where there is a mayor, his or her role is primarily ceremonial. In about one-half of the communities that have this form of government, the mayor is selected by the council from among its own membership; the remaining communities elect their mayor by popular vote.

Drawing on the experience of Staunton, Virginia—where, in 1908, pragmatic experimentation led to the creation of the post of "general manager"—Richard Childs, founder of the council-manager plan, formulated a system to separate policymaking from administration. Childs drew on the experience of the commission form of government, notably its integrated structure and nonpartisan short ballot features, and added the idea of a professional general manager, a concept stemming from private business. In essence, the council would propose and the manager dispose. In practice, as the council-manager form grew in popularity over the ensuring decades, this distinction was not always so clear-cut. The manager's powers—appointing and removing ranking administrators, preparing and executing the budget, making recommendations to the council—imply that the professional manager cannot help exercising some degree of influence on policy. Political scientists seem to agree that the most successful managers have always been formulators of policy, although this role must be exercised with great skill and delicacy.[18] The professional manager, after all, must always be aware that he or she serves at the pleasure of the council.

Supporters of the council-manager plan note that it allows for administrative and supervisory responsibility to be centralized in a single individual, and that it allows for that individual's expertise to be encouraged and developed. Critics contend that the plan may fail to generate effective political leadership, especially in the problem-ridden larger cities. Professional managers, they argue, do not have the necessary political resources to mediate among such contending political forces as powerful unions, business interests, and ethnic and racial groups.

In recent years, the council-manager form of government has achieved widespread popularity. As Table 1–2 shows, by the 1980s it was the preferred form of government in some 2,308 cities with a population of 2,500 and over. Although this form existed in only 5 of the 23 cities of 500,000 and over (the remainder being governed by mayor-council systems), it was clearly the most popular form in cities of 25,000 and over. In this population range, 589 communities had adopted the council-manager plan in comparison with 406 local governments with the mayor-council form and 46 communities with the commission form of government.

Organizing for financial administration

The remainder of this chapter will discuss organizational models for financial administration and will conclude by focusing more sharply on the essential characteristics of financial decision making in local government.

The historical perspective

The drive to improve financial administration in the United States has been inextricably related to the government reorganization movements already described. Thus, for example, when prevailing sentiment decreed that local government should be decentralized through many independent offices and agencies, administration of the financial functions underwent related structural changes. Similarly, when the strong mayor or the council-manager form of government became popular, unification of the hitherto fragmented functions of financial administration was, in general, also achieved.

The civic reform movement associated with the founding of the National Municipal League in 1894 had significant influence in ensuing years. Espousing values of executive leadership, the league's model municipal code included a budget system that was to be directed by the mayor rather than by the city council. This concept was further developed by the New York Bureau of Municipal Research, which was established in 1906. The bureau viewed municipal budgeting as a major tool for achieving responsibility in government: budgeting would realize economies, eliminate dishonest practices, and set fixed and objective standards of accountability. Furthermore, with the chief executive responsible for recommending revenues and expenditures, coordination of goals, programs, and services would be achieved. Many communities eventually adopted these budget proposals, encouraged by the strong support of business leaders who called for demonstrable economy and efficiency in government.

In subsequent decades, city and state governments began to upgrade and to interrelate other important components of financial administration—accounting, auditing, purchasing, tax administration, and treasury management, for example. Gradually, the idea of a centralized department of finance serving the chief executive as a vital instrument of municipal management emerged and took shape. As one observer concluded, "by the mid-1920's most . . . American cities had undergone a more or less thorough reform in municipal financial practices and had established some sort of a budget system."[19]

By the 1980s it appears that where values of representativeness prevail, certain fiscal officers—notably treasurers and controllers—are still independently elected. Where the values of nonpartisan, technical competence remain entrenched, it is possible to find a variety of autonomous or semiautonomous fiscal agencies, ranging from boards of tax appeal to boards of assessors. Nevertheless, the idea of a fully integrated financial system under the chief executive has won increasing favor, even if implementation of the practice varies.

The integrated system

The model city charter suggested by the National Municipal League describes a fully integrated financial system. Figure 1–4, a representation of it, indicates that the city manager, appointed by the council, assumes overall responsibility

Figure 1–4 General organization chart, department of finance.

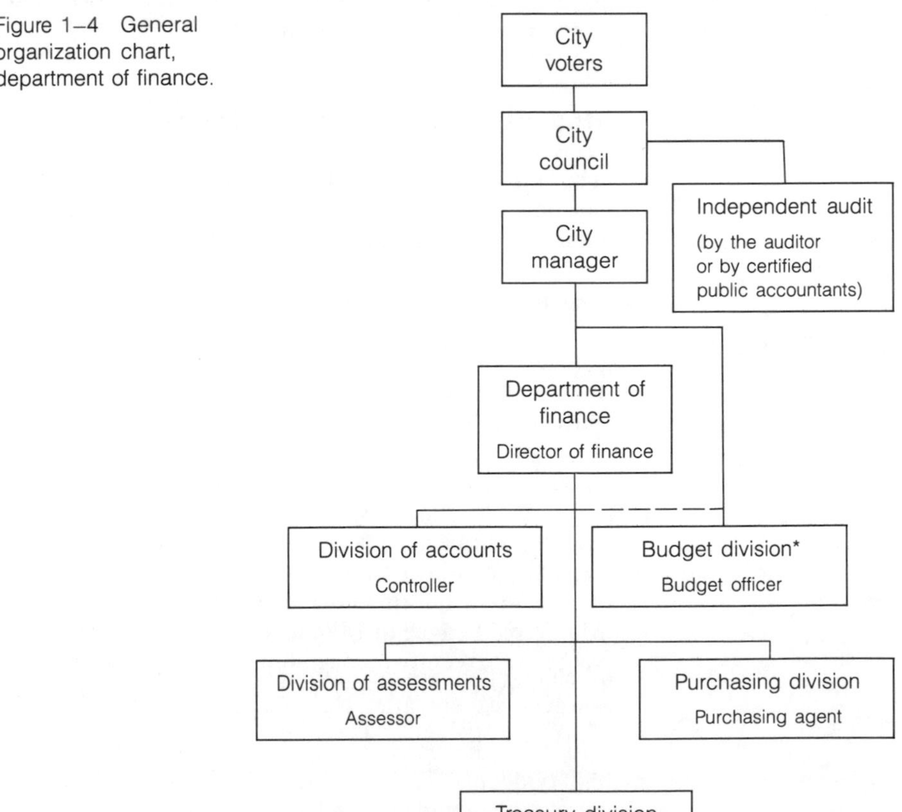

*The dotted line between the director of finance and the budget officer indicates that the latter is often primarily responsible to the chief administrator (and physically located in the finance department) to prevent the duplication of records. In many cities the finance director handles the budget.

for financial affairs. (In mayor-council governments, the mayor would perform an equivalent role.) In this model the finance department is divided into five areas of control—accounts, budget, assessments, purchasing, and treasury. The director of the finance department, often called the finance director or finance officer, is appointed by the manager and serves at the manager's pleasure; division heads, in turn, are appointed by the finance director. Figure 1–4 also indicates that the model city charter provides for an independent outside audit as well as a preaudit performed by the accounts division. The preaudit is conducted before the payment of all claims and includes a daily check of all revenues and receipts. The independent audit, or postaudit (taking place after payment), serves as a check on officials in the executive branch by ascertaining whether any errors have been made or whether any illegal expenditures have occurred. The objectivity of the independent audit would, of course, be in question if it were to be administered by persons from the branch that authorized the expenditures. In only a small number of cities, in fact, is this function carried out by an independently elected auditor or controller.

Within this overall framework it is possible to delineate specific components of financial management. Figure 1–5 illustrates a possible division of responsibility for those components, which may be characterized briefly as follows:

Director of finance As a department head the finance director supervises and coordinates the administration of major financial services. As a managerial aide to the chief executive—mayor or manager—the director advises on fiscal policy and other related concerns such as debt and investment management. In some cities this officer may also be the chief budget officer.

Accounts After the council has adopted a budget for the forthcoming fiscal year, the division of accounts administers the budget through the preaudit function. This division assures each department of permission to spend—within authorized guidelines. The division also keeps accounts, maintains inventory records of municipal property, and furnishes financial information needed in the preparation of the next budget.

Assessments In theory, assessment does not involve decision making; it is conceived as the mechanical application of state and local laws to the evaluation of property for tax purposes. In the uncompromising reality of contemporary local government, however, assessors often function as important decision makers with discretion in computing property values. Because these assessments can be a matter of judgment, where the state does not provide a means of handling appeals on disputed assessments, the municipality usually establishes a board of appeals or a board of equalization that can perform this function.

Treasury The treasury division collects the taxes and pays out the monies that, taken together, are the lifeblood of local government. Payments cannot be made, however, except after the preaudit and after appropriate certification by the controller. In many municipalities, the treasury is also empowered to issue licenses, administer sales taxes, and invest idle funds.

Purchasing Most of the supplies, material, and equipment for the city or county are procured (and then stored) through the purchasing division. This division, particularly if the government is a large one, can thus make the savings that are likely to accrue from large-scale centralized purchasing. The division can also administer appropriate quality control procedures, specifying standards against which purchases are then tested and inspected. In addition, the purchasing division usually manages risk protection through insurance and risk reduction programs.

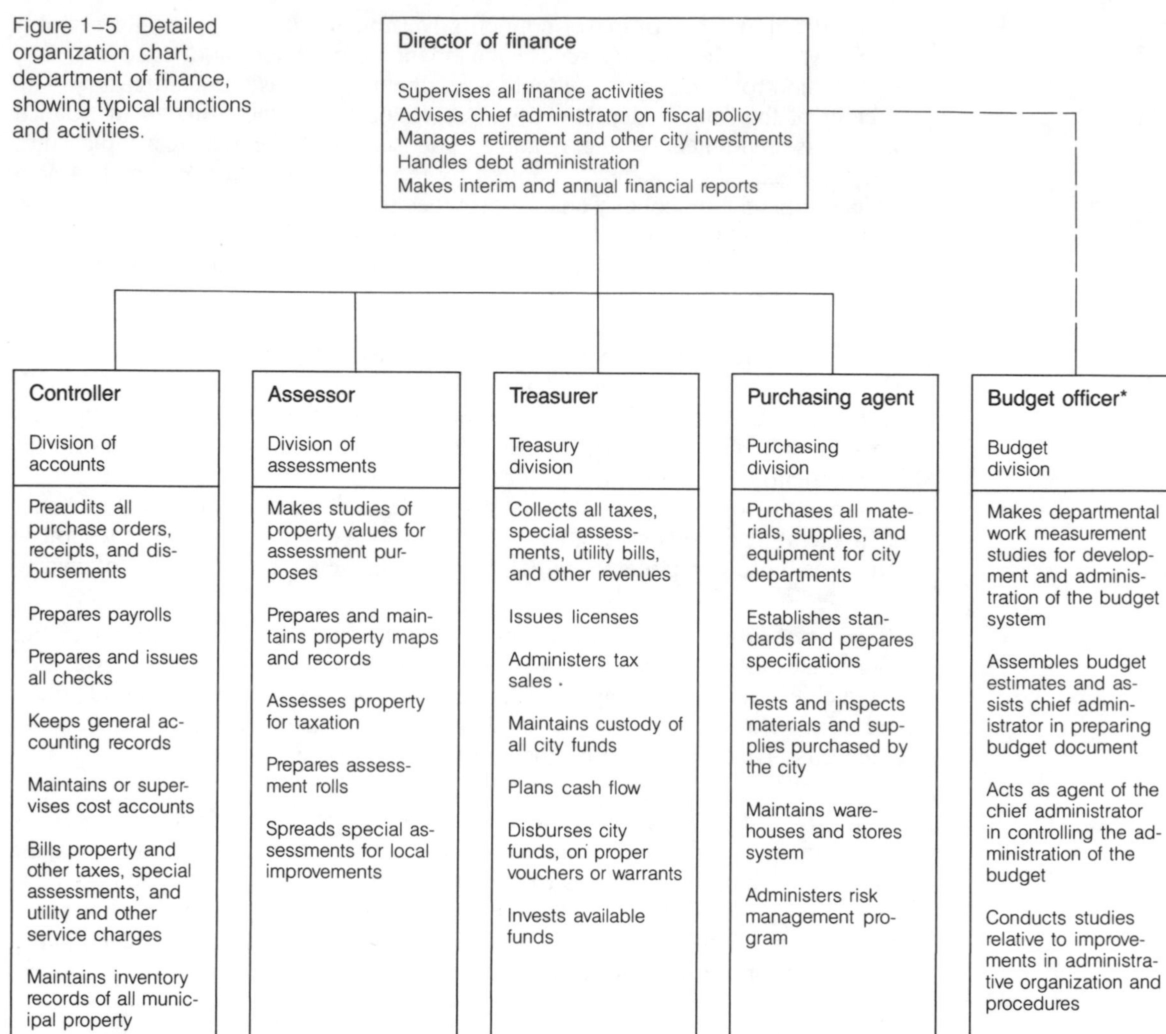
Director of finance
Supervises all finance activities
Advises chief administrator on fiscal policy
Manages retirement and other city investments
Handles debt administration
Makes interim and annual financial reports
Controller
Division of accounts
Preaudits all purchase orders, receipts, and disbursements
Prepares payrolls
Prepares and issues all checks
Keeps general accounting records
Maintains or supervises cost accounts
Bills property and other taxes, special assessments, and utility and other service charges
Maintains inventory records of all municipal property
Assessor
Division of assessments
Makes studies of property values for assessment purposes
Prepares and maintains property maps and records
Assesses property for taxation
Prepares assessment rolls
Spreads special assessments for local improvements
Treasurer
Treasury division
Collects all taxes, special assessments, utility bills, and other revenues
Issues licenses
Administers tax sales
Maintains custody of all city funds
Plans cash flow
Disburses city funds, on proper vouchers or warrants
Invests available funds
Purchasing agent
Purchasing division
Purchases all materials, supplies, and equipment for city departments
Establishes standards and prepares specifications
Tests and inspects materials and supplies purchased by the city
Maintains warehouses and stores system
Administers risk management program
Budget officer*
Budget division
Makes departmental work measurement studies for development and administration of the budget system
Assembles budget estimates and assists chief administrator in preparing budget document
Acts as agent of the chief administrator in controlling the administration of the budget
Conducts studies relative to improvements in administrative organization and procedures

Figure 1–5 Detailed organization chart, department of finance, showing typical functions and activities.

*The dotted line between the director of finance and the budget officer indicates that the latter is often primarily responsible to the chief administrator (and physically located in the finance department) to prevent the duplication of records. In many cities the finance director handles the budget.

Budgeting The budget division occupies a position of paramount importance in the overall functioning of the city or county. Where the executive budget has become established, the head of the budget division usually becomes one of the principal aides to the chief executive. In cases where the budget officer is not in fact the director of finance, he or she is usually placed in the office of the chief executive so that the latter may be assured of a direct line of communication. Because of the wealth of knowledge that is acquired in the course of preparing the budget, the chief budget officer may well know more about governing operations than any other local official, including the mayor or the manager. Because the budget officer should possess expertise extending beyond purely fiscal concerns, he or she may be expected to contribute to studies and proposals involving administrative organization and management planning. The budget officer and his or her staff also assist the chief executive in administering the budget once it has been approved by the council. The budgeting amounts involved are subsequently turned over to the accounting division, which preaudits expenditures.

Organization for financial administration tends to vary from community to community. Usually, the larger the community, the more specialized are the organizational components that function within an integrated framework. Smaller communities are likely to be less specialized while tending to rely more on independent boards and elected officials. These organizational configurations are important not only because they influence how financial functions are carried out, but also because they help structure the nature of financial decision making.

Financial decision making

At the heart of the local government fiscal system is the decision-making process. It energizes and directs the system, and all administrators are expected to abide by its mandates. The finance officer must be viewed as both administrator and decision maker. The two roles are often inextricably related because information conveyed by the finance officer for making decisions is largely contingent on his or her values and perspectives. Furthermore, it is not unusual for policymakers to request specific policy proposals from administrators, thereby using their expertise. Perhaps most important, policymakers usually are not able to provide for all exigencies in the course of making policy. Generally the more technical the subject, the more the policymakers are inclined to delegate discretion to administrators during the implementation phase.

To perform effectively as a decision maker, the finance director must understand the political and administrative system of which he or she is a part. The roles and responsibilities of the job are shaped by underlying social and economic conditions in society at large as well as by formal rules established by government. The finance director must deal also with representatives of other public agencies (federal, state, and local) and interest groups, each of which has special stakes in making and carrying out fiscal policies. Responsiveness to the political system is just as critical as efficiency in the effective performance of the finance function. Reconciling these two concerns can be very difficult in all areas of administration, but it is especially difficult in financial management.

Figure 1–6 illustrates the process of financial decision making, showing the factors involved and the interrelationships among the factors.[20] Social and economic conditions (box 1) refer to community needs and resources. Particularly important here is the extent to which communities are undergoing resource expansion or decline and whether changing needs are being met. For example, when the levels of elderly dependents rise at the same time that average personal income declines, communities are usually faced with a reduced capacity to raise revenues to meet the growing needs of the elderly. Where there is severe

Figure 1–6 A model of financial decision making.

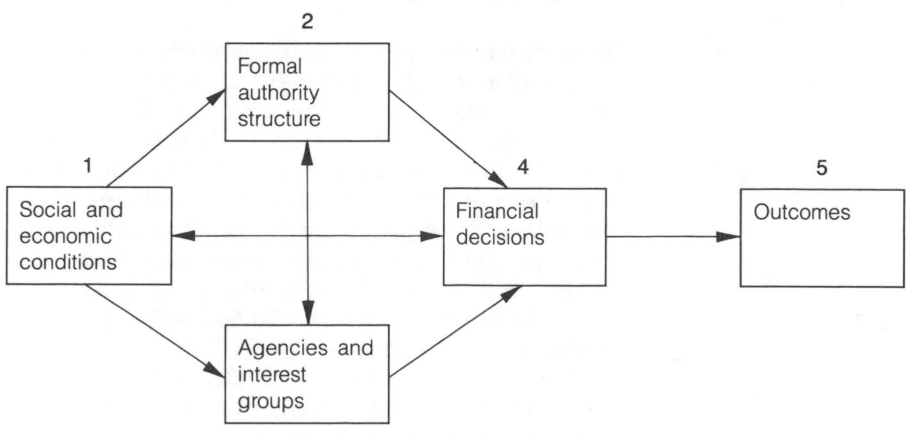

economic decline, local government is not likely to be able to fund its programs at previous levels.

The formal authority structure (box 2) refers to the amount of formal power legally granted to local officials through the home rule provision in the city charter and state statutes that structure state-local relations. Particularly important here is the amount of authority conferred on local government to manage such matters as debt, taxes, and expenditures. The charter also specifies the powers of the council, mayor, manager, and other officials relative to financial decision making—executive initiation of the budget, the power to appoint or remove finance officers, and the power of review over the budget. This, in turn, determines the degree to which the financial management system is either integrated or dispersed in the implementation of financial functions. Also important here is how state and local law structures a division of labor among the different agencies that administer fiscal policies.

The third component of the model (box 3) is interest groups and other local government agencies, such as business organizations, labor unions, civic groups, and ethnic and racial groups. Some groups attempt to work alone in developing political strategies, but most are inclined to form coalitions with other groups as a way of better asserting themselves. Local government agencies are usually very much a part of interest group politics, since they generally see themselves in competition with other agencies in the pursuit of their share of the funding pie. It is not unusual for them to seek ties with clientele groups for support in the course of requesting or defending budgetary allocations. Usually, as issues change, so will coalitions.

Ultimately, all of these factors affect financial decisions (box 4) and outcomes (box 5). How decision makers respond to changing conditions and evolving needs is largely a reflection of who the decision makers are, how they perceive their role, and the political and organizational environment in which they function. Where political pressure from interest groups and other agencies is substantial and where decision makers have little or no professional orientation, decisions are likely to be based more on the need for political accommodation than on criteria of effectiveness and efficiency. On the other hand, where political pressures are moderate, and decision makers have strong professional backgrounds, there is greater likelihood that decisions will reflect a more concerted effort at achieving effectiveness and efficiency through rational planning. More often than not, real-life decision making lies somewhere in between these two extremes. In light of this, it would be useful to review some theories that attempt to explain decision making in different settings. The best demonstration lies in the area of public budgeting.

Financial decision making as incrementalism

In the incremental model, decisions evolve through cautious steps based on what is already accepted as policy.[21] Rather than strive for broad or comprehensive change in dealing with problems, decision makers usually settle for small adjustments to existing policy. In their search for solutions, decision makers often find that time and money constrain them from identifying the full range of alternatives and likely consequences. Furthermore, it is easier to negotiate with and obtain agreement among different interests when the proposal being considered represents only marginal change over the previous settlement. In essence, this means that "the existing level of funds is accepted as the legitimate base for future decisions. Next year's budget is based upon this year's, as this year's budget was based upon last year's."[22]

Many social scientists are critical of the incremental approach to financial decision making. They contend that incremental budgeting is likely to occur in terms of percentages rather than in terms of content. As Ira Sharkansky has observed: "The criteria employed by financial decision-makers *do not* reflect a primary concern with the nature of the economy, the platforms of political parties, or articulated policy desires. . . . The criteria of financial decision makers are non-ideological and frequently non-programmatic."[23] Those who accept incrementalism argue that it is unavoidable in the real world of politics; particularly with regard to budget making, which "lies at the heart of the political process."[24] Defenders also contend that cost-benefit ratios for alternative policies cannot be accurately calculated where many diverse political, social, and economic values are at stake.

Financial decision making as rational planning

While the incremental model is useful for understanding the many constraints on decision making posed by the organizational environment, it has little to say about how to achieve efficiency through systematic analysis. The rational planning model (as illustrated in Figure 1–7) is the key here:[25] The organization or individual (1) recognizes a need; (2) defines the problem in light of this need; (3) identifies value preferences as goals and objectives; (4) searches for and identifies different alternatives for achieving goals and objectives; (5) estimates costs and benefits for each alternative; (6) compares and ranks alternatives using the criterion of expected maximum benefits over least costs; and, finally, (7) recommends the preferred alternative as a solution.[26]

Of late, the rational planning approach to financial decision making has received special emphasis as pressures for fiscal austerity continue. Here the budget is seen as the optimal solution to the problem of allocating scarce resources. This approach is characterized by PPB (planning-programming-budgeting) system and, more recently, by ZBB (zero-base budgeting) systems. Derived from operations research, PPB uses a long-term planning model to determine comprehensively the costs and benefits of expenditures on all program objectives. Variations of this method have been attempted by governmental bodies on all levels. In zero-base budgeting, every ongoing program and activity must be justified from the bottom up each year. A program that has been

Figure 1–7 The rational planning model for decision making.

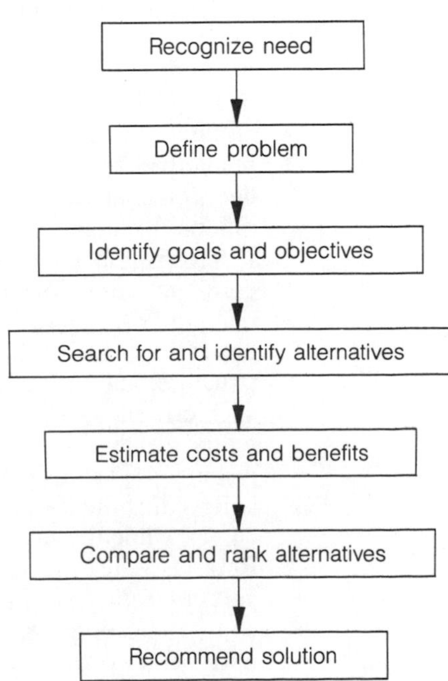

funded in the past will not necessarily be funded in the future; its value cannot be taken for granted.

Both PPB and ZBB are worthwhile concepts, but both have encountered strong obstacles. Some administrators believe they are fads and not likely to last. Others complain that the terms lack precision because so many budgeting approaches have been labeled PPB or ZBB, while still others criticize the wide gap between idealized concepts and actual government practices. Other obstacles are rooted in relations between the administrative agencies and the legislature or city council. A change desired by the manager or an agency head may not have high priority among council members who represent different constituencies and have a different professional role orientation. Changing budget-making procedures will not necessarily change the use to which the budget is put and so may have no real effects.

Finally, one observer of budgeting claims, most of the obstacles are bureaucratic:

> The unwillingness of agency personnel to develop meaningful work units, to learn the skills of the cost effectiveness analyst, to accept the system analyst into the decision-making circle, and the general unwillingness to change time-hallowed practices all militate against budget innovation. Additionally, lack of resources in the agencies reduces the likelihood of any kind of change.[27]

Although the PPB and ZBB approaches have not been adopted widely, their many variations have made important contributions to "program budgeting" practices. The major actors in the budgetary process—the council, the chief administrative officer, department heads, program administrators, the finance and budget staffs, and major interest groups—have been forced to deal with fiscal issues in terms of service levels, programs, and other activities likely to contribute to greater efficiency.

Financial decision making as "satisficing"

Thomas D. Lynch has described "satisficing"[28] as a mode of decision making in which decision makers develop their own criteria to determine acceptable alternatives for dealing with a given problem.[29] Rather than consider the best possible alternative, as based on the criteria of maximum benefits and minimum cost, decision makers settle on an alternative that appears to be "good enough." Supporters of this approach point out that with deadlines to meet, it is often too time-consuming to collect all necessary information about every possible alternative and its likely consequences. Furthermore, they claim, rational planning requires a vision of the future, extremely difficult to achieve in a field where predictive capabilities are neither sophisticated nor very accurate. Consequently, decision makers have chosen to "satisfice"—to be only as systematic and rational in their search for solutions as is feasible.

Referring back to the model in Figure 1–6, it is now necessary to consider consequences or outcomes (box 5) as a way of assessing the efficacy of decision making. While outcomes may be defined as the results of decisions made by key actors, they also reflect the influence of environmental conditions, governing structure, and interest groups. Generally, outcomes are assessed on the basis of such criteria as *efficiency, responsiveness,* and *equity.* Efficiency, for example, refers to whether government is able to deliver services with more or fewer resources. Various polls indicate that in recent years many citizens have come to believe that the costs of administering government have been increasing significantly, while the quality and quantity of public services have been decreasing.[30] Responsiveness refers to how well government is able to meet the needs of particular groups in the community. For some time now, for example, elderly and handicapped persons have complained that their more specialized needs have been overlooked. Equity refers to the distribution of resources to various sectors of the community, that is, which neighborhoods receive more and which neighborhoods receive less. In many communities, low-income minority neighborhoods have complained that they tend to receive less.

The role of the finance officer

What is the appropriate role of the finance officer in decision making? There are no simple answers to this question for the role tends to vary with circumstances. Lynch identifies four ideal types worthy of consideration: the true rational believer, the pure reactive person, the finance-wise person (or cynic), and the wise finance person.[31]

The true rational believer The true rational believer tries to follow the rational planning approach outlined in Figure 1–7. While this approach holds the most promise for achieving efficiency, the decision maker should be aware of its limitations as well. In many instances, public agencies are not able to define specific goals and objectives because of the need to achieve political compromise among competing interests: agreement comes easier where goals and objectives are not stated very clearly. Furthermore, an exhaustive examination of all alternatives and their likely consequences is usually not feasible. In the real world of public affairs, the budget calendar cannot wait until an analysis has been completed.

The pure reactive person The pure reactive person defines the job of finance manager in very limited terms—namely, performing the formal requirements of the job description and responding to specific requests made by policymakers and ranking administrators. Other than providing information of a technical nature, this individual does not see himself or herself as a decision maker. The hazard of this approach, according to Lynch, is that potentially foolish mistakes are not avoided, particularly in the budgeting process. He explains:

> The budget person has a unique vantage point and can often understand both the political actors' viewpoints as well as the workings of government. By merely reacting, the government loses the important insight of the budget expert. Thus more errors are likely to occur.[32]

The finance-wise person (or cynic) The "cynic" views government decisions as based entirely on political criteria. Such persons are keenly aware of the trade-offs that occur among different interests in the course of negotiating decisions and they believe that information and advice from the professional staff are not taken seriously by the policymakers. To corroborate their belief, they perpetuate stories of conflict of interest and corruption. While this may be the pattern in some government settings, it is not universal, especially in recent years when citizens have developed strong expectations for improved productivity and efficiency in the public sector.

The wise finance person The wise finance person recognizes the importance of politics and expertise in the decision-making process—if government is to attain a high level of efficiency. The sheer complexity of financial decision making demands that mayors and council members seek such financial expertise. The wise finance person recognizes the need for:

1. Hard work
2. Mastery of detail
3. Honesty
4. Exercising tight control over taxpayers' money
5. A rational approach to financial management
6. Adaptability to political exigencies

7. Informing and updating policymakers
8. Establishing trust
9. Discretion.

Conclusion

As outlined in this chapter, how local governments manage finances depends on such factors as population movement and development in the urban environment; governmental structure, including the intergovernmental system; organizational structure; and the nature of financial decision making. Central to the functioning of a local government is the finance manager who makes the fiscal system work. For the finance manager to perform successfully, he or she must not only understand the interaction of shaping and contributing factors, trends, and urban and governmental processes, but he or she must come equipped with the knowledge and skills needed to make and implement decisions.

These functions of the fiscal manager and the stage on which he or she performs are covered fully in this book on local financial management. The chapters that follow elaborate further—from a theoretical as well as practical perspective—the local government setting, management tools, revenue sources, and financial management principles and techniques.

1 See Charles H. Levine and Irene Rubin, eds., *Fiscal Stress and Public Policy* (Beverly Hills: Sage Publications, 1980); Katharine L. Bradbury, Anthony Downs, and Kenneth A. Small, *Urban Decline and the Future of American Cities* (Washington, D.C.: The Brookings Institution, 1982); and Nancy Humphrey, George E. Peterson, and Peter Wilson, *The Future of Cleveland's Capital Plant* (Washington, D.C.: The Urban Institute, 1979).

2 This is discussed in Bradbury, Downs, and Small, *Urban Decline,* Chapter 2.

3 National Urban Policy Advisory Committee, *Urban America 1984: A Report Card,* report prepared for the Subcommittee on Investment, Jobs, and Prices of the Joint Economic Committee of Congress (Denver: University of Colorado at Denver, 1984), pp. 8–10.

4 See Karen Benker and Daphine Kenyon, "The Tax Revolt—Round II?" *Intergovernmental Perspective* 10 (Summer 1984): 14–24.

5 See President's Commission for a National Agenda for the Eighties, *Urban America in the Eighties* (Washington, D.C.: GPO, 1980).

6 See Pat Choate and Susan Walter, *America in Ruins: The Decaying Infrastructure* (Durham, N.C.: Duke University Press, 1981).

7 Jean Gottmann, *Megalopolis: The Urbanized Northeastern Seaboard of the United States* (New York: Twentieth Century Fund, 1961), p. 5.

8 This is discussed in detail by Jack Meltzer, *Metropolis to Metroplex* (Baltimore: Johns Hopkins Univ. Press, 1984), pp. 13–22.

9 U.S. Bureau of the Census, *1980 Census of Population,* Metropolitan Statistical Areas, Supplementary Report (PC 80-81-18), (Washington, D.C.: GPO, December 1984), p. 11.

10 Elizabeth M. Moen and Walter T. Martin, "On Moving Out of the Metropolis," Working Paper Number 13a (Paper presented at the annual American Sociology Association Meetings, San Francisco, Cal., 1978).

11 Herrington J. Bryce, "Current Trends in Financing Smaller Cities," in *Local Distress, State Surpluses, Proposition 13: Prelude to Fiscal Crisis or New Opportunities?,* U.S. Congress, House Committee on Banking, Finance, and Urban Affairs, Subcommittee on the City, and Joint Economic Committee, 95th Cong., 2d sess., July 25–26, 1978, pp. 95, 96.

12 John F. Dillon, *Commentaries on the Law of Municipal Corporations,* 5th ed. (Boston: Little, Brown, 1911), vol. 1, section 237.

13 Advisory Commission on Intergovernmental Relations, *An Agenda for American Federalism: Restoring Confidence and Competence* (Washington, D.C.: GPO, 1981), p. 3.

14 Ibid.

15 Advisory Commission on Intergovernmental Relations, *A Catalog of Federal Grant-in-Aid Programs to State and Local Governments: Grants Funded FY 1984* (Washington, D.C.: GPO, 1984) pp. 1–3.

16 Herbert Kaufman, *Politics and Policies in State and Local Governments* (Englewood Cliffs, N.J.: Prentice-Hall, 1963), Chapter 2.

17 On the national level, the Articles of Confederation provided for no executive at all. Historians have held that the creation of a strong presidency at the Philadelphia Convention of 1787 could be attributed to atypical qualities of the delegates.

18 See, for example, Stanley T. Gabis, "Leadership in a Large Manager City: The Case of Kansas City," *Annals of the American Academy of Political and Social Science* 347 (May 1963): 52–63; and Keith Mulrooney, ed., "Symposium on the American City Manager: An Urban Administrator in a Complex and Evolving Situation," *Public Administration Review* 31 (January/February 1971): 6–46.

19 Jesse Burkhead, *Government Budgeting* (New York: John Wiley & Sons, Inc., 1956), p. 14.

20 This model has been adapted from Charles H. Levine, Irene S. Rubin, and George G. Wolohojian, *The Politics of Retrenchment* (Beverly Hills, Calif.: Sage Publications, 1981), pp. 35–43.

21 See Charles E. Lindblom, "The Science of 'Muddling Through'," *Public Administration Review* 19 (Spring 1959): 79–88; and Aaron B. Wildavsky, *The Politics of the Budgetary Process,* 3d ed. (Boston: Little, Brown, 1979).

22 Lewis A. Friedman and Bryan T. Downes, "Local Level Decision-Making and Budgetary Outcomes: A Theoretical Perspective on Research in Fourteen Michigan Cities" (Paper presented at the Annual

Meeting of the American Political Science Association, Chicago, Ill., September 7–11, 1971).

23 Ira Sharkansky, *Spending in the American States* (Chicago: Rand McNally, 1970), p. 13.

24 Wildavsky, *The Politics*, p. 5.

25 See Thomas D. Lynch, *Public Budgeting in America* (Englewood Cliffs, N.J.: Prentice-Hall, 1979), pp. 23–26.

26 Leonard Ruchelman, *The Formation and Presentation of Alternatives for Public Programs* (Croton-on-Hudson, N.Y.: Policy Studies Associates, 1984), pp. 1–4.

27 John Wanat, *Introduction to Budgeting* (North Scituate, Mass.: Duxbury Press, 1978), p. 105.

28 This term was first used by Herbert Simon who combined the words "satisfy" and "suffice" to develop the idea of "satisfice." See his article, "Theories of Decision Making in Economic and Behavioral Science," *American Economic Review* 49 (June 1959): 262–64.

29 Lynch, *Public Budgeting*, p. 23.

30 Advisory Commission on Intergovernmental Relations, *Changing Public Attitudes on Government and Taxes* (Washington, D.C.: GPO, 1980), p. 2. Also see Advisory Commission on Intergovernmental Relations, *Changing Public Attitudes on Government and Taxes* (Washington, D.C.: GPO, August 1984).

31 Lynch, *Public Budgeting*, pp. 100–102.

32 Ibid., p. 101.

The fiscal problems of the fragmented metropolis

A metropolitan area—comprising central cities and suburbs—is a complex, fluid network of interrelated activities. It has the resources and stability to feed, house, transport, and take care of the daily household and business needs of hundreds of thousands or millions, but just a few decades of change can transform it beyond recognition. Seemingly arbitrary boundaries define governments that serve populations with different levels of income, mixes of industry, inherited infrastructure, and personal characteristics. Whereas on the one hand, technological, demographic, and value changes drive the metropolis to constant reconstruction and renewal, on the other hand government boundaries and institutions remain relatively fixed. The result is (1) uneven distribution of benefits and costs among governments and (2) political problems. Reactive public policies sometimes intensify the problems so that all too often "solutions" simply create more problems.[1]

The most dramatic change in metropolitan areas has been the surge of population and economic activity into the cities and then out to the suburbs. There has also been a constant regional shifting of people and economic activity nationally. Less visible but equally dramatic in their influence on urban life have been changes in political participation, attitudes toward equity, and family behavior.

Governmental structures have changed as well (but more slowly than organizational forms in the private sector). Boundaries have shifted, new governments have been created, and functions have been redistributed. In general, older central cities suffer more than suburbs, but the poorer suburbs have been the most fiscally troubled of all localities.

The technology and culture of a new period usually clash with the technology and culture of the past. The tendency of capital and governmental institutions to stay put only aggravates any possible adjustment. Too often the resistance to change is so strong that only a perception that urban governments are in crisis will mobilize a community for action. Change does take place, but the unintended consequences of a shift in policy often seem to dwarf the anticipated results.

Given this complex sociohistoric context, the economic and fiscal problems of the metropolis are understandably complex. This chapter discusses the demand for and supply of local government services from the perspective of efficiency analysis and redistribution of resources. Market and games models are presented, as well as such issues as cost considerations and economies of scale. When appropriate, the concepts are applied to central cities and suburbs as distinct entities. Finally, the chapter looks at the changing federal role and the effect of the tax limitation movement on the ever changing and fragmented metropolis.

The fragmented metropolis

The metropolis is a product of its history, reflecting current objectives and know-how as filtered through a decades-long obstacle course of goals and institutions. Because metropolitan areas develop and grow over different periods, those that were founded in the era of the automobile, for example, are very different from those that were established during the age of the tall ships. Changing technology, social values, governmental roles, individual preferences, and demographics all leave their mark. Changes in the technology of production, energy sources and uses, communications, and transportation, for example, have altered the relative advantages of location in different regions of the country and within metropolitan areas. Less important, but still significant, are such social changes as an increase in leisure time, which gives workers more time to commute and an incentive to invest more heavily in a home away from the central city.

All metropolitan areas are continuously adapting, but the burdens of change are very unequal among them. In older metropolitan areas changes have created a massive redistribution of activities over space. As a result, major capital resources have been scrapped and whole neighborhoods have vanished or have been altered drastically as streets, utility networks, and buildings, built for an earlier technology, have been relocated.

Since metropolitan areas are part of a competitive market economy, those with greater adjustment costs suffer the most. Obsolescent urban capital results in costly production processes, leads to higher taxes, discourages business and residential investment, and causes losses in tax revenues. This process then inhibits public improvements, thereby furthering obsolescence—a destructive cycle that ends, finally, in decline and abandonment (although it may be succeeded by renewal sometime in the future). Newer metropolitan areas are spared the enormous burdens created by an obsolescent capital stock. Their turn may come, however, as technological change continues to alter relative geographical advantages, and still newer cities are born to compete with older ones.

Older central cities and troubled suburbs

The fiscal health of a city is related to its age. Older cities usually have a greater accumulation of physical and social problems than newer cities, which have been active in annexation so that new industries and suburban growth are located within their borders. In 1977 Richard P. Nathan and Charles Adams compiled an index of urban health indicators for the central cities of the major metropolitan areas.[2] The index is a composite of ratios of central city social and economic indicators to those of their suburbs. The numbers range from 422 for Newark (in very poor shape) to 67 for Seattle (in great shape). Table 2–1 shows the index number for each city. If the set of cities were divided into three age groups, the unweighted mean index of the oldest group would be 209; of the middle group, 143; and of the youngest group, 127. The age of the city was measured from the census year in which the city reached a population of at least 200,000. The population of the oldest group reached that size by 1900, while that of the youngest group reached it in 1930 or later. The contrast is seen most sharply in comparing the oldest group of cities with the younger groups. Only one city in the younger group had an index that was poorer than the mean for the oldest.

The relative cost of renewal versus new development on clear land is dramatically evident in the metropolitan area. As a consequence, the central city of a declining metropolitan area will suffer more grievously the burden of competitive disadvantage than will other parts of the area. Disadvantages are magnified since the costs of relocating among sites within a metropolitan area are small and movement is relatively frequent; therefore, cumulative processes are accelerated. All changes, especially the dynamic trends advantageous to newer suburbs, are generally magnified by the existence of old boundaries. The advantages to a new suburb are contained within its boundaries; the losses are suffered by the older city (see Table 2–1).

Table 2–1 Index of central city disadvantage relative to balance of SMSA, by age group of central cities, 1972.

Oldest		Middle age		Younger	
Newark	422	Atlanta	226	Dayton	211
Cleveland	331	Rochester	215	Richmond	209
Baltimore	256	Youngstown	180	San Jose	181
Chicago	245	Columbus	173	Miami	172
St. Louis	231	Akron	152	Fort Worth	149
New York	211	Kansas City	152	Sacramento	135
Detroit	210	Denver	143	Birmingham	131
Philadelphia	205	Jersey City	129	Oklahoma City	128
Boston	198	Indianapolis	124	Grand Rapids	119
Milwaukee	195	Providence	121	Tampa	107
Buffalo	189	Toledo	116	Syracuse	103
New Orleans	168	Los Angeles	105	Omaha	98
Louisville	165	Portland	100	Dallas	97
Cincinnati	148	Seattle	67	Houston	93
Pittsburgh	146			Phoenix	85
Minneapolis	131			Norfolk	82
San Francisco	105			San Diego	77
Mean	209	Mean	143	Mean	127

Sources: Central City Disadvantage Index from Richard P. Nathan and Charles F. Adams, Jr., *Revenue Sharing: The Second Round* (Washington, D.C.: Brookings Institution, 1977), p. 86. The index is a composite of city-suburban relationships in regard to unemployment, education, dependent population, income, crowded housing, and poverty. The oldest group of cities reached 200,000 population before 1900, the younger reached that size after 1930, and the middle cities, unsurprisingly, were in between. Population was from various U.S. Censuses of Population.

It is accurate to emphasize the tensions and differences between the central city and the suburb, but it is important to remember that suburbs range from exclusive country club communities to the poorest of neighborhoods.

There have always been poor outlying communities that became engulfed in the wave of metropolitan expansion but remained poor, because it was more profitable to develop new areas. Many suburbs have the same problems as central cities. They have a disproportionately large share of low-income population, large or fast-growing minority populations, population loss, old housing stock, low educational levels, high crime rates, elderly population, and high unemployment. Furthermore, suburbs have become more heterogeneous. The central city has remained relatively fixed while the urban area has grown, with the suburbs absorbing more of the average cross section of the population.

Just as every central city has poor and affluent neighborhoods, every metropolitan statistical area (MSA) has distressed and opulent suburbs. Though troubled suburbs can exist in any MSA, they tend to be associated with declining central cities, where urban growth is concentrated in the fringe suburbs and in the nonmetropolitan area bordering the MSA.[3]

In fact, distressed suburbs are usually worse off than central cities; the latter usually have some posh neighborhoods and enough space to add new industry, whereas the former have no such capacity. Even when a new industry locates in the suburbs, the central city still has a large industrial base and low transportation costs, making it advantageous for workers to locate in the central city if they can find a reasonable neighborhood. Those who work in the central city may choose to live there because of congestion and long distances to the border. However, commuting to the borders of a suburb is relatively easy, and it is not costly for workers to move beyond the borders of the suburb where they work. Since movement costs out of the suburb are relatively low, the process of cumulative decay can proceed more rapidly there, if the conditions are ripe.[4]

Technological, political, and social change

Governmental boundaries and intergovernmental fiscal relations are influenced by technological, political, and social change, each of which affects the relative prosperity of the various jurisdictions in a metropolitan area.

Technological change Technological change not only determines the location and nature of industrial development, but also changes the relations among governments; however, the scientific and technological advances that have spurred the private sector to develop large plants and firms have moved government much more slowly. Although one might expect large government units to arise to exploit new technologies and manage large public service plants more effectively, this has not been the case. Instead, the boundaries of general governments have remained fixed; limited, special-purpose governments have emerged; and an increasingly complex set of exchange relations among governments has resulted. What might have become a single metropolitan service, if new technology with economies of scale had free rein, has become a complex structure of small local services with contractual or service relationships with large units. Even when new technology has been introduced, the overlapping sets of governments are ill-equipped to adopt it.

Technology has played a role on the demand side of government as well. Improvements in transportation and communications have reduced the costs of influencing higher and more distant levels of government, and they have made it easier for citizens to voice their concern about policy choices in these arenas. Since there are political pressures for governments to treat all districts within their jurisdiction equally, the shift to higher levels results in more uniformity in local services.

Political change Political constituencies have changed and so has the urban political economy. Democratization in participation and policy has brought all of society into city hall; equalization has changed the distribution of services and taxes; and the scope of government has been greatly expanded by the growth of welfare services. Given the new political economy, the preferences, wealth, and activities of neighbors who share in the collective choice become very important in determining the influence of the government on the individual. Moving just a few blocks across an "arbitrary" political boundary, for example, may put a citizen into a collective choice group of a very different social composition. The result is a mosaic of governments facing citizens, who may find it easier to move to a government of their choice rather than incur the political costs of changing their current government. The rich, in particular, have become mobile.[5]

Such political changes have increased metropolitan problems. As more local and national governments have become increasingly responsive to the demands of lower income groups, they have found it more difficult to respond efficiently to technological change.

Social change Two major social revolutions in the 1970s and 1980s have been the movement of women into the marketplace and overall changes in the structure of the family. The early post–World War II period was characterized by marriage, motherhood, and the nuclear family living in a detached house with space for the family to grow. Personal investment was concentrated in the house and its furnishings. Public investment was concentrated on amenities to support suburbanized families. Dramatic changes occurred over the next decades: children matured; women entered the labor force bringing with them a lifetime commitment to careers outside the home; government replaced women as supporters of aged parents and of the sick; and household size shrank. The drastically changed family altered the supply of labor and the demand for housing. Demographic changes have been almost as dramatic as technological changes in altering the relative merits of location in different parts of the metropolitan area. Spacious backyards, for example, can become a burden to a working couple whose income allows them to adopt an active life-style. With the virtues of yesteryear becoming passé, new areas just outside of the MSAs may find themselves transformed.[6]

Political boundaries

Boundaries define institutions, constrain policy, and nurture nostalgia and vested interests in such a way that many persons have a stake in their retention. Neither boundaries nor the mix of activities within borders are part of any natural order. Drawing a boundary is a policy decision influenced by the workings of the political economy, the reshuffling of functions among levels of governments, the transfers of revenues among these levels, and the introduction of new layers of special governments. Drawing, retaining, and reconstituting boundaries are among the most difficult tasks in the political process. To the legislator, the number of those injured by a change often seems to equal the number of those benefiting.

Boundaries often represent institutional obsolescence that may inhibit efficiency as much as do narrow streets, ancient subways, or corroding sewers. Whereas the man-made topography of metropolitan areas (e.g., road networks and settlement densities) has changed dramatically, the lines defining the political jurisdictions of the region have barely shifted in comparison. The persistence of rigid political boundaries is not only a manifestation of institutional sluggishness; it can also be an instrument of defense against the high redistributive taxation that an influx of low-income groups into the local government unit may cause. Sharing a community with the poor means paying for their social services and considering their preferences in collective decision making. Thus boundaries become protective barriers when zoning ordinances are enacted to discourage the entry of the disadvantaged. However, excluding the disadvantaged from some communities in a metropolitan area means a relative increase in their proportions in others. The result is increasing fiscal disparity among the communities. In a period of strong political movement toward equalization, these disparities have led to greater reliance on central taxation and intergovernmental transfers to equalize services and payments for services.

The possibility of boundary changes—a more direct response to the problem and sometimes a more efficient solution—is usually ignored. One prominent study of urban problems concludes:

> Nearly all U.S. metropolitan areas have failed to reform those institutions and practices that perpetuate or aggravate the problems of urban decline for one reason: too many people benefit from the existing arrangements. That is why radical restructuring of urban areas seems so unlikely. Hence it forms an unsuitable foundation for any realistic program for improving urban conditions.[7]

The fixed boundaries of the older central cities are a major factor in their decline relative to the growth of suburbs. They have remained stable while newer cities in the Sun Belt have grown by annexation at their peripheries. Between 1950 and 1970, 188 already large cities almost doubled in area. However, Northeastern cities increased in area by only 2 percent, Western cities by 68 percent, North Central cities by 82 percent, and Southern cities by 224 percent. The regional differences persisted into the 1980s. In 1980–83 New England and Middle Atlantic cities accounted for only 0.2 percent of annexations despite the fact that they contained 16 percent of the population.[8]

There is no theory of boundaries explaining where boundaries are drawn, but there is a theory of the size of governments, of assignment of functions, and of transfers among governments that can explain why boundaries are established and maintained and the consequences of their existence. This theory, part of welfare economics, is derived from a study of the failures of the market to achieve a social optimum. Public policies are built solely around the correction of market shortcomings, not the feasibility of public intervention. Although weak on the discussion of the institutions that would be necessary or useful for implementing policy (there is no body of analysis that incorporates decision making about costs and benefits at the legislative and administration levels), the theory shows that government failure will equal or exceed the market failures that the government programs are supposed to correct.[9]

Individuals and firms can cross local boundaries easily and, in fact, most economic exchanges do cross local geographic borders. The permanent movement of occupants is usually a mixed blessing because while in-migrants increase the volume of taxable resources, they also increase costs. The residents of a municipality or a school district are a tax-sharing collective; new members help pay the costs of the services, but may also cause the costs to increase. Thus, a new resident imposes fiscal economies and diseconomies on all current residents. The most desirable in-migrant is wealthy, disdains using public services, and votes with the majority.

The economics of metropolitan areas

The following section discusses issues that affect the demand for and supply of public services in a metropolitan area. Demand factors depend on the characteristics of the residents—their preferences, incomes, and collective choices. The supply factors are costs of services and economies of scale, and externalities or spillovers in production and consumption. This analysis also considers the decision making of policymakers and those issues that seem to be main determinants of change in the near future.

Demand for local government services

The analysis of demand for public services includes simultaneous consideration of two major roles of government: (1) efficiency in matching services and tastes (a predominant role in the suburbs) and (2) redistribution of resources to the deprived (predominant in the central cities).

Efficiency analysis of the suburbs Suburbs are often viewed by public choice analysts either as the source of metropolitan fiscal problems or (less commonly) as a model of future urban life. Some critics see suburbs as draining the central city of its wealth and suburban residents as exploiting the central city's infrastructure. These critics maintain that the fragmented governments serving the suburbs inhibit the development of an orderly and effective policy for the metropolitan area.[10] In contrast, defenders of the suburbs view them as a competitive market of many governments from which citizens can choose a package of taxes and services best suited to their needs. These defenders view competition among suburbs for shopping centers or subdivisions not as anarchy but as a healthy spur to make a city more attractive.

Efficiency analysis, in its simplest form, views the metropolis as a set of competing communities, all of which are similarly located with respect to jobs, shopping, topography, and other features. The analysis focuses on only two of the many factors that enter into an individual's choice of residential location: the value of the public services to a resident and the tax price he or she must pay.

The tax price is the taxes paid by the household divided by the quantity of government services provided to it. It is assumed that each suburb offers a different package of public services at a different tax price.[11] The simple prediction of this analysis is that individuals will sort themselves into cities of homogeneous groupings where everyone is pleased with the public package he or she receives. This prediction is farfetched if it is supposed to reflect reality; nevertheless, efficiency analysis should not be summarily rejected because, as the following discussion shows, it does in fact capture some important behavioral characteristics of the suburban world. Furthermore, it is an influential force in the discussion of metropolitan policy.

In the theoretical suburban "utopia," individuals have sorted themselves among communities according to their preferences for such services as police, recreation, and education. The theory holds that a commodity bought at any uniform price (the tax price) will be purchased by individuals in amounts sufficient to meet their marginal needs. Therefore, every purchaser in the community reveals the same preference. Because preferences are related to levels of education and income, homogeneity should extend to socioeconomic class characteristics as well. For some economists this "clublike" picture of suburbs represents an optimal world.

In the suburban utopia, the government represents the citizenry, making sure that an optimal set of public services is provided. The government need not produce the services itself, however. For instance, instead of employing street cleaning crews, the government could mount an antilitter campaign, impose fines for littering, or contract with a private firm or another government to clean the streets. The decision to allocate resources (public or private) to clean streets is a collective governmental decision, but how to deliver the service should be decided on grounds of efficiency. Some argue that the smaller the suburb the more efficient the choice of level and quality of services and method of production. They assert that a smaller city with a more homogeneous population would be able to rely on persuading a cooperative citizenry to curb their dogs or do whatever else is necessary to reduce the need for public services. A further argument holds that the level of public services is a compromise among groups with very different preferences. As a consequence, the argument goes, too much service may be provided. Political minorities who have to be cajoled into joining the majority coalition receive benefits far beyond what might have been efficient for most residents. Therefore, it is argued, a heterogeneous community with a government formed by a coalition of minorities will be larger and less efficient than a homogeneous suburb.

The three conditions necessary to approximate the "utopian" world of suburbs are summarized below:

1. If economies of scale in production exist, then an institutional mechanism is necessary to foster efficiencies in the smaller cities.
2. User charges or a tax based on the marginal costs of service should be used, rather than the ad valorem property tax. This would ensure that all citizens pay a tax price that conforms to the costs of the services provided.
3. A zoning mechanism is necessary since the marketlike sorting out of persons will be unstable. Government controls also are necessary to prevent negative fiscal spillovers from in-migrations, a source of instability.

Economies of scale in public services are one factor operating against the suburban utopia. If there were significant economies of scale, governments would grow very large, cities would become few in number, and households would be unable to find a community that would provide their preferred service and tax-price package. Advocates of the competitive local government model suggest that this problem could be bypassed with the adoption of contractual arrangements among governments. If significant economies of scale are possible, a county or a large city could produce the service and supply varying amounts to the smaller communities in the area. The charge for the service would be determined by the supplier and each community. While this is now being done, more common is the creation of regional bodies or the use of counties to provide areawide services, ranging from the complete handling of a function to assisting locals. In the suburban utopia model, the city or county becomes a cooperative purchasing agency for public services rather than a producer of them. The objective is to achieve efficiency in supply and to provide smaller communities the opportunity to consume only as much as they want or need. Otherwise, these smaller areas would be bound by the collective decision of a larger, more heterogeneous population of divergent preferences.

Economies of scale Economies of scale are cost savings or other returns that increase on a per-unit basis with the size of the production effort. Quite simply, some services—water supply is a good example—are provided most efficiently on a large scale, as the total cost of production is spread out over a greater number of consumers.

A second factor that operates against the suburban utopia is the local tax system. Local governments rely heavily on the ad valorem property tax, which is based on the value of a house. A person with a more highly valued house pays a higher tax price than a person with a lower valued house. Both receive the same amount of street maintenance and educational and recreational services. Thus, the wealthier person may find it advantageous to move to a city that has more wealthy residents to share the cost of public services. For example, two towns may have identical public services costing a total of $100,000. In the wealthier community are 100 families with houses valued at $50,000. To support $100,000 in public services, the tax rate is 2 percent on property worth $5 million. In the poorer community are 99 families with $10,000 homes and 1 family with a $50,000 home. To support the same level of services, the tax rate is 9.5 percent on a tax base of $1.04 million. The family with the $50,000 home in the poorer community is paying a tax of almost $5,000. The families with $10,000 houses are paying the same 9.5 percent tax rate, but due to their lower-valued homes their actual payments are only $950. If the wealthy family moves to the wealthy community, where the tax rate is 2.0 percent, they will pay $1,000 on a $50,000 house. Thus, the use of an ad valorem property tax might break the expected homogeneity by preference groups in favor of a greater homogeneity by income classes. Residents would sort themselves according to income rather than tastes. Of course, those who argue the efficiency of the suburban utopia prefer taxing according to benefits received rather than wealth, which, in the case of homogeneous communities, would be a uniform price.

Mobility is the third force operating against the attainment of the suburban utopia. The flight of the middle and upper classes to the suburbs poses a serious problem for the central city. But the poor also can move.[12] A poor person might find that a wealthy suburb provides more public services than he or she prefers; however, at the lower tax rate it may be advantageous to live there.

This kind of mobility is discouraged by fiscal zoning, by which suburbs authorize the land use that has the highest public revenues less the increase of public costs. This tends to zone out low-value housing structures. Thus, while mobility is not forbidden, the price of moving into an upper-income suburb is increased due to the zoning restrictions.

A natural consequence of this tendency toward segregation is fiscal disparity among communities, frequently deplored because it hinders local efforts to redistribute resources. Local governments cannot be expected to perform a redistributive role if the poor and the rich are not members of one community. Only the central city is likely to remain heterogeneous, because it extends over a large area and encompasses a large population of all socioeconomic classes.

Although the theory of the differentiation among suburbs and homogeneity within a suburb is well developed, there is little to support it. In fact, the one careful study of homogeneity among suburbs found that while a sorting of socioeconomic groups does exist, it is a far cry from the "clublike" suburb implied in the model of efficient suburbia. For instance, Howard Pack and Janet Rothenberg Pack found that only 11 percent of suburban towns in Pennsylvania were homogeneous in regard to income. Forty percent of the towns were homogeneous with respect to either occupation, education, or household type.[13] If a "clublike" community is considered homogeneous in regard to at least three of the five qualities of income, education, occupation, age, and household type, then only 15 percent of the Pennsylvania suburbs would qualify. It is interesting to note that the Packs found that the most homogeneous communities are best characterized as family communities with blue-collar, poorly educated, and relatively low-income residents; the least homogeneous communities are professional towns, with well-educated and relatively high-income residents.

Redistribution of resources in the central city Redistribution is carried out most frequently in the central city rather than in the suburbs, and it is one of the factors contributing to the relative decline of the central city. In general the wealthy pay more in taxes than the value of the public services they receive. Therefore, there is an incentive for them to leave any city that responds to the political mood of redistribution. The out-migration of the wealthy makes it difficult for a typical city to carry on redistribution with its own resources. At one time the central city had adequate fiscal resources. Over time, however, the in-migration of the poor was so large and the out-migration of the wealthy so extensive that even with the vast commercial and industrial activity within its borders, the central city foundered under its redistributive tasks. At the same time the suburbs often adopt antigrowth policies to prevent lower-income residents from moving into their precincts.

The forms of income redistribution are (1) equalization of government services across neighborhoods; (2) increased services to the poor to correct their inadequate capacity to earn income; and (3) cash transfers to the poor to compensate them for their low incomes. These three forms of redistribution have very different bases in political support and different program implications, but all of them complicate the governance of the metropolitan area.

Redistribution by equalization of services across neighborhoods has significant fiscal effects. The ideal of the suburban utopia came close to realization in an earlier, pre-redistributional age by a simple choice of neighborhoods within a central city. The streets of the well-to-do were better lighted and cleaned more regularly. Their parks were better maintained. Their schools were better staffed. The wealthy paid more to the community and they received more from it. Since then, discrimination in services to the rich and poor has been reduced, increasing the unfavorable spread between tax costs and public service to the wealthy. Of course, some countervailing forces have reduced the fiscal burden on the wealthy. The property tax has become less significant for central cities, assessment biases tend to underestimate the assessed values of the more expensive properties, and deductibility of property tax on federal income taxes has historically resulted in a relatively lower net tax price for the upper-income groups.

Redistribution by providing increased services to the poor has taken the form of public investment in health, education, and welfare. Much of this activity is a simple transfer of resources in kind with the objective of providing those services by which the poor can rise above their poverty. Often these services are provided by the county rather than the municipality, with the burden remaining heaviest on the county that encompasses the central city.

For the central city, the losses of economic wealth due to equalization are compounded by the fact that the costs of equal education, health, and police services are greater for the poor than for the average resident. The central city spends far more per capita than do the suburbs on noneducational services. The central city urban poor are culturally differentiated. The delivery costs of human services are increased because these services bear the extra tasks of integrating minorities into the dominant culture. If the services to the poor were made equal to those of the well-to-do, the budget and taxes would have to rise considerably. Otherwise, equality could be achieved only at a lower service level for the entire community and with a significant reallocation of the service budget from wealthy to poor neighborhoods. In reality, costs have risen and the level of services has fallen. Relative to that of the suburbs, the fiscal base of the central cities has been steadily declining, and the tax rate has been growing at a higher rate. One consequence has been a further decline in the desirability of the central city as a place of residence for the upper- and middle-income groups. Another consequence has been the greater burden placed on the suburbs. Although the incremental costs of providing central city services will not appear explicitly in the local tax bill of the suburban resident, the price to the suburbanite is an increase in the state and federal taxes required to support the burden of the central city. Though relatively more state and federal aid goes to central cities, their relatively greater expenditures have resulted in a much greater tax burden.[14]

Redistribution by cash transfers to the poor has taken the form of income assistance to a variety of disadvantaged groups. Aid to Families with Dependent Children, Supplemental Security Income, and unemployment insurance are cases of cash transfers. The basic Old Age and Survivors Insurance is not means tested but the pension formula provides for a significant redistribution to the lower incomes. These cash transfers are supplemented by significant in-kind transfers such as Medicare, food stamps, and housing assistance. The higher incidence of the problem population in the central city ensures that as transfers to individuals grow (while fiscal support to governments declines), governments with a higher proportion of disadvantaged will have a more advantageous fiscal balance with the federal government.

In general, the sources of "overspending" by central cities are not clearly understood, and policymakers find it difficult to shape a policy to reduce the fiscal disparity when lacking adequate explanation.[15] Nevertheless, the central city remains a vital part of the metropolitan area, both in its key downtown services and its function in the absorption of new members of the labor force. The in-migration to the metropolitan area may have been a shock to the older residents, but the new population is there, and it must be housed, educated, doctored, policed, and employed.

Supply of local government services

Many of the same forces of supply and demand that characterize the private sector apply to the local public sector as well. Whereas it may seem unusual to apply the economic language of private markets to the supply of goods and services provided by a set of governments in a metropolitan area, the market metaphor is useful.

The private market supply of goods is considered to be the various amounts that are produced at different prices. The relationship between the quantity of output and the price depends on the costs of input, the technical characteristics of production, the entrepreneurial goal of profit maximization, and the structure of competition among the entrepreneurs. These factors, taken together with the characteristics of demand, will determine the amounts of different commodities produced, their prices, and their distribution.

Certainly the behavior of local governments depends on input costs, production conditions, and competition among governments. The major difference is that the objective of government decision makers cannot easily be represented as profit maximization. Furthermore, the demand for public services is not registered by discrete sales, and the maze of legal constraints on government behavior is much greater than that facing the private firm.

The market and games models Two models have been proposed to explain the decisions of a local government: the market model and the games model.[16] The market model views the government as analogous to a firm and equates the marginal benefit of each service to the marginal cost. The games model views the government as an arena of conflicting groups, each seeking the allocation of services and costs that would be to its advantage. The test of leadership is to control the conflict and create a coalition that keeps a party in office. There is no firm evidence to suggest which model is generally applicable, or which type of government the models approximate.[17] However, there is a strong tendency to associate the market model with suburbs and the games model with central cities.

The market model has been implicitly discussed earlier in the description of suburbs as "clublike" communities. But why should local leadership respond to marketlike forces? And how do these forces work to implement residents' demands? The answer is found in the way citizens express their preferences—either by voting for the candidates who are more likely to provide the preferred public service tax package, or by moving to a jurisdiction that more closely approximates the desired package. Given the great frequency of moving and the low incidence of political participation in the suburbs, it is likely that "voting with one's feet" is the more important mode of expression.[18]

The link between individual mobility and the incentives for the political leadership to satisfy residents' demands is land values. If the community public service tax package is attractive, the demand for residences will increase and land values will rise. On the other hand, if public services are not satisfactory, demand will decline, land values will fall, and residents will leave. This will stimulate political action to change the service package.

Although a rise in land values is a boon to most residents, it can be a bane to others. Bitter conflicts often arise between environmentalists (antigrowth) and developers (pro-growth). For example, where improved local services and growth programs lead to increases in land values, they are often accompanied by higher density and loss of some amenities. Local residence usually encourages the adoption of zoning ordinances that curb and reduce development in order to preserve and enhance environmental amenities.

In the games model as applied to the central city, an increase in jobs rather than an increase in land values is the goal; jobs satisfy the demands of the disadvantaged, who are so great in number. Public jobs should be viewed as costs necessary to produce useful outputs, but in the arena of city governmental politics, expenditures that create jobs become the "benefits" over which to fight. Instead of minimizing costs (which would enable the city to become more competitive), expenditures for jobs expand costs to provide jobs and stability to agencies. Survival, not efficiency, dominates the political agenda. In central cities, the defenders of many massive spending programs have not been able to find any benefits other than increased employment. Nevertheless, these created jobs are sufficient to attract powerful constituencies.

The distinction between the models for suburbs and big cities is so extreme that it may appear to be a caricature. Certainly, suburbanites have their moments of fighting over shares, and many urban areas have undergone a remarkable renaissance as the efficiency of the core of the central city improves. However, the contrast captures the distinctive features of suburban competitive behavior and the central city's preoccupation with distribution.

Cost considerations and economies of scale Costs are the value of the resources necessary to produce a service (output). With different production technologies, average (or unit) costs may decrease, remain constant, or increase as output increases. For most production processes, however, it is believed that initially unit costs decrease sharply as output increases; a long period of constant unit costs follows, and then, as output increases beyond a critical point, unit costs begin to increase. Big cities that grow beyond a certain point will find that their unit costs rise as population rises, not decrease as would be expected. In 1982–83 the per capita general expenditures of cities over 1 million population were $1,388, whereas for cities under 50,000, they were only $396.[19]

Regarding economies of scale, it is difficult to define an efficient scale for a service; it is clear, however, that there is often a mismatch between sizes of jurisdictions and efficient units of production. The interest in economies of scale focuses on a set of related problems: (1) determination of the optimal-sized jurisdiction; (2) assignment of functions to levels of government; and (3) optimal pattern of decentralization.

Economies of scale can be realized for functions that can be effective only if they are carried out for an entire system. In these instances, as the number of municipalities entering into a common planning and decision making unit rises, the quality of output rises per unit of input. For example, the roads in a metropolitan area need to be consistent in vehicle capacity and direction because they go through many cities. On the negative side, air pollution controls also must be consistent; they make little sense if each municipality monitors only its own facilities and pays little attention to the activities of other cities.

Economies of scale also are possible for functions requiring heavy capital investment, especially in distribution systems. Water supply and sewage disposal are classic examples of services few suburban municipalities can perform cost effectively on their own. Instead, they may turn to multipurpose metropolitan-wide special districts. Or they may contract with a large government for that part of the production process that has economies of scale. For instance, a smaller municipality may purchase its water from a central city whose system is large enough to justify dams and extensive pipelines; the local police department may purchase crime analysis from a sophisticated county or state laboratory; or the local government may contract with another government instead of providing services itself. The local government, as a residents' representative, would specify the terms of the contract and then monitor the service. Flexibility in intergovernmental contracting can frequently sever the relationship between economies of scale and size of government.

Figure 2–1 summarizes the results of some historic studies of economies of scale in local public services. The one clear point that emerges is that there is no unique size at which a community can be called efficient. Many services that are characterized by constant costs could be packaged together in municipalities of different sizes without any loss of efficiency. Other services can be produced efficiently only by a larger jurisdiction or one that has the capacity to market its excess output. In general, all services in a central city have reached at least the lowest point on their average cost curves and some are in the stage of increasing costs. However, there is likely to be more variety in the suburbs because many small cities cannot produce all of the services.

Studies of economies of scale in local public services are inconclusive, however. While most studies measure expenditures on a per capita basis, this measure is incomplete because quality varies. For instance, low public per capita expenditures on streets may lead to high private costs if congested streets lead to inefficient traffic flow. Without an accurate measure of public output holding everything reasonably constant as the size of a facility or a jurisdiction increases, it is difficult to relate variation in expenditures with size of output or even with level of activity. For big central cities an increasing per capita (unit) cost usually implies that production should be decentralized. For small suburbs it implies that some services should be centralized.[20]

Because of the variation of economies of scale, an amazing number of special districts, regional authorities, commissions, local offices of state agencies, and bureaus have proliferated in metropolitan areas. In fact, the many small governments of suburbia are viable primarily because these organizations have been created to take advantage of economies of scale. These may operate as independent governments or as arms of other governments. They can be fully integrated suppliers of services or they can be contractors to other governments. The diversity is so great that it has been difficult for the Census of Governments to

Figure 2–1 Results of studies of scale economies in local public services.

Average costs are declining:
- Electricity[1]
- Sewage plants[2]
- Gas[3]
- Water[4]

Average costs are about horizontal:
- Elementary schools[5]
- Police protection[6]
- Refuse collection[7]

Average costs are U-shaped with trough at different points:
- High schools[8]
- Fire protection[9]
- Hospitals[10]
- School administration[11]

Sources: Adapted from Werner Z. Hirsch, *Urban Economics* (New York: Macmillan, 1984), pp. 270–74.

1 Marc Nerlove, *Returns to Scale in Electricity Supply* (Stanford, Cal.: Institute for Mathematical Studies in the Social Sciences, Stanford Univ., 1961), p. 11; and Jack Johnston, *Statistical Cost Analysis* (New York: McGraw-Hill, 1960).

2 Walter Isard and Robert E. Coughlin, *Municipal Costs and Revenues* (Wellesley, Mass.: Chandler-Davis, 1957), p. 76.

3 K. S. Lomax, "Cost Curves for Gas Supply," *Bulletin of the Oxford Institute of Statistics* 13 (1951).

4 Lawrence G. Hines, "The Long-Run Cost Function of Water Production for Selected Wisconsin Communities," *Land Economics* 45 (1969): 133–40; and James R. Marsten et al., "The Large-Scale Regional Planning Hypothesis: Discriminant Analysis," *Water Resources Research* 11 (1975): 1013–17.

5 H. J. Kiesling, "Measuring and Local Government Service: A Study of School Districts in New York State," *Review of Economics and Statistics* 49 (August 1967); and Werner Z. Hirsch, "Determinants of Public Education Expenditures," *National Tax Journal*, March 1960.

6 N. Walzer, "Economies of Scale and Municipal Police Services," *Review of Economics and Statistics* 54 (1972): 431–38.

7 W. Z. Hirsch, "Cost Functions of an Urban Government Service: Refuse Collection," *Review of Economics and Statistics* 47 (February 1965).

8 J. Riew, "Economies of Scale in High School Operation," *Review of Economics and Statistics* 48 (August 1966); and J. C. Hambor et al., "Optimal Community Educational Attainments: A Simultaneous Equation Approach," *Review of Economics and Statistics* 55 (1972): 98–103.

9 R. E. Will, "Scalar Economies and Urban Service Requirements," *Yale Economic Essays* 5 (Spring 1965); and W. Z. Hirsch, "Expenditure Implications of Metropolitan Growth and Consolidation," *Review of Economics and Statistics* 41 (August 1959).

10 K. K. Ro, "Determinants of Hospital Costs," *Yale Economic Essays* 8 (Fall 1968); and H. A. Cohen, "Variations in the Cost among Hospitals of Different Sizes," *Southern Economic Journal* 33 (January 1967).

11 W. Z. Hirsch, "Expenditure Implications of Metropolitan Growth and Consolidation," *Review of Economics and Statistics* 41 (August 1959).

find an adequate definition of government to measure and classify the organizations it surveys.

Table 2–2 shows the number of "official" local governments inside and outside of metropolitan areas. Special districts are the most numerous of these local governments, especially in MSAs. They have the attributes that many analysts would assign to efficient public operations. For instance, they rely on contracts or sales of output rather than taxes.[21] In general, the special district is restricted to one function (87 percent of district expenditures are in single function districts) and thereby less subject to the vagaries of political logrolling. The adaptation of a service area to the technical characteristics of production, the relative insulation from the political hurly-burly, low public visibility, and the use of user charges perhaps imply a more businesslike and efficient service. (User charges and special districts are discussed in detail in Chapter 11.)

Jurisdiction size and public policy Jurisdiction size is a major factor influencing public policy toward local government supply of services and public spending. Whereas an efficiency analysis requires a clear distinction between benefits and costs, in the public sector a clean separation between benefits and costs is not always made. Costs of a program are the inputs (labor and materials) necessary to produce outputs. To the resource owners, the purchase of the inputs (the costs) are *gains*. The resource owners, then, try to influence public decision makers in favor of the programs they supply and, of course, for specific contracts in their favor. If the community is small the resource owners are likely to reside outside the community and their influence may be restricted to political contributions. If the community is large there is much more chance that the resource owners are residents and therefore also voters and members of the many organizations that influence the political system. If the beneficiaries of the costs are "internal" to the jurisdiction, then it is likely that the costs would not be fully and properly interpreted as losses, but partially, at least, as gains. A smaller jurisdiction, where the resource owners are "external" to the jurisdiction, is more likely to view costs in their full negative value. For those who assign importance to efficiency, this is an argument in favor of smaller jurisdictions for decision making.

One of the implications of the above policy would be a relative neglect of distributional values in the smaller jurisdictions. Of course there would still be a concern about the distribution of the outputs but at least the receipt of the costs would not be politically relevant. Therefore, in a world of smaller jurisdictions resource owners would appeal to the central government for a policy that would give weight to their gains. And, in fact, at the national level a great deal of attention is given to the lobbyists of the contractors, professional associations, unions, and so on. The conspiratorial role assigned by some to the military-

Table 2–2 Number of local governments inside and outside metropolitan areas, 1982.

Type of government	Inside MSA	Outside MSA
County	670	2,371
Municipality	7,018	12,058
Township	4,756	11,978
School district	5,692	9,159
Special district	11,725	16,683
Total	29,861	52,429

Source: U.S. Department of Commerce, Bureau of the Census, 1982 Census of Governments, vol. 1 *Governmental Organization*, part 1, *Governmental Organization* (Washington, D.C.: GPO, 1983), p. 42.

industrial complex captures the essence of the role of the supplier in influencing public policy about supply. The belief held by some that a return of more services to self-finance at the local level would lead to a reduction in the scale of services would seem to have support in theory.

Jurisdiction size also influences public policy regarding stabilization programs. Public spending to overcome unemployment is extremely ineffective for a small jurisdiction because much of the impact would leak across the borders. In a large jurisdiction there may be significant contained multiplier effects so that every dollar of public spending would be respent several times within the jurisdiction and would have a magnified effect on sales and employment. For a small jurisdiction the expenditure dollar is quickly spent outside the borders and so has no further beneficial employment effects within the jurisdiction, except to the supplier.

Externalities and spillover effects

When a jurisdiction is small or is restricted in its functions, its taxes or services are likely to impose costs or generate benefits for persons outside its boundaries. When governments adopt programs and policies according to perceived benefits and costs, they are primarily influenced by the benefits and costs that are generated in their jurisdiction and only slightly influenced by those that appear elsewhere. Nevertheless, if externalities become large, overall inefficiencies will emerge.

The three major sources of externalities are (1) the migration of population, (2) the consumption and production activities of commuters, and (3) the costs and benefits from consumption and production activities that operate within narrow city boundaries. Migration externalities are, for example, the costs to educate youth who then move to another city to work and live. Commuter spillovers are the externalities that cause the greatest concern because they are associated with a general feeling that suburbanites "exploit" the central city by using its infrastructure while paying property taxes to their own residential suburb. Nevertheless, the central city gains from commuters through property taxes on the places where they work and shop and through sales taxes on their purchases. Thus, the direction of gains is uncertain. The externalities caused by consumption and production activities pose the most difficult problems. Air or water pollution in one city easily spreads to neighboring cities. Vigilant policing in one city can motivate criminals to move on to neighboring cities. An attractive park will invite usage from neighboring cities.

Innovative governmental responses to externalities have taken several forms, but voluntary agreements among cities are rare. Differences over the contribution from each and feelings of local pride create very difficult bargaining situations. Common solutions include agreements among governments, creation of special bodies to plan and influence the behavior of the individual governments, intergovernmental grants, the reassignment of functions among levels of government, and the creation of commissions with varying degrees of power to encourage or impose overarching solutions in areas where externalities exist. Economists favor open-ended matching grants, which encourage communities to expand their services beyond the level warranted by any perceived internal benefits, because there is no limit on the amount contributed. In principle, the matching grant is supposed to reflect the division of benefits between the local area and the nation or state. In practice, the matching ratio is a political decision. The state or federal agency that grants the funds usually has only a vague idea about the amount of external benefits and so the matching ratios usually bear little relationship to division between internal and external benefits.

The most common response to externalities is an increase in the territorial size of local governments, generally by annexation. Governments rarely merge or create an overall metropolitan government. There have been no systematic studies to evaluate how well these various innovations have succeeded in overcoming externalities, but casual empiricism indicates that it is a mixed story, varying with sources of externality and institutions adopted.[22]

Policy implications

Critics are prone to characterize the governance of metropolitan areas as balkanized and chaotic, suggesting that current systems grew without rhyme or reason. On the contrary, there is a huge body of state and federal legislation directed toward the governance of metropolitan areas, although admittedly many programs conflict with one another.

Federal policy

Governments, especially national governments, have grown dramatically since World War I, and government services and regulations have extended to almost every sector of society—transportation, housing, sewerage, and health services, for example. Major federal policy thrusts have been in three directions. First, federal policies have dealt with the living and working conditions of the poorest members of the population, who occupy the central city in disproportionate numbers. Massive programs, using the city as a contractor to supply services for poverty groups, were developed and categorical grants-in-aid increased the flow of funds to cities (and central cities in particular)—but they were designed to satisfy national redistributional policies, not to improve the urban situation. Federal support peaked in 1978 and under the Reagan administration significant shifts took place. Many categorical programs were consolidated into block grants, with the states playing a more significant allocational role, and the total number of grants was reduced. Public welfare grants have not been reduced as much as grants to support other local programs. The percentage of federal grants going to individuals increased from 31 percent in 1978 to 45.4 percent in 1984.[23] It is too early to proclaim this a major policy shift, but it is a change worth monitoring closely.

Second, grant programs have been designed to create fiscal equity—to redistribute resources to communities with fewer fiscal resources, greater financial problems, and a consequent inability to supply adequate services. For example, the countercyclical economic stimulus package, which included such programs as the Comprehensive Employment and Training Act (CETA), was targeted to hardship cities. This city targeting has been changing to fiscal assistance to communities that provides a broadly defined set of human service programs. Now this too may be a transitional phase as the federal grants shift toward the states and large blocks rather than to the cities and for specific programs. Between 1978 and 1983 federal aid to states as a percentage of state general revenue from own sources fell by 17 percent, while to cities the percentage fell by 37 percent. The absolute amount of federal grants to states rose by 32 percent over this period, while the federal grant level to cities was essentially stationary.[24] The state response to the cutback by the federal government and the continuing need in the metropolitan areas will press the states to maintain the older programs, but future paths can take many other directions.

Third, federal policy has promoted efficiency. Subsidies to public services that are characterized by externalities and economies of scale (e.g., transportation and waste disposal and treatment) were followed by federal support of regional planning and coordinating bodies. At a local and state level there was the proliferation of intergovernmental service supply contracts and the creation of special districts to respond to the same needs. In the seven years between 1977 and 1984, the general revenues of special districts increased by 148 percent, while the general revenues of all local governments increased by 81 percent.[25]

Each of these major policy orientations, although somewhat successful, has exacerbated the problems addressed by other policies. Antipoverty programs have often served as little more than income transfer programs keeping the poor inside the central cities and heightening the fiscal imbalance between the central cities and the suburbs. Fiscal support of central cities has provided some relief, but is has not improved the competitive position of the central city. The innovations in regional planning and special districts have reduced the pressures to correct fiscal imbalances; however, they have not led to the consolidation of services proposed by many reformers.

From the beginning, many federal programs were designed and implemented without consideration of their spatial effects, whereas other programs intentionally fostered regional dispersal and a deconcentration of jobs and population—albeit with little foresight. For example, federally supported freeways and sewerage systems underwrite new suburban shopping centers, but these centers compete with the central city's commercial district, which must then obtain funds from the federal government for downtown renewal.

The most important influence of the federal government on older metropolitan areas has been its encouragement of new private investment. The tax laws have made building new capital facilities more advantageous than maintaining old ones, thereby encouraging new construction on the peripheries of the urban area. Although the underlying motivation was not to move jobs away from the city center, the new laws have had just that effect.

Equally destructive of older urban centers are regulatory policies that discourage the use of rail and highway construction policies that encourage trucking. The central cities, especially the older ones, are less adaptable to trucking. Moreover, the federally underwritten highway program also encourages residential dispersal.

Federal Housing Administration (FHA) and Veterans Administration (VA) mortgage guarantees were a major component in the flight to the suburbs from the central city by the middle classes. These subsidies to finance housing were extended by the income tax provision that allowed the deduction of interest and local tax payments. The subsidy to the new areas was increased by federal grants that reduced the local public capital required for new sewage and water treatment facilities.

The governance of metropolitan areas thus is beset with problems and proposed solutions.[26] Too often the patchwork that exists has not solved all the problems and it is assumed that a larger and administratively more tidy entity would do so. Despite the huge outpouring of writing on urban problems, there is no authoritative understanding of how the problems are linked and therefore no foresight into the consequences of new reform policies. Consolidation creates order, but it generates inefficient uniform distribution of services among diverse areas and dilutes the political power of the poor. Is there a partial solution? Can the patchwork of communities be improved to accommodate diverse objectives, not with the hope of eliminating all problems but to do better? Although there is still no consistent federal urban policy, there has been an increasing awareness of the consequences of various programs and a conscious effort to counteract the unanticipated effects of earlier programs.

The tax limitation movement

By the 1970s the tide of the tax limitation movement appeared to be swelling. In each state the attack on the fiscal system took a different form, such as a limit on specific taxes (e.g., the property tax); a limit on total taxes, expenditures, or appropriations with many different formulas to define the limits; and the specification of procedures to make it difficult to increase expenditures.[27] During this period property tax revenues nationally fell from 3.7 percent of GNP in 1972 to 2.6 percent in 1983.[28]

By the mid-1980s the tax expenditure limitation movement had peaked, state and local taxes had begun to increase again, and the property tax leveled off as a percentage of GNP. Growth was not as rapid as in earlier decades but it was clear that government was not being liquidated. While federal taxes were a declining percentage of GNP through the 1980s, state and local taxes have become an increasing percentage. Overall government taxes declined, but state and local revenues survived the revolt.

State role In many states the limits on the property tax heralded a shift of power to the state government with an increase in state aid. The greatest shift was for school districts, the governments most dependent on the property tax. Thus, although the tax revolt was heralded as a reaction to an unresponsive government, it had the unforeseen effect of increasing the centralization of government and therefore a more distant bureaucracy.

Regulation A second major effect of the tax limitation movement was that governments began to seek to achieve their objectives by regulations rather than by budgetary allocations. This trend became apparent in land development as some developers were required to provide streets, parks, and other elements of the infrastructure as a condition for development permission. Instead of taxing and providing services, the government began to demand the services of private parties. In practice, the percentage of local activity attributable to government policy may be greater under regulation than under public provision of services. The public's conservative drive to limit government may result in a much greater scope for government.

The replacement of public production by regulation raises problems far beyond the scope of this chapter. The vast increase in regulation at the federal level has given rise to an intensive analysis of regulatory practices and their effects on local governments. Nevertheless a fully satisfactory understanding of the regulatory process, the response of the private sector to regulations, or the best way to design regulations is still in the future. The effects of tax and expenditure limits will be felt slowly and the substitution of regulations will be gradual. There will be time for adjusting local management policies.

User charges A third consequence of the tax limitation movement has been an expansion of user charges. In principle and in practice, user charges are not taxes because they are voluntary prices paid by users for the public services they consume. Since user charges are exempt from most tax limitation programs, they are likely to become an increasingly popular form of local government finance. A shift to user charges will sharply reduce the redistributive effect of a local budget by allowing citizens in any community to choose and pay for the services they prefer. Therefore, the fiscal advantages of a flight from the central city and the formation of segregated clublike suburbs will lessen.

The trend toward user charges is also likely to lead to a change in government structure. Some limitation formulas encourage the organization of districts (without taxing powers) and the transfer to some of these districts of functions that had been routine municipal services in the past. For instance, a parking special district, rich with resources from parking fees, might absorb an unprofitable municipal bus service or street maintenance service.

The important point for local financial planners to know is that changes will become necessary and that there will be an increasing need to consider innovations and their implementation across areas. The analysis of the design of user charges for conventional public services is still in its infancy, but the large volume of literature on optimal pricing of public enterprises could help.

The Reagan years

Each presidential administration announces a new federalism policy, often indistinguishable from its predecessors. It is possible, however, that as a consequence of indirect and direct policies the Reagan administration may lead to a significant change in the structure of federal relations and, therefore, of local government.

The Reagan administration had a strong ideological bent toward the reduction of government at all levels and a transfer of responsibility for many social programs to the states and to local governments. Although this trend had begun earlier, the special thrust of the Reagan administration resulted in its reinforcement. The Reagan fiscal policy was to cut income tax rates, increase military expenditures, and force Congress and the administration to cut the civilian part of the budget. Couple these policies with an attitudinal shift toward grant consolidation and simplification and the stage is set for a historic reversal.

The Reagan proposal was to swap some programs, such as a federal absorption of Medicare, for the state and local responsibility for welfare. In addition, there would be a shift from categorical grants to block grants, primarily to the states, and eventually a cutback in federal funding of the grants. In Reagan's first term the number of categorical grants was reduced by more than 25 percent and block grants became 15 percent of federal outlays for grants.[29] Even if you believe that the changes are not massive, it is reasonable to conclude that there has been an impressive reversal of what many would have proclaimed an inexorable trend. However, it is much too early to claim that the trend is more than a cyclical adjustment or to identify the effect on the structure and behavior of local government of the efforts to make the states a more dominating influence.[30]

An epilogue on the future

In a sense, all public policies are deficient because they are designed to deal with *future* problems. A persistent error in social science analysis of which policymakers must be aware is the projection of trends to the distant future, particularly if the projection is based on only a few years of experience. Beginning in the 1960s, for example, the federal government took the initiative in introducing and banking on an enormous array of new programs, and social scientists predicted continued growth of central government. Then all of this peaked in the mid-1970s. Federal aid as a percentage of GNP fell dramatically and total federal expenditures as a percentage of GNP leveled, maintained primarily by growth in defense and Social Security expenditures.[31] It is premature to say yet that the earlier trends have been reversed, but it is clear that the predictions were too firm.

A further complication in planning for the future is that the future behavior of public policies that are planned for are based on a study of past behavior. The most serious case of misapplied knowledge is when military policy is set by generals who were trained to fight the last war. Firm knowledge is limited to past events, but the future may be dominated by forces that were unimportant in the past. This dilemma is as true for metropolitan policy as for any other. Family size has shrunk and working wives are far more evident. The relative costs of energy have changed, the computer revolution rages on, the taxpayer revolt may have weakened but its spectre is everpresent, and environmental concerns have been rising. Each of these trends and many more were in their infancy when current metropolitan governance was shaped. Policymakers, who are necessarily future-oriented, have had to evaluate how these changes may affect costs, preferences, objectives, and alternatives for the future. The analysis of the past has to be sufficiently general to plug in these changes, and the politics of the future will reflect them. The education of those who will determine policy should be sufficiently general so that they may absorb the implication of future technology and life-style.

1 Perspectives from several disciplines can be found in Paul E. Peterson, ed. *The New Urban Reality* (Washington, D.C.: Brookings Institution, 1985). An undauntingly pessimistic view about the efficacy of solutions is taken by Edward C. Banfield in *The Unheavenly City Revisited* (Boston: Little, Brown & Co., 1974). The Advisory Commission on Intergovernmental Relations is one of the many organizations that is persistently optimistic in proposing solutions. See Advisory Commission on Intergovernmental Relations, *Improving Urban America: A Challenge to Federalism,* M–107 (Washington, D.C.: GPO, 1976). A moderate position is presented by Katherine L. Bradbury, Anthony Downs, and Kenneth A. Small, in *Urban Decline and the Future of American Cities* (Washington, D.C.: Brookings Institution, 1982).

2 Richard P. Nathan and Charles Adams Jr., *Revenue Sharing: The Second Round* (Washington, D.C.: Brookings Institution, 1977), p.86; a comparison among the studies of fiscal distress is contained in Roy Bahl, *Financing State and Local Government in the 1980s,* (New York: Oxford, 1984), pp. 58–59; and Robert W. Burchell, et al., *The New Reality of Municipal Finance* (Rutgers, N.J.: Center for Urban Policy Research, 1984), pp. 29–39.

3 Data for this section are taken from Judith Fernandez and John Pincus, *Troubled Suburbs: An Exploratory Study,* A Rand Note, N–1759–HUD (Santa Monica, Cal.: Rand, June 1982). Scanning the most recent data in the U.S. Department of Commerce's annual *County and City Data Book* reveals no changes since then.

4 Fernandez and Pincus, *Troubled Suburbs;* and Bradbury, Downs, and Small, *Urban Decline.*

5 See J. R. Aronson and E. Schwartz, "Financing Public Goods and the Distribution of Population in a System of Local Governments," *National Tax Journal* 26 (June 1973): 137–60.

6 Bradbury, Downs, and Small, *Urban Decline.*

7 Ibid., *Urban Decline,* p. 295.

8 Richard L. Forstall, "Annexations and Corporate Changes Since the 1970 Census: With Historical Data on Annexation for Larger Cities for 1900–1970," in *The Municipal Year Book, 1975* (Washington, D.C.: International City Management Association, 1975), p. 28; Joel C. Miller and Richard L. Forstall, "Annexations and Corporate Changes: 1970–1979 and 1980–83," in *The Municipal Year Book 1984* (Washington, D.C.: International City Management Association, 1984), p. 99; and Joel C. Miller, "Municipal Annexations and Boundary Changes: 1980–83," in *The Municipal Year Book 1985* (Washington, D.C.: International City Management Association, 1985), p. 81. Note that the survey included only 19 Western cities for which data were available for the extended time period covered by the study (1900–70). Several Western cities of more recent rapid growth were *not* included.

9 The new field of public choice aspires to fill the gaps among economic, political, and organizational analysis. See various issues of the journal, *Public Choice,* and Charles Wolf, Jr., "A Theory of Nonmarket Failure: Framework for Implementation Analysis," *Journal of Law and Economics* 12, no. 1 (April 1979).

10 Anthony Downs, *Opening Up the Suburbs* (New Haven, Conn.: Yale Univ. Press, 1973); and Edwin S. Mills and Bruce W. Hamilton, *Urban Economics,* 3d ed. (Glenview, Ill.: Scott, Foresman & Co, 1984).

11 Central cities have taken to the notion of packaging services to be more responsive to the different groups in the city. There was a period, highlighted by the Model Cities program of the Johnson administration, when the goal was to decentralize city hall. It was hoped that a neighborhood political constituency would develop to influence a decentralized administrative structure to make public services more responsive to the different needs of the neighborhoods. This movement was politically popular, but ultimately not very successful.

12 If the poor and the rich are equally mobile, an equilibrium in population distribution between local communities may not exist. For details, see Aronson and Schwartz, "Financing Public Goods."

13 Howard Pack and Janet Rothenberg Pack, "Metropolitan Fragmentation and Suburban Homogeneity," *Urban Studies* 14, no. 2 (June 1977): 191–201.

14 Advisory Commission on Intergovernmental Relations, *Fiscal Disparities: Central Cities and Suburbs, 1981* (Washington, D.C.: GPO, August 1984), p. 12. In 1981 the ratio of per capita aid of central city to outside central city was 163 percent; the ratio of per capita general expenditures of central cities to outside central cities was 139 percent; and the ratio of per capita taxes of central cities to outside central cities was 129 percent.

15 Ibid.

16 Lyle C. Fitch, "Fiscal and Productive Efficiency in Urban Government Systems," in *Metropolitan America,* eds. Amos Hawley and Vincent Rock (New York: Halsted Press, 1975).

17 For a test and review of the arguments, see Robert P. Inman, "The Fiscal Performance of Local Governments: An Interpretive Review," in *Current Issues in Urban Economics,* eds. Peter Mieszkowski and Mahlon Straszheim (Baltimore, Md.: Johns Hopkins Univ. Press, 1979); and Daniel Rubinfeld, "Local Public Economics: A Methodological Review," in Martin Feldstein and Alan Auerbach, eds. *Handbook of Public Economics* (Amsterdam: North-Holland, 1985).

18 On the average, less than a third of the adults vote in municipal elections. See Albert K. Karnig and B. Oliver Walter, "Municipal Elections: Registration, Incumbent Success, and Voter Participation," in *The Municipal Year Book, 1977* (Washington, D.C.: International City Management Association, 1977), pp. 65–72.

19 U.S. Bureau of the Census, *City Government Finances in 1982–83* (Washington, D.C.: GPO, 1984), p.4.

20 For a summary of these studies, see Werner Hirsch, *Urban Economics* (New York: Macmillan, 1984), pp. 270–74; and Advisory Commission on Intergovernmental Relations, *Substate Regionalism and the Federal System,* vol. 4, *Governmental Functions and Processes: Local and Areawide* (Washington, D.C.: GPO, 1974).

21 U.S. Department of Commerce, Bureau of the Census, *1982 Census of Governments,* vol. 4, *Governmental Finances,* no. 2, *Finances of Special Districts* (Washington, D.C.: GPO, 1984), p. 1. In 1982, 7 percent of special district revenues came from property taxes; 27 percent from intergovernmental grants; 28 percent from charges; and 22 percent from utility revenue.

22 The multivolume report of the Advisory Commission on Intergovernmental Relations, *Substate Regionalism and the Federal System* (Washington, D.C., 1974), is an excellent source of information about practices and proposals, but it is, unfortunately, replete with casual evaluation.

23 Advisory Commission on Intergovernmental Relations, *Significant Features of Fiscal Federalism, 1984 Edition* (Washington, D.C.: GPO, March 1985), p. 21.

24 Ibid., p. 62.

25 U.S. Bureau of the Census, 1982 Census of Governments, vol. 6, no. 4, *Historical Statistics on Governmental Finance and Employment* (Washington, D.C.: GPO, 1985), p. 38; and U.S. Bureau of the Census, 1982 Census of Governments, *Governmental Finances in 1983–84* (Washington, D.C.: GPO, 1985), p. 51.

26 For a summary of proposals and arguments, see Peterson, ed., *The New Urban Reality;* Advisory Commission on Intergovernmental Relations, *Improving Urban America;* Alan Campbell and Roy Bahl, eds., *State and Local Governments: The Political Economy of Reform* (New York: Free Press, 1976); Hawley and Rock, eds., *Metropolitan America;* Robert W. Burchell and David Listokin, eds., *Cities Under Stress: The Fiscal Crises of Urban America* (New Brunswick, N.J.: Center for Urban Policy Research, Rutgers Univ., 1981); James H. Carr, ed., *Crisis and Constraint in Municipal Finance* (New Brunswick, N.J.: Center for Urban Policy Research, Rutgers Univ., 1984); U.S. Congressional Budget Office, *The Federal Government in a Federal System: Current Intergovernmental Programs and Options for Change* (Washington, D.C.: GPO, August 1983); and Bradbury, Downs, and Small, *Urban Decline.*

27 The Advisory Commission on Intergovernmental Relations regularly reports on developments in tax expenditures limitation activities in its journal, *Intergovernmental Perspective.*

28 Advisory Commission on Intergovernmental Relations, *Significant Features of Fiscal Federalism, 1984 Edition,* p. 48.

29 Advisory Commission on Intergovernmental Relations, *A Catalog of Federal Grant-In-Aid Programs to State and Local Governments Funded FY 1984* (Washington, D.C.: GPO, 1984), pp. 2–3.

30 Steven D. Gold, *State and Local Fiscal Relations in the Early 1980s* (Washington, D.C.: Urban Institute Press, 1983), p. 223.

31 Advisory Commission on Intergovernmental Relations, *Significant Features of Fiscal Federalism, 1984 Edition,* p. 18.

Fiscal structure in the federal system

The public sector in the United States, Canada, and most other federal countries is a highly fragmented system of governmental units. These units function within the context of a constitution that defines only roughly the scope of responsibility and authority at different levels of government. On a conceptual level, a federal model might be conceived of as a tidily organized structure in which there exists a clearly recognized *and* constitutionally specified separation of powers among the levels of government. Within and among different levels, agencies would pursue their activities independently. In the late nineteenth century James Bryce described such a federal system as "a great factory wherein two sets of machinery are at work, their revolving wheels apparently intermixed, their bands crossing one another, yet each set doing its own work without touching or hampering the other."[1]

Federal systems, however, have evolved far differently. The activities of levels of government in the modern federal system overlap and intertwine in such fundamental and complex ways that political scientists now characterize our age as one of "cooperative federalism." Some would contend that assigning functional responsibility among levels of government is a vacuous issue. As Michael Reagan puts it, "Those things are national and justify grant programs which the Congress *says* are national. The concepts of local and national interest are squishy at best."[2]

In spite of this apparent chaos and absence of principle in the functioning of federal fiscal structures, the economic roles of different levels of government can and should be considered systematically. This chapter describes the division of functions among levels of government from an economic perspective and examines the structure and development of the intergovernmental fiscal system in the United States and in other federal countries. Of central interest are intergovernmental transfers, which probably have played a more basic role in shaping the modern federal system than have any other fiscal instruments. Finally, this chapter examines the so called "New Federalism" movement in the United States, aimed at a fundamental restructuring of the grant system and a realigning of functional responsibilities among levels of government.

The division of functions

In economic terms, there are three functions of government: (1) stabilizing the economy at high levels of output and employment without creating excessive inflationary pressures; (2) establishing an equitable distribution of income; and (3) providing certain public goods and services directly and introducing regulations or incentives to correct for significant distortions in the market-determined allocation of resources. While these functions refer to the public sector as a whole, the peculiarly federal role is assigning these functions to different levels of government.

Economic stabilization

The macroeconomic function of stabilizing the economy at high levels of output and employment without creating excessive inflationary pressures rests with the central government, which controls the creation and destruction of money. If each local government had monetary control, there would be a powerful incentive to create new money to purchase real goods and services from other jurisdictions, in lieu of raising money by local taxation. The result would be excessive creation of money with a consequent rapid price inflation. Moreover, the limited scope of local countercyclical budgetary measures, and the "openness" of local economies in particular, severely constrain local fiscal policy.

If, for example, a local authority were to undertake a substantial tax cut to stimulate the local economy, it would find instead that most of the newly generated spending would flow out of the jurisdiction in payment for goods and services produced elsewhere—with ultimately little effect on local levels of employment.

In short, the absence of monetary prerogatives and the "openness" of regional or local economies (implying the limited scope of local countercyclical budgetary measures) suggest that the potential for effective macroeconomic stabilization policy is extremely limited at the local level. Yet states (and perhaps even local governments) can take some countercyclical measures. Through tax-stabilization funds, for example, reserves are built up through fiscal surpluses during expansionary periods and drawn down during recessions in order to stabilize spending over the course of the business cycle. Ultimately, however, the central government, with its monetary and fiscal instruments, must assume primary responsibility for macroeconomic stabilization.

Income distribution

The income distribution function also requires a major role of the central government. The national economic system places real constraints on the capacity of local governments to redistribute income. The high degree of mobility of economic units among local jurisdictions implies that one municipality, for example, cannot tax a particular group significantly more heavily than it is taxed elsewhere without creating incentives for emigration. If such a municipality were to undertake an aggressive program to reduce inequality in the distribution of local income through subsidies for the poor and steeply progressive tax rates for the rich, for example, relatively high-income households would tend to leave and settle in jurisdictions where they would obtain more favorable fiscal treatment, while poorer families would migrate into the community. A more equal distribution of income may result, but it would be because of the out-migration of the well-to-do and the in-migration of lower-income families.

Studies suggest that in the United States there have been significant movements of low-income households across states and metropolitan areas in response to differentials in welfare payments—and that this has led to decisions to hold down levels of support payments. This mobility problem was recognized explicitly under the Poor Laws in England.[3] Although the care of the poor (dating back to pre-Elizabethan times) was designated as a local (parish) responsibility, this care extended *only* to the parish's own poor. Under the Law of Settlement and Removal, paupers from other parishes were deported (often rather cruelly). Without such strict "residency requirements" (which, incidentally, are now unconstitutional in the United States), an effective system of local poor relief probably would not have been feasible. Writing in the nineteenth century, Edwin Cannan concluded:

Measures adopted to produce greater equality are, however, exceedingly unsuitable for local authorities. The smaller the locality the more capricious and ineffectual are likely to be any efforts it may make to carry out such a policy. It seems clearly desirable that all such measures should be applied to the largest possible area, and that subordinate authorities should be left to act, like the individual, from motives of self-interest.[4]

This is not to imply that local governments cannot redistribute income to any extent at all; they can and do. Nevertheless, the mobility of households and firms imposes real constraints on the character and level of local taxation and transfer payments. The result is that the central government must not only stabilize the economy but also assume a primary responsibility for income transfer programs designed to establish a more equitable distribution of income. That responsibility, however, does not preclude an extensive role for localities in actually administering and operating programs; it simply recognizes that levels of redistribution cannot vary widely among local jurisdictions and that localities cannot be expected to fund the bulk of redistributive programs from their own sources.

Provision of goods and services

With regard to the remaining function of the public sector encompassing the direct provision of public goods and services, decentralized levels of government have their basic economic rationale. Certain public goods, such as national defense, are intended to benefit all members of society, and the federal government is unquestionably the appropriate agent for providing such truly national public services. In contrast, many other services with collective characteristics are primarily local. Refuse disposal and sewer systems, fire and police protection, libraries, and recreational resources are but a few examples. In these cases, a compelling argument can be made for the localized provision of services according to local preferences, particularly because centralized control tends to result in uniform levels of output across all jurisdictions, even though this uniformity can entail substantial losses in consumer well-being. Econometric estimates of demand curves for various local public goods can measure the potential losses in consumer surplus when everyone is required to consume the same level of public services. Studies suggest that the magnitude of these losses can be quite substantial.[5] Wherever possible, then, levels of consumption should be adjusted to the tastes of individuals or groups of individuals.[6] These studies suggest that decentralized provision of services, being more sensitive to local consumers' willingness to pay, is most likely to achieve this goal.

"In great centralized nations the legislator is obliged to give a character of uniformity to the laws, which does not always suit the diversity of customs and of districts."

—Alexis de Tocqueville

The economic literature on local finance over the past 20 years has emphasized the role of consumer mobility in realizing consumer gains from locally determined service levels. In 1956 Charles Tiebout introduced a model of local finance in which individuals seek a community that provides the level of public output best suited to their tastes.[7] The outcome closely resembles the market solution for private goods.

Just as the consumer may be visualized as walking to a private market place to buy his goods, the prices of which are set, we place him in the position of walking to a community where the prices (taxes) of community services are set. Both trips take the consumer to market. There is no way in which the consumer can avoid revealing his preferences in a spatial economy. Spatial mobility provides the local public-goods counterpart to the private market's shopping trip.[8]

The Tiebout model thus envisions a system of local finance in which consumers sort themselves out according to their demands for public goods. As in the private market, individual consumers "purchase" their preferred basket of services based on their tastes and the cost of these services.

The Tiebout model does entail a number of heroic assumptions, in particular, one of footloose consumers moving costlessly among localities and choosing a community of residence solely on the basis of fiscal considerations. Nevertheless, subsequent research suggests that the mobility model is useful. Numerous studies have found, for example, that local property values vary directly with levels of local services. People do appear to pay more for houses of the same size and quality in order to live in communities that provide such amenities as better schools for their children and greater safety from crime.[9]

This should not come as a surprise. Households in the United States move with considerable frequency. The 1980 census, for example, found that only about one-half of the families sampled were living in the same house as they were in 1975. Surely the vast majority of these moves were not motivated primarily by fiscal considerations but by changes in employment or family status. Whatever the motivation for the move, however, the process of choosing the new community in which to live is likely to involve serious consideration of local services and taxes. An individual working in a metropolitan area, perhaps in the central city itself, has a wide range of choices among suburban communities in which to reside. The quality of such local services as education and safety is likely to be a significant factor in this choice.

In assessing the implications of the local finance literature, it is most important to distinguish between the descriptive and the prescriptive. The mobility model does isolate an important set of forces that have had a profound effect on the evolution of metropolitan areas. Families with high demands for public services tend to live in suburban communities with high levels of amenities; households with lesser demands for public outputs tend to live together in jurisdictions with a lower quality of services. From a descriptive perspective, these models can "explain" the development of metropolitan areas into systems of relatively small suburban communities, each with a relatively homogeneous population when compared with that of the urban area as a whole.

From a prescriptive point of view, however, things are somewhat more complicated. Purely in terms of consumer choice, the Tiebout model suggests that such an outcome has real appeal. A variety of communities permit individual consumers to purchase the quantity of public services that they desire at a tax-price equal to cost. But from a broader social perspective, there are some troublesome matters. Because the demand for services is positively correlated with income, the "sorting-out" process tends to generate a system segregated by income class. A spectrum of communities emerges, ranging from high-income jurisdictions with high levels of services to low-income jurisdictions with low levels of services. While this may not be objectionable to some, certainly court decisions and a general societal concern for equality (busing to achieve racial balance, for example) do not favor such an outcome. Whatever the implications of this apparent tension between local choice and social justice, the mobility model illuminates a powerful set of forces that must be dealt with in the design of social and economic policy.

Intergovernmental transfers

Alexis de Tocqueville observed that "the federal system was created with the intention of combining the different advantages which result from the magnitude and the littleness of nations."[10] Economic analysis provides some support for his claim. A centralized authority is necessary to implement macroeconomic stabilization policy, to accomplish socially desirable income redistribution, and to provide those goods and services whose pattern of benefits is national in scope. At the same time, the "littleness" of local fiscal jurisdictions offers compelling advantages in terms of tailoring the provision of certain public services to local tastes.

Even in countries with unitary governments, there is considerable de facto budgetary choice at decentralized levels of the public sector. In an economic sense, government sectors in *all* nations are "federal" because to a greater or lesser degree, discretionary budgetary activity is exercised at several levels of the governmental system.

Although the assignment of functions outlined in the preceding section can provide a framework for thinking about federal fiscal structure, it is a bit too neat and tidy. The macroeconomic and redistribution functions are not *solely* centralized responsibilities. State and local governments undertake some explicitly countercyclical and redistributive measures. Moreover, some services (e.g., education), although primarily of local interest, have important national dimensions or "spillover effects." It is unclear how best to structure the provision of such services. As one observer of federal government puts it:

> There is and can be no final solution to the allocation of financial resources in a federal system. There can only be adjustments and reallocations in the light of changing conditions. What a federal government needs, therefore, is machinery adequate to make these adjustments.[11]

The federal system has several levels and determining the appropriate level of government to provide a particular service is often ambiguous.

Federal governments have found intergovernmental grants-in-aid to be a piece of fiscal "machinery" well suited for dealing with the continuing budgetary tensions among different levels of government. Nearly all federal countries have come to place a growing reliance on these grants. In the United States, William Young contends, "the most powerful engine in the century for reshaping national-state relations has been the grant-in-aid system of national financing of state and local activities."[12] The operations of federal, state, and local governments interact with and overlap one another to such a degree that a basic problem is integrating budgetary and other decisions of different public units into a coherent and consistent set of policies. From this perspective, intergovernmental grants have proved to be highly flexible fiscal instruments, capable of assuming a number of different forms to promote varied objectives in the public sector, from expansion of specific activities to equalization of fiscal capability.)[13] In the 1980s, grants function as a basic fiscal link among the budgetary structures of the different levels of government.

Grants take one of two major forms: conditional or unconditional (lump-sum). A conditional grant is contingent on some specified behavior on the part of the recipient. In general, the funds must be used for a particular purpose. Conditional grants may take a matching form, under which the grantor agrees to pay some fraction of the unit cost of the recipient. Under one-to-one matching, for example, the state or locality would receive one dollar in grant monies for each dollar it expended from its own funds. Such a grant effectively cuts in half the costs of the service to the locality. Moreover, the only way the locality can increase its grant money is by increasing its own spending. Unlike a fixed sum for some specified purpose, the matching grant reduces the effective price and provides a direct inducement to expand the service. Unconditional or lump-sum grants have no strings attached; the recipients are free to use the funds however they wish. Other grants such as formula and block grants are discussed later in the chapter.

The following section will explore the rationale, magnitude, distribution, and design and effects of intergovernmental grants.

The rationale for intergovernmental grants

Intergovernmental grants in their various forms serve a number of functions: they alleviate external effects, equalize fiscal status, and promote fair taxation via revenue sharing.

Alleviation of external effects Whenever the choices of one individual (or group of individuals) impinge significantly on the welfare of others outside the market, there is potential for distortion in economic decisions. A classic example is the factory spewing forth smoke that imposes external costs on the neighboring laundry. In this case, the decision makers (the factory owners) have no incentive to take into account the costs (the dirty laundry) they generate. Third parties are not considered, so the economic choices of the immediate decision makers fail to incorporate the full range of relevant social costs. In certain instances where the affected parties are able to come together and negotiate an agreement, voluntary private decisions can yield an efficient outcome.[14] However, voluntary resolution of externalities relies on a number of quite restrictive assumptions, such as low transaction costs and an absence of strategic behavior, suggesting that its relevance is limited to cases involving only a very small number of participants.[15] More likely is a distorted pattern of resource use consisting of excessive levels of activities that generate external costs and inappropriately low levels of activities that involve spillover benefits.

External effects are not limited to decisions by private consumers or firms, for the programs adopted by one local or state government may have important implications for the well-being of residents of other jurisdictions. A good system of roads in one locality, for example, provides services for travelers from elsewhere. Likewise, medical research funded in one state may produce new treatments or cures of widespread interest. In such instances, the state or locality can hardly be expected to use its own resources to expand its activity to levels for which outsiders would be willing to pay if a payment mechanism existed. From the perspective of the federal government, the perfectly rational but myopic decisions of the states and localities are a matter of serious concern when considering the adequacy of programs that have important external effects.

As a representative of the national interest, the federal government could, in principle, simply take over the whole function and thereby "internalize" all relevant costs and benefits. However, this response often is politically infeasible or simply unconstitutional. But, even if it were a viable alternative, centralization is frequently a cure that may be worse than the disease. Decentralized provision of public services can be a means to use resources efficiently because the state or local government is in a position to fashion its programs according to the particular tastes of its constituency.

How then does the federal government influence state-local services involving external effects across jurisdictions, without at the same time preempting the states and local governments? It employs intergovernmental grants. *Conditional grants* are particularly useful for encouraging expansion of a particular service (e.g., medical research). However, the funds must not only be earmarked for the intended purpose, but they must not be substituted for local revenues that would otherwise have been spent on the service. Even if a grant is conditional (in the sense that the recipient is required to use the monies for a prescribed function or program), it does not follow that the grant will increase spending for the function. For example, a locality that receives a grant to expand local police services might use these funds—especially in periods of rising budgets—to cover planned budgetary increments that would otherwise have been financed with locally raised revenues. In effect, the grant funds would be available indirectly for use in other programs or, alternatively, for local tax cuts. In short, this "fungibility" of grant funds may allow states and localities to use conditional grants in the same way that they would employ monies with no strings attached, thereby frustrating the intent of the federal grant program. A case in which this is not true is where the state or locality would have expended none of its own funds (or less than the sum of the grant) on the aided program. For example, "demonstration grants" may induce expenditures that would not have taken place without federal assistance.

The appropriate form of grant when both local and external benefits are involved is a *matching grant*. In theory, the matching terms should reflect the magnitude of the spillover effect. If, for example, two dollars of local expenditure generates one dollar of benefits for residents of other jurisdictions, then the granting government's share should be one-third or one-to-two matching. This would effectively induce the recipient to take account of the external benefits. In practice, it may be difficult to determine the precise shares of local and external benefits, but the analysis does provide some guidelines. It suggests that where the purpose of the grant program is to encourage state and local provision of particular services that are also beneficial elsewhere, the appropriate instrument is the matching grant. Moreover, where the spillover benefits are considered large relative to local benefits, the grant program should offer relatively generous matching terms. These grants, incidentally, should involve "open-end matching"; the matching terms should be available to the recipient at whatever level of spending is selected. If the matching stops at some level of local expenditure on the program, the grant no longer has a price effect and may have the same effect as an unconditional, lump-sum grant.[16]

The federal government in the United States has used matching grants to state and local governments extensively under several programs for which spillover benefits would appear to be quite important. For example, federal matching grants to the states have supported the construction of a national network of highways. Federal agencies also have employed matching grants for various educational programs that have a clear national interest. The actual evolution of federal systems of intergovernmental grants will be examined later in this chapter, but these examples suggest that the "economic principles" of grant design can provide a rationale for the structure of some grant programs.

Fiscal equalization Typically, federal systems of government have relied on intergovernmental grants to correct geographical inequities as well as to improve the allocation of resources. One rationale for these grants stems from perceived geographical differences in fiscal well-being. Some jurisdictions have relatively large tax bases and populations that require comparatively little in the way of social services. Adequate service levels can be provided with relatively low tax rates in these localities. Other areas have significantly higher tax rates and a lower level (or quality) of services. Central governments in dozens of countries have tried to eliminate or decrease such geographical fiscal differences with equalizing grants.[17] The stated purpose of such grants is to establish a fiscal environment in which each state or locality can provide a satisfactory level of key public services with a fiscal effort that is not discernibly greater than that of other jurisdictions. To achieve this goal, the central government bases the allocation of grant funds on the measured "need" and "fiscal capacity" of the decentralized units of government. In this way, jurisdictions with populations requiring large public expenditures or with comparatively small tax bases (or with an unfortunate combination of the two) receive proportionately larger sums.

Three points concerning equalizing grants are worthy of special emphasis. First, the appropriate grant form in this case is an unconditional (lump-sum) grant, intended to equalize fiscal capability, not to stimulate public spending. From this perspective, it would be inappropriate to employ a matching grant, which would effectively lower the cost of services to each jurisdiction and thereby directly encourage increased spending. The implication is that fiscal equalization grants should vary with a jurisdiction's need and fiscal capacity, but should not depend on the fiscal response of the jurisdiction.

Second, although equalizing grants may reduce fiscal differentials among *jurisdictions,* they are not an effective device for achieving the socially desired distribution of income among *individuals*. Typically such grants will channel funds to poorer areas, but they are very clumsy instruments for interpersonal redistributive purposes. Most low-income areas have some wealthy residents and most high-income areas have some poor residents. Therefore, transfers from rich to poor *areas* through the medium of equalizing grants are bound to have some unfair redistributive elements.

Unconditional equalizing grants are not a full substitute for a national program designed to achieve an equitable distribution of income among individuals.

Third, the scope and design of equalizing grants should not overlook the powerful market forces that compensate automatically for some of the apparent inequities in a federal fiscal system. The case for equalizing grants is sometimes made in terms of the principle of horizontal equity: people in equal positions should be treated equally. At first glance, it would appear that a system of decentralized finance is likely to violate this principle because the size of the tax base per capita will vary from one jurisdiction to the next. It also appears that different tax rates will be required to raise the same amount of revenue per person. A resident of a locality with a relatively large tax base will thus face a lower tax rate and have a lower tax bill than his or her counterpart in a district with a smaller tax base. This apparent source of inequity was, incidentally, one of the grounds (in 1973) for declaring the system of school finance in the state of New Jersey to be unconstitutional.

However, where households are highly mobile among jurisdictions, market forces themselves will eliminate any horizontal inequities. Suppose, for example, that one jurisdiction has a notable fiscal advantage over the others (e.g., a relatively large tax base or a lower cost of maintaining clean air in a town located on a hill). In an environment of mobile individuals, the value of such differences will be capitalized into local property values. Consumers will bid for places in the fiscally advantaged community until the increased price of property exactly offsets the fiscal gain. Thus, an individual considering the purchase of a residence in a community with a relatively high tax *rate* will find that the high tax liability is approximately offset by the lower price of the property, as compared with an equivalent property in a jurisdiction with lower tax rates.[18] Mobility, therefore, promotes the equal treatment of equals. Whatever fiscal advantages are enjoyed will be paid for in the form of higher actual (or imputed) rent; conversely, higher taxes will be offset by lower prices of property. In the mobility model, horizontal equity tends to be self-policing, which suggests that significant horizontal inequities may be ironed out by market forces within the metropolitan economy. This may not be true, however, at the regional level, where the mobility model appears less applicable. Here the obstacles to mobility may permit unequal treatment of equals to persist. Moreover, sudden changes in the fiscal position of a particular community will generate a once-and-for-all set of windfall gains or losses to reflect the new fiscal circumstances.

Taxation and revenue sharing Another important rationale for intergovernmental grants is the need to establish an efficient and fair system of taxation for the public sector as a whole. There is some evidence that the federal tax system is basically more just and less distorting than state and local tax systems. The federal income tax, for example, is probably a good deal more progressive than state and local income, sales, and property taxes.[19] Moreover, taxes at the more decentralized levels of government have a greater potential for distorting the flow of resources in the economy. To take one example, federal taxes cannot be avoided by a change of location within the national economy; therefore, this source of taxation will not create direct incentives for locational distortions. At state and local levels, however, similar taxes may chase capital from high-tax to low-tax jurisdictions, resulting in inefficiencies in resource allocation and a subsequent reduction in output. The relatively high mobility of both goods and people across state or local boundaries implies that there may be much more sensitivity to state and local fiscal differentials than to those at the national level.

In addition, states and localities often shift a substantial portion of their tax burden onto residents of other jurisdictions. Taxing certain production activities in one jurisdiction, for instance, may result in higher prices, which are paid largely by outsiders. For example, the burden of taxation of Michigan's auto industry falls largely on purchasers of new automobiles nationwide. Areas that draw heavy tourist populations frequently meet much of their local tax needs through substantial excise taxes on hotel and restaurant bills. And these are not isolated examples. Charles McLure has estimated that, on average, state governments in the United States are able to "export" approximately 20 to 25 percent of their taxes to residents of other states.[20]

The federal government, in contrast, has a greater opportunity to rely on fairer, more wide-reaching programs, such as progressive taxation, or a national uniformity of tax rates whereby it can avoid the distortions in resource allocation generated by state and local tax differentials. Finally, a greater reliance on centralized taxation provides some economies of scale in tax administration. Data for the United States indicate that the cost of administering the federal individual income tax system amounts to only about 0.5 percent of the revenues received. At the state level, the administrative costs for income or sales taxes are typically 1 percent to 2 percent of revenues.[21]

It would appear, then, that the equity and efficiency of the federal-state-local tax system as a whole might be improved by shifting more of the taxation function to the central government. However, as has been discussed previously, retaining state and local discretion over the size and composition of their expenditures has important benefits. One way to retain state and local as well as federal control is through a program of revenue sharing, by which federal taxation can be substituted for state and local taxes. In a sense, the federal government acts as a tax-collection agent for states and localities by collecting tax revenues in excess of its own needs and distributing this excess in lump-sum form to state and local treasuries. The appropriate form in which to transfer these funds is the unconditional grant. If the purpose of these monies is to alter the overall revenue system and *not* to encourage state and local expenditure on particular functions (or spending in general), the revenue-sharing grants should have no strings attached. In other words, recipients should not be required to spend the funds as a condition for receiving them.

An implicit assumption in this discussion is that the central government can function as a tax collector for state and local governments without intruding on state and local expenditure prerogatives. As long as the transfers of funds to states and localities are truly unconditional, there is no reason *in principle* why the recipients should feel any constraints about how these resources are used. This assumption, however, is naive; if the central government is a major supplier of state and local funds, political pressures and opportunities can be expected to induce central agencies to use this leverage to achieve some of their own objectives. In the United Kingdom, for example, central government grants (primarily unconditional) account for approximately two-thirds of local authority revenues. Widespread concern over the erosion of local autonomy has resulted, generating renewed interest in additional sources of tax revenues at the local level.[22] Likewise, the extensive reliance on centrally raised revenues in the Australian federal system has, in the view of several observers, undercut the fiscal independence of state and local governments. In short, a "modest" revenue-sharing program may contribute to the effectiveness of the tax system, but over the long run, heavy reliance on such programs may undermine the fiscal discretion of decentralized levels of government.

Although revenue sharing offers a mechanism to improve the total tax system, political realities suggest limitations on the extent of its use.

We have, thus, two potential roles for unconditional grants: fiscal equalization and an improved overall system of taxation. On a pragmatic level, there is no reason why the public sector cannot pursue both of these objectives at the same time through a system of unconditional grants (revenue sharing) in which the size of the per capita grant varies with the fiscal characteristics of the jurisdiction. The United States has attempted to do just this with the general revenue-sharing (GRS) program.

The magnitude of intergovernmental grants

The growth in the size and complexity of the public sector generated a striking expansion in the use of intergovernmental grants from the 1950s to the early 1980s. Such transfers have provided a policy tool capable of promoting a number of quite different and important government objectives. Table 3–1 documents this growth in the United States. Federal grants to state and local governments increased from about $3 billion in 1955 to $94 billion in fiscal year 1983. In 1983 about 12 percent of federal expenditures took the form of grants-in-aid to states and localities. Until 1981, this growth also manifested itself in a rapid increase in the number of federal grant programs. As column (5) indicates, the estimated number of such programs rose from 132 in 1960 to 539 in 1981. The growth in federal grants then started to decline after 1981—both in real terms [see column (3)] and as a fraction of federal outlays. The number of grant programs also declined in the early 1980s. This reversal will be examined later in this chapter in the section on the New Federalism.

As column (6) in Table 3–1 indicates, state governments in the United States obtain grants from the federal government equal to about one-third of the revenues they generate from their own sources (i.e., they get about 25 percent of their total revenues from federal grants). Local governments in turn have become increasingly reliant on the states. Column (7) shows that, in the aggregate, state grants to local governments rose from $6 billion in 1955 to almost $100 billion in 1983. Local governments in 1983 received in grants, both from the federal government and their states, revenues equal to about two-thirds

Table 3–1 Intergovernmental grants in the United States for selected years (dollar amounts in billions).

(1) Year	(2) Federal grants to state and local governments	(3) Federal grants in constant (1972) dollars	(4) Federal grants as % of federal outlay	(5) Estimated number of federal grant programs	(6) Federal grants to states as % of state's own general revenue	(7) State grants to local government[a]	(8) Intergovernmental revenue to local government as % of local own general revenue[b]
1955	$ 3.2	$ 5.3	4.7	N.A.	20.9	$ 6.0	43.1
1960	7.0	10.2	7.6	132	31.0	9.5	44.1
1965	10.9	14.7	9.2	379	32.3	14.0	46.9
1970	24.0	26.2	12.2	N.A.	33.5	26.9	57.5
1975	49.8	39.6	15.3	448	37.3	51.1	73.5
1980	91.5	51.2	15.8	N.A.	36.6	81.3	78.8
1981	94.8	48.6	14.4	539	36.2	89.0	76.5
1982	88.2	42.6	12.1	441	32.1	95.0	71.0
1983 est.	94.0	43.5	11.8	409	33.4	98.4	66.7

Source: Advisory Commission on Intergovernmental Relations, *Significant Features of Fiscal Federalism, 1982–83 Edition* (Washington, D.C.: GPO, January 1984), Tables 75 and 76, pp. 120–21.

[a] State grants to local government include substantial sums of federal aid that is passed through the states. Such aid in 1980 was estimated at $17 billion.
[b] Includes intergovernmental revenue from federal and state governments.

of their own-source revenues—that is, they received about 40 percent of their total revenues in the form of intergovernmental transfers.

These transfers support a wide variety of public programs. Table 3–2 indicates the breakdown of federal grants by categories of aid for fiscal year 1983. Note, in particular, the diversity of purposes for grant funds. A substantial chunk (41 percent) of federal intergovernmental transfers is for public welfare. As discussed earlier, there is a sound rationale for this because it is difficult for states, and especially for localities, to engage in aggressive redistributive programs to help lower-income households. As a result, the federal government has used intergovernmental transfers extensively for redistributive purposes.

Certain of these grants provide a stimulus for state-local programs that confer benefits on residents of other areas. Federal grants for highways and for various educational activities are good examples; the population of the United States has an important interest both in a good system of national roadways and in an educated electorate. Conditional intergovernmental grants provide a mechanism for higher-level governments to represent the broader concern of the citizenry through budgetary incentives.

Distribution of intergovernmental grants

Typically, conditional grants involve some kind of cost-sharing between the federal agency and the recipient state or locality such that the effective price at which the recipient purchases the aided good or service is lowered. This is accomplished either through an explicit grant formula that specifies the respective shares of the grantor and recipient, or through an application and negotiation procedure for a "project grant" under which the state or local share is determined in the process itself. In both instances, the federal government includes equalizing elements by providing more generous matching terms to jurisdictions with less fiscal capacity. This is accomplished by using "variable matching grants" in which the fiscal circumstances of the jurisdictions enter into a formula that determines the federal matching share. Under project grants, the

Table 3–2 Federal intergovernmental expenditure by function, 1982–83 (in millions).

Function	Amount
Education	$12,528
Grants-in-aid	8,938
Elementary and secondary education	2,703
Human development	1,266
School breakfast and school lunch program	795
Occupational, vocational, and adult education	715
Education for the handicapped	1,120
School assistance in federally affected areas	538
Payments for services	3,590
Scientific research and development	3,434
Tuition payments	156
Public welfare	36,282
Medical assistance	19,030
Maintenance assistance	7,793
Social and child welfare services (n.e.c.)[a]	2,490
Child nutrition	2,201
Low-income energy assistance	2,374
Food stamp program—administration	626
Child support enforcement	497
Refugee assistance	545
Work incentives (n.e.c.)[a]	280
Nutritional support for the aging	361
Housing and urban renewal	5,583
Community development training and block grants	3,452
Low-rent public housing	1,530
Urban development operating subsidies	444
Health and hospitals	3,682
Special supplemental food programs—women's, infants', and children's programs	1,164
Health Services Administration	875
Alcohol, drug abuse, and mental health programs	500
National Institutes of Health	489
Natural resources, parks and recreation	2,220
Department of Energy—conservation programs	314
Land and water conservation	287
Mineral Leasing Act	535
General revenue sharing	4,620
Highways	8,851
Social insurance administration	2,452
Other and combined	12,321
Labor and manpower (n.e.c.)[a]	3,176
Water and sewage facilities	3,212
Urban mass transportation	3,695
Unemployment compensation for federal employees, ex-servicemen, and temporary extended benefits	233
Airport development	459
Contribution to District of Columbia	427
Civil defense and disaster relief	249
Other	870
Total federal intergovernmental expenditures	88,539

Source: U.S. Department of Commerce, Bureau of the Census, *Governmental Finances in 1982–83* (Washington, D.C.: GPO, 1983), Table 12, p. 20, and Table 10, p. 18.
Note: Categories listed under individual functions are not fully exhaustive; spending by categories adds up to less than the function total.
[a] n.e.c.—not elsewhere classified

federal administrator of a particular program takes local fiscal capacity into consideration in determining the local contribution. During the 1960s and 1970s, formula grants and matching grants played a central role in the federal grant system. Formula grants—primarily to the states—accounted for about two-thirds of federal grants. Federal transfers to local governments were mainly project grants and made up about 20 percent of federal intergovernmental transfers.[23] As will be shown later in this chapter, the New Federalism programs of the 1980s involved consolidating many of these programs into broad "block grants," thereby allowing considerably more discretion on the part of recipients.

In addition to its extensive system of conditional grants, in 1972 the United States instituted general revenue sharing with state and local governments. The accepted view of revenue sharing as a purely unconditional form of intergovernmental transfers is not quite accurate in this case. The U.S. Congress adopted both a House formula and a Senate formula, allowing each state to select the formula under which its entitlement is determined. The two revenue-sharing formulas are rather complicated and allocate these monies on the basis of a number of criteria.[24] For example, a state's entitlement to revenue-sharing funds depends not only on its population but also on its level of per capita income, its fiscal effort (measured by total state and local taxes as a percentage of aggregate personal income), and its level of income-tax collections. The revenue-sharing program in the United States is modest in size and its political future is uncertain. Because of fiscal stringency at the central level, states were excluded from revenue-sharing payments beginning in 1980. In contrast, several other federal countries rely heavily on unconditional grants. In both Australia and Canada, for example, the central government acts as a revenue-raising agent for other levels of government by distributing to them large, unconditional sums.

The design and effects of intergovernmental grants

Thus far, this chapter has presented the economic principles of grant design and related them to the existing structure of the intergovernmental transfer system. A closer examination of federal transfers to state and local governments, however, reveals a number of anomalies; this should not be too surprising because the design and enactment of grant programs is, in part, the result of an interaction of governors, local government officials, and various special interest groups with federal legislators. Such interaction is frequently characterized by a tension between the grant administrator's desire to restrict the use of funds to realize the agency's own objectives and the recipient's efforts to minimize any strings attached to the monies. The grant program that finally emerges reflects some degree of compromise.

It is interesting to explore a bit further the extent to which the structure of grants appears consistent with our economic criteria for grant design. As discussed earlier, a primary justification for intergovernmental grants is the existence of external benefits across governmental jurisdictions for such state and local services as highways and educational programs. For these programs, a system of matching grants (where the respective matching shares would reflect the extent of the spillover benefits) would be desirable. Yet, from this perspective, certain characteristics of the federal grant system are quite puzzling. Under most matching grants, federal matching ceases at some modest level of transfers (the major exceptions being federal grants for public assistance and Medicaid). This implies that the states and localities at maximum funding levels receive no inducement to take into account the spillover benefits that their fiscal decisions generate. In principle, matching grants should be open-ended. Their provisions should apply to any potential *extensions* of budgetary programs if state and local officials are to be induced to consider the spillover effects associated with the program.

Moreover, it would appear very difficult to justify the actual matching shares under a number of programs by the extent of external benefits. For example, the federal share for interstate highway construction has been 90 percent of cost, although it would seem very unlikely that 90 percent of the value of the interstate highways passing through a particular state accrue to out-of-state drivers. To an even greater degree, the benefits from sewage waste treatment systems are largely local. Neighboring jurisdictions may benefit in some instances, but hardly enough to rationalize the existing federal share of 75 percent of construction costs. More generally, a study by the Advisory Commission on Intergovernmental Relations (ACIR) reveals that most federal grant programs require either low (less than 50 percent) or *no* matching on the part of the recipient state or local government. Only about 5 percent of federal grant monies are in programs requiring high matching (over 50 percent from the recipient).[25]

For many programs, external benefits themselves appear inadequate to justify the magnitude of the federal matching share.

In addition to the issue of the matching share itself, other elements in grant design can impair the effectiveness of a particular grant program. One important illustration is the federal subsidy program for waste treatment plants to reduce water pollution under which the federal government has provided several billion dollars for the construction of new waste treatment facilities. As various studies have shown, the failure to link the grants directly to their intended purpose—the reduction of water pollution—has seriously undercut their efficacy. In particular, the subsidies support only a specific technology (waste treatment) even where a less costly and more effective alternative exists. Moreover, by subsidizing only the *construction* of treatment plants, the program has provided no incentive for the efficient *operation* of these facilities. One study found that in over half of the plants studied, services were substandard either because of poor operating procedures or because the plants were not designed to treat the waste load delivered to them.[26]

Intergovernmental grant programs seem to have had a significant—and, in some instances, a surprisingly large—expansionary effect on state and local spending.

Any evaluation of federal grant programs must actually observe and attempt to measure the effect of the programs on the decisions (budgetary and otherwise) of state and local officials. There has been some effort in this direction, although general understanding of the effects of federal grants is quite spotty. Despite considerable variation in estimates from one study to the next, most research findings suggest that federal grants have stimulated state and local expenditures substantially. Grant monies have not been used simply to substitute for state and local tax revenues.[27] Moreover, the evidence supports the expectation that conditional grants generate a larger expenditure response (dollar for dollar) than do purely unconditional transfers, with high federal matching providing a greater stimulus than that of low matching.

In general, these grants induce a surprising degree of budgetary expansion. Consider, for example, the case of an unconditional grant to a local community. Because such grants contain no explicit incentives for budgetary expansion, the members of the community may be expected to treat these monies as a kind of windfall, a supplement to their wealth or income. In principle, it should not really matter that the monies flow into the local government treasury, for if local officials are responsive to the preferences of their constituencies, it should make little difference whether the grant goes to the local government or into the pockets of local residents directly. From this perspective, an unconditional intergovernmental grant is simply a veil for a direct federal tax cut to individuals.[28]

The implication of the "veil hypothesis" is that the additional local public spending generated by a dollar of lump-sum grants to the local government should be approximately the same as the increment to public expenditure resulting from a one-dollar increase in private income in the jurisdiction. In both cases, aggregate income in the jurisdiction has risen by a dollar so that the desired increase in public spending should be about the same. However, existing empirical work suggests that this is not the case. In particular, if the present size of the state and local sector (10 to 15 percent of GNP) is any guide to desired marginal adjustments, increases in private income should induce additional state and local expenditure on the order of 10 to 15 cents per dollar of additional income. The evidence indicates, however, that the stimulative effect of unconditional intergovernmental transfers is much larger than this; it is closer to 40 to 50 cents on the dollar. The evidence comes from a number of sources, including various econometric studies and an actual "monitoring" of the general revenue-sharing program.[29] There are, however, some important qualifications attached to these results (involving both measurement problems and issues in interpretation), so they should not be regarded as the last word on the subject.

Economic analysis provides a number of important insights into the as yet incomplete understanding of the workings of intergovernmental grants. In particular, the federal government in the United States has found these grants to be an attractive policy tool to encourage state and local programs that also serve the broader national interest (for example, the promotion of an improved distribution of income and the establishment of a more efficient and equitable tax system). However, to accomplish their intended objectives at the least cost to society, individual grant programs must take the requisite form and must provide the appropriate incentives for state and local decision makers. By carefully evaluating grant programs both in terms of the economic principles of grant design and available evidence on the relevant magnitudes, fiscal analysts can contribute significantly to the evolution of a more effective intergovernmental transfers system that promotes the objectives of public policy.

Historical trends in federal fiscal structure

Historically, state and local levels of government have relied increasingly on intergovernmental transfers from the central government. This trend raises the broader question of whether the expansion of such grants reflects a continuing tendency over time toward the centralization of fiscal structure. Over a century ago, de Tocqueville predicted that "in the democratic ages which are opening upon us, . . . centralization will be the natural government."[30] Referring to the federal form of government in particular, Edward McWhinney has cited Bryce's Law, the proposition that "federalism is simply a transitory step on the way to governmental unity."[31] That is, a public sector that relies substantially on decentralized budgetary choice is *unstable* and will, over time, move toward more reliance on a central government.

Although the next section will show departures from this trend in the 1980s, a case can be made for centralization over a longer period. Rising incomes, improved transportation, and new modes of communication have linked regions and localities in the modern nation-state much more closely together, fostering increased mobility and interdependence. As a result, decisions made in one part of the country spill over into other areas. For example, the services provided in one jurisdiction have an "option value" to people who currently reside in other areas, who *may,* at some future date, choose to move.[32] Clearly, certain basic features of economic growth promote increased centralization of government. As Michael Reagan writes: " . . . Many more problems today than in the past are national in the sense of being affected by developments elsewhere in the nation or having their own impact upon other parts of the nation."[33]

However, the case for the centralization thesis is far from ironclad. As the mobility model of local finance suggests, individuals seek out communities that provide the public services they want. From this perspective, improved urban transportation and mobility may permit the local public sector to perform its functions more effectively. Economic growth, then, can facilitate the congregation of individuals with similar demands for local public goods and, in this way, generate potentially powerful forces (in both economic and political terms) for a continued substantial reliance on local budgetary choice.

To the extent that diverse local jurisdictions can cater to the particular demands of their own relatively homogeneous populations, there will exist strong support for local government to play a major role within the public sector.

Examining the fiscal indices of public-sector concentration may suggest the direction of movement toward or away from reliance on central government and the role of affluence on centralization. But first, the ambiguities inherent in any measure of government centralization should be acknowledged.[34] There is no single, satisfactory measure of the "quantity" of decision-making power at different levels of government; even if there were, it would be impossible to weight the roles of the federal, state, and many local governments to produce a single index of fiscal centralization. Nevertheless, certain summary measures may at least suggest tendencies in the hierarchical structure of the fiscal system.

Table 3–3 presents a historical profile of public expenditure in the twentieth century by level of government in the United States. The first four columns show absolute spending; the last three indicate percentage shares. The federal

Table 3–3 Public expenditure by level of government for selected fiscal years (dollar amounts in billions).

Year	Total public expenditure	Federal	State	Local	Percentage share Federal	State	Local
1902	$ 1.7	$ 0.6	$ 0.2	$ 0.9	34.5	10.8	54.8
1913	3.2	1.0	0.4	1.9	30.2	11.6	58.3
1922	9.3	3.8	1.3	4.3	40.5	13.6	46.0
1932	12.4	4.3	2.6	5.6	34.3	20.6	45.1
1940	20.4	10.1	4.5	5.8	49.3	22.3	28.5
1950	70.3	44.8	12.8	12.8	63.7	18.2	18.1
1955	110.7	73.4	17.4	19.9	66.3	15.7	18.0
1960	151.3	97.3	25.0	29.0	64.3	16.5	19.1
1965	205.7	130.1	35.7	39.9	63.3	17.4	19.4
1970	333.0	208.2	64.7	60.1	62.5	19.4	18.1
1975	560.1	340.5	122.2	97.4	60.8	21.8	17.4
1980	958.7	615.4	191.8	151.4	64.2	20.0	15.8
1981	1,109.8	717.4	220.5	171.9	64.6	19.9	15.5
1982	1,196.9	785.8	230.3	180.8	65.7	19.2	15.1
1983	1,350.5	874.3	263.6	214.4	64.7	19.5	15.9

Sources: Tax Foundation, Inc., *Facts and Figures on Government Finance, 22nd Biennial Edition* (Washington, D.C., 1983), Tables 9 and 10, pp. 21–22. Data for 1983 are from U.S. Bureau of the Census, *Governmental Finances in 1982–83* (Washington, D.C.: GPO, 1984), Table 9, p. 17.

share of total public expenditures may be regarded as a kind of "centralization ratio" that reflects the extent of fiscal centralization in the United States.

A cursory examination of Table 3–3 provides strong support for the centralization thesis. The federal share of total spending rose from about one-third to two-thirds from 1902 to 1983. The state government share of total spending almost doubled from about 11 percent to 20 percent. These increases in the federal and state shares came, by definition, at the expense of local governments, whose relative share in public expenditure fell from over 50 percent to only 16 percent. Substantial fiscal centralization appears to characterize the twentieth century in the United States.

However, a closer study of Table 3–3 suggests some important qualifications to this finding. In particular, after 1950 the federal share levels off, and federal spending in 1983 as a percentage of total public expenditure was about the same as in 1960. State and local shares likewise changed only a few percentage points. Although a strong tendency toward fiscal centralization characterized the first half of this century, it seems to have weakened in the last 25 years.

It is important to note that Table 3–3 attributes intergovernmental transfers to the grantor so that the dramatic growth in federal grants shows up implicitly as an expansion of federal spending. It is not clear how these funds should be allocated to measure the extent of fiscal centralization. They should, perhaps, be attributed to the government units that actually spend the funds for goods and services (particularly for unconditional or block grants). If, in fact, intergovernmental transfers are attributed to the recipient (see Table 3–4), the centralizing tendencies in the fiscal structure of the United States are less pronounced. Since 1950, federal, state, and local shares have remained fairly steady.

Fiscal data from other countries reveal similar trends. As shown in Table 3–5, the share of the central government in Canada has declined noticeably since 1950. In a study of fiscal patterns in several countries over the period 1950–70, Werner Pommerehne found that the central share had declined in every instance (see Table 3–6). This was not a sudden or dramatic shake-up in fiscal structure, but rather a gradual and continuing shift away from centralization over the entire 20-year period.

The picture that emerges from the fiscal data is a fairly complex one, but it does not support any sweeping hypothesis of a pervasive and continuing tendency toward a more centralized fiscal structure. On the contrary, over the past three decades the trends would seem to be in the opposite direction, indicating

Table 3–4 Percentage shares of expenditure with intergovernmental transfers attributed to recipient level of government.

Year	Federal (%)	State (%)	Local (%)
1902	34.0	8.2	57.8
1913	29.8	9.2	61.0
1922	39.2	11.7	49.1
1932	32.4	16.3	51.3
1940	45.0	17.4	37.6
1950	60.4	15.4	24.2
1960	59.7	14.6	25.7
1965	57.9	15.3	26.8
1970	55.5	16.9	27.6
1975	52.4	18.7	28.9
1980	55.2	18.0	26.8
1981	56.4	17.8	25.8
1982	57.6	17.2	25.2
1983	58.2	17.2	24.6

Source: Calculated from data in Tax Foundation, Inc., *Facts and Figures on Government Finance, 22nd Biennial Edition* (Washington, D.C., 1983), Table 9, p. 21, Table 149, p. 173.

Table 3–5 Canadian percentage shares of public expenditure by level of government.

Year	Federal (%)	Provincial (%)	Local (%)
1900	57.1	N.A.	N.A.
1910	50.0	27.6	22.4
1920	59.2	17.0	23.8
1930	32.1	24.6	43.3
1938	34.3	36.1	29.6
1950	52.2	25.2	22.6
1960	50.5	24.1	25.4
1965	43.1	28.7	28.2
1971	37.1	37.9	25.0
1975	40.1	37.0	22.9
1980	36.0	41.0	23.0

Sources: Data through 1971 are from Werner W. Pommerehne, "Quantitative Aspects of Federalism: A Study of Six Countries," in *The Political Economy of Fiscal Federalism,* ed. W. E. Oates (Lexington, Mass.: Lexington Books, 1977), p. 311. For 1975 and 1980, figures are calculated from data in United Nations, *Yearbook of National Account Statistics, 1978* (New York, 1983), vol. 1, part 1, pp. 225, 227.

Note: Intergovernmental transfers are treated as expenditures by the recipient government.

Table 3–6 Central government expenditure as percentage of total government expenditure for four countries, 1950–1970.

Year	France (%)	Germany (%)	Switzerland (%)	United Kingdom (%)
1950	85.6	48.4	32.9	76.6
1955	80.5	44.3	33.4	75.0
1960	83.2	39.9	30.7	68.0
1965	81.7	40.3	26.9	60.6
1970	79.3	37.9	26.2	60.0

Source: Werner W. Pommerehne, "Quantitative Aspects of Federalism: A Study of Six Countries," in *The Political Economy of Fiscal Federalism,* ed. W. E. Oates (Lexington, Mass.: Lexington Books, 1977), p. 307.

that local government is alive and well. This should not be too surprising because the local provision of certain services offers such important advantages that it would seem quite unlikely that the local sector would simply wither away.

Although a simplistic version of the centralization thesis does not seem tenable in light of the evidence, the evolution of the public sector both in the United States and elsewhere exhibits some intriguing elements. In particular, as the public sector grows as a whole, there seems to be a tendency to form new sorts of units and jurisdictions for public decision making. The government sector seems to be evolving into a more complex and highly specialized set of institutions, taking different forms in different countries. In the United States, its most dramatic manifestation is the rise of special districts. As Table 3–7 indicates, the number of special districts more than tripled during the period from 1942 to 1982. This reflects an increasing specialization in the public sector, for most of these districts are single-function entities. Moreover, the services provided by special districts are diverse, including highways, sewers, housing, libraries, fire protection, natural resources, hospitals, and cemeteries. However, there has been a large reduction in the total number of governmental units. This is primarily the result of consolidating smaller school districts and some small townships.

Yet, the creation of new jurisdictions and units has not been limited to single-purpose public agencies. In fact, public sectors in the western industrialized

Table 3–7 Number of governmental units in the United States, 1942–1982.

Government	1942	1952	1962	1972	1982
U.S. government	1	1	1	1	1
States	48	48	50	50	50
Local governments	155,067	116,694	91,186	78,218	82,290
County	3,050	3,049	3,043	3,044	3,041
Municipal	16,220	16,778	18,000	18,517	19,076
Township and town	18,919	17,202	17,142	16,991	16,734
School district	108,579	67,346	34,678	15,781	14,851
Special district	8,299	12,319	18,323	23,885	28,588
Total	155,116	116,743	91,237	78,269	82,341

Source: U.S. Bureau of the Census, *Statistical Abstract of the United States, 1984* (Washington, D.C.: GPO, 1983), table 447, p. 272.

economies repeatedly show evidence of the establishment of "new" levels of government to cope with new demands on the public sector. Metropolitan governments have been created in some urban areas in the United States, in Toronto, Canada, and in several European urban centers. The goal is to integrate fiscal decision making between suburban residential communities and the central cities that serve them. At the same time, the inability of a central government to meet certain "regional needs" has led to the establishment of regional governments in Italy and to proposals for Scottish and Welsh assemblies in Great Britain. In Britain, Alan Peacock contends, the "deviation in individual and group preferences from those reflected in the existing amount and pattern of government services has become more marked [and has resulted in] the growing demand for devolution. . . ."[35]

Moreover, the formation of new governments has not been restricted to the lower tiers. A totally new level of government whose jurisdiction is the entire membership of the European Economic Community (EEC) is emerging in Europe. It is not yet clear what the ultimate range of responsibilities and powers of the new government will be, but the contrast between a newly created European level of government and the move toward devolution in certain member countries does suggest the diversity of pressures operating on the public sector.

The implications of these historical changes on the trends and future of federal fiscal structure are not clear. However, any simplistic notion of continuing centralization and of the eventual extinction of local government seems highly unlikely and inconsistent with recent fiscal trends. Local government will continue to contribute to the functioning of the public sector. This by no means implies a static view of local structure and its role in the federal system, for local government has shown itself quite capable of taking new forms in response to changing demands. It is interesting to speculate on the growing specialization that these new forms represent. The general growth of the public sector has no doubt made it feasible to increase the degree of specialization in the government sphere. Here may be a principle for the public sector that parallels Adam Smith's famous dictum for the private sector: "The division of labour is limited by the extent of the market."

The New Federalism

The preceding section explored broad tendencies in federal fiscal structure. In the 1980s a significant restructuring of the fiscal system has occurred in the United States under the banner of the "New Federalism." Table 3–1 showed, for example, that the historic tendency toward increasing reliance on federal grants to states and local governments seems to have reversed itself around 1980. Since that time, federal grants have declined significantly in number, in real dollars, and as a fraction of federal outlays. This is the result of a deliberate program under the Reagan administration to extricate the federal government from its extensive involvement in what the administration sees as essentially state and local matters.

The New Federalism of the 1980s seeks to reorder the roles of the different levels of government. This is being accomplished largely through a reform of the federal grant system—consolidating many specific grant programs into a few more broadly defined block grants. Such block grants provide much wider budgetary discretion to the states and localities.

The New Federalism program for restructuring the U.S. federal system was initially embodied in four proposals:

1. The assumption by the states of full responsibility for the basic welfare programs: Aid to Families with Dependent Children (AFDC) and the Food Stamp Program. In return, the federal government proposed to take on the full burden of administering and funding the Medicaid program (which provides health care for low-income households).
2. A "turnback" to the states and localities of a variety of existing federal programs in the areas of education and training, social services, transportation, and community development.
3. The consolidation of a large number of specific categorical grant programs into more broadly defined "block" grants. Proposed block grants included child welfare, training and employment, rental rehabilitation, welfare administration, vocational and adult education, education for the handicapped, and rehabilitative services.
4. The creation of a "Federalism trust fund" from which the federal government would earmark the revenues from certain excise taxes and the windfall profits tax on oil for use by the states. This fund would eventually be phased out and would disappear after 1991, leaving the states the option of imposing their own excises to replace these funds or, alternatively, of cutting their spending.

This set of proposals reflected the administration's contention that the federal government was intervening in matters in which it had no legitimate business. In particular, the evolution of an elaborate system of categorical grants had produced an intergovernmental fiscal system of "bewildering complexity." It was the view of the President that "this massive federal grant-making system has distorted state and local decisions and usurped state and local functions." The thrust of the New Federalism is a move toward devolution, a move to disengage the federal government from its involvement in a broad range of domestic programs.[36]

The New Federalism initiative has met with mixed success. The first component of the proposals, that of shifting full responsibility for AFDC and food stamps to the states, met intense opposition and was subsequently abandoned. The President argued that state and local governments should provide for the poor. But there emerged a strong consensus that the federal government should retain an active role in funding the major welfare programs. As discussed earlier in this chapter, there is a strong sense that the problem of poverty is a national problem and that for reasons of both equity and effectiveness, the burden of financing welfare benefits should be shared by society as a whole.

In contrast, the New Federalism has made real headway in restructuring the federal grant system. As noted earlier, the period from 1950 to 1980 was one of striking growth in federal grant programs. Not only did the total sum of such aid grow rapidly, but there was a dramatic expansion in the number and variety of programs. As Table 3–1 shows, grant programs grew from 132 in 1960 to over 500 in 1981. This created a maze of overlapping and sometimes conflicting programs, which was not only hard to rationalize but required extensive "grantsmanship" efforts on the part of state and local officials. The administration contended that it was time to simplify the federal grant system and to extricate the federal government from the detailed management of state and local affairs. This would be accomplished by consolidating many specific categorical grant programs into a set of broad "block grants." Such grants would define in only very general terms the use of the grant funds and, hence, would permit state and local agencies much greater discretion in the deployment of these revenues.

Under the Omnibus Budget Reconciliation Act of 1981, the U.S. Congress responded to the New Federalism initiative by consolidating about 80 categorical grant programs into nine block grants encompassing a broad range of domestic functions. Four block grants provide funding for health services, and one each for social services, low-income energy assistance, education, community development, and community services. Furthermore, federal funding levels declined somewhat relative to earlier levels under the categorical programs.

Compared with categorical grants-in-aid, the block grant programs have given state and local officials broader authority to set priorities and determine the use of funds. A study by the General Accounting Office (GAO) has found, not surprisingly, that in the first two years of the new block grant programs, there was a growing diversity across states in the use of federal grant monies.[37] For certain programs, many of the states have drawn on their own funds to offset losses in federal funding. In the aggregate, however, spending on these programs has declined. The GAO found that in real terms, between 1981 and 1983, total program expenditure fell in about three-quarters of the states that they examined. This also is not surprising. As noted earlier, econometric studies have suggested that, generally, grant programs stimulate spending, and categorical (particularly matching) programs stimulate spending more effectively than do unconditional programs. Broadly defined, block grants are obviously closer to the unconditional end of the grant spectrum than are more narrowly targeted categorical grants. The expectation is that a program that both cuts the total level of grant funding and reduces the conditions attached to the funds will significantly reduce state and local spending in the program areas—and this does seem to be happening.

Finally, though, while there is certainly much too be said for efforts to simplify and rationalize the federal grant system, the consolidation of grants should not be pursued indiscriminately. As discussed earlier, many categorical grant programs have a sound rationale—encouraging state and local activities that serve the broader national interest. To fold such programs into the umbrella of block grants effectively undermines their ability to focus local spending. What is needed is a careful program-by-program assessment to determine which categorical grant programs are the proper subject for consolidation (or extinction) and which have a legitimate role to play in the intergovernmental system. Such an assessment of the grant system still needs to be made.

Summary

The fiscal structure of the federal system does not involve a clearly delineated separation of functions among levels of government. Nevertheless, economic analysis provides some insights into the appropriate roles of different levels of the public sector. It suggests that the central government must assume the major responsibility for macroeconomic stabilization of the economy, for socially equitable distribution of income, and for the provision of certain national public goods and services (such as national defense). Decentralized levels of government make their major contribution by providing important local public goods and services.

There is, however, some inevitable overlap in the workings of different levels of government. The intergovernmental grant system has proved a flexible and widely employed mechanism for integrating the operations and interests of the different levels of government. Such grants are used to supply state and local governments with incentives to provide services that benefit those residing in other jurisdictions, to equalize fiscal capacity among jurisdictions, and to achieve a more efficient and fair tax system. Because types of intergovernmental grants vary, individual grant programs must select the appropriate form (e.g., conditional or unconditional, matching or nonmatching) to perform their function effectively.

The historical record of fiscal structure reveals a pronounced trend toward centralization of the public sector over the first half of the twentieth century. The role of the central government during this period rose dramatically at the expense of the state and local sectors. However, there is evidence from several countries that the centralization trend has leveled off since the 1950s and, in some instances, even reversed itself. Whatever the trend, the Reagan administration under its "New Federalism" proposals sought to shift the balance of fiscal responsibilities toward state and local government. The central thrust involved consolidating many specific categorical grant programs into broad block grants that allow more discretion in the use of funds at state and local levels. In addition, levels of grant support have declined, and there has been a phasing out of general revenue sharing. The ultimate effects of the New Federalism are not yet clear, but the evidence suggests that these measures have resulted in significant reductions of state and local spending on programs that were previously supported in part by federal grant monies.

1 James Bryce, *The American Commonwealth* (New York: Macmillan, 1896), p. 324. 2 vols.

2 Michael D. Reagan, *The New Federalism* (New York: Oxford Univ. Press, 1972), p. 81.

3 Geoffrey W. Oxley, *Poor Relief in England and Wales, 1601–1834* (North Pomfret, Vt.: David & Charles, 1974).

4 Edwin Cannan, *The History of Local Rates in England,* 2d ed. (London: P. S. King & Son, 1912), p. 185.

5 See, for example, David Bradford and Wallace Oates, "Suburban Exploitation of Central Cities and Governmental Structure," in *Redistribution Through Public Choice,* eds. Harold Hochman and George Peterson (New York: Columbia Univ. Press, 1974), pp. 43–90; and Michael Boss, "Economic Theory of Democracy: An Empirical Test," *Public Choice* 19 (1974): 111–15.

6 See the discussion of the "Decentralization Theorem" in Wallace E. Oates, *Fiscal Federalism* (New York: Harcourt Brace Jovanovich, 1972), pp. 33–38, 54–63.

7 Charles Tiebout, "A Pure Theory of Local Expenditures," *Journal of Political Economy* 64 (October 1956): 416–24.

8 Ibid., p. 422.

9 See, for example, Wallace Oates, "The Effects of Property Taxes and Local Public Spending on Property Values: An Empirical Study of Tax Capitalization and the Tiebout Hypothesis," *Journal of Political Economy* 77 (1969): 957–71; and Gerald S. McDougall, "Local Public Goods and Residential Property Values: Some Insights and Extensions," *National Tax Journal* 29 (December 1976): 436–47. For an alternative approach involving the study of fiscally induced patterns of migration, see J. Richard Aronson and Eli Schwartz, "Financing Public Goods and the Distribution of Population in a System of Local Governments," *National Tax Journal* 26 (June 1973): 137–60.

10 Alexis de Tocqueville, *Democracy in America,* the Henry Reeve text as revised by Francis Bowen, further corrected and edited by Phillips Bradley (New York: Vintage Books, Alfred A. Knopf, 1945), vol. 1, p. 168.

11 Kenneth C. Wheare, *Federal Government,* 4th ed. (London: Oxford Univ. Press, 1963), p. 117.

12 William H. Young, ed., *Ogg and Ray's Introduction to American Government,* 13th ed. (New York: Appleton-Century-Crofts, 1966), p. 62.

13 See Oates, *Fiscal Federalism,* Chapter 3.

14 Ronald Coase, "The Problem of Social Cost," *Journal of Law and Economics* 3 (October 1960): 1–44.

15 William Baumol and Wallace Oates, *The Theory of*

Environmental Policy: Externalities, Public Outlays, and the Quality of Life (Englewood Cliffs, N.J.: Prentice-Hall, 1975), Chapter 2.

16 Oates, *Fiscal Federalism,* Chapter 3.

17 For a careful examination of equalizing grants and their use in federal countries, see Russell L. Mathews, ed., *Fiscal Equalization in a Federal System* (Canberra: Centre for Research in Federal Financial Relations, 1974).

18 For some findings on the capitalization of fiscal differentials into local property values, see Oates, "The Effects"; McDougall, "Local Public Goods"; and Aronson and Schwartz, "Financing Public."

19 For a good summary of the evidence on the incidence of various taxes in the United States, see Joseph A. Pechman, *Who Paid the Taxes, 1966–1985* (Washington, D.C.: Brookings Institution, 1985). As Pechman makes clear, any conclusions on overall tax incidence must be hedged by a number of important qualifications.

20 Charles McLure, "The Interstate Exporting of State and Local Taxes: Estimates for 1962," *National Tax Journal* 20 (March 1967): 49–77.

21 Joseph Pechman, *Federal Tax Policy,* 4th ed. (Washington, D.C.: Brookings Institution, 1983), p. 61; and J. Richard Aronson and John L. Hilley, *Financing State and Local Governments,* 4th ed. (Washington, D.C.: Brookings Institution, 1986), p. 101.

22 See R. J. Bennett, *Central Grants to Local Governments* (Cambridge: Cambridge Univ. Press, 1982), Chapter 3.

23 See Advisory Commission on Intergovernmental Relations, *Federal Grants: Their Effects on State-Local Expenditures, Employment Levels, and Wage Rates,* A–61 (Washington, D.C.: GPO, 1977). This study uses data for 1972.

24 For a careful analysis of these formulas, see Robert Reischauer, "General Revenue Sharing: The Program's Incentives," in *Financing the New Federalism,* ed. W. E. Oates (Baltimore: Johns Hopkins Univ. Press, Resources for the Future, 1975), pp. 40–87.

25 Advisory Commission on Intergovernmental Relations, *Federal Grants,* pp. 26–28.

26 A. Kneese and Charles L. Schultz, *Pollution, Prices, and Public Policy* (Washington, D.C.: Brookings Institution, 1975), Chapter 3.

27 For useful surveys of the empirical work on the budgetary impact of intergovernmental grants, see Edward M. Gramlich, "Intergovernmental Grants: A Review of the Empirical Literature," in *The Political Economy of Fiscal Federalism,* ed. W. E. Oates (Lexington, Mass.: Lexington Books, 1977), pp. 219–40; and Advisory Commission on Intergovernmental Relations, *Federal Grants.*

28 For a formal presentation of the veil hypothesis, see David F. Bradford and Wallace E. Oates, "The Analysis of Revenue Sharing in a New Approach to Collective Fiscal Decisions," *Quarterly Journal of Economics* 85 (August 1971): 416–39.

29 See Gramlich, "Intergovernmental Grants"; and Richard P. Nathan and Charles F. Adams, Jr., *Revenue Sharing: The Second Round* (Washington, D.C.: Brookings Institution, 1977). For a useful collection of papers exploring this whole issue, see Peter Mieszkowski and William Oakland, eds., *Fiscal Federalism and Grants-in-Aid* (Washington, D.C.: Urban Institute, 1979).

30 De Tocqueville, *Democracy in America,* vol. 2, p. 313.

31 Edward McWhinney, *Comparative Federalism,* 2d ed. (Toronto: Univ. of Toronto Press, 1965), p. 105.

32 On option value in local finance, see Burton Weisbrod, *External Benefits of Public Education* (Princeton, N.J.: Industrial Relations Section, Princeton Univ., 1964).

33 Reagan, *The New Federalism,* p. 77.

34 On this issue, see Oates, *Fiscal Federalism,* Chapter 5.

35 Alan Peacock, "The Political Economy of Devolution: The British Case," in *The Political Economy,* ed. W. E. Oates, p. 51.

36 For a useful description and analysis of the New Federalism proposals, see Claude E. Barfield, *Rethinking Federalism: Block Grants and Federal, State, and Local Responsibilities* (Washington, D.C.: American Enterprise Institute, 1981).

37 U.S. General Accounting Office, *Block Grants Brought Funding Changes and Adjustments to Program Priorities* (Washington, D.C., 11 February 1985).

Local government expenditures and revenues

This chapter lays out a framework that local officials might use in setting or reviewing the underlying goals and constraints on their budgets. First, the discussion applies economic theory to resource allocation and distribution—the fiscal roles of government. The chapter then focuses on expenditures and revenues—at both a prescriptive level (how *should* governments make their expenditure and revenue decisions?) and a descriptive level (how *do* they actually spend and tax?). Next the chapter emphasizes the need for fiscal planners to ask whether their expenditure practices meet and serve budget goals and to understand the determining and shaping factors in expenditure decision making. After focusing on the core of this process—designing a local tax system and structure—the chapter concludes with a look at future trends and factors, from national economic performance and demographics to federal policy.

The fiscal roles of government

Richard Musgrave, in his classic book *The Theory of Public Finance,* provides a useful simplification of the fiscal functions of government.[1] Setting the public budget, according to Musgrave, involves an allocation decision (what services will be provided?), a distribution decision (who will get the benefits and bear the burdens?), and a stabilization/growth decision (what levels of growth in income and prices are acceptable?). Local government financial planners might begin their evaluation of alternative fiscal actions by considering each of these possible objectives.

Allocation

The most important fiscal role of local government is to decide on the level and mix of taxes and expenditures that best match the preferences and needs of the local population. That local governments take this allocation function seriously is evidenced by the wide variety of choices they actually make. When apportioning their budgets, local governments can choose among programs that benefit different economic groups: low-income residents benefit from social services; all residents theoretically benefit, directly or indirectly, from programs that protect the environment; and middle- and upper-income residents are likely to benefit from programs that reduce traffic congestion or improve airports. In some cases, it is even possible to predict which choices will improve the equality of income distribution, that is, which decisions will primarily benefit the low-income population. In other cases, it is not—such as the choice between spending more for social services (subsidized housing and welfare) or spending more for economic development programs that ultimately produce more jobs. The debate on such issues is endless and there are no easy guidelines.

An example of the variety of responses to allocation decisions is the share of current expenditures devoted to education in metropolitan areas that varies from 29 percent in New York to 66 percent in Tulsa; similarly, the share of local expenditure for police varies from 3.3 percent in the northeast Pennsylvania metropolitan area to 9.5 percent in Miami; and average effective property tax rates vary from 0.14 and 0.35 percent in various localities in Mobile County, Alabama, to 2.33 and 4.63 percent in Suffolk County, New York.[2] Underlying such variations are a number of important allocation decisions that have been made by local governments; for example, the decisions whether to hire more fire fighters or pay a higher wage, whether refuse collection will be public or private, and whether a CAT scanner or a school bus will be purchased.

In making such choices about levels of service, local government officials and managers can be guided by three general criteria: economic efficiency, technical efficiency, and net social benefit when jurisdictions or interests overlap.

Economic efficiency Economic efficiency requires that government fiscal decisions match local preferences for public services. In short, it means that the government should try to deliver the package of government services and taxes that the population wants. This "preferred" package differs from city to city. Syracuse requires more snow removal than does St. Petersburg, which requires more services for the elderly. Cleveland and Buffalo must maintain an aging stock of public capital, whereas growing cities in the South and West must allocate more to new infrastructure development. Large cities must address a mass transit problem that small cities may not have.

Public service packages may also vary with the "tastes" of the local population. New York and California residents have historically preferred a relatively large government sector and a progressive tax system; Texas and Florida residents seem to prefer smaller public sectors, no income taxes, and a smaller allocation to public education. In some states these differences are actually legislated, such as the greater fiscal dominance of the state government over the localities in North Carolina and Hawaii, and the relatively greater fiscal dominance of local government in Ohio and Pennsylvania.

In order to meet the criterion of economic efficiency, local government decision makers need to recognize citizen preferences as well as changes in taste. This may look easy, since voters make their wishes known through school budget votes, bond referendum votes, and general elections. Yet local officials can easily misread a community's complex preferences. Voters may have mixed views on what they want, and they may not be able to reveal preferences on every issue (e.g., there is no separate vote on the police budget).

Furthermore, preferences may change; favorable votes on tax limitation referenda were the rule in the late 1970s, but the exception in the early 1980s. An interesting example of how preferences can change comes from two surveys of public opinions on taxes by the Advisory Commission on Intergovernmental Relations (ACIR).[3] The 1972 survey showed that 45 percent of respondents thought the property tax was the least fair tax and only 19 percent identified the federal income tax as the least fair. A repeat survey in 1985 showed that only 24 percent thought the local property tax was least fair, but 38 percent thought that the federal income tax was the worst tax.

Finally, reading preferences is difficult because voters may be "unreasonable" in their expectations; for example, given the choice between lower taxes and better public services, voters almost inevitably choose *both* of the above.

Technical efficiency Technical efficiency refers to the provision of services at least cost. Local officials may take a number of actions to lower the cost of operations:

1. Increase the productivity of workers through training, recasting job rules, or initiating new management and work procedures
2. Institute long-range planning improvements

3. Substitute capital for labor in government operations
4. Reduce interest costs on local debt
5. Capture economies of scale in service delivery
6. Contract with private organizations for service delivery.

However attractive each option may be, none is without its social or economic price. Improvement in productivity, for example, is especially appealing because it arouses little political opposition (who could oppose a more productive public-sector labor force?). But the cost of improved productivity may be the elimination of "excess" public workers. Whereas this may help the budget, it may harm the local employment situation and may be politically unattractive.

Examples of improved planning include establishing a scheduling procedure for maintenance of the capital stock or instituting a multiyear fiscal planning model. In the long run, such actions can significantly improve the efficiency of government operations and probably the unit cost of output, but they necessitate a potentially large outlay to establish and maintain the planning models.

Examples of substituting capital for labor are computerization, newer police cars and fire trucks, less labor-intensive refuse collection systems, and even relocation of certain public facilities, such as fire stations. While all these could be cost savers, they imply a substantial initial capital outlay.

Interest costs might be reduced by taking actions that would lead to a higher bond rating or to improved marketability of an issue. The attractiveness of an issue could be increased by dedicating a portion of general revenue to debt repayment, purchasing bond insurance, or installing put options. However, these actions also entail costs: a dedicated revenue stream would weaken the general fiscal base available for other purposes; bond insurance is purchased for a fee; and put options increase the future budget uncertainty for the local government.

Economies of scale can be realized by expanding the geographic area over which a public service is delivered.[4] These economies—particularly for hardware-type services such as public utilities—are a principal reason that regionwide and consolidated service districts have become common, particularly water and sewer districts, health and hospital districts, park districts, and health and physical planning activities. However, even though regionwide provision of service usually lowers unit costs, it also entails some loss of local control and, consequently, more difficulty in satisfying particular local preferences.

Finally, technical efficiency can be improved through privatization of public services—refuse collection being the most common example. Numerous services seem to be amenable to either public or private delivery and it may be worthwhile for a local government to see whether private firms can provide them more efficiently. On the one hand, turning a service over to the private sector to produce and deliver can offload some responsibility from the government budget. On the other hand, if such services have a broad social purpose, and privatization reduces the level of output, then privatization may impose a substantial social cost. Moreover, it is by no means certain that all services can be delivered more inexpensively through the private sector. The use of private contracting involves increased government administration and monitoring in addition to payment of contractors' fees.[5]

Net social benefit Local governments need to consider total net social benefit when "externalities" or spillover effects and costs are involved. In seeking to address community preferences, local officials and managers need to accommodate the interests of society at large, not only of their particular constituency. For example, a community may choose to control its air and water pollution at a level that does not satisfy adjacent communities; the unbridled growth of a suburban community may increase the number of commuters to the central city until central city services are unduly congested; and one community's failure or inability to provide adequate primary and vocational education opportunities may lead to another community's crime problem. All these local decisions may impose spillover costs on other sectors of the society.

Policymakers typically respond in the following three ways to deal with the spillover problem: (1) the federal or state government may either coerce or induce local governments to take total social costs and benefits into account; (2) local governments may engage in some form of intergovernmental compact to compensate one another for social costs incurred or social benefits received; or (3) a local government may expand its service boundaries so as to "internalize the externalities."

Trade-offs The essence of this discussion is that local government officials—even if guided by sound economic reasoning—face some difficult choices in allocating services. Economic efficiency is best served by units of government that are small enough to allow preferences to be taken into account. In fact, one economist has suggested that a theoretically ideal metropolitan governance arrangement would consist of many different local governments offering different packages of public services and taxes.[6] In this consumer-sovereign world, consumer-residents could "vote with their feet" in choosing a community whose public service package best matched their own preferences.

In contrast, considerations of technical efficiency and net social benefit seem to argue for placing less emphasis on local preferences and greater emphasis on the larger governmental unit. In such a case, local officials will confront residents with the possibility of relinquishing some local control over their service package in order to obtain (perhaps) a reduced unit cost and the consolation of knowing that they have paid their social as well as private dues. These are the arguments that underlie the movement toward consolidation of services and metropolitan governance.

Distribution

Distribution is another major role of local government. Distribution decisions concern how the benefits and burdens of local budgets should be divided among residents. Economics and history have shown that local governments cannot successfully use transfer payments to redistribute income, because people are relatively free to move across local boundaries. This does not mean, however, that local government officials should totally eschew any income redistribution role. After all, nearly 20 percent of all government taxes are collected by local governments and 25 percent of all expenditures are made by local governments.

One of the three major ways local governments might affect income distribution is their choice of *where* to deliver services. Many public services are delivered directly to *locations* rather than directly to persons. For example, a city might decide to increase the frequency of refuse collection in lower-income areas, to locate special park facilities in those areas, to increase police protection services in high-crime areas, and to establish neighborhood health clinics. Such decisions can be, in essence, a subsidy to low-income neighborhoods. Note that these types of decisions can be made even after the overall size of the budget has been settled.

Another way local government can affect income distribution is through its system of user charges. It can decide, for example, what proportion of local transit system expenditures will be financed by fares and what proportion by general local tax revenues.

Income distribution also can be affected by decisions on what kind of taxes to levy and on the specific structure of these taxes, but these decisions generally are made at the state level. The decision to allow a "circuit breaker" in the property tax that will provide relief to the elderly and to low-income families is a state government decision, as are decisions to levy local sales or income taxes, or to include food, medicine, and clothing in the local sales tax base.

Stabilization/development

Local budget planners often ask whether their particular local government can do much to stabilize local economic fluctuations and to promote economic development. On the surface, it would appear that the local government sector is large enough to have a significant influence on the national economy. After all, local government expenditures account for about 8 percent of the gross national product (GNP). Yet, the answer to the *stabilization* question is a clear "no." Local governments can do little to affect interest rates, consumer prices, or, except for very brief periods, the unemployment rate. Whereas the federal government can use deficit financing or its control of the money supply to affect the level of unemployment or the rate of inflation, local governments do not have control over the money supply. The resources local governments control are limited, their economies are too open to permit the use of deficit spending to increase employment within the local area, and the benefits of any actions they take independently will not remain in the area but will "leak out" to the rest of the country.

When it comes to *development,* however, local governments have considerable ability to stimulate local economic development through autonomous actions. Virtually every local government has some sort of development agency and/or Chamber of Commerce that is dedicated to promoting the local economy. Whereas study after study has shown that factors such as the availability of a skilled labor supply, location and transportation facilities, and energy costs are far more important in industry location decisions than are local tax and expenditure policies,[7] the level and types of taxes in a locality may be an important determinant of business location *within* the metropolitan area and for the location decisions of small businesses. Whatever the effect of the fiscal environment, local officials try to do what they are most capable of—to influence location decisions through the fiscal system.

It is difficult to develop a prescriptive guideline for action in this area. Even if in the final decision tax concessions are deemed unimportant, local government officials are very aware that other communities offer such incentives. Not to do so is to signal that the "climate is hostile" for development. Thus, tax concessions may be a necessary defensive action.

What this comes down to is another choice. How much is a local government willing to charge its current citizens—in the form of higher taxes or lower public services—to provide tax incentives for economic development? The right answer to this question depends on the local officials' evaluation of the probability that the fiscal incentive will work, the need for jobs in the local area, and the potential effect of any new industry on local revenues and costs.

Expenditures

How do governments actually spend their funds? What patterns are "average" or "normal"? To what extent are allocation, distribution, and growth objectives served? Local government expenditures can be examined in three ways:

1. By looking at the functions or purposes for which local governments expend their funds—police, fire, education, and so on
2. By classifying expenditures in terms of object—wages and salaries, materials and supplies, and interest payments, for example
3. By considering how much of the expenditures are for current items (such as wages and supplies) versus longer-lived capital projects (such as roads or buildings).

In examining these patterns, a word of caution is in order about the comparability of the data among different localities. Cities, counties, and special districts have been given different expenditure responsibilities in different states, and these are reflected in the "norms" described below.

The magnitude of local expenditures

The relative size of local government expenditures is shown in Table 4–1. Local governments accounted for about 25 percent of *total* government expenditures, but they accounted for about 68 percent of all education expenditures and more than 40 percent of expenditures for highways and for health. These data reinforce a long-known fact, that the major single function of local governments is primary and secondary education (mainly administered through semi-independent school districts). The data also emphasize the labor-intensive nature of local services. Local governments accounted for about 45 percent of all government employee wages and salaries but for less than 10 percent of all income transfers and insurance payments, which mostly represent expenditures made for the purpose of income redistribution.

Table 4–2 shows the distribution of these expenditures by type of local government. The second column shows how local governments as a whole spend their resources, including 13.8 percent for capital outlay and 5.5 percent for highways. The remaining columns show how these totals are divided among cities, counties, and special districts. These data show that over 40 percent of local government resources are allocated to education, with no other function coming close. It is not surprising, therefore, that special districts, which include school districts, also account for over 40 percent of local government spending—more than the percentage accounted for by either cities or counties.

Selected indicators of trends in local government expenditures over two decades are described in Table 4–3. After rising from 1964 to 1974, real per capita expenditures of local government had not increased markedly by 1983. If

Table 4–1
Government expenditures by object and function, 1983.

Expenditure category	Total federal, state, local (in billions of dollars)	Local expenditures as % of total
Total by object[a]	$1,351	24.8
Current operation	693	37.2
(wages and salaries)	(314)	(45.8)
Capital outlay	149	30.0
Assistance and subsidies	74	9.2
Interest on debt	138	12.7
Insurance benefits and repayments	297	1.7
Total by function	1,000	28.4
Education	177	67.7
Highways	37	41.7
Welfare	83	18.4
Health	56	41.9
Interest on general debt	133	9.7
Other, including defense	518	18.6

Source: U.S. Bureau of the Census, *Governmental Finances in 1982–83,* series GF83, no. 5 (Washington, D.C.: GPO, 1984), computed from Tables 9 and 10.
Note: Because of rounding, detail may not add to totals.
[a]Includes expenditures on utilities, liquor stores, and insurance trusts.

Table 4–2 Percentage distribution of local government expenditures by function, object, and spending unit, 1983.

Expenditure category	Distribution of local expenditures (%)	Distribution by type of government (%)		
		City[a]	County	Special district[b]
Total by object[c]	100.0	39.2	21.4	40.9
Current operation	77.2	36.7	20.2	43.1
Capital outlay	13.8	45.7	16.4	37.9
Assistance and subsidies	2.1	26.8	73.2	—
Interest on debt	4.8	40.6	17.4	42.0
Insurance benefits and repayments	1.5	78.5	16.1	5.4
Total by function[c]	100.0	34.7	23.4	41.9
Education	42.1	10.2	7.7	82.0
Highways	5.5	59.4	39.0	1.6
Welfare	5.4	31.2	68.8	—
Police and fire protection	8.1	78.2	19.4	2.4
Health	8.3	24.8	50.4	24.8
Interest on general debt	4.5	42.2	25.1	32.7
Other[d]	24.1	58.3	29.0	12.6

Sources: U.S. Bureau of Census, *Governmental Finances in 1982–83*, series GF83, no. 5 (Washington, D.C.: GPO, 1984), Tables 10 and 23; and *1982 Census of Governments, Compendium of Governmental Finances*, vol. 4, no. 5 (Washington, D.C.: GPO, 1984), Tables 2 and 48.

Note: Table is compiled from 1982 and 1983 data.

[a]Including municipalities and townships.

[b]Including school districts.

[c]The allocations across local governments by object and function *are not the same* because some expenditures could not be allocated by function.

[d]Including expenditures for environment, housing, and government administration.

intergovernmental transfers are not counted, local government expenditures from own sources actually declined from 25.3 percent of total government expenditures in 1964 to 22.6 percent in 1983. Rows 3 and 7 show the growing fiscal responsibility of state governments relative to local governments. It is interesting to note that much of this growth in state fiscal responsibility occurred during a time when there was increased emphasis on direct federal-to-local assistance. Row 10 shows that local governments continue to account for more than half of all public employment in the United States.

Determinants of local expenditures

The level and mix of local government expenditures are determined both by economic and demographic factors that are mostly beyond the control of the local government and by policy choices. Even if the major influence on local public expenditures is a high rate of inflation, local decision makers still have some degree of choice. They can raise taxes or lower the level of services provided, depending on their own preferences and those of the voters.

The job of local fiscal planners is to identify the determinants of public spending, estimate their potential effects on local budgets, and somehow present the available fiscal choices to the public. This can be done most effectively if the local finance officer has a framework within which to consider the factors that determine the level and mix of items in the government budget.

The determinants of local government spending might be thought of in the familiar demand-supply framework. After all, each year's budget is an attempt by local officials to balance demand (the quantity and quality of public services local residents would like to have) and supply (the quantity and quality of services the local government can provide at given levels of revenue, or "tax prices").

Table 4–3 Trends in local government expenditures.

Item	1964	1974	1983
Local expenditures from own sources			
1. Per capita in 1972 dollars	$216	$282	$287
2. As a % of GNP	4.7	4.8	4.4
3. As a % of state expenditures[a]	108.2	75.7	71.4
4. As a % of total government expenditures[a]	17.1	15.0	12.4
Local expenditures after intergovernmental transfers			
5. Per capita in 1972 dollars	$319	$524	$524
6. As a % of GNP	7.0	9.0	8.0
7. As a % of state expenditures[b]	185.8	169.9	155.8
8. As a % of total government expenditures[b]	25.3	28.0	22.6
Local employment			
9. Per 10,000 population	241[c]	325[d]	332
10. As a % of total government employment	52.9	56.2	57.0

Source: Advisory Commission on Intergovernmental Relations, *Significant Features of Fiscal Federalism, 1984 Edition*, (Washington, D.C.: GPO, 1984), Tables 1, 2, 82.
[a]From own sources
[b]After intergovernmental transfers
[c]1962
[d]1972

Demand factors The demand for public services, as expressed in community preferences, is affected by four major factors:

1. Population shifts
2. National economic performance
3. The relative price of services
4. Changes in income level.

Population shifts The community's preferences for public service may shift with a change in the composition of the population. Rapid in-migration has brought new populations with new demands to such booming areas as South Florida. Moreover, growing cities in general face a changing set of public service demands that can cause budgets to escalate rapidly. New industry and annexation creates pressure to expand the infrastructure and carry a heavier debt burden, higher income in-migrants and newly arrived companies often agitate for an improved education system, and the cost of managing and maintaining a city increases at a faster rate than city population. Even in a conservatively financed setting, such as Houston in the 1970s, population increased by 29 percent between 1970 and 1980, while city operating expenditures increased by almost two and one half times between 1973 and 1978.[8]

National economic performance Some have argued that the prolonged period of slow economic growth and high inflation that characterized the 1970s and early 1980s shifted the interest of local citizens toward tax limitations and away from services that tended to redistribute income. Public goods and income distribution are much more acceptable, it would seem, when there is economic growth and a substantial surplus to redistribute.

Relative price A change in the relative price of a public service will cause a change in the quantity demanded. It stands to reason that if the cost of public recreation services increases relative to other costs, citizens will reduce their demand for those services.

Changes in the relative price of publicly supplied goods is only half the story, however. The other half is the extent to which local governments actually respond to changes in these relative prices. A great deal of research on public-sector behavior indicates that the governmental response is not very great. For instance, when wages of public employees increase, local governments do not appear to cut back public employment in proportion to those increases.

Inflation can also increase the relative price of public goods if the price of government services is driven up faster than the local tax base. For example, the local property tax base is usually not increased at the same rate as inflation. As a result, the purchasing power of local government revenues is reduced. Apparently, higher rates of inflation can lead to a lower rate of growth in real expenditures,[9] especially in older cities where property values are relatively stable and little new construction is underway.

Changes in community income levels Research has shown that public services are "income elastic"; that is, the demand for such services increases more than the proportion to the increase in personal income. As their income increases, citizens seem to want more and better services from local governments, such as better schools, better parks, and better road maintenance.

While it is clear that local officials must plan a budgetary response to such expected increases or decreases in community income, the appropriate response may vary depending on local circumstances. For example, certain types of income growth are less powerful than others in influencing the growth in public expenditures. Substantial increases in welfare-related transfer payments and Social Security benefits do not yield the same amounts of local tax revenue as other sources of income and therefore may not exert the same stimulus on public expenditure growth. Moreover, some changes in community income are brought on by federal government actions such as reductions or infusions of federal grants and (potentially) reduced federal tax rates and measures such as the elimination of state and local government tax deductibility under the federal income tax.

Each of these four factors will affect the demand for public goods and services and ultimately the growth in local public expenditures. The response of local budgets to changes in any of these factors will differ across communities, dependent as they are on local preferences, the persuasiveness of local politicians, and the ability of local officials to inform voters about the choices available to them. Because changes in income, relative prices, and preferences also appear to be variable across local governments, it is impossible to make an unambiguous statement about how changes in the local economy affect the growth of public expenditures. What local government fiscal planners must do is answer such questions as: What changes in "tastes" for local public goods are in the offing? What changes in population composition and/or income are likely? Will increasing public employee wages raise the relative price of services and should employment be reduced accordingly? Such changes can be anticipated, and local financial planners should take them into account in budgeting multi-year expenditures.

Supply factors The level of local government expenditures is also determined by supply factors. These factors affect the cost of providing a given level of public service and determine whether the relative price of a service will rise or fall:

1. Costs of labor and capital
2. Economies of scale
3. Indexation
4. Long-term costs associated with capital investments
5. Employee productivity.

Costs of labor and capital The relative price of local government goods can be driven up if the wage paid to local government workers is increasing faster than the wage paid to workers in general. Similarly, expenditures can grow if the cost of capital to local governments is rising faster than the cost to other users. However, in the mid-1980s such differentials did not occur. The general inflation rate is lower than it was in the mid- and late 1970s, and labor costs in the public sector have been growing more slowly than those in the private sector. The major factors that will affect relative wage costs in local government employment in the future are the growth in employment opportunities and wages in the local private sector and the strength of local government employee unions.

Local government capital costs are largely influenced by borrowing rates for state and local government bonds; these have increased substantially in the 1980s. Under conditions of inflation, the nominal interest rates rose faster than local government revenues, hence the capital investment purchasing power of state and local government revenues fell. The reduction in federal capital grants also has had the effect of increasing the relative cost of capital goods by increasing the proportion of the cost that must be covered from local resources.

Economies of scale Economies of scale can allow local governments to reduce the unit cost of producing increased levels of service. The politically feasible opportunities to capture such economies are generally limited to public utilities and other hardware-type services, and perhaps to planning. Most local government services, however, are labor intensive and there is much less opportunity to substitute capital for labor as local government output expands.

Indexation Some welfare and medical services and even some collective bargaining contracts are indexed so that they rise with the rate of inflation. Local expenditures in these areas rise accordingly.

Long-term capital commitments An important and often neglected source of expenditure increase is the long-term recurrent cost commitments that grow out of capital projects. Building an auditorium today will lead to debt-servicing requirements in the future as well as maintenance and operating costs of the new capital facility. As local governments respond to the need for infrastructure improvements, these long-term expenditure commitments will become even more important.

Employee productivity As noted earlier, local government activities are labor intensive with relatively little opportunity to increase productivity by substituting capital for labor. Yet, public workers may receive increases in salary and benefits that parallel those received in the goods-producing private sector—the latter often being related to real productivity gains. The result of such a situation, it has been argued, is to cause government to claim an increasing share of private-sector income.[10] This, of course, is an oversimplification because (1) private-sector wages do not necessarily reflect real productivity gains; (2) the private sector is becoming increasingly service oriented; and (3) the measurement of productivity changes in the public sector is next to impossible in any case. Yet the basic idea is useful. If local government remains labor intensive and oriented more toward people than toward products, and if technological improvements and productivity gains are tied to capital, then the relative cost of delivering a given quantity and quality of service will increase.

All five of these supply factors raise the cost of local government services over time. Although some are uncontrollable, others can be affected by policy actions. As with demand factors, the most important thing local officials can do is anticipate and plan for cost changes in their long-range fiscal planning.

External factors In addition to these demand and supply determinants of local expenditures, certain external factors can affect expenditure levels. They can be thought of as shocks to the system. A national or regional recession, for example, or the closing of a local plant can have a major effect both on the amount of fiscal resources available to the local government and on the level of expenditures such as unemployment compensation and public assistance. Such changes can also create uncertainties and thereby foster more caution on the part of state and local government officials. This in turn can lead to a much lower level of spending. A good case in point is the post-1975 reaction to the New York City financial collapse. The new nationwide financial conservatism that subsequently arose can be considered in large part to be a response to this particular crisis.

Other shocks that might affect the level and growth rate of government expenditures are state legislated mandates, such as expenditure requirements for education and health, or busing requirements imposed by the courts. These are uncontrollable from the point of view of the local government and can increase the cost of local services. Another prominent kind of shock is that induced by changes in federal government fiscal policy. The retrenchment in federal grants starting in the late 1970s and the elimination of federal revenue sharing no doubt slowed the growth in local government expenditures. Provisions in federal income tax laws such as deductibility of state and local government taxes and marginal tax rates could also dampen the level of state and local government spending.

Revenues

Local governments receive revenues from user charges, taxation, intergovernmental transfers, and borrowing. This section of the chapter outlines some general principles that can guide the fiscal planner in designing the right mix of taxes and other revenue sources for financing local government services. One might start by noting that the appropriate assignment of revenue sources depends on the expenditure responsibilities of the local government.

1. User charges are the most efficient revenue instrument for public goods and services. Benefits accrue only to those who pay for them directly. User charges are appropriate, for example, in the cases of public utilities and public transit.
2. Local taxes are the best source of revenue for other local services such as general administration, traffic control, street lighting, and police and fire services whose benefits accrue to the entire local population; individual pricing cannot be applied.
3. State or federal intergovernmental transfers should contribute to financing services such as health and education where substantial spillovers into neighboring jurisdictions occur. Purely local financing—user charges or taxes—would lead to an underprovision of these services from a regional or national perspective.
4. Borrowing is an appropriate source of financing for long-lived capital investments.

Of course, these guidelines are based on economic efficiency, which is not the only value that may influence a local financing system. There are also equity, political, legal, and administrative concerns. User charges may be an efficient way to finance local transit system, but a general revenue subsidy may also be justified on the grounds of reducing the burden on low-income families who are most dependent on public transit. Higher local taxes may be the most appropriate way to finance a recurrent budgetary shortfall, but short-term borrowing or a drawdown from local asset balances often turns out to be more politically acceptable. Without a clear statement of the underlying goals of local budget policy, it is not possible to argue how the local financing structure ought to look.

Designing a local tax system

Five criteria are typically considered in structuring a revenue system: yield, equity, neutrality, administrative ease, and political feasibility. (Only the first three of these criteria will be discussed here.) It is necessary to emphasize that although each of these criteria is important in evaluating every tax, policymakers must recognize that there is no perfect tax. Not every tax will be equitable, yield adequate revenues, and be free of heavy administrative cost. Policymakers must consider the trade-offs involved. When designing the tax system, they should focus on the whole rather than on the individual parts and select a tax structure that in the aggregate will meet the desired criteria.

Yield The most important goal in structuring a tax is to raise adequate revenue. Generally, this means that either the tax base must be broad or the rates must be high. One can think of any number of "desirable" objects of taxation whose base is simply too small to generate an adequate revenue flow—industrial polluters, or luxury jewelry or gourmet food purchases. To raise significant funds from such bases, the nominal tax rates would have to be unrealistically high. The alternative is to search for broader bases, such as aggregate consumption, earnings, and property wealth.

In addition to having a broad base, a tax should have adequate income *elasticity.*[11] That is, tax revenues should grow in proportion to the growth in local real personal income and inflation: Revenues should grow sufficiently to cover expenditures and should not require annual discretionary rate or base adjustments. What is the right level of elasticity? It depends on the anticipated growth rate of expenditures. If elasticity is too low, then local officials will be forced to return to the voters the next year to seek a rate increase; this is commonly the case with school budgets in areas where the growth in the property value base is inadequate to meet increasing expenditure needs. However, if elasticity is too high, then the tax burden will automatically rise each year and could conceivably generate voter dissatisfaction; some think that the high elasticity of the local property tax in California was a precipitator of Proposition 13. Moreover, higher elasticity also implies that revenues will be much more unstable over the business cycle.

Structuring the tax system to achieve the target elasticity can be done in two ways. The first defines a tax base that grows approximately as fast as personal income and inflation—the sales tax, for example, particularly if it includes services; the individual income tax; even the local earnings tax. In principle, the local property tax in many communities might have an income elastic base—property values may be growing faster than income—but assessors in most local areas are unwilling to allow assessed value to keep pace with the growth in market value. Moreover, in some central cities the growth in property values is quite low and much of the tax base is exempt because it is used by governmental, charitable, or nonprofit organizations.

The second way to increase elasticity is to introduce a progressive rate structure in the tax system, that is, to build in a possibility of "bracket creep." Although some state governments have structured progressive income tax rates, local governments find it most difficult to do so. Of the 11 states that do have local income taxes, 3 use state surcharges and a graduated tax and the remainder levy flat rate taxes.

Equity Equity or fairness in taxation can mean several things. User charges are fair according to a benefits-received principle in the sense that they charge beneficiaries for the services they receive—a bus fare and a water meter charge are examples. However, these charges might be viewed as unfair in the sense that they do not take into account a person's income level, that is, everyone riding the bus pays the same fare regardless of how poor or rich he or she might be. An alternative to the benefits-received principle is to tax people for services according to their ability to pay. This raises the issue of *vertical equity:* are those with a greater ability to pay charged a greater tax burden?

Most concerns about local tax systems have centered on the vertical equity issue and on the possibility that local taxes might be *regressive*—lower income people pay a greater percent of their income in taxes. As is discussed in later chapters of this book, conclusions about the vertical equity of local taxes are not so easily reached. For example, the property tax on rented residential units is probably divided between renters—in the form of higher rents—and landlords—in the form of a lower return on their investment. To the extent that landlords bear part of this burden, and the evidence suggests that they do, the property tax may even be *progressive*—higher income taxpayers pay a higher percentage of their income in property taxes.[12]

Yet another question of fairness in taxation is *horizontal equity:* are equals treated alike? Assessment variations on homes of similar value are a particularly objectionable form of horizontal inequity. Many communities attempt to measure the fairness of their assessment practices by estimating ratios of assessment dispersion,[13] and in many states there have been challenges to the classification practices associated with the property tax—the differential treatment of residential and nonresidential properties.

What are the equity goals that local governments can realistically attain with their revenue structures? It is unlikely that local governments can achieve a great amount of progressivity through their tax systems because the base of local earnings taxes is not sufficiently broad nor the rate structure sufficiently progressive. Since the local government tax structure—property and sales taxes—is approximately proportional—that is, one whose effective rate remains constant across all income classes—local governments might concentrate on making these taxes as horizontally fair as possible. They might strive for maximum equality in property tax assessment ratios and exempt necessities from the sales tax. In general, however, redistributional objectives must be left largely to the state and federal tax system.

Neutrality The neutrality principle in tax design holds that economic choices should be distorted as little as possible by the tax structure. In other words, the tax system should not affect location decisions, employment decisions, or consumption decisions. In theory, there are some taxes that do not affect relative choices, but in practice taxes do affect economic behavior. Sales taxes distort the choice between taxable consumption and other forms of consumption and savings; income taxes distort the choice between work and leisure; and property taxes distort the choice between holding wealth in the form of real property or in some other form.

Local government fiscal planners should design their tax systems with neutrality in mind. The general rules to be followed are (1) avoid those distortions that would seem most harmful, and (2) pass up the temptation to try and fine tune the structure of local taxes to achieve particular goals.

In the local government context, three tax neutrality issues come to mind in particular. The first is the establishment of differential tax rates among neighboring or competing jurisdictions. People and businesses will travel short distances in order to save on their tax bills. The New York/Connecticut disparity in income tax rates—New York's was the highest in the nation while Connecticut had no income tax—undoubtedly contributed to the movement of jobs and people away from New York City. Sales tax differentials among communities within a single metropolitan area are hard to live with, and research suggests that industrial location choices within metropolitan areas are significantly influenced by variations in the level and types of taxation.

A second, related issue is the use of tax incentives to attract industry. In fact, this is a different kind of violation of the tax neutrality principle in that one community attempts to influence the location choices of industry by making its burdens more bearable. Even if tax subsidies do not make much of a difference overall, they may still have to be granted for defensive purposes, that is, as a competitive measure.

A third important neutrality issue relates to the practice of assessing both land and improvements for property tax purposes. This introduces a tax penalty for investing in structures, by comparison with a land value tax that would yield equal revenue without rewarding or penalizing such investments. The desire to remove some of the disincentives to property improvements has led many countries and a handful of U.S. cities to tax structures at a lower rate than land.

Local government finances in practice

How do local governments structure their finances? As Table 4–4 shows, local governments raised from own sources nearly 20 percent of all government revenues in the United States and nearly all property tax revenues. They also raised approximately 17 percent of general sales tax revenues and 31 percent of all user charges. Income taxes, however, were not a major local revenue source.

The percent distribution of local government revenues is described in Table 4–5. These data show that local governments depended on intergovernmental assistance, primarily from state governments, for about 32 percent of all their resources. They depended on taxes (primarily the property tax) for nearly 30 percent of revenues raised from own sources. And they depended on user charges (17 percent) for most of the remaining revenue raised.

There is a wide variation in practice around these averages. States differ in the degree of local control granted over sales and income taxes, and local governments vary in the mix of taxes and in rate and base structures. ACIR reports that local sales taxes are levied in 29 states, but in only 11 states do general purpose local governments have "exclusive authority."[14] Regardless of the degree of

Table 4–4 Government revenues by source, 1983.

Revenue category	Total for all governments (in $ billions)	% raised by local governments
Total[a]	1,181	28.6
Own source	1,181	18.5
Taxes	666	17.0
Property	89	96.3
Individual income	344	1.6
Corporate income	51	2.2
General sales	65	17.3
Selective sales	71	7.2
Other	46	9.7
User charges	213	31.0

Source: U.S. Bureau of the Census, *Governmental Finances in 1982–83,* series GF83, no. 5 (Washington, D.C.: GPO, 1984), computed from Table 4.

[a]Including intergovernmental transfers, utility revenue, insurance trust revenue, and liquor store revenue.

Table 4–5 Percentage distribution of local government revenues, 1983.

	As a percentage of:		
	Total revenues	Current revenues	Taxes
Total revenues	100.0		
Current revenues	89.1	100.0	
Intergovernmental	31.5	35.3	
Federal	5.6	6.2	
State	25.9	29.1	
Own source[a]	57.6	64.7	
Taxes	29.8	33.5	100.0
Property	22.6	25.4	76.0
Income	1.7	1.9	5.7
Sales	4.3	4.8	14.4
User charges	17.4	19.5	
Capital revenues[b]	10.9		
Long-term	6.7		
Short-term	4.2		

Source: U.S. Bureau of the Census, *Governmental Finances in 1982–83*, series GF83, no. 5 (Washington, D.C.: GPO, 1984), computed from Tables 4 and 18.
[a]Own-source totals do not add up. Minor categories omitted.
[b]Estimated as total short-term debt issued and the net change in total long-term debt issued.

control, they report, over 6,000 local governments (of which about 40 percent are in Texas and Illinois) levy a local sales tax. A more limited use of income taxes is reported for local governments. Only 11 states permit local income taxation, and if Pennsylvania's 2,758 levying jurisdictions are excluded, only 707 local governments in the remainder of the country levy local income taxes.

Because of the degree of variation in the practice, it is difficult to construct a general profile of local tax structures. One can, however, make some generalizations. Local sales taxes tend to follow their respective state structures—flat rates and a base that usually excludes housing, services, and food. Local income taxes tend to be flat rate. Finally, the property tax, the major local revenue source, dominates the overall local tax structure.

The outlook for local finances

Local governments faced problems of fiscal and economic adjustment in the late 1970s and early 1980s. These problems reflected five major factors that will continue to affect local government finances in the future:

1. The performance of the United States economy
2. Regional shifts in population and economic activity
3. Demographic changes such as changing age structure of the population
4. Tax limitation in the form of voter resistance to "big government" and perceived excessive governmental regulation
5. Changes in federal budget and federal grant policy.

National economic performance

The performance of the U.S. economy is the major determinant of the fiscal health of state and local governments. No one can predict precisely the future course of the U.S. economy, but several scenarios are possible. Continued expansion at low inflation rates would generate a rising tide of stable economic activity. On the other hand, if the combination of a large federal deficit and a strong dollar should choke off expansion, the state and local government surplus would be likely to fall markedly, as it did in the recession of 1976.[15]

Uncertainty about future national economic performance is an important issue in local financial planning. Cutbacks and threatened cutbacks in federal grant programs further accentuate the uncertain fiscal environment. How would prospects of unstable economic growth and fewer grants affect the fiscal decisions of state and local governments? One could expect local governments to hold larger precautionary financial balances, spend less, and levy higher taxes than they would in a more stable economic environment. State and local governments could well shy away from commitments to long-term programs and new activities and attempt to reduce the proportion of uncontrollable expenditures in their budgets.

Uncertainty has a greater effect on the finances of some local governments than on others. Cities that are operating with the smallest margin of revenue coverage of their obligations and perhaps those whose credit ratings are lowest would have to take the most conservative fiscal stance. Growing cities can afford to gamble somewhat more, because their errors are partially made up by natural economic growth and because they are likely to have a greater reserve surplus on which to draw. But as the mid-1980s have taught many local governments in the South and West, continued growth is not certain.

Regional shifts

Regional economic shifts mean that the relative performance of local governments will vary over the next few years. Although the shift of population and jobs to the Sun Belt slowed in the early 1980s, it may resume unless declining regions make major improvements in their relative locational competitiveness. If the regional shifts of the 1970s and early 1980s continue, many formerly rich states will have to increase their efforts to bring fiscal activities into line with new, relatively lower levels of income. This retrenchment will probably mean reduction of public-sector services in many states, particularly those in the Northeast and North Central regions. On the other hand, the growing regions, where the less developed public sectors are located, will also face fiscal adjustment problems. In response to a growing population, local governments in the South will face a continuing need to deal with rural poverty, expand infrastructure, improve school and health systems, deal with water shortages, and ameliorate environmental problems.

Demographic changes

Demographic changes also affect the financial requirements of local governments. Declines in fertility rates have had the effect of pushing the nation toward a zero population growth, an increasing concentration of the elderly, and a declining proportion of school-age children. At the same time, the children of the "baby boom" have been moving through the labor force and the rate of household formation has increased. The effects of these changes on the finances of some local governments could be quite significant.

Slower population growth surely implies less pressure for the expansion of public services and therefore less pressure on public budgets overall. However, a growing elderly and retired population could have an offsetting effect by causing shifts in social service expenditures and by putting pressure on the financing of retirement needs and health care. An important pressure on local government budgets may come from the problems of financing government employee pension plans. Demographic trends also affect the revenue side of the budget. Retirees earn less and therefore have less to spend on taxable consumer goods and housing; hence, one might expect a dampening of revenue growth. On the other hand, the increasing rate of household formation among the baby boom generation suggests more property units, perhaps a greater buoyancy for the property tax, and perhaps even an increase in the taxable consumption share of total community income.

Tax limitation

The late 1970s saw the beginnings of a series of legal actions to roll back property tax rates and limit future growth in taxes. The outlook for local government finances will be affected by whether the tax limitation movement continues. The enthusiasm for such measures as Proposition 13 (California), Proposition 2½ (Massachusetts), and the Headlee Amendment (Michigan) seemed to have waned in the early 1980s. The limitations movement may have served its purpose by calling attention, in a rather dramatic way, to some features of local financing systems that many citizens found objectionable: too much property tax, too much welfare expenditure, and perhaps too little work effort from the public sector. The slower rate of growth in local government budgets may have been a response to this sentiment.

Federal policy

A final consideration, and perhaps the most important of all, is federal policy. After they peaked in the late 1970s, federal grants to state and local governments began to decline. There is every indication that this decline will continue, and therefore more pressure will be put on local governments to find their revenues elsewhere. Policies relating to the federal deficit, federal taxes, and state and local tax deductibility all affect local governments. One can only speculate on the effects of any particular action, but many potential federal moves would have the effect of shrinking the size of local government budgets.

1 Richard A. Musgrave, *The Theory of Public Finance; A Study in Public Economy* (New York: McGraw-Hill, 1959).

2 These illustrative differences are taken from the U.S. Bureau of the Census, *Census of Governments, 1982,* vol. 2: *Taxable Property Values and Assessment—Sales Price Ratios* (Washington, D.C.: GPO, 1984), Table 22; and *Local Government Finances in Selected Metropolitan Areas and Large Counties: 1982–83,* series GF 83, no. 6 (Washington, D.C.: GPO, 1985), Table 2. Note that some portion of the variations reported here are due to differing splits of expenditures responsibility between the state and local governments.

3 Advisory Commission on Intergovernmental Relations, *1985 Changing Public Attitudes on Governments and Taxes,* S–14 (Washington, D.C.: GPO, 1985), p. 1.

4 Economies of scale show up in a lower average cost as output is expanded. A review of the literature on this subject is in William Fox, *Economies of Size in Local Government: An Annotated Bibliography,* Rural Development Research Report 9 (U.S. Department of Agriculture, Economic Statistics Cooperative Service, 1979).

5 Donald Fisk et al., *Private Provision of Public Services: An Overview* (Washington, D.C.: Urban Institute, 1978).

6 Charles M. Tiebout, "A Pure Theory of Local Expenditures," *Journal of Political Economy* 64 (October 1956): 416–24.

7 Michael J. Wasylenko, "Business Climate, Industry Location and Employment Growth." (Paper presented at the Seventy-eighth Annual Conference of the National Tax Association Tax Institute of America, Denver, Col., 1985.) Forthcoming.

8 Susan A. MacManus, *Federal Aid to Houston* (Washington: Brookings Institution, 1983), Chapter 1.

9 This is discussed in Roy Bahl, "The Effects of Business Cycles and Inflation," Chapter 4, in *Financing State and Local Government in the 1980s* (New York: Oxford Univ. Press, 1984).

10 This thesis was developed by William Baumol in "The Macroeconomics of Unbalanced Growth: The Anatomy of Urban Crisis," *American Economic Review* 57 (1967): 415–26.

11 The revenue-income elasticity of a tax is the percent increase in revenues (net of any discretionary changes) associated with each 1 percent increase in personal income.

12 See Henry J. Aaron, *Who Pays the Property Tax?: A New View* (Washington, D.C.: Brookings Institution, 1975).

13 The common measure is the coefficient of intra-area dispersion; that is, the mean of the absolute values of the deviations of assessment-sales ratios about their median divided by the median.

14 Advisory Commission on Intergovernmental Relations, *Significant Features of Fiscal Federalism: 1985–86 Edition*, M–146 (Washington, D.C.: GPO, 1986), Tables 63, 64, pp. 94–98.

15 Roy Bahl, *Business Cycles and the Fiscal Health of State and Local Governments,* Occasional Paper No. 92, Metropolitan Studies Program, The Maxwell School (Syracuse, N.Y.: Syracuse Univ., January 1985).

Part two: Management tools

5 Forecasting local revenues and expenditures

The preceding chapter on local revenues and expenditures presented both a theoretical foundation and an empirical review of the revenues on which local governments rely and the services such revenues support. This chapter focuses on the methods by which local governments try to forecast the future levels of these revenues and expenditures. Forecasting provides public planners and financial managers with the tools to make sound financial policy—for the future—and to avoid fiscal crises to whatever extent is possible.

While local governments probably rely less on formalized forecasting for planning purposes than do private businesses, all public bodies do engage in some type of forecasting. The annual budget, for example, is essentially a forecast of expected revenues and expenditures. Other types of forecasts include short-range cash flow projections (up to one year), medium-range forecasts (from two to five years), long-range fiscal impact analyses (five years and over), and projection models that illustrate the potential effects of such alternative public policies as new transportation systems or land development schemes.

This chapter describes the major models of fiscal forecasting—short-, medium-, and long-range—emphasizing in particular medium-range forecasts. Most of the principles discussed, however, apply as well to short- and long-range projections. Examined in great detail are the various forecasting techniques, their application to revenue and expenditure forecasting, and the specific data requirements used in the projections. These techniques operate under a set of consistent assumptions regarding how the economy is likely to perform and what policy initiatives will be undertaken. Finally, this chapter presents the administrative and political issues associated with medium-range forecasting in the public sector.

Forecasting models

The different forecasting models can be classified most conveniently by the length of the forecast period.

Short-range forecasts

Short-range (up to one year) forecasts are principally used to prepare the annual budget and to manage cash flow.[1] It is fiscally prudent that the flow of cash be predicted, particularly in a time of high interest rates when borrowing money even for short periods is costly and money-market investments can yield positive returns for periods as short as one day.

Preparing the annual budget requires forecasting the revenue streams that are likely to be realized during the following fiscal year as well as forecasting variables on the expenditure side. If a particular level of real inputs must be used to derive the desired level of service, the prices for these inputs must be predicted so that expenditures can be estimated.

Medium-range forecasts

One of the principal uses of medium-range forecasts is to project fiscal "gaps" or revenue shortfalls. Given a set of assumptions, forecasters project revenues and expenditures independently. If the projections suggest a major shortfall of revenues compared with expenditures, policy decisions can be made to balance the two sides of the budget.

Medium-range forecasting also plays a major role in formulating policy decisions that extend beyond the current budget period. For example, wage negotiations involving multiyear contracts have fiscal implications extending beyond the current year, as do government grants. Whether an existing grant will be renewed or not must be considered by managers as they plan the budget for subsequent years. Expenditures for capital projects extend beyond the current budget year as well, the most obvious being capital debt service charges. In addition, capital projects incur lifetime operating and maintenance expenses. Analyzing these longer-range cost implications is an important function of medium-range forecasts.

Thus, by anticipating future budgetary problems, medium-range forecasting averts potential problems. It helps avoid the crisis situations that all too often characterize public-sector financial management. For example, failure of fiscal managers to plan for periods longer than the traditional budget year often results in "management by crisis" and hasty remedies, such as emergency expenditure cutbacks and tax increases.

Finally, it is important for those who make and use forecasts to realize that projections are not unalterable prophecies but guides to be adjusted as necessary. When steps are taken to eliminate the fiscal gap, actual revenues and expenditures should not and will not be the same as those forecasted. The altered figures do not reflect "errors" in the initial forecast but rather show the forecast at work and justify its very undertaking.

Long-range forecasts

A major function of long-range forecasting is to determine whether fiscal problems are on the horizon. When planning the long-range forecast for a community, the financial analyst should first determine the past and present state of the local fisc and economy and examine recent trends among the following components: population (size, age, skills, and education), income structure, and employment mix in the area. Each of these variables is related (directly or indirectly) to the capacity of local residents to pay taxes and to their requirements for public services.

A variety of systematic techniques has been devised to aid the local government analyst in carrying out such a review. In general these techniques are designed to provide an early warning signal of something amiss. Nearly always they rely heavily on consideration of past trends in fiscal and economic indicators applicable to the city.[2] There are, in addition, more detailed techniques available designed to describe the local economic base.

Location quotient analysis One popular forecasting technique is *location quotient analysis*.[3] Briefly, location quotients are based on a comparison of the industrial composition of local employment (local employment in an industry divided by total local employment) with national employment in the same industry (divided by total national employment). If a locality has *relatively* greater numbers of employees in one industry than the nation has as a whole, its location quotient for that industry is greater than 1, and the locality can be regarded as specializing in that industry. Specialization in one industry may suggest that industrial diversification would be useful to avoid swings of boom-and-bust that often characterize particular industries. On the other hand, specialization may be used as an inducement to attract complementary industries to the area.

Shift-share analysis Whereas, the location quotient provides information on a local economic base for a given point in time, *shift-share analysis* attempts to describe how local employment (classified by industry) has changed over a period of time vis-à-vis changes in national employment.[4] This technique categorizes observed changes in local industrial employment into three components: overall national growth in employment; the particular industrial mix within the area; and the share of total national employment growth in the locality by industry. The industrial mix suggests whether employment in the locality is predominately in slowly growing or rapidly growing industries. Changes in the locality's share of employment growth relative to that of the nation show whether the locality is remaining competitive with other areas of the country. If the results show that local employment is predominately in relatively slow-growth industries, decision makers may decide to take steps that will attract to the area new industries with brighter long-range futures. Likewise, if it appears that the locality has an unfavorable competitive position relative to other areas, decision makers can at least consider *why* this situation has occurred.

Shift-share analysis does not, however, explain the underlying causes of change; it is only a descriptive analytical technique. The causes of change in fact may lie outside the powers of local decision makers (e.g., a declining regional population or pressures that have made local wages noncompetitive), yet local policies may be able to alter the competitive balance. Tax breaks, special services to new industries, or aggressive promotion of the area by government officials may yield positive results.[5] In any event, shift-share analysis can be an important step in initiating a long-range planning process.

Fiscal impact analysis Because neither location quotient computation nor shift-share analysis can be used for explicit long-range projections of the local economy, a third technique, *fiscal impact analysis,* is used. Forecasters project the long-range implications of changes in population, income, and land use on the local fiscal situation.[6] The rationale underlying fiscal impact models is that as the size and composition of the population shift, as income levels and distribution change, and as land-use patterns vary, revenues and expenditures will change accordingly. For example, a large parcel of vacant land might be ripe for development of low-density residential housing, apartments, or commercial buildings. Policymakers use information about land development options and their fiscal implications when reviewing present zoning classifications and petitions for zoning change.

Although any use of the land may require new capital investment to provide streets and sewer and water services, these requirements are likely to differ for commercial and residential land use. Moreover, different levels of police and fire protection will be required for the alternative uses. Taxes, and thus the revenue yield, will also depend on the type of land use chosen.

Even within a general land-use category, a choice may have to be made concerning the specific type of use permitted. For example, residential housing may be single-family detached houses, apartments, or condominiums. Obviously, population density and public service costs will differ for these forms of housing. Furthermore, the population and income levels of the groups demanding these different types of housing will differ. The number of school-age children who live in apartments is likely to differ from the number in single-family homes. Given the population mix, the levels of tax revenue may depend on the specified land use.

If the effect of different population groups, income groups, and land uses on government revenues and expenditures can be roughly calculated, then the budgetary effects of zoning policies can be projected under alternative policy scenarios. Revenues and expenditures under each of the zoning alternatives for future use of vacant land may be projected as well. Furthermore, because development may require a different time schedule for each type of land use, the flow of revenues and expenditures—including debt financing—can be forecasted and compared.

Complete consideration of the revenue and expenditure implications under a variety of scenarios is most easily accomplished with the help of a computer. Given the substantial interest in fiscal impact analysis, it is not surprising that several computer packages are currently available to derive such estimates. These packages, however, have different capabilities and data requirements and the initial cost ranges from $20,000 to $75,000.

One model, the Municipal Impact Evaluation Systems (MUNIES) model, is basically an accounting system that compiles the expected costs and revenues of a particular policy change.[7] The program uses substantial amounts of locally prepared data concerning the timing of the proposed change, the anticipated changes in population and employment by homogeneous groups, and the estimates of revenues and expenditures associated with the different types of employment and population. The program calculates the budgetary implications of the proposed decision (including a breakdown of capital and current expenditures) and, if applicable, it projects the changes in tax rates necessary to achieve a balanced budget.

A second model (actually a set of models) is the Fiscal Impact Analysis System (FIAS).[8] Whereas MUNIES uses accounting as its base, FIAS uses historical data from the jurisdiction to relate changes in policies to changes in population, employment, and income. The projected changes in the structure of the local economy are then used to project revenues and expenditures.

As with any management or policy tool, these fiscal impact models are not capable of *making* decisions; they only provide information for decisions. The principal advantage of the computer-assisted approach is the speed and accuracy with which the projections can be prepared. However, the models do require that a significant amount of data be entered into the system. In addition, they are unlikely to be general enough to incorporate all of the major variables that affect local revenues and expenditures over the long term. The models focus primarily on the long-range effects of general policies rather than on the shorter-range effects of changes in economic conditions. Thus, although the models could be tailored to concentrate on two- to five-year budget forecasts, that has not been their primary use. For such projections, the techniques described in the following section are more likely to be inappropriate.

Medium-range forecasting techniques

This section focuses on the four principal techniques used to project revenues and expenditures from two to five years into the future.[9] The methods differ primarily in terms of their complexity. In general there is a trade-off between the cost of assembling a detailed forecast and the amount and accuracy of information provided from using different methods. The simpler methods require less data, less time to produce, and, possibly, less expertise on the part of the forecaster. The more complex methods can incorporate the effects of a larger number of forces acting on revenues and expenditures, are more amenable to systematic analyses. and are likely to provide more useful information for considering particular policy choices, but they take longer to produce and are more costly. The size of the community and complexity of the fiscal problems should influence the choice.

Judgmental or expert forecasts

Few generalizations can be made about producing "expert" forecasts because there is no single best method used in forecasting.[10] Probably the key to successful expert forecasting is finding *the* expert. Often such expertise is gained only through experience; thus, the successful expert forecasters are those who know their own system extremely well and also know where they can obtain additional information. For example, local finance directors may be responsible for annual forecasts of all revenue streams. If these individuals know their sources, they may be more able to derive an accurate "best guess" of what the revenues will be during the following year—without a formalized, explicit method. Drawbacks to this technique include an inability to evaluate *why* the forecast was correct or incorrect. Furthermore, if the forecaster were to leave, the "model" would be lost. Finally, the lack of an explicit model limits the use of the technique for estimating the effects of a variety of discretionary policy changes or of external factors. Nevertheless, an important advantage is that it is an inexpensive technique.

Trend techniques

For some revenues and expenditures, fairly accurate predictions may be obtained simply—by basing projections on the recent past. These projections, based entirely on previous levels of the variable (an expenditure or revenue source), are termed trend techniques.

Different forms of these time-dependent relationships are possible to predict: the variable will not change in the projection period; the variable will change next year by the same absolute amount that it changed during the current year; or the rate of growth will be the same in the future period as it was in the immediate past. For example, if property taxes grew by 7 percent during the previous period, they would be forecast to grow by 7 percent during each of the subsequent periods.

Providing a stronger basis for time-trend techniques is the longer history of the revenue or expenditure variable. A review of nearly equal annual increments in a series over the past 6 to 10 years provides strong evidence for the constant absolute growth assumption.

Graphical analysis is often helpful in spotting historical trends. In Figure 5–1 time has been plotted on the horizontal axis and the variable to be forecast

Figure 5–1 Time trend chart.

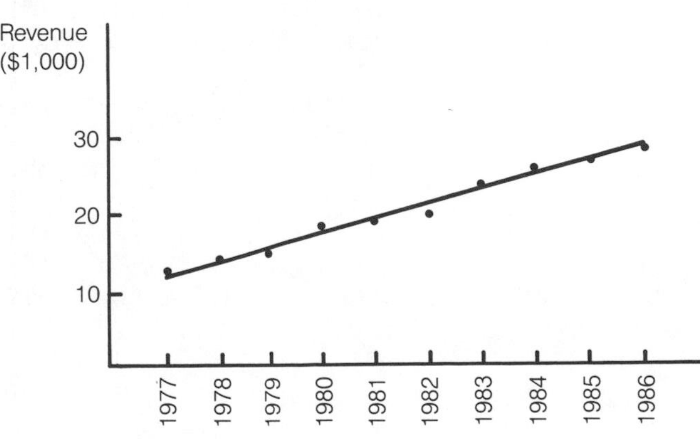

plotted on the vertical axis. Because all points lie approximately on a straight line, the constant absolute growth assumption is reasonable. Projections of future levels of the variable would be plotted simply by extending the line. (Note that such a relationship means that the *rate* of growth in the variable is slowing.)

If, on the other hand, the plotted points appear to follow a nonlinear path concave from above, a constant growth *rate* may be the more reasonable assumption. This assumption can be verified easily by determining past annual growth rates in the variable. These rates are determined as

$$g_t = \left(\frac{V_t - V_t - 1}{V_{t-1}}\right) 100, \text{ where:} \qquad (1)$$

g = the percentage growth rate in the variable

V = the variable

t = the period of time.

Thus, if property taxes in 1985 yielded \$5.1 million and in 1986 taxes yielded \$5.7 million, the annual growth was 11.76 percent. If annual growth for each period from 1980 through the present yields similar rates, in the range from 10.0 percent to 12.0 percent, for example, an 11.0 percent annual growth rate might be assumed in forecasting the future.

These figures can be checked graphically as well, especially through the use of "semi-log" graph paper. As shown in Figure 5–2, on semi-log paper the vertical axis is constructed such that equal distances represent equal percentage changes. That is, the distance from 10 to 20 (a 100 percent increase) is equal to the distance from 20 to 40 (also a 100 percent increase). The horizontal axis is the same as it is in Figure 5–1 and is used here to denote time periods. Because all points lie near the plotted line, the assumption of a constant growth rate is reasonable. Projections can once again be obtained from the extension of the line to the right.

Although time-trend analysis may be useful for deriving quick, relatively short-range forecasts, it will never predict a "turning point." Time-trend analysis will only project increases or decreases throughout the projection period regardless of what may occur in the local economy.

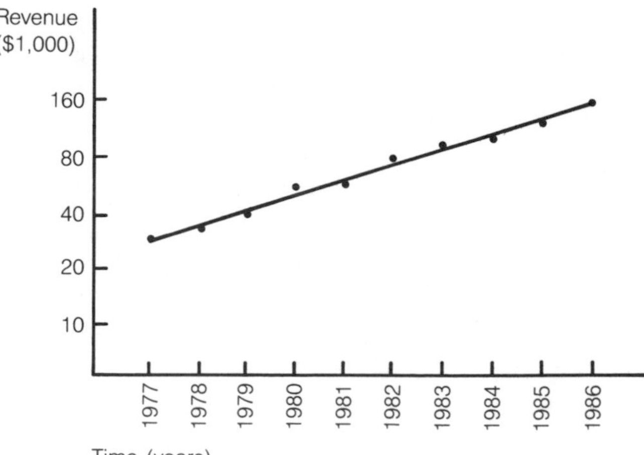

Figure 5–2 Time trend chart, semilogarithmic scale.

Deterministic techniques

Unlike time-trend forecasts, in which only time is used to project revenues or expenditures, deterministic techniques allow for other variables as well. The most common deterministic technique is the use of a preestablished formula to forecast revenues or expenditures. For example, if a city knows it will obtain $600 per pupil in state education aid, total aid can be determined as the product of the projected future school enrollment times $600.

Deterministic forecasting is especially useful when considering the expenditure side of the budget. For example, the state may mandate that no more than 30 students be assigned to a single teacher. If it is anticipated that 1,000 new residents will include 150 school-age students (and all are assumed to enroll in the public schools), then a deterministic estimate of the number of new teachers who must be hired is 5 (150 students divided by 30). If analysis of personnel positions shows that, on average, 40 support personnel (administrators and staff) are required for every 100 teachers in the school system, then the additional 5 teachers projected would require an additional 2 support personnel (5 teachers times 0.4 support personnel per teacher).[11]

Implicit in each of these examples are particular assumptions that should be examined before proceeding with the deterministic approach. One assumption concerns the level of service being provided and another the combination of resources required to produce that service. The requirement of one additional teacher for each 30 additional students assumes something about the level of service—that it be held at a minimal level, or, if in line with what is already being provided, that it be held at a constant level. Likewise, the support personnel projection is based on the assumption that the ratio of support personnel to teachers is inflexible.

Another assumption concerns the use of averages. The projection in the example was based on averages (40 support personnel *per* 100 teachers) even though the projections were in terms of five additional or *marginal* teachers. The preferred method is to base marginal projections on marginal relationships. For example, rather than state that *on average* a city allocates one fire station per 15,000 residents, it is preferable to state that if 1,000 new residents are attracted to a new subdivision located in close proximity to a group of residents for whom fire service is only minimal, an additional fire station will be allocated to serve both groups. Thus, one additional fire station would be allocated even though the average (1 fire station per 15,000 residents) would call for only 0.07 fire stations.

Still another issue is the applicability of the deterministic approach to cities that are experiencing a growth or decline in population. Although cities are certain to hire more public service employees in response to a growth in population, the assumption that the work force will be reduced proportionately in response to a decline in population may be less realistic. In any case, each of the assumptions behind the forecasts should be examined carefully by policymakers.

Econometric forecasting

Econometric forecasting combines economic principles with statistical techniques. Conceptually somewhat more complex than deterministic forecasting, econometric forecasting is capable of yielding more useful information to both the forecaster and the policymaker. It allows the investigator to consider the simultaneous effects of several variables that ultimately determine the level of a revenue or expenditure stream.

Regression techniques—a multistep process The most common econometric approach is to forecast the series independently using regression techniques drawn from statistical theory. The approach is likely to involve a multistep process similar to the one detailed below.[12]

Linear regression analysis Linear regression analysis is a statistical technique that allows an investigator to estimate how one variable, called a dependent variable, is related to one or more other variables, termed independent variables. For example, one might expect that sales tax revenues of a city would be related to the personal incomes of city residents and to the rate of the local sales tax relative to that in neighboring jurisdictions. The computational technique of regression analysis allows one to use past observations on the dependent and independent variables to estimate how changes in the independent variable(s) would affect or be related to changes in the dependent variable. Such relationships can then be used to forecast future changes in the dependent variable based on expected changes in the independent variables. For a simple treatment of the rudiments of linear regression analysis, interpretation of results, and a discussion of some major issues associated with the technique, see Larry D. Schroeder, David L. Sjoquist, and Paula Stephan, *Understanding Regression Analysis, An Introductory Guide* (Beverly Hills: Sage Publications, 1986).

First, for a given revenue source, one or more "independent" or causal variables are hypothesized. Economic theory rather than eclectic or empirical approaches should be used to choose the independent variables, because economic theory is more likely to result in relationships that will hold true in the future. For example, economic theory would suggest that incomes, relative prices, tastes, and number of consumers are variables affecting the demand for taxable consumer goods, which, in turn, determine the sales tax revenues.

In contrast, an empirical approach simply uses the variables that provide the "best fit" to the historical revenue series. This approach usually involves estimating numerous relationships via statistical regression techniques and then choosing the "best" one based on some set of criteria. Yet, the past historical relationship may have been a fluke and may not continue into the future. In any case, if an empirical approach is used, thought should be given to the realism and implications of the resulting relationship.

Second, forecasters should consult the internal records of the city or county for all historical data pertaining to a particular revenue series. They must ensure, however, that the data truly reflect what they purport to measure and that data compilation methods have been consistent over the entire period. For example, minor revenue sources such as service fees or charges may not have been reported consistently in the past. To the extent possible the data must be adjusted to yield a time series that most closely reflects the current definition of the revenue source. (This aspect of forecasting is described in more detail later in this chapter.)

At this point, lack of data on the variables suggested from economic theory may require substitution of proxy variables. For example, many cities find that there is no reliable time series of data on city income; thus, county, state, or national income data must be used as a proxy.

Third, forecasters will determine a statistical relationship among variables, preferably using least squares linear regression analysis. In linear regression analysis, the dependent variable denoted Y is specified as a linear function of the *independent* variables:

$$Y = a + b_1X_1 + b_2X_2 + \ldots + b_kX_k, \quad \text{where:} \tag{2}$$

$X_1, X_2, \ldots, X_k$ = K different independent variables

$a, b_1, b_2, \ldots, b_k$ = parameters to be estimated using regression techniques.

For example, in forecasting local sales taxes (*ST*) the analyst may specify that these revenues depend on real personal income (*I*), the consumer price index (*CPI*), and the population of the community (*POP*). The regression equation to be estimated is

$$ST = a + b_1I + b_2CPI + b_3POP. \tag{3}$$

Least squares regression analysis finds numerical estimates of a, b_1, b_2, and b_3.

Assume that local sales taxes are hypothesized to be a linear function of local income and that the values of these two variables have been plotted on the graph as shown in Figure 5–3. (Each point on the graph represents the observed values of the two variables in one year.) Least squares regression then finds the *unique* line passing through these points that *minimizes* the sum of the *squared* vertical distances between the line and all observed pairs of values. This unique line can be expressed algebraically as

$$ST = a + bI, \quad \text{where:} \tag{4}$$

a = the "intercept term" or the value of *ST* when *I* equals zero

b = the slope of the line.

The slope can be interpreted as the change in *ST* associated with each unit change in *I*. For example, if the analysis yields the result

$$ST = 16.221 + .013I \tag{5}$$

the implication is that for each dollar increase (decrease) in income, sales tax revenues are estimated to increase (decrease) by \$.013. (The 16.221 term has no reasonable interpretation since it suggests positive tax revenues even with an income of zero; yet it is necessary to ensure that the least squared distance criterion is satisfied.)

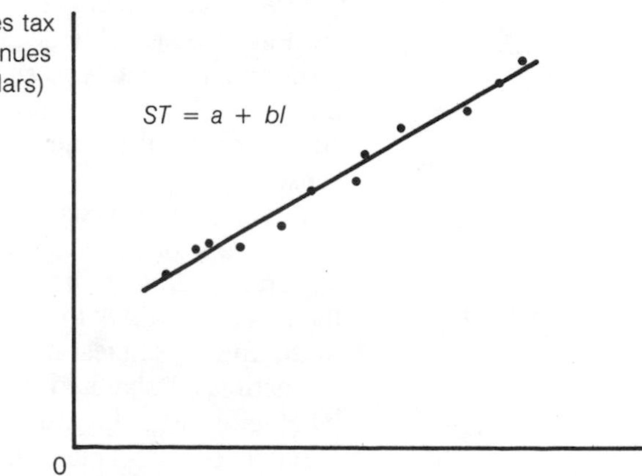

Figure 5–3 Least squares regression analysis.

Several major features of regression analysis must be kept in mind when using this technique.[13] Most often revenue equations include two or more independent variables rather than the single variable used in equation (4). In such cases, the individual regression coefficients are estimates of the change in the dependent variable associated with a one unit change in the particular independent variable—*with the remaining independent variables held constant*. The sign on the coefficient indicates whether the two variables tend to vary in the same or opposite direction.

Consider the following example of a multiple regression equation of the form specified in equation (3):

$$ST = 10.315 + .011I + 1.614CPI + 3.215POP. \qquad (6)$$

These results imply that even if prices (*CPI*) and population (*POP*) remain constant, each dollar increase in real incomes is estimated to result in an increase of sales taxes by \$.011. That the two variables are expected to move in the same direction follows from the plus sign (+) on the coefficient of *I*.

Whereas each of the examples presented here has used a linear relationship of dependent and independent variables, the same technique can be applied to nonlinear relationships among variables. The most commonly used nonlinear relationship is a logarithmic transformation of one or more of the variables. A change in the logarithm of a variable is the same as a percentage change in the variable. For example, consider the equation

$$ln(CIG) = 5.33 + 1.007\, ln(CIGR) + 0.970\, ln(ILAG), \quad \text{where:} \qquad (7)$$

$ln(CIG)$ = the natural logarithm of cigarette taxes

$ln(CIGR)$ = the natural logarithm of cigarette tax rates

$ln(ILAG)$ = the natural logarithm of real personal income, with a lag of one year.[14]

The equation implies that, with cigarette tax rates constant, a 1.0 *percent* increase in lagged real income is associated with a 0.970 *percent* increase in cigarette tax revenues. Note that equations in this form yield direct estimates of *elasticity* as discussed in the previous chapter. In this case, the lagged income elasticity of cigarette tax revenue is 0.97.

The example also illustrates another transformation useful in revenue forecasting—the use of "lagged" variables. The equation relates revenue in the *current* year to income of the *past* year, rather than relate current revenue to current income. This is often appropriate when taxpayers are not expected to respond immediately to changes in such variables as income or prices. Although these transformations (and others) are extremely useful, the analyst should consider carefully whether the function chosen makes theoretical and practical sense.

Regression analysis yields other statistics that can be used to judge the final results. One of these is the coefficient of determination (R^2), which can take on any fractional value from zero to one; higher R^2 values suggest a "closer" fit of the observed points to the regression equation, and, if the relationship will hold in the future, suggest that a more accurate forecast will result. Another statistic, the estimated standard error of the regression coefficient, can be used to test whether a particular independent variable is statistically related to the dependent variable (i.e., whether the regression coefficient is equal to zero). This is especially important when the regression results are used to analyze policy questions that focus on a particular independent variable.

The cigarette tax example may be used to illustrate these two statistics. A complete reporting of the regression results shows

$$ln(CIG) = \underset{(1.26)}{5.33} + \underset{(0.172)}{1.007}\, ln(CIGR) + \underset{(0.163)}{0.970}\, ln(ILAG) \tag{8}$$

$$R^2 = 0.965$$

where the number below each regression coefficient is its estimated standard error and the coefficient of determination is 0.965. The latter statistic means that over 96 percent of the variation in the natural logarithm of cigarette taxes can be attributed to variation in the two independent variables. Thus it appears that these variables offer a good "explanation" of cigarette tax revenues.

The estimated standard errors suggest that changes in each of the independent variables are significantly related to changes in the independent variable; nevertheless, if the estimated standard error on the *I* variable had been found to be as large as, say 0.6, rather than 0.163, there would have been insufficient evidence to conclude that changes in the natural logarithm of *I* were significantly related to changes in the natural logarithm of *ST*. Even if real income increased, there is not sufficient statistical evidence to conclude that cigarette tax revenues would respond.

Finally, the fourth step in this process occurs once the final equation is chosen. The forecaster must then obtain observed values of each independent variable for the projection period. This step may produce errors in the projections since the resulting forecast of the dependent variable is based on variables that are, themselves, forecasted and, therefore, subject to forecasting error (this difficulty is discussed in more detail later in this chapter).

Advantages and disadvantages The econometric or statistical approach to forecasting has relative advantages and disadvantages compared with the expert, trend, and deterministic techniques. An econometric model bases estimates on behavioral relationships that have a theoretical foundation and that can be evaluated by the user of the forecast—an attribute missing in expert forecasts. Furthermore, time-trend techniques forecast in only one direction, while regression techniques have no such limitations.[15] For example, if real incomes were to fall, the cigarette tax equation in (7) would project decreases in revenues.

Unlike their deterministic counterparts, statistical techniques can test whether an observed relationship between variables is, in fact, statistically significant. For example, on average, there may be a linkage between income in a city and the amount of revenues collected from fines; however, this relationship may have varied so greatly in the past that there are no statistical grounds on which to base predictions.

Purely deterministic approaches usually include only one causal variable (e.g., population), while the statistical regression approach uses several independent variables simultaneously. Thus, it is possible to estimate the effect that a change in one independent variable (e.g., tax rate) will have on revenues while holding the other variables (e.g., real income) constant—an especially useful feature for policy analysis. Alternatively, each of the independent variables can be altered simultaneously to estimate the net effect of such changes on the dependent variable.

A major disadvantage to the statistical approach is its cost. Specifying the forecasting equations usually requires the skills of a person trained in economics and statistics, skills less important to the other techniques. Data collection, too, can be costly since greater quantities of data are needed for regression analysis than for the alternative techniques. Finally, although the statistical approach yields results that can be evaluated systematically, the forecasts may contain errors. In fact, each of the four steps in this analysis contains potential for error: the equation may be improperly specified; the data may not be appropriate for the use intended; the estimate can create particular statistical difficulties;[16] and the values of the independent variables used to generate the econometric forecasts may, themselves, be in error.

Given the available techniques for medium-range forecasting of revenues and expenditures, the analyst may find that no single technique is most appropriate for forecasting all revenue and expenditure streams. In fact, some combination of techniques is usually most desirable. Those revenue streams that are most sensitive to fluctuations in the local economy are best forecast using statistical techniques. Trend or expert projections may be most applicable to revenues that are insensitive to local economic conditions or are so unstable that no underlying causal relationship can be specified. Expenditure projections are best forecast with some variant of the deterministic approach to ensure that both are realistic and amenable to policy analysis. Nevertheless, before undertaking a forecasting project, the various traits of the different techniques should be considered carefully, as should the needs of the jurisdiction, the revenues and expenditures to be forecast, and the cost associated with each method.[17]

Revenue and expenditure forecasting—data requirements

This section applies in detail the four forecasting techniques discussed above to revenue and expenditure forecasting.

Revenue forecasting

When analyzing the effects of specific policies or economic changes on revenue structure, the three types of revenue to consider are tax revenue, nontax local revenue, and intergovernmental revenue. No single projection technique is necessarily most appropriate for each of these revenue sources, but whichever approach is selected, separate or disaggregated forecasting (of each revenue source) is recommended. The aggregated model, which lumps together the various revenue sources, introduces a "hodge-podge" of data. The result is a complicated and confused analysis. The disaggregated model, on the other hand, includes only those independent variables considered theoretically important to the particular revenue source in question. Furthermore, it provides for more extensive analysis of the source of errors in the forecast.

Tax revenues Most tax revenues are sensitive to fluctuations in the local economy. Econometric forecasting is most useful for examining the effects of these projected changes. The first step is to specify the independent variables to be used in the regression equations. The purchasing power of the community as measured by income (or some proxy thereof) is generally the most significant variable and, in fact, it appears to be the principal one used by local governments that actually forecast revenues.

Choosing from among several measures of income can be problematic, however, because few sources provide income data for cities on a timely basis. The Bureau of Economic Analysis (BEA), U.S. Department of Commerce, collects income data for counties; however, the data are available only after a time lapse of at least one year. This means that if, for example, the data were needed for a regression equation, the forecast would have to ignore the most recent year. A considerable amount of relevant information is thus lost, especially since many cities can obtain historical revenue data series for only 15 years or so. In addition, county data may not be appropriate for a city that does not coincide closely with the county's political boundaries or for a city that is a wealthy enclave in a relatively poor county. However, for revenues such as the retail sales tax, the relevant income area may be that of the entire market area, which may very well coincide closely with the county.

States can provide another source of income data via income estimates, at least at the county level. Such data may be available on a more timely basis than those from BEA, but the underlying source and definition of the state data series must be reviewed carefully. For example, data based on state income tax returns may use a definition of income that differs considerably from that of the U.S. Department of Commerce. Transfer payments, including both Social Security income and unemployment compensation, are likely to be excluded from data based on income taxes although these income sources are included in BEA income estimates. On the other hand, realized capital gains are generally included in income tax data, but they are excluded by the BEA. Because transfer payments are an important component of the overall purchasing power of the community, their exclusion from the income measure can yield inaccurate results if, over time, such payments constitute differing proportions of total income.

Even if local income data are available and can be used in econometric models, projections of local income have to be made in order to yield revenue forecasts. If no econometric model is available that produces these income projections, then a method linking local revenues (county or MSA) to more accessible projections of *national* income must be employed. Predicted values of national income are used to forecast local income, and these projections are then formulated as revenue equations. For example, the city of New Orleans regressed local personal income (LPI) on national personal income (NPI) to obtain the following linkage equation:

$$LPI = 4147 + 23.105\,NPI \tag{9}$$

The projections of *NPI* are inserted into the operation to derive the estimates of *LPI* values, which are then used in the revenue estimating equations.[18]

Another approach is to use national income as an independent variable in the regression equation. However, not all local economies experience recessions and expansions in exactly the same pattern as does the nation as a whole. For example, manufacturing industries are more vulnerable to economic cycles than are consumer-oriented and service-based industries. Consequently, communities with an economic base that consists primarily of manufacturing may lead the nation in decline. Other communities with a service-based local economy may be more resistant to a national recession. Thus, choosing the most appropriate form of the national-local linkage requires careful consideration of the advantages and disadvantages of each method.

Another problem arises when using population forecasts. If national income data (which encompass effects of changes in national population) are used directly in the tax equation, an adjustment must be made for relative changes in local population. To the extent that local population grows more rapidly (or slowly) than the national population, changes in local population can stimulate (or retard) the growth of the revenue source. One solution to this problem is to estimate all data in per capita terms and then multiply by the projected estimates of the local population. A second solution is to use local population directly in the estimate. Both approaches require availability of detailed data on the population for each year of the observation and projection periods.

Projecting the property tax, an important revenue source for many localities, is often extremely difficult. The crux of the problem lies with the discretionary nature of assessment administration.[19] Where assessment practices are such that assessed values are not revised continually to reflect current market conditions, simple time-trend techniques (or even expert methods such as the judgment of the chief assessor) may be superior to econometric models.[20]

Where assessed values do change to reflect changes in the market, the property tax base generally responds positively to economic conditions—although maybe not in all neighborhoods. Income, prices, population, and measures of local building activity are again the variables for possible use in property tax equations. Furthermore, the forecaster can choose between projecting the property tax base (to which an assumed tax rate can be applied to estimate revenues) or projecting the total tax revenues directly. Projecting the base is more flexible because policymakers can estimate different tax yields associated with alternative tax rates.

Where assessment practices are such that new properties are the prime source of growth in the property tax base, data on new building activity should be used as a primary independent variable in the statistical relation. If these data are not available, projected increments to population may constitute a proxy variable for new building activity.[21]

Jurisdictions with property tax limitations may find deterministic methods most applicable for forecasting property tax revenues. Thus, if the total tax levy can be increased by only 6 percent annually, a deterministic method of projection will show a growth rate of 6 percent.[22]

Nontax local revenues For such diverse nontax revenue sources as charges and user fees, fines, and interest, forecasters often require a variety of projection techniques to derive reasonable projections. Econometric forecasting techniques are most appropriate for projecting some of these revenues. Certain user fees may be closely related to economic activity, in which case assumptions similar to those used for projecting taxes can be applied in forecasting revenues. For example, sewer connection fees may depend on new building activity.

Other nontax revenues can often be projected fairly accurately by using simple time-trend projections or by relying on estimates from experts. Thus, fees from such activities as the sale of maps by the planning department can be most accurately projected by persons in the planning department. Nevertheless, the department-level forecaster must be given a set of assumptions on which to base the projections; and these assumptions should be consistent with the assumptions underlying the other revenue projections.

One of the more complex nontax revenue sources to project is interest income, primarily because of the difficulties in forecasting both the liquid-asset position of the city and the short-range interest rates. The forecaster usually will find that here expert-based projections (e.g., consulting with the finance director) will be as effective as econometric projections. Even major econometric forecasters have difficulties projecting a series as volatile as short-range interest rates.

Intergovernmental revenues Because intergovernmental aid and grants are often important revenue sources for local government, accurate predictions of total revenues require that these grants be projected. Unfortunately, the primary determining variables for projecting intergovernmental revenue are the political decisions made at higher levels of government. Even so, several nonstatistical methods can be useful in estimating these funds.

One commonly used assumption is that the dollars involved in intergovernmental grants will remain constant over the forecast period. A less conservative estimate is to assume that grants will rise at the rate of inflation over the period. A more conservative forecast is obtained by assuming that those aid programs scheduled to be phased out during the forecast period will not be renewed, and that other grants will remain constant in money terms.

The forecaster may find it helpful to elicit "expert" opinions on particular types of intergovernmental aid programs. Legislators at the state or federal level may provide useful information regarding the probability of continuation or termination of major grant programs.

A more thorough method for forecasting formula-based grants calls for simulating the distribution of revenues, which is based on probable funding levels and projected changes in the variables that enter the allocation formula. For example, if state aid for education is based on school enrollments, projections of the number of school-age residents could be used to forecast future levels of aid. The difficulty with this approach is that the formulas for obtaining aid are often stated in terms of relative amounts, such as the size of school enrollment vis-à-vis all schools in the state. Thus, a complete projection requires a forecast of the city's *share* of the statewide variable as well as assumptions concerning overall funding levels. In any case, projection of grants first requires some study of the statutory and administrative details of the grant programs.

Expenditure forecasting

The deterministic or "accounting identity" approach seems to work best for expenditure forecasting. Expenditures are classified by type of spending (e.g., personnel, materials, and debt service) and then projected according to a consistent set of assumptions about service levels, productivity, and price level changes. While projections of some of the disaggregated expenditures may be amenable to econometric or trend techniques, it is unlikely that a city will find the benefits of a full-scale econometric model to be worth its costs. The general categories of expenditures are discussed in the following sections.

The deterministic approach outlined here starts with a disaggregation of each type of expenditure into subcategories: (1) expenditures by agency or department and (2) expenditures by object (e.g., labor or materials). These subcategories can be further divided into units within agencies or departments (e.g., uniformed and nonuniformed personnel expenditures within police departments) and sub-objects within objects (e.g., utilities or contractual expenditures within nonpersonnel expenditures). The forecast of these detailed expenditures can be as fine as desired, or at least as fine as the accounting or management system allows.[23]

Personal-service expenditures The total cost of labor can be divided into direct labor expenditures and fringe benefits. Cost projections are made on the basis of a functional area (e.g., budget unit, department, or program) and the relatively homogeneous groups of employees (e.g., uniformed officers or white-collar professionals) within that functional area. If this large amount of detail is impossible to achieve (or deemed unnecessary), the approach can be applied to broader categories, such as departments in the aggregate, or total personnel spending.

A straightforward accounting identity approach shows that the product of the wage rate multiplied by the number of employees will be equal to the direct cost of labor, and represented as

$$L_t = W_t N_t, \quad \text{where:} \tag{10}$$

L = labor costs

W = the wage or salary level of employees (relatively homogeneous labor) in the functional area

N = the amount of labor

t = the year under review.

Stated this way it is obvious that the projections of direct labor expenditures, L_t, require forecasts of W_t and N_t throughout the projection period.

Derivations of projected levels of employment are considered first. The amount of a particular type of labor employed depends on several factors, including the level of service desired or mandated, the productivity of the labor, and the wage of this type of labor relative to other wages and prices.

Expenditure projections are generally made using a baseline assumption of service levels. The usual assumption is that of a "constant service-level budget." This term suggests that no discretionary changes in service levels are built into the forecasts; however, in practice there seems to be little agreement about what this means. In communities where the population being served is increasing, the usual assumption is that employment in the functional area will increase proportionately. This assumption may be reasonable for direct-service functions such as police and fire, but it may be less applicable for projecting the service level of staff functions.

Some have pointed out that categorical federal grants impose major "hidden" costs—namely, the operating and maintenance expenditures necessary to keep a project in operation after it is begun. Forecasting that takes explicit account of such expenditures should determine whether the categorical grant is really a "worthy" project in an environment of fiscal constraint.

Legislated changes in service levels should be factored into labor usage projections. Such changes may be mandated by higher levels of government or may result from local policies. If productivity improvements are foreseen, possible reduction of the labor force should also be factored into the forecast.[24]

Capital projects scheduled for completion may affect the required level of labor. For example, if a new recreation center is supposed to open in 1987, projections made in 1985 should include the operating and maintenance costs required to keep the center in operation from 1987 through the end of the projected period.

Estimates of the effects on employment of changes in the local population, legislated programs, new capital projects, and productivity can be calculated in at least two ways. One approach calls for centralizing the estimates, within the office of the manager or budget officer, for example. While this approach may yield more consistent estimates, it increases the chances of overlooking major changes, such as scheduled state-mandated expenditures. The other approach calls for department units or budget centers to project personnel needs. Department administrators must take this task seriously and not use these longer-range plans to compile an unrealistic "wish list" of projects. To ensure that the projections are realistic and consistent with the assumptions underlying the forecast, the centralized forecasting unit must review the projections made by the departments.

Wage levels also should be considered in projecting labor expenditures. The usual approach is to use the same set of assumptions concerning the level of wages for all city employees. One method assumes that money wages will increase at the same rate as prices, that is, that real wages will remain constant. Another method assumes that increases in money wages will lag behind price increases by one year; however, the forecaster should analyze historical changes in wages to justify these assumptions. Whenever wage changes are based on projected price changes, the price projections are most accurate if they are consistent with the macroeconomic assumptions used on the revenue side of the forecast. A third method forecasts the possibility of varying wage changes by type of employee. For example, the bargaining strength of uniformed personnel may be assumed to be greater than that of nonuniformed employees; thus, larger wage increments will be obtained by the uniformed officers. The problem with such an assumption is that it must not be made public or the forecast itself may hinder the bargaining process.

A final approach to wage level projections ignores the issue entirely and simply assumes that wages will not change. Although this approach is likely to underestimate labor expenditures, it may be desirable in a collective bargaining environment because it limits the amount of information available to unions regarding the long-range fiscal plans of the city.[25] On the other hand, if the public assumes that the local government can remain fiscally sound even with a 5 percent annual wage increase, the union usually will not be willing to settle for anything less than a 5 percent increase in wages.

Direct wages and salaries may constitute the bulk of labor expenditures, but the level of fringe benefits is becoming increasingly important. The major fringe benefits are retirement contributions, Social Security, and insurance expenditures. The first two are likely to be related directly to the wage bill (total direct labor expenditures), while insurance expenditures usually depend on the number of people employed. Once contribution rates for the benefits have been assumed (or projected) and the levels of employment and wages have been forecasted, fringe benefit costs are projected easily using the deterministic method.

Social Security contribution rates can be assumed with considerable certainty; retirement contribution rates projected into the future may be obtainable from a retirement system if the local government does not have a self-administered retirement program. There is, however, the additional question of what actuarial assumptions go into these projections and whether they are consistent with the remainder of the forecasting exercise.

Other benefits to be considered by the forecaster are such fringes as vacation and sick leave. If these benefits are projected to increase and service levels and productivity are projected to remain constant, changes in personnel must occur. One way to account for these changes in fringe benefits is to use full-time workers or labor hours, rather than the number of workers on the payroll, as the measure of employment.

Other current expenditures Other expenditures include a multitude of items ranging from stationery and gasoline to contractual services. As with labor expenditures, costs of supplies, materials, and equipment can be *projected* for each agency by using some degree of disaggregation. That is:

$$O_t = P_t Q_t, \text{ where:} \qquad (11)$$

O = other current expenditures

P = price

Q = the quantity of materials projected to be purchased

t = the year in which the expenses are to be incurred.

The degree to which these expenditures are disaggregated depends on the desired detail of the projection, the ability of the local government to disaggregate materials into relatively homogeneous groups of goods, and the price indexes of the different types of supplies. Projections of changes in quantities of materials are usually tied to projected alterations in staffing levels. (The assumption is that the quantity of materials will change in proportion to changes in manpower.) The unavailability of disaggregated price indexes is generally the primary constraint to a full disaggregation of other current expenditures. There is no good series of price indexes for many categories of goods used in governmental production; thus, either proxy variables or judgmental opinions are used to project these prices. The principal proxy variables for projecting prices include the producer price index, the consumer price index (CPI), and the components thereof. If particular materials and supplies (e.g., utility expenditures) are expected to increase at a rate faster or slower than the general level of prices for consumers and producers, differential inflation rates should be used in the forecast.[26] Again, each of these additional assumptions should be explicitly considered and reviewed.

Transfer expenditures Transfer payments to particular segments of the population (e.g., the blind and disabled) are not part of the budgetary responsibility of most cities although they often affect county budgets. Where the local government does not have responsibility for such payments, applying trend or econometric projection techniques may be appropriate. For example, the caseloads of social welfare programs probably increase when local economic activity slows. Techniques similar to those used for projecting tax revenues would apply in these instances. Predicted caseloads multiplied by an assumed or mandated level of payment determine these expenditures.[27]

Debt service Debt service—interest and debt retirement—can be one of the easier expenditures to forecast. If no change in the overall level and composition of the debt is projected over the relevant time period, future debt service expenditures are known with certainty. It is more likely, however, that there will be additions to debt as the result of a long-range capital plan, and the analyst must make assumptions about the structure and rates at which the new debt will be issued. The costs of servicing short-range debt and bond- or tax-anticipation notes must also be forecast. Projections from a cash management model, together with interest rate forecasts obtained from external sources, can be used for these cost estimates.

Interfund transfers Local governments that focus their forecasts on the general fund must consider transfers to and from this fund. Such projected transfers can be based on judgmental techniques. For example, when individual departments "rent" autos or other capital equipment from other local government agencies, a special fund is created with interfund transfers included in the overall expenditure forecasts.

If the details of the fiscal activity of all funds are forecast, interfund transfers (based on current policies concerning such transfers can be built into the overall forecast. For example, it may be common practice for a community to transfer all excess revenues obtained from a sewer fund into the general fund. If revenue surpluses in the sewer fund are forecast, these excess funds are projected as a source of revenue to the general fund.

Managing projected shortfalls

Given the projections of revenues and expenditures, the forecaster can construct a table or chart that compares the absolute levels of each for the entire forecast period. The purpose of the chart is to focus on projected revenue shortfalls, or fiscal "gaps." Using a set of assumptions about economic conditions and revenue and expenditure policies, the forecaster may note which types of policies are likely to close the projected shortfalls. For example, rescheduling long-range capital projects may sufficiently alter current expenditures (by changing debt-service schedules or delaying the operating and maintenance costs associated with the projects) to avoid budget deficits. Projected shortfalls may also be eliminated by increasing property tax rates or by reducing city services. The consequences of various policies can be very important in the policymaking process, particularly when viable alternatives need to be considered.[28]

Once the baseline projections have been completed, a range of budgetary forecasts can be produced using different underlying assumptions. For example, alternative sets of assumptions on important variables such as the rate of inflation or the growth rate in the local economy can be studied; and five-year economic projections under "most likely" and under "less vigorous" growth assumptions may be used in the budget forecasts that relate the fiscal health of the city to the economic conditions of the nation.

Implementing a forecast Implementing a multiyear projection model is not particularly difficult and certainly not beyond the capabilities of most city governments, but it does require availability of data, time to assemble the data and to construct the model, and some thought and planning. Nearly all local forecasters recommend, however, that when initiating a model-building effort, one should start at a simple level and attempt to make the model more complex only after some experience is gained.

The increased availability of microcomputers with their spreadsheet and statistical analysis capabilities simplifies the overall task. Once data are assembled, spreadsheet programs lend themselves quite easily to producing deterministic expenditure forecasts. Base year spending by function and/or object can be inserted in the program and then "rolled forward" using whatever assumptions the forecaster needs regarding changes in prices and real levels of resources. Statistical packages available for micros usually have regression capabilities useful for estimating revenue forecasting equations economically. Given the availability of these computer resources, probably the greatest effort required to complete the initial forecast will go into data collection. It is necessary to obtain data from both within and without the governmental body.

Internal data Both econometric and time-trend techniques require historical data for the projected series. While a series of at least 10 to 15 years of observations is best for obtaining reasonable regression results, data are not always accessible in this form. Two major problems inherent in working with historical information are changes in definitions and changes in the rates and bases of revenue sources that occur over a time period.

Although major revenue sources usually are reported on a consistent basis, the same is not true of minor revenue sources. For example, during some periods, a local government may have aggregated all fees into a single amount and reported them as such in both the budget document and the annual financial report. In other periods, the same fees may have been reported separately. Thus, the disaggregated amounts must be combined to form a single consistent time series or an attempt must be made to disaggregate the series during the time the fees were reported as a single number. The first approach is less complex but loses information; the second approach requires more of an effort to reconstruct the series from historical documents but may be more accurate.

Accounting for the discretionary changes in the rate or base of a tax (especially the major tax revenue sources) creates a more complex problem for the forecaster. For example, a particular tax may have yielded $1 million in revenues for two or three years after which the yield suddenly increased to $1.5 million. A 50 percent increase suggests that either the tax rate was increased or the tax base was broadened. To attribute these changes in revenues to changes in the economic or demographic variables used in the regression equation would be misleading and would lead to biased results. Thus, it is necessary to "clean" the data series for purely administrative changes.

Different methods are available for this cleaning operation.[29] Essentially, they attempt to factor out the effects of discretionary changes in tax rates or base definitions by estimating what revenues *would have been* without the changes. Not only is substantial investigation of the legal bases and rates of revenue sources required, but considerable computational effort is involved as well. Thus, many forecasters opt to clean only the major revenue series.[30]

In this respect, then, statistical forecasting is a less than satisfactory technique for expenditure forecasts. After all, historical changes in expenditures nearly always arise from a combination of external factors (such as price increases) and internal policy changes (such as the addition of new police officers). To attribute all previous variations in spending to economic factors, as would be assumed if expenditures were regressed on economic variables, would confuse the effects of the economic variables with the effects of policy initiatives. On the other hand, to "clean" these expenditure series for all such policy changes would be extremely difficult and probably not worth the effort in terms of providing forecasts that are any more useful than those produced under a deterministic approach.

A lack of correlation between the fiscal year of the local government and the time period of the available external data (which is usually the calendar year) arises when using statistical techniques. When time periods do not correspond, it is often necessary to adjust the series to the base of one or the other. It is best to adjust the external data to fit the definition of the fiscal year since it is the internal data that is being forecasted; however, data preparation costs may increase as a result of the adjustment. Except in cases with dramatically fluctuating series, these adjustments are generally not worth the effort. Nevertheless, when specifying the equations, the forecaster should consider the varying time periods. For example, if the 1987 fiscal year (FY87) runs from 1 July 1986 to 30 June 1987 and the data used for the independent variables are for calendar years, whether FY87 revenues are made a function of the 1986 or 1987 calendar year variables may make considerable difference in the specification. Since many economic decisions involve time lags, probably the more reasonable specification is to assume that FY87 revenues are a function of the economic data of calendar year 1986. It is crucial, of course, that those collecting the data be aware of any differences in the definitions of the time period used by those preparing the data for analysis.

External data External data generally do not require cleaning, but they do carry their own set of problems. (Forecasters, however, should examine the exact definitions used by the reporting agency, lest observed changes in the series be the result of altered definitions.) The problem most frequently associated with externally collected data is the lack of available information sources. This holds true for both historical data and projections of series into the future.

The federal government does not, at least on a timely basis, provide large amounts of data for cities; therefore, proxies are often necessary. State agencies such as the labor department, tax or revenue department, and commerce department may also have useful information. Some local firms, chambers of commerce, banks, and universities have considerable information on a locality. These organizations may also have economic forecasting units that can make data available to the budget forecaster.

Finally, subscribers to major national econometric forecasting units may obtain and utilize the data compiled by the service. Subscription services can provide many of the independent variables required for econometric revenue

Federal data sources Many kinds of statistical data are compiled by the federal government. Among the most important for financial analyses are those covering income, population, and the labor market and prices. The sources for these data areas are summarized in the following paragraphs.

The principal agency that collects income data in the United States is the Bureau of Economic Analysis of the United States Department of Commerce. The *Survey of Current Business*, published monthly by this bureau, contains estimates of income for the entire nation, including estimates of gross national product, national income, and personal income. Periodically, this source also publishes income estimates for states, counties, and areas within states. See, for example, "County and Metropolitan Area Personal Income," *Survey of Current Business* 64 (April 1984) and "State Personal Income," *Survey of Current Business* 64 (August 1984).

The Bureau of the Census, also within the United States Department of Commerce, is the primary source of population data at the federal level. While the decennial Census presents detailed demographic information for localities, the primary source of small area data on an annual basis is from Series P–25 of the Current Population Reports, *Population Estimates and Projections*. There are approximately 70 reports issued annually, including reports for estimates of county populations and projections of state populations.

The Bureau of Labor Statistics (BLS) of the United States Department of Labor compiles labor market and price information. The *Monthly Labor Review* is published by the BLS and contains nationwide data on labor market conditions, including those on employment, unemployment, earnings, and prices. A compilation of historical data collected by the BLS is found in the *Handbook of Labor Statistics 1977, Bulletin 1966* (Washington, D.C.: GPO, 1977) with detailed definitions of the measures provided in *BLS Handbook of Methods for Surveys and Studies Bulletin 1910* (Washington, D.C.: GPO, 1976).

forecasting. In addition, they provide access to the expertise of a staff of forecasters. Of course, such subscriptions are expensive, costing several thousand dollars a year.

If such a service is not used (and only a few cities are currently using one), estimates of the independent variables for the forecast period must be obtained in another manner. Most often, local governments use data from the major national macroeconomic models, even without formal subscriptions to their services. The national income, gross national product, and price projections from the models are publicized in business publications such as the *Wall Street Journal* and *Business Week,* for example. Each year the Federal Reserve Bank of Richmond, Virginia, publishes a booklet summarizing projections from nearly three dozen judgmental and econometric forecasts. Some cities have also found it useful to assemble a group of local economic experts (e.g., bankers, academic economists, business economists) to discuss the probable future course of the local economy. Not only can such a group provide good information, but it can provide all members of the group with a better understanding of the fiscal issues faced by the locality.

Another set of projections is available from the Congressional Budget Office (CBO), which produces five-year forecasts of the national economy. The forecasts include projections of national income and prices in alternative scenarios that deal with the general rate of growth. Furthermore, because these are five-year forecasts, they are perhaps more useful than most of the forecasts from the other major econometric models.

Given the variety of macroeconomic forecasts available, the analyst should be cognizant that while econometric forecasts tend not to differ *greatly* in their final projections, different forecasters may use different assumptions. For example, one analyst may assume that a major strike by coal workers will dampen the overall growth rate of the economy during a portion of the upcoming year and, may, therefore, project lower growth rates than another forecaster who assumes the strike will be settled quickly. Use of national income projections from one model and price projections from the other would involve inconsistent forecasts and could lead to forecast errors as well.

Administrative and political issues in forecasting

In addition to the technical matters involved in forecasting, there are administrative and political issues that forecasters should consider when evaluating the feasibility of a forecasting project.[31]

Administrative issues

Included among the management issues that may arise are (1) the role of the chief administrative officer (CAO); (2) the assignment of responsibility for the forecasts; and (3) the presentation of the projections.

Role of the chief administrative officer The chief administrative officer (mayor, or city or county manager), the finance director, and the planning director are not likely to be forecasters, yet, their role in forecasting is far from passive. The chief administrator, for example, must ascertain the most appropriate type of forecast to undertake. That decision demands a thorough understanding of the forecasting process, for the administrator must be able to evaluate and coordinate forecasting needs, financial resources, availability of data, data access, and available staff.

The role of the manager in the process is probably most important when expenditure forecasts are based on data submitted by department heads. Compiling projections of labor and national costs under a set of assumptions and mandates that are likely to affect the department can be time-consuming. If they believe that projections probably will not be used, or that the CAO has little interest in the final product, time-pressed department heads may be unwilling to devote much effort to the process. However, if the manager encourages his or her staff, forecasting can become a welcome plus—stimulating department heads to be more "forward-thinking." Conducting a systematic review of what is likely to occur over the next two to five years encourages department chiefs to develop longer-range perspectives on the operations of their departments. Moreover, reviewing the overall projections for the city or county may help administrators themselves develop a broader perspective of the entire organization. One basic requirement does persist, however; all those involved in forecasting must recognize its usefulness as a tool, not a panacea; as a means, not an end. Armed with this understanding and with sustained professional commitment and involvement, managers, administrators, and their staffs can make forecasting work effectively and efficiently in shaping public policy.

Responsibility for forecasts Responsibility for forecasting may fall to a variety of offices depending on the organizational structure. In most cities, however, forecasts originate in the budget office,[32] since budget personnel are the most intimately involved with the flow of expenditures and with the operations of individual departments. Projections of revenue, on the other hand, can be made by the budget department or a tax-oriented department such as finance. Personnel in the finance department generally have the expertise necessary to clean data series. They are also likely to have experience in projecting different revenue series for individual budget years.

A division of effort between the budget office and the finance office may be the least costly way to produce a forecast, but it raises some potential management issues. Because the revenue and expenditure projections are to be compared, a single set of assumptions concerning the course of the local economy should be used in both projections. The CAO must see to it that such coordination occurs.

Another management issue centers on the decision to use internal staff or outside consultants to produce the forecast. Although the latter are likely to have greater technical expertise, they may lack an intimate understanding of the financial or organizational structure of the local government. Furthermore, once a model is constructed, it should be more than just a once-a-year exercise producing a single set of numbers. Having the forecast model produced in the organization facilitates its use as an ongoing management tool.

Whether done internally or externally, forecasting is likely to be costly, both in the time expended by city employees and as a budget outlay to consultants. If it is done internally, the city should support the effort fully and not be content to have individuals construct and operate the model in their "spare" time.

Presentation of projections The CAO should be responsible for presenting the forecasts effectively. It is crucial to go beyond a simple description of projected revenues and expenditures. Especially if a revenue shortfall is being projected, the rationale for the entire exercise should be presented in language that is readily understandable. Readers of the projection should know the assumptions under which the budgetary projections are made—assumptions about the future state of the local economy, the revenue structure, costs of services, and service levels. If a revenue shortfall is projected, the forecast document should make it clear that this does not necessarily mean the local government will resort to deficit financing during the projection period. The forecasted shortfall does imply that some form of action will be taken (or at least planned) to avoid the financing problem.

Some cities take the forecast one step further when a revenue gap has been forecasted and specify, at least for the near future, exactly what actions can be taken to avoid a deficit. Tax increases, increases in intergovernmental aid, and expenditure cutbacks can restore the desired balance to the budget.

Political issues

As with nearly all governmental decisions, political issues shape the forecasting process. For example, should the forecast be made public? If the projection is to be used solely as an internal document, useful to the CAO, it will have little effect on policymaking. Only if it is released to publicly elected officials will it become a tool for policymaking; however, this public knowledge can have both negative and positive effects.

Some citizens may view a forecast of a fiscal crisis as an indication of poor management or poor political leadership, a perception (especially if seized upon by the press) that could seriously disrupt the overall operation of the local government. For example, as noted earlier in this chapter, publishing projected levels of compensation for public employees greatly erodes the collective bargaining position of a local government.

On the other hand, making forecast results public can be advantageous. When it comes to collective bargaining, a published projection of fiscal problems may lower the bargaining demands of the employees' association. The union will know that the local government's lack of ability to pay is, in fact, true. Furthermore, while a forecast of revenue shortfalls can create negative publicity, voters may be impressed when policymakers react to these projections with informed decisions based on a forecast. Bond rating organizations are also favorably impressed with forecasting as a management technique. Thus, even when fiscal problems are projected, the fact that a forecast was produced suggests that the local government is attempting to stay on top of its financial problems and is better equipped to handle them. Finally, some cities use projections of fiscal problems to lobby for more aid from higher levels of government.

Conclusion

This chapter has presented the three modes of financial forecasting in local government—short-range cash management, medium-range forecasting of from two to five years, and long-range forecasting of general trends in the city—each of which feeds into the budget-making task (discussed in the following chapter).

Medium-range forecasting can proceed via several techniques, differing in data requirements, cost, and accuracy. Consequently, the ultimate choice of method should be made only after a complete study of the respective costs and potential benefits. Finally, the nature of forecasting is not only technical since, if it is to be truly useful, its success depends on the cooperation, commitment, professionalism, and encouragement of both management and policymakers.

1 For a complete discussion of cash management, see Chapter 14 of this volume.

2 A good review of the bulk of these several indexes is found in J. Richard Aronson, *Municipal Fiscal Indicators* (Washington, D.C.: U.S. Department of Housing and Urban Development, Office of Policy Development and Research, 1980). Specific guidelines for carrying out one such analysis can be obtained in the five-part handbook, Sanford M. Groves and Maureen Godsey Valente, *Evaluating Financial Condition: A Handbook for Local Government* (Washington, D.C.: International City Management Association, 1986).

3 For a more complete discussion of location quotient, see Charles Mills Tiebout, *The Community Economic Base Study* (New York: Committee for Economic Development, 1962). Location quotients sometimes are used to estimate the "multiplier" effects of additional spending in a community. Tiebout also discusses this use of the technique.

4 Shift-share analysis is described more thoroughly in Harry W. Richardson, *Regional Economics: Location Theory, Urban Structure, and Regional Change* (Urbana, Ill.: Univ. of Illinois Press, 1979), pp. 202–6.

5 The efficacy of many location incentive policies is, however, questionable. For a review of the theoretical and empirical literature, see Michael Wasylenko, "The Location of Firms: The Role of Taxes and Fiscal Incentives," in *Urban Government Finance, Emerging Trends,* ed. Roy Bahl, vol. 20, *Urban Affairs Annual Reports* (Beverly Hills, Calif.: Sage Publications, 1981), pp. 155–90.

6 For a thorough discussion of techniques associated with such studies see Robert W. Burchell and David Listokin, in collaboration with Robert W. Lake et al., *The Fiscal Impact Handbook: Estimating Local Costs and Revenues of Land Development* (New Brunswick, N.J.: Center for Urban Policy Research, 1978). A review and critique of methods are contained in William H. Dutton, Kenneth L. Kraemer, and Martha S. Hollis, "Fiscal Impact Models and the Policy-Making Process: Theory and Practice," *The Urban Interest 2* (Fall 1980): 66–74.

7 For a brief discussion of this model, see Robert W. Rafuse, Jr., *State Economic Modeling,* State Planning Series, No. 13 (Washington, D.C.: Council of State Planning Agencies, 1977). The MUNIES model is marketed by Tischler, Marcou and Associates, Inc., Washington, D.C., and has been used by the Metropolitan Washington Council of Governments; the Southeast Idaho Council of Governments; Greenwich, Connecticut; and San Diego, California, among others.

8 For a discussion of the use of FIAS in Orange County, California, see "Fiscal Impact Analysis Forecasts Effects of Policy Changes," *State and County Administrator* 3 (October 1978): 14–15. The model is marketed by Decision Sciences Corporation, Jenkintown, Pennsylvania.

9 Numerous books devoted to forecasting methods provide a greater degree of detail concerning use of these methods, especially with reference to business situations. See, for example, Jon Scott Armstrong, *Long-Range Forecasting: From Crystal Ball to Computer*, 2d ed. (New York: John Wiley & Sons, 1984); and Spyros G. Makridakis and Steven C. Wheelwright, *Forecasting: Methods and Applications* (New York: John Wiley & Sons, 1978). For further information on econometric forecasting methods, see Robert S. Pindyck and Daniel L. Rubinfeld, *Econometric Models and Economic Forecasts,* 2d ed. (New York: McGraw-Hill, 1981).

10 Armstrong, *Long-Range Forecasting,* provides a very readable account of the strengths and weaknesses of various judgmental forecasting techniques.

11 Note that this approach is not unlike that used in many fiscal impact models.

12 Since revenue forecasts are most amenable to this technique, examples are restricted to such series.

13 It is beyond the scope of this chapter to provide much detail on regression analysis. The underlying statistics of regression as well as interpretation of results

are provided in nearly all statistics and econometrics books. See, for example, Thomas H. Wonnacott and Ronald J. Wonnacott, *Introductory Statistics for Business and Economics*, 3d ed. (New York: John Wiley & Sons, 1984).

14 This equation was in fact used to project cigarette taxes in San Diego. See Financial Management Department, City of San Diego, *Long Range Planning: Revenue Projection Model: FY 1979–84* (San Diego, Calif., February 1978). The San Diego model as well as several other large-city forecasting models are reviewed in Roy Bahl and Larry Schroeder, *Forecasting Local Government Budgets*, Occasional Paper no. 38, Metropolitan Studies Program (Syracuse, N.Y.: Syracuse Univ., 1979).

15 Time trends also can be estimated using regression analysis with time as the sole independent variable. The resulting model will still be incapable of predicting turning points, however.

16 Among the statistical problems encountered in econometric projections are autocorrelation, multicolinearity, and simultaneity across independently estimated equations. Discussion of these problems is beyond the scope of the present chapter, but they are considered in nearly all econometrics books. See, for example, Jan Kmenta, *Elements of Econometrics* (New York: Macmillan & Co., 1971); or, Pindyck and Rubinfeld, *Econometric Models*.

17 Steven C. Wheelwright and Spyros Makridakis, *Forecasting Methods for Management*, 2d ed. (New York: John Wiley & Sons, 1978) pp. 206–7, present an extensive discussion of criteria to be considered when choosing a forecasting technique, and they include a convenient tabular summary of several methods available for forecasting, judged according to these criteria.

18 This and several other linkage techniques are discussed in more detail in Larry Schroeder, *Effects of Business Cycles on City Finances—Insiders' Views*, Occasional Paper no. 93, Metropolitan Studies Program (Syracuse, N.Y.: Syracuse Univ., 1985).

19 John L. Mikesell, "Property Tax Assessment Practice and Income Elasticitics," *Public Finance Quarterly* 6 (January 1978): 53–65.

20 Trend or judgmental techniques are used to project property taxes in many cities. See, for example, Office of the Commissioner's Court, Dallas County, Texas, *Long Range Plan for Dallas County: Fiscal Years 1983–87* (Dallas, March 1983); or, Department of Budget and Research, City of San Antonio, *Long Range Financial Forecast: Fiscal Years 1983–88—Summary Document* (San Antonio, April 1983).

21 This approach was used in New Orleans. See L. E. Madere, *Municipal Budget Projections, Econometric Revenue Forecasting* (New Orleans, Office of Economic Analysis, 1977).

22 See City of Vancouver, Washington, *Five Year Financial Forecast, 1984–88* (Vancouver, September 1983).

23 See City of San Antonio, *Long-Range Financial Forecast*.

24 Productivity is, unfortunately, easier stated than measured. See John P. Ross and Jesse Burkhead, *Productivity in the Local Government Sector* (Lexington, Mass.: Lexington Books, 1974).

25 This is the approach that was used by New York City in Office of Management and Budget, City of New York, *Four-Year Financial Plan, Fiscal Years 1979–1982* (New York, 1979), pp. II–10. The city argued (and its various fiscal oversight groups agreed) that the bargaining strength of the city would be eroded by publishing projections using a particular set of wage rate increase assumptions.

26 A wide variety of differential inflation rates has been used by different forecasters. See Schroeder, *Effects of Business Cycles*.

27 This approach is used in Washington, D.C., one city with responsibilities for transfer functions. See Roy Bahl et al., *Local Government Revenue and Expenditure Forecasting: Washington, D.C.*, Occasional Paper no. 51, Metropolitan Studies Program (Syracuse, N.Y.: Syracuse Univ., 1981).

28 The Dallas County forecast, *Long Range Plan for Dallas County*, presents very detailed estimates of the fiscal impacts of alternative policies.

29 For discussions of different methods of cleaning revenue series, see Roy Bahl, "Alternative Methods for Tax Revenue Forecasting in Developing Countries" (Unpublished Paper, International Monetary Fund, Fiscal Affairs Department, 1972); Robert Harris, *Income and Sales Taxes: The 1970 Outlook for States and Localities* (Washington, D.C.: Council of State Governments, 1966); and A. R. Prest, "The Sensitivity of the Yield of Personal Income Tax in the United Kingdom," *Economic Journal* 72 (September 1962): 576–96.

30 Regression forecasting techniques provide another method for cleaning revenue series via the use of "dummy" independent variables. Such variables take on the value 0 before a revenue rate (base) is changed, and a value of 1 after the change is made. The technique is especially useful when only one or two major administrative changes have been made in a tax source. For discussion of the dummy variable technique, see Wonnacott and Wonnacott, *Introductory;* Kmenta, *Elements;* and Pindyck and Rubinfeld, *Econometric*.

31 These issues are discussed in more depth in Larry Schroeder, "Local Government Multi-Year Budgetary Forecasting: Some Administrative and Political Issues," *Public Administration Review* 42 (March/April 1982): 121–27.

32 The use of multiyear forecasting models in the annual budget process is considered in Roy Bahl and Larry Schroeder, "Multi-Year Forecasting in Annual Budgeting," *Public Budgeting and Finance* 4 (Spring 1984): 3–13.

6 Budgeting

The role of public budgeting is to harness financial and organizational resources to pursue such goals as alleviation of community problems and provision for community needs. A public budget can be viewed as a financial plan prepared for a given fiscal period that enables government officials to pursue these politically chosen goals.[1] This chapter examines the fiscal context and major characteristics of budgeting, the role of budgeting in attaining goals, the activities of various players in the budget cycle, and the types of budgets used and adapted by local governments.

Fiscal context and major characteristics

Local government budgeting takes place in a legal, political, and organizational setting that is substantially different from budgeting in the private sector. Budgeting practices are established and constrained by state law, local ordinance, accepted standards, and local tradition.

Scope and content of budgets

A local government budget specifies the resources that are expected to be available to cover the estimated expenditures for carrying out government programs and services. The budget is generally broken down into a *current* budget showing operating expenditures and a *capital* budget showing the financing plans for long-term capital improvements, facilities, and equipment. The two budgets may be consolidated for certain purposes. The consolidated budget indicates the amount of estimated revenues available for the current period and the amount of new debt to be incurred for financing projects in the capital budget.

In most local governments, the initial responsibility for budget formulation rests with the executive (mayor or city manager), who submits a proposed budget to a governing body (city council or county board) for legal approval. The council or board generally has the power to amend or revise the executive's revenue and expenditure estimates, but the executive may have power to veto the entire budget or specific items. After the council or board approves the proposed budget through a budget ordinance, the newly adopted or enacted budget becomes a legally binding document for the executive's administration.

The period for which a budget is authorized spans a fiscal year (FY) that may correspond to the calendar year or to some other twelve-month period, most commonly July 1 to June 30. Some cities use biennial budgets spanning two years. In most annual budget reports, revenue and expenditure figures are presented for three time periods: (1) the actual revenues and expenditures compared to the budgeted figures for the prior fiscal year, (2) the estimated revenues and expenditures for the current fiscal year, and (3) the proposed revenues and expenditures for the next fiscal year. The budget document summarizes the financial plans for all funds and shows all expenditures either by department or by object. Figure 6–1 shows a typical consolidated local government budget.

Funds and budget types

Most government budgets include a number of subbudgets for individual funds set up within a fund accounting system[2] (see Chapter 7). A fund is an independent fiscal entity with assets, liabilities, reserves, a residual balance or equity, and revenues and expenditures for undertaking activities. Funds may be *expendable,* meaning that authorization for spending expires at the end of the fiscal period, or *nonexpendable* or *revolving*. To facilitate legal compliance, the National Council on Governmental Accounting (NCGA) calls for the use of

Figure 6–1 Sample consolidated budget for all funds, fiscal year ending December 31.

	(1) Prior FY	(2) Prior FY	(3) Prior FY	(4) Current FY	(5) Next FY
	Budgeted 1991–92	Actual 1991–92	Variance favorable (unfavorable)	Budgeted 1992–93	Proposed 1993–94
Revenues					
1. Taxes	$ 8,858,790	$ 8,870,970	$ 12,180	$ 9,038,630	$ 9,832,740
2. Licenses and permits	3,313,350	3,481,730	168,380	3,829,910	4,212,900
3. User charges and fees	369,150	336,490	(32,660)	370,140	407,150
4. Intergovernmental revenue	1,082,730	1,056,050	(26,680)	1,161,660	1,277,820
5. Special assessments	680,670	687,050	6,380	755,860	831,330
6. Miscellaneous revenue	421,060	402,220	(18,840)	442,440	486,580
7. Total revenues	$14,725,750	$14,834,510	$108,760	$15,598,540	$17,048,520
Expenditures (by department)					
8. General government	358,690	357,540	1,150	368,060	438,740
9. Health	601,540	600,940	600	611,460	691,280
10. Welfare	1,992,260	1,974,180	18,080	2,093,960	2,409,340
11. Public safety	2,132,890	2,139,050	(6,160)	2,260,550	2,560,520
12. Education	3,983,620	4,080,320	(96,700)	4,290,840	4,540,630
13. Sanitation	1,499,630	1,552,270	(52,640)	1,576,720	1,826,890
14. Highways and streets	3,244,830	3,246,020	(1,190)	3,266,540	3,736,410
15. Recreation and cultural	902,110	884,190	17,920	894,710	924,720
16. Total expenditures	$14,715,570	$14,960,580	$(245,010)	$15,462,840	$17,128,530
17. Excess of revenues over/(under) expenditures, or budget surplus (deficit)	$ 10,180	$ (126,070)[a]	—	$ 135,700[b]	$ (80,010)[d]
18. Cumulative amount available for appropriations (or unreserved fund balance) from prior fiscal year	$ 258,660	$ 258,660	—	$ 132,590[c]	$ 268,290[e]
19. Unreserved fund balance (to be used) for appropriations	—	—	—	—	$ 80,010[f]

[a]Actual budget deficit, which is covered by the unreserved fund balance of $258,660 (line 18, column 2).

[b]Estimated budget surplus.

[c]Unreserved fund balance of $258,660, from prior fiscal year (line 18, column 2) minus budget deficit of $126,070 in prior fiscal year (line 17, column 2).

[d]Proposed budget deficit to be financed from the unreserved fund balance of $268,290 (line 18, column 5).

[e]Current year surplus of $135,700 (line 17, column 4) plus unreserved fund balance of $132,590 (line 18, column 4).

[f]The amount of the available fund balance used to cover the budgetary deficit of $80,010 (line 17, column 5), shown formally here as a source of revenues to partially finance estimated expenditures. A deficit is intentionally incurred to use up some of the available fund balance, which is considered to be too large (line 18).

Figure 6–2 Fund structure of local governments.

	Governmental funds				
	General	Special revenue	Capital projects	Special assessment[a]	Debt service
Component funds	General fund	School aid Library book purchase City hospital emergency services State gasoline tax (roads)	Solano School Building Aaron Medical Center Street and road construction Brams Bridge Storm sewer construction	New housing development Commercial/ industrial support Improvement district no. 1 Improvement district no. 2	General improvements Nora Hospital Linn High School
Major resources	Property taxes Sales taxes Licenses and permits Intergovernmental grants Charges	Earmarked taxes Sales Property Intergovernmental grants Charges	Intergovernmental grants Proceeds of general obligation bond sale	Special assessment levies Proceeds of special assessment bond sale	Taxes Intergovernmental grants Proceeds of refunding bond issue
Major expenditures	Personnel services Materials Supplies Contractual services Equipment	Personnel services Materials Supplies Contractual services Equipment	Construction contracts Engineering services	Capital outlays Bond principal retirement Bond interest	Bond principal retirement Bond interest

eight different types of funds, which can be grouped into three broad categories—governmental funds, proprietary funds, and fiduciary funds—according to the resources employed and the activities required.

Governmental funds Most local government activities are conducted through five governmental funds (see Figure 6–2):

1. The general fund, which supports all services (e.g., police, fire, welfare) not assigned to other funds
2. Special revenue funds, which provide services to be financed from specifically designated revenues (e.g., recreation financed by fees earmarked for such use)
3. Capital projects funds, which are usually obtained from long-term debt and intergovernmental grants and are used for the acquisition of major long-term assets that have a useful economic life greater than one year
4. Special assessment funds, which are made up of revenues from assessments on properties in order to finance services or improvements directly beneficial to the designated property owners (e.g., water and sewer connections, sidewalk construction)
5. Debt service funds, which receive resources from other funds (or proceeds from refunding bond issues) to pay the principal and interest on the government's long-term general obligation debt (municipal bonds).

All but debt service funds support the traditional services and capital goods provided by the public sector.

Figure 6–3 summarizes a typical balance sheet and budget of a governmental fund. The balance sheet shows (1) what is owned by the fund (assets) and (2) what is owed by the fund (liabilities), plus *reserves* or monies set aside for

Figure 6–2 (cont.)

	Proprietary funds		Fiduciary funds			
	Enterprise	Internal service	Nonexpendable trust[c]	Expendable trust[c]	Public employee retirement[c]	Agency[c]
Component funds	City water and sewer Refuse collection Alexis Park facilities Amy Civic Center	Motor pool Stores Equipment replacement	Economic development loan Venture capital Myrna Arts Endowment	Myrna Arts Endowment Adam Childrens' Playground	Teachers' annuity Clerical retirement Managerial employees retirement	Liquor tax collection (for schools) Lottery fund (for aid to the elderly)
Major resources	User charges	User charges	Contributions Interest on investment gifts	Contributions Interest on investment gifts	Contributions Interest on investment gifts	Taxes Inter-governmental grants
Major expenditures	Operating expenses Personnel services Contractual services Materials, supplies Depreciation[b] Utilities Nonoperating expense Fees Interest Rents	Operating expenses Personnel services Contractual services Materials, supplies Depreciation[b] Utilities	Loans Transfers	Benefits, awards	Benefits, payments	Transfers

[a] As this book went to press, special assessment funds were eliminated for financial reporting purposes, and the activities accounted for in special assessment funds are to be reported in other fund types and account groups.

[b] Includes construction contract, bond retirement, bond interest.

[c] A subcategory of fiduciary funds.

contingencies and potential liabilities. The difference between these amounts is either an *unreserved fund balance* or *surplus,* as shown in the figure, or a *fund deficit*. These balance sheet accounts are affected by budgetary transactions. Revenues increase assets, and expenditures create liabilities or establish reserves.

If revenue collections exceed expenditures for the fiscal period, the result is a budget surplus, which increases the fund balance; if expenditures are greater than collected revenues, a budget deficit results and decreases the fund balance. An accumulated unreserved fund surplus can be used to cover a budgetary deficit or to finance the expenditures of a subsequent budgetary period (also see Figure 6–1).

Each fund has a fixed budget, and the council or board approves appropriations that authorize spending on particular items. The budgeted amounts cannot be exceeded unless additional appropriations are approved. Under annual fixed budgets, governmental funds are expendable; if spending is to be continued in the next fiscal period, a new budget must be adopted. These budgetary characteristics permit the council or board to supervise fiscal administration, since it can assess whether the appropriated monies were spent on the designated items within the stipulated time period.

Figure 6–3 Structure and operations of balance sheet and budgetary accounts of expendable funds.

Balance sheet December 31, 1992	
Assets	
Cash	$1,560,000
Taxes receivable	330,000
Accounts receivable	452,000
Due from other funds	285,000
Inventory	220,000
Total assets	$2,850,000
Liabilities	
Vouchers payable	$1,250,000
Contracts payable	780,000
Due to other funds	210,000
Reserves	380,000
Unreserved fund balance	230,000[a]
Total liabilities, reserves, and fund balance	$2,850,000

Actual budget FY ending December 31, 1993	
Revenues	
Taxes	$6,136,000
Licenses	405,000
Intergovernmental	1,302,000
Charges	832,000
Total revenues	$8,675,000
Expenditures	
Personal services	$4,445,000
Materials and supplies	495,000
Contracts	2,050,000
Capital outlays	1,560,000
Total expenditures	$8,550,000
Surplus (deficit)	$ 125,000[a]

Balance sheet December 31, 1993	
Assets	
Cash	$3,020,000
Taxes receivable	437,000
Accounts receivable	618,000
Due from other funds	399,000
Inventory	405,000
Total assets	$4,879,000
Liabilities	
Vouchers payable	$2,980,000
Contracts payable	960,000
Due to other funds	194,000
Reserves	390,000[b]
Unreserved fund balance	355,000[a]
Total liabilities, reserves, and fund balance	$4,879,000

[a]Ending unreserved fund balance, 1992 ($230,000), plus budget surplus, 1993 ($125,000) equals ending unreserved fund balance, 1993 ($355,000).
[b]This amount could be made available for appropriation in the 1994 budget.

Proprietary funds Two types of proprietary funds—enterprise funds and internal service funds—can be used when a government engages in activities analogous to private commercial operations (see Figure 6–2). Enterprise funds are maintained to control electric utilities, water and sewer systems, and other entities providing continuing public services financed through customer user fees. Internal service funds are used for governmental organizations that provide services to other units within the government for fees that cover cost of operations (e.g., motor pool, materials, and supplies).

The main purpose of these business-type organizations is to provide services to consumers at a price that will cover both the current cost of operations (expenses) and the maintenance and financing of necessary capital assets. Net income (revenues less expenses) or net loss at the end of the fiscal period either adds to or reduces the fund's residual equity in the form of retained earnings (see

Figure 6–4). Unreserved or unrestricted retained earnings can be used to cover an operating deficit in the current fiscal year or to finance operations in the subsequent year. The equity of these funds may also include contributed capital (i.e., money, equipment, and facilities) from the local government itself, higher-level governments, or the private sector.

Proprietary funds have a flexibility not found in governmental funds. Although expenditures are fixed for each unit of service—for example, 10 cents per kilowatt-hour of electricity—total spending varies according to demand. In contrast to governmental funds, when expenditures under proprietary funds rise because of increased production to satisfy demand, revenues also increase. Moreover, capital outlays and long-term debt transactions of proprietary funds are not controlled by separate funds but are accounted for within the proprietary fund itself. Because governmental commercial entities are supposedly self-sustaining, budgetary authority is nonexpendable or revolving—that is, authorization for collecting revenues and incurring expenses neither lapses at the end of the fiscal period nor requires renewal at the beginning of the next period. Since budgetary authorization is continuous, legal compliance with budgetary estimates is not an issue for the council or board, whose main concern is assessing operational performance as reflected in the earning of an adequate net income. Thus, the budget is a major tool for planning and evaluating operational efficiency in responding to different levels of service demand.

Fiduciary funds In the operation of a fiduciary fund (see Figure 6–2), government acts as a custodian of assets that must be disbursed to individuals, private and public entities, and other funds. These fiduciary, or trust and agency funds, receive resources that are to be passed through to designated individuals, entities, or other funds: retirement trust funds, funds for donations to local government (e.g., park commemorations), funds for taxes to be forwarded to other governmental units, or funds for nontax resources held by the government. These funds may be conduits to collect revenues shared by several governments (e.g., state lottery proceeds distributed to local governments), or to receive grants to be held temporarily for distribution to the appropriate participating jurisdictions, (e.g., federal revenue sharing grants). Because the funds merely pass through an agency, budgeting to establish for financial accountability is unnecessary.

Trust and agency funds may be expendable or nonexpendable. Expendable funds ensure that endowments or contributions from a private or public donor or grantor are spent in accordance with the donor's specification—to fund a library or scholarships, for example. Since the assets are to be expended over a specific time period, a fixed budget authorizes the receipt of an estimated amount of assets and the expenditure of a maximum amount of the assets to be used for stated purposes.

Nonexpendable funds account for both the principal, or received assets, and the income generated from the principal. Like proprietary funds, they have flexible budgeting. These funds are in continuous operation beyond a particular fiscal period. For example, in the case of a loan fund for economic development, loans would be made with the capital, and the fees (interest) charged would yield earnings and cover lending expenses; the income would in turn be available for relending. If only the principal should be designated as nonexpendable, and earned income could be disbursed, then two funds should be set up: (1) a nonexpendable fund for the maintenance of the principal, and (2) an expendable fund that would receive the earnings from the former fund. If the assets are to finance certain levels of activity when certain criteria are met—students with various incomes are to be lent different amounts—a flexible budget would be more useful than a fixed budget.

Figure 6–4 Structure and operations of balance sheet and budgetary accounts of nonexpendable funds.

Balance sheet December 31, 1992	
Assets	
Current	$ 1,309,000
Restricted	1,106,000
Property, plant, equipment	16,334,000
Less: accumulated depreciation	178,000
Net property, plant, equipment	16,156,000
Total assets	$18,571,000
Liabilities	
Current payables	$ 1,911,000
Long-term debt	8,076,000
Total liabilities	9,987,000
Fund equity	
Contributed capital	1,989,000
Retained earnings	6,595,000
Total equity	8,584,000
Total liabilities and equity	$18,571,000

Actual budget FY ending Dec. 31, 1993	
Revenues	
Operating	
Billings	$668,000
Charges	64,000
Nonoperating	
Rents	8,000
Interest	7,000
Total revenues	$747,000
Expenses	
Operating	
Personal	$130,000
Contracts	20,000
Depreciation	270,000
Other	18,000
Total expenses	438,000
Net income (loss)	$309,000[a]

Balance sheet December 31, 1993	
Assets	
Current	$ 1,572,000
Restricted	1,509,000
Property, plant, equipment	18,001,000
Less: accumulated depreciation	206,000
Net property, plant, equipment	17,795,000
Total assets	$20,876,000
Liabilities	
Current payables	$ 2,153,000
Long-term debt	9,820,000
Total liabilities	11,973,000
Fund equity	
Contributed capital	1,989,000
Retained earnings	6,914,000[a]
Total equity	8,903,000
Total liabilities and equity	$20,876,000

[a]Ending retained earnings, 1992 ($6,595,000), plus net income, 1993 ($309,000), equals ending retained earnings, 1993 ($6,914,000).

Finally, public employee retirement funds—the most important municipal trust fund—hold pension contributions from the government and its employees and the earnings on invested contributions. Whether or not both the principal and income of the fund are expendable depends upon the enabling legislation of the pension system. Since pensions are awarded to individuals or families on the basis of stated criteria, flexible budgeting is necessary.

Fiscal practices

Institutional forces have produced considerable variation in fund structures and budgets among cities. State constitutions and statutes as well as local charters and ordinances may place requirements or restrictions on revenue collection and spending, in addition to specifying how revenues and expenditures must be accounted for. A city may be required to have trust funds to accept and pay out state grant monies, (e.g., school aid). Likewise, according to municipal ordinance, a portion of local property taxes may be set aside in a capital projects fund to finance particular services such as street repairs. Thus, as demonstrated in Figure 6–5, a service could be financed from more than one fund. For instance, current education expenditures for salaries and supplies could be provided through the general fund, while school construction could be subsumed under a capital projects fund, and both the school meals program and school repairs could be supported through special revenue funds via earmarked sales taxes.

Fund structure A fund structure facilitates financial responsibility by restricting the amount and use of resources (current revenues and borrowed monies), assets, and residual balances to those spending purposes which have been legally authorized. The fund structure is a manifestation of historic political choices regarding what services should be provided and how they should be financed. Fund structures reflect policy orientations about the equity of local government activities because they determine who bears the costs of services and who obtains the benefits. In some cities, water or sewer services are supported solely by property taxes and financed through the general fund. In other localities these services are operated through utility or enterprise funds as self-sustaining fee-for-service commercial operations. In still others, separate utility enterprises may be partially subsidized by monies from the general fund or special revenue funds so that users do not pay the full cost of service. Conversely, if charges exceed costs, "excess" profit or revenues may be transferred to other funds. If so, users of the utility subsidize other governmental activities.

The relationship of costs and prices is likely to be obscured when many revenue-producing services are collapsed into the general fund and lose their separate identities. For this reason, services that directly benefit distinct property owners, such as sidewalk repair and installation and trash collection, are generally segregated into individual funds. It is appropriate to finance such activities by special taxes, fees, charges, or assessments so that the amounts paid by the beneficiaries correspond to the cost of serving them. This makes for a more efficient allocation of resources and provides a more equitable allocation of costs according to benefits received.

Even though fiduciary responsibility can be facilitated substantially by separate funds, the NCGA points out that a proliferation of funds and fund types could produce administrative inefficiently and organizational rigidity in service delivery and could complicate the budgetary process.[3] Such difficulties can be alleviated in several ways. First, all funds should be on the same budget cycle. Second, the fund structure should be simplified whenever possible consistent with the scope and nature of the government's fiscal activities. In practice, small municipalities do consolidate revenue and expenditure activities into a few governmental funds, and for many cities, trust or fiduciary activities, debt service, and capital outlays are recorded as major accounts within the general fund. Third, even where numerous funds exist, the budgetary process need not be complex. Enterprise funds are not generally budgeted extensively, because the primary legislative concern is to oversee the enterprise's financial performance. Since the management of fiduciary funds is regulated by governmental

Figure 6–5 Consolidated line-item budget by funds, proposed expenditures.

Function	General	Special revenue	Capital projects	Special assess-ment	Debt service	Enter-prise	Internal service	Trust/ agency	Total estimated expenditures[a]
General government	$ 344,445				$33,740			$60,555	$ 438,740
Health	390,015	$ 100,465	$ 200,800						691,280
Welfare	800,460	1,608,880							2,409,340
Public safety[b]	1,463,565	456,825	640,130						2,560,520
Fire department	483,115	148,860	315,865						
Inspection	154,915	25,300							
Investigation	77,560								
Fire and rescue	250,740	123,560	315,865						
Police department	980,450	304,965	324,265						
Investigation	120,660								
Traffic	125,880		45,605						
Patrol	733,910		378,660						
Personal services	496,820								
Salaries	405,610								
Wages	24,100								
Sick pay	21,090								
Social security	46,020								
Materials and supplies	142,080								
Office supplies	16,625								
Uniforms	11,055								
Gasoline/oil	65,800								
Heating and power	35,600								
Telephone	13,000								
Equipment	45,010	304,965							
Communications		110,330							
Weapons	5,090	80,555							
Auto		114,080							
Office furniture	39,920								
Contractual services	50,000								
Youth clubs	50,000								
Capital outlays			378,660						
Construction			262,780						
Patrol cars			115,880						
Education	3,066,275	421,335	1,053,020						4,540,630
Sanitation	318,015		673,860	332,695		502,320			1,826,890
Transportation	826,775	974,780	983,620	951,235					3,736,410
Recreation	829,035		95,685						924,720
Total expenditures	$8,038,585	$3,562,285	$3,647,115	$1,283,930	$33,740	$502,320		$60,555	$17,128,530

[a] Total estimated expenditures for the eight categories shown here by source of funding are taken from the consolidated budget shown in Column 5 of Figure 6–1.

[b] Although not shown here because of space limitations, other functions would be similarly classified by department, organization, objects, and items.

policy, custom, and/or donors' legal stipulations, it does not require budgetary decision making. Fourth, greater coordination in fiscal and economic planning can be achieved by integrating the individual budgets of each fund into two comprehensive budgets, the annual operating budget and the capital budget.[4] Together these two budgets form the government's consolidated or current budget for the current fiscal year, shown schematically in Figure 6–6.

Operating and capital budgets The annual operating budget is a financial document setting forth expenditures for personal services, materials and supplies, contractual services, lighting, heating, power, and other resources needed

Figure 6–6 Consolidated budget and its components.

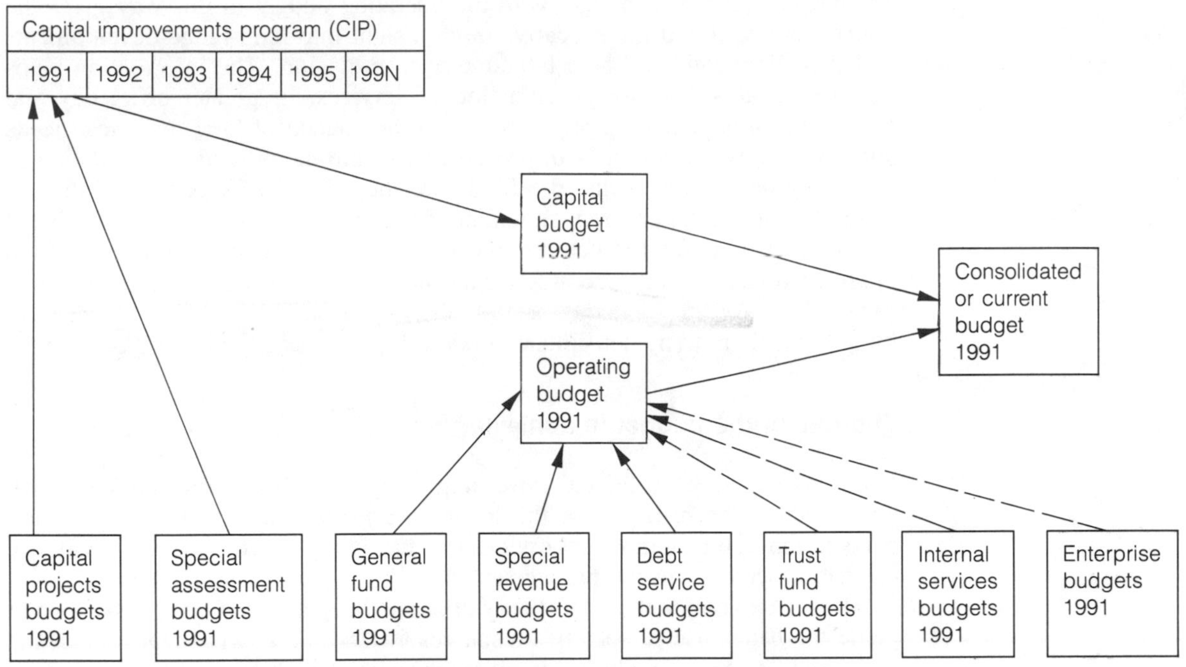

——— May not be integrated into the operating budget.

to provide public services for the fiscal year. The operating budget is an aggregation of the individual budgets of the general fund, special revenue funds, debt service funds, and if so budgeted, the various enterprise funds and fiduciary funds as well.

The capital budget, on the other hand, covers outlays for the acquisition of major long-lived assets, including assets to be purchased from restricted monies, and the resources (current monies and debt) to be employed for purchase of the assets. The capital budget should reflect the city's capital improvements program (CIP), which schedules projects over a five- to ten-year period, provides an economic justification for projects, presents fiscal projections of the interest and debt amortization required to finance the projects, and shows the effect of debt service on the operating budget (see Chapter 17 on capital budgeting). The capital budget should be an aggregation of the costs and financing of all capital projects. However, many small and short-lived capital assets such as furniture, fixtures, and small equipment, can be budgeted as current expenditures in the general fund and special revenue funds.

Unless there are legal requirements or an important need to control certain types of capital investments, the capital outlays of proprietary funds should not be included in the comprehensive capital budget. For enterprises and internal service organizations, the cost of capital outlays are amortized and recorded as current expenses through depreciation charges that spread the cost of the asset over its useful economic life. Enterprises and internal service organizations are self-sustaining entities, "closed" decision-making units. Decisions about investments in fixed assets are based on assumptions that the capital outlays will yield sufficient revenue to cover interest costs and that the annual depreciation will yield sufficient revenue charge over the life of the account.

Although the capital budget extends over a number of years, it should be updated every year to show what projects are already on line, what projects will need funds in the current year, and what projects will be started in the current year. This section of the capital budget should be submitted to the executive and the council or board at the same time as the operating budget. Coordinating the comprehensive capital budget with the operating budget in this way gives the council or board and the executive more insight into long-range developments and their implications for costs and service provision. The information helps decision makers improve coordination of services for greater efficiency and assess short-run financing requirements in the context of long-run fiscal needs and constraints. A caveat is in order here. Coordination and consolidation in budgeting do not mean that the funds are intermingled. Specifically, monies raised for the capital program should not be diverted into the operating budget.[5]

Whatever their fund structures, most local governments apply the line-item approach (discussed later) to produce an annual consolidated budget as shown in Figure 6–5. As the following section shows, the fund structure and line-item budget together strengthen financial control in the budgetary process.

The role of the budget in achieving goals

In its policymaking role, the governing body sets short-term and long-term goals, which are reflected in the local government budget. These goals are pursued through programs or services that can be provided more efficiently by the public sector than the private sector.

Although no comprehensive theory of public budgeting has been developed to guide the better use of society's resources,[6] B. Verne Lewis suggests that the economics of resource allocation, although somewhat abstract and limited, does yield a theoretical basis for governmental budgeting.[7]

A rational budget decision model

The economic theory of budgeting is rational in that means (incremental costs or inputs) are explicitly tied to—and supposedly produce—certain ends (outcomes or benefits). Public budgeting can promote economic efficiency by allocating resources to those programs and services that (1) generate greater benefits—in accordance with residents' preferences and valuations—than any alternative and (2) result in incremental benefits greater than incremental costs. Net benefits can be increased by judging each budget decision against three criteria:

Intersector efficiency The incremental spending on any government activity should yield more net benefits than would be obtained if the resources were left with individuals and organizations in the private sector

Interprogram efficiency When resources must be allocated among competing government programs, they should go to the one that produces the greatest net benefit.

Intraprogram efficiency For each program, the inputs should be combined so as to maximize the net benefits from any given increment of expenditure. For example, a given amount of money can be spent on personnel and materials for in-house service delivery, or it can be spent on contracting out.

The rational budget decision model is difficult to implement, however. Human limitations, organizational and fiscal structures, and government processes all impose obstacles to the rational attainment of goals through budgeting. What follows is a practical, prescriptive methodology for budgetary analysis that helps achieve established goals while taking these restrictions into account.

Executive budgeting

To use resources efficiently through budgeting, the executive must (1) organize the budget units along programmatic lines that relate to organizational goals, (2) establish funding levels to guide budget units in preparing their alternatives, and (3) approve alternatives in the form of programs. Each of these decision points is discussed below.

Program structure The budget must yield data that will allow the executive and council or board to see how budget units propose to achieve organizational goals with the funding they receive. This end can be facilitated by a program budget format.[8] In this format, government activities are organized according to programs so that the budget units that plan and subsequently undertake those activities can be held solely responsible for pursuing clearly defined goals. A program format can have three or more levels, as illustrated in Figure 6–7. The accomplishment of goals at the lower (right-hand) levels of the program struc-

Figure 6–7 A sample program budget format.

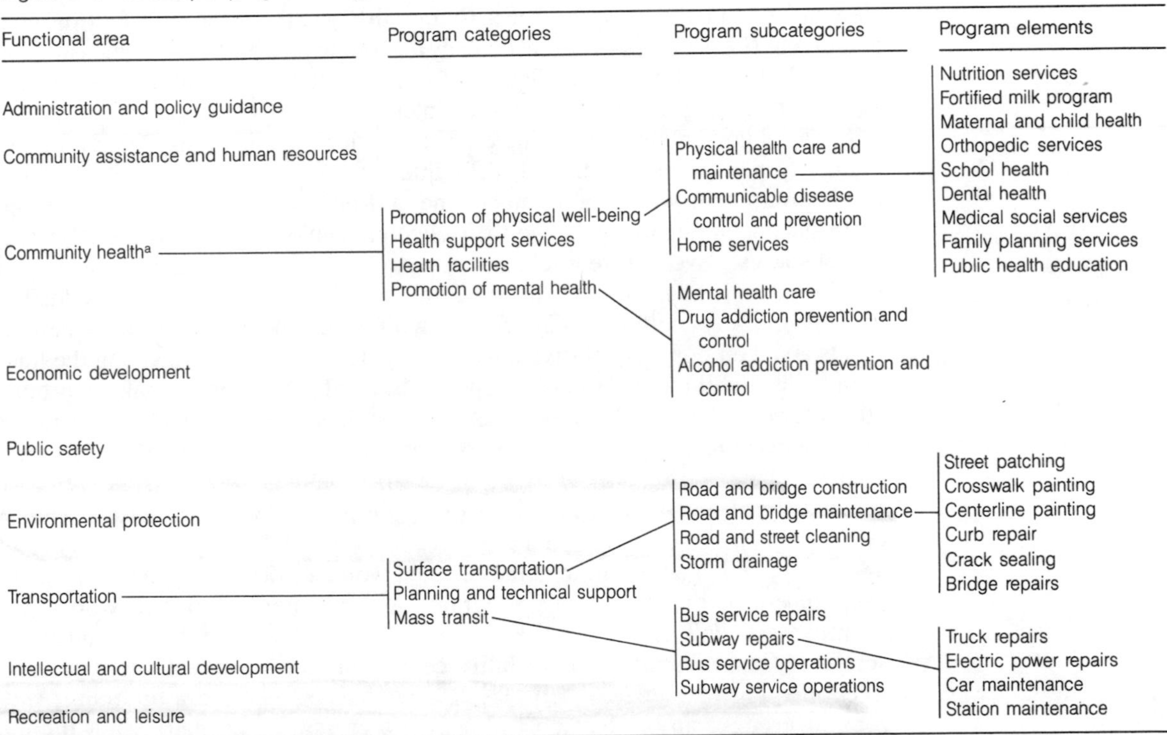

[a] Functional area—Community health
Goal: To provide freedom from debilitating disease and illness for all residents.

Program category—Promotion of physical well-being
Goal: To provide the necessary mechanisms and facilities for treatment and prevention of physical illness and diseases.

Program subcategory—Physical health care and maintenance
Goal: To decrease the incidence of physical illnesses among city residents.

Objective measures: Number of infant mortalities
Number of maternal deaths
Number of children suffering from nutritional deficiency
Number of adults with specific illness
Number of children with specific illness

Program element—Maternal and child health services
Output measures: Number of doctor visits by indigent pregnant women for prenatal care
Number of doctor visits by indigent children between birth and three years old.

ture are considered means to achieving the ends associated with the higher (left-hand) levels. At the highest level in the structure are the broad functional areas that reflect the basic needs and purposes of the government. Each area has its own goals and is made up of distinct program categories of related services or client groups. Program subcategories identify one or more services that are directed at a particular clientele or that have other characteristics in common. These program subcategories are the major policy concern and the analytical focus of budgeting; they are most commonly called "the programs" of government for which direct budgetary actions are undertaken. Subsumed under the program subcategories are *program elements* or subunits, the main building blocks of the program structure. The elements are organizational and administrative mechanisms and processes that are used by budget units to put programs into operation and accomplish discrete outcomes.

Each program element is a separate cost center encompassing all the costs required to produce an identifiable and distinct outcome.[9] Each element is also a responsibility center and budget decision points under an individual manager. Thus responsibility centers (budget decision points) would be coterminous with cost centers (program elements). If desired outcomes are assigned monetary values or benefits (discussed more extensively below), managers of program elements can identify the mix of activities that has the greatest effect on goal attainment (i.e., intraprogram efficiency). Moreover, with benefits measured at the level of the subprogram, high-level decision makers can allocate resources among competing programs to ensure interprogram efficiency.

For local governments, aligning existing service organizations with a program budget format poses substantial difficulties. Structurally reorganizing a large local government would be cumbersome and quite costly. In addition, vested interests among departments and their clientele could present substantial political obstacles. Even if reorganization were possible, changing goals would require periodic adaptation of the structure. Local governments seem wedded to the object-of-expenditure budget format with government organized by departments and their component divisions (see Figures 6–1 and 6–5). Using the line-item budget, still the most popular approach, local governments make appropriations for commodities to be purchased by the departments and divisions rather than their being assigned to subunits that produce separate and distinct outcomes. Thus a single program may be split among two or more separate organizational units. For example, to provide prenatal care, a welfare agency could be in charge of identifying and screening potential patients, while a health agency could diagnose and treat the selected women. Moreover, one department may undertake more than one program: A department of public works, for example, may deliver refuse collection, street maintenance, and water and sewer services. Consequently, responsibility centers do not mesh with cost centers.

Despite this discrepancy between the line-item budget and a program structure, efficiency can be fostered by creating a crosswalking matrix showing the relationship of line-item departmental appropriation accounts to program categories, subcategories, and elements, as demonstrated in Figure 6–8.[10] The expenditures of those separate departmental subunits (or responsibility centers) that contribute to each specific output can be aggregated into cost centers that form program elements.[11] Consequently, all resources that are likely to produce a distinct objective and benefits can be compiled into a separate program subcategory. The capability of producing such a cross-classification of accounts requires a sophisticated and costly accounting system; nevertheless, it forces a conscious linkage between government activities (program elements) and desired goals, thereby matching the costs and benefits of government actions.

Funding levels Next, the executive must establish funding levels for the preparation of budgetary alternatives. For example, the executive may direct budget units to propose programs at several levels above and below the current funding level (e.g., 80 percent, 90 percent, 100 percent, 110 percent, 120 percent). The number of funding levels should be limited; otherwise budget units will have to examine so many alternatives that the quality of analysis may suffer. The size of the funding intervals should be sufficiently large (e.g., 5 percent or 10 percent) so that the amount of resources to be added or withdrawn by the funding increment can be expected to measurably influence the achievement of goals. Small funding intervals can discourage budget units from performing extensive analyses because their efforts would be rewarded with insignificant additions to resources. When a new program is under consideration, the budget unit must first demonstrate that more is to be gained by undertaking the program than by leaving the money needed to finance it in the private sector. Once a new program can be justified, alternative funding levels can be applied.

The fund structure used in governmental accounting complicates the determination of funding levels and the selection of programs. The resources encompassed by the total budget may not be available for spending on all programs. For example, the executive and the budget units do not have discretion to move monies out of special revenue funds and divert them to other programs; these funds contain earmarked revenues that must be spent on particular functions and activities. Thus a share of a locality's taxes may be earmarked for spending on roads and streets, and a portion of property taxes may be earmarked for the maintenance of library buildings. Sometimes earmarked revenues could provide more benefits to the community if they could be allocated to nonearmarked activities. If this is the case, more efficient use of resources could result from (1) widening the scope of earmarking to related areas (e.g., gasoline taxes for mass transportation as well as roads, and library "taxes" for book purchases as well as library building repairs); (2) eliminating earmarking altogether to allow complete discretion; and (3) reducing earmarked revenues and leaving them in the private sector instead of spending them simply because they are available for earmarked purposes. Likewise, matching grants that commit the local government's own resources to purposes deemed less beneficial than those of programs not eligible for grants should not be pursued or accepted. The grant plus local resources for a given purpose may yield less benefit than if the local resources alone were allocated to an alternative purpose.

On the other hand, capital projects funds (or the capital improvements fund) and special assessment funds pose no problems for applying funding levels and fiscal constraints. As with non-earmarked revenues, borrowing by way of issuing long-term debt to finance capital outlays can merely be adjusted to the specified funding levels. Resources can be approved and then expended in accordance with the estimated effect of the funding increments on the project's net benefits. Since they are not required for repayment of bonds, the unreserved fund balances of capital projects funds could be transferred to the general fund, and the balances of the special assessments funds could be used to reduce levies against property owners. Because of their stated purpose, the resources of debt service funds should be committed to the payment of bond principal and interest. The amount of required payments has a first claim against the estimated budget revenues. Since these payments are contractual obligations for past services (sunk costs), which should have been evaluated previously for their resource efficiency, existing debt service should be excluded from the evaluation of current program alternatives.

Finally, proprietary funds may have unreserved retained earnings at the beginning of the fiscal year. These unattached monies should not be employed for producing services unconnected with the enterprises. Proprietary enterprises are most efficient when prices charged for their services are sufficient to cover the cost of operations, necessary reinvestment, and any external social costs of

Figure 6–8 Crosswalk matrix of a program structure and a line-item format:
Translating the contribution of health and social services departments to various "programs" (subcategories).

	Program structure Promotion of physical well-being (program category)										
	Physical health care and maintenance (program subcategory)									Communicable disease—control and prevention (program subcategory)	
Departmental line-item budget format	Nutrition services	Public health education	Maternal and child health	School health	Dental health	Orthopedic services	Medical social services	Family planning services	Fortified milk program	Communicable disease	Chronic diseases control
Health department											
Division of hospitals			X			X	X			X	X
Personal services			X			X	X			X	X
Supplies			X			X	X			X	X
Contracts						X	X				
Equipment			X			X	X			X	X
Capital outlays			X				X			X	X
Other											
Division of health care	X			X	X	X	X	X		X	X
Personal services	X			X	X	X	X	X		X	X
Supplies				X	X	X	X	X		X	X
Contracts							X	X		X	X
Equipment				X	X	X		X		X	X
Capital outlays											
Other											
Division of public health								X	X	X	X
Personal services									X	X	X
Supplies											

Departmental line-item budget format	Nutrition services	Public health education	Maternal and child health	School health	Dental health	Orthopedic services	Medical social services	Family planning services	Fortified milk program	Communicable disease	Chronic diseases control
Contracts											
Equipment											
Capital outlays											
Other											
Social service department											
Division of aging	X						X				
Personal services	X										
Supplies	X										
Contracts											
Equipment											
Capital outlays											
Other											
Division of handicapped							X				
Personal services							X				
Supplies							X				
Contracts											
Equipment							X				
Capital outlays											
Other											
Division of assistance	X		X			X	X	X			
Personal services	X		X			X	X	X			
Supplies	X										
Contracts											
Equipment											
Capital outlays											
Other											
Total estimated expenditures											

operating the enterprises (e.g., limiting pollution caused by production of electricity). When the price yields excess revenues, then prices in subsequent years should be reduced. If excess retained earnings are transferred to other funds, users of the services are subsidizing the cost of other programs from which they may not benefit in direct proportion to their subsidy.

Approval of alternatives Finally, program alternatives should be chosen by the executive, starting with those that promise the largest net incremental benefits at given funding levels until the available resources are exhausted.

As with zero-base budgeting (discussed below), an executive's comparison of submitted program alternatives could be accomplished through priority ranking. Lower-level managers submit their program alternatives, in accordance with the specified funding levels and intervals, to higher-level managers who in turn rank the alternatives of those programs for which they are responsible. Program decision makers need to consider not only a program's value but the ways in which different administrative, financial, and organizational mechanisms are likely to affect gains achieved by the program. The executive, who must be committed to using these estimates and evaluations, then generates a comprehensive priority list of all program alternatives by further ranking them, integrating the alternatives into one list without rearranging the order assigned by the individual higher-level managers. Afterward, alternatives are funded in accordance with the rankings until the accumulated costs of the selected alternatives reach the limit of the budget.

For this selection process to work, program goals must first be quantified in the form of objectives, and then benefits must be derived by assigning monetary values or prices to the objectives. When a uniform presentation of benefits for all alternatives is unavailable, managers usually make subjective evaluations, assigning greater or lesser values to one alternative, but without knowing the net value that another could yield. The dangers in this kind of evaluation are twofold. First, the ranking process can take on a veneer of objectivity that is then used to support choices made for limited political purposes. Second, decision makers may substantially misallocate societal resources because they do not have enough information to be sure the most valuable services are provided. Consequently, the credibility of the public sector as a capable problem solver suffers in the long run due to the failure to contribute effectively to the fulfillment of community needs.

To avoid these dangers, managers must strongly encourage, if not require, estimated monetary valuation of various program alternatives, even where benefit measurement is difficult; in the latter situation, explicit justification and the basis of evaluation must be supplied along with the problems encountered in making the estimates. Obviously, such benefit estimates should be supplemented with data on objectives and unit cost where they are relevant. In order for the ranking process to be even minimally effective decision makers must be provided with at least descriptive and qualitative information on what is to be gained by each alternative. The presentation of such quantitative and qualitative information on programs—especially benefits—orients executives and higher-level managers and aids them in their critical judgments of a program's contribution to societal goals.

Budgetary analysis by the budget unit

Clearly, preparation of a proposed budget for consideration by the executive and the governing body requires careful analysis by the budget unit. This section outlines the major steps: determining service needs; setting goals, objectives, and targets; assessing clientele and demand; considering alternatives; presenting estimates; and planning the workload.

Needs The first step in budgetary analysis is to prepare an issue paper on community needs and problems.[12] This task can be accomplished using both objective and subjective data. First, hard or objective data on social, economic, demographic, and physical conditions should be collected on a regular basis, and data interpretation should be guided by up-to-date literature in economics, sociology, psychology, and public finance. Second, information on community conditions should also be provided through surveys that ask citizens' opinions of the quality and effectiveness of service and identify problem areas. These survey findings can be supplemented when government officials interact with civic groups (through public and other forums).

Goals and objectives Goals are normative or value-laden statements of intended results to be achieved in response to a particular need or problem.[13] After community issues are clarified, the second major step in budgetary analysis is to link community needs and problems to the budget through the formulation of goals. For example, with respect to crime rates, a defined goal might be "to ensure the protection of individuals and property in the city against criminal activities."

Objectives quantify the measures by which to achieve the goals (see Figure 6–9). Objectives should not describe a means or a process, but rather a desirable end. For example, if traffic congestion plagues a commuter road, an objective might be to facilitate commuting by reducing travel time from point *A* to point *B* by 20 minutes. (Widening the road is one *means* to obtain the desired outcome, but it is not an objective.) Likewise, if a defined goal is to ensure protection

Figure 6–9 Examples of goals, objectives, and outputs

1. Fire protection

Goal
To protect against personal injury, loss of life, and property damage caused by fires in commercial and residential units.

Objectives
1. To reduce the amount of fire damage to property in both residential and commercial units by 20%
2. To reduce the loss of life due to fires by 50%
3. To reduce personal injury due to fires by 60%
4. To reduce medical costs by 60%.

Outputs
Number of responses to fires
Number of ambulance responses
Number of fires investigated
Number of housing units inspected

2. Employment opportunity

Goal
To provide the unemployed and the employed with income below the poverty level with opportunities to attain adequate family income.

Objectives
1. To have 70% of the unemployed youth obtain a permanent full-time summer job
2. To have 60% of the unemployed adults gain full-time employment above the stated poverty level income standard
3. To have 40% of the employed adults with incomes below the poverty level to gain full-time employment above the stated poverty level income standard.

Outputs
Number of workers trained
Number of jobs developed
Number of job placements for adults
Number of job placements for youths

against crime, one objective might be to reduce the crime rate by 12 percent. Increasing the number of police car patrols would be one means of achieving this objective. To be effective, goals and objectives should be a product of collective decision making among representative citizen groups, governmental operating units, the budget office, and the executive.

Given a particular goal, the budget analyst can consider multiple objectives as measures of achievement. The goal to improve traffic conditions, for example, might have two objectives: (1) to reduce travel time from point *A* to point *B* by 20 minutes, and (2) to reduce traffic accidents by 40 percent. Sometimes two objectives can conflict. If widening a road were selected as the means to achieve the objectives of reducing commuter travel time, more accidents might result from faster moving vehicles on the renovated road, thus increasing rather than decreasing the accident rate. Assuming that the conflict cannot be resolved, the analyst must trade off gains in one objective against losses in another. Such a decision can be made easier if objectives are assigned monetary values. The choice of alternatives can then be based on the maximum incremental net benefits derived when the dollar losses of one objective are weighed against the dollar gains of the other.

Targets Since many goals are unlikely to be realized in a short period of time, the budget unit must set targets that specify a series of interim sequential results.[14] For instance, for the objective of a 12 percent reduction in crime, an interim target could be "to reduce crime rates by 2 percent every six months." For each objective there may be numerous targets, each of which contributes over time to the selected goal. Like objectives, targets should be selected after evaluating the available alternatives in terms of the varying resources and types of inputs.

Targets are an inherent part of planning.[15] Establishing these short-term objectives orients the efforts of budget units toward their long-term purposes. With clear targets, managers can assess and monitor progress toward goals and, where necessary, make organizational and financial adjustments. Furthermore, executives and program directors can judge the performance of employees in their departments and hold them accountable for the management of programs under their direction. Finally, the chain of goals, objectives, and targets eliminates duplication in government activities by identifying common threads running through different programs and budget units.

Clientele and demand Objectives and targets can be made more precise by designating the population group that receives the service. For some programs, the target population or clientele is readily identifiable. For example, if needy elderly households are the target population for an assistance program, an objective should state explicitly the group to receive benefit: All elderly households with annual incomes of $8,000 or below should receive one free hot meal five days a week. In fact, many government programs—those dealing with criminal activity, air pollution, traffic congestion, and traffic accidents, for example—serve and target heterogeneous populations because they are attempting to alleviate negative conditions that prevail over much or all of the entire community. Knowledge of the target population and of detrimental conditions affecting that population provides a basis for estimating the extent of the demand and/or potential workload of the program. These data can be built into needs assessments and used for continual monitoring of program effectiveness.

Determining the size and characteristics of the clientele or target population is necessary because clients within this population could have different socioeconomic characteristics and, as a result, they may value government service differently. In the example of meals for the needy elderly, the value of benefits derived by households with annual incomes below $8,000 might vary according to income level, marital status, and homeownership. The benefits derived from relief of traffic congestion would depend on the distance traveled, the cost of travel, the value of time, and the loss of income of road users with different occupations and income levels. Once the relevant subdivisions of clientele have been identified, a monetary value must be assigned to measure the gain in dollars that would accrue to each. Numerous economic methods of measuring benefits and costs (e.g., cost savings, time savings, loss of life and limb, and pricing mechanisms) have been developed.[16] For example, one measure of the benefit of free meals provided to the needy elderly might be the estimated savings on the costs of groceries, which would vary with income level and marital status. Similarly, the monetary benefits of relieving traffic congestion could be approximated by valuing the amount of time saved by road users in different income classes. Figure 6–10 shows some possible measures of benefits provided by fire protection and employment opportunity programs. Admittedly, for some government activities measurement of benefits is problematic, making intraprogram resource efficiency somewhat difficult to judge.

Alternatives Measurement problems aside, the benefits that can be produced by a program depend on the chosen alternatives. Conceptually, alternatives are proposals that link resources with desired objectives and benefits. In practice, alternatives are merely different sets of program elements expected to be financed at different funding levels specified by the executive for the realization

Figure 6–10 Objectives, benefits, and benefit measures.

1. Fire protection[a]

Objective	Benefit	Benefit measures
Reduction in property damage	Value of property damage prevented from occurring	Assessed market value of property destroyed and/or cost to repair and restore damaged property
Reduction in deaths	Value of lives saved	Income that would have been lost by potential victims in accordance with their occupations
Reduction in personal injury	Value of injuries prevented	Income that would have been lost by potential victims in accordance with their occupations
Reduction in medical costs	Value of medical care cost saved	Cost in medical care that is avoided by preventing death and injury

2. Employment opportunities

Objective	Benefit	Benefit measures
Youth summer employment	Additional income gained	Earnings from employment
Full-time employment of formerly unemployed	Additional income gained	Difference between job earnings and unemployment compensation payments
Full-time employment of employed with poverty incomes	Additional income gained	Difference between new job earnings and earnings from prior job

[a]Some information can be obtained from fire department and insurance company records.

of objectives. Resources in the form of estimated expenditures must be used to purchase personal services, supplies, and other items necessary to carry out the program.

Identification To attain intraprogram resource efficiency, the budget analyst must determine which program design would yield the greatest net benefits for each incremental level of funding. These decisions involve the following considerations. First, a moderate number of alternatives should be considered. Resources for the analysis itself are limited; even the time needed to determine all possible means to achieve objectives is insufficient. In fact, given the very complexity and amount of information that would need to be generated to evaluate each alternative, full-scale analysis generally is undertaken before implementation of all new programs and only periodically thereafter. Decision makers may simply not be able to consider every option.

Second, alternatives should be identified in large part on the basis of existing knowledge about the causal relationships between social factors and the measures by which achievement of objectives is judged. By establishing causal relationships, budget analysts can determine what factors can be affected by programs and what factors are outside governmental control. In some cases, theoretical knowledge and empirical evidence are so limited that budgeters cannot accurately predict the effect of budgetary inputs on objectives; thus, unforeseen consequences can occur. Where knowledge is limited, rigorous analysis is particularly important. Otherwise, causal relationships will be assumed incorrectly, programs will be executed without direction, and budgeting is unlikely to further he attainment of goals.

The predicted causal relationships should guide the choice of activities that are likely to produce desired outputs or end products. These outputs are a product of the expenditures for which the budget unit manager requests an allocation. As a consequence, these activities become cost centers. However, as explained earlier, cost centers and responsibility centers are not necessarily coterminous in the line-item budget format common to many local governments. In this case, the objects of expenditure of separate responsibility centers within organizational units must be aggregated as shown in Figure 6–11. A program coordinator or, better yet, a program manager should direct the program's organizationally separate activities. To coordinate the program effectively, the higher-level manager and executive must be informed of how all units that contribute to the program's objectives will be funded.

Determining program elements or cost centers is accomplished by comparing alternatives in terms of various mixes of incremental costs and incremental benefits. With a given mix of objects of expenditure to produce an element, the budget unit manager can use one or more of the following options: in-house delivery, contracting out, grants and subsidies, vouchers, and volunteers. For example, to reduce crime rates, the alternatives could be increased car patrol, increased foot patrol and car patrol, or increased foot and car patrol together with the use of volunteer neighborhood crime watch groups. For any program, the "best" alternative is the one in which the incremental costs generate the greatest net benefits in accordance with the allowed funding levels.

Spillover effects In considering alternatives, the budget manager must be aware of nonfinancial or social costs and benefits, as well as monetary ones. Once a program is implemented, its effects may spill over to nontargeted groups. The value of these unintended benefits or costs should be calculated in evaluating each alternative; and, even if they cannot be assigned a monetary value, they should still be considered qualitatively. An example of intended effects and benefits is a widened roadway that benefits drivers by saving them time and reducing the number of accidents. When neighboring land and housing

Figure 6–11 Cost centers and responsibility centers in a program for prevention and treatment of alcohol addiction.

Cost centers		Responsibility centers		
Activity	Nature of workload	Organizational unit or subunit	Object of expenditure	Estimate
Administration	Supervision of program	Alcohol Abuse Division, Health Department	Personnel Supplies Overhead	$ 15,000 1,000 2,000
	Clientele identification and referral	Social Work Division, Human Resources Department	Personnel Supplies Overhead	$ 10,000 2,000 3,000
Alcohol clinic	Medical care	Outpatient Treatment Services, Hospital Department	Personnel Supplies Rent Equipment	$ 35,000 40,000 60,000 65,000
	Counseling	Social Work Division, Human Resources Department	Personnel Supplies Overhead	$ 18,000 1,000 4,000
Male halfway houses	Provision of living quarters	Alcohol Abuse Division, Health Department	Personnel Contracts	$ 11,000 15,000
	Counseling	Social Work Division, Human Resources Department	Personnel Supplies Overhead	22,000 1,000 5,000
Female halfway houses	Provision of living quarters	Alcohol Abuse Division, Health Department	Personnel Contracts	16,000 10,000
	Counseling	Social Work Division, Human Resources Department	Personnel Supplies Overhead	$ 14,000 1,000 3,000
Driving while intoxicated	Counseling	Social Work Division, Human Resources Department	Personnel Supplies Overhead	$ 5,000 1,000 1,000
Total budget estimate for program				$361,000

values increase as a result of an improved road, these are unintended spillover benefits to nontargeted groups. If neighborhoods are destroyed to make way for the road, these are unintended spillover costs to former residents—even if they are compensated for the market value of their properties—because their lives may be disrupted and adversely affected.

Trade-offs In the comparison of benefits associated with various alternatives, budget unit managers can make trade-offs among such factors as timeliness, responsiveness, levels of service, and quality of materials. These trade-offs can raise or lower the cost of alternatives and therefore should be incorporated into the calculation of benefits. For example, a possible trade-off in a meals program for needy elderly persons would be to reduce the quality of food and use the cost savings to serve more participants. In this way, a large number of participants receive fewer benefits, instead of a small number of participants receiving larger benefits. The response time of police and fire departments can be viewed similarly. While quick response time may produce increased benefits in public safety, it may require additional costs in the form of personnel, equipment, and capital facilities.

Unquantifiable benefits When benefits cannot be measured satisfactorily, program alternatives can be assessed in terms of their potential furtherance of objectives. In cases of a single objective the best program design is the alternative that yields the greatest incremental gain in the achievement of the objective. For goals with multiple objectives, intraprogram efficiency is difficult to determine. The trade-offs do not necessarily reveal the value of gains and losses entailed in the increments and decrements of the different objectives. For example, with a program to alleviate traffic congestion for which assignment of benefits is lacking, it is unclear what amount of travel time reduction is equivalent in value to the rise in the number of accidents that involve deaths, personal injury, and property damage caused by increased automobile and truck speeds.

Moreover, whether a program involves a single objective or multiple objectives, a problem is encountered with trade-offs among programs, or interprogram efficiency, because the units that compromise the objectives of separate programs are not comparable in value. For instance, the executive must subjectively choose between funding for additional recreational activities or additional spending on disease control. Judgments about intersector efficiency are also problematic. While it may be easy to assess the quantity of one or several objectives that can be achieved by a program alternative, such analysis does not indicate that the gains in the objectives are greater in value than the costs incurred by the alternative.

Unquantifiable objectives When the effect of governmental actions is not measurable in objectives, unit cost is a possible substitute for evaluating program alternatives.[17] Operationally, unit cost is merely the total cost of an activity divided by the total output of that activity. In principle, as illustrated in Figure 6–12, unit cost can be calculated for the individual cost centers of a program as well as for the entire program. All expenditures (including depreciation and inventories) accrued in the fiscal year should be allocated through a cost accounting system to the appropriate cost centers or program elements. When the program elements or cost centers are combined, they should produce an identifiable and measurable workload or end product that furthers the program goal and is directed toward a homogeneous or uniform clientele.[18] For example, unit cost could be compiled for refuse collection if such efforts are considered to further the goal of a clean urban environment. However, separate unit cost

Figure 6–12 Unit cost of three alternatives for refuse collection.

Two-worker truck		One-worker truck		Contracting out	
Input mix	Cost[a]	Input mix	Cost[a]	Input mix	Cost[a]
10 Trucks	$250,000	6 Trucks	$240,000	Contract	$478,000
20 Personnel	300,000	6 Personnel	108,000	Supervision	10,000
Truck service	25,000	Truck service	20,000	Overhead	2,000
Supervision	20,000	Supervision	20,000		
Overhead	10,000	Overhead	8,000		
Total cost	$ 605,000		$ 396,000		$ 490,000
Total output (tons collected)	4,000,000		4,000,000		4,000,000
Unit cost (cost ÷ output)	15.1¢/ton		9.9¢/ton		12.3¢/ton

[a] Should include the discounting of outlays over the period covering the useful life of the equipment.

measures should be calculated for residential and commercial collection if the characteristics of these two types of services differ substantially.

Presumably, unit cost measures the technical efficiency of an activity; lower unit costs than would reflect improved productivity. It is sometimes argued, therefore, that alternatives can be selected on the basis of unit costs alone, since lower costs produce a greater achievement of program goals per unit of resources. However, a budgetary analysis based solely on unit cost as a measure of economic efficiency is complicated by conceptual and operational shortcomings.[19] First, like objectives, some outputs or end products of governmental activities are not readily measurable, so unit costs cannot be determined. Second, some declines in unit cost are the result of decreases in quality. For example, using less expensive materials in road construction might cut immediate costs but might then require more repairs and cause more property damage to automobiles. This would reduce short-term governmental expenditures at the expense of increased long-term costs to both the government and the private sector. Third, some outputs are only a rough measure of program goals. For example, the unit cost for the tons of garbage collected is not indicative of the quality of the cleanliness of city neighborhoods and streets. Fourth, unit cost is not always an adequate index of program results. For example, with programs directed at alleviating a social ill or correcting detrimental conditions (e.g., disease, crime, pollution), unit cost may rise, not fall, as the level of social ill decreases.

Thus, as a decision tool, unit cost is only a limited measure of efficiency. In terms of intraprogram efficiency, lower cost may reflect a lower level of goal achievement. Even if unit cost is considered a suitable measure of goal attainment, some technical issues must still be addressed. First, selecting a program design with the lowest unit cost does not guarantee that the cost is as low as it should be. Costs can be compared, however, with unit costs for similar activities conducted by other governments. Second, costs may change with inflation from one fiscal year to the next; consequently, unit costs must be adjusted with appropriate price indices if they are to be compared over time. Unit cost also has shortcomings as a measure of intersector efficiency because, although it can indicate improved productivity, it does not reveal whether the value gained with government output is greater than the cost incurred to produce it. Finally, assessing interprogram efficiency is hampered since decreases in unit cost among different programs do not indicate which programs produce a greater net value for society.

Presentation of estimates For each program, expenditure estimates of chosen alternatives should be prepared for the different funding levels and intervals specified by the executive. These estimates should show the expected incremental benefits that are to result from changes in the amounts of proposed spending for the program elements or cost centers. At the same time, if the appropriation structure is based on a line-item format, the expenditure estimates should be cross-referenced to program activities. Information should be provided on any interconnection between the budget unit's proposed action and the activities of other governmental subunits. The budget estimates should also show the source of financing for the proposed program alternatives.

Work planning A final task in budget analysis is the preparation of management and workload plans for the budget unit. As critical linkages between the objectives and resources of a program, these plans should be multiyear and, in theory, geared to the life cycle of the program. However, to restrain budget units from presenting unrealistic estimates and projections, the schedule of proposed future actions should be tied to continued funding at expected levels beyond the budget year. The plans should stipulate the goals and objectives of the program together with guideposts in the form of targets, the resource levels needed to reach the targets, and a timetable of steps to be undertaken and completed. Each step should be described in terms of (1) the organizations responsible for executing the required activities, (2) the amount of work to be completed to meet deadlines, (3) the proposed use of resources, and (4) a schedule of obligations or encumbrances and expenditures. A management plan orients program directors to the attainment of goals and allows higher-level managers to hold program directors accountable for achieving agreed-upon objectives. Moreover, such a plan with its benchmarks for determining the level of program performance provides a basis for establishing a managerial monitoring system.

Conclusion

The rational budget decision model is integrated and holistic because it employs the same principle of efficiency at each level of resource allocation (intersector, interprogram, intraprogram) by focusing on the incremental costs (inputs) and benefits (objectives) associated with alternative uses of revenues. Because accurate quantification of costs and benefits can be elusive, the theory is not always easy to apply; nevertheless, it is valid on its own terms because it provides (1) a proper method of calculation when costs and benefits can be quantified and (2) a qualitative framework for judgment when they cannot be quantified but when decisions must still be made. In other words, cost-benefit analysis is a thought process as well as a technical analytical tool for implementing budget theory.

In sum, the rational decision-making theory as integrated with practical economic principles produces 10 steps to follow in the budgeting process.[20]

1. Select and define goals that are derived from a perception of existing social problems and needs. Then design a program for each goal and analyze potential programmatic actions by an organizational unit that would be or is responsible for the program's implementation.
2. Put the goals into operation and translate them into one or more objectives.
3. Assign weights to each objective by giving it a monetary value and, in so doing, determining the benefits to be gained from pursuit of the selected objective.
4. Select criteria to (1) judge the best alternative for each program aimed at achieving the selected goal, and (2) choose which programs to finance. The most appropriate or optimal alternatives and programs are those that provide the greatest additional benefits for additional resources (i.e., provide the greatest net benefits).
5. Determine all possible alternatives for achieving each program goal. To analyze alternatives, select funding levels and funding intervals. The funding levels can be set below and above the current level of funding of existing programs. Alternatives may include continuing existing programs, varying these programs, or trying entirely new approaches.
6. Allow for alternatives; many objectives can only be realized over a span of time.
7. Evaluate alternatives in terms of their contribution to additional gains in benefits for each funding increment. Calculate the benefits to be realized by each program along with the costs to be incurred by the alternatives. Within each funding level the social costs incurred by an alternative must be added to its financial costs. Included in this analysis should be an assessment of both the benefits gained or lost due to conflicts among objectives, and the likelihood of the alternatives to produce the objective (or beneficial outcome).

8. Compare alternatives and select the one that yields the greatest additional benefits for the additional costs incurred per increment in funding levels. In some cases greater benefits would be produced if the resources that would be used to finance the alternatives were left in the private sector.
9. Compare all the chosen alternatives of every program. Usually only limited resources—estimated revenues, estimated borrowing, and unreserved fund balances—are available for financing services in the proposed fiscal year. Within the budget constraint, the manager should choose program alternatives in descending order of net benefits until the available funding is exhausted.
10. Award financing to programs when the rankings have been confirmed by a chief executive. The awarded amount is the sum of the costs of all the alternatives that have been approved for a particular program in the ranking process. Consequently, those alternatives must be implemented in conducting the programs.

The practical difficulties of applying the rational theory of budgeting furnish a partial foundation for an alternative theory of public budgeting, incrementalism or successive limited comparisons. This approach offers a description and explanation of how the budget process is actually conducted. The number of alternatives that can be considered are not only subject to human analytical limitations on rational decision making, but they are also limited by the conservative political and organizational environment of budgeting. The feasible alternatives that remain are evaluated and chosen according to their acceptability by relevant decision makers. Decision-making criteria are easily derived from the need to reach consensus among interested parties and active participants in government policymaking. Decisions are a product of conflicts between budget makers and clientele, and among budget makers themselves, often ultimately resolved by bargaining, negotiation, and other strategies.

The budget cycle

Four major political players are involved in the budget cycle: the executive, the council or board, the departments, and the clientele who are affected by the public goods and services provided by government.[21] The clientele may be the public at large or groups of citizens who benefit from specific programs. In either case their welfare may be reduced or enhanced in the budgeting process. The complex and dynamic interactions among these institutional players are determined by organizational structure and budget procedures, which vary in cities or counties of different population size, scale of services, and form of government (council-manager or mayor-council). However, many basic principles apply across the board.

The budget cycle for a fiscal year has four phases:[22]

1. *Preparation,* when the budget units and the executive estimate their resources and expenditures
2. *Adoption,* when the executive's budget estimates are submitted to the council or board for approval
3. *Implementation,* when the adopted budget is executed throughout the year
4. *Evaluation,* when implementation is assessed.

These phases are common to the budgets of every fund and apply to line-item, performance, program, and zero-base budgeting. As shown in Figure 6–13, the budget cycle covers a time period beyond the fiscal year for which it is adopted and implemented. Moreover, budget cycles for separate fiscal years overlap. The following sections not only describe the four phases but also prescribe proce-

Figure 6–13 Annual budget cycle for fiscal year 1990.

	July 1	Months of FY	June 30
FY 1989	Preparation of FY 1990		Adoption of FY 1990
FY 1990	Implementation of FY 1990 ⟶		
FY 1991	Evaluation of 1990		

dures, practices, and actions that affect financial control and attainment of goals. Unfortunately these two budgetary purposes often conflict, for the need for control may hamper the ability of executives to respond to changing situations.

Preparation

During the preparation phase, revenue and expenditure estimates are developed by the executive, who initiates and completes this phase, and the budget units, which are the initial sources of the estimates. Because the estimates submitted by the executive to the council or board for adoption include a statement of how policy goals are to be achieved, the preparation stage should include major planning and programming for service delivery.

Executives must pursue operational goals while at the same time holding down expenditures within feasible limits. They must maintain financial control over appropriated funds to prevent negligence or fraud. The executive's central budget office must prepare *estimates* of appropriable resources—those that are available for the budget year. The budget office forecasts the monies likely to be collected under the existing revenue structure. Added to these estimated revenues are the unreserved surpluses that may be available from different funds. The executive then estimates the total allowable expenditures, which reflect changing population demands and social and economic conditions. In addition, an assessment of the city's or county's future fiscal condition, along with the revenue forecast, can indicate whether the government should consider issuing long-term debt in the budget year.

If estimated revenues exceed estimated expenditures, the predicted budgetary surplus can be used to expand services, reduce revenue levies, or create a financial safety net (a reserve for contingencies). Too large a surplus, however, may lead to political criticism, to the effect that the government is unnecessarily taxing citizens. A surplus may hamper intersector resource efficiency, as well, because too much money is being extracted from the private sector. However, when estimated revenues are less than estimated expenditures, the resulting budgetary deficit can be avoided by cutting expenditures, raising additional revenues, or drawing on available unreserved fund balances.

Revenues and expenditures should be forecasted for each month of the budgetary year so that cash flow requirements can be predicted. Because tax receipts do not coincide with the beginning of the fiscal year, revenues may be temporarily insufficient to cover cash payments. Thus the executive must decide on the amount and timing of short-term borrowing to cover revenue insufficiencies. However, the executive should make considerable efforts to (1) close out tax and nontax revenue anticipation notes at the end of each fiscal year, and (2) avoid using short-term debt to finance a continuing deficit. A sound budget rule is that current expenditures should be financed by current revenues. Political and managerial unwillingness of local officials to "live within their fiscal means" can prove detrimental to a government's credit rating.

Next comes the budget call for departmental spending estimates and for estimates of such obligations as interest and principal payments due on outstanding indebtedness and pension payments. Instructions are sent to budget units stipulating how budget forms are to be completed and outlining a budget calendar of decision steps and deadlines prior to adoption. The executive also issues a policy statement giving details of the expected fiscal situation, stating a general position of retrenchment or of expansion, and perhaps offering views on program orientation. The executive may supply information and data on economic, financial, and social trends (e.g., price levels, pay policies) that will affect the cost of programs.

Two features of the budget call can further the attainment of goals. First, the executive can require that the estimates of budget units be compatible with a program budget structure. The executive can ask departmental managers to prepare budget estimates under both line-item and program formats so that the executive and council or board can identify program costs, make policy judgments, and evaluate programmatic performance. Second, the executive can stipulate the processes by which budget analyses are to be conducted and the amounts of financing that can be requested. As suggested earlier, budget units should be required to submit alternative budgets, that is, estimates of different funding levels that link incremental spending amounts to incremental benefits of programs.

Several other options are available to executives as they call for budget estimates.[23] Open-ended budgeting is a "bottom-up" approach that allows the budget units to submit any amount they consider essential to execute their activities. Unfortunately, this approach presents two problems. First, higher-level managers have less knowledge about specific program activities and, therefore, cannot assess the effect of spending cuts in case funding levels must be lowered. Second, a single estimate does not provide information on which to judge the relative value of programs within and across budget units.

Another option is to establish a fixed ceiling on estimates from the budget units. In this "top-down" approach, higher-level managers judge the validity of financing demands before they have information on the needs and likely performance of the various programs. In effect, executive judgment supersedes the expertise located in the budget units. Moreover, the fixed ceiling encourages budget units to request the maximum amount allowed by the ceiling. The resulting estimates do not permit comparative evaluation of programs to determine whether some monies could be allocated more efficiently.

Still another option is to require the budget units to submit, along with a single budget estimate, a priority listing of activities that can be eliminated if funding is unavailable. Again, however, priority listings do not permit the executive to compare the relative value of lower-priority items among different budget units.

After the budget units conduct their budgetary analyses, their requests are forwarded to the executive's budget office to be reviewed for mathematical accuracy and compliance with budget instructions. The budget office analysts should review the appropriateness of requests by examining audits and other reports on the budget unit's past performance, and departmental managers should be allowed to defend their expenditure recommendations. At the same time, the estimates of appropriable resources should be updated for any significant changes since the initial forecast. Both sets of estimates are then sent to the executive for decisions on final funding levels. At this stage the executive must make trade-offs among programs and may, if appropriate, decide to raise or lower the estimated budget level.

When this evaluation is completed, the executive writes a budget message and the proposed budget document is prepared for the council or board. The budget message presents information on past and current trends together with the executive's major programmatic emphasis for the coming fiscal year. The budget document contains the following:

1. Summaries of the estimated receipts and outflows of all funds as well as the expected status of the funds at the beginning and end of the fiscal year
2. Estimates of the revenues and expenditures by department and program for the consolidated budget
3. Revenue and spending estimates of the operating and capital budgets
4. A statement of the actual cash position of the government and cash flow requirements for the budget year
5. A statement of the estimated level of short-term borrowing and its repayment schedule during the fiscal period.

The council or board should receive along with the budget a draft of the property tax levy ordinance as well as a draft of the budget ordinance which, if approved, makes the proposed budget the legally adopted budget of the city.

Adoption

The second phase of the budget cycle involves the council's or board's review and approval of the executive's proposed budget. Council or board adoption of the budget entails the legal approval of both expenditures and financing authority. Some revenues (e.g., interest on investments) accrue without current legal authorization, and collection of some taxes (e.g., licenses, fees, sales, and income taxes) stems from past legislative approvals. But the right to levy property taxes must be authorized for every budget period. In addition to authorizing current revenues and short-term borrowing, the council or board must also approve long-term borrowing in the form of municipal bonds. The latter finances capital outlays, which may be submitted through capital projects funds, through a capital improvements fund, or through the operating budget. The financing authorization would direct bond proceeds to particular funds to safeguard the collected monies.

To authorize spending by the departments, the council or board passes a *budget ordinance* that specifies appropriations for expendable funds (i.e., governmental funds and some trust funds). Appropriations are not needed for nonexpendable funds (i.e., proprietary funds and some trust funds), since they are self-sustaining, but their integration into the budget process increases financial control over governmental resources.

Through the appropriations ordinance, departments are granted new obligational authority during the budget year to make commitments to spend in the form of contracts, purchase orders, and salary obligations.[24] As these commitments are made, an encumbrance is charged against the pertinent appropriation so that the required amount of money is reserved for expenditures when the commitments are fulfilled. Encumbered monies are those that have been committed but not spent, while unencumbered monies are those that have not yet been committed. Additional commitments, and, concomitantly, additional spending can come only from the unencumbered monies. With the completion of commitments, the relevant encumbrances are canceled and the value of the fulfilled commitments is charged against the appropriation as expenditures. The amount of an appropriation that has been spent is the expended portion; the remainder, or the unexpended portion, is made up of encumbered and unencumbered monies.

In any given year the council or board can establish three types of obligational authority: lapsing, continuing, and implied appropriations.[25] Most appropriations are lapsing, where any unexpended portions of the appropriations (encumbered and unencumbered) that expire at the end of the budget year are unavailable for the next year's expenditures. For most local governments, authorization for all unexpended funds (including encumbrances) expires at the end of the fiscal year, but the government legally stands by the commitments made during the budget year. The encumbrances of the current year must be charged against the appropriations of the following year. This is accomplished by maintaining a reserve for encumbrance account at the end of the budget year so that the executive and council or board are notified that they are required to appropriate resources in the following year to cover past commitments.

For activities that require several years to complete (e.g., capital construction projects), continuing appropriations are employed. In some cases only the encumbered portions of the unexpended monies are carried over to the following year and the remaining unexpended authorizations lapse. This carryover is signified by reducing the unreserved fund balance of the pertinent funds and by establishing an appropriation fund balance account, shown on the balance sheet, equivalent to the value of the nonlapsing encumbrances. Thus the executive and council or board are informed that only the unreserved fund balance can be appropriated, and that some of the equity of a fund is legally committed. Therefore, it does not need further approval to finance expenditures in the following year so as to meet obligations incurred in the prior year. For other continuing appropriations, authorization for all unexpended balances, including encumbrances, is carried over to the next budget year. As in the prior case, the unreserved fund balances of the relevant funds are reduced to account for the amounts carried over.

Finally, some appropriations are implied each year through the passage of authorizing legislation, most commonly debt interest and principal redemption.

Unfortunately, lapsing appropriations provide an incentive for inefficient use of resources, for when unexpended (encumbered and unencumbered) appropriations are about to lapse, administrators may engage in ill-considered spending before the end of the fiscal year—to avoid losing unexpended appropriations. Such behavior is less likely if the authorization of unexpended funds continues into the following year, because decision makers know that monies will be available when needed. This promotes more efficient use of resources. In effect, "control" over the resources can be obtained by linking them with the achievement of goals, objectives, and targets by managers and their units.

Another kind of appropriation that trades off some financial control in the interests of attaining programmatic goals is lump-sum appropriations. With lump-sum appropriations, an amount of monies is authorized for a stated purpose, department, or category of expenditure without detailed specification of the use of these monies. The decision makers of the operating units or programs denoted by the appropriations are given discretion to spend the budgeted monies on those items and activities that they deem most fruitful. Given that the basis of appropriations is to provide resources for program goals, this kind of flexibility in the use of monies helps decision makers achieve maximum program effectiveness. While stringent financial control by the council or board must be relinquished through lump-sum appropriations, accountability can still be retained through the exercise of financial, managerial, accounting, and reporting controls that are external and internal to departments and agencies during budget implementation. These controls can also foster managerial responsibility for the effectiveness of operating unit activities.

Implementation

Implementation of the adopted budget, the third phase of the budget cycle, involves management of both revenues and expenditures. Financing program activities requires resources obtained from current revenues or from borrowing via municipal bond issues. Current revenues must be collected so that cash will be available to pay expenses. This can be achieved by establishing policies and procedures that:

1. Promote prompt revenue collection
2. Minimize revenue delinquencies and nonpayments
3. Foster quick deposit of revenue in government bank accounts to maximize interest income.

To accomplish these goals, the budget office should refer to the monthly revenue, expenditure, and cash forecasts made in the preparation phase, monitor the actual results, and compare them with the estimated figures. If revenue shortfalls seem imminent, the executive has several options:

1. Improve revenue collection
2. Raise additional revenues
3. Reduce expenditures (a task made easier if alternative funding levels were specified during the preparation phase)
4. Finance the revenue and/or cash deficiency through a reserve for contingency account
5. Use short-term borrowing to cover the temporary shortfall.

On the expenditure side of the budget, the executive has two responsibilities. First, encumbrances and expenditures must be monitored to ensure that monies are used according to appropriations.[26] Second, spending should be directed to those items and activities that contribute to program objectives. The extent to which these two responsibilities conflict and require trade-offs depends on the nature of the appropriations, whether a line-item or program format is used, and the executive's perspective on managerial responsibility.

The executive can initiate expenditure controls by requesting budget units to submit allotments and/or allocations. An allotment controls the rate of spending authorized by an appropriation, while an allocation controls the specific use of the monies that have been appropriated. Since the budget ordinance generally does not specify *when* expenditures are to be made during the fiscal year, the executive can divide an appropriation into bimonthly, monthly, or quarterly time segments. Such an allotment limits a budget unit's legal authority to incur obligations and make expenditures within the stated time frame. In the case of detailed appropriations that restrict spending to specified amounts on particular authorized objects, an allotment is the only step necessary for an executive to retain financial control over the rate of spending. In the case of lump-sum appropriations that allow managerial discretion in spending, the executive can still make allotments, but first he or she must designate the use of the appropriated monies through allocations that establish tight or loose financial control over budgetary spending. For example, if the city's fire department were given a lump-sum appropriation for all of its nonpersonnel goods and services, the executive could merely confirm this discretion by a lump-sum allocation and then periodically allot the appropriation for the year. On the other hand, if the transportation department has a lump-sum appropriation for highway expansion, the executive could maintain control by stipulating that spending must or must not entail purchases of certain personal services, materials, or equipment.

By spreading appropriation authority over the fiscal year, overspending can be forestalled, short-term borrowing can be minimized, and the need for supplemental appropriations can be avoided. At the same time, departmental managers are legitimately concerned that their programs receive enough resources on a timely basis to allow delivery of services as needed. While no optimal solution to this dilemma exists, better decisions on allotments can be made if the departments have prepared workload plans that reflect service demands and/or the impact of various input mixes on the achievement of objectives. Allotments should not be uniform across budget units or within a program. Demand may vary seasonally (in education or public works, for example). Workloads may change with increases or decreases in the client population brought about by programmatic actions. For example, although timing of equipment needs may vary for many programs, some seasonal programs such as recreation need equipment earlier in the fiscal year than other programs. Flexibility in responding to changing program needs and resources can be attained if allotment periods are established more frequently during the fiscal year (e.g., bimonthly or monthly instead of quarterly).

Additional executive financial control can be exerted through various budgetary and accounting practices. First, the approved allotments and allocations are recorded by the budget office in the pertinent allotment-expenditure ledgers in accordance with the specification of appropriations. With a ledger, as shown in Figure 6–14, the executive and budget office can monitor the use of funds authorized in the allotment periods. The ledger is opened with the amount allotted for the time period (column 9) and carried over to column 10 to show an unencumbered allotment balance available for spending. When a commitment is made via contract or purchase orders, the amount of the obligation is recorded as an encumbrance (column 4); the unencumbered allotment balance is then reduced by the value of the encumbrance, reflecting the new amount available for expenditures and encumbrances. After a commitment is fulfilled or completed, the pertinent encumbrance is canceled and expenditures are made. At any time, the ledger shows the value of the allotted funds that have been expended (column 8), and the amount of allotted funds that are encumbered for potential payment (column 6). When these two figures are added together and then subtracted from the value of the allotments (column 9), the result is the unencumbered allotment balance (column 10), the amount the manager has available for further commitments.

Figure 6–14 Illustrated allotment-expenditure ledger.

Allotment for June, 1990 — City of Springfield

Function: Health
Organization: Department of Environmental Protection
Division: Bureau of Pollution Control
Activity: Drainage and spraying
Character: Current expenses
Object: Materials and supplies

		Encumbrances				Expenditures			
(1) Date	(2) Item	(3) No.[a]	(4) Issued	(5) Completed	(6) Balance	(7) Amount	(8) Total expenditure	(9) Total allotment	(10) Unencumbered allotment balance
6/1	Allotment	—	—	—	—	—	—	25,000	25,000
6/2	Detergents	1	1,300	—	1,300	—	—	—	23,700
6/3	Uniforms	2	800	—	2,100	—	—	—	22,900
6/4	Detergent	1	—	1,300	800	1,300	1,300	—	22,900
6/4	Chemicals	3	14,000	—	14,800	—	1,300	—	8,900
6/6	Office supplies	4	2,200	—	17,000	—	1,300	—	6,700
6/8	Chemicals	3	—	14,000	3,000	14,000	15,300	—	6,700
6/28	Uniforms	41	900	—	1,500	—	22,100	—	1,400[b]
6/30	Closing entry							(1,400)	

[a] Number assigned to items as they are encumbered and unencumbered.
[b] This amount may be impounded by the executive since it has not been encumbered by the bureau.

Control over allotments can be strengthened further by preauditing procedures that require budget office approval before obligations are incurred by the budget unit. Transactions involving commitments are submitted for review in the form of written documents such as purchase orders, requisitions, and contracts. Preauditing permits the budget office to determine the availability of uncommitted funds and whether the proposed commitments and the methods of making them are consistent with the allotment authorizations and existing statutes. Additional scrutiny by both the operating manager and the budget office can be obtained with a voucher system whereby all disbursements for completed commitments must be approved by the budget office through the submission of a voucher. This document verifies that the budget unit has received the goods and services, that prices are consistent with the commitment, that the expenditure can be charged to the allotment, and that the allotment is not exceeded.

Financial control is also strengthened by periodic reports from the budget office on the use and status of allotments. Information is presented on encumbrances, expenditures, and available balances. Such reports should be distributed to budget unit managers on a frequent and timely basis so that they can ascertain the amount and type of resources available to carry on unit activities and to take corrective action when funds are inadequate. For example, monthly allotment reports should be prepared with considerable lead time before the end of the monthly allotment period; otherwise, budget unit managers will not have time to take corrective action.

Budget implementation does not always go as smoothly as planned, especially when prices of goods and services rise and demands for service increase. These circumstances can be planned for by a reserve for contingency account (if the reserve is legally available for such use) or by requesting a supplemental appropriation through the executive. Additional authorization for financing services should be avoided unless it is accompanied by additional generation of revenue; otherwise, it represents deficit spending or causes a drawdown of unreserved fund balances.

Excessive reliance on either short-term borrowing or supplemental appropriations may be avoided through executive impoundment of the unencumbered allotment balance of each budget unit at the end of each allotment period. Thus the balances would not be carried forward, and spending authorization in the next allotment period would include only the amounts specified according to the previously approved allotment schedule. The impounded balances could be allocated to reserve accounts consistent with the original appropriations. For example, if a detailed appropriation stipulated the use of monies for a particular object of expenditure by a specific agency, then a reserve fund could be established only in accordance with that specified purpose. When the agency required additional money for the object covered by the reserve fund in the following allotment periods, a request could be made to the executive for an amount from the pertinent reserve fund. On the other hand, if a lump-sum appropriation had been granted for one entire department, program, or activity, a reserve fund could be set up to correspond to the wide authorization of the appropriation, even though the expiring allotment balances had been allocated for some particular object. Thus, program managers could request monies to be released from the reserve fund, and if approved by the executive, the released monies could be employed for any goods and services covered by the lump-sum appropriation.

Program implementation can also be facilitated by management action and workload plans, which were described previously. Managers can monitor progress in their programs by comparing actual performance levels with planned targets and by determining whether particular activities have been accomplished in accordance with the planning schedule. Such monitoring should be conducted frequently, (e.g., bimonthly, monthly) with periodic reports. If variances from programmatic plans are found, program managers can undertake prompt corrective measures to prevent inadvertent diversion of resources away from program goals. In addition, if decision makers have agreed to the plans, upper-level managers and the executive can hold program directors responsible for achieving the targets of the budget year. Accountability is also increased by the publication of an annual report that summarizes the accomplishments of programs within the framework of their specified objectives.

Evaluation

The final phase of the budget cycle is evaluation, when the performance of governmental units is assessed for their implementation of the budget during the fiscal year. A *financial and compliance audit* is conducted to determine whether the budget has been executed consistently with appropriations; the purpose of this audit is to control fraud, waste, and mismanagement of funds. An *economy and efficiency audit* indicates whether departmental managerial and administrative practices have been economical or cost efficient, and, if not, identifies the reasons for cost inefficiencies. Finally, a *program results audit* reveals whether departments have achieved program objectives and have employed the most cost-effective alternatives.

Conclusion

During the budget cycle many accounting and budgeting mechanisms are employed to increase managers' financial control over appropriated resources. These controls, however, may be so strict that they actually hinder the achievement of programmatic goals. Nevertheless, it is possible to maintain financial accountability and control while also providing managerial flexibility.

1. A program structure can encourage the executive, the operating unit managers, and the council or board to examine activities in terms of societal needs.
2. Through the establishment of program elements or cost centers, goal statements, objectives, benefits, and unit costs, decision makers in operating units can consider the linkages involving the final impacts of their units' activities.
3. Lump-sum appropriations and allocations provide more discretion to program directors to adapt programs to changing conditions.
4. Appropriations, allocations, and allotments can be tied to performance factors (targets, unit cost) rather than to objects of expenditures.
5. Budget reports should pertain to objectives and workloads, and only secondarily to expenditure items.
6. Preaudits of an operating unit's expenditures by the budget office should be restricted to checking the availability of authorized spending balances.
7. Program directors should have considerable power to re-allot funds to adapt to changing program needs.

All these suggestions entail some shift in control from the budget office to the operating units. One argument for budget office control is that it can prevent budget units from overspending appropriations and incurring deficits. However, program decision makers have more information and experience with the substantive issues involving service delivery. If the budget office imposes burdensome control over finances and becomes involved in programmatic decisions, program directors will lose their initiative and take less responsibility for program activities. A better alternative is to shift the role of the budget office from preaudit to postaudit evaluation and, simultaneously, hold program managers accountable for program effectiveness and efficiency, as well as financial integrity. The reward system and the authority to remove ineffective managers are then linked to the budget and the attainment of program goals.

Budgetary approaches

The previous sections have focused on two sometimes conflicting purposes of public budgeting: goal attainment and financial control. A third purpose of budgeting is managerial productivity.[27] The different budgetary approaches used in local governments reflect the political importance of these various purposes at any given time. Financial control has been associated with line-item budgeting; managerial productivity with both performance budgeting and zero-base budgeting (ZBB); and goal attainment or planning with both program budgeting and planning-programming-budgeting (PPB) systems. Because there is considerable variation in practice, these budgetary approaches are described as "ideal types" in the following discussion.

Line-item budgeting

The line-item budget (which is still the predominant form) was, for all practical purposes, the only budgetary approach employed by local governments until the 1950s. Developed as a response to the substantial governmental corruption that prevailed at the turn of the twentieth century, the line-item budget was designed to assure financial accountability of public officials who were in charge of public monies.[28] With the line-item budget, financial control is exerted mainly through an objects-of-expenditure format that designates what is to be purchased. Generally, the objects are classified by character—current items (operating costs), long-term items (capital outlays), and past services (debt service). The separate organizational units and subunits are usually required to submit their budget expenditure estimates in accordance with these objects-of-expenditure classifications, as shown in Figure 6–5. Line-item budgets are generally fixed budgets with monies appropriated only for a particular time period, most commonly one year. The discretion of the executive can be limited further if the council or board makes appropriations more detailed. Appropriations can be approved for different classes of expenditure (e.g., personal services, supplies), subclasses of expenditure (e.g., wages, salaries, travel, overtime compensation, stationery supplies), or even very specific separate items (e.g., the pay scales for individual positions, supplies of pencils and paper). The council also exerts financial control by setting overall spending limits and by financial audits of the executive branch.

The major responsibility for exercising financial control shifts to the executive in the preparation and implementation phases of the budget cycle. Decision making by the executive, the budget office, and the operating units is uncoordinated, however. The executive initiates the budget by clarifying a general policy orientation and spending guidelines. Operating units prepare estimates independently for the services for which they are responsible and submit requests for spending on particular objects. If open-ended estimates are solicited, the executive may cut them back. After the council or board adopts the budget, the executive secures control over the operating units' budget implementation by establishing allotments for the funded objects and preauditing expenditures in accordance with allotments or appropriations. The budget office authorizes encumbrances and spending only for items that fall within the scope of applicable allotments and may refuse expenditures on grounds that the spending is not suitable for the service. Finally, bimonthly and monthly financial reporting provides information on the legality of spending and on spending trends that could interfere with achieving a balanced budget.

Because information is organized according to inputs, budgetary analysis in the line-item approach is focused on what is purchased and ignores the importance of governmental actions to achieve goals. Program elements may not be coordinated; evaluation of alternatives is not encouraged, and the budget estimates submitted to the executive do not contain information on intersector or intraprogram efficiency. There is no incentive for such analysis because executive budget allocations are not made on the basis of the most efficient alternatives. Since, in a strict line-item approach, no information is given on what is to be accomplished with the requested expenditures, the executive and council or board cannot ascertain whether the service is being provided cost-effectively or even effectively. The executive has no criteria for cutting requests because he or she does not know what will be lost or gained with different amounts of expenditures. Consequently, efficient trade-offs among services are impossible; the executive simply cuts spending on particular objects and makes subjective judgments on effectiveness. Such decisions presuppose that the executive has greater expertise on service issues than the operating unit managers.

Performance budgeting

The major impetus for performance budgeting originated in the late 1940s with the Hoover Commission Report on federal government budgeting. Performance budgeting was viewed as a mechanism to improve the management of service delivery, with cost-efficiency being the indicator of managerial effectiveness.[29] This orientation required that governmental managers design their budgets to correspond to functions and activities that further goals. In a performance budget format, government activities are divided into major functions, each encompassing a number of programs. In turn, programs are made up of a number of activities, each of which is undertaken by separate *performance units*. A unit can be an entire department, a division, or a workgroup, and any one of them may be responsible for more than one activity. Each activity must yield an identifiable output, sometimes referred to as workload or end product, and each is produced by a mix of objects of expenditure. To obtain the required program structure, the program format is adapted to the existing structure of the line-item budget, as shown in Figure 6–15.

The initiative in budget preparation lies with the performance unit. Output or workload measures are developed for each activity of a performance unit by

Figure 6–15 Illustration of performance budget format.

Function	Community health	Community health
Program	Environmental protection	Public health care
Performance unit	Division of public works	Division of hospitals
Activity	Street cleaning	Vaccination for contagious diseases
End product	Miles of street swept	Number of vaccinations
Objects	Personal services Materials and supplies Equipment Other services	Personal services Materials and supplies Equipment Other services
Performance unit	Bureau of pest control	Bureau of school health
Activity	Spraying of contaminated areas	Health examination of children
End product	Acres sprayed	Number of examinations
Objects	Personal services Materials and supplies Other services	Personal services Materials and supplies Equipment Other services

counting the work units that can be accomplished in each activity during the budget year. Then the total cost and the unit cost are estimated for each activity. Unit cost is used as a criterion for choosing the most appropriate alternatives; a performance unit manager may consider different mixes of objects of expenditure, entailing different costs and different levels of output, and then choose the alternative with the lowest unit cost. To obtain a budget estimate for the service activity of a performance unit, the number of units of output is estimated and multiplied by the chosen unit cost figure. Along with budget estimates, a performance unit submits a narrative statement that (1) describes how the activity pertains to the department's service responsibilities and goals, (2) outlines the tasks to be performed in carrying out the activity, (3) demonstrates how the appropriation will facilitate the activity of the performance unit, and (4) sets forth a workload plan specifying guideposts for workload/output units to be accomplished during the budget year and a schedule of the type and amount of work to be undertaken to reach the guideposts.

Accepting unit cost–based figures as budget estimates means that the appropriations should authorize spending for each activity undertaken by a performance unit. Likewise, allotments should parallel the appropriations. In addition, preauditing by the budget office should be limited to the checking of allotment or appropriation balances rather than routine approval of encumbrances. This restrained executive oversight allows performance unit managers to exercise more discretion in overseeing activities and gives them responsibility for service provision. Managerial accountability and effectiveness are reinforced by a performance reporting system. The activities of a performance unit can be monitored by collecting data on workload and outputs and comparing these data with the guideposts in the performance plan. Through monthly reports managers can determine the need to make adjustments in the timing, quantity, or mix of inputs to keep the performance unit on track with its guideposts. Finally, managerial accountability can be fostered through performance audits.

Performance budgeting has several weaknesses. First, as explained previously, unit cost measures are meaningless for many activities. Second, the separate activities assigned to performance units may not include all organizational actions that contribute to a particular output. As a result, total costs are not compiled accurately and unit cost is a misleading indicator of cost efficiency; moreover, authority over governmental services is fragmented and diffused. Third, since benefits are not measured, unit cost does not indicate intersector efficiency. Fourth, interprogram efficiency cannot be established because unit cost does not indicate the net value yielded by each competing program. Finally, since only one funding level is submitted for each activity, executives have no basis for cutting the requested funding of competing activities if reductions in budget requests are required.

Program budgeting

The most elaborate form of program budgeting was the planning-programming-budgeting (PPB) system initiated by the federal government in the early 1960s.[30] Scaled-down variations of PPB have been adopted by many state and local governments. The program budgeting process is more centralized than other budget approaches. Executives provide explicit formal guidance during the preparation phase by clarifying goals. Based on the goals, a program structure is designed, as illustrated in Figure 6–7, to show how the goals will be achieved organizationally. With a program format, all potential alternatives that contribute to the attainment of goals are examined systematically. The intent is to reexamine past programmatic commitments to determine whether they should be continued or whether their resources should be reallocated to new programs.

The alternative with the greatest net benefits for a given cost becomes the budget request of a program.

Evaluation of alternatives is conducted within the context of long-range planning. Consequently, multiyear plans are prepared along with the budget estimates. These plans describe how resources will be used to meet specified targets over the life of the program. For each program element the executive receives one funding request. Funding is awarded according to the greatest net benefits or, if benefits cannot be calculated, greatest gains in objectives. While funding choices are being made, the executive reviews forecasts of revenues and expenditures for three to five years to establish potentially available resources and the demands on them so that future revenue needs can be determined.

When funding requests for program alternatives are submitted to the council or board, the budget should be authorized through lump-sum and continuing appropriations for each program alternative so that program managers have the flexibility to mix objects of expenditure compatible with long-range planning goals. Similarly, while the appropriations have to be allotted to be consistent with revenue flow, executive allocations to program elements should be lump-sum, merely mirroring the appropriations. Equally important in reserving discretion for program managers, executive preaudit controls should be restricted to determining unencumbered balances available for commitments. Executives can hold program managers accountable for their spending actions through (1) comparing the targets in the program's multiyear plan with actual achievement of objectives and (2) using program results audits to assess programmatic effectiveness. With their multiyear plans, managers can adjust programmatic actions when variances occur with respect to targets and workload requirements.

Several difficulties are encountered with a program budget. First, goals are difficult to define and formulate. Second, goals are subject to change, and program structure must be changed concomitantly. Third, for many goals, it is impossible to measure benefits and objectives. Fourth, alternatives cannot be evaluated systematically because of human limitations, time constraints, and the expense of extensive analysis. Fifth, while the analysis of program alternatives in terms of costs and benefits can yield information for the determination of intersector and interprogram efficiency, the executive has limited information regarding intraprogram efficiency; a single budget request does not provide alternatives for reducing or expanding a program in line with the overall budget.

Zero-base budgeting

Zero-base budgeting (ZBB) originated in the private sector and gained popularity with the Carter administration in 1972.[31] ZBB arose from the managerial concern with cost efficiency of government services. With ZBB, outputs are the basis for assessing the usefulness of an activity, and annual reviews of budgeted activities focus on the effect of increments in financing. These alternative funding levels are used for setting priorities among activities.

The first step in ZBB is to establish decision units—organizational subunits with a designated manager who has responsibility and authority for a specific set of activities. With a program format, decision units would be the program elements. However, in practice, decision units have merely been grafted on the existing objects of expenditure format. A department or division may have more than one decision unit.

The second step is to devise decision packages for each decision unit at alternative levels of funding. A package should identify the mission and goal of the unit, outline different ways to deliver the services, and describe the benefits of each alternative. Generally, the manager of the decision unit selects among the options in each package on the basis of the greatest gain in outputs. In most cases, funding levels are stated in percentages of current year funding (e.g., 90 percent, 100 percent, 110 percent), and decision packages generally encompass three different levels of funding—minimum, current, and improved.

The minimum level is the amount of funding needed to keep the activities viable. Difficulty in determining the level of viability has led to requiring as a minimum either an 80 percent, 85 percent, or 90 percent funding level. When the current level of funding is specified, the decision unit requests 100 percent of its last year's expenditures. For example, if $2 million had been received in the previous year, then the decision unit's budget request for the next fiscal year would also be $2 million. Finally, an improved level of funding would obtain if the decision unit were permitted or required to submit requests for more than 100 percent of its previous year's expenditure. For example, with an improved level of funding stated at 110 percent, the decision unit that received an appropriation of $2 million in the previous year could request a maximum appropriation of $2.2 million for the next fiscal year.

The third step in ZBB is to rank the selected packages of the decision units. First, upper-level managers rank the separate packages of the decision units under their authority in priority order. Packages from all decision units are in turn arranged in priority order by the executive, producing a ranked list of all organizational decision packages. The packages to be funded in the budget are those at the top of the list, starting with the highest-ranked package and continuing down until the cumulative total of costs equals the maximum allowable spending for the budget year. Packages falling farther down the list are not funded. This total budget with its ranked packages is then submitted to the council or board.

Although the literature provides little insight into implementing ZBB, lump-sum appropriations would provide managers of decision units with flexibility to adapt to changes that affect cost and output levels; likewise, this flexibility would be furthered by allotments and allocations that correspond to council or board authorizations and by executive preaudits limited to checking unencumbered balances.

Several major criticisms can be raised regarding the suitability of ZBB. First, without measurement of costs and benefits, the executive and council or board cannot judge intersector or interprogram efficiency. Second, without a program structure, decision makers cannot conduct a coherent analysis of alternatives. Third, authority over services is diffused since activities in several decision units may contribute to the same output.

Conclusion

The line-item budget is still perhaps the most popular approach to local government budgeting. The other approaches have been adopted by a large number of governments since the 1950s, but in their pure form they have not been very successful. As ideal types, performance, program, and zero-base budgets require large amounts of paperwork and administration, considerable supervisory time, and high costs for accounting, information collection, and analysis. This complexity and expense are probably unnecessary for small local governments. Nevertheless, many concepts embodied in these approaches have been incorporated into line-item budgeting, and in many places hybrids have been implemented successfully. It is difficult to say which of the four budget approaches is the most appropriate for local governments. Each approach has conceptual, measurement, and operational strengths and deficiencies. This chapter has provided the finance officer with the basic information needed to make sound decisions regarding the scope and types of public budgeting methods and approaches.

1 Much of the discussion in this section can be found in Municipal Finance Officers Association, *Governmental Accounting, Auditing, and Financial Reporting* (Chicago, 1980); Edward S. Lynn and Robert J. Freeman, *Fund Accounting: Theory and Practice,* 2d ed. (Englewood Cliffs, N.J.: Prentice-Hall, 1983); Leon E. Hay, *Accounting for Governmental and Nonprofit Entities,* 7th ed. (Homewood, Ill.: Richard D. Irwin, 1985); and Harry D. Kerrigan, *Fund Accounting* (New York: McGraw-Hill, 1969). Also see John L. Mikesell, *Fiscal Administration: Analysis and Applications for the Public Sector* (Chicago: Dorsey Press, 1986).

2 The authoritative position on these matters is given by the MFOA in *Governmental Accounting,* often referred to as GAAFR.

3 GAAFR.

4 GAAFR.

5 For analysis of capital budgeting, see J. R. Aronson and John L. Hilley, *Financing State and Local Governments* (Washington, D.C.: Brookings Institution, 1986), Chapter 10.

6 V. O. Key, Jr., "The Lack of a Budgetary Theory," *American Political Science Review* 36 (1940): 1137–44; B. Verne Lewis, "Towards a Theory of Budgeting," *Public Administration Review* 12, no. 1 (Winter 1952); and Aaron B. Wildavsky, *The Politics of the Budgetary Process* (Boston: Little, Brown and Co., 1964).

7 B. Verne Lewis, "Towards a Theory of Budgeting."

8 For many excellent articles in this area, see Freemont J. Lyden and Ernest G. Miller, eds., *Public Budgeting: Program Planning and Implementation,* 4th edition (Englewood Cliffs, N.J.: Prentice-Hall, 1982); and Robert D. Lee, Jr., and Ronald W. Johnson, *Public Budgeting Systems,* 3d ed. (Baltimore, Md.: University Park Press, 1983).

9 Francis E. McGilvery, "Program and Responsibility Cost Accounting," *Public Administration Review* 28, no. 2 (March/April: 1968): 148–54; Lee and Johnson, *Public Budgeting Systems;* and David Novice, ed., *Current Practice in Program Budgeting (PPBS): Analysis and Case Studies Covering Government and Business* (New York: Crane, Russak & Co., 1973).

10 C. West Churchman and A. H. Schainblatt, "PPB: How Can It Be Implemented?" *Public Administration Review* 29, no. 2 (March/April 1969): 178–89.

11 McGilvery, "Program and Responsibility Cost Accounting."

12 Frederick O'R. Hayes et al., *Linkages: Improving Financial Management in Local Government* (Washington, D.C.: Urban Institute, 1982), Chapter 7; Thomas D. Lynch, *Public Budgeting in America,* 2d ed. (Englewoods Cliffs, N.J.: Prentice-Hall, 1985), Chapter 6; and E. S. Quade, *Analysis for Public Decisions* (New York: American Elsevier, 1975).

13 O. Lynn Deniston et al., "Evaluation of Program Effectiveness and Program Efficiency," in Lyden and Miller, eds., *Public Budgeting;* Hayes et al., *Linkages;* and Quade, *Analysis for Public Decisions.*

14 O. Lynn Deniston et al., "Evaluation of Program Effectiveness and Program Efficiency"; and Lee and Johnson, *Public Budgeting Systems.*

15 Lee and Johnson, *Public Budgeting Systems;* and Lyden and Miller, eds., *Public Budgeting.*

16 For example, see E. J. Mishan, *Cost-Benefit Analysis,* 3d ed. (Boston: George Allen & Unwin, 1982); Robert Sugden and Alan Williams, *The Principles of Practical Cost-Benefit Analysis* (New York: Oxford Univ. Press, 1978); Mark S. Thompson, *Benefit-Cost Analysis for Program Evaluation* (Beverly Hills: Sage Publications, 1980); Steven E. Rhoads, ed., *Valuing Life: Public Policy Dilemmas* (Boulder, Col.: Westview Press, 1981); and Edward M. Gramlich, *Benefit-Cost Analysis of Government Programs* (Englewood Cliffs, N.J.: Prentice-Hall, 1981).

17 For the classic discussion of the use of unit cost in public budgeting, see Jesse L. Burkhead, *Government Budgeting* (New York: John Wiley & Sons, 1956), Chapters 5, 6, and 7.

18 Ibid.

19 Ibid.

20 Charles E. Lindblom, "The Science of Muddling Through," *Public Administration Review* 19 (Spring 1959): 79–88; David Braybrooke and Charles E. Lindblom, *A Strategy of Decision: Policy Evaluation as a Social Process* (New York: Free Press, 1970); and Herbert A. Simon, *Administrative Behavior: A Study of Decision-making Processes in Administrative Organization,* 3d ed. (New York: Free Press, 1976).

21 Lynch, *Public Budgeting in America,* Chapters 2 and 5; see also Wildavsky, *The Politics of the Budgetary Process.*

22 Lynn and Freeman, *Fund Accounting,* Chapters 3 and 4; Hay, *Accounting for Governmental and Nonprofit Entities,* Chapters 2–5; and Lynch, *Public Budgeting in America,* Chapters 4–8.

23 Lewis, "Towards a Theory of Budgeting."

24 Kerrigan, *Fund Accounting,* Chapters 7–10; Lynn and Freeman, *Fund Accounting,* Chapters 3–6; and Hay, *Accounting for Governmental and Nonprofit Entities,* Chapters 2–5.

25 Ibid.

26 Lynn and Freeman, *Fund Accounting,* Chapters 5 and 6; and Hay, *Accounting for Governmental and Nonprofit Entities,* Chapters 4 and 5.

27 Allen Schick, "The Road to PPB: The Stages of Budget Reform," *Public Administration Review* 26, no. 4 (December 1966): 243–58.

28 Schick, "The Road to PPB." Also see GAAFR; Lynn and Freeman, *Fund Accounting;* Hay, *Accounting for Governmental and Nonprofit Entities;* Kerrigan, *Fund Accounting;* and Mikesell, *Fiscal Administration.*

29 Burkhead, *Government Budgeting,* Chapters 5–7.

30 See Schick, "The Road to PPB."

31 Peter A. Pyhrr, "The Zero-Base Approach to Government Budgeting," *Public Administration Review* 37, no. 1 (January/February 1977): 1–8; Robert N. Anthony, "Zero-Base Budgeting Is a Fraud," *The Wall Street Journal,* 27 April 1977; Allen Schick, "Zero-Base Budgeting and Sunset: Redundancy or Symbiosis?" *The Bureaucrat* 6 (Spring 1977); and Allen Schick, "The Road from ZBB," *Public Administration Review* 38, no. 2 (March/April 1978). Also see Mikesell, *Fiscal Administration,* Chapter 4.

Financial accounting, reporting, and auditing

Financial accounting and reporting by local governments is on the brink of dramatic change. The Single Audit Act of 1984 has become law, and the new Governmental Accounting Standards Board is addressing an agenda loaded with major projects. Financial reporting and auditing have assumed positions of substantially increased significance, a response to the near financial failure of several of the nation's largest cities and the resultant heightened interest in cost, level, and quality of various governmental services. Public administrators have recognized the need for adequate accounting systems with multiple reporting capabilities—to communicate with citizens and other interested parties, to plan and control operations, and to ensure accountability.

As this chapter will demonstrate, local government financial management differs from private business practice in major ways (although the latter is beginning to have a beneficial influence on the way government is run). A private firm is relatively free to operate in the economic arena, and its operations, revenues, and costs can vary considerably. The commercial accounting system reports not only on a firm's return to investors, but also reflects to a degree its *adaptability* to the market. Local government operations, on the other hand, are not as flexible or variable; rather, they are specified and constrained by the budget and a host of regulations.

The budget is the heart of administering public resources, and governmental accounting is central to the budget-making process. The historical accounting records furnish the best data for forecasting the ongoing revenue sources used in constructing the budget, and it provides a fix on the costs of such standard operations as police, fire protection, and street cleaning and maintenance. Accounting records also furnish data on existing debt and debt service charges and serve as a basis for estimating the city's fiscal capacity to finance additional capital improvements. Finally, good accounting reports provide timely information as to when the budget plans are going amiss, when capital funds are diverted to operations, when expenditures are outrunning revenues, and when the local government is incurring financial obligations beyond its fiscal capacity. In this chapter, specific governmental accounting techniques are presented in detail. They facilitate keeping track of, controlling, and reporting the sources and uses of financial resources.

Financial and management reporting play central roles in local government financial management. As this chapter shows, financial statements provide information on fiscal and budgetary compliance, funds flow, and liquidity. Administrators use the information contained in these reports to plan and evaluate operations as well as to comply with a variety of regulatory and granting authorities.

Finally, this chapter addresses auditing. Traditionally, auditing activities have been concerned primarily with financial and compliance issues. But it is now quite clear that the audit function holds substantial promise for municipal managers attempting to improve the efficiency and effectiveness of a variety of programs. In fact, a broad concept of auditing is particularly useful in governments—where a direct profit motive is usually, by necessity, lacking.

Underlying the accounting, reporting, and auditing concepts described in this chapter is a set of standards and techniques accepted by the profession for managing finances responsibly. Before proceeding with a closer look at accounting, reporting, and auditing, this chapter will first present those standards and describe the users of the financial reports.

Accounting and reporting standards

The accounting profession has developed a set of rules, standards, and practices to guide financial reporting. Derived from generally accepted accounting principles and referred to as GAAP, they have been described by a subcommittee of the Financial Accounting Standards Board as follows:

> Generally accepted accounting principles are primarily conventional in nature. They are the result of decisions; they represent the consensus at any time as to how the financial accounting process should operate and how financial statements should be prepared from the information made available through the financial accounting process.
>
> Inasmuch as generally accepted accounting principles embody a consensus, they depend heavily on notions such as "general acceptance" and "substantial authoritative support," which have not been and probably cannot be precisely defined. There is concurrence, however, that the notions of "general acceptance" and "substantial authoritative support" relate to the propriety of the practices, as viewed by informed, intelligent, and experienced accountants in the light of the purposes and limitations of the financial accounting process.[1]

The accounting profession in the United States has followed this rationale in creating bodies capable of establishing GAAP (see accompanying sidebar describing the organizations that set and safeguard accounting standards). Standards and practices representing GAAP for state and local governments have been developed since the 1930s by the National Council on Governmental Accounting (NCGA) and the predecessor committees sponsored by the Government Finance Officers Association (GFOA). More recently, a Governmental Accounting Standards Board (GASB) has been formed and is currently recognized as the authoritative organization for setting financial accounting and reporting standards for state and local governments. The first authoritative pronouncement of the GASB recognized and adopted all existing authoritative literature published by the now defunct NCGA. Therefore, until altered by the GASB, NCGA statements and interpretations continue to describe GAAP for state and local governments. An audit guide dealing, in part, with state and local government financial accounting practices was issued in 1986 by the American Institute of Certified Public Accountants (AICPA), which has been active in formulating such standards since 1974.

Financial reporting is a complex communication form, related primarily to the transmission of economic data about an organization to concerned individuals and institutions.

The GASB is made up of five members, (currently two full-time and three part-time) who are experts in governmental accounting and financial reporting and who are supported by research and administrative staffs. Under this structure, emerging issues can be addressed more quickly, due process established more readily, and research conducted more efficiently and directly than was possible under the NCGA, which was composed of 21 part-time members with little technical and administrative support.

Ultimately, the overriding criterion of success for financial communication is the usefulness of the information provided, not the reporting process itself.

Sources of state and local government accounting principles The organization primarily responsible for establishing, reviewing, and changing accounting standards for state and local governments is the Governmental Accounting Standards Board (GASB). The standards established by this group provide for uniform accounting and financial reporting for citizens, the bond market, state and federal granting agencies, and public accounting companies.

GASB was created to replace another long-standing organization, the National Council on Governmental Accounting (NCGA). NCGA was a group of 21 part-time volunteer members from local, state, and federal governments and the academic and private sectors. The group operated with the financial support of the Government Finance Officers Association (GFOA). NCGA had been operating since 1934, originally as the National Committee on Municipal Accounting.

Generally accepted accounting principles (GAAP) were established by NCGA in its 1968 publication, *Governmental Accounting, Auditing, and Financial Reporting*. This publication was superseded by NCGA Statement 1, *Governmental Accounting and Financial Reporting Principles*, published in 1979. Following Statement 1, 6 additional statements, 11 interpretations, and 1 concepts statement were issued by NCGA before that organization was replaced by GASB. In 1980, GFOA published *Governmental Accounting, Auditing, and Financial Reporting*, not as an authoritative statement but as an interpretation of NCGA Statement 1. The GASB has codified all existing NCGA pronouncements and has issued three statements of Governmental Accounting Standards and one interpretation.

Financial accounting and reporting should be tailored to the goals and objectives of different users, and the financial statements should reflect those differences. The 7 statements and 11 interpretations originally issued by the NCGA and adopted by the GASB and the recent GASB pronouncements recognize this concept of usefulness by specifying the various types of reports to be prepared by governments, some of which are presented in this chapter.

Users of accounting, reporting, and auditing information

Government accounting systems provide data to many users—categorized here as external, internal, and internal/external users—whose varied information needs should be anticipated and met to the fullest extent possible.

External users

External users include interested citizens, long- and short-term creditors, suppliers, and many others transacting business with the governmental unit. They need financial information because they frequently have or contemplate having a direct financial interest in the operations and financing of the governmental unit. Yet, functioning outside the governmental unit, they lack either implicit or explicit authority to prescribe the nature, timing, content, and extent of the financial information they receive.

To assure external users that similar economic events are accorded similar accounting treatments, to provide for a common understanding of published financial statements, and to assure that relevant and reliable financial information is being transmitted, the accounting profession has established GAAP.

The American Institute of Certified Public Accountants (AICPA) influences accounting principles for state and local governments, particularly through its *Audits of State and Local Governmental Units*, an industry accounting and audit guide published in 1986 by the AICPA State and Local Government Committee.

The Financial Accounting Standards Board (FASB), a standard-setting body for the private sector, also influences state and local governments and their independent auditors as a source of generally accepted accounting principles. The GASB Codification, for example, requires that proprietary funds of a government follow GAAP that are applicable to business enterprises. In addition, *Audits of State and Local Governmental Units* identifies certain FASB and AICPA pronouncements as those to be followed by state and local governments.

State and local government accounting practices are influenced by federal government accounting and reporting requirements for grant programs and by state laws covering financial reporting for state and local governments.

The Governmental Accounting Standards Board is a separate and independent accounting standards board established to set standards of accounting for governments. The organization has a full-time staff and financial backing and represents a broad range of groups in public and private sectors concerned with state and local government accounting standards. In addition, the Financial Accounting Foundation provides oversight and fundraising for GASB, and the Governmental Accounting Standards Advisory Council, a group of 20 or more persons, advises GASB on a wide range of problems and issues.

Internal users

Internal users are managers and administrators responsible for planning, organizing, executing, and reviewing the operations and strategies of the governmental unit. They need a variety of financial information to prepare forecasts and budgets, to control expenditures, and to apply techniques such as cost-benefit analysis to the decision-making process.

Unlike the external users, most internal users have access to a large amount of financial information, and they are able to specify in detail the assumptions and practices underlying that information. Some of the information may be in the form of published external financial statements, but much of it is not available from the external reports prepared in conformity with GAAP. Instead, that information is provided by other functions of the accounting and reporting system.

Although most reports to decision makers and managers are prepared on a recurring basis, the system must also be flexible enough to meet unique or nonrecurring reporting demands. Managerial accounting and analytical techniques such as flexible budgeting, standard costing, and variance analysis—commonly applied in business enterprises—have only recently begun to assume a significant position in many governmental operations. While they are not yet as robust and advanced in their application as might be desirable, the benefits of using such procedures in governmental administration seem clear.

Internal/external users

A third category of users is those who are not directly involved in day-to-day operations but who have significant authority over the governmental entity, such as granting authorities, governing boards, legislative bodies, closely related governmental units, and other significant providers of resources. These organizations may require compliance reports to show that grant funds were properly used, and they may set specifications for the information they seek. The reporting task may not be too onerous because the reports, once established, tend to remain formalized and constant for a relatively long period of time.

The fund basis of accounting and reporting

To a person familiar only with business financial accounting and reporting practices, governmental accounting represents a radical change. Business enterprises prepare GAAP-based reports for the total organization (defined in terms of the overall organization, not the separate parts), whereas state and local governments prepare more narrowly focused reports. The GASB Codification of NCGA pronouncements defines a fund as:

> . . . a fiscal and accounting entity with a self-balancing set of accounts recording cash and other financial resources, together with all related liabilities and residual equities or balances, and changes therein, which are segregated for the purpose of carrying on specific activities or attaining certain objectives in accordance with special regulations, restrictions, or limitations.[2]

The fund basis of accounting recognizes that most governmental assets are not fungible, and that data on budgetary compliance are an exceptionally important part of the stewardship responsibility of government. Distinct *fund* accounting and reporting is necessary to control resources and to demonstrate compliance with the various legal and budgeting constraints affecting government. Information on the flow and use of financial resources is the most significant feature of government financial reports, and the primary operating statement should reflect the inflow and the related outflow of financial resources for each type of fund.[3]

The GASB Codification has established eight generic fund types divided among three separate fund categories (i.e., governmental, proprietary, and fiduciary).

Governmental funds

1. The *general fund* is normally the most important fund of a municipality. It accounts for all resources not otherwise devoted to specific activities, and it finances many of the basic municipal functions, such as general administration and police.
2. *Special revenue funds* account for the receipts from revenue sources that have been earmarked for specific activities. For example, a city with a special property tax levy for parks might have a park fund.
3. *Capital projects funds* account for the acquisition of capital facilities, which may be financed out of bond issues, grants-in-aid, or transfers from other funds. This type of fund, which is most closely related to the capital budgeting process, is limited to accounting for the receipts and the expenditures on capital projects. Any bond issues involved will be serviced and repaid by the debt service funds.
4. *Debt service funds* account for the financing of the interest and the retirement of the principal of general long-term debt. Where single maturity, sinking fund bonds have been issued, a debt service fund accounts for the sinking fund set up to retire the bonds.
5. *Special assessment funds* account for the financing and construction of those public improvements that benefit a specific group of properties. For

example, the costs of a street-paving project or of a sewer extension may be assessed against the abutting properties, rather than charged against the taxpayers as a whole. Those funds are a special type of capital project fund that handles both the financing and the expenditure. Special assessments are often paid by abutting property owners in installments over a number of years. In order to finance the immediate construction, the funds often issue bonds that are paid off by the proceeds of these future assessments.[4]

Proprietary funds

6. *Enterprise funds* account for business-type activities supported largely by user charges, such as municipal utilities, golf courses, swimming pools, and toll bridges.
7. *Internal service funds* are similar to enterprise funds except that the services, rendered to the general public, are for other governmental units within the same governmental jurisdiction. For example, if a central photocopying machine is financed out of one budgetary line item and is available free to all departments, there is little incentive for the department heads to economize on its use. This is not true, however, if a central duplicating service department charges each department on the basis of use. The operations of such departments as municipal garages, central purchasing offices, and even municipal office buildings have been placed under this type of fund to account for the costs of services they provide and to encourage economy in their use.

Fiduciary funds

8. *Trust and agency funds* account for assets held for others or nontax resources held by the government under specific trust instructions. Taxes collected for (and to be forwarded to) other governmental units are accounted for in agency funds. The most important municipal trust funds are those associated with retirement systems. Another example of a trust fund is the money donated to the local government to buy park equipment as a commemoration. Such a donation would be accounted for as a trust fund although it is similar to a special revenue fund.

Generally, local government activities (e.g., police and fire protection) are financed by taxes and other fixed or restricted revenue sources, and expenditures are controlled by various budgetary processes. Certain business-type activities of governments (e.g., airports, utilities, and golf courses) are operated so that the costs incurred can be recovered by charging fees to the specific users of those services. These activities are controlled by matching revenues to expenses, thereby ensuring that the user charges are adequate to maintain the service. Because of these differences in supporting revenues and operating and financing objectives, accounting and reporting practices for proprietary activities differ from those for standard governmental activities.

Budgetary accounting and control

The GASB Codification states that every governmental unit should adopt an annual budget, that the account system should provide the basis of appropriate budgetary control, and that a budget-to-actual expense comparison should be included as part of the appropriate financial statements. Frequently the budget itself is made part of the formal accounting system by entry into the general ledger. Governmental budgets represent a mandate for requiring as well as limiting expenditures; of course, expenditures may be subject to some revision if economic or operating circumstances change significantly. Budgeted revenues are referred to as *estimated revenues* or anticipatory assets, and budgeted expenditures are termed *appropriations* or anticipatory liabilities. Formal budgets exist for almost all funds and fund types, but usually the budget-to-actual comparison reports are prepared only for the general and special revenue funds.

Accounting for governmental funds

Because budgetary compliance is of such significance in managing governmental activities, and because expenditure overages may endanger the fiscal health of the whole city if allowed to accumulate, techniques have been adopted to ensure conformance with budget specifications. One such technique is encumbrance accounting.

Encumbrance accounting Administrators must know how much of an available appropriation has not yet been expended or otherwise committed to the acquisition of any particular good or service. As in commercial accounting, an expenditure and its related liability should be recognized only when the governmental unit incurs an obligation that must be paid or otherwise satisfied. However, once a manager or department head reports an intent to purchase a particular object—even prior to incurring a definite liability—an encumbrance of funds should be recorded.

Encumbrance accounting is especially desirable for governmental funds in which a maximum budget limit is set for each period (usually a year), for it provides an early warning system when expenditure maximums are approached. It also ensures that no unexpected liabilities that must be paid from the current year's budget emerge after the end of the year. In such a case, a reported encumbrance would signify a lingering commitment.

Encumbrances are frequently recorded as estimates based on quotes from manufacturers. Expenditures reflect the actual amounts paid. Even though encumbrances appear in the accounting records, they should not be reported in the financial statements as expenditures or liabilities. They are entered as a reduction of the unreserved fund balance. The reserve for the encumbrances account should be reported as a reservation of the fund equity that has been committed to a particular future expenditure. This is, of course, consistent with the nature of encumbrances and enhances the representational faithfulness of the financial statements. Thus the local government's fund balance should not show a positive balance without accounting for encumbrances. If an encumbrance lapses (i.e., the proposed expenditure is never completed), the amount in the reserve for the encumbrances account should be returned to the unencumbered portion of the fund balance account.

The importance of a proper encumbrance system cannot be overemphasized. If administrators do not record encumbrances for orders and commitments, for example, they may appear to stay within their budget—by encouraging suppliers to delay rendering goods or services until the next budget period. However, these obligations then become a burden on the next period and may exhaust that period's appropriation prematurely. The payments due on later bills may be delayed again and again, and eventually the deferred payments can constitute a large and not fully recognized floating debt.

Nevertheless, one of the problems of budgetary control is that most governmental units are eager to use up their unencumbered balances at the end of the fiscal year. Otherwise, the unused appropriation may expire at the end of the budgetary period. This eagerness can lead to a rush of purchase orders in the last days of a fiscal period. Where this practice is abused, the local government manager should examine closely the outstanding encumbrances at the end of the year and, if necessary, cancel them.

Other equity reserves Keeping track of other equity reserves is another means of achieving budgetary control. The unreserved fund balance of a governmental fund should reflect its residual equity in assets that are available for future commitment and expenditure. The reserve for the encumbrances portion of the equity section of a fund's balance sheet is not available for expenditure; it reflects the estimate of the resources that have been committed to a particular objective. Other reserve accounts are often necessary to achieve the goal of reporting the appropriate uncommitted fund balance. For example, when a fund expends cash to acquire supplies, any unused supplies are shown as assets in the financial statements even though they are not, as such, expendable. Therefore, it is necessary to reduce the unreserved equity of the fund in expendable assets by establishing a balancing "reserve for inventory." Other equity reserves include contingencies, non-current repayable advances to other funds, and future expenditure limitations. An example of the reporting for fund equity is provided in Figure 7–1 as part of the balance sheet for a governmental fund.

Fixed assets and long-term debt Fixed assets acquired by regular governmental funds are reported in the general fixed assets account group. Long-term debts incurred by governmental funds are reported in the general long-term debt account group, with one exception—the special assessment funds that must account for their own long-term debt (as the debt will be serviced from revenue derived from the special assessments made on the users of the improvement). Long-term debts are treated as a source of revenue, not as a liability of the fund in question because budgetary reporting focuses on resources not assets. Account groups serve as a means of securing and maintaining effective accounting control over those assets and liabilities that are excluded from the reporting components of the individual governmental funds.

Accounting for proprietary funds

When a municipal enterprise is run on a fully self-supporting, independent basis, the financial accounting and reporting parallels that found in business enterprises. Because proprietary funds must cover all operating costs through user charges for the service, an income determination/capital maintenance accounting model is employed. In such an accounting model, *expenses* as well as *expenditures* are measured. An expenditure reflects the cost of acquiring a

Assets			Liabilities and fund equity	
Cash		$ 15,000	Liabilities	
Short-term investment (at cost			Accounts payable	$10,000
market value $123,000)		120,000	Payroll taxes payable	2,000
Property taxes receivable	35,000		Total liabilities	12,000
Less: allowance for				
uncollectable taxes	3,000	32,000	Fund equity	
			Reserve for encumbrances	7,000
Due from other funds		1,500	Reserve for inventory of	
			supplies	10,000
Inventory of supplies		10,000	Undesignated fund balance	149,500
			Total fund equity	166,500
Total assets		$178,500	Total liabilities and equity	$178,500

Figure 7–1 General fund balance sheet, Trojan City, 31 December 198_.

good or service. An expense may represent in addition the expiration of the value of the good or service. Thus, as with accounting for governmental funds, accounting for proprietary funds calls for a statement of changes in financial position reflecting the sources and application of resources. However, also required is an income statement matching revenues and expenses.

Since recognition of all expenses is required for proprietary funds, accounting for fixed assets and their related depreciation is also necessary. The cost of fixed assets (which represent an expenditure of resources at the time of acquisition) must be allocated over the estimated life of the asset to properly match the cost of the asset with the revenue it helps to generate.

A balance sheet must also be prepared to communicate information about the resources and obligations of the fund at a particular point in time. The balance sheets of proprietary funds differ from those of governmental funds in at least two significant practices. First, the fixed assets employed in rendering the proprietary service net of an allowance for accumulated depreciation are reported as assets of the fund. Second, the long-term debt incurred by a proprietary fund is reported as a liability of that fund.

Funds that render services to other elements or units of government should also apply proprietary fund type accounting practices. One objective of those funds should be to "break even," to cover costs with the revenues charged for services. This objective places many of the profit-oriented incentives for efficiency and effectiveness into the conduct of governmental operations.

Accounting for fiduciary funds

Accounting and reporting for fiduciary trust and agency funds should follow either governmental or proprietary practices. For example, if a tax agency fund is used to collect and remit sales taxes for several different levels of government, then the operating and reporting emphasis is on the strict accountability for inflow and outflow of monies. However, if the operation of a fiduciary fund is designed to break even, then the income determination/capital maintenance accounting and reporting model of proprietary funds should be employed.

Financial reporting

Two types of financial statement packages are recognized in the GASB Codification: (1) general purpose financial statements that provide an overview of the financial position and the results of operations of all fund types; and (2) comprehensive annual financial reports that contain the general purpose financial statements, an introductory section, supporting statements, and a statistical section.

Figure 7–2, reproduced from the GASB Codification, shows the relationships of the elements in the financial accounting and reporting system and the degree of fund and fund type aggregation considered necessary for the two types of financial reports.

Examples of simplified summary financial statements are presented in Figures 7–1 and 7–3. These are designed to reflect the accounts usually presented for general purpose financial statements for a single governmental fund or fund type.[5] Such reports present detailed information about fiscal and budgetary compliance, funds flow, and current liquidity. The operating statement (Figure 7–3) is prepared on a functional or program basis rather than on an object of expenditure basis. That is, expenditures are classified by activity (e.g., public safety or education) rather than by nature (e.g., salaries or supplies). Comparing the statement of revenues and expenditures with budgeted amounts provides users of the financial statement with necessary information on the government's resources and the application of these resources to specific programs or ac-

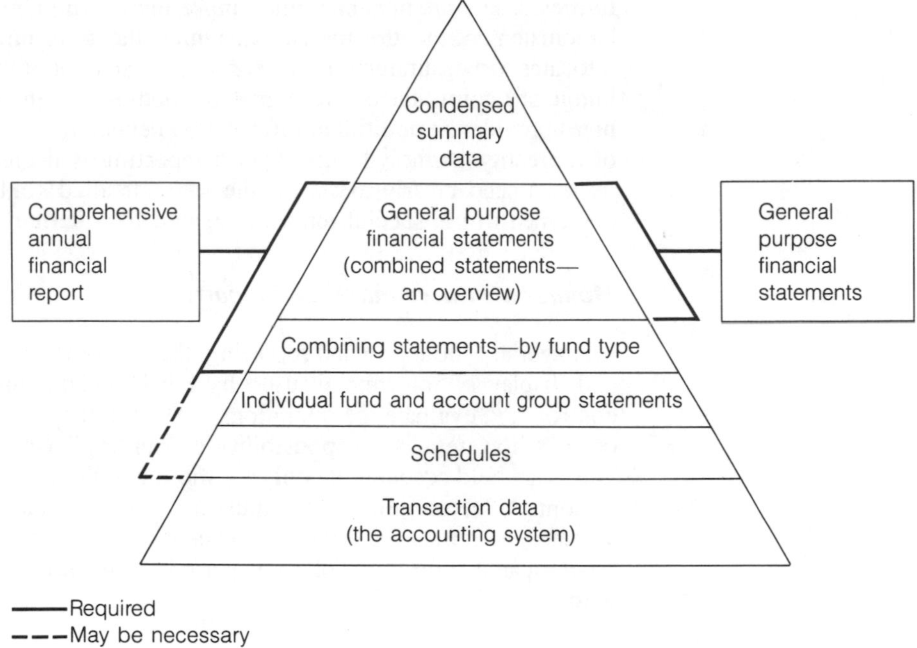

Figure 7–2
The financial reporting pyramid.

Figure 7–3 General fund statement of revenues, expenditures, and changes in fund balance, budget and actual. Trojan City, year ended 31 December 198_.

Classification	Budget	Actual	Actual over-(under-) estimated
Revenues			
Taxes	$240,000	$290,000	$50,000
Licenses and permits	30,000	36,000	6,000
Intergovernmental revenue	120,000	90,000	(30,000)
Charges for services	40,000	45,000	5,000
Fines and forfeitures	6,000	9,000	3,000
Miscellaneous	4,000	10,000	6,000
Total revenues	440,000	480,000	40,000
Expenditures (current)			
General government	45,000	41,000	4,000
Public safety	100,000	98,000	2,000
Highways and streets	60,000	60,000	—0—
Sanitation	40,000	39,000	1,000
Health	20,000	18,000	2,000
Welfare	30,000	25,000	5,000
Culture—recreation	16,000	13,200	2,800
Education	14,000	12,600	1,400
Capital outlay	75,000	75,000	—0—
Debt service	25,000	25,000	—0—
Total expenditures	425,000	406,800	18,200
Excess of revenues over expenditures	15,000	73,200	58,200
Fund balance (beginning of year, 1 Jan.)	76,300	76,300	—0—
Undesignated fund balance (end of year, 31 Dec.)	$ 91,300	$149,500	$58,200

tivities. Users are in a position to make their own judgments and form their own conclusions about the manner in which the government collects monies and allocates expenditures. The operating statement also reveals the degree of budgetary compliance. Furthermore, footnotes to the statement (not presented here) provide the additional information needed to assess the financial condition of the entity. Although this type of reporting is deemed adequate for external users, a need clearly exists for the more detailed kinds of information that are contained in the special reports prepared for internal management.

Management accounting and reporting

Managerial accounting and reporting deal with the capture, retention, summary, and display of information used by local government administrators to plan, control, and evaluate the operations for which they are responsible. At the heart of such a system is "responsibility accounting" wherein individuals and programs are held accountable only for those conditions under their direct influence or control. Determining and evaluating costs associated with various programs, services, activities, or work units is central to this system. Such costs may then be compared with those of prior periods, with estimated or standard costs, or with alternative costs.

Cost determination Cost determination is central to measuring the economic endeavor needed to deliver a given service or perform a certain function. For most of the business-type activities of local governments (e.g., utilities and airports), cost determination is relatively straightforward and primarily involves reclassifying existing expense (expired cost) data that have been generated routinely for financial reporting. This reclassification usually involves transferring costs from a general responsibility center to a function or activity center that provides direct services to constituents. This process may be accomplished manually, using relatively simple work sheet procedures, or electronically through the use of computer routines.

Cost determination for activities contained within a general fund is more difficult and requires additional procedures. Data prepared for financial reporting purposes on an expenditure basis must be converted to expense or cost data in a form useful for managerial reporting purposes. In addition, the expense or cost data must be reclassified to the functional areas benefited. Data from several funds may need to be considered because a single government function may be financed and accounted for through several funds. For example, the cost of maintaining public roads and streets may be financed partly from a special gasoline tax revenue fund and partly from general fund expenditures.

Cost accounting, cost finding, and cost evaluation (which will be discussed later) are useful procedures for allocating resources in a rational manner and evaluating the efficiency and economy of particular government functions.[6] *Cost accounting* is the continuous and routine process of analyzing, classifying, capturing, and summarizing cost data within the confines and control of a single accounting system. Results are reported to users on a regular basis. The GASB Codification, in defining cost accounting, notes that cost accounting assembles and records " . . . all the elements of cost incurred to accomplish a purpose, to carry on an activity or operation, or to complete a unit of work or a specific job."[7] *Cost finding* is a less formal method of program or activity cost determination. It is conducted on an irregular basis for special purposes.

In determining costs, there are three components of the total cost of any product or service:

1. Direct materials, the cost of items used directly in the production of a good or service (e.g., asphalt in a street-paving project)

2. Direct labor, the salaries and other costs of employees related directly to a product or service (e.g., wages of employees working in a street-paving project)
3. Overhead, the indirect costs associated with the production of a good or service (e.g., employee benefits).

Accounting records are frequently available for determining the first two costs, although, as previously mentioned, the data may be contained in several funds. Determining overhead costs, however, may involve substantially greater effort, for there are at least two major problems in attempting to allocate overhead costs to particular projects or services. First, cost or financial data may be unavailable. For example, the cost of machinery used to pave a street may be unknown, and surrogates for depreciation (e.g., use allowances) must be adopted. Second, some costs benefit more than one project and sophisticated allocation techniques may be required. For example, the cost of a personnel department operated from the general fund benefits every department of the government that hires employees. Therefore, the cost of the personnel function should be allocated to the various service or production departments on a rational basis whereby each one is charged an appropriate share of the costs. Cost-finding techniques are useful in these situations.

Some costs involved in rendering a service are not readily apparent and require careful study to detect and allocate properly. For example, fringe benefits (e.g., the pension costs of employees) may be paid from the general fund; if such expenses are not considered, the full cost of a particular activity may be understated. Care must be exercised to ensure that all costs relating to a given project or service are, in fact, allocated to that service.

There are several methods of resolving each of these problems,[8] but one particular technique is used in general purpose financial reporting as well. Internal service funds (ISFs) are used by state and local governments to account for the provision of goods and services by one department (the provider) to other departments (the consumers) of government. These service activities are set up like business enterprises, although they are operated by one government office for other government entities on a fee-for-service basis.

Most professional literature confines discussion of ISF operations to the effects on the department providing the service, such as the problems of matching revenues with expired costs to determine income and to measure capital, and the management incentives created for the providing department when an independent service department fund is established. However, the literature has not considered in detail the effect on the consuming department.

With full cost accounting, space-consuming departments are charged for space occupied, thereby encouraging departments to use only as much space as is efficient for operations.

The use of space in a municipal building provides a good illustration. If a municipal building is accounted for through the general fixed assets group of accounts and building expenses such as utilities and maintenance are paid through the general fund, then no vehicle exists to charge departments for the building space they occupy. Consequently, the total or full costs of operating the various departments are understated. Building space, then, is essentially treated as a "free good," thereby providing a disincentive for efficient operation because the user departments tend to ask for additional space without considering costs.

On the other hand, if the provision of building space is accounted for through a service department, the total cost of operating the building is computed in the routine of ISF general ledger accounting, thus obviating the need for cost finding. The real cost of operating each department, including space, is then easier to determine. Finally, the goals of responsibility accounting are achieved by holding the property manager accountable for the quality and financial success of building operations. An important by-product of ISF operation is that full cost information by each user department is generated as a routine bookkeeping function.

Regardless of the manner by which cost information is accumulated, program cost determination is only a beginning in understanding the operating and financial characteristics of various activities. Careful cost evaluation is a necessary corollary to cost determination.

Cost evaluation Whenever a set of costs can be related to an activity or function, that activity should be assessed from the perspective of efficiency and economy. Standards established during the planning and forecasting phase will be useful for evaluating performance characteristics and volume of activity.

Analyzing performance characteristics usually calls for classifying costs as either fixed or variable. Fixed costs remain constant in total over a relevant range of activity levels, whereas variable costs change with changes in the activity level. An example of a fixed cost is building rental, which remains constant with the lease regardless of the activity taking place in the building. An example of a variable cost is the cost of fuel to run vehicles; this changes with the amount of vehicle use. Variable costs tend to remain constant per unit of activity over a given activity range, but the fixed costs per unit of activity change as activity levels change. Fixed costs per unit decrease over a given range as output increases, and increase as output decreases. However, production cannot be expanded indefinitely because of the limited capacities of any facility. This relevant range of capacity establishes the range of activity levels to be considered.

Static, line-item budgeting is the traditional method for controlling expenditure levels. The expenditure lines are prepared for a single level of activity. Although revisions may be made as necessary throughout the budgetary period, a specified maximum expenditure level is established and operating results and expenditures are compared with this budget, regardless of any differences between actual activity levels and estimates underlying the original budget. This method is unsatisfactory, however, for program evaluation and management control.

An improvement on traditional budgeting is the flexible budget, which recognizes the financial effect of fluctuations in actual activity levels. Expenses under flexible budgets may vary according to service levels. Flexible budgets are designed for many levels of activity rather than for one single level. This facilitates evaluating the financial aspects of an operation by comparing what the estimated costs should have been at a given activity level with the costs actually incurred.

Three separate and distinct steps are necessary to set up flexible budgeting procedures.

1. First, a static budget is prepared based on a relevant measure of anticipated future activity. This is accomplished prior to the operating period.
2. Second, a flexible budget is developed based on the *actual* activity level during the operating period. The differing behavior of fixed and variable costs must be considered when tailoring the original static budget to a flexible budget for the actual activity level. This step is accomplished after the operating period.
3. Third, actual expenses incurred are compared with the amounts allowed in the flexible budget. Any significant variance from the flexible budget

levels should be analyzed to determine the need for corrective executive action.

Variance analysis is the process of evaluating deviations between the flexible budget and the actual costs incurred. It can take many forms and the type suggested below should not be viewed as necessarily the right one for all situations. At least three component subvariances should be considered:

1. *Spending* The analysis of spending variance compares actual costs incurred with those predicted in the flexible budget for the activity level achieved. Fixed costs included in this variance are the same as those in the static budget because they are not, by definition, expected to change with activity. The spending variance reveals only the effect of differences between costs expected and costs incurred at the actual activity level.
2. *Usage* Volume variances in costs are affected by fixed costs only. These variances reflect the economies (or diseconomies) of use resulting from spreading the same total fixed costs over greater (or fewer) units of activity. For example, if the activity level exceeds that planned in the static budget, then each productive unit of activity absorbs a smaller fixed cost. Volume variance summarizes the economic impact of using a facility more or less intensively than was originally anticipated.
3. *Efficiency* The time variance relates to how many hours were required to accomplish the total activity relative to how many hours should have been required according to the flexible budget. For example, if the flexible budget indicates that it should take 100 hours for each 1 million gallons of sewage processed, but 120 hours were actually required, then the time variance will be unfavorable. The variance is then translated into dollars so that the economic consequences will be clear.

Even when detailed variance analyses are conducted, however, management will still be required to conduct additional studies to determine the underlying or hidden causes of the variances. Spending variances, for example, may be due to a rate of inflation that is faster than expected and may thus represent a forecasting deficiency, not an operational shortcoming. Efficiency variances may be the result of activities that are more severe or complicated than anticipated and may indicate a need to allocate additional resources, not to initiate punitive action. At times, a careful analysis of unfavorable variances will show a level of performance that was higher than anticipated. In general, the combination of flexible budgeting and detailed variance analysis provides a powerful tool for evaluating efficiency.

Variances demonstrate only the degree of departure from management plans. They are "attention getters" or "red flags" that require further study.

Compliance reporting

The accounting and reporting systems of local governments should be capable of providing specified information to a variety of regulatory or granting authorities. Such reporting capabilities should be considered and anticipated when developing an accounting system so that all financial, managerial, and compliance reporting requirements can be met by a single accounting system.

Accounting reports to granting or regulatory authorities generally apply specific and restricted resources to the performance of specified functions or activities. Many of the general aspects of financial and managerial reporting may be applicable to compliance reporting as well. However, there are several notable differences. For example, granting agencies frequently reimburse the recipient government for the costs incurred in administering the grant program, but the costs that are refundable under the terms of the grant may be defined in a manner that requires the application of special cost-finding techniques. An allowable or refundable cost is expressed generally as a necessary cost of administering a particular program. It is important to determine carefully all of the costs related to a grant program and to establish a cost-accounting system capable of capturing data conforming with the grant provisions.

Frequently, grant provisions require the recipient government to provide matching contributions to the grant program. Whereas cash, supplies, or services are easily recognized in determining the municipal contribution, other contributions—especially those made in kind—are more difficult to trace. For example, the depreciation of equipment used in a program may qualify as a matching contribution. The labor effort expended on the program may also qualify as a matching contribution even if employees do not devote all their time to the grant program. Carefully documented accounting records and sound allocation practices will help ensure the reimbursement of all allowable costs for matching contributions.

Thus, managerial accounting techniques provide a dynamic basis for predicting, understanding, and controlling operations. Employed intelligently, such controls can provide an early warning system against adverse economic and operational events. Budgets, prepared on a static basis, cannot provide the data necessary for an adequate evaluation of just how efficiently and effectively a government is being run. The management practices recommended here are designed not as substitutes but as supplements to standard budgeting. They are designed to provide compliance and legal control of expenditures and financial reporting in accordance with GAAP.

Auditing

The Single Audit Act of 1984 was a major step toward providing uniform entity-wide audits of the governmental recipients of federal financial assistance. In essence, this act requires single audits of all governmental recipients of federal funds in excess of $100,000 in any fiscal year. Recipients of less than $100,000 but more than $25,000 must either have a single audit or they must comply with other requirements concerning audits contained in federal statutes or regulations. Recipients of less than $25,000 are exempt from audit requirements although financial accounting records must be maintained. Generally, audits are to be conducted annually but exceptions are provided for units of government whose constitutions or statutes mandate biennial audits.

Each single audit shall determine and report whether the financial statements present fairly the financial position and results of operations in accordance with GAAP, the unit's compliance with applicable laws and regulations, the unit's establishment of an adequate system of internal accounting control, questioned costs, and any instances of fraud, waste, or abuse.

The General Accounting Office (GAO) of the federal government has been active in developing auditing standards. Specifically, the GAO recognizes three necessary elements in a full-scope audit.

1. *Financial and compliance* Determines whether financial operations are properly conducted, whether the financial reports of an audited entity are presented fairly, and whether the entity has complied with applicable laws and regulations.
2. *Economy and efficiency* Determines whether the entity is managing or

utilizing its resources (personnel, property, space, and so forth) in an economical and efficient manner and determines the causes of any inefficiencies or uneconomical practices, including inadequacies in management information systems, administrative procedures, or organizational structure.

3. *Program results* Determines whether the desired results or benefits are being achieved, whether the objectives established by the legislature or other authorizing body are being met, and whether the agency has considered alternatives that might yield desired results at a lower cost.[9]

Modern auditing techniques are capable of addressing these elements and providing valuable management tools for both asset control and project evaluation. Although independent external auditors are available to provide evaluation services on a contract basis, it is frequently desirable to maintain complete internal auditing departments as well. On the other hand, because internal auditors are employees of the governmental unit, it is important to establish controls to ensure the independence and competency of the internal audit department and the adequacy and quality of the audits it conducts. Figure 7–4 summarizes the provisions of an internal audit, acts as a self-evaluation guide, and suggests certain standards that must be considered when establishing an internal audit function. The AICPA has revised its audit guide for state and local governments to help practicing CPAs plan and execute efficient and effective audits in accordance with generally accepted auditing standards.

The use of performance auditing techniques is increasing, but generally accepted standards for conducting audits with a broad scope have not yet been established at the level that exists for financial and compliance audits. The limitations as well as the potential of performance auditing should be considered carefully by municipal managers before establishing audit programs and objectives.

Summary

Accounting and reporting systems for state and local governments, like the information systems in commerce and industry, must be capable of meeting many diverse requirements and diverse operational reporting objectives. With GAAP standards as their underlying framework, they should assist in external decision making; provide operational information to management; provide adequate internal accounting controls to monitor expenditures; and demonstrate financial and fiscal compliance with the legislated budget, various laws, regulations, and grant requirements. The usefulness of accounting data is limited only by the imagination and creativity of the information users and the reporting capabilities of the system. It would be worthwhile for accounting professionals to determine the information needs of the users so that an effective system responsive to those needs can be designed. For example, electronic data processing (EDP) would seem to offer considerable advantages to local government managers. However, employment of EDP may be more costly than a manual system and should be made only after careful analysis of the number of reporting objectives, the volume of transactions, and the complexity of the organization.

Budgetary accounting practices strengthen the controls over governmental fund expenditures. Encumbrance accounting and the use of equity reserves support other budgetary control measures to help ensure compliance with the budget, laws, and regulations.

Cost accounting and cost finding represent valuable tools for government managers attempting to evaluate performance and program effectiveness. The

Figure 7–4
Audit standards.

General standards

Audit scope
1. Authority to conduct audits
2. Fulfillment of audit responsibilities
3. Consideration of user needs

Staff qualifications
1. Audit staff education requirements
2. Professional achievements of audit staff
3. Continuing education programs for audit staff
4. Appraisal systems
5. Use of consultants

Independence
1. Organizational placement of the head of internal audit
2. Organizational independence of internal audit staff
3. Freedom to audit
4. Level of management reported to
5. Audit report availability

Professional care
1. Clear definitions of authority and responsibility
2. Written policies for planning, conducting, and reviewing audits, and other quality control measures

Examination and evaluation standards

Audit planning
1. Isolate problems
2. Avoid redundancies
3. Determine personnel needs
4. Develop audit programs
5. Establish detailed steps
6. Review procedures

Staff supervision
1. Level of supervision required
2. Supervisor availability
3. Supervisory reviews
4. Preparation of time budgets
5. Evaluation of performance

Internal control, evidence, and compliance
1. Adequacy of description, documentation, and evaluation of internal control
2. Appropriateness of audit evidence procured
3. Procedures based on evaluation of internal control
4. Compliance with operating policies
5. Restrictive regulation—related evidence gathered for the above steps

Audit conduct
1. Procedures associated specifically with each of three audit types: (a) financial and compliance, (b) economy and efficiency, and (c) program results audits
2. Weaknesses detected in each of aforementioned areas
3. Adequacy of work papers as to form, content, clarity, and relevance

Reporting standards

Form and distribution
1. Medium used (written, oral, etc.)
2. Formats employed
3. Distribution policies

Timeliness
1. Meeting reporting deadlines
2. Other general considerations of frequency and timing of reporting

Content
1. Clarity, convenience, objectivity, tone, and scope of the report
2. Adequacy of supporting evidence offered in report
3. Adequacy of underlying audit evidence not cited in report

Financial reports
1. Whether financial statements present what they purport to present
2. Whether all disclosures are included
3. Appropriateness of auditors' opinion or disclaimer

use of such accounting control tools as flexible budgeting, standard unit costing, and detailed variance analysis is being adopted by increasing numbers of local government units.

The rise of intergovernmental financial activity has required more sophisticated reporting systems. Intergovernmental grants, contracts, and other resource transfers necessitate special purpose compliance reports and have resulted in higher standards of accountability.

Finally, the increased use of operational auditing has complemented traditional financial and compliance auditing to make the audit function more valuable to local government managers. Audits that report on the efficiency and economy of operations as well as on program effectiveness have become popular as government officials respond to tighter budgetary constraints. Full-scope audits provide evidence and support for decisions on resource allocations and program funding levels. The results of such audits are useful in communicating the quality of management to taxpayers and to bond holders.

1 Marshall S. Armstrong, "Some Thoughts on Substantial Authoritative Support," *Journal of Accountancy,* April 1969: 50.

2 Governmental Accounting Standards Board, *GASB Codification,* Section 2100 (Stamford, Conn., 1985).

3 The *GASB Codification,* Appendix A, however, defines financial reporting much more broadly. Rather than focus on the fund basis of accounting reports, it requires that resources, obligations, and operating activities of one governmental organization be included in the financial report of another—if the latter unit of government exercises oversight responsibility over the former. Oversight responsibility relates to the dominance of one unit of government over the activities and net resources of another—specifically, to the ability of the dominant unit of government to select the governing authority, designate the management, and influence the operations of the subservient unit. This definition of the financial reporting entity is, in some respects, a response to accounting and financial reporting abuses. For example, previously, some governments established "special districts" to issue bonds and transfer monies to the oversight unit of government. By omitting the special district, the oversight unit could avoid reporting the debt in its financial statements.

4 As this book went to press, special assessment funds were eliminated for financial reporting purposes, and the activities accounted for in special assessment funds are to be reported in other fund types and account groups.

5 The *GASB Codification,* Appendix A, shows more detail for these summary financial statements.

6 At least four specific steps are necessary:

1. Activity identification, the selection of a meaningful measure of productivity for a project
2. Cost identification, the isolation of costs incident to conducting the activity in (1)
3. Cost and activity data accumulation, the capture, retention, and reporting of information specified in (1) and (2)
4. Evaluation, the analysis of the data to uncover the relationship of outputs as measured in (1) and inputs as measured in (2).

This chapter concentrates on steps (2) and (4).

7 *GASB Codification,* Appendix B.

8 For example, see Robert J. Freemen, Harold H. Hensold, and William W. Holder, "Cost Accounting and Analysis in State and Local Governments," in *The Managerial and Cost Accountant's Handbook,* eds. Homer A. Black and James D. Edwards (Homewood, Ill.: Dow Jones-Irwin, 1979), pp. 794–839.

9 U.S. General Accounting Office, Comptroller General of the United States, *Standards for Audit of Governmental Organizations, Programs, Activities, and Functions* (Washington, D.C.: GPO, 1972), p. 2.

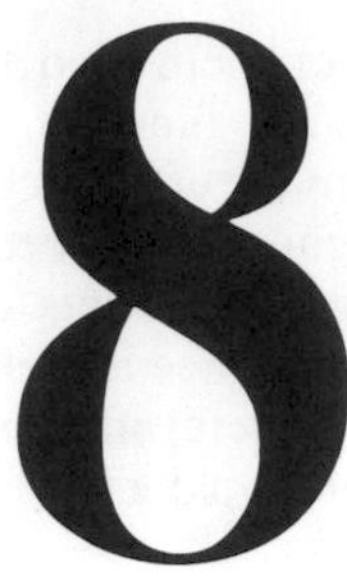

Computer applications

Local government officials need sophisticated financial information to support both day-to-day operations and long-run decision making. The information system must be flexible to accommodate frequent changes in information needs. And the information itself must be accurate, complete, timely, and economical. If it is not, the information is at best useless, and at worst, misleading and dysfunctional to the decisions and operations that it is intended to support.

The key to a properly specified information system is to identify the needs of the manager or managers, who best understand the operating problems to be solved and the decisions to be made. In the traditional (manual) data processing environment, management assumes full responsibility for defining output report formats, specifying sources of data, selecting the appropriate accounting rules to be applied, and establishing the controls necessary to maintain the integrity of the system.

With the introduction of computer-based systems, however, many managers have become uncertain of their technical competence and have turned over their traditional responsibility to data processing professionals who know much more about computers than about the operations of the organization. The result is information systems designed entirely by individuals who are far removed from departmental operations and who may not fully understand the manager's needs. The resulting misfit of systems and needs can be disastrous, and many documented failures stand testimony to the potential hazards of badly defined systems.

Computer-based systems require nothing less of management than do manual systems. Although the technology has changed and is sometimes intimidating, the objectives of an information system still revolve around the needs of the users, whose input into systems design decisions is essential to the system's success. Managers should recognize and accept their role in systems development or risk misinterpretations and faulty judgments by those who assume this responsibility for them.

This chapter guides the manager—specifically the financial manager—through this relatively new area of responsibility. Because of the scope and interdisciplinary nature of information systems, the chapter focuses on the following three areas: (1) the relevant technology and "buzz words" that often inhibit effective communications with computer professionals; (2) the system features that effective and responsive software packages should have; and (3) a methodology for assessing information system needs and evaluating alternative software packages to satisfy those needs.

The basics of computer technology

It is essential that even the nontechnically oriented financial manager understand the basic principles of computer technology and data management. The following sections provide a primer on data structure, hardware, software, data management concepts, data processing modes, and centralization issues.

The structure of data

Computers are machines that communicate only in their own language. In order for data to be accepted as input to the computer and processed, they must be structured in the computer's *binary* language in a form the computer recognizes. The basic building block of computer data is the *bit*. This term is an acronym for BInary digiT. A bit can assume one of two mathematical values—0 or 1.

Unique combinations of bits (most commonly groups of eight) are used to represent all characters. Figure 8–1 is an example of a common binary coding scheme. Bits grouped together in this way to represent a character are collectively referred to as a *byte*. Thus, eight bits make up a byte and a byte is any character such as a letter of the alphabet, a special character (*, &, %), or a digit (0 through 9). All symbols needed for written communication are represented through this eight-bit code.

The next level in the data hierarchy is the *field,* a logical grouping of bytes that forms an element of data related to a particular entity. To illustrate, consider the example of a taxpayer. Three separate fields would be required to represent the name, address, and account number of a taxpayer on the tax roll. Although each of these fields is a separate datum they are all logically related to the same entity—the taxpayer.

At the next level, logically related fields are grouped to form a *record*. A simple tax roll record might contain the following fields: name, address, account number, current taxes payable, taxes past due, and due date.

The highest level in the data hierarchy is the *file,* a collection of records that are logically related to one another. For example, the tax roll file would contain one record for each individual on the tax roll. Each taxpayer record would contain the same types of data elements (fields), but the values would be different for each taxpayer. The entire file is stored by the computer as a series of 0's and 1's. Although meaningless to most people, these bits are a logical representation of data that can be interpreted unambiguously.

Hardware

The term *hardware* refers to the physical computer itself and all the peripheral devices with which it must interface. *Software,* which will be discussed later, refers to the programmed instructions that control and direct the hardware.

The hardware system is made up of three integrated elements: (1) input/output devices, which provide access to the computer; (2) the computer itself, which stores and processes data according to programmed instructions; and (3) secondary storage devices such as magnetic tapes and disks, where data files and programs are kept until they are needed by the computer operator. The general arrangement of these elements is illustrated schematically in Figure 8–2.

Input/output (I/O) devices Because computers process data in binary form, some sort of "translation" must occur. Input and output communications must be encoded and decoded according to the requirements of both the particular computer and its human users. This human-computer-human interface is provided by input/output devices, which enable commands and data to be submitted to the computer and output to be received back.

Figure 8–1 A common binary coding scheme.

Character	Binary code
Letter A	11000001
Letter B	11000010
Digit 5	11110101

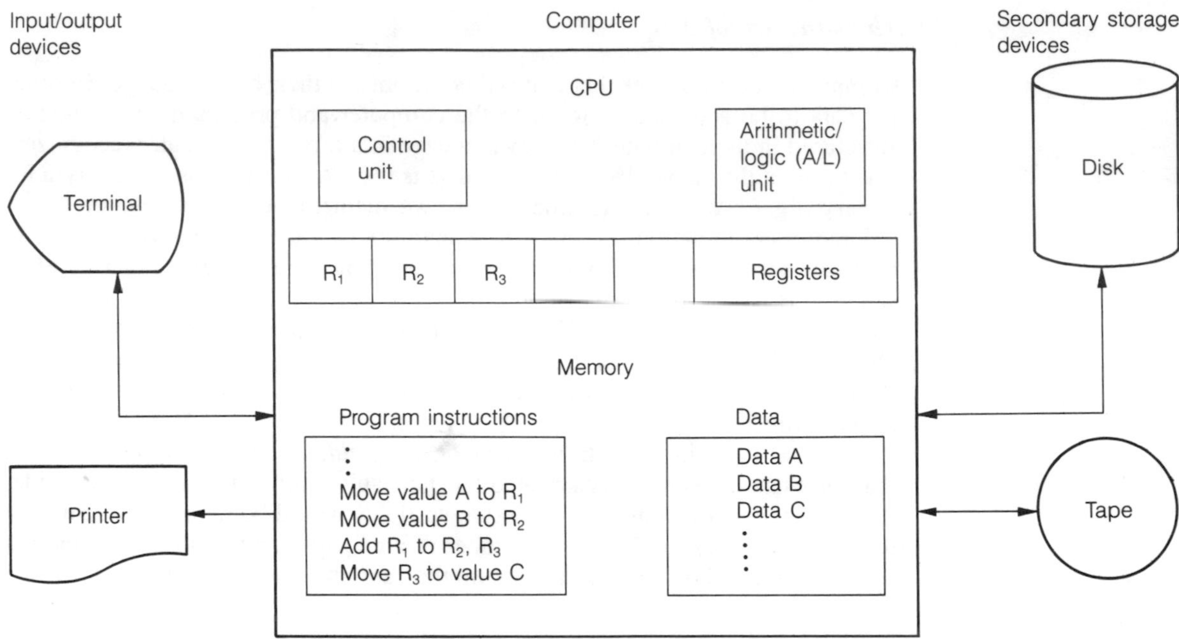

Figure 8–2 The relationship of hardware components.

The most common type of I/O device is the terminal. Input is entered through the keyboard and output is received on the screen. *Input-only* devices include card readers, magnetic ink character readers, and optical character readers. *Output-only* devices include printers with a wide range of capabilities.

The computer A computer has three functional units housed in one package: the central processing unit (CPU), the memory or primary storage area, and the registers or internal work locations.

CPU The CPU is actually made up of two subunits: the control unit and the arithmetic/logic (A/L) unit. The control unit interprets coded computer instructions one at a time as they are encountered. The A/L unit performs or executes these instructions.

Programmed tasks (such as adding together two values) are broken down into a series of detailed subtasks or instructions, which are then individually processed in sequence. First, the control unit analyzes the instruction and determines what is to be done; then the A/L unit takes control and activates the appropriate circuits to accomplish the subtask. Interpretation and execution take only a few nanoseconds.[1] Computers perform subtasks sequentially, one at a time, but at astounding speeds. Complex tasks are performed in small pieces, each in a fraction of a second.

Memory The memory of the computer is made up of thousands (or sometimes millions) of separate locations where the program instructions and the data to be processed are stored. Most microcomputer systems accommodate only one program and its data in memory at a time. After the program is completely executed, another program can be loaded into memory and executed.

In larger computers, the memory is partitioned into smaller areas to allow the simultaneous storage of many programs and associated data. The CPU moves from program to program, executing a single instruction from each. Thus, the computer may serve the needs of many users concurrently. This is called multiprogramming.

Registers Registers are temporary storage areas that provide a "workbench" for the CPU. Special-purpose registers are needed, for example, to store the instruction that is currently being executed and to accumulate vital control data. General-purpose registers store data values to be used in mathematical calculations, comparison, and other operations. The data are first stored in memory and then transferred as needed to registers where the specific operation is actually performed. Results are then transferred back into the main memory.

Hardware: an integrative example The following example illustrates the relationship of the computer's component parts in the execution of the following single task:

Add data A to data B to give a new value: data C.

Assume data A and data B are locations that contain the values "6" and "8," respectively. These values were entered into memory from a terminal or were retrieved from secondary storage in a previous step. Data C contains no value at this point. Through a special software program, called a language translator, this task is first reduced to a series of simple instructions to the computer. In this case four instructions are required:

1. Move data A from memory to register R-1.
2. Move data B from memory to register R-2.
3. Add R-1 to R-2 and store results in register R-3.
4. Move contents of R-3 to memory and store it at data C.

The first of these instructions is placed in a special register, where it is interpreted by the CPU control unit. Once the control unit identifies the memory location of data A and the location of R-1, control is passed to the A/L unit, which activates the path between the two locations. A copy of data A follows this path and is stored at R-1. This register now contains the value "6." Note that the original data A still resides in memory. Thus data A may be used many times in different operations without being destroyed. At this point control passes back to the control unit.

The second instruction is likewise interpreted by the control unit and executed by the A/L unit. The value "8" is now at R-2.

The third instruction adds R-1 (6) to R-2 (8) and stores their sum (14) at R-3.

The fourth and last instruction in this series transfers the contents of R-3 to the predefined memory location called data C. The computed value (14) in data C may now be processed further. It can be used in additional calculations, printed in a report, displayed on a terminal screen, or placed in secondary storage for future reference. Of course, any further processing would require additional detailed instructions beyond those shown in this illustration.

Secondary storage devices Computers have limited internal storage (memory) capacity. Therefore data files and programs that must be saved for use at a later date are removed from memory and stored outside the computer in secondary storage. The most common forms of secondary storage are magnetic tapes and magnetic disks.

Magnetic tapes Magnetic tapes are made of plastic with an oxide coating that can be magnetized. Physically, they are either 1,200 or 2,400 feet long and one-half inch wide and they are wound on reels 10½ inches in diameter. Along the entire length of a magnetic tape run nine channels or tracks for storing data (see Figure 8–3). A fully loaded tape can theoretically store 180 million bytes of

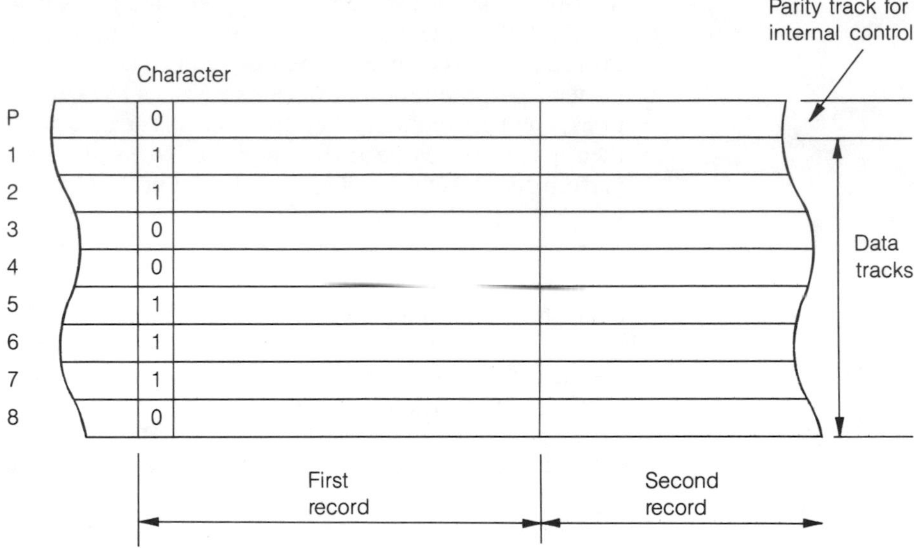

Figure 8–3 Technique for storing data on magnetic tape.

data. At a cost per tape of about $30, tapes represent an efficient and inexpensive storage medium.

Magnetic tape has two characteristics that limit its use to certain types of applications. First, it is strictly a sequential access device—that is, accessing any record on a tape file requires a search of all preceding records. For example, if a tape file contains 5,000 records and the user wants to access record number 4,000, he or she must access and reject 3,999 unwanted preceding records to get it. This can be very slow. Second, tapes are off-line devices much like a book—that is, they are not always connected to the computer but are stored in a tape library on a shelf. When required, the tape is taken from the library by a computer operator and mounted onto a tape drive. Thus, access to tape files takes time and human involvement.

Despite the availability of more versatile magnetic disks for smaller installations, tapes are still used extensively in large installations for file backup and for other applications where the following three conditions exist. First, the file must be large enough for the cost savings of tape storage to be material. Second, because human intervention is required each time a tape file is accessed, the application must accommodate scheduled, periodic file access rather than random or continuous access. Third, because of the tape's sequential characteristics, the percentage of records on the file being processed with each access (the file activity ratio) must be fairly high. Generally speaking, an activity ratio of 20 percent or greater is considered high. An illustration of a good use for tape storage is payroll. The payroll file usually is large, it is accessed periodically (weekly or monthly), and the file activity ratio is extremely high (100 percent of the payroll records are processed each time the file is accessed). In contrast, it would be expensive and chaotic to load and read sequentially an entire file of 5,000 records at frequent and irregular intervals throughout the day to process only one record each time. When the limitations of tape storage adversely restrict the information system, a direct access technique is required.

Magnetic disks Magnetic disks are the most popular form of direct access storage device (DASD). In appearance, disks resemble phonograph records, but instead of grooves several hundred magnetic tracks form concentric circles of data on the surfaces of the disk. Figure 8–4 illustrates how direct access to specific records is possible. Each record storage location on the disk has a unique address.

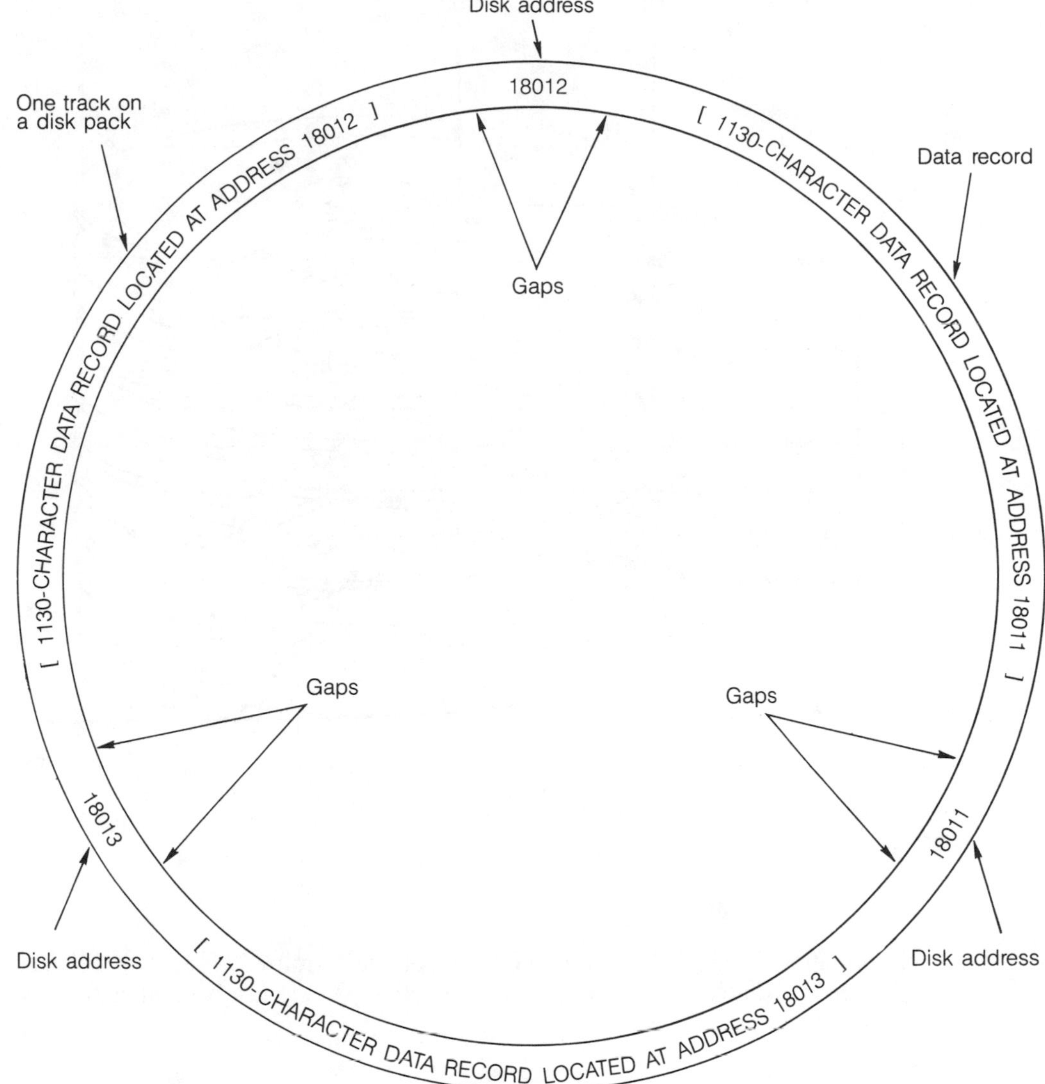

Figure 8–4 Record addresses on a disk track.

Disks are often stacked together in groups of 11 to provide a mass storage capability. These disk packs are portable and can be used to store data off line. Most often, however, they are used as on-line devices connected directly to the computer, so that access to data on the disks is unimpeded by the need for human intervention.

A disk pack is mounted on a disk drive, which rotates it at a constant velocity. Access to data records is provided by a set of read/write heads (one for each disk surface). Figure 8–5 shows a disk pack and access mechanism arrangement. When a particular record is desired, its storage address (disk, track, surface, and record number) is first determined by a computer program. All read/write heads are then moved to that same track on each disk surface, but only the head for the appropriate disk surface is activated. With the activated read/write head positioned over the track, the desired record is then read (or written) as it rotates under the head.

Although prices are constantly falling, the cost per unit of disk storage is many times that of tape. However, this high cost is often outweighed by the advantages of flexibility and direct access. In a department where on-line

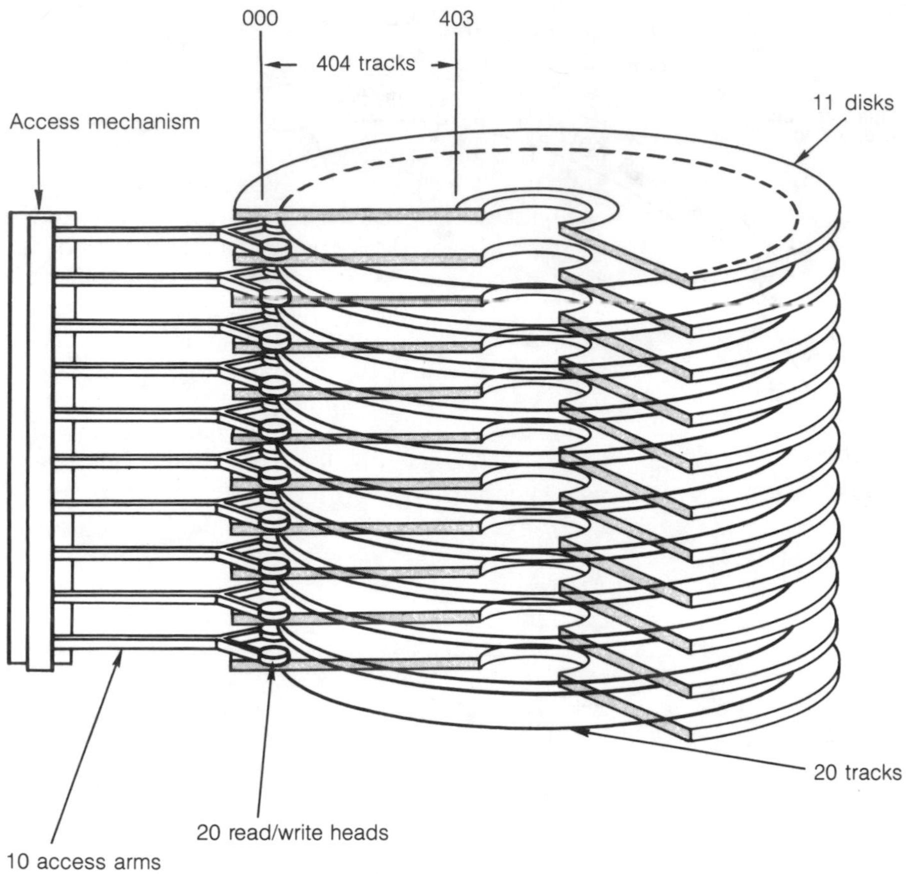

Figure 8–5 A disk pack and access mechanism.

information is needed to respond to telephone inquiries, for example, disk storage is essential. For these reasons magnetic disks are fast becoming the most popular storage medium.

Software

Computer software falls into two categories, systems software and applications software. Systems software consists of programs that control the general operations of the computer. It includes the operating system, language translators, and utility programs. Applications software consists of programs developed to serve specific purposes such as payroll processing or accounts payable. Applications for local governments are covered later in this chapter. The focus here is on the various types and purposes of systems software.

The operating system The operating system is a group of support programs that reside in the primary memory at all times and control the various functions of the computer. The tasks performed by these programs vary among computers according to their level of sophistication. Large-scale mainframe computers require more elaborate operating systems than single-user microcomputers. For example, a sophisticated multi-user environment would require support for such functions as allocating space in the main memory for each program and its data to protect the many users from each other; assigning a CPU time limit and an execution priority to each program to achieve an efficient and equitable allocation of computer resources to the users; and allocating input/output devices to programs to prevent the mixing of data of different users.

Language translators Language translators (compilers and interpreters) convert programs written in high-level languages like FORTRAN or COBOL into the detailed instructions the computer needs to function. Language translators are stored until needed in secondary storage on disks in the program library. Each high-level language must have its own compiler or interpreter to translate programs to instructions the computer can interpret.

High-level languages were developed to make the programming task easier and the programs themselves computer independent. High-level languages have a relatively simple syntax to master. Without them, programs would have to be written directly in the detailed instructions (machine language) of the specific computer in use. Apart from being an exceedingly technical and complex task requiring special skills, programs written in machine language are compatible only with the model of computer for which they are originally written. This would tend to tie users to a single hardware manufacturer. High-level languages provide program portability. For example, to run a COBOL program originally written for an IBM on any other computer requires only that the compiler convert COBOL to the machine language for that computer.

Utility programs Utility programs perform routine tasks and thus ease the programming burden. Like language translators, utilities are stored in the program library and are accessed when needed. Transfer utilities are used to transfer data from one medium to another—for example, from cards to tape or from tape to disk. Sort utilities sort data files alphabetically or numerically by one or more fields in the records. Code conversion utilities translate data files from one code scheme to another and make files created on one type of computer readable by another.

Data management concepts

Data may be managed in several ways—in separate files kept by individual users (the traditional approach), or in common files accessible by all users (the data base approach).

The traditional approach In the traditional approach, the organization's data resources reside in independent (private) files. Users of the data maintain exclusive rights to these data files and, generally speaking, there is no sharing. If the same data are needed for multiple purposes, each user must independently create, store, and maintain a separate set of files. This concept is illustrated in Figure 8–6. Data in "common" use (illustrated as data B in Figure 8–6) must be replicated in different files for each user. This redundancy creates several problems for data management. First is the problem of physical storage. Multiple tape and disk files must be created, catalogued, documented, and physically secured and maintained. While it is impossible to remove all data redundancy, excessive redundancy represents a severe drain on the information system resources of the organization.

Second is the problem of updating data stored in multiple locations. For instance, if there is a change in the name and address data for an individual who is carried in several different files, each file must be separately updated. Ensuring the currency of such common data requires a great deal of coordination and communication among the various users involved. To complicate matters, different users may well refer to common data by different names. The lack of standard data names for all applications makes it extremely difficult to communicate changes to all potentially affected users. The potential for error due to outdated data is high in this sort of environment.

Third is the problem of maintenance and modification of application programs. A user's information requirements change over time. Legislative

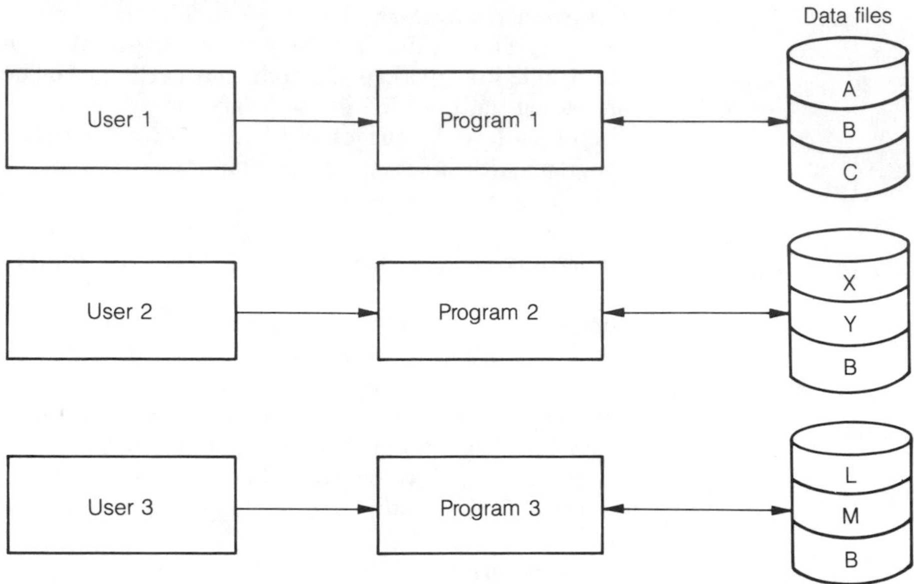

Figure 8–6 The traditional file approach.

changes, new government programs, and changes in tax laws all create pressure for new and timely information. New data must be gathered and existing application programs modified accordingly. In the traditional environment this is particularly difficult, because application programs are data dependent—that is, each application is tailored specifically to its data files; configuring to new data files is difficult and expensive. Furthermore, the emergence of yet another file to be maintained only intensifies the problems of redundancy and updating. Consequently, the traditional approach tends to foster an environment in which information needs over time are never completely satisfied.

The data base approach In the data base approach, illustrated in Figure 8–7, the data files of all users are gathered together in one file for common access, thereby avoiding some of the major drawbacks of the traditional approach: (1) data redundancy is reduced by consolidating files for all transactions and applications in one data base; (2) file updating is simplified (when one element changes—for example, if a taxpayer moves to a new address—the change is made once, and all other users who subsequently access this element retrieve the new data); and (3) program maintenance is enhanced. Because programs in a data base environment are independent of their data files and readily available, data base programs may be modified, updated, and maintained with relative ease. Data files do not have to be recreated, nor do programs have to be redesigned when data change. This is especially important because program maintenance can be as much as 50 percent of the total cost of a program. The data base approach, then, facilitates program maintenance.

The data base approach has four components: (1) the user's application programs; (2) the data base management system (DBMS); (3) the data base administrator (DBA); and (4) the data base.

Applications Application programs fall into two classes: routine applications and ad hoc applications. The bulk of the demand on the information system is for routine data. Users receive information about the economic or financial events for which they are responsible in the form of regularly scheduled reports. Here a data base system has no great advantage over the traditional system; routine information is produced in much the same way.

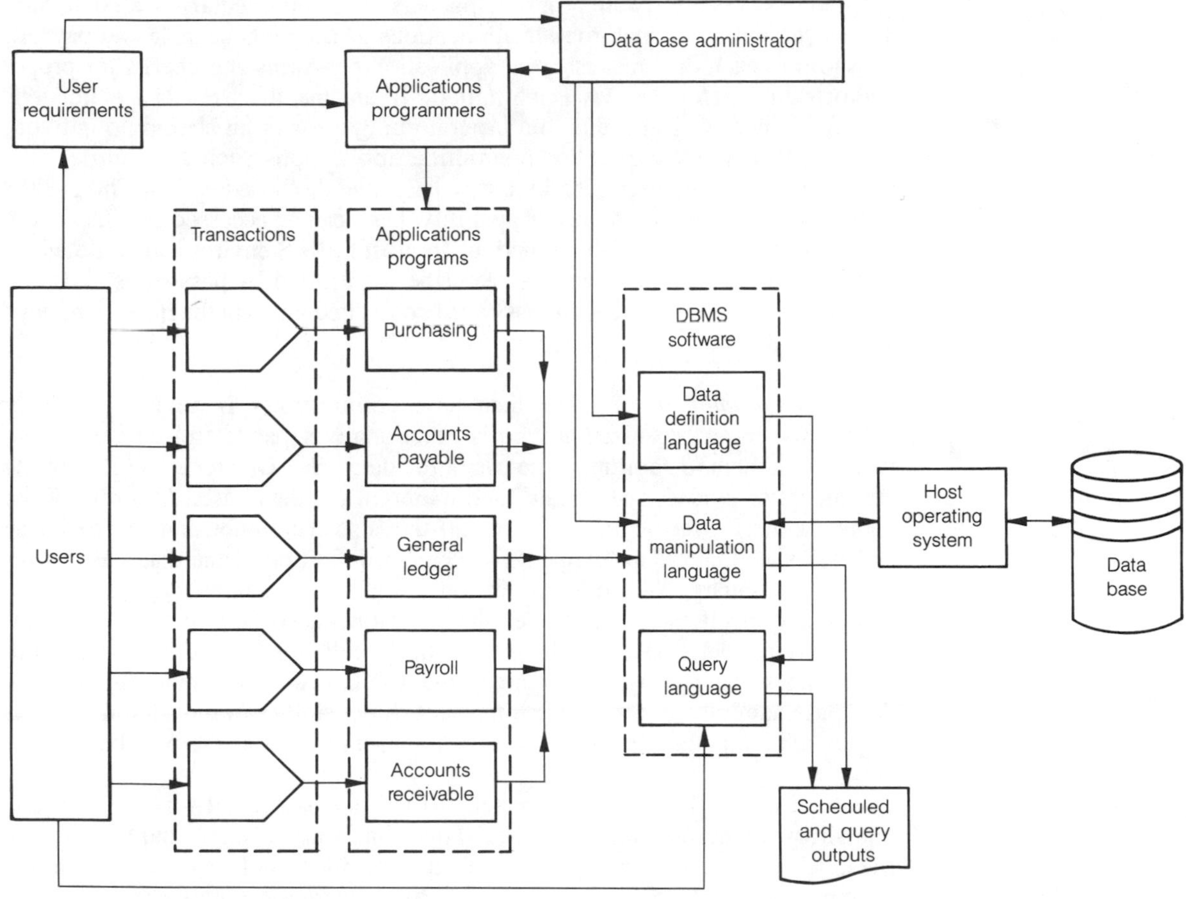

Figure 8–7 The data base approach.

Increasingly, however, users must respond quickly to demands for "one-time" information to produce special reports that have never been produced before and may never be produced again. For the most part, these demands go unsatisfied in the traditional environment because of time and data constraints. Even if the data are available, development of the applications to produce the reports often cannot be accomplished in time to satisfy the need.

The data base approach is far better equipped to deal with ad hoc information. Through a query language built into the data base system, users interface directly with the system to access the entire data base and to generate the information they need in whatever report format they desire. The query language structure is recognizable as English, consisting of verbs, objects, and modifiers. For example, the command, "Select name address phone from taxfile where overdue > 90" will generate a listing of the names, addresses, and phone numbers of all taxpayers whose taxes are delinquent by more than 90 days.

Data base management system Having a single data base is analogous to putting all your eggs in one basket. It is important to take very good care of that basket through careful control measures: restricting access to authorized users, limiting access by each program to those data elements necessary to perform its prescribed tasks, and maintaining a segregation of incompatible functions. Unauthorized access may result in data elements being changed, deleted, or added to the data base. This control function is the role of the data base management system (DBMS).[2]

The DBMS is a software program that acts as an intermediary in all data base access attempts. For such routine applications as accounts payable and payroll, it examines each data request from application programs and checks for proper authorization before access is permitted. If an unauthorized data element is called for by a program, due to a programming error or an attempt to defraud, the DBMS denies access. For nonroutine applications such as inquiries, the DBMS provides the user-friendly query language discussed earlier. The DBMS limits this access to "read only" capability. Data can be accessed and displayed, but not changed, through this function. In most DBMS environments, access to sensitive or confidential data can be further controlled by passwords. Without proper authority, even access to password controlled data via the query language would be denied.

Data base administrator The data base administrator is an individual (or group) within an organization who is functionally separate from the users but works with them to coordinate the use of the data base. One responsibility of the administrator is to define, create, and maintain the data base. All users of the data base must agree on the data elements they use in common and how to define and delineate them. This element by element definition of the data base forms the data dictionary. No user's application can gain access to the data base unless it properly specifies each data element it requires according to this document. All additions, deletions, and changes to the data dictionary and the corresponding changes to the physical structure of the data base are the responsibility of the data base administrator. Another important responsibility of the administrator is to provide the authorizations necessary for users to access the data base.

The data base The final component—the data base itself—is the physical repository of the organization's data. Functions such as direct inquiry into all files, ad hoc report preparation from multiple files, and data sharing among multiple users require a high degree of file integration within the data base. Therefore, the data base must reside entirely on direct access storage devices such as magnetic disks. Magnetic tapes are used only for backup purposes. Typically, the production data base—the data base used in normal, day-to-day operations—is copied onto magnetic tape daily. In the event of its loss or destruction, the production data base can then be reconstructed from the tape.

Data processing modes

Transactions are processed in either *batch* mode or *real-time* mode. Batch processing is the periodic (hourly, daily, weekly) processing of groups of similar transactions that flow as a single unit through the entire processing cycle. This mode of data processing is efficient and easy to control. It is most common in applications that involve posting to ledger accounts large volumes of transactions, such as payroll processing, vouchers payable, cash disbursements, and billings.

Real-time systems process a single transaction at a time (often as the economic event occurs) in an interactive session with the user. Whereas batch programs occupy the computer only for a few minutes at the time the batch is scheduled to be run, real-time programs reside in the computer's main memory for the duration of the interface session with the user. In some applications this approaches permanent residency and requires dedicated computer resources.

The advantages of the real-time mode include up-to-date data files, reduced data entry errors through visual screen editing of transactions, and direct inquiry capability. Real-time systems are preferred wherever there is a need to capture immediately the effects of transactions. Many modern batch systems have a real-time data collection interface to control against data entry errors. The primary disadvantage of this approach is the cost of dedicated computer resources and expensive secondary storage.

Degree of centralization

In early data processing systems, all data and data requests were referred to a centralized location for processing by the central computer facility; output in the form of hard copy reports was distributed back to the users. This centralization provided the organization with both physical control of the data and economies of scale. Such completely centralized systems are becoming a thing of the past, however. The modern approach, distributed data processing (DDP), is to distribute some or all of the data processing responsibility and resources throughout the organization or department. DDP offers many options, each having different hardware and software implications. The challenge for the manager is to identify the level of DDP that is most desirable under the circumstances.

In its simplest form, DDP uses the shared logic approach, distributing only the input/output (I/O) function to various users. A central computer is connected via communication lines to terminals in the users' areas. Data are collected, converted to magnetic form immediately, and then transmitted to the central facility for processing. Output from processing is transmitted back to the user's terminal in the form of a video screen display or as hard copy. All data files, programs, and computing capability are maintained centrally and shared by users.

At the other end of the DDP spectrum is the distributed logic approach. Here a central computer and central files are still a part of the system. In addition, however, users have their own computers (not just "dumb" terminals but minis or micros), their own data files, and their own programs. Data processing actually occurs at each user's site. These smaller computers, tied to the central computer and perhaps to each other through communications lines, form a network. Data may be transmitted from the central computer to the local computer (downloaded) for processing by the user. Processed data can then be transmitted back to the central computer (uploaded) for consolidation and further processing.

Local government applications

In general, the applications software market is characterized by frequent changes of vendor products. It seems that as soon as one package comes into the marketplace, it is made obsolete by another, more sophisticated and complex, package. User demand for more timely, more accurate, and more cost-effective information is the driving force behind this technological state of flux. The government sector of this market, dominated by a handful of large vendors, is volatile as well, although perhaps less so than the rest of the market.

Any survey of existing applications conducted under these conditions runs the risk of being dated, if not made obsolete, by the time it finds its way into print. Yet, as a starting point for software acquisition decisions, prospective buyers need to know the structure and composition of this market and the available options. The following discussion avoids the special features of specific applications (such as report formats, screen layouts, and specific commands) that are subject to change and may clutter the decision process. Rather, this section focuses on the system characteristics and features that constitute the real differences among various software products—what decision makers must consider and match against their specific needs and circumstances. The two classifications of features discussed here are general system features and specific application features.

General system features

General system features include systems architecture, hardware compatibility, modularity and integration, real-time versus batch processing, distributed systems versus centralized systems, and data bases versus traditional files.

Systems architecture Systems architecture (the technical and logical construction of the system) is the primary basis on which vendors differentiate their respective products and develop their marketing strategies. Architecture can be viewed as a continuum. At one end are "turnkey" systems, designed as a series of integrated, pretested, general purpose modules. These systems are fully tested and documented prior to delivery to the user and they require no additional programming to tailor them to the user's existing system. Interfacing these systems to government or business accounting structures is accomplished through the inherent flexibility of the application logic when the system is installed by the vendor's technical representatives at the user's site. An example of this approach is the packages offered by Management Science America (MSA).

At the other end of the continuum are custom-tailored systems, designed entirely for clients with unique needs too complex to be adequately served by turnkey systems. Engagements for custom-tailored systems are typically large scale and require specialized implementation and support. Vendors of these tailored systems may provide a resident support team during the installation and training phases of the project and access to on-site or hotline technical support thereafter. An example of this approach is the Peat Marwick system.

A number of vendors serve the market from a middle ground position between the two extremes described above. Their approach is to produce a standard package that may, or (more often) must, be tailored through programming to meet client needs. For example, the Integrated Financial Information System (IFIS/III) produced by Systems & Computer Technology Corporation (SCT) is a large-scale system designed to meet the general needs of local government. As it stands, the system is complete and could in theory be implemented without change. In practice, however, moderate to extensive reprogramming is necessary to tailor the system to the individual user.

Integral to SCT's approach is a high level of vendor support. They provide facilities management services for their clients. This includes providing all programming and operations functions for clients who do not possess the in-house resources necessary for tailoring the general application provided. As part of their support approach, SCT provides other services as well that allow users to share computing solutions with each other, pool their resources, and take advantage of economies of scale. Users receive discounts through group purchases of hardware and software, for example.

The architecture of a system affects flexibility of use, timeliness of information, speed of operation, user friendliness, vendor support, and price. For example, the development costs of general purpose applications are spread over a large user base. Therefore, these applications are usually less expensive than systems designed specifically for individual clients. Where user needs are particularly complex or unique, they may be met only by tailoring prewritten applications or by designing entire systems from scratch. Tailoring is usually less expensive than new design. However, where extensive tailoring is involved the added costs can become prohibitive and the system's performance may be impaired. In view of these implications, an awareness of the architectural alternatives available and how they may pertain to the user's specific situation is vital.

Hardware compatibility In the perfect world, managers would first choose software and then hardware. In reality, however, a local government generally has hardware already in place and must choose new software that is compatible. The buyer must bear in mind that past hardware decisions represent sunk costs that must not play a part in software selection decisions. To select only from those packages that are compatible with existing hardware may leave some needs substantively unsatisfied. The only relevant considerations are the future benefits from the package versus the current and future costs of its acquisition and maintenance.

Modularity and integration In modular systems, individual functions such as accounts payable and utility billing are separate from one another instead of being parts of a larger program. The major advantage of modular systems is that they can be expanded and changed as needs dictate; they do not need to be scrapped and redesigned.

Integration describes the way individual program modules interface with each other and with their respective data files. Integrated systems usually comprise a series of subtask modules integrated with a core financial module. The core system, for example, contains the accounting rules that are to be applied and performs posting and reporting functions. This enables transactions to pass directly from modules to core to update all relevant files directly and automatically. In nonintegrated systems each file must be updated separately. For example, a change in a name and address maintained in multiple files would require separate updates for each file involved. Redundancy results and, to the extent there is a time lag between the updates, the yet unchanged files contain outdated data. In a fully integrated system, these problems would be avoided. Changes would be made only once and the data would be updated in each location automatically, thus providing timely data to all users immediately.

Most software packages on the market are both integrated and modular. This is an efficient way to design a system because it allows subsystems to reside in the background and to be invoked as needed rather than to be included in the main application module. Also, this approach adds a degree of flexibility to the system. Optional subsystems may be purchased, or not, as desired. In this way the initial user is not encumbered with unneeded functions, such as fixed asset accounting or inventory control systems, but has the option of later adding these functions to the core system.

Batch processing versus real-time processing To select the appropriate processing mode, the user must determine the need and requirements for current data. The primary drawback of batch processing, compared with real-time processing, is that it does not fully support the integrated approach. Batch files do not reflect current transactions as they occur. Files contain old data until the batch programs that update them have been run. In some applications, this approach imposes severe limitations on the user. In others it does not, however. For example, payrolls are often processed in batch because the more expensive real-time approach is not justified by the demand for immediate and current payroll information.

The major drawback in real-time processing is its excessive cost, regarding (1) the application software—because it is so difficult and complex to design; (2) the overhead of the complex operating system; and (3) the storage devices.

Centralized systems versus distributed systems The degree of centralization in a computer system is influenced by the organizational structure of the government unit. Centrally structured units that use large common files may best be served by a shared logic system. Decentralized organizations in which users have private data files at the local levels but also need to consolidate information centrally for planning or reporting can take advantage of the distributed logic approach.

Distributed data processing requires specialized software to download and upload data files. Most vendor packages now support DDP by providing specific microcomputer applications for local processing or by downloading files into formats that can then be processed by such general packages as Lotus 1-2-3 and dBASE III.

Data bases versus traditional files Most software vendors support both data base management systems (DBMSs) and traditional files. In large government units, a DBMS is almost essential, but in smaller units or where there is little sharing of common data, this is not the case. The organization need not have a DBMS to have an effective information system. However, taking full advantage of the features inherent in an integrated system requires that traditional files be on line and organized for direct access processing.

Specific application features

Virtually all of the major software packages support financial and governmental accounting in conformance with GAAFR (Governmental Accounting, Auditing, and Financial Reporting), GASB (Governmental Accounting Standards Board), and AICPA (American Institute of Certified Public Accountants) requirements. Other standard functions include the generation of comparative financial statements for current and prior year activity, accounts payable, budget preparation, cash disbursements, project reporting, and revenue accounting. Most packages on the market perform essentially similar basic tasks; however, depending on their architecture, the packages perform these standard functions in slightly different ways and each has special features that enhance the package and facilitate the performance of the specific task in question. The following sections consider these special features broadly, in terms of the minimum requirements and capabilities, so that the decision maker can perform a realistic needs analysis.

In general, state-of-the-art software should have features that support ease of use, flexibility, and control. The package should perform routine tasks automatically and employ, to the extent possible, a single-entry concept. In addition, in order to deal with special case transactions, the system should provide the user the flexibility to override automatic task performance where necessary, without sacrificing accountability and control. For example, a cash disbursement function might have the following special features:

1. The system automatically verifies available funds prior to establishing payables and encumbrances.
2. Before payments fall due, the system advises the user of the invoices that will be paid automatically if no action is taken.
3. On the due date the system subtracts discounts, prints checks, updates the appropriate accounts, and liquidates the encumbrance automatically.
4. The user may add, change, or delete vendor information, void checks, and process manual checks interactively.
5. The system provides for checks issued and checks paid by the bank to be reconciled through a batch job from magnetic tape input provided by the bank.

User friendliness Successful implementation of a system depends in great part on its level of user friendliness. The system must not threaten, intimidate, or impede nontechnical users and must facilitate a smooth transition from the old system. The natural tendency of users to resist a new system is reinforced if they perceive the new system as too rigid in its requirements and unforgiving of errors. User-friendly systems are usually menu-driven and have "back out" or abort capability, pause and help functions, and flexible inquiry capability.

Menu-driven The interactive portion of the system should be menu-driven—that is, it should display on the screen a list of task options from which the user selects one by typing a number or letter. Menus promote efficient use of applications without the user's having to remember complicated access codes. The menu capability should be designed to allow unimpeded movement forward and backward through and among the various menus. This will improve the user's learning process and facilitate the correction of errors.

Back out or abort capability The ability to back out of transaction begun in error is a useful feature, for it is particularly frustrating after selecting the wrong option to be forced to complete the entire cycle in order to get back to the main menu.

Pause function A pause function allows the user to interrupt data entry to do something else, such as look up an unknown vendor code, and then return to the same transaction to resume data entry.

Help function A particularly useful feature during the transition to the new system is an on-line "help" or tutorial function. When faced with a problem, the user can seek assistance on the screen rather than refer to printed documentation. The help function should be accessible from virtually any point in the application at the press of a key.

Flexible inquiry Inquiry functions help reduce the need for printed reports and provide quick responses to questions. Flexible inquiry is most useful when transactions can be displayed using any of a number of key fields. For example a record may be displayed based on transaction type, action code, processing period, range of budgetary account codes, range of vendor codes, or range of dollar amounts.

Control Another determinant of success is the ability of the system to accommodate the organization's control standards and procedures. Some packages are deficient in this regard because they either force the user to conform to a single prescription for controls or require additional programming to handle the user's special needs. For example, a user may desire to budget by organization or activity and to control expenditures against expense budgets, appropriations, or allotments. Some users may even want no controls at all. In such a case a desirable feature of the system is the ability to select those control procedures that will accommodate the specific needs of the user.

Data coding structure A responsive system must be able to classify, record, and report financial data in terms of the specific codes of the user's organization. The required codes should be those common to local governments: fund, department, and account. Additional optional coding schemes might include unit of appropriation, agency organizational unit, and activity. It is particularly useful to have the chart of accounts keyed by fiscal year. This allows for changes to the code structure from year to year and yet still keeps historical data intact for reporting purposes.

Report writer A key requirement of a financial system is a user-friendly report writer. This feature uses predefined values for format elements such as page size, column spacing, margins, location of date, and so on. Thus, managers can quickly and easily generate ad hoc reports and financial statements through a few simple commands. These packages also have sophisticated programming capabilities for more complex reporting requirements. Often users will want to create their own reports to satisfy internal reporting requirements. However, many report writer modules include a set of predefined reports in common use. These reports can also be modified to the user's specifications.

On-line budget preparation On-line budget development with simultaneous multiyear budgeting capability is an essential feature of a state-of-the-art package, for it permits the user to begin budget development at any time. The system should provide, on-line, current and past period budget information to facilitate long-range planning and modeling for future periods. In addition, the system should automatically perform a "roll forward" of the current budget to create a starting point or first version of the next year's budget. This improves productivity and promotes user acceptance of the system by vastly reducing start-up effort with each new budget period. The system should also support real-time interaction in the budget building process. This feature enables personnel in budget units to enter and update revenue and expenditure requests interactively and to monitor the budget's status through on-line inquiry.

A word of caution here is appropriate. The prospective user should also be aware of what functions are *not* included in the core system of the package under consideration. More than one package is generally required to provide all the necessary local government support functions. For example, payroll processing, tax roll accounting, and cost accounting functions may be separate from the core system. In most cases these additional packages can be integrated, at least partially, with the core, although products vary in this regard.

Software selection

Much of the software in use throughout government and the private sector has been developed "in-house" by individual users; the remainder is "canned" software supplied by vendors. However, with the emergence of industry-specific vendors, the general decline in the cost of computer resources, and a growing demand for automation from small buyers who cannot afford to develop systems in-house, the vendor sector of the market is now expected to grow at a relatively greater rate.

Current practice in the mid-1980s is shown in Table 8–1, based on a 1984 survey. In finance, depending on the application, from 45 to 70 percent of the respondents indicated that they developed applications in-house for central computer systems, but the percentages were generally lower for microcomputer systems, for which governments tended to purchase software.

Development of software in-house has two major advantages. First, the programs can be tailored to exact specifications. Often the user's needs are unique and so complex that no commercially available software package adequately meets them. Second, applications can be altered as needed to meet changing information needs.

However, these advantages are substantially offset by the disadvantages of high cost and lengthy development time. In-house development costs must be totally absorbed by one organization and may result in a total cost four or five times that of a commercially available equivalent. In addition, months or sometimes years may pass from inception to implementation of an application. Unless the organization successfully anticipates its future information needs and

Table 8–1 Current application software sources.

	Central systems								Microcomputer systems							
	Have the application		Developed in-house		Contracted programming		Purchased software		Have the application		Developed in-house		Contracted programming		Purchased software	
Finance application	No. (A)	% of respondents	No.	% of (A)	No.	% of (A)	No.	% of (A)	No. (B)	% of respondents	No.	% of (B)	No.	% of (B)	No.	% of (B)
Accounting	886	86	396	45	189	21	301	34	79	8	23	29	10	13	46	58
Budgeting	809	78	420	52	162	20	227	28	121	12	55	45	12	10	54	45
Purchasing	514	50	266	52	110	21	138	27	38	4	11	30	6	16	12	32
Payroll	875	85	432	49	186	21	257	29	40	4	9	23	10	25	21	53
Fixed assets	570	55	344	60	93	16	133	23	39	4	18	46	2	5	19	49
Business licenses	408	40	287	70	71	17	50	12	24	2	11	46	5	21	8	33
Accounts receivable	597	58	351	59	113	19	133	22	39	4	9	23	7	18	23	59
Investment management	208	20	134	64	35	17	39	19	117	11	65	56	10	9	42	36

Source: *The Municipal Year Book, 1986 Edition* (Washington, D.C.: International City Management Association, 1986), p. 36.

Note: The reported percentages are based on the total number of survey respondents (1,032).

schedules application development accordingly, it may suffer long periods without needed software.

In contrast, the development costs of a vendor-produced package are spread across many users. Hence, these products are available at a fraction of the cost of in-house development and can be purchased and installed quickly once a need is recognized. In addition, alterations can be made in packaged software so that it meets the purchaser's needs more precisely. For many general or common applications, packaged software should be seriously considered.

Once a decision has been made to purchase a vendor package, the department faces the major task of choosing the package that best satisfies its needs. Although the quality of individual products varies considerably, products may seem comparable to the prospective buyer, with no clear-cut best choice. The financial manager may choose to hire a consultant to help with this process. The step-by-step procedure that follows provides a framework and criteria for evaluating vendor software.

Needs analysis

A philosopher once said that when a sailor does not know what harbor he wants, any wind is the right wind. In other words, without a considered objective, one has no basis for choosing among alternatives. Likewise, objectives for application software must be carefully considered and formulated before a rational comparison of competing alternatives is possible. For example, the stated objectives of the package may be to:

1. Support the accounting and reporting requirements of diverse functions
2. Provide timely and efficient access to information
3. Simultaneously support both accrual accounting and fund accounting systems
4. Increase transaction processing capacity
5. Reduce the cost of current operations.

Once objectives are established, specific performance criteria for evaluating competing packages can be identified.

Specification of features

The system specifications should be as detailed as the user's technical background permits, for detailed specifications enable the user to narrow the search to those packages most likely to satisfy the department's needs. Although computer literacy is a distinct advantage in this step, as the section on applications has demonstrated, the technically inexperienced user may still compile a useful list of desirable features that the system should possess. The user should address such items of importance as compliance with accounting conventions, special control requirements, capacity limitations and, to the extent possible, the more technical features of system configuration and architecture.

Request for proposals

System specifications are summarized in a document called a request for proposals (RFP) and sent to each prospective vendor. A letter of transmittal accompanies the RFP to explain to the vendor the nature of the problem, the objectives of the system, the performance criteria, and the deadline for proposal submission. The RFP provides a format for vendor responses and thus a comparative basis for initial screening. Some vendors will choose not to respond to the RFP and others will propose packages that clearly do not meet the specifications. Through initial screening the user should attempt to reduce the number of proposals to five or less.

Vendor evaluation

The vendor proposals that survive initial screening must be evaluated methodically to determine the one that best satisfies the user's needs at the lowest cost.

Benchmark problems One common technique for measuring the relative performance of competing systems is to establish a benchmark problem typical of the transactions or tasks that are required of the system. Each vendor's system is then tested on the same benchmark problem; performance in solving the problem is compared with regard to speed, accuracy, and efficiency.

Vendor support The functional differences among vendor packages may not always be the decisive factor, for the final decision may rest on other considerations such as vendor support. The range of support options is wide. At one end of the spectrum are vendors who provide full service support including client training, user and technical documentation, warranties, maintenance programs to implement system enhancements, toll-free hotline numbers, and even annual user seminars to obtain user input and to apprise users of new developments. At the other end of the spectrum, support is virtually nonexistent.

The level of support desired or needed by the user deserves careful consideration. Some want and need a high level of support; others do not. Although prospective buyers must be sure they will get the support they need, they should recognize that the difference in the support provided by different vendors accounts for a large portion of the price differential between their products. Support is a large overhead item for vendors, and the cost is passed on to customers. The buyer should be wary of a proposal that seems too good to be true—it probably is. To avoid "dump and run" vendors, the buyer must be prepared to pay for support.

Vendor presentations At some point during the review, vendors should be invited to the user's premises to make formal presentations of their systems. At these presentations, vendors usually give technical demonstrations using modified versions of the packages on microcomputers. This provides the prospective purchaser with an opportunity to evaluate the capabilities of the system, assess the vendor's personnel, and obtain answers to detailed questions. Sufficient time should be allotted for an in-depth demonstration followed by a question-and-answer period.

If the vendor's representatives are unable or unwilling to demonstrate the full range of system capabilities or to deal with specific questions, this may be a clue to a functional deficiency of the system or to technical incompetence on the part of the representative. If the representative does not understand the system or the user's problem, the decision maker and users should question the vendor's ability to deliver and support a quality product. There is no reason to suspect that support from the vendor will exist at a level beyond the technical capabilities demonstrated by support personnel.

References An important part of analyzing a software package is to contact references supplied by the vendor. It is important that the reviewer, not the vendor, select the references. This provides for a more objective appraisal and reduces the possibility of receiving biased information from model or "show-case" installations. A representative selection should be made of users with the latest version of the package, users in the same geographic location, and users with similar computer configurations. A standard set of questions directed to each will expedite the information gathering process and allow subsequent comparisons among packages. The following list is an example of the type of questions that should be asked.

When did you purchase the package?
Which other vendors did you review?
Why did you select this package?
Are you satisfied with the package?
Are you satisfied with the vendor support?
Does the system perform as advertised?
Were modifications required?
What type of training did the vendor provide?
What is the quality of the documentation?
Have any major problems been encountered?
Do you subscribe to the vendor's maintenance program?
If so, do you receive enhancements?[3]

Analysis of the findings The final phase in the selection process is to analyze the data gathered in the previous steps. A popular technique for analyzing qualitative variables is the "weighted factor matrix" demonstrated in Table 8–2. For illustrative purposes, Table 8–2 compares only two vendors. In practice the approach would be applied to all vendors under consideration.

The table lists the relevant decision criteria and assigns each one a weight that reflects its relative importance to the user, a most critical step. Because the factors represent all relevant decision criteria, their weights should total 100 percent. These weights may well vary among decision makers. One may consider vendor support an overriding factor in the ultimate decision, while another may consider support unimportant relative to hardware compatibility.

After weights are assigned, each vendor package is evaluated according to its performance in each factor category. Based on the information gathered in previous steps, the individual factors are scored using an arbitrary scale of, say, 1 to 5, where 1 is poor performance and 5 is excellent.

Next, weighted scores are computed by multiplying the raw score by the weight for each vendor. To use the example in Table 8–2, a weight of 15 for vendor support is multiplied by a score of 4 for Vendor A and 3 for Vendor B to give weighted scores of 60 and 45 respectively. The weighted scores are then totaled for each vendor to produce a composite performance index for each. Table 8–2 shows a higher score for Vendor B (391) than for Vendor A (372),

Table 8–2 Weighted factor matrix.

Factor	Weight	Vendor A Raw score	Vendor A Weighted score	Vendor B Raw score	Vendor B Weighted score
Response time	10	5	50	4	40
Compatibility	9	3	27	5	45
Reputation and experience	5	3	15	5	25
Ability to deliver on schedule	7	4	28	5	35
Range of capabilities	15	4	60	4	60
Modularity	12	4	48	3	36
User friendliness	15	4	60	3	45
Supports data base	9	2	18	5	45
Supports DDP	3	2	6	5	15
Vendor support	15	4	60	3	45
Total	100		372		391

Source: Joseph W. Wilkinson, *Accounting and Information Systems* (New York: John Wiley & Sons, 1986), p. 884.

indicating that Vendor B slightly outperforms Vendor A on the factors considered so far.

Next the analysis must be taken a step further to include financial considerations. For example, assume the proposal from Vendor A costs $150,000 and that from Vendor B costs $190,000. An overall performance/cost index can be computed as follows:

$$\text{Vendor A:} \quad \frac{372}{\$150{,}000} = 2.48 \text{ per } \$1{,}000$$

$$\text{Vendor B:} \quad \frac{391}{\$190{,}000} = 2.06 \text{ per } \$1{,}000$$

When financial considerations are brought into the analysis, Vendor A provides 2.48 units of performance per thousand dollars versus only 2.06 units per thousand dollars from Vendor B. Therefore, Vendor A provides greater value for the cost.

The option with the highest performance/cost ratio is the economically feasible choice. Of course, this analysis rests on the user's ability to identify all relevant decision factors and assign to them weights that reflect their relative importance to the decision. If relevant factors are omitted or their individual weights misstated, the results of the analysis will be misleading. Further complicating the choice is the fact that the majority of the data collected is qualitative in nature and does not lend itself to easy, objective comparison. And the qualitative characteristics important to the decision will probably be found to some degree in each of the systems examined. Therefore, even with all the analysis, no clear-cut "best choice" is likely to emerge.

Conclusion

Computers are a basic tool for financial management in local government. The increasingly sophisticated information systems under their control can be used to improve the efficiency with which local jurisdictions provide and deliver services. The results of a 1985 survey on computer use conducted by the International City Management Association and John Scoggins and Associates, Inc., indicate that "major problems associated with computer technology in local governments are not technical but organizational, managerial, and financial."[4] Consequently, even the nontechnically oriented finance director needs a sound understanding of information management principles, system design, applications, vendor selection, and staff training. Only in this way will these increasingly expensive and complex systems be used as effectively and efficiently as possible.

As this chapter has demonstrated, new computer applications and enhanced versions of existing software packages enter the marketplace almost daily—and the financial manager needs to stay abreast of this market by referring to computer-oriented periodicals and directories of software applications.

The manager should bear in mind, however, that despite the ongoing changes, many of the basics outlined in this chapter remain constant. By following the guidelines presented here, the manager will be well prepared with a solid foundation for making informed decisions about computer use.

1 A nanosecond is one thousand millionth (1/1,000,000,000) of a second.

2 For a review of the leading microcomputer data base management systems, see *Datapro Report on Microcomputers,* vol. 2, no. 9 (Delran, N.J.: Datapro Research Corporation, September 1985).

3 Steven J. Weinberg, "Why Choose an Accounting Software Package?" *Management Accounting,* February 1980: 45.

4 *The Municipal Year Book, 1986 Edition* (Washington, D.C.: International City Management Association, 1986), p. 44.

Part three: Revenue sources

9 The property tax

The property tax, an annual tax on the values of certain properties (principally real estate), is levied and administered almost exclusively by local governments. State property taxes have been significant in the past, but for more than 25 years states have collected less than 5 percent of total property tax revenue, and they have not been an important source of revenues. There is no federal property tax. Because real property is the least mobile of tax bases, it is especially appropriate as the main source of revenues for local jurisdictions with relatively fixed boundaries.

Although the property tax has been the source of considerable economic autonomy for local communities, there has been a growing hostility to local property taxation in recent years. In the late 1970s, after inflation caused rapid increases in the real burden of the tax, special limits on increases in property taxes were enacted in California (Proposition 13) and some other states. This temporarily slowed the increase in overall revenues from property taxation; as local governments turned to other revenue sources, the percentage of total revenues collected as property taxes decreased. Still, the property tax remains the most important source of local tax revenues, and a basic and thorough explanation of property taxation is crucial to an understanding of policies of local government finances.

Several criteria may be used to decide whether to impose a tax and to judge its equity, efficiency, and long-range effectiveness:

1. Fairness. A tax should reflect the ability to pay of those who bear its burden, or the tax burden should be matched by the benefits taxpayers receive. In general, taxes that take a higher percentage of the income of the poor (regressive taxes) are considered unfair.
2. Certainty. The rules of taxation should be clearly stated and evenly applied. In the case of the property tax, appraisal of property should reflect its market value without bias.
3. Convenience. A tax should be convenient to pay, with billing dates that coincide with the income streams of taxpayers. Although the property tax is due as a lump-sum payment each year, the opportunity to make monthly escrow payments (under mortgage contracts) and quarterly payments has made payment of the tax more convenient for many taxpayers.
4. Efficiency. Fair administration should be feasible and efficient. The administration and collection costs should not be out of proportion to the revenues. A tax should be appropriate for its geographical jurisdiction; it should be neither easy to avoid nor too costly to enforce.
5. Productivity. A tax should produce sufficient, stable revenue.
6. Neutrality. A tax should not distort the way a community would otherwise use its resources—unless it is very clear that such a change is socially desirable.

These criteria are fundamental to the origin, development, and scope of the property tax, the continuing issues surrounding the property tax, and the administration of the property tax.

Background

The property tax is not a tax on all wealth; it is a tax on certain types of personal or business wealth, represented by real or personal property. Real estate is the main element in the tax base, although the property of some owners (other governments and nonprofit institutions) is exempt. The tax rate is applied to the assessed value of a taxable property owned on the assessment date. Ideally, the assessed value reflects the gross value of the property; no reduction is made in the assessed value because of a mortgage or other debt carried on the property.

Origin and development

In the colonial period, various categories of property were listed as part of the property tax base, with a specific tax rate for each category. Only those types of property specifically cited by the law were included. However, by the middle of the nineteenth century, the tax had evolved into a general property tax. All property was considered part of the tax base unless specifically exempted by law, and a uniform rate, specified by a state law or constitution, had to be applied to all property within each district. Property ownership was considered an indicator of the ability to pay taxes, an equity ideal that precluded discrimination among types of property as well as among taxpayers.

The evolution of the tax to a general property tax and the development of uniform rates were thought to be reform measures designed to remedy the ills of special property taxes. Recently, however, some states have introduced property tax classifications and provided different rates for different categories of property. Now these measures are considered reforms. In some cases, different rates have been established for residences, farms, and businesses, creating differentials in the distribution of the tax burden. Low rates are sometimes set for agricultural land and open space in an attempt to slow the development of farmland and open areas.

Figure 9–1 Categories of real and personal property.

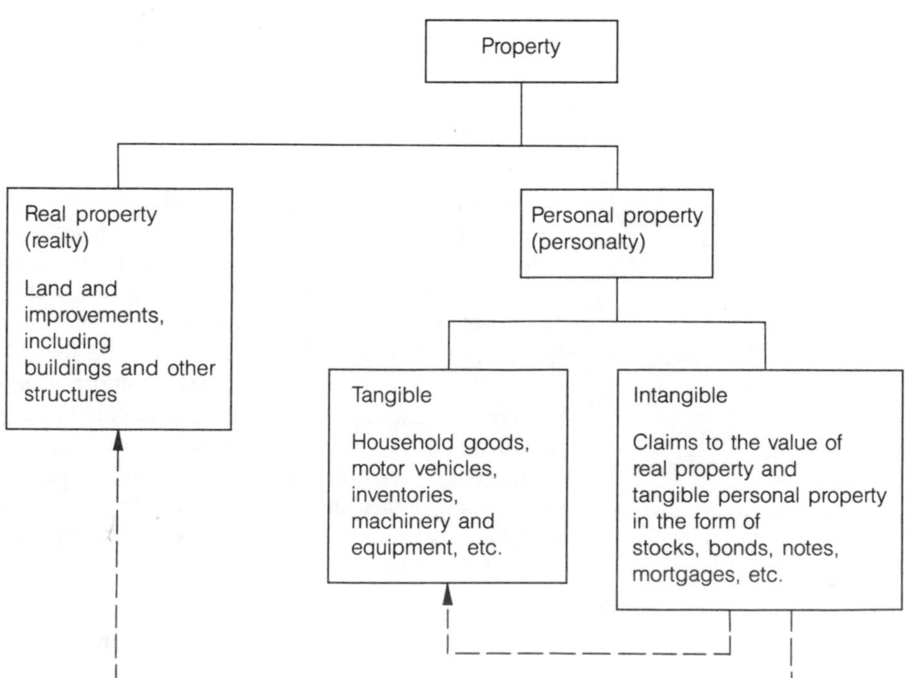

Scope

In few places is there a truly general property tax that covers and taxes all properties at uniform rates.[1] Although some states have as many as 25 classes of property subject to the tax, the tax base and the revenues are derived overwhelmingly from realty, that is, real estate consisting of land, improvements, and structures. The rest of the tax base of assessed property values (and only in some jurisdictions) is personalty—personal property that is not real estate (see Figure 9–1).

Intangible property—claims in the form of stocks or mortgages, for example—is generally exempted from taxation or taxed at low rates. There are many practical problems with discovering, assessing, and applying a property tax to intangible personal property. A tax on intangibles is easy to avoid and costly to administer fairly. Besides, it can be argued, in many cases an intangibles tax involves double taxation of the same property. Thus, while some have proposed taxing intangibles at relatively low rates, others argue that from both a practical and theoretical viewpoint it is wisest to eliminate intangible property from the property tax base altogether.[2]

The tax base is described in Tables 9–1 and 9–2, which show the increasing annual growth of the base. State-assessed property, which includes utilities and railroads, was about 5 percent of the tax base in 1981, having declined from about 8 percent in 1956. Personal property was about 9 percent of locally assessed property in 1981, having declined from nearly 17 percent in 1956. The

Table 9–1 Gross and net assessed property values, selected years, 1956 to 1981 (in $ billions).

Assessed value type	1956	1961	1966	1971	1976	1981
Total gross assessed value	280.3	365.9	499.0	717.8	1,229.1	2,958.2
Total net assessed value (net locally taxable)	272.2	354.0	484.1	694.6	1,189.4	2,837.5
State-assessed property	22.5	27.8	41.6	53.5	84.7	159.0
Inside SMSAs, including state-assessed	(NA)	244.6	342.2	507.9	854.0	2,092.4
Outside SMSAs, including state-assessed	(NA)	109.3	141.9	186.7	335.5	744.9
Locally assessed property	249.7	326.1	442.5	641.1	1,104.7	2,678.4
Real property	202.8	269.7	378.9	552.7	959.1	2,406.7
Personal property	46.9	56.5	63.6	88.3	145.6	271.7

Source: 1982 Census of Governments, *Taxable Property Values and Assessment–Sales Price Ratios*, vol. 2 (Washington, D.C.: GPO, 1982), p. x.
Note: Because of rounding, detail may not add to totals.

Table 9–2 Gross and net assessed property values, average annual percentage change, selected years, 1956 to 1981.

Assessed value type	1956 to 1961	1961 to 1966	1966 to 1971	1971 to 1976	1976 to 1981
Total gross assessed value	5.5	6.4	7.5	11.3	19.2
Total net assessed value (net locally taxable)	5.4	6.5	7.5	11.3	19.0
State-assessed property	4.0	8.4	5.2	9.6	13.4
Inside SMSAs, including state-assessed	(NA)	6.9	8.2	10.4	19.6
Outside SMSAs, including state-assessed	(NA)	5.4	5.6	12.4	17.0
Locally assessed property	5.5	6.3	7.7	11.5	19.4
Real property	5.9	7.0	7.9	11.5	20.2
Personal property	3.5	2.1	6.8	10.5	13.3

Source: 1982 Census of Governments, *Taxable Property Values and Assessment–Sales Price Ratios*, vol. 2 (Washington, D.C.: GPO, 1982), p. x; average annual percentage changes were calculated from data.
Note: Because of rounding, detail may not add to totals.

dollar amounts in these categories grew by less than those in the other categories, especially from 1966 to 1981. The continued decline in the relative importance of personal property in the tax base is partly the result of the discontinuation of such assessments in several states. Real estate property values, on the other hand, grew by increasing annual rates from 1956 to 1981, especially in the last five years of that period, and they accounted for about 85 percent of locally assessed property by 1981. The $120.7 billion difference between the net and the gross totals of assessed values represents exemptions granted by circuit breaker provisions (described later).

Since 1961, there has generally been greater growth in the proportion of assessed values in urban areas than in rural areas; in 1981 about 75 percent of the values were in urban areas. Tables 9–3 and 9–4 show the distribution of gross assessed values of real estate by use categories from 1956 to 1981. Nonfarm residential real estate grew in importance over most of the period, and it accounted for more than 60 percent of the total of gross assessed values in 1981. The growth was most marked in single-family homes, which were 53 percent of the 1981 total, but the proportionate value of farm property and of commercial real estate values declined.

Revenue growth

Total gross assessed values of locally assessed realty grew by more than 150 percent from 1976 to 1981, with increases in all of the use categories.[3] This

Table 9–3 Gross assessed values of locally assessed realty, by use categories, selected years, 1956 to 1981 (in $ billions).

Use category	1956	1961	1966	1976	1981
United States total, all use categories	209.8	280.5	393.2	992.5	2,514.9
Acreage and farms	29.1	32.7	43.4	117.6	247.8
Vacant platted lots	4.8	7.0	10.2	38.0	109.4
Residential (nonfarm)	113.5	162.5	236.3	587.3	1,520.0
Single-family houses only	95.1	135.5	196.7	495.3	1,328.7
Commercial and industrial	58.0	74.5	97.2	239.8	549.3
Commercial	34.8	44.2	60.0	166.0	353.5
Industrial	22.6	30.3	37.1	73.7	195.8
Other and unallocable	4.4	3.8	6.0	9.8	88.3

Source: 1982 Census of Governments, *Taxable Property Values and Assessment–Sales Price Ratios*, vol. 2 (Washington, D.C.: GPO, 1982), p. xiii.

Table 9–4 Gross assessed values of locally assessed realty, by use categories, percentage distribution, selected years, 1956 to 1981.

Use category	1956	1961	1966	1976	1981
United States total, all use categories	100.0	100.0	100.0	100.0	100.0
Acreage and farms	13.9	11.7	11.0	11.9	9.9
Vacant platted lots	2.3	2.5	2.6	3.8	4.4
Residential (nonfarm)	54.1	57.9	60.1	59.2	60.4
Single-family houses only	45.4	48.3	50.0	49.9	52.8
Commercial and industrial	27.7	26.6	24.7	24.2	21.8
Commercial	16.6	15.8	15.3	16.7	14.1
Industrial	10.8	10.8	9.4	7.4	7.8
Other and unallocable	2.1	1.4	1.5	1.0	3.5

Source: 1982 Census of Governments, *Taxable Property Values and Assessment–Sales Price Ratios*, vol. 2 (Washington, D.C.: GPO, 1982), p. xiii.

growth in assessed values was the result of several factors: (1) rising market values of existing properties; (2) increased number of developed parcels; (3) additional investments in buildings and improvements; and (4) rising ratios of assessment values to market values. The resulting increase in the value of the realty tax base has been the major factor in explaining the continued rise in property tax revenues, despite the generally lower average effective rates (the ratios of property tax liability to the market value of the base) in recent years, as shown in Table 9–5.

Table 9–5 National average effective property tax rates on existing single-family homes, selected years, 1958–1983.

Year	Percentage of full market value
1958	1.34
1966	1.70
1971	1.98
1977	1.67
1981	1.26
1982	1.26
1983	1.31

Source: Advisory Commission on Intergovernmental Relations, *Significant Features of Fiscal Federalism, 1984* (Washington, D.C., 1985), pp. 106–107.

Note: The effective property tax rate is the tax liability as a percentage of the market value of a home. The 1.31 percentage rate for 1983 suggests that the average tax bill would be $1,310 on a house with a full market value of $100,000.

From 1957 to 1984, aggregate property tax revenues rose for both state and local levels of government in every year. As Table 9–6 shows, the rise was from $13 billion in 1957 to an estimated $98 billion for 1984. Most of the property tax revenue (almost 95 percent) goes to local governments.

Despite their growth, property tax revenues represent a low percentage of total state tax revenues. Over the long term, the downward trend in the importance of state property tax revenues is pronounced. In 1902, state collections of $82 million in property taxes were 52.6 percent of total state tax revenues. By 1957, the states had largely left property tax collection to local governments and relied primarily on income, sales, and excise taxes. Although state property tax revenues were $479 million by 1957, they represented only 3.3 percent of total state tax revenues. The trend continued over the next 25 years. In 1983, state

Table 9–6 Property tax revenues by level of government and as a percentage of total tax revenues, selected years, 1957 through 1984.

	Revenues ($ billions)			As a % of total tax revenues	
Period	Total	State	Local	State	Local
1957	12.9	0.5	12.4	3.3	86.7
1962	19.1	0.6	18.4	3.1	87.7
1967	26.0	0.9	25.2	2.7	86.6
1972	42.9	1.3	41.6	2.1	83.7
1977	62.5	2.3	60.3	2.2	80.5
1979	64.9	2.5	62.5	2.0	77.5
1981	75.0	2.9	72.0	2.0	76.0
1982	81.9	3.1	78.8	1.9	76.0
1983	89.2	3.3	86.0	1.9	76.0
1984 est.	98.0	5.0	93.0	2.5	75.0

Source: Advisory Commission on Intergovernmental Relations, *Significant Features of Fiscal Federalism, 1980–81* (Washington, D.C., 1981), pp. 42–44; and Advisory Commission on Intergovernmental Relations, *Significant Features of Fiscal Federalism, 1984* (Washington, D.C., 1985), pp. 48–51.

property tax collections of 3.3 billion were only 1.9 percent of total state tax revenues.

As a percentage of total revenue, the property taxes of local governments show a trend similar to that of the states. In 1932 local property taxes were more than 97 percent of local tax revenues. By 1957, with revenues of $12.4 billion, local property taxes were 86.7 percent of local tax revenues, but only 43.4 percent of revenue from all sources, reflecting the increased significance of state grants to local governments. By 1984, it was estimated that local property tax revenues would be $93 billion—75 percent of total local tax revenue. These changes also reflect the public pressures against property taxation that have led local governments to meet their spending needs with other taxes and charges.

The pressures to reduce reliance on the property tax are revealed by the data in Table 9–7. Over the 30-year period from 1953 to 1983, the average annual increase in property tax revenues was 7.8 percent. In the breakdown by periods, the average growth rates for property tax revenues have generally been higher than those for gross national product (GNP) in current dollars and higher than the rates of inflation as reflected in the consumer price index. The exceptions were in the 1970s. After the limitations introduced during the "tax revolt" of 1973 to 1978, the average annual rise in property tax revenues fell to 4.0 percent whereas GNP rose at the rate of 10.9 percent, and consumer prices at the rate of 11.7 percent. Property tax revenues again rose at higher rates in the early 1980s, but the overall decline in their relative importance as part of total local government tax revenues indicates that collections from other sources rose even more.

Table 9–7 Average annual rates of increase in local property tax revenues, gross national product, and consumer price index, selected periods, 1953 through 1984.

Period	Local property tax revenues	Gross national product (current $)	Consumer price index (1972–73 weights)
1953–58	8.4	4.1	1.6
1958–63	7.2	5.8	1.2
1963–68	7.0	7.9	2.6
1968–73	10.4	8.7	5.0
1973–78	7.8	10.3	8.0
1978–81	4.0	10.9	11.7
1981–82	9.4	3.8	6.1
1982–83	9.1	7.7	3.2
1983–84 est.	8.1	10.9	4.3

Source: Advisory Commission on Intergovernmental Relations, *Significant Features of Fiscal Federalism, 1984* (Washington, D.C., 1985), p. 45.

These trends cannot be extended to predictions of the future or applied to all places. John Shannon of the Advisory Commission on Intergovernmental Relations (ACIR) cites several caveats. The decline in the relative importance of property taxes has been greater for city governments than for counties, and greater for counties than for school districts. The effects also differ widely among states. Furthermore, the relative importance of property tax revenues may increase again with future declines in some other revenue sources, such as interest on investments (given declining interest rates). For these reasons, Shannon suggests, the property tax is likely to remain a vital part of local government finance for some time to come.[4]

Despite the decline in the relative importance of the property tax, the absolute level of collections by local governments has increased steadily. As Table 9–6 shows, local property tax collections rose from $12.4 billion to an estimated $93 billion from 1957 to 1984, a 650 percent increase. Even after the tax limitation measures of the 1970s, local government property tax collections rose about 50 percent—from $62.5 billion in 1979 to an estimated $93 billion in 1984.

Continuing issues

As a local tax used to support local services, the property tax is a highly visible levy whose costs can be related directly to the benefits of local government programs. Yet, despite its importance to local governments, the property tax has for a long time been one of the least popular sources of public revenue.[5] Its visibility makes the tax an easy target for attack and may account for the emergence of the following controversial issues surrounding the tax: (1) the discriminatory potential of property taxation when used as the basis for local expenditures on public education; (2) the momentum of the general movement to limit the burden of property taxation along with the level of local government spending; and (3) the differential effects of the tax and its incidence on persons of various income classes.

Detractors of the property tax have said that the property tax, unlike a tax on net wealth or income, does not fully reflect ability to pay; appears to impose unreasonable burdens on the poor; and encourages urban blight, suburban sprawl, and unfair disparities in local government services. As the following sections will show, however, changes in state laws and local practices have reduced some of the regressivity, and in general there is enough evidence from recent analyses to challenge the largely negative view of the property tax.

Financing education

In a state school program that relies on local property taxes, the quality of a child's education would depend on the relative property values of the community. A child in a poor community, then, would receive an education of lesser quality than a child in a wealthy community. In 1971, the California Supreme Court ruled in *Serrano* v. *Priest* that a local government system for financing public education that discriminates among students on the basis of wealth in the school district violates the equal protection clause of the United States Constitution.[6] The *Serrano* case, and others that followed in other localities, made it clear that the wealth or income of the state as a whole—not the particular locality—should determine the level of spending for every child in the state.

The court decisions required the end of discrimination against any definable group, called for more intrastate equalization of educational spending, and delegated the responsibility to the state legislature. The property tax was not discarded as a major source of school support, however, nor was there any attempt or directive to equalize educational spending on a national (rather than intrastate) basis,[7] even though reform of the system of financing public education was a matter of national concern.

Among the ways that states could respond to the move for reform was to increase their efforts under equalization and support programs for public schools. From 1962–72, the national average of state shares for the support of public elementary and secondary school education rose only from 40.5 percent to 42.0 percent of total local school costs. However, by the 1983–84 school year, the state share had risen to 48.3 percent. State governments now provide the financing for the major share of local expenditures of schools.[8] With the rising contributions from the states and from general revenue sharing in the 1970s, there was a decrease in the pressure on local property taxation for the support of the schools.

Table 9–8 Restrictions on state and local government tax and expenditure powers, October 1985.

State	State imposed limits on local governments[a]			
	Overall property tax rate limit	Specific property tax rate limit	Property tax levy limit	General revenue limit
Total number	12	31	21	6
Alabama	CMS***	CMS*		
Alaska	CMS**		CM**	
Arizona			CM***	
Arkansas		CMS*	CMS***[1]	
California	CMS***			
Colorado		CS*	CM*	
Connecticut				
Delaware		S**	C***[1]	
District of Columbia				
Florida	CM***	CMS*		
Georgia		S*		
Hawaii				
Idaho		CMS*	CMS***	
Illinois		CMS*	CMS***	
Indiana			CMS***	
Iowa		CM*		
Kansas		[3]	CM**	
Kentucky	CMS*	CMS***		
Louisiana		CMS**	CMS***[1]	
Maine				
Maryland				CM***
Massachusetts			CMS***	
Michigan	CS*	M*	CMS***	
Minnesota		CMS*	CMS**	M*
Mississippi		CMS*	CMS***	CMS***
Missouri		CMS*		CMS***
Montana		CMS*		
Nebraska		CMS*		CMS***[5]
Nevada	CMS*	S*	CM**	
New Hampshire				
New Jersey			C**	
New Mexico	CMS*	CMS*	CMS***	
New York		CMS*		
North Carolina		CM**		
North Dakota			CMS***	
Ohio	CMS*		CMS**[1]	
Oklahoma	CMS*	CMS*		
Oregon			CMS*	
Pennsylvania		CMS*[4]		
Rhode Island			M	
South Carolina				
South Dakota		CMS*		
Tennessee				
Texas		CMS**		
Utah		CMS*		
Vermont				
Virginia				
Washington	CMS**	CMS**	CMS**	S**
West Virginia	CMS*	CMS*		
Wisconsin		CMS*		
Wyoming		CMS***		

Source: ACIR staff calculations based on surveys of state revenue departments. Advisory Commission on Intergovernmental Relations, *Significant Features of Fiscal Federalism, 1985–86 Edition* (Washington, D.C.: GPO, 1986), pp. 146–47.

Notes: C—County, M—Municipal, S—School district, *—Enacted before 1970, **—1970 to 1977, ***—1978 and after, Const.—Constitutional, Stat.—Statutory.

[a] For an explanation of column headings, see third page of table.

Table 9–8 (continued)

State	General expenditure limit	Limits on assessment increases	Full disclosure	Limits on state governments
	State imposed limits on local governments			
Total number	6	7	13	18
Alabama				
Alaska				Const.***
Arizona	CMS***	CMS***		Const.***
Arkansas				
California	CMS***	CMS***		Const.***
Colorado	S**		CMS***	Stat.**
Connecticut				
Delaware				
District of Columbia			C	
Florida			CMS**	
Georgia				
Hawaii			C**	Const.***
Idaho				Stat.***
Illinois			CMS***	
Indiana				
Iowa		CMS***	CMS*	
Kansas	S**			
Kentucky			CMS***	
Louisiana				Stat.***
Maine				
Maryland		CM**	CM**	
Massachusetts				
Michigan			CMS***	Const.***
Minnesota	S**			
Mississippi				
Missouri				Const.***
Montana			CMS**	Stat.***
Nebraska				
Nevada				Stat.***
New Hampshire				
New Jersey	MS**			
New Mexico		CMS***		
New York		CM***[2]		
North Carolina				
North Dakota				
Ohio				
Oklahoma				
Oregon		CMS***		Stat.**
Pennsylvania				
Rhode Island			M	Stat.**
South Carolina				Stat.***
South Dakota				
Tennessee			CMS***	Const.***
Texas			CMS***	Const.***
Utah				Stat.***
Vermont				
Virginia			CM**	
Washington				Stat.***
West Virginia				
Wisconsin				
Wyoming				

[1] Limits follow reassessment.
[2] Applicable to only New York City and Nassau County.
[3] Only for selected districts (fire, library, cemetery, etc.).
[4] Jurisdictions with home rule charters are not subject to limits.
[5] Expired 31 December 1984.

(continued on next page)

Table 9–8 (continued)

Explanation of column headings

Overall property tax rate limit The maximum rate that may be applied against the assessed value of property without a vote of the local electorate. The rate is usually expressed as millions per dollar of assessed value. The overall limit refers to the *aggregate* tax rate of all local governments—municipal, county, school districts, and special districts (if applicable).

Specific property tax rate limit Same as above, except the specific rate *limit* refers to *limits* on individual types of local governments (i.e., *separate* limits for cities, counties, etc.) or limits on narrowly defined services (excluding debt).

Property tax levy limit The maximum revenue that a jurisdiction can raise from the property tax. This is typically enacted as an allowed annual percentage increase in the property tax levy.

General revenue limit The total amount of revenue, from both property and nonproperty tax sources, that a local government is allowed to collect during a fiscal year.

General expenditure limit The maximum amount that a jurisdiction can either appropriate or spend during a fiscal year. This is usually legislated as an allowed annual percentage increase in operating expenses.

Limits on assessment increases Self-explanatory. Such limits force local governments to increase tax rates for needed additional revenue, instead of relying on the automatic revenue windfall caused by rising property values.

Full disclosure or truth in property taxation A procedure designed to promote public discussion and political accountability requiring local governing bodies to advertise and hold public hearings on proposed tax rate increases.

The tax limitation movement

From the mid-1970s on, there has been a growing movement to enact restrictions on the growth of taxes through limitations on revenues, expenditures, or both. Sometimes the limits have come in the form of amendments to state constitutions; sometimes they are simply acts of the legislature. This tax limitation movement, which began in California with an attack on the property tax spearheaded by Harold Jarvis and culminated (in 1978) in voter passage of the Jarvis-Gann Amendment—Proposition 13—has had effects lasting well into the 1980s. Proposition 13 restricted the property tax rate to 1 percent of assessed value, put limits on the assessed value of properties, and required approval of new taxes or increases in existing taxes (except property taxes) by two thirds of the legislature in the case of state taxes, or by two thirds of the voters in the case of local taxes.

Table 9–8, compiled by ACIR, shows the extent of the tax limitation movement. The number of states with levy limits on the property tax has increased dramatically, from 3 prior to 1970 to 21 in 1985.

Although initial voter approval of the Jarvis-Gann Amendment caused considerable trepidation among officials, the actual belt tightening and cutting of programs was less than anticipated (at least for the time being) because the state government had a considerable surplus, which it parceled out to the local governments. However, not all states have surpluses to act as a fiscal cushion against the new limits, and it is unlikely that tax limitation pressures will be relieved by increased state and local reliance on federal aid. State and local governments will be forced to continue efforts to increase productivity, make greater use of fees and charges, and shift some services to the private sector. Significantly, Proposition 13 was followed by the passage of Proposition 4, which restricted overall increases in governmental spending, not just property taxes. Although the Jarvis movement and Proposition 13 were directed mostly against the property tax, there is some evidence that the voters in California were registering as well a general protest against the size of the public sector as a whole.

Tax incidence

Statistical studies show that those with lower incomes spend a higher percentage of their incomes for consumption (specifically for shelter) than do those with higher incomes. If this observation is coupled with the idea that much of the property tax burden is shifted through higher prices for goods and services, including housing, it appears that people with lower incomes bear a proportionately greater tax burden as a percentage of their incomes.

ACIR studied the tax burdens of families residing in the largest city in each state. For the four income levels noted in Table 9–9, the median of property taxes paid in each income class may be taken to represent a "typical" city family with two adults and two dependents in that income class. These estimates indicate that a family with $17,500 in 1982 income paid 2.89 percent of its income in property taxes. As the income level rises to $25,000, $50,000, and $100,000, the property taxes paid by the median family with that income fall to 2.47, 1.96, and 1.44 percent of income, respectively. This suggests that the property tax burdens of city homeowner families with $100,000 in income is typically about half of the burden of those with $17,500.[9] Given the assumptions that relate the tax burden to capital owners, these estimates indicate that the property tax is regressive for lower-income classes and that the burden declines as income rises.

Henry Aaron and others have challenged the traditional view of the regressivity of property taxation. Aaron suggests that measuring the tax burden in relation to current income rather than permanent income may be misleading. Even if property taxation is viewed as an excise tax on housing, some measures indicate that the effective incidence of the tax shows progressivity for homeowners and proportionality for renters, rather than regressivity. Aaron views the property tax as a kind of national tax on owners of capital. He concludes that property taxes are thus borne by all owners of capital in the nation in proportion to their ownership of capital. Because ownership of capital and levels of income are correlated, he concludes that the incidence of the property tax is, in the long run, progressive.[10]

The ability of capital owners to shift the burden of the tax to others (in rental fees or in prices charged for products) has been viewed as critical to determining whether the property tax is progressive or regressive. Richard Musgrave has noted that different conditions in various markets lead to different conclusions about shifting the tax burdens for rental housing and shifting the burdens for

Table 9–9 Median property tax burdens for families residing in the largest city in each state, 1982, for selected income levels.

Annual income level ($)	Assumed ratio of property value to annual increase[a]	Property value ($)	Median tax ($)	Payment as a % of income
17,500	2.8	49,000	505	2.89
25,000	2.4	60,000	618	2.47
50,000	1.9	95,000	979	1.96
100,000	1.4	140,000	1,442	1.44

Source: Advisory Commission on Intergovernmental Relations, *Tax Burdens for Families Residing in the Largest City in Each State, 1982*, Staff Working Paper 3R (Washington, D.C., August 1984), pp. 37–46.

[a] ACIR assumed property values that were based on the median of the property values in each of these levels of income as reported in the 1980 Census of Housing.

different types of business property. However, he agrees with Aaron's assertion that the use of lifetime income patterns would make the distribution of the property tax burden less regressive, and he concludes that the property tax on housing is *progressive*.[11] Clearly, there are those who believe that the property tax may be less regressive than was originally thought.[12]

Homestead exemptions and circuit breakers

To relieve some of the presumed regressivity of the property tax, many states have enacted homestead exemptions and circuit breakers. However, ACIR has noted that homestead exemptions and other programs of property tax relief may not have very significant effects on the regressivity of the tax. A homestead exemption excludes a determined amount from the assessed value of a single-family home before the tax rate is applied. The problem, however, is that in many states the excluded amount (sometimes up to $5,000) is the same for all households, no matter what their income. In place of the homestead exemption, ACIR has recommended the use of circuit breakers, financed by the state government and specifically designed to provide relief for low-income homeowners and renters who may be overburdened by property taxes.[13]

Circuit breakers The circuit breaker provision for property taxes is an attempt to relieve persons of tax burdens that are excessive in relation to their incomes or ability to pay. This provision is analogous to a circuit breaker to prevent electrical overloads. It is designed to protect the poor from a "tax overload" without affecting the property tax revenues from those who are able to pay. This is usually done by providing relief at the expense of state, rather than local, government. The relief (available to the elderly, the poor, or both—depending on the program) gradually phases out as the income of the taxpayer rises; it is not available for those above stated income levels.

A property tax burden is considered excessive when it exceeds a stated proportion of household income. This varies among the states, from 4 to 7 percent. Many states provide ceilings—on incomes, the value of eligible property, and the amount of rebate or relief—and relief only for those above 62 or 65 years old. Some states provide relief for renters as well as for homeowners, assuming that a stated proportion of rent (varying among these states from 10 to 30 percent) is for property taxes.

The U.S. Advisory Commission on Intergovernmental Relations considers this approach superior to homestead exemptions because the circuit breaker recognizes degrees of need for relief from the property tax. Because it is state financed, the circuit breaker does not burden local governments, especially those where the elderly and poor may be concentrated. However, some object to the provision on several grounds: (1) it fails to recognize fully the ability of the eligible taxpayers to pay with savings, securities, or other assets; (2) it protects the estates of the elderly, whereas permitting deferral of tax payments would not; (3) it permits elderly owners to keep properties off the market, preventing potentially better uses and making property more expensive and more difficult to obtain for the young; and (4) it encourages greater local government spending by making local officials less sensitive to the income pressures of taxpayers. Of course, proponents of the circuit breaker offer responses to each of these arguments.

Source: Adapted from Advisory Commission on Intergovernmental Relations, *Financing Schools and Property Tax Relief—A State Responsibility,* A–40 (Washington, D.C.: GPO, 1973), pp. 43–59.

The first circuit breaker was adopted by Minnesota in 1964. By 1984, 30 states and the District of Columbia had adopted circuit breakers, and 7 states had low-income eligibility provisions for homestead relief.[14] Circuit breakers vary substantially among the states. Most states specify income limits that range from $2,500 to $10,000 per couple; the most common limits are between $4,000 and $6,000. In most circuit breaker plans, the amount of relief declines as income rises, and no relief is offered once the income limit is reached. Some states include only homeowners in their programs; others also cover renters. Many programs are restricted to the elderly, with eligibility beginning at 62 or 65 years of age, and some offer state tax rebates or credits. ACIR has determined that, in general, these special provisions have made the property tax less regressive.[15] It has been argued that circuit breakers may favor those who are only temporarily poor and those with large amounts of property who may not be poor—even if their current income levels are relatively low. Moreover, the elderly, who might otherwise liquidate or trade down the value of their homes, may be induced to stay in them if the market values are not fully reflected in the property taxes levied on them as homeowners.[16] A deferral of all or part of tax liabilities until a set future date or until a future sale or transfer of property may be a better alternative to circuit breaker relief provisions for the aged.[17]

Capitalized value of income

Both income and property ownership can be viewed as separate bases of ability-to-pay taxation. Income, however, is viewed as a flow over a period of time, while capital, or property, is perceived as a stock of wealth owned on a particular date. These concepts are related because the property is expected to yield income over a future period. One way to determine the value of an asset is to capitalize the value of its expected earnings. For example, assume that a property is expected to yield $500 a year for an indefinite period of time and that the market rate of return on capital is 10 percent a year. The capitalized value of the property is then $5,000, the same as any other asset expected to yield $500 a year given a 10 percent rate of return. The owner of that property is subject to an ability-to-pay tax equivalent to the tax on a person who has an income of $500 from another source. A tax of 1 percent on the property value, then, imposes an annual burden of $50, the equivalent of a 10 percent tax on $500 of other income.

Whenever there is a change in the tax, the difference may be capitalized and reflected in the property's market value. In this example a property yielding $500 in income was valued at $5,000. If, with no other changes, an annual property tax of $100 were levied, the effect would be to reduce aftertax income to $400. As a result, the value of the property would fall to $4,000, reflecting the capitalization of the tax increase. However, if a tax has the effect of reducing the tax base (assessed property values) by an amount reflecting this capitalization, a higher tax rate is required to raise the same amount of revenue. In the example, a 1 percent tax rate produced $50 in revenues from a property valued at $5,000. If capitalization reduces the assessed value to $4,000, a tax rate of 1.25 percent would be needed to raise the same $50. This alters the relationship between effective property tax rates and tax rates on gross income from property, both of which can affect property market values.[18] However, such changes in market values are not always reflected in the tax base. Especially if many similar properties are involved, a change in market values may result in a change in the ratio of assessment to market values, with little or no change in the assessed values as such. Moreover, if a tax increase is accompanied by additional services (e.g., improved education or recreation), this could increase the demand for such property and offset the effect of the tax increase. A tax decrease (with no drop in services) could be expected to increase the after-tax income and the capitalized value of the taxed property.

Capitalization of the property tax has been cited as a cause of urban sprawl—the spread of residential and commercial structures to lower-taxed outlying areas. In some places, central city tax rates have risen more rapidly and are higher than those in suburban areas. The effects are greater tax burdens on property owners in the city and a decline in the value of city property. Although city land and existing structures would have lower values, those planning new construction may nevertheless buy more expensive land in the lower-taxed suburbs—and still receive a lower tax bill and lower overall costs when the improvements and new buildings are counted.

Classification by use

Several different approaches have been taken in response to the problems of inner city deterioration and urban sprawl. All states and the District of Columbia have some provisions that classify and tax property for agricultural, open-space, and related benefited uses.[19] As a result, open land such as that used for agriculture may be taxed at a lower rate. A change to urban uses would result in higher property tax rates and thereby slow the growth of urban sprawl. Tax classification is also used to realign the tax burden by placing higher rates on business properties than on farms or homes.

Another tax reform using classification provides a lower rate for improvements to deteriorated properties. A 1977 Pennsylvania state law permitted several cities in that state to allow property tax exemptions for a number of years for improvements to deteriorated properties or to properties in deteriorating areas.[20] The purpose of these exemptions is to encourage redevelopment of properties and renovation of neighborhoods.

In California and several other states, special programs have been designed to slow conversion of agricultural land to other uses. The landowner agrees to maintain the land in agricultural use for 10 years; in return, the property tax assessment is based on the capitalized, rather than market, value of the land. The owner may incur a substantial tax obligation if he or she cancels the agreement. Critics have noted that this arrangement carries special benefits for the owners and that it is an insufficient inducement to prevent development in the urban-rural fringe areas. Some have suggested land-use zoning instead of differential property tax assessment as a more effective planning tool.[21]

Property tax administration

Many criticisms and proposals for reform of property taxation deal with administration, for the property tax is not easy to administer. Property tax administration involves discovery of the tax base, preparation of an inventory or property list, appraisal and assessment of property value, recognition of exemptions, determination of the tax levy, and collection. Fundamental to accomplishing these tasks, of course, are the establishment of a highly qualified staff and organization, the establishment of procedures and forms, and the provision of a system—generally computerized—to maintain records and retrieve information on the location of land, the nature of improvements, assessed value, and other data.

Discovery

Discovery of the tax base involves discovery of both real and personal property. Discovery of real property is relatively straightforward. The property exists in situ, subject to easy canvass, and there is a conventional system for recording both its description and its ownership.

Discovery of personal property is more complicated, particulariy in the case of intangible property. The major practical impediment to taxing intangibles is the difficulty of finding such assets as cash, bank deposits outside the assessment district, and other assets for which ownership is not subject to registration and records. Discovery is likely to be limited to the declaration of the owner and to reliance on other uncertain data (e.g., federal income tax returns) or specific legal actions (e.g., probating an estate) that yield a property listing. The discovery of intangible property may depend largely on the compliance and self-assessment of individuals who may feel that by revealing their assets they incur a tax burden that many others forgo. Discovery is difficult and uncertain; enforcement costs for full compliance are prohibitive; and high rates of taxation on intangible property represent double taxation. Abolishing the tax on intangibles, rather than attempting to improve its administration, may be the best solution to its theoretical and administrative problems.

Discovery of tangible personal property, other than automobiles, also is difficult and incomplete, and assessors have tended to be cautious in enforcing this part of the tax. Moreover, there are some theoretical arguments against the taxation of movable properties such as inventory. Briefly, on a given assessment date, property value may not represent an annual value because various inventory policies may minimize the value on the assessment date. First, deliveries themselves may be delayed. Second, seasonal variations in inventory may differ among industries so that different taxpayers may have different burdens. Third, different policies for inventory valuation can yield different values on the same property. And finally, some values may have to be set on the basis of self-assessment because they are beyond the assessor's experience and for some items cannot be otherwise determined. Thus the principal efforts to improve property tax administration are likely to continue to focus on real property.

Inventory

To prepare an inventory or property list, parcels (tracts or plots of land) are identified on the basis of drafting and mapping, and on the basis of a numbering system designed to permit revisions that could result from consolidation or subdivision of properties. Aerial photographs may be used to confirm the location and identify parcels and improvements, establish relationships among different areas, and check for changes. Such aerial photographs have led to the discovery of land areas that had been omitted from tax rolls for many years.[22]

Appraisal and assessment

Once discovery and inventory are completed, the property may be appraised. Appraisal and assessment are the heart of property tax administration, for in this process, the share of the tax burden is determined for each property owner.

Assessment is complex and often controversial. Assessors carry heavy responsibilities, particularly for the equitable treatment of all taxpayers. The assessment process is facilitated when the variables making for value and assessment classification are clearly delineated and the techniques employed make full use of the latest statistical tools and methodologies.

Officials of primary assessing jurisdictions totaled over 13,000 in 1981—all of them at the county, municipal, and township levels (except in Maryland and Montana where state employees perform the assessment function). These officials have the primary responsibility for setting and recording assessments. John O. Behrens notes that they have the task of "dealing with individual realty parcels on a mass basis."[23] Improving the process would involve greater use of cadastral (tax plot) maps, greater use of computers for inventory and assessing functions, and greater involvement of the states in auditing the assessment process. This would allow local jurisdictions to pay more attention to the tax base as a whole and to work toward updating reappraisals.

The assessor establishes a valuation for each parcel and ultimately the total value of the property in the district. Assessment may not yield to rule-of-thumb appraisal or arbitrary judgment; both equity and law require that each valuation be defensible. The assessor is frequently called on to defend the accuracy of a valuation as well as the uniformity of the method of appraising the value of properties.

IAAO policy statements The International Association of Assessing Officers believes that the property tax is an essential part of any truly balanced and equitable local tax system. The property tax is a stable and reliable source of local government revenue because property values reflect long-term economic considerations, not short-term economic fluctuations. The property tax cannot be replaced by any other tax or combination of taxes without causing dramatic and unpredictable shifts in individual tax burdens and in the revenue-producing capacities of local units of government. The property tax also captures for local government some of the increases in property value that are partially created by public expenditures. The association also believes that this visibility of the property tax serves to focus attention on the overall quality of governance.

It is incumbent on the local jurisdictions that rely on the property tax to see that assessment systems are administered in a professional, equitable, and open manner. Key elements of modern, cost-effective assessment systems include: (a) an adequate budget, a well-organized, well-trained staff, and sufficient computing resources; (b) effective management procedures and internal controls, including assessment-ratio studies; (c) adequate, accurate, and accessible information and data for identifying and describing properties, appraising them, linking them to their owners, determining taxable status, and satisfying their owners and others that assessing officers are conversant with the properties in their jurisdiction; (d) effective appraisal programs utilizing the sales comparison, cost, and income approaches to value; (e) open public relations; and (f) accessible and effective appeal procedures.

It is incumbent on all government officials who administer and participate in the tax to avail themselves of every opportunity to improve their professional qualifications and conduct themselves in such a manner that the tax will be perceived as a fair and equitable means of producing revenue by the taxpaying public.

The International Association of Assessing Officers further believes that property tax systems should adhere to the following basic principle: Assessments should be based on current market values. The property tax is generally conceived to be an ad valorem tax, which means that a tax levy is apportioned among taxpayers according to the value of each taxpayer's property.

The International Association of Assessing Officers believes that exemptions should be kept to an essential minimum and that other forms of property relief should be based on tax abatements or credits rather than limits on assessment increases, other-than-market-value assessment standards, and the like.

Source: Abridged from *IAAO Policy Statements,* published by the International Association of Assessing Officers, 1313 E. 60th Street, Chicago, Illinois 60637-9990.

The assessor's goal generally is to value the land and improvements of each parcel at the market price (variously characterized as actual, fair, true, cash, or money value) and then set the assessment on each parcel at market value or at least at some uniform percentage of market value. This is not an easy task. Only a very small proportion of the property on a tax list during any fiscal period is subject to a transaction where an actual price is assigned to it. Even when there is direct evidence of a sale price on a parcel, the assessor must be sure that the price reflects the market and is not the result of a forced sale or of a transaction between relatives where underevaluation may reflect a gift or other special circumstances.

Because of practical difficulties, many assessors can only hope to appraise and reassess a fraction of the existing taxable properties in any given year. Simply making sure that new construction is added to the current tax list may be a major task.[24] Consequently, most assessors do not attempt to reflect annual changes in market price levels. Instead, they try to maintain uniformity in the fraction of current market value at which each parcel is assessed. Even in states where the law specifies that assessments should be at 100 percent of market value, the actual average assessments will vary from this mark. The rationale is that as long as a uniform assessment percentage is applied to all market values, the shares of total property tax revenues borne by each property owner are not distorted. This rationale has been countered by arguments that such underassessment distorts the true tax rate and complicates the administration of state equalization programs that may be related to the assessed property values of districts. The latter problem, however, is generally solved through sampling techniques. State equalization boards, using the results of their sample surveys, adjust the local assessment ratios for the purposes of state programs.[25]

Methods of valuation The problem of establishing and updating the market value of property may be approached in several ways. Among the most common methods are use of sales data, regression analysis, replacement cost, and capitalized value. None of these valuation methods is likely to be used exclusively, however. Rather, it is the combination of these methods with existing and developing analytical techniques that provides adequate bases on which the assessor can determine reasonable estimates of true values in all but the most extraordinary situations.

Use of sales data Where there is an active, competitive real estate market, market forces will establish a going price that can be used by assessors and other appraisers to estimate the value of the properties that were not sold. Current market price data are the most direct evidence of current property values and should be relatively accurate, even for properties that have not recently changed hands. It is important to note, however, that each property is in some way unique and its market value cannot be directly estimated from transactions on other parcels without accounting for the differences and similarities among them. Nevertheless, even when a small proportion of properties in a particular area is sold during a period of observation, the prices of these transactions provide useful information on the values of other parcels in the area.

Sales data have been used by assessors and other appraisers for a long time. In some jurisdictions, the sale of a property is a signal for the reassessment of that property based on its most recent price; the data in such cases are clear, current, and direct. However, a reevaluation of the properties in the area or district as a whole should follow. Otherwise, the higher prices registered for recently sold properties will result in higher property tax burdens on these properties relative to others in the area. A lag in the reassessment of unsold parcels can result in the redistribution of the property tax burden—solely on the basis of the timing of a sale. If a small staff or other constraints preclude annual review and reassessment of all properties, it would be more equitable to postpone the reassessment of any properties sold on the market until the number of transactions yields sufficient evidence (and there is enough time) for a general reassessment.

Regression analysis A somewhat more sophisticated method for placing a value on property is multiple regression analysis, essentially a statistical technique for correlating independent variables with a dependent variable to predict market value.

In using this method for appraisal, the characteristics of properties may be used as independent variables in an equation where the dependent variable is the estimate of property value. The coefficients for the independent variables indicate the expected changes in property value from a change in the independent variable (e.g., the nature of improvements).[26]

Multiple regressions for property values A multiple regression for assessing property values takes the form of:

$$\hat{y} = a + b_1x_1 + b_2x_2 + b_3x_3 + \ldots + x_n, \text{ where:}$$

$\hat{y}$ = the estimated market value of properties

$x_1, \ldots, x_n$ = the values of the independent variables

$b_1, \ldots, b_n$ = the coefficients or parameters for the independent variables

a = the intercept value, or the estimated value if zero values were associated with the independent variables.

For this purpose, the independent variables would be the characteristics of the properties in the sample. Examples of such variables would include lot size, location, front footage, type of building, type of construction, number of rooms, and square feet. The data used to estimate the property value would be the market value (dependent variable y) and the property characteristics (independent variables x) for each parcel in the sample of recorded sales.

To see how the equation would be interpreted, let us assume that the equation is related to single-family homes, that x_1 is the independent variable representing the number of bathrooms, and that b_1 (the coefficient for x_1) is $800. On this basis, with all other property characteristics or values for independent variables held constant, the estimated sales price (y) would increase by $800 for each unit increase in the value of x_1 or for each additional bathroom. If the equation is in logarithmic form, the value for b_1 would be expressed as a percentage change in the value of the estimated sales price for a change in the value of the independent variable. Applications of this equation could include the prediction of different levels of prices associated with different neighborhoods in the community as well as the prediction of different property values within the neighborhood that are associated with differences in lot size, size and type of structure, and other characteristics of the property. If the capitalization argument is followed, however, the tax rate also has an impact on the property value which, in turn, has an impact on the tax. If these interrelationships are not taken into account, the estimated coefficients will be biased. Multiple regression analysis must be used very carefully.

Replacement cost Another approach is to estimate the replacement cost for improvements on the property. The replacement value approach involves estimating the value of an existing improvement or structure on the property based on the current cost of construction, less a depreciation allowance for the age of the building. The size, number of rooms, building materials, and similar characteristics of the structure are specifically taken into account, and the estimate of replacement cost is made according to current building costs.

The depreciation factors, classified by type of structure, permit the value of the building to be adjusted for age and condition. Subtracting depreciation from the cost of reconstruction yields a net replacement value, which may be roughly checked against available current prices for alternative buildings, even though the buildings may differ somewhat in construction, age, or condition.

The land value of the building site is estimated separately by noting sales prices of parcels that are similar in terms of zoning, general location, size, and any other factors that might affect desirability and price. Both front footage and square footage of the site may serve as bases for determining the lot value. The values derived may be roughly compared to market transactions for vacant land. Finally, the total of land value plus the depreciated replacement cost of the structure may be compared to the recent sales prices of other properties in order to test the combined estimate. Although sales prices are used to confirm the estimated assessed value, the other steps are required because no one property is exactly similar to another.

When buildings are clustered in housing developments or industrial parks, estimating property values may be relatively easy since location differences will tend to be minor. In addition, the external checks for market prices may be applied to determine whether the separate assessment valuations for the properties in the group are within a likely range.[27]

Capitalized value As explained earlier, yet another method of estimating the market value of property is to capitalize the estimated net income obtainable from the property by discounting the net income at a weighted average of the going rate of interest and the desired rate of return on the equity investment in the property. Although this approach is seldom used as the sole basis for assessment, it is useful in checking the values derived by the other approaches.[28] Direct capitalization is particularly helpful when the market for a type of property (e.g., hotels and theaters) is imperfect or limited. The success of direct capitalization hinges on the availability of reliable estimates of annual income or rent, accurate estimates of operating expenses, and allowances for depreciation. The availability of such estimates permits calculation of the income for the property. The income or annual rent after operating expenses may then be divided by a current discount rate to estimate the property value. For example, if the net cash flow from a property is $100,000 and the required rate of return is 12.5 percent, then the estimated property value would be $800,000.

The capitalization method leads to underassessment, however, if the property is not used in a way that will yield its highest possible income. An example is a property being held primarily for speculation on future appreciation in value. Such cases should be revealed in the process of checking the results of the capitalization method with available market data. Any large disparity in estimates of market value—in the absence of specific zoning, classification, or other provisions to the contrary—should be resolved by using the estimate reflecting highest possible return. The higher value, indicated by sales data, would reflect the market estimate of the capitalized value of the property in its highest, most profitable use.[29]

Exceptions Extraordinary cases do exist where the methods of valuation do not apply. For example, properties such as an operating railroad or public utility that serve an area larger than a particular district are not appropriate for local assessment. If the assessment is left to each jurisdiction, anomalies arise and the whole operation may be overtaxed. Estimates of the values of the separate parts of a system may make little sense compared to a valuation of the system as a whole. It is questionable whether a locality that has a portion of the total system—the railroad yards and terminals, for example—in its boundaries should impose a cost on all riders. It is also questionable whether utilities should be required to pay a property tax that is built into the utility rates for all users—especially when there are general overall taxes on utility revenues in most states. Thus many state governments assume responsibility for the assessment of railroad and utility property. In some instances, the states apportion the centrally assessed value among the districts; in others, they collect the tax for themselves.[30]

For some industries, alternative taxes have been developed in lieu of the property tax because the effects of the property tax could conflict with public policy. For example, property taxes on the value of forests may induce earlier cutting than would otherwise be economically justifiable. In many jurisdictions a severance tax, which is levied on the value of timber when it is cut and sold or used by the owner, has replaced the property tax.[31] The severance tax does not require annual payments, which might force the owners to cut timber prematurely in order to raise cash to pay taxes. The severance tax has also been used in extractive industries.[32]

Periodic reassessment Adjusting the assessment of each parcel of taxable property—ideally on an annual basis—is necessary to maintain a reasonable relationship between the assessment base and market values. The problem is not simply to keep the tax base at an appropriate level but, more important, to keep individual properties in line. Although market trends may be clear for real estate prices as a whole, the rate and direction of the trends are unlikely to be uniform. For example, there can be many declining neighborhoods in a central city that is surrounded by exuberant suburban developments; during any time period, market values could be declining in one neighborhood and rising in another. Periodic reassessment must be frequent enough to reflect these changes. The longer the time between reassessments, the greater the variations between the assessed and market values for particular properties, and the greater the dispersion in the ratios of assessed to market values among properties and neighborhoods.

The reassessment should result in a substantial reduction in the coefficient of dispersion for the district; this is a measure of how close the ratios of assessed values to market price of different properties are to each other. It serves as an index of the amount of inequity in the assessments. (The coefficient of dispersion is described in more detail in the next section.)

In large assessment districts with well-staffed offices, periodic reassessment is a continuing function; every property is assessed every few years using a combination of mass appraisal, site-visit techniques, and sampling and statistical methods. There may be, of course, some lag in the adjustments for different areas, but the judicious rotation of areas should permit an organized staff to deal with this problem, in spite of the budgetary constraints that may preclude annual reassessment of all areas and parcels.

In small districts, staff limitations (in both numbers and competence) may preclude the frequent reassessment of existing parcels. The principal effort may be devoted to recording new properties and construction and noting new prices reflected in transfers. In such cases, the passage of time nurtures inequity.

The problem of infrequent assessments can be relieved in several ways. One method that has been used to some degree in recent years is consolidating small assessment districts to achieve economies of scale. The result has been a decline in the number of assessment districts and a concomitant increase in the areas served by full-time assessors.

A second and perhaps better solution lies in periodic reassessment of smaller districts by outside agencies, preferably by professionally qualified consulting firms. This requires a new assessment of all areas and properties in the district.

Frequent reassessment also can be facilitated by use of the computer. The assessor can code and transfer most of the information on the property records—including property descriptions and assessed values—to computer files. The assessor can, similarly, record all property transactions by noting the price that is stated when the deed is recorded. In localities where the full purchase price is not required to be written on the deed or reflected by transfer tax stamps, the information can be obtained by contacting the participants in the transaction.

The sales files may then be listed by the identification number of the parcel (which will also indicate its location), the date of the transaction, the assessed value, and the sale price or adjusted market value. This procedure permits calculation of an assessment ratio—the ratio between the current assessed value and the market price. This process has been used not only by local tax bodies, such as counties or school districts, but also by state tax equalization boards and the Census of Governments.[33] If the assessment process has been reasonably accurate and the property market stable, the assessment to market price ratio will be close to the official assessment ratio of the jurisdiction.

Separate samplings may be developed for different areas of the district and different types of property, for each zone, or for any other relevant characteristic. The assessment ratios may serve as the basis for updating assessments in each relevant category of similar properties. Adequate sales data should permit this procedure to be carried out annually at a reasonable cost with a minimum amount of on-site appraisals.[34]

After giving property owners adequate notice of the new values, a procedure for extensive review and appeal is usually established before the results of the reassessment are used to determine the tax levy. After all, the less frequent the reassessment, the more heroic the final adjustments will be and the greater the stress on individual property owners. Sharp changes in value will surely raise opposition to the implementation of reassessment; such opposition is less likely if changing values are accommodated more gradually. On the other hand, in boom areas such as California, for example, when the assessor keeps assessment values abreast of rising property values, the property tax escalates faster than income and local governments ride a curve of rising revenues. In fact, the revolt against the property tax stemmed from the combination of proportionately greater growth of property values relative to income and the increasing employment of computer technology that keeps assessments up-to-date.

The difficulty individual property owners may have in meeting sharply rising tax levies during a period of rapid value changes may lead to calls for special classification of land for agricultural use, or for a moratorium on the implementation of the new assessments on old holdings. On the other hand, such measures may be opposed by the owners of new homes who, when old properties are reassessed, benefit from the equalization in the tax burden.[35]

Evaluating the assessment How is the quality of the assessment itself to be evaluated? As this section shows, several problems related to assessment accuracy—discrimination regarding assessment of various classes of properties, or overassessment—can be tested objectively by calculating the average coefficient of dispersion, that is, the deviation from the mean of the assessment ratios for different individual properties or property classes. The coefficient provides an estimate of how accurately the assessor apportioned the property tax burden among owners of different properties according to their "true value"; a lower coefficient indicates a more consistent assessment. While more sophisticated statistical techniques can be used, historically the coefficient of dispersion has been the accepted measure of uniformity in assessment practice and probably serves its function well enough.

The coefficient is calculated in four steps, illustrated in Table 9–10. The first, based on bona fide sales prices, is to determine the assessment ratio for the parcels in a sample of recently sold properties. The second is to determine the mean (average) or median of the assessment ratios for the sample of transactions. The third is to compute the average deviation of the individual property assessment ratios from the mean or median. The final step consists of relating the average deviation to the mean or median. The result is the coefficient of dispersion.[36]

In Table 9–10, the coefficient of dispersion is 19.8 percent. A coefficient of dispersion of 20 percent or less might be explained by imperfections in the raw data and by problems inherent in valuation procedures. A coefficient of less than 20 percent is generally considered quite good.

A problem in some localities is apparent discrimination against or in favor of some classes of properties, such as industrial, commercial, rental residential, or homeowner. Private dwellings, for example, may be assessed at 60 percent, rental properties at 50 percent, commercial at 40 percent, and industrial at 30 percent. If there are enough representative sales in each category, the assertion of bias can be tested objectively. The test is similar to the coefficient of dispersion, but the average assessment ratio of each *category* is substituted for the assessment ratios of the *separate properties*. This procedure permits the calculation of a coefficient of dispersion relating the average assessment ratios of the different classes of property to the overall ratio for the district.[37] The different assessment ratios may not be the fault of the assessor but may reflect the accepted political view of the tax-bearing capacity of different properties.

Another occasional problem is overassessment of low-value properties relative to higher-priced properties. Sometimes called regressive assessment, this may occur because the assessor is more familiar with the values of lower-priced properties, which are generally sold more frequently. On large properties, which

Table 9–10 Illustrative table for coefficient of dispersion (hypothetical values).

Property	Recent price ($)	Assessment value ($)	Assessment ratio[a]	Deviation from mean[b]
Parcel A	100,000	37,000	37%	55 − 37 = 18
Parcel B	80,000	40,000	50%	55 − 50 = 5
Parcel C	75,000	30,000	40%	55 − 40 = 15
Parcel D	70,000	42,000	60%	55 − 60 = 5
Parcel E	65,000	41,000	63%	55 − 63 = 8
Parcel F	60,000	33,000	55%	55 − 55 = 0
Parcel G	35,000	28,000	80%	55 − 80 = 25
Mean assessment ratio			55%	Average deviation 10.9%

$$\text{Coefficient of dispersion} = \frac{\text{Average deviation from mean assessment ratio}}{\text{Mean assessment ratio}} = \frac{10.9}{55.0} = .198 \text{ or } 19.8\%$$

[a] The assessment ratio is the assessment value as a percentage of the recent price. The average for the seven parcels is calculated at 55 percent. For this illustration, the mean or average value is equal to the median value associated with Parcel F. Use of the median is an alternative to use of the mean value and, where the values are different, the results may vary.

[b] The calculation of the deviation is for the absolute value and disregards the sign, or whether the assessment ratio on a parcel is above or below the mean or median.

often are unique, the assessor may give the benefit of the doubt. The assessment ratios in Table 9–10 roughly reflect a condition of regressive assessment. The average assessment is 55 percent. The properties with sales prices of $75,000 or more are assessed below the average; those with lower prices are assessed at or above the average.

The problem of regressive assessment also may be exposed by calculating the price-related differential in the assessment ratios. The first step is to calculate a weighted aggregate assessment ratio (the total value of all assessments divided by the total values of the parcels in the sample). The second step is to calculate an unweighted average of the assessment ratios. The means of the unweighted assessment ratios divided by the aggregate assessment ratio give the price-related differential. If the two ratios are equal, the price-related differential will be 1, or 100 percent. If the price-related differential is substantially greater than 100 percent, it suggests underassessment of higher-priced properties. A value considerably less than 100 percent would indicate the underassessment of lower-priced properties. In Table 9–10, for example, the total of the prices of parcels listed is $485,000 and the total of assessed values is $251,000. The weighted assessment ratio is $\frac{251}{485}$ or 52 percent, while the mean (unweighted assessment ratio) is 55 percent. Thus, the price-related differential is $\frac{55}{52}$ or 106 percent, reflecting underassessment of higher-priced properties.

The existence of a price-related differential may be more important for properties within a given category than for properties in different categories.[38] Political problems may arise if there is a price-related bias in the assessment ratios of residences in general, or if one section of the city or district is overassessed relative to others. A lower assessment of industrial properties (as compared to residential or commercial properties), however, may be the result of a deliberate policy to attract industrial employers and to stimulate economic development.

In spite of improvements, evidence suggests the need for better property tax administration in a substantial majority of districts. Behrens has noted that the 1982 Census of Governments survey found only 16 states with the median of coefficients for different assessment districts within the state lower than 20 percent. Nationally, the median of coefficients, which fell from 29.9 percent in 1956 to 19.2 percent in 1966, rose again to 21.3 percent in 1981. Apparently more than half of the assessment authorities fell below the quality criterion and had excessive ranges in the ratio of assessments to market value among different properties.[39]

Exemptions

Some properties and owners are eligible for exemptions. These exemptions, which may be partial or complete, are granted under law on the basis of the use of the property (e.g., hospitals, homesteads, and educational and religious institutions) or on the basis of the status of the owners (e.g., the elderly, veterans, persons with low income, and firms with industrial development incentives), and they vary in their financial impact. If a high proportion of the land is held by large universities, churches, hospitals, public housing authorities, or state and federal government agencies, the impact on the jurisdiction can be severe. Even when these organizations make payments in lieu of taxes, the payments seldom equal the amount that would be obtained through property taxes. ACIR has estimated that local governments lose $3.65 billion a year in taxes that would otherwise be collected on federally owned property. In 1982, the Committee for Intergovernmental Tax Equity, which was formed by local officials to encourage a program of federal payments in lieu of property taxes on federal property, estimated the 1978 value of such property at $279 billion.[40] Of course, the tax-exempt entities may return services and economic value to the community in excess of the taxes forgone. In general, though, it may be better to subsidize such activities directly rather than by tax exemption.

Many exempt properties do not carry even a shadow assessment. The failure to assess these properties has prevented full knowledge of the costs of the exemptions. Recommendations for improvement are to assess such property, repeal permanent exemptions, use exemptions only on a limited basis, and estimate the revenues lost by exemption of certain properties (including the exemptions used to attract industry) at a cost to owners of taxable properties.[41] A review of the uses of exempt property, to ensure that such uses are in the public interest, has also been recommended as a way to reduce the controversy surrounding property tax exemptions.[42] As part of a package to aid localities, Connecticut has authorized special grants to "distressed municipalities" for 75 percent of the taxes lost in exempting certain manufacturing properties.[43]

Many states and localities offer industrial exemptions as part of their economic development programs, the principal goal of which is to expand or sustain local levels of employment. This goal appears justified because local taxpayers have something to gain by bearing a higher property tax burden to subsidize new industry. Higher employment helps maintain the value and prices of local property and, ultimately, adds to the local tax base. However, critics of these inducements note that exemption policies invite retaliation or imitation by other jurisdictions; so many areas now offer exemptions that there may no longer be any competitive advantage in doing so.[44]

Determining the levy

To determine the required property tax levy, budget officers usually subtract the forecasted amounts of local government revenues (derived from sources other than the property tax) from the total estimated expenditures. The property tax rate is then obtained by dividing the required levy by the total value of property assessments and adjusting for anticipated delinquencies and estimated tax collections from past delinquencies. The resulting tax rate is expressed in mills per dollar (or tax dollars per thousand dollars) of assessed value.[45]

Collection

The amount of tax due on each piece of property is the tax rate times the assessed value of the parcel. Bills reflecting the tax assessment, tax rate, total liability, and terms of payment (dates and discount and penalty rates) are sent by the tax collector to the property owner of record. In some states, billing and collection are centralized by the county; in others, the cities, counties, and school districts may all collect these taxes separately. The tax traditionally has been collected in one annual payment in the year after the assessment, but use of quarterly and semiannual installments has become increasingly popular.

The imposition of penalties and interest charges for late payments is part of the program of enforcing collection. In many jurisdictions, however, the penalty interest rate is below the market interest rate. This encourages delinquencies because in a sense owners may obtain relatively low-cost loans by delaying payment. Liens against the property are imposed when the tax remains unpaid for a long period. Continued delinquency may lead to seizure and eventually to the forced sale of the property to recover the delinquent taxes.

Although the functions of the tax collector and the assessor may be separate, their offices should be well coordinated. Both should have access to the information on the tax roll, and both must be prepared to defend their actions in assessment appeals or enforcement procedures.

Site-value taxation

There has long been an argument that the property tax should be based on land values alone, regardless of improvements. Proponents of this view argue that a tax on improvements discourages capital investment. They note that land values as distinct from building and improvement values are derived from community investment and development of public facilities (e.g., sewers and roads), so that a land-value tax is an appropriate way to recapture some of that investment. A tax on land value is also neutral, because it does not discriminate for or against any particular land use; the most profitable use is the same before and after a land tax.

Some site-value taxation proposals would exempt improvements (partially or wholly) in order to encourage building, achieve more intensive land use, and reduce urban decay and housing costs by encouraging the replacement of deteriorated buildings on valuable sites.[46] Such proposals, however, have been seriously questioned on the basis of revenue adequacy; improvements are a major part of the current tax base. There have also been questions about equity in the subsequent shifts of the property tax burden. Current owners of land may be penalized because they paid prices based on a long-standing tax system. In addition, the need to alter state laws and constitutions imposes serious political obstacles.[47]

An empirical study of the effects of implementing a site-value or land-value tax has indicated that such a tax would lead to substantial investment in improvements in the long run.[48] The total exemption of improvements, however, would require very high site-value assessments or high tax rates on land to maintain property tax revenues. Other empirical studies indicate that on this basis only partial exemption of improvements would be feasible. Otherwise, it would be necessary to supplement property tax revenues from other nonproperty tax sources.[49]

Conclusion

There is, then, no panacea to eliminate the problems of property taxation. Most programs for reform give highest priority to "maintaining uniform assessments through frequent and regular reevaluation of property" as a way to address the issues of poverty and urban decay.[50] ACIR calls for market value appraisal by professionals, under strong state supervision or direct state administration of the assessment system, and with disclosure of assessment ratios so that the fairness of the system can be judged. ACIR also calls for state financing of circuit breaker provisions, state payment of some state-mandated local expenditures, and in-lieu payments for state-mandated property tax exemptions. To avoid further imposition of the severe restrictions required under tax limitation measures, ACIR recommends moderation in the use of and reliance on property taxation. Use of alternative taxes and of state support as sources of revenue that appear more equitable would relieve pressures to restrict local government programs.[51]

Some of the responsibility for the improvement of property tax administration has been assigned to state governments. The Advisory Commission on Intergovernmental Relations, for example, once suggested that the states reform the tax laws to remove such elements as intangible personal property, which is theoretically suspect and impossible to administer; to review exemption laws; to consolidate small assessment districts; to improve assessment personnel standards; and to provide strong state supervision, coordination, and appeal procedures.[52]

The case for more active state supervision is based in part on the feeling that state supervision to achieve efficiency and equity in local tax administration is just as important as a state presence in activities such as education and health.[53] However, more supervision involves more costs and may not be worthwhile in all cases.

Improvements in administration have been noted at both the state and local levels of government. Some states, for example, have extended technical and advisory consulting services to local assessment districts in addition to taking over the assessment of some categories of property. Assessment districts have been made larger by designating the county as the assessment unit and by consolidating small districts. The use of the computer and of mass reappraisal techniques have been extended.

Nevertheless, some of the basic problems in property tax administration remain. As noted earlier, research has tended to confirm a bias toward a lower rate of assessment on properties with higher values, making the property tax somewhat more regressive than need be.[54]

Past surveys of public attitudes toward various types of taxation have shown the property tax to be the least popular. In a 1978 survey, the property tax was favored least by 32 percent of the participants, but the federal income tax was not far behind, favored least by 30 percent. The difference is not very large, and since 1978, the federal income tax has been cited in surveys as the "least fair" or worst tax. The 1985 ACIR survey, in fact, showed the widest gap since 1972 between the federal income tax as worst (38 percent) and the property tax as worst (24 percent).[55] ACIR feels that such results give "little credence" to the notion that people are getting fed up with property taxes.[56] However, in its study of school financing, ACIR cites several reasons for the unpopularity of the property tax:

1. No other tax is so harsh on persons with low incomes and so "capriciously" related to ability to pay.
2. The tax appears to be antihousing when compared to the preferential treatment accorded housing outlays under both the income and sales taxes.
3. The tax is on unrealized capital gains, because increased property values are taxed prior to increases in spendable income.
4. Administration, particularly assessment of the tax base, is more difficult and subjective (especially during inflation) than for any other tax, and the shock of reassessment is "without parallel" for other taxes.
5. Less frequent payment (for those who do not pay monthly to escrow accounts) makes the cost more apparent and "painful" than the current payment of sales and income taxes.[57]

How does the property tax stack up in terms of the criteria noted at the beginning of this chapter?

Fairness The property tax has been criticized as regressive and unfair. Different analyses, based on different assumptions, have reached alternative conclusions concerning the distribution of the burden of the tax. To some extent that distribution has been changed by circuit breaker provisions, although, as noted above, such provisions have been subject to criticism. Property tax classification and equalizing grants (especially for school finance) by state government also have altered the distribution of the tax burden.

Certainty Property tax administration has been criticized as biased and costly. Certainly the variations in assessment practices would not be acceptable for other tax bases, such as income. However, improved state supervision, increased professionalism, and new techniques promise improvements.

Convenience Provisions for more frequent payments through lending institutions and collection procedures have made payment of the property tax much more convenient for many people.

Efficiency The property tax can be administered efficiently by local governments. This is not generally the case for other major taxes, such as income and sales taxes.

Productivity New construction and rising property values in most areas have increased the tax base and provided a fairly stable source of tax revenues despite some fluctuations in income and employment. Local governments require stable, continuing sources of tax revenues to meet locally desired levels of expenditure.

Neutrality The property tax has been criticized for its adverse effects on housing and on capital investment. A land or site-value base would be more neutral although difficult to implement.

In spite of its faults, the property tax does have distinct advantages. Overall, it is a stable and acceptable source of local government revenue that is particularly well suited for local administration. Clear evidence of the property tax on an annual bill permits the property owner to evaluate the costs of locally provided services. The tax enables local governments to capture some of the property value created by the community at large. All in all, since there are substantial problems in finding substitute sources of local government revenue, the local property tax is likely to remain a substantial basis for local government autonomy.[58] And finally, as the volume of federal grants-in-aid is reduced, pressure may build to make even greater use of the property tax.

1 Most of the data in this section are from U.S. Department of Commerce, Bureau of the Census, 1982 Census of Governments, vol. 2, *Taxable Property Values and Assessment—Sales Prices Ratios* (Washington, D.C.: GPO, 1984).

2 J. Richard Aronson, "Intangibles Taxes: A Wisely Neglected Revenue Source for States," *National Tax Journal* 19, no. 2 (June 1966): 187–86.

3 Most of the data cited in this section are from tables in Advisory Commission on Intergovernmental Relations, *Significant Features of Fiscal Federalism, 1984 Edition* (Washington, D.C.: GPO, 1985).

4 John Shannon, "The Property Tax Paradox," *Intergovernmental Perspective* 9, no. 4 (Fall 1983): 30.

5 Advisory Commission on Intergovernmental Relations, *Significant Features of Fiscal Federalism, 1985–86 Edition* (Washington, D.C.: GPO, 1986), p. 138.

6 *Serrano* v. *Priest*, 5 Cal. 3d 584, 487; P.2d 1241; 96 Cal. Rptr. 601 (1971).

7 Advisory Commission on Intergovernmental Relations, *Financing Schools and Property Tax Relief—A State Responsibility*, A–40 (Washington, D.C.: GPO, 1973), pp. 3–4.

8 Advisory Commission on Intergovernmental Relations. *Significant Features of Fiscal Federalism, 1985–86 Edition*, pp. 38–39.

9 Advisory Commission on Intergovernmental Relations, *Tax Burdens for Families Residing in the Largest City in Each State, 1982*, Staff Working Paper 3R (Washington, D.C., August 1984), pp. 37–46.

10 Henry J. Aaron, "A New View of Property Tax Incidence," *American Economic Review* 64, no. 2 (May 1974): 212–21. This view is fully explained and its implications discussed in Henry J. Aaron, *Who Pays the Property Tax?: A New View* (Washington, D.C.: Brookings Institution, 1975).

11 Richard A. Musgrave, "Is a Property Tax on Housing Regressive?" *American Economic Review* 64, no. 2 (May 1974): 222–29.

12 George E. Peterson, comment, *American Economic Review* 64, no. 2 (May 1974): 234–35.

13 Advisory Commission on Intergovernmental Relations, *Financing Schools*, pp. 40–41. These are more fully described in Advisory Commission on Intergovernmental Relations, *Property Tax Circuit-Breakers: Current Status and Policy Issues* (Washington, D.C.: GPO, 1975).

14 Advisory Commission on Intergovernmental Relations, *Significant Features of Fiscal Federalism, 1984 Edition*, pp. 108–15.

15 Ibid., pp. 3, 64–68.

16 Henry Thomassen, "Circuit Breaking and Life-Cycle Lock-In," *National Tax Journal* 31, no. 1 (March 1978): 59–65.

17 Anita A. Summers, "Proposition 13 and Its Aftermath," *Business Review* (Federal Reserve Bank of Philadelphia), March-April 1979: 11.

18 For an explanation of capitalization and formulas for relating these tax rates, see J. Richard Aronson, *Public Finance* (New York: McGraw-Hill, 1985), pp. 333–35.

19 Several types of approaches to special provisions for different uses of land are described by state in U.S. Department of the Census, *1982 Census of Governments*, vol. 2, pp. 269–73.

20 *Citizens Business*, no. 2 (Philadelphia: Pennsylvania Economy League, 26 July 1979), p. 497.

21 Hoy F. Carman, "California Landowners' Adoption

of a Use-Value Assessment Program," *Land Economics* 53, no. 3 (August 1977): 275–87.

22 Mason Gaffney, "Adequacy of Land as a Tax Base," in *The Assessment of Land Value,* ed. Daniel M. Holland (Madison: Univ. of Wisconsin Press, for the Committee on Taxation, Resources, and Economic Development, 1970), pp. 175–76.

23 John O. Behrens, "Taxable Property Values 1 to 6—Matters of De Facto." (Paper prepared for delivery at 17th Annual Conference on Taxation, Nashville, Tenn., 25–28 November 1984.

24 John Shannon, "Conflict between State Assessment Law and Local Assessment Practice," in *Property Taxation—USA,* ed. Richard W. Lindholm (Madison: Univ. of Wisconsin Press, 1967), pp. 39–40.

25 Ibid., pp. 40–61.

26 Paul B. Downing, "Estimating Residential Land Value by Multivariate Analysis," in *The Assessment of Land Value,* ed. Daniel M. Holland, pp. 101–23.

27 Kenneth Back, "Land Value Taxation in Light of Current Assessment Theory and Practice," in *The Assessment of Land Value,* ed. Daniel M. Holland, pp. 38–39.

28 Ibid., p. 38.

29 James M. Buchanan and Marilyn R. Flowers, *The Public Finances,* 5th ed. (Homewood, Ill.: Richard D. Irwin, 1980), pp. 473–76.

30 James A. Maxwell and J. Richard Aronson, *Financing State and Local Governments,* 3d ed. (Washington, D.C.: Brookings Institution, 1977), pp. 134–65.

31 W. David Klemperer, "An Economic Analysis of the Case Against Ad Valorem Property Taxation in Forestry," *National Tax Journal* 30, no. 4 (December 1977): 469.

32 See, for example, Tax Institute of America, *The Property Tax: Problems and Potentials* (Princeton, N.J., 1967), pp. 143–204.

33 See, for example, *30th Certification of the Pennsylvania State Tax Equalization Board* (Harrisburg, 30 June 1978); and U.S. Bureau of the Census, *1982 Census of Governments.*

34 Ted Gwartney, "A Computerized Assessment Program," in *The Assessment of Land Value,* ed. Daniel M. Holland, pp. 125–41.

35 *Philadelphia Evening Bulletin,* 4 August 1972, p. 5. This account describes the activities, including a protest march, of organizations formed in response to a new reassessment in Bucks County, Pennsylvania. Such protests were by no means uncommon in the 1970s.

36 A technical point worth noting here is that the value of the coefficient will differ if the median rather than the mean is used in this calculation in cases where they are not equal, because that inequality results from a skewed distribution.

37 These issues are discussed extensively in Karl E. Case, *Property Taxation: The Need for Reform* (Cambridge, Mass.: Ballinger Publishing Co., 1978).

38 Harold F. McClelland, "Property Tax Assessment," in *The American Property Tax: Its History, Administration and Economic Impact,* ed. George C. S. Benson et al. (Claremont, Calif.: Institute for Studies in Federalism, Claremont Men's College, 1965), pp. 109–10.

39 Behrens, "Taxable Property Values."

40 Advisory Commission on Intergovernmental Relations, *Intergovernmental Perspective* 8, no. 3 (Summer 1982): 6.

41 Aaron, "A New View," pp. 84–85.

42 Summers, "Proposition 13," p. 11.

43 *Intergovernmental Perspective* 5, no. 1 (Winter 1979): 17.

44 Paul E. Alyea, "Property-Tax Inducements to Attract Industry," in *Property Taxation—USA,* ed. Richard W. Lindholm, pp. 139–58.

45 Bernard P. Herber, Modern Public Finance, *The Study of Public Sector Economics,* 2d ed. (Homewood, Ill.: Richard D. Irwin, 1971), p. 230.

46 Dick Netzer, *Economics and Urban Problems,* 2d ed. (New York: Basic Books, 1974), pp. 256–58.

47 Advisory Commission on Intergovernmental Relations, *Financing Schools,* p. 72.

48 Richard L. Pollock and Donald C. Shoup, "The Effect of Shifting the Property Tax Base from Improvement Value to Land Value: An Empirical Estimate," *Land Economics* 53, no. 1 (February 1977): 67–77.

49 Richard W. Douglas, Jr., "Site Value Taxation and Manvel's Land Value Estimates," *American Journal of Economics and Sociology* 37, no. 2 (April 1978): 217–23.

50 Summers, "Proposition 13," p. 11.

51 John Shannon and Carol Weissert, "After Jarvis: Tough Questions for Fiscal Policymakers." *Intergovernmental Perspective* 4, no. 3 (Summer 1978): 1–18.

52 Advisory Commission on Intergovernmental Relations, *The Role of the States in Strengthening the Property Tax,* vol. 1 (Washington, D.C.: GPO, 1963); and Robert J. Cline and John Shannon, "The Property Tax in a Model State-Local Revenue System," in C. Lowell Harriss, ed., *The Property Tax and Local Finance* (Proceedings of the Academy of Political Science) 35, no. 1 (1983), pp. 42–56.

53 Maxwell and Aronson, *Financing State and Local Governments,* pp. 155–56.

54 David E. Black, "Property Tax Incidence: The Excise-Tax Effect and Assessment Practices," *National Tax Journal* 30, no. 4 (December 1977): 429–34.

55 Advisory Commission on Intergovernmental Relations, *Significant Features of Fiscal Federalism, 1985 Edition,* p. 138.

56 Advisory Commission on Intergovernmental Relations, *Significant Features of Fiscal Federalism, 1984 Edition,* p. 139.

57 Advisory Commission on Intergovernmental Relations, *Financing Schools,* p. 30.

58 Ibid.

Sales taxes, income taxes, and other nonproperty tax revenues

The single most important tax levied by local governments is the property tax. However, over 50 percent of the revenue collected by local governments from their own sources is derived from local sales and income taxes, various other taxes and charges, and miscellaneous general revenue. Reliance on property tax revenues has been declining steadily over the past 30 years, with the sharpest five-year drop in history occurring between 1976 and 1982 (see Table 10–1). In this period the share of property tax revenue in own-source general revenue fell from 59 percent to 48 percent. This decline was accompanied by an almost equivalent increase in the use of charges and miscellaneous sources of revenue, such as school lunch sales, hospital fees, and interest earnings. Reliance on these sources rose from 26.8 percent to 36.9 percent over the same period. Local governments as a whole continued to rely on sales taxes, income taxes, and other types of nonproperty tax levies—the third major category of local general revenue—to about the same degree as in the mid-1970s.[1]

This chapter focuses primarily on nonproperty taxes, the two most important being sales and income taxes. Local governments use nonproperty tax revenues to (1) obtain additional revenue while avoiding increases in the property tax, (2) achieve a wider distribution of the local tax burden among those who benefit from public services, (3) make the tax structure more flexible so it can be tailored to fit local conditions, (4) obtain greater responsiveness of local revenues to rising costs and service demands, and (5) reduce the relatively high rates of taxation that can arise in overlapping jurisdictions when all rely on the property tax as their major revenue source.

First the chapter describes the general significance of local nonproperty tax revenues in the overall local government revenue picture. Then sales taxes and income taxes are discussed in terms of features, extent of use, administrative procedures, and major issues. A brief evaluative conclusion follows each section. The chapter concludes with a description of other miscellaneous tax

Table 10–1 Percentage of local government revenues from own sources, selected years, 1957 to 1981–82.

Revenue source	1957	1962–63	1966–67	1971–72	1976–77	1981–82
General revenue, total	100.0	100.0	100.0	100.0	100.0	100.0
Taxes	80.0	78.3	76.4	75.9	73.2	63.1
Property	69.3	68.5	66.2	63.5	59.0	48.0
Sales and gross receipts	5.8	5.6	5.1	6.5	8.1	9.0
Income	1.1	1.1	2.4	3.4	3.7	3.7
License and other	3.8	3.1	2.7	2.5	2.5	2.4
Charges and miscellaneous	20.0	21.7	23.6	24.1	26.8	36.9

Sources: U.S. Department of Commerce, Bureau of the Census, *1977 Census of Governments*, vol. 6, *Topical Studies*, no. 4, *Historical Statistics on Governmental Finances and Employment* (Washington D.C.: GPO, 1979), pp. 52–53; and U.S. Department of Commerce, Bureau of the Census, *1982 Census of Governments*, vol 4, *Governmental Finances*, no. 5, *Compendium of Governmental Finances* (Washington, D.C.: GPO, 1984), p. 4.

revenues. Though statistical information and operating details of a sample year in the early 1980s are used, the general principles involved can be expected to remain applicable throughout the 1980s and beyond.[2]

Importance in the revenue structure

The overall importance to local governments of nonproperty tax revenue sources, as well as the composition of these revenue sources, is indicated in Table 10–2. In 1981–82, 82,615 local governments (counties, municipalities, townships, school districts, and special districts) received revenue of over $315 billion. Of this, local general revenues amounted to over $164 billion, with property tax receipts of almost $79 billion. The remainder, composed of various nonproperty taxes and charges and miscellaneous general revenues, accounted for more than 50 percent of local general revenue.

Table 10–1 shows the trend in the percentage of local general revenues from each major source from 1957 through 1981–82. Aside from the relatively modest upward trend in reliance on sales taxes, the most noticeable trends are the marked decline between 1976–77 and 1981–82 in the share of property taxes in local general revenue and the corresponding rise in the share of charges and miscellaneous revenue.

Use of the different revenue sources varies substantially among types of local government. As Table 10–3 indicates, the property tax is used predominantly by school districts and townships, whereas user charges are used extensively by special districts, and sales and income taxes are used predominantly by municipalities.

Table 10–4 looks at reliance on revenue sources from a different perspective, answering such questions as "What type of local government accounts for the bulk of the sales taxes that are raised?" For example, municipalities collected 68.6 percent of all the sales tax revenues received by local governments and

Table 10–2 Local government revenues from all sources, 1981–82.

Revenue source	Revenue (in millions)	% of general revenue
Total	$315,322	
Own sources, total	198,703	
General revenue, total	164,426	100.0
Taxes, total	103,783	63.1
Property	78,952	48.0
Sales, gross receipts, and customs	14,824	9.0
Income	6,097	3.7
License and other	3,909	2.4
Charges and miscellaneous, total	60,643	36.9
Current charges	35,877	21.8
Interest earnings	13,701	8.3
Miscellaneous	11,065	6.7
Other than general revenue, total	34,277	
Utility and liquor store	29,100	
Insurance trust	5,176	
Intergovernmental sources, total	116,619	
From states	95,363	
From federal	21,256	

Source: U.S. Department of Commerce, Bureau of the Census, 1982 *Census of Governments*, vol. 4, *Governmental Finances*, no. 5, *Compendium of Governmental Finances* (Washington, D.C.: GPO, 1984), p. 4.

Note: Due to rounding, totals and percentages may not equal 100 percent.

81.6 percent of all the income tax revenues. Since municipalities received 36.3 percent of all local general revenues raised, municipalities are disproportionately heavy users of sales and income taxes. Table 10–4 also shows that school districts received 26.7 percent of all local general revenues but received 43.6 percent of all property tax revenues, reflecting the disproportionately large reliance of school districts on property taxes.

Why was there such a large decrease in the property tax share and such a correspondingly large increase in the charges and miscellaneous category over the period from 1976–77 to 1981–82? One contributing factor is that counties, municipalities, and special districts raised a higher proportion of own-source local revenue in 1981–82 than five years earlier (whereas school districts and townships raised a lower proportion). Accordingly, their revenue sources would be expected to grow in relative significance (with the reverse being true for the important revenue sources of school districts and townships). Moreover, between 1976–77 and 1981–82 there was a rapid growth in the number of special districts—an increase of more than 2,700, or 10.5 percent—and special districts raised over 80 percent of their revenue from charges and miscellaneous revenues (Table 10–3).[3]

Table 10–3 Percentage distribution of general revenues collected by types of local government, 1981–82.

Revenue source	Counties	Municipalities	Townships	School districts	Special districts
General revenue, total	100.0	100.0	100.0	100.0	100.0
Taxes	59.4	62.2	79.6	81.0	18.3
Property	45.9	32.7	74.6	78.4	14.6
Sales and gross receipts	9.5	17.1	0.2	1.0	3.4
Income	1.7	8.3	2.0	0.8	—
Licenses and other	2.3	4.0	2.8	0.8	0.3
Charges and miscellaneous	40.6	37.8	20.3	19.0	81.7
Charges	25.5	21.0	9.2	9.5	56.1
Interest earnings	8.2	8.5	5.7	5.9	16.1
Other miscellaneous	6.9	8.4	5.6	3.6	9.5

Source: U.S. Department of Commerce, Bureau of the Census, *1982 Census of Governments*, vol. 4, *Governmental Finances*, no. 5, *Compendium of Governmental Finances* (Washington, D.C.: GPO, 1984), p. 4.

Note: Due to rounding, percentages may not equal 100 percent.

Table 10–4 Percentage distribution of local government general revenues, by type of local government, 1981–82.

		Taxes					Current charges and miscellaneous		
Type of local government	Total	Total	Property	Sales and gross receipts	Income	License and other	Total	Current charges	Miscellaneous general revenue
All	100.0	100.0	100.0	100.0	100.0	100.0	100.0	100.0	100.0
Counties	23.5	22.1	22.5	24.8	10.7	23.0	25.9	27.5	24.0
Municipalities	36.3	35.7	24.7	68.6	81.6	61.6	37.2	34.9	45.2
Townships	4.1	5.2	6.4	—	2.2	4.9	2.3	1.7	3.3
School districts	26.7	34.2	43.6	2.9	5.5	9.4	13.8	11.6	14.2
Special districts	9.4	2.7	2.9	3.6	—	1.2	20.9	24.3	13.3

Source: U.S. Department of Commerce, Bureau of the Census, *1982 Census of Governments*, vol. 4, *Governmental Finances*, no. 5, *Compendium of Governmental Finances* (Washington, D.C.: GPO, 1984), p. 4.

Note: (—) indicates negligible amount or not used.

The changing revenue significance of different types of local government is not, however, a complete explanation for the shift in revenue shares. Consider Table 10–5, which shows the same information as Table 10–3, but for 1976–77. A comparison of these tables shows that every type of local government reduced reliance on the property tax over the five-year period and increased reliance on charges and miscellaneous sources of revenue. Moreover, all derived a larger share of revenue from interest and from other miscellaneous sources, and all but special districts increased their reliance on charges. These shifts in the revenue shares for all types of local government may have been the result, at least in part, of the tax and spending limitation movement.

Another factor contributing to the shift in revenue shares is the relatively high rate of price inflation that occurred over the period. Between 1976–77 and 1981–82, prices rose by about 60 percent. If assessments of property are not continually revised to match increases in market value, property tax revenues will tend to rise at a slower rate than prices and money incomes. Furthermore, high rates of inflation also bring high interest rates (as lenders build expectations of rapid inflation into the interest rates they require borrowers to pay). Inflation has therefore contributed to the increased share of revenues every type of local government derives from interest earnings.

Table 10–5 Percentage distribution of local government general revenues by revenue source, 1976–77.

Revenue source	Counties	Munici-palities	Townships	School districts	Special districts
General revenue, total	100.0	100.0	100.0	100.0	100.0
Taxes	69.8	71.2	88.2	86.8	24.8
Property	56.7	42.7	80.8	84.6	22.7
Sales and gross receipts	8.7	15.8	3.0	0.6	1.9
Income	1.7	8.5	1.6	0.6	—
Licenses and other	2.7	4.2	2.7	0.8	0.2
Charges and miscellaneous	30.2	28.8	11.8	13.2	75.2
Charges	22.2	18.6	6.0	8.6	60.9
Interest earnings	3.0	3.6	1.6	2.2	7.7
Other miscellaneous	4.9	6.6	4.3	2.4	6.6

Source: U.S. Department of Commerce, Bureau of the Census, *1977 Census of Governments*, vol. 4, *Governmental Finances*, no. 5, *Compendium of Governmental Finances* (Washington, D.C.: GPO, 1979), p. 24.

Note: Due to rounding, percentages may not equal 100 percent.

Local general sales taxes

The first local general sales taxes[4] were adopted in the 1930s, a time when significant reductions had occurred in local revenues as a result of the Great Depression. New York City adopted a sales tax in 1934, followed by New Orleans in 1938. In 1950 Mississippi adopted a system of state-administered local sales taxes, an innovation that significantly enhanced the feasibility of the tax for a large number of local governments.

The most rapid period of expansion in the use of local sales taxes occurred in the 1960s, when the number of states authorizing local sales taxes increased from 12 in 1963 to 25 in 1970. By the early 1980s, local governments in 27 states and the District of Columbia were levying sales taxes. In addition, three other states (Florida, Kentucky, and Wisconsin) had authorized the sales tax for use by local governments, although none had chosen to levy it. Most local sales taxes are authorized by state legislation, although some are based on home rule charter or general licensing powers. Among the 27 states where local governments levy the sales tax, the tax rate ranges from a low of 0.25 percent in some Utah localities and in Albuquerque, New Mexico, to a high of 4 percent in New

York City. (These figures exclude Alaska, which has no state sales tax.) The combination of local rates and the state rate can become substantial. In cities of over 100,000 population, such combined rates in the early 1980s ranged from a low of 3.5 percent in some Nevada and Kansas cities to a high of 8.25 percent in New York City and Yonkers, New York. The number of local governments using the tax ranges from a high of more than 1,300 in Illinois to a low of only 1 municipality in the states of Minnesota and Mississippi.

In 1981–82 sales and gross receipts tax revenue amounted to $14.8 billion (see Table 10–2), of which $10.2 billion represented general sales tax receipts and $4.6 billion represented receipts from selective sales taxes on particular goods and services. Thus, general sales tax receipts represented about 6.2 percent of the general revenues for all local governments; however, for municipalities the percentage was considerably larger at 10.6 percent.

Revenue yield

The revenue yield of any tax depends on the tax base and the tax rate applied to this base. For a given tax rate, the yield will vary as the base (sales subject to the tax) varies. Important to local government managers and finance directors are the questions of what revenue yields can be expected from a newly imposed local sales tax, how the yield can be expected to grow with the local economy and fluctuate over the business cycle, and how exemptions, especially for food, will affect the yield.

In states having a sales tax, local jurisdictions can estimate the revenue expected from a local sales tax by obtaining information about recent state sales tax receipts in the local government jurisdiction. If there is no state sales tax, a less precise estimate can be made based on the experience of other local jurisdictions of similar size, economic characteristics, and retail outlets, making allowance for differences in tax rates and exemptions. In either case, if the sales tax is to be applied in a locality adjacent to a nontax area to which retail sales may be diverted, the estimates may be excessive. Some actual experience with the tax will be necessary to determine the expected revenue yield.

Sales tax receipts vary with fluctuations in business activity and income of the local economy. Numerous studies have attempted to estimate the effect of changes in income on the yields of major state and local taxes. The results have been assembled by the U.S. Advisory Commission on Intergovernmental Relations (ACIR).[5] The estimates are for state rather than local taxes, but they constitute the best proxy evidence available on the question of yield variability of local sales taxes. The studies of state sales taxes show that a 1.0 percent change in total income causes a change in sales tax revenue of between 0.8 and 1.27 percent, with the most frequent estimate in nationwide studies being 1.0 percent. Thus, sales tax revenues fluctuate with income and grow over time at about the same rate as income grows. This contrasts with personal income taxes, whose yields are estimated (in all studies) to fluctuate (or grow) more than proportionately to changes in income. Property tax revenues, on the other hand, are found in most studies to fluctuate less than income. Hence, the sales tax lies somewhere between these other local taxes in the variability of its yield relative to changing economic conditions.

Exemption of food consumed at home significantly reduces the yield of a sales tax between 15 and 20 percent.[6] Thus, a 5 percent sales tax with no food exemption would generate about the same revenue as a 6 percent tax with a food exemption. The major reason usually given for exempting food is to make the sales tax less regressive. While the exemption of food does achieve this objective, there are other methods that can be used in many situations to achieve a similar effect without sustaining the increased costs of compliance and administration that the food exemption entails.

Features

For all their differences, local sales taxes share a number of important features. First, virtually all general sales taxes are *ad valorem* rather than *per unit* taxes. That is, the tax is computed as a percentage of the value of a transaction rather than as a fixed amount per unit of the good exchanged (as is the practice with cigarette and gasoline taxes).

Second, the tax is levied on retail, not wholesale, purchasers. The law requires vendors to collect and pay the tax to the local government via the consumer; hence, the tax is often called the "consumers' sales tax." (The question of who actually bears the burden of the local retail sales tax, referred to as the *incidence* of the tax, will be discussed later.) Most states having state sales taxes require, or at least encourage, separate quotation of the tax from the price. Presumably, this requirement extends to sales taxes levied by local governments within states having such laws. Furthermore, almost every state prohibits sellers from advertising the absorption of state sales taxes. Again, such prohibitions presumably extend to local sales taxes in those states as well.

Because sales taxes are intended to be paid at the retail level, resale items are usually not taxed. Thus, raw materials to be incorporated into a finished product destined for ultimate sale to the consumer are not taxed. However, sales of such items as tools and coal, which are used or consumed in manufacturing and not incorporated into the product to be sold, usually are taxable. Thus, a phenomenon known as *tax pyramiding* (i.e., adding taxes on a tax) does occur when such items as tools and coal are taxed. It is more pronounced in some products and services than in others.

A third common feature is the disallowance of deductions for losses or necessary business expenses permitted under net income taxes, hence the name "gross proceeds taxes"; the retailer is responsible for collecting and remitting the sales tax regardless of whether the business enjoys a positive accounting profit. Similarly, the sales tax does not take into account the personal circumstances of the consumer, as an income tax often does through exemptions and deductions. Thus, a sales tax is sometimes described as an *in rem* rather than a *personal* levy. Because of this, the sales tax is frequently criticized for being horizontally inequitable (failing to treat persons or families having the same incomes equally) and vertically inequitable (failing to discriminate appropriately among those having unequal incomes). However, as will be discussed later, the *in rem* character of sales taxes is neither inevitable nor necessary.

A fourth common feature is that sales taxes are imposed directly *on* sales at the point of sale, and thus may be distinguished from the gross proceeds, occupation, or license taxes that are frequently measured *by* sales. Both the sales tax and license and occupation taxes may be directly related to sales and they may be passed on to the consumer through higher retail prices; however, the amount of the sales tax is expressed as a separate part of the bill at the time of sale and is tax deductible by consumers who itemize federal income tax returns.[7] Gross receipts, occupation, and business privilege taxes are not expressed separately in transactions, nor are they deductible by consumers on individual federal income tax returns.

Except in states where some local jurisdictions administer their own taxes (Alabama, Arizona, Colorado, and Louisiana), the base of a local general sales tax is almost always mandated to be the same as the base of the state sales tax. Considerable diversity exists in state sales tax bases, but all have certain exclusions of goods purchased for business rather than personal use, as well as exemptions of specific consumption goods and services. Twenty-six of the 45 states levying sales taxes exempt food purchased for home consumption; 41 exempt prescription drugs; and 5 exempt clothing. By taking these and other exemptions into account and deducting other categories of consumer expenditures not subject to the retail sales tax (the major item being housing), one can calculate that only slightly more than 37 percent of all consumer expenditures are subject to a general sales tax.[8] Hence, local general sales taxes (like state sales taxes) have a base much narrower than all consumer spending. Nevertheless, the base for a *general* sales tax is still far broader than that of various *selective* sales taxes (often called *excise* taxes) on specific categories of goods such as alcoholic beverages and tobacco products.

To deter residents of a local jurisdiction from making purchases in outside areas where there are no sales taxes or taxes with lower rates, the local sales tax is often accompanied by a *use* tax levied on goods bought outside the jurisdiction and used inside it. The use tax is levied in 23 of the 30 states authorizing local sales taxes. In theory, the use tax, coupled with the assignment of tax liability at the point of delivery (which frees nonresident purchasers from paying the tax), insulates local retailers from loss of sales to either residents or nonresidents. In practice, however, both of these features of local sales taxes have only generated difficult enforcement and compliance problems which will be considered in more detail later.

Extent of use

There is a bewildering variety of local sales taxes. As noted earlier, the extent of use of the tax by local governments varies considerably by state. In addition, responsibility for administration in some states is at the state level and in others at the local level. In 23 of the 30 states authorizing the use of local sales taxes, only the state may administer (i.e., collect and enforce) any local sales tax; in 3 states all administration is done locally; and in 4 states there is a mixture of state and local administration.

Three other features of local sales tax use are (1) the method of local tax coordination, (2) the location of liability, and (3) the method of distributing collected tax revenues back to local governments in states where there is state administration.

The problem of tax coordination arises when sales tax jurisdictions overlap. Whereas some states allow sales tax rates to overlap one another fully, others have tried to eliminate or at least minimize the problem. Some states have established exclusive jurisdictions, allowing only municipalities or only counties to levy the sales tax. Others allow the tax paid in one jurisdiction to be credited against the amount owed in another. However, some states limit the maximum total rate that can apply, and a local government given first priority, such as counties in Tennessee and Kansas, can levy the maximum rate and thereby preclude any other unit of government from levying the tax. The state of New York follows a different procedure, allowing cities and counties each the right to levy half the maximum rate permitted by state law.

Location of liability establishes whether purchases made in a jurisdiction are subject to the tax in that jurisdiction or whether the tax, if any, is to be levied where the purchased item is to be delivered. In the early 1980s, liability was at the retailer location in local jurisdictions in 18 states and at the point of delivery in 9 others. In the former case the jurisdiction receives the sales tax on all purchases made within it, whether the purchases are made by local residents or by persons residing outside the jurisdiction. Under the point-of-delivery system, the jurisdiction where merchandise is delivered receives the revenue generated by its own tax on goods delivered there.

Where the local tax is administered by the state, revenues are sent to the state (usually monthly) by the firms collecting them; the state then distributes the revenues back to the local governments. In most states the revenues are distributed back to the location where the tax liability was incurred, with no *redistribution* of the sales tax revenue among jurisdictions.

Administrative procedures

Setting up and operating a local sales tax involves four steps: preparing and updating a list of local vendors or tax roll, preparing return forms, mailing returns, and auditing returns to ensure compliance.

If there is a state sales tax, the state's tax roll can be used to identify local retailers. Otherwise, local directories, rolls for license taxes, and other sources must be used. Registration forms are then sent to a list of vendors, and a number is assigned to each form as it is returned. Additional field checks may be necessary to determine whether any vendors have been overlooked.

Vendors must file tax return forms when they pay the tax. Most cities levying a sales tax require such returns to be filed monthly. Examples of two such forms

Figure 10–1 Sales and use tax return, Duluth, Minnesota.
(Top portion is front side of card; bottom portion is reverse of card.)

DUL-T1 (REV. 1/84)

CITY OF DULUTH, MINNESOTA
DEPARTMENT OF FINANCE AND RECORDS
SALES AND USE TAX RETURN
READ INSTRUCTIONS BEFORE COMPLETING RETURN
IF NO TAXABLE TRANSACTIONS WERE MADE DURING THE PERIOD, WRITE "NONE" ON LINES 1 AND 4, SIGN AND RETURN TO SALES TAX DIVISION.

MAILING ADDRESS

SALES & USE TAX PERMIT NUMBER

PERIOD OF RETURN

DATE DUE

LOCATION OF THE BUSINESS TO BE REPORTED ON THIS RETURN.

I hereby declare under the penalties of criminal liability for willfully making a false return, that this return has been examined by me and to the best of my knowledge and belief is true and complete for the period stated.

SIGNATURE ______

TITLE ______ DATE ______

IF YOU USE THE ACTUAL TAX METHOD (SEE INSTRUCTIONS) CHECK HERE. ☐

1	Gross Sales	◆	
2	Deductions (From Line 26)	◆	
3	Net Sales (Line 1 Minus Line 2)		
4	Purchases Subject To Use Tax	◆	
5	1% Sales Tax (1% of Line 3)		
6	Add.'l 1% Tax (1% of Line 3)		
7	3% H.M. Excise Tax (3% of Line3)		
8	1% Use Tax (1% of Line 4)		
9	Total Tax Due (Lines 5+6+7+8)	◆	
10	A. Penalty		
	B. Interest		
	C. Adjustment(s)	◆	
11	Total Amount Remitted	◆	

MAKE CHECKS PAYABLE TO: "CITY OF DULUTH" 1-218-723-3273

MAIL TO: SALES TAX DIVISION P.O. BOX 29 105A CITY HALL DULUTH, MN 55802

CHECK ACCOUNTING METHOD USED IN REPORTING GROSS SALES
CASH ☐ ACCRUAL ☐

AVOID PENALTIES

THIS RETURN MUST BE FILED ON OR BEFORE THE 25TH OF THE MONTH FOLLOWING THE CLOSE OF THE PERIOD.

NEW OWNERS

DO NOT USE PREVIOUS OWNER'S FORM TO FILE YOUR RETURN—ANY CHANGE OF OWNERSHIP ORGANIZATION OR ADDRESS REQUIRES A NEW PERMIT.

(SEE INSTRUCTIONS)

DD-T 17665-0R3

DEDUCTIONS

12	SALES FOR PURPOSE OF RESALE		
13	SALES TO CHARITABLE, EDUCATIONAL, RELIGIOUS AND GOVERNMENTAL ORGANIZATIONS		
14	SALES OF MATERIALS FOR USE IN AGRICULTURAL OR INDUSTRIAL PRODUCTION		
15	SALES OF FOOD PRODUCTS		
16	SALES OF CLOTHING AND WEARING APPAREL		
17	SALES OF GASOLINE		
18	BAD DEBTS (only when on an accrual basis)		
19	SALES OF GOODS DELIVERED OR MAILED OUT OF CITY		
20	RECEIPTS FROM LODGING (Over 28 Days)		
21	SALES TO BUILDING CONTRACTORS FOR USE OUT OF CITY (must comply with all requirements)		
22	RECEIPTS FOR SALES UNDER MINIMUM		
23	OTHER AUTHORIZED DEDUCTIONS (List separately)		
24			
25			
26	TOTAL DEDUCTIONS (Enter on line 2)		

are provided in Figures 10–1 and 10–2. Once returns are mailed, it is necessary to make follow-up contacts with delinquents and nonfilers.

The final step is auditing returns to ensure compliance. Some cities have a large enough staff of trained personnel for auditing, but many have too few, and

Figure 10–2 Sales and use tax return, New Orleans, Louisiana.
(Form mailed out with postal indicia, not shown here, printed in top right-hand corner.)

CITY OF NEW ORLEANS
DEPARTMENT OF FINANCE
BUREAU OF REVENUE
ROOM 1W09, CITY HALL, CIVIC CENTER 70112

RETURN POSTAGE GUARANTEED

LOCATION OF BUSINESS

CITY AND SCHOOL
SALES AND USE TAX RETURN OF

MONTH	YEAR

1. Sales by Cash and Credit		
2. Sales by Food Stamps		
3. Cost of Tangible Property used or consumed		
4. Total (Lines 1, 2 & 3)		
ALLOWABLE DEDUCTIONS		
5. Sales to Registered "W" Wholesalers		
6. Sales for Further Manufacturing		
7. Sales to "M" Multi-Parish Businesses		
8. Sales to State of Louisiana & U. S. Government		
9. Cash Discounts, Sales Returns & Allowances		
10. Sales in Interstate Commerce		
11. Sales of Gasoline		
12. Sales delivered in Jefferson Parish		
13. Sales delivered elsewhere in Louisiana outside of City of New Orleans		
14.		
15. Total Deductions		
16. Amount Taxable (Line 4 less Line 15)		
17. Tax: 3% of Line 16		
18. Excess Tax Collected (Over 3%)		
19. Total (Line 17 plus Line 18)		
20. Less Vendor's Compensation, if not delinquent		
a. 1% of Tax on Retail Sales		
b. 2% of Tax on Wholesale Sales		
c. Total Lines 20a. and 20b.		
21. Amount of Tax Due (Line 19 less Line 20c.)		
22. Less Credit Sales Tax: (New Orleans Advance retail dealers' tax paid to wholesalers on purchases for resale at retail: Amount of Purchases__________)		
23. Net Tax Payable (Line 21, Less Line 22)		
24. Interest - 1% per month from due date until paid.		
25. Penalty - 5% for each 30 days or fraction thereof not to exceed 25%		
26. Total Tax, Interest & Penalty (Lines 23, 24 and 25)		

Gross Business Reported to State ____________

FOR OFFICE USE ONLY	TYPE PAYMENT	
	CASH	
	CHECK	

Date	Sign Here	Signature of Preparer Other than Taxpayer

Make Your Remittance Payable to CITY OF NEW ORLEANS

To avoid penalties Return must be filed on or before the 20th day of the month following the period covered.
DO NOT use any other taxpayer's return as this will result in improper credit.

WARRANTY

NO RETURNS WILL BE ACCEPTED UNLESS SIGNED BY TAXPAYER OR AUTHORIZED AGENT.

IT IS HEREBY WARRANTED THAT THIS RETURN, INCLUDING THE ACCOMPANYING SCHEDULES AND STATEMENTS (IF ANY) HAS BEEN EXAMINED BY ME, AND TO THE BEST OF MY KNOWLEDGE AND BELIEF, IS A TRUE AND COMPLETE RETURN MADE IN GOOD FAITH, ON THE BASIS OF THE BRACKET SYSTEM, FOR THE TAXABLE PERIOD AS STATED, PURSUANT TO CHAPTER 56 OF THE CODE OF THE CITY OF NEW ORLEANS, AS AMENDED AND RESOLUTION ADOPTED BY ORLEANS PARISH SCHOOL BOARD LEVYING A 1% SALES AND USE TAX.

DID ANYONE PREPARE OR ASSIST IN PREPARING THIS RETURN OR SUPPLY ANY DATA INCLUDED HEREIN? YES NO

HENRY G. SIMMONS
DIRECTOR OF FINANCE

ORIGINAL

some smaller cities have no audit staff at all. The experience of states with sales taxes indicates that one auditor per thousand accounts is the bare minimum for reasonable enforcement and that one per six hundred accounts is more nearly optimal.[9]

Major issues

The local sales tax has created problems and raised issues in four major areas: administration, revenue allocation, incidence and equity, and locational effects.

Administration Problems arise whether localities or states administer the sales tax. In the early 1980s, seven states had local governments that were levying and administering their own sales taxes. In Alaska local administration occurred by default since the state did not levy a sales tax. Louisiana and Minnesota had exclusive local administration, duplicating the administrative apparatus at the state level for collecting the state sales tax. Alabama, Arizona, Colorado, and Illinois had a dual system in which the state administered the taxes of some local governments and the local governments themselves administered the balance.

Experience suggests that local sales tax administration results in higher costs for both vendor compliance and governmental administration. With state administration the same amount of revenue can be collected at a lower overall cost, or more revenue can be collected at the same cost. State administration also entails a lower cost primarily because it avoids duplicating tax collection efforts and vendor compliance costs. Other costs and enforcement problems that characterize locally administered sales taxes are the following:

1. Dissimilar state and local tax bases that create additional recordkeeping, enforcement, and auditing costs.
2. Uncoordinated tax rates within a state, which increase the complexity and cost for compliance and enforcement and may bring tax-induced shifts in retail purchases and retail outlet migration from higher to lower tax areas. Although relocation depends on tax rate differentials, not state or local administration, experience suggests that state administration produces greater coordination of rates and makes large rate differentials less likely.
3. Severe enforcement problems, which are encountered when local governments designate the place of delivery as the point for imposition of the sales tax. Such a designation is an awkward attempt to keep local merchants from losing sales to persons living outside the taxing jurisdiction. Sellers are required to keep sales records by geographic area or jurisdictional boundaries, and such records are frequently inaccurate. The point-of-delivery rule almost invites actual or bogus shifts of purchases to destinations outside the jurisdictional boundaries. Use taxes, the natural complement of the delivery rule, also are notoriously difficult to enforce.
4. Low quality and lack of enforcement staff, which reduce yield and multiply inequities and enforcement problems.

Are there any advantages to local administration? If not, the question is, why do pockets of local administration still exist? Since the publication of Charles Tiebout's famous paper on local expenditure,[10] economists have recognized that the existence of many local governments provides individuals with some ability to choose the mix of taxes and local public services they prefer—by "voting with their feet." State administration of local sales taxes may reduce this range of choice and so impose some costs on citizens. For example, state administration virtually always requires the local tax to have the same base as the state tax. This may force a local government to give up certain exemptions (e.g., for food) or to stop applying user taxes to intrastate sales, thereby causing a loss of revenue. (This revenue loss may be more than offset, however, by revenue gains arising from more effective enforcement of the tax.) There may also be loss of local control over tax rates, as states with local administration tend to have wider ranges of local rates than do states with state administration. However, in the context of the many other dimensions of choice not affected by the issue of local versus state tax administration, it seems unlikely that the lost freedom entailed in state administration is significant enough to warrant enduring the problems associated with local administration. The trend over the years has been toward state administration.[11]

Other administrative issues that will be discussed briefly are identification and assignment of vendors to taxing jurisdictions, charges for state collection, and vendor compensation. Verifying and updating the location of vendors relative to the boundaries of the taxing jurisdiction is necessary not only to ensure tax compliance but also to determine, with state administration, how to distribute tax revenues back to local governments. Special problems arise when the vendor has multiple outlets, no fixed place of business, more than one place of business, or a place of business outside the state.[12]

Only five states provided free collection of local sales taxes in the early 1980s: Arizona, Colorado, Kansas, Mississippi, and Virginia. The rest charged for local collection, basing the charge on cost, on a fixed percentage of total revenue collected, or on cost up to some maximum percentage of revenue. States charging a fixed percentage have set the rates from as low as 1 percent (Georgia, Missouri, and Nevada) to rates as high as 3 percent (Nebraska). Actual administration costs of *state* sales taxes (averaged over all states) have been estimated by John Due and John Mikesell to be 0.73 percent of sales tax revenue.[13] Assuming that this same estimate applies to state-administered local sales taxes, it appears that states charging a fixed percentage apply a rate that exceeds their administration costs.

Regarding vendor compensation, some states compensate vendors for collecting and remitting both state and local taxes. These payments are calculated as a percentage of revenue collected (rather than actual cost), though compensation may be greater for early payment and may be forfeited if payment is late. Some states also reduce the percentage compensation if revenue exceeds a given amount. The only available study of vendor compliance costs was done by J. C. Yokum.[14] Based on a sample of 526 Ohio stores in eight major classes of retailing, he found an average compliance cost of 3.93 percent of tax liability.

Revenue allocation Local sales tax receipts are usually returned to the jurisdiction in which they were collected. The jurisdictions that receive the most sales tax revenues, however, may not be those that incur the greatest expenditures for public services. Such problems are most apparent in metropolitan areas where some jurisdictions have few residents and many retail stores and others have few shopping areas but many residents. One possible solution is to allocate the tax receipts back to local governments by a formula that takes into account the economic and social characteristics of various local jurisdictions. However, because of the consequent loss of revenue and local autonomy only a handful of states with local sales taxes use such formulas.

Incidence and equity The traditional view is that sales taxes are shifted to consumers of the taxed goods and services through higher prices, even though the tax is legally imposed on vendors (or vendors are liable for collecting it). The essential reasoning behind this view is as follows: when the sales tax is imposed, either the taxed good must rise in price or prices of the factors of production used to make the taxed product must fall. The latter result is unlikely, especially in the long run; with over 60 percent of the products and services that consumers buy (not to mention tax-exempt capital goods) already exempt from the sales tax, producers will simply produce more of these untaxed products—if offered lower returns in the taxed industries. Hence, factor prices are unlikely to fall. Instead, it is more likely that prices of taxed products will rise and that consumers of the taxed products will bear the burden of the sales tax.

This relatively simple story becomes more complicated when the local sales tax applies to a very limited geographic area adjacent to other easily accessible locations where no sales tax applies or where sales tax rates are substantially lower. Consumers who make purchases in the lower sales tax area can escape a portion of their sales tax burden. In response to this border tax problem, business firms may alter their location decisions.

These border tax cases aside, consumers generally bear the local sales tax in proportion to their expenditures on the taxed goods and services. Using this conclusion about tax incidence, it is possible to evaluate the local sales tax by applying two basic principles: benefits-received and ability-to-pay. Do persons who pay more sales tax benefit to a greater extent from local public services (fire, police, sanitation, education, public works) than those who pay less? If so, how close is the match between taxes and benefits? Although studies of the relationship between income of the residents of a local jurisdiction and the demand for local public services are rudimentary, they suggest nevertheless that benefits—as measured by willingness to pay (demand)—rise with income, but not in proportion to it.[15] To comply with the benefits-received principle, taxes, then, should also rise with income, but less than proportionately to it (i.e., the taxes should be somewhat regressive). The ratio of sales tax to income does fall as income rises (because expenditures on the items subject to sales tax do not rise in proportion to income); hence, it may be tentatively concluded that a sales tax is broadly consistent with the benefits-received principle.

The sales tax does not fare as well when evaluated by the ability-to-pay principle. Ability to pay is related to both horizontal and vertical equity. When two persons with the same income spend different amounts of money on taxed items and so pay different amounts of sales tax, the sales tax is horizontally inequitable. When persons with lower income pay a higher proportion of that income in sales tax than do those with higher incomes, this tax is regressive and would be regarded by many as vertically inequitable.

Eliminating regressivity is perhaps the major argument for exempting food consumed at home from sales taxation, and thereby making sales tax paid more or less proportionate to income, except at the very lowest income levels. However, eliminating regressivity by exempting food creates problems in retailer compliance and auditing procedures. Arbitrary decisions must often be made about what is considered food consumed at home and what is not (e.g., hot take-out food from the deli, chewable vitamins, candy, soft drinks). To apply the tax correctly, grocery clerks must discriminate between food and nonfood items, a task that can increase checkout time, nuisance, and errors in stores that do not have electronic scanning checkout systems. Moreover, stores have an incentive to overstate the proportion of sales that are food items, necessitating increased auditing to prevent them from evading their full tax liability.

Many regard the rebate approach as a superior alternative. It allows a tax-free amount of food expenditures, the exact size of which may be determined by estimating the cost of a "minimally necessary" amount of food. (The U.S. Department of Agriculture has considerable experience in setting up schedules indicating such amounts for various family and age groups.) As an example, if the "minimally necessary" amount of food for an individual costs $2,000 per year and the sales tax rate is 4 percent, then each eligible person would be entitled to a check from the taxing authority for $80, or each eligible person could be given a credit of $80 against any other tax, such as the state income tax, local income tax, or local property tax. The former procedure has the advantage of allowing coverage of all persons whether or not they owe any other tax to the taxing authority.

The rebate (or credit) approach illustrates how a sales tax can be structured to allow for the differing personal circumstances of taxpayers. (Note that the rebate approach could be extended to other "necessities" in addition to food.) Compared with the exemption approach, it has two basic advantages. First, the rebate can be targeted just to people with incomes below a certain level, such as the official U.S. government poverty line. Such targeting substantially cuts the revenue loss that a food exemption entails and would permit lowering the overall sales tax rate while still obtaining the previous level of tax revenue. In addition, such targeting puts tax relief in the hands of those persons who need the help of the food exemption without at the same time helping the affluent. Second, the compliance and administration costs of the sales tax are reduced when no items are exempt.

Locational effects If a local jurisdiction imposes a sales tax, and if shoppers can travel freely to adjacent nontax jurisdictions to take advantage of tax-created price differentials, then the taxing jurisdiction may lose sales of taxable items. While a perfectly enforced use tax in conjunction with an assignment of tax liability at the point of delivery would completely neutralize the effect of such a tax on local retail sales, such an arrangement is difficult to enforce. The size of the retail sales loss is determined in part by the extent to which local sales taxes are used by neighboring jurisdictions. In states like California where local sales taxation is universal and set at uniform rates, the problem is largely nonexistent (except for possible loss of sales to other states). On the other hand, in metropolitan areas where only one municipality imposes the tax, some shoppers are likely to cross municipal borders to escape it. The effect on shopping decisions depends on how much shoppers can save by changing purchase locations when compared with the costs incurred (principally in extra travel time and gasoline costs) to obtain these savings. These benefits and costs depend on the size of the tax rate differential and the accessibility and comparative quality of competing shopping areas. If the potential saving is great, a tax may not only affect shoppers but may also induce new retail shopping centers to be built just beyond the boundaries of the taxing jurisdiction to capitalize on the tax-induced price differentials.

Economists call these changes in location decisions "deadweight efficiency loss," that is, a loss in welfare caused by a misallocation of resources. If the local government were to offer a given shopper a refund of the sales tax that would be paid if shopping were done in the sales tax jurisdiction (rather than in an adjacent no-tax jurisdiction), both the jurisdiction and the shopper would be better off. The local taxing jurisdiction would have no less revenue than in the case where the shopper bought outside the taxing jurisdiction and therefore paid no sales tax in it, and the shopper would save in extra travel time and auto expenses entailed in shopping outside the taxing jurisdiction.

Several studies have been made dealing with the "border city" sales tax problem. They examine losses in cities near state borders where purchases may be shifted to avoid a state sales tax and in cities where city-suburban tax rate differentials exist. Harry E. McAllister's study of three border cities in Washington (Vancouver, Walla Walla, and Pullman) found that, "in every case for the three cities . . . , the trade pattern is different from what would be expected if the sales tax were not a factor in buying decisions."[16] For New York City, William Hamovitch found that an increase of 1 percentage point in the city sales tax reduced sales in the city by about 6 percent,[17] and Harry Levin found that the city lost sales of taxed goods and gained sales of untaxed goods.[18] Finally, Mikesell conducted a more general study of the effect of city-suburb sales tax differentials and found that a 1 percent increase in the ratio of city to suburban sales tax rates caused per capita retail sales to fall by 1.69 to 10.97 percent.[19] Little or no work has been done to investigate how these induced changes in shopping behavior have affected retailer location decisions. So far study results suggest that to minimize distortion of locational choices, sales tax rates should be uniform throughout as wide an area as possible, as in Illinois, California, and Virginia.

In 1985 New York and New Jersey drew up a compact (effective January 1, 1986) designed to reduce the amount of tax avoidance (and evasion) achieved by crossing borders and by mail order sales.[20] Under the terms of this agreement, sales and use taxes are to be collected and administered jointly, with each state collecting the other state's use tax on goods purchased out-of-state. This agreement greatly reduces evasion of the use tax because the purchaser's state cannot legally require an out-of-state seller to collect the use tax. John Baldwin, Director of the New Jersey Division of Taxation, estimated that the compact would result in additional tax collections of about $50 million per year. In addition, the compact would protect law-abiding businesses from competitors who offer customers illegal tax scams to gain an unfair competitive advantage. (The two states have filed criminal charges against firms allegedly falsifying records to make in-state purchases of furs and pianos appear as if they were shipped out-of-state, thereby exempting these sales from the sales tax in the seller's state.)

Major elements of the New York/New Jersey agreement are as follows:

1. Businesses registered under the joint program collect tax on items shipped to the other state if those items are taxable in both states. When a tax is imposed, it will be at the rate of the state and locality to which the goods are delivered.
2. Businesses registered under the joint program file returns only in the state in which they are located. Each state remits to the other the funds it has collected for its neighbor.
3. Participation by a business in the joint program is voluntary. A business choosing not to collect tax for the state into which it is shipping is subject to each state's administrative and legal action.
4. The two states share all information.
5. Businesses registered under the joint program are subject to a single audit by taxing authorities. Businesses separately registered are subject to audits by both states.

Evaluation and summary

Local sales taxes are an important revenue source for many local governments. The tax offers extra autonomy in setting local revenue and expenditure levels, and it offers a way for local governments to collect taxes for services provided to nonresidents, which may correspond roughly with the benefits-received principle.

Desirable features of a local sales tax are as follows:

1. State (rather than local) administration is more efficient for operating the tax and for coordinating tax rates and bases in different locations.
2. To avoid complicating compliance and auditing, the base of the local tax should be the same as that of the state sales tax (if a state tax exists, as it does in 45 states).
3. Locating the tax liability with the vendor rather than at the point of delivery and limiting use taxes to out-of-state purchases facilitates compliance.
4. Tax rates should be uniform over as large a geographic area as possible (i.e., countywide is better than citywide) to ensure against adverse locational effects.

5. When allocating local sales tax revenue between counties and municipalities, decision makers should consider the division of local government functions (and hence relative expenditures of each) and the revenues available to the respective local governments from other sources.

On the negative side, there are three major problems with a local sales tax. First, unless applied uniformly over a wide geographic area, the tax will have adverse effects on locational decisions. Second, the tax runs counter to widely held views of horizontal and vertical equity, though the vertical equity problem could be remedied at least partially by special tax credits or rebates for taxes paid on food (either of which is superior to exempting food altogether). Third, tax proceeds are almost always distributed by sales location and hence may not match the demands of constituents for provision of public services. The first and third problems have led some observers to conclude that when additional revenues are to be provided to local government, increasing local sales tax rates would be distinctly inferior to increasing the state sales tax rate (to be accompanied by a redistribution of the extra revenue to local governments on the basis of a formula that embodies various criteria of local need, such as population and average income). This argument could be carried further to recommend eliminating all local sales taxes and substituting increases in state sales tax rates, or even replacing all state sales taxes with a national sales tax. Such sweeping changes, however, would result in a substantial loss of local autonomy for local governments relying heavily on sales tax revenue. They would probably also lead to an increase in income redistribution among geographic areas and, ultimately, individuals.

Local income taxes

Local income taxes were being levied by approximately 3,300 local governments in the mid-1980s.[21] Producing about 3.7 percent of all own-source local general revenue, the local income tax was somewhat less important in the aggregate than the local sales tax, which produced 6.2 percent. As Table 10–6 shows, use of the tax was not uniformly distributed over the country; rather, the tax was used by local governments in only 13 states and it generated appreciable

Table 10–6 Use and importance of local income taxes, by state and for municipalities within states, 1981–82.

(1) State	(2) Local government revenue from own sources (in thousands)	(3) Local income tax revenue (in thousands)	(4) Income tax revenue as % of own-source revenue	(5) Municipal income tax revenue (in thousands)
Alabama	$ 1,850,063	$ 34,586	1.9	$ 34,586
Arkansas	904,206	11	—	11
Colorado	2,770,418	3	—	3
Delaware	248,698	12,213	4.9	12,213
Indiana	2,907,844	52,779	1.8	0
Kentucky	1,092,439	201,693	18.5	126,461
Maryland	3,111,422	638,932	20.5	79,109
Michigan	7,819,488	295,145	3.8	295,145
Missouri	2,925,276	125,285	4.3	125,285
New York	21,174,200	2,187,755	10.3	2,187,755
Ohio	6,953,996	959,199	13.8	959,199
Pennsylvania	7,493,970	1,178,211	15.7	744,823
Virginia	3,085,452	136	—	0

Sources: U.S. Department of Commerce, Bureau of the Census, *1982 Census of Governments*, vol. 4, *Governmental Finances*, no. 5, *Compendium of Governmental Finances* (Washington, D.C.: GPO, 1984), p. 24 and p. 26; and U.S. Department of Commerce, Bureau of the Census, *1982 Census of Governments*, vol. 4, *Governmental Finances*, no. 4, *Finances of Municipal and Township Governments* (Washington, D.C.: GPO, 1984), p. 6.

revenue (more than 1 percent of own-source local general revenue) for local governments in only 10 states. The local income tax was used mainly by municipalities (Table 10–4); for some municipalities (e.g., Philadelphia) in states relying heavily on the income tax, it provided almost half of own-source revenues.[22]

Typically, local income taxes have been adopted in response to fiscal pressures, without having been subjected to close scrutiny assessing equity and revenue implications. The exceptions are New York City, Detroit, and Maryland counties. Many income tax provisions reflect attempts to circumvent legal hurdles or constitutional limitations imposed by state governments, rather than attempts to adhere to widely recognized canons of taxation. Nevertheless, the local income tax is useful because of its revenue potential, certainty of incidence, adjustability to the personal circumstances of taxpayers, and ability to achieve a reasonably close correspondence between tax liability and benefits received from local public services.

History of the local income tax

The first modern income tax was adopted by the city of Philadelphia in 1938 under the 1932 Sterling Act, by which the state permitted the city to tax any nonproperty sources not already taxed by the state.[23] In 1939 the Philadelphia tax was declared unconstitutional by the state supreme court for violating the uniformity requirement of the Pennsylvania constitution, which precluded a progressive income tax. The Philadelphia flat-rate tax was progressive because it exempted the first $1,000 of income. The following year the city adopted a flat-rate tax on all earned income within its boundaries (i.e., wages, salaries, and net income of professions, partnerships, and unincorporated businesses), with no personal deductions or exemptions. Major features of this tax—flat rate, exclusion of property income and capital gains from its base, and lack of personal exemptions and deductions—have been retained, and it has served as the model for other local governments in Pennsylvania, and for localities in Alabama, Kentucky, Missouri, and Ohio.

Between 1940 and 1962 the income taxes adopted by local governments were the Philadelphia type of earned income taxes. In 1962 Detroit introduced the first change by levying an income tax on all forms of income, including dividends, rental income, interest, and capital gains. Two years later Michigan adopted the Uniform City Income Tax Ordinance incorporating the provisions of the Detroit tax. The tax base was essentially adjusted gross income as defined in the federal Internal Revenue Code.

The next major development came in 1966 when New York City introduced a personal income tax very similar to the federal levy. As in Michigan cities, the resident tax base was essentially the same as the federal base and personal exemptions were allowed. In addition, however, income was taxed at graduated rates (ranging from 0.4 percent to 2.0 percent), and the taxpayer was permitted to take personal deductions. (Married couples were allowed to file separately and assign their combined deductions to the spouse with the higher income.)

A final major development occurred in Maryland in 1967, when the state enacted a law under which Baltimore City and each county were required to levy a local income tax on residents at not less than 20 percent and not more than 50 percent of the state income tax liability. Increases or decreases in rates between these limits had to be in increments of 5 percent. Nonresidents could not be taxed.

Extent of use and features

By the early 1980s, local income taxes were being used by local governments in 13 states (Table 10–6). Of these, Arkansas, Colorado, and Virginia receive only negligible amounts of revenue from the tax, leaving 10 states where local governments receive significant revenue. Like local sales taxes, local income taxes display considerable diversity. The following discussion focuses on local income taxes levied on individuals and excludes local corporate income taxes.[24]

Tax rates Except in Maryland, Michigan, and New York, local governments with income taxes impose those taxes at a flat rate. These rates range from 0.25 percent in some Kentucky, Ohio, and Pennsylvania municipalities to 4.96 percent in Philadelphia. The flat rate in Philadelphia exceeds the highest rate in Maryland counties (where rates range from 0.4 percent to 2.5 percent), in Michigan municipalities (where rates range from 1.0 to 3.0 percent), and in New York City (where the range of rates is 0.4 to 2.0 percent). For taxpayers with adjusted gross income between $15,000 and $20,000, New York levied a 5 percent surtax in 1983 and a 2.5 percent surtax in 1984; for taxpayers with adjusted gross income above $20,000, the surtax was 10 percent in 1983 and 5 percent in 1984.

Alabama and Delaware municipalities tax residents and nonresidents at the same rate. In Indiana counties, nonresidents pay a maximum rate of 0.25 percent (compared with resident rates ranging from 0.5 to 1.0 percent). Larger Kentucky cities tax nonresidents at lower rates. Maryland counties and the city of Baltimore do not tax nonresidents. Michigan municipalities tax nonresidents at half the rate applied to residents. In New York City, nonresidents pay a flat tax of 0.45 percent of wages earned in the city. In Ohio, nonresidents are liable for the portion of the tax that is collected by the city, but not the portion collected for school districts.

Double taxation The possibility that the same income will be taxed twice, once at the place of work and once again at the place of residence, cannot arise in Maryland counties, where only residents are taxed. Nor can this happen in the local jurisdictions of Alabama and Kentucky, where income taxes are technically "occupational license" taxes levied only on economic activity within the taxing unit, residency being irrelevant for determining tax liability. Even in states where double taxation might occur, it is virtually always precluded by crediting the tax paid in one local jurisdiction to that owed in another. For example, in Pennsylvania (with the notable exception of Philadelphia) residence is given priority; a taxpayer is allowed to credit the tax paid to the place of residence against a tax levied by the jurisdiction of employment.

Philadelphia, on the other hand, has a prior claim to the earnings taxes it collects from nonresidents, who are permitted to credit this tax against any levied where they live. Philadelphia has no rate limit and has set a rate of 4.96 percent; other local governments, however, are limited by state law to 1.0 percent (save for home rule localities, which have no rate limit for taxes on residents). Many of Philadelphia's suburban "bedroom" communities have chosen not to levy an earnings tax because most of the tax base represented by their residents' earnings belongs to Philadelphia.[25] The reverse circumstances have arisen in other metropolitan areas of Pennsylvania (e.g., Pittsburgh, Scranton, Johnstown, and Erie), where local jurisdictions have a prior claim to earnings tax collections from their residents. Following the adoption of income taxes in the cities where many suburban residents work, suburban communities around these areas have quickly enacted local earnings taxes. For example, when Pittsburgh enacted a local income tax in March 1954, 130 local governments within 25 miles responded by enacting their own taxes by the end of the year.[26]

Michigan localities have followed the Pennsylvania pattern. In Ohio, however, taxes paid at the place of employment remain with that jurisdiction, but they are credited against the tax liability owed in the locality of residence.

Little overlapping of local income taxes has occurred even where several jurisdictions overlap because most states limit the use of the tax to one type of local government (e.g., counties in Maryland and Indiana, cities in Michigan and Missouri). In Pennsylvania each of two overlapping jurisdictions is limited to half the maximum rate of 1 percent, except for Philadelphia, Pittsburgh, Scranton, and a few other municipalities and townships with home rule.

Tax base Local jurisdictions in Alabama, Delaware, Kentucky, Missouri, and Pennsylvania limit the base of the local income tax to earned income: wages, salaries, and the net income of unincorporated businesses. The tax base excludes property income (rental income, capital gains, dividends, and interest) and disallows personal exemptions and deductions. In Maryland counties, Michigan cities, New York City, and Ohio the local tax base is the same as the state income tax base, which is essentially the same as the federal tax base, and, therefore, includes property income. All four also allow personal exemptions, and New York City and Maryland counties permit personal deductions.

Property income has been excluded from the tax base in most localities primarily because of the greater administrative collection and enforcement costs entailed in a tax on this income source. The almost universal practice of employer withholding from wages and salaries does keep these costs low, but the administrative costs for processing returns for business and professional income (where there is no withholding for salaries and wages) are much higher. Putting other types of nonwithheld property income (rent, dividends, interest, and capital gains) into the tax base can also raise administrative costs.

Administrative procedures and collection costs When local governments adopt an income tax, state administration is recommended to minimize administrative and taxpayer compliance costs and avoid the limitations that characterize local collection.[27] However, except in Maryland, local income taxes are administered by local taxing bodies. (Optional state administration is available in Kentucky and New York, but no local government has chosen it.) In Maryland, state administration is mandated with the use of local "piggyback" income taxes. State and local income taxes are collected using one return, and each county pays a prorated share of the cost of operating the Maryland Income Tax Division.

In Ohio, Pennsylvania, and Kentucky, local taxing jurisdictions combine taxes on a single return submitted to a joint collection agency. In Pennsylvania a single return is used to collect the 1 percent earnings tax levied by school districts and coterminous cities, townships, and boroughs. Ohio has achieved many of the cost-saving advantages of state administration by delegating three agencies—located respectively in Cleveland, Columbus, and Dayton—to collect income taxes for surrounding local governments using a single return and one collection staff.

As with sales taxes, where a tax is administered locally, the local government must establish a tax roll, prepare tax return forms, hire clerical and audit staff, and monitor taxpayers to ensure compliance. Collection costs for a local income tax tend to be lower when (1) a high proportion of the tax is collected by withholding; (2) a large percentage of the locality's employees work for a few employers; (3) the intensity of tax enforcement is low; and (4) a relatively small number of taxpayers is employed outside the taxing jurisdiction (because employers outside the local jurisdiction may not voluntarily withhold the tax).

Because successful operation of the income tax depends heavily on employer withholding (the bulk of all local income tax revenues is collected in this manner), a major effort must be made to obtain employer cooperation.[28] Monthly remittances are usually required from employers with large work forces and quarterly remittances from others. Quarterly declarations of other taxable income and quarterly payments of the associated taxes are commonly required.

Revenue potential and elasticity Local governments in states with income taxes tend to rely on the tax for a substantial portion of their tax revenues (in some Ohio jurisdictions, as much as 80 percent), often substituting it for reliance on the property tax.[29] The revenues collected from a local income tax depend on the tax rate, income components, allowable exemptions and deductions, economic characteristics of the community, and administrative procedures. The best way to estimate the revenue potential of a tax to be used for the first time is to examine the size of the relevant income components of the state income tax base in the local jurisdiction. Applying the proposed tax rate to the proposed income components in the local base (assuming no income types not in the state base are to be taxed locally) also produces an estimate, but without accounting for local tax revenues collected from nonresidents.

Cities and local governments in states without a state income tax can make crude revenue estimates by comparing local economic characteristics with those of jurisdictions that have a local income tax or by surveying local employers to get some measure of local wage and salary payrolls. At best, such estimates are likely to be inaccurate, and they may be seriously awry if local business conditions change substantially in a short period of time or if tax administration is poor and fails to gain the cooperation of local employers in withholding the tax. (However, those experienced in collecting the tax will find forecasting techniques useful for projecting revenues.[30])

Because local income tax revenues change automatically when local economic activity changes, it is important to measure revenue *elasticity.* A flat-rate income tax with a comprehensive base equal to gross income would necessarily have an elasticity equal to 1. That is, revenues will rise proportionately with gross income. A tax with exemptions, deductions, or credits (which do not adjust automatically as gross income changes) will generate revenues that rise more than proportionately to increases in taxable gross income. The same will be true of a tax with graduated rates, because a rise in average incomes pushes taxpayers into higher brackets and raises the effective average tax rate. Hence, the New York City income tax and the Maryland county income taxes, with their exemptions, deductions, and graduated rates, are more elastic than the taxes levied by Pennsylvania and Kentucky localities, which do not have these features.

Relatively high elasticity of the income tax is desirable, however, only when local income rises more or less continually and is subject to only mild downward fluctuations—a set of circumstances not within the control of local authorities. Downward fluctuations in income will produce more than proportionate reductions in revenue and could be a source of embarrassment to local officials who may have to cut expenditures. Fortunately (and somewhat paradoxically), actual experience suggests that the local income tax is a highly reliable and stable revenue source. One study of the revenue fluctuations of Philadelphia, Detroit, Columbus, and Dayton, Ohio, showed that revenues never declined by more than 0.1 percent (between successive years) over the time studied (either since the tax was initiated or since World War II) in spite of recession periods in these cities when the unemployment rate was well above the national average.[31]

Major issues

There are five major issues in local income taxation: (1) defining taxable income and equity; (2) incidence; (3) taxation of nonresidents; (4) revenue allocation; and (5) locational effects.

Defining taxable income and equity In most local jurisdictions that levy an income tax, taxable income is simply gross earned income. Nonbusiness deductions and exemptions are not usually allowed and property income is not included in the tax base. This definition of income raises two questions: Should property income be included in the tax base? How does widening the tax base affect distribution of the income tax burden by income class, the amount of revenues generated, and administrative costs?

Equity considerations provide the strongest argument for taxing nonlabor income, for failure to tax this income raises equity problems whether equity is defined by ability to pay or by benefits received. These problems can be clearly illustrated by the following situations involving two taxpayers, who shall be called Mutt and Jeff. In the first situation, suppose that in a given year Mutt and Jeff each receive a total income of $10,000. Suppose that Mutt receives $8,000 in wages and $2,000 in interest income, whereas Jeff receives $3,000 in wages and $7,000 in interest income. If each must pay an earnings tax of 1 percent on wage income, then Mutt has a tax liability of $80 whereas Jeff owes only $30. Because $10,000 buys the same goods and services regardless of the source of the income, the principle of horizontal equity based on ability to pay would call for both to pay the same tax. In addition, provided that Mutt and Jeff have the same preferences for public services, a concept of equity based on benefits received also would prescribe equal taxes. Now, suppose that Jeff receives an income of $20,000—$6,000 in wages and $14,000 in interest—while Mutt's income remains at $10,000 as before. With the same 1 percent earnings tax levy, Mutt still pays $80 and Jeff now pays $60. Jeff still pays less than Mutt even though he has twice Mutt's total income.

Results like these, permitted by excluding property income from the tax base, violate the principle of vertical equity based on ability to pay. Moreover, because taxpayers with higher incomes probably have higher demands for all types of goods and services, including local public services (i.e., they are willing to pay more dollars per unit for a given good), failure to tax property income can lead to serious violations of the benefits-received principle as well.

A second advantage of including property income in the tax base is that the same total revenue can be collected with a lower tax rate. A lower rate is desirable because it gives taxpayers less incentive to modify their behavior solely to reduce their tax liabilities, thereby reducing deadweight losses. Typically, local income tax rates are very low anyway, so this advantage may at first seem trivial. However, local income taxpayers are almost always subject to state and federal income and Social Security taxes as well. Reducing local income tax rates knocks a small chunk off a combined federal-plus-state-plus-local marginal tax rate of over 20 percent for even the poorest taxpayers.

A third advantage in taxing property income is that it simplifies tax enforcement by making the local tax base identical to the state or federal tax base. Identical tax bases can facilitate the exchange of information appearing on federal, state, and local returns.

The major disadvantage of taxing property income is higher collection and enforcement costs. As noted earlier, all local income taxes, except those in Maryland, are administered locally. Taxing property income would create a significant additional burden, especially for small jurisdictions whose local tax administration funds are limited. Furthermore, because property income is not subject to withholding, the incremental administrative costs of adding property income to the tax base would have to be borne by the local government. The average cost of collecting a dollar of tax on property income is several times as large as that of collecting a dollar of tax on wages, for two reasons. First, auditing efforts must be significantly expanded because there are many more taxpayers than employers, and second, the greater discretion given to individual taxpayers in reporting, computing, and paying tax on property income means that this part of the tax must be collected actively rather than received passively.[32] The desirability of taxing property income, together with the burdens entailed, provides an excellent argument for state administration. In Maryland's "piggyback" tax system, for example, rental income, interest, dividends, and capital gains are included in the local tax base (because they are included in the state tax base), and the costs of duplicative local administration and taxpayer compliance (from having to complete a local tax return) are avoided. Of course, these advantages must be weighted against the losses of local fiscal autonomy.

Incidence When there is no economic shifting of a local income tax, the incidence of a flat-rate earned income tax that allows no personal exemptions is regressive: tax liabilities as a percentage of income fall as total income rises. Factors contributing to regressivity are deductibility of the local income tax on federal individual tax returns and exclusion of property income from the tax base. Progressive federal rates imply that the higher the taxpayer's income, the more valuable the deduction for local income taxes. Hence, for federal taxpayers itemizing deductions, effective rates of flat-rate local earnings taxes decline as income rises. Excluding property income from the local earnings tax base contributes to regressivity because dividends, interest, rental income, and capital gains tend to be received by persons in the upper income groups. Therefore, a tax on earned income as a percentage of total income falls as total income rises.

Nonresidents Three major unresolved questions in the treatment of nonresidents are (1) should nonresidents be taxed? (2) if so, at what rate? and (3) should taxes paid in one jurisdiction be allowed as a credit toward taxes paid in another? In fact, as noted earlier, nonresidents are almost always taxed (Maryland counties and the city of Baltimore being the sole exception), though sometimes at a lower rate than residents. Also, crediting taxes paid to prevent double taxation is virtually universal.

The benefits-received principle provides some insights here. Undeniably, commuters who work or shop in a local jurisdiction reap benefits from local government services. Some degree of taxation of nonresident income may therefore be justified, especially if the incremental cost arises mostly from working commuters and if no low-cost system of user charges can be established. More difficult to determine is what the nonresident tax rate should be. A study by William Neenan concluded that Detroit's 0.5 percent tax on nonresident income represented full compensation for benefits received by nonresident commuters.[33] However, benefit estimation is more of a treacherous art than a hard science. One could argue that the total of all taxes levied on resident workers should be greater than that levied either on residents who work elsewhere or on nonresident workers. But since the resident worker is taxed in other ways—via the property tax, for example—it is difficult to justify taxing resident workers at higher rates than nonresidents. Indeed, in localities with relatively heavy property taxation, a lower income tax rate for resident workers might be justified. Moreover, taxing nonresidents at the same rate as residents, rather than at a lower rate, would eliminate the incentive to migrate to neighboring jurisdictions for tax savings.

The benefits-received principle does not necessarily support granting tax credits to prevent double taxation. If a commuter receives benefits from a local jurisdiction (or imposes costs on its residents), there is no real basis for giving a tax credit. Such credits (clearly demonstrated in Pennsylvania cities other than Philadelphia) eliminate the possibility of using the income tax as a means of assessing nonresidents for benefits received. Substitute methods of taxing nonresidents (e.g., sales taxes, amusement taxes) are thereby encouraged, and these methods are likely to be less closely related to the benefits that nonresident employees actually receive.

Revenue allocation The income tax collections of a jurisdiction depend on the size of its tax base, which in turn depends on the level of economic activity, the incomes of persons subject to tax, and the assignment of tax liability to place of residence or employment. Given the tax rate, localities with large tax bases collect large amounts of revenue, and those with small tax bases do not. Hence, the income tax does not easily serve as a method of income redistribution between high- and low-income jurisdictions. It should be noted, however, that revenue distribution among jurisdictions produced by a system of local income taxes is likely to be much more consistent with constituents' demands than is the pattern of revenue distribution derived from a system of local sales taxes. Localities with large populations, for example, will collect relatively large amounts of income tax revenue with which to meet relatively high demands for expenditures, but if such localities have few sales outlets, a sales tax would yield much less revenue to meet the same demand for expenditures.

To redistribute income from high- to low-income jurisdictions, state or federal funding of local expenditures is more effective than any type of local taxation. Distributing state or federally collected revenues back to local governments can then be based on a formula that favors poorer jurisdictions. In part, the controversy over the extent to which local taxation should be used to fund local expenditures focuses on how much income redistribution among local governments is desirable, how much should be accomplished by giving income transfers to the poor directly, and how much should be provided by transfers of resources to the local governments in areas where the poor are more heavily concentrated.

Locational effects Several factors that affect individual and business location decisions are (1) the size of the geographical area in which such an income tax is used and the rates applied in neighboring jurisdictions; (2) differentials among jurisdictions within a given metropolitan area (these are likely to cause greater locational adjustments than are those between one state or region and another); and (3) changes that accompany the adoption of a local income tax or a change in the income tax rate, such as higher local expenditures for services or lower rates for other taxes such as the property tax.

The locational effects of local income taxes have not been researched as extensively as have the effects of a local sales tax on shopping decisions, and the sparse research thus far has found little effect on location decisions.[34] Models of locational choice are necessarily quite complex and difficult to test, and no firm conclusions have yet been drawn. Nevertheless, it seems safe to say that local governments are no doubt influenced by fears of emigration in response to any type of tax, including the local income tax.

Evaluation and summary

The local income tax is a productive and stable revenue source for many local governments. Despite some early fears, the tax has also proven to be administratively expedient, not only when applied just to earned income and collected in large part through employer withholding, but also when a more nearly comprehensive tax base corresponding to that of the federal income tax is used. Unfortunately, the widespread local administration of the tax has tended to limit the base to earned income. This restriction causes the tax to violate criteria of vertical and horizontal equity, whether these criteria are grounded in the principle of benefits received or that of ability to pay. The treatment of nonresidents is based more on what the law allows and on revenue considerations than on any close adherence to taxation principles. Broadening the tax base to include property income and implementing state administration to achieve economies in compliance, collection, and enforcement are reforms that have considerable merit.

Other revenues

The remaining nonproperty sources of local general revenue include (1) selective sales and gross receipts taxes; (2) licenses and other taxes, including occupational and business privilege levies, per capita taxes, occupation taxes, and taxes on real estate transfers; (3) current user charges for such services as education, hospital care, sewage disposal, parking, rental of public housing, parks, and museums; and (4) general revenues from special assessments, sales of property, interest earnings, fines, and forfeits. When combined, these sources generated over two-fifths of local general revenues from own sources in 1981–82.

Although economists and other fiscal experts differ about the appropriateness of various items in this disparate bundle of revenue sources, some consensus exists. The excise and head taxes in the first two groups have often been criticized for being inefficient, inequitable, or both. A kind word is sometimes uttered, however, for excise taxes levied on goods that are essential complements of public services, such as local taxes on motor fuels. These taxes resemble user charges because they are linked to the benefits from the use of local streets. In contrast with excise and head taxes, direct user charges have been viewed more favorably than taxes for allocating goods and services more efficiently and for providing closer conformance to the benefits-received principle.

The following discussion, based on 1982 census data, is limited to the above-mentioned tax components. Fees, user charges, and other nontax revenues that finance special districts, public authorities, and municipal enterprises are covered in Chapter 11.

Importance in the revenue structure

The overall significance of the four major sources of local general revenue for all local governments in the early 1980s is shown in Table 10–7. The importance of the first two categories, selective sales taxes and licenses and other

Table 10–7 Importance of miscellaneous sources of local government general revenues, 1976–77 and 1981–82.

Revenue source	1976–77 Revenue (in millions)	1976–77 % of total general revenue	1981–82 Revenue (in millions)	1981–82 % of total general revenue
Total	$32,721	32.0	$69,160	42.1
Selective sales taxes	2,807	2.7	4,608	2.8
Licenses and other taxes	2,552	2.5	3,909	2.4
Current user charges	19,097	18.7	35,877	21.8
Miscellaneous general revenue	8,265	8.1	24,766	15.1

Sources: 1976–77 data are from U.S. Department of Commerce, Bureau of the Census, *1977 Census of Governments*, vol. 4, *Governmental Finances*, no. 5, *Compendium of Governmental Finances* (Washington, D.C.: GPO, 1979), p. 82; and 1981–82 data are from U.S. Department of Commerce, Bureau of the Census, *1982 Census of Governments*, vol. 4, *Governmental Finances*, no. 5, *Compendium of Governmental Finances* (Washington, D.C.: GPO, 1984), p. 4.

taxes, changed little as a percentage of revenue over the five-year period, between 1976–77 and 1981–82. However, the last two categories, user charges and miscellaneous revenue, became more important in the overall revenue picture—the miscellaneous category nearly doubling its share from 8.1 percent to 15.1 percent.

A more detailed breakdown of three of the four categories is shown in Table 10–8. (A revenue breakdown of licenses and other taxes, which includes an assortment of items, is not readily available.) This table is largely self-explanatory. The major findings are the following:

1. The bulk of all revenues from selective sales and gross receipts taxes came from taxes on public utilities.
2. More than one-third of all user charges came from hospitals. The growth in the share of hospital charges is partly explained by the rising relative cost of medical care services. Education and sewerage charges were the next most important single sources of user charge revenues.
3. The largest miscellaneous source of revenue was earnings from interest-bearing assets. Interest earnings quadrupled between 1976–77 and 1981–82, accounting for much of the growth in the share of the miscellaneous general revenue category as a whole. The increase in interest earnings is attributable to the unusually high nominal interest rates that prevailed over much of this period.

Table 10–8 Selective sales taxes, current user charges, and miscellaneous revenues of local governments, 1981–82.

Classification	Revenue (in millions)	%
Selective sales taxes, total	$ 4,608	100.0
Motor fuel	147	3.2
Alcoholic beverages	225	4.9
Tobacco products	178	3.9
Public utilities	2,818	61.2
Other	1,240	26.9
Current user charges, total	35,877	100.0
Education	5,165	14.4
School lunch sales	2,299	6.4
Institutions of higher education	1,725	4.8
Other	1,141	3.2
Hospitals	12,700	35.4
Sewerage	4,949	13.8
Sanitation other than sewerage	1,427	4.0
Local parks and recreation	1,156	3.2
Natural resources	215	0.6
Housing and community development	1,429	4.0
Airports	2,074	5.8
Water transport and terminals	667	1.9
Parking facilities	394	1.1
Highways	651	1.8
Other	5,049	14.1
Miscellaneous general revenues, total	24,766	100.0
Special assessments	1,557	6.3
Sale of property	536	2.2
Interest earnings	13,701	55.3
Other (includes fines and forfeits)	8,972	36.2

Source: U.S. Department of Commerce, Bureau of the Census, *1982 Census of Governments*, vol. 4, *Governmental Finances*, no. 5, *Compendium of Governmental Finances* (Washington, D.C.: GPO, 1984), p. 4.

Description and evaluation

This section evaluates a number of local taxes using the criteria of equity, efficiency, administrative ease, and revenue potential and elasticity. The taxes examined are per capita (head) taxes; occupational and business privilege taxes (licenses); real estate transfer taxes; and selective sales (excise) taxes on alcoholic beverages, tobacco products, motor fuels, and public utilities.

Per capita taxes Per capita taxes are commonly referred to as "head taxes" (from the Latin *per,* meaning "by," and *capita,* meaning "head"). The per capita tax (also called a residence or poll tax) was used much less frequently in the early 1980s than earlier, when many political jurisdictions had levied the tax for the privilege of voting.[35] When the tax was still being used, it was usually levied annually on all adult residents of the taxing jurisdiction at a fixed amount (typically between 1 and 10 dollars). The tax is almost perfectly neutral (i.e., efficient) because it cannot be avoided by modifying spending, saving, or work choices, and taxpayers are rarely motivated to move out of a taxing jurisdiction to escape a yearly 10 dollar tax. The tax guarantees that all adults make a minimum direct contribution to the cost of government; the tax yield is stable; and the tax is visible, predictable, and simple to report and pay.

The major shortcoming of the tax, which has led many local governments to abandon it, is its low yield relative to administration costs. A tax of one dollar per capita is hardly worth collecting; even a five dollar levy may incur collection costs of 30 to 50 percent of revenues. The problem grows worse over time if the tax is not increased to match increases in wages and prices. Were it not for the low amount of the tax, an additional serious difficulty would be its regressivity in relation to income. Some local governments exempt all persons with annual incomes below a certain level. Finally, the non-deductibility of the tax for federal income tax purposes and the use of the tax by several overlapping jurisdictions (as in Pennsylvania, for example) have confused and annoyed taxpayers and have caused the levy to be labeled a "nuisance" tax. All things considered, this appears to be an apt description.

Occupational and business privilege taxes Historically, taxes on occupations or on the privilege of engaging in an occupation or business were considered property taxes because in seventeenth-century England taxes were levied on the many offices created by grant or letter of appointment (which could sometimes be sold or transferred). Although transferability is no longer typical (seats on the stock and commodity exchanges being notable exceptions), many occupations still require membership in a professional association or labor union. Hence, there is still some basis for regarding occupation taxes as taxes on a property right, though now the tax is more often construed as a levy on the privilege of operating a business or practicing an occupation or profession. Local taxes on occupational and business privileges go by several names, are levied in several forms, and are intended for (or are rationalized by) various purposes. The occupation taxes discussed here are lump-sum taxes and taxes on business gross receipts.

Lump-sum taxes Lump-sum taxes on individuals engaged in occupations and on individual business owners and corporations resemble per capita taxes. The levy is a flat annual amount, invariant to the income or net profit of the taxpayer and thus unrelated to ability to pay. The tax may vary, however, by type of occupation or business.

The tax raises equity issues because actual earnings or net profits do not affect tax liability. Moreover, even though lump sum, the tax is not neutral if individuals are induced to shift among differently taxed occupations or out of the taxing jurisdiction to avoid the tax. Where the tax is small (e.g., 10 dollars per year), the significance of these negative features is small. Moreover, if the tax is subject to employer withholding (as is true, for example, of the 10 dollar occupational privilege levy in many Pennsylvania localities), the administration costs are considerably lower than for per capita taxes, which require a periodic census to update tax rolls.

On the positive side, flat-rate occupation taxes also can serve as a vehicle (in some cases one of the few available to a jurisdiction) for requiring nonresident workers to contribute toward the cost of local public service. Localities having substantial numbers of employees within their boundaries can derive large amounts of revenue from these taxes, and the revenue yield is comparatively stable because the tax is paid annually and is not subject to seasonal employment fluctuations.

Gross receipts taxes Local taxes on the gross receipts of incorporated and unincorporated businesses function in most respects either as general sales taxes, if applied uniformly to a wide class of businesses (e.g., all retail and wholesale establishments), or as selective sales (i.e., excise) taxes, if applied to only one or a few types of businesses (e.g., telephone service). Such taxes are generally shifted to customers of the taxed firms. The major differences between the gross receipts and the explicit sales taxes are that (1) customers may be less resentful of the tax because it is hidden and not calculated as a separate part of the total sales price, and (2) the tax paid by customers is not deductible on federal individual income tax returns.

Most of the issues and problems that arise with the general sales tax also apply to the gross receipts tax. Because the tax is on gross receipts rather than net income, it has been criticized for discriminating against businesses with a low ratio of net profit to sales. But this criticism is based on the assumption that the incidence of the tax is on the businesses legally liable to pay it. If the tax is shifted to customers, the true question (as with the general sales tax) concerns the equity of the burden among customers. Some local jurisdictions allow firms to pay a tax on net income (at 10 times the rate applied to gross receipts, for example), in lieu of the gross receipts tax. Assuming the tax is shifted forward simply causes greater administrative complexity—without making the tax any more equitable. Of course, if there is some uncertainty about the incidence of the tax, then this extra administrative burden may be sensible. Where the tax is imposed on both wholesale and retail businesses, the tax may be discriminatory between vertically integrated and nonintegrated businesses.

The revenue potential of the gross receipts tax depends on its base and the rate applied. Local jurisdictions with large concentrations of businesses can reap substantial revenues, as with the general sales tax. If the tax is shifted to purchasers, it may serve to exact a contribution from nonresident shoppers as well. Where the tax is not levied on all businesses, disputes arise over where to draw the line; such disputes may require resolution through the courts. Pennsylvania's local mercantile tax on wholesale and retail businesses, for example, has been held to apply to persons who buy and resell, but not to persons who sell what they make.[36]

Gross receipts taxes have been levied by some local governments on nonprofit institutions that are exempt from other local taxes. Gross receipts taxes also share with sales taxes the problem of allocating sales made inside and outside the taxing jurisdiction. Whether a broad-based gross receipts tax should play a role in financing local governments depends on an assessment similar to that required for the local sales tax.

Real estate transfer taxes Some types of exchanges are much more visible and easily taxed than others, and this appears to be the major explanation for the existence of the real estate transfer tax. Also referred to as the deed transfer tax, it was used in the early 1980s by local governments in 10 states and the District of Columbia.[37] Localities in California and New York taxed only the difference between the sales price and the amount represented by assumed mortgages, or just the equity of the real estate exchanged. All other jurisdictions imposed the tax on the full sales price. The tax rate ranged from 0.05 percent to 1.0 percent. Revenues from the tax tend to be volatile, because they fluctuate with the pace of real estate and construction activity. Hence, revenues were largest in urban areas where there was considerable economic growth and turnover of real estate. Administrative practices varied greatly in the use of stamps and provisions for recording and transmitting sales prices. Because seven state governments also imposed a transfer tax, there was some tax overlapping.

The real estate transfer tax is an excise tax on the exchange of one type of property. The rationale for such a narrowly based tax, aside from permitting relatively easy and low-cost collection of revenue, is not apparent. Some users of the tax have justified it as an "initiation fee" for new residents to an area, a kind of user charge imposed for the benefits provided by public capital financed by taxes on older residents. Whatever the merits of this argument, the transfer tax, though modest in size, discriminates against real property transactions and raises their cost relative to transactions of other kinds.

The incidence of the tax is not confined to those who actually exchange real estate, because a tax penalizing exchanges usually hurts potential as well as actual buyers and sellers by preventing some mutually advantageous exchanges from ever occurring. Because the tax rate is low, however, the number of exchanges prevented is probably small. (No studies of the effects of this tax on purchase or location decisions appear to have been made.) As for the question of whether the buyer or seller bears the real burden of the tax, in most cases both bear a portion of it regardless of where the legal liability is placed. Hence, there is no validity to the argument sometimes made that where the tax is imposed by both the state and a local government, duplicate taxation is avoided if one level of government taxes the buyer while the other taxes the seller. Finally, while the tax has little to recommend its use, it does provide immediate revenues to finance service demands in rapidly expanding communities and it compensates to some extent for lags in beginning property tax collections on new housing.

Excise taxes Excise taxes are levied by local governments on a wide variety of individual products and services, but the major taxes are those on alcoholic beverages, tobacco, motor fuels, and public utilities. Excise taxes may be expressed as a percentage of the sales price or as a given amount per unit of the product or service. The former is called an *ad valorem* tax, and the latter is called a *unit* tax. Because of their narrow base, excise taxes are generally viewed as running afoul of both equity and efficiency criteria. Taxpayers in the same economic circumstances will pay different amounts of the tax if they consume different amounts of the taxed items. Moreover, to the extent that consumption of a taxed good does not rise in proportion to income, the tax is regressive.

In an otherwise competitive economy with no other distorting taxes, an excise tax alters choices by making the relative prices of taxed and untaxed goods depart from relative costs of production; it gives consumers false signals about true relative scarcities; and the choices based on the incorrect prices cause deadweight efficiency loss. This deadweight loss grows larger if the excise tax causes people to divert their purchases from sellers in one jurisdiction to those in another—to avoid paying the tax.

Although in general excise taxes cause equity and efficiency problems, excise taxes on alcohol, tobacco, and motor fuel are not necessarily undesirable. Given the costs that consumers of these products may impose on third parties, taxes on alcohol and cigarettes could be justified as improving upon an otherwise inefficient allocation of resources. Similarly, congestion and pollution costs resulting from automobile use have sometimes been the basis for justifying motor fuel taxes. The argument has also been made that this tax functions as a user charge for the use of local streets. While evaluating the merits of these various arguments would take this discussion too far afield, suffice it to say that if consumption of a good harms third parties, an excise tax on the good may be the most appropriate response to the problem in some situations, but not in others.

Alcoholic beverages A few municipal and county governments tax distilled spirits, beer, and wine, either by excise taxes or by occupational license taxes. Municipalities in 11 states and the District of Columbia taxed alcoholic beverages in 1981–82. Those in just three states—Georgia, Tennessee, and New York—raised over 82 percent of all municipal tax revenue from alcoholic beverages.[38] County governments in seven states taxed alcoholic beverages, and, again, counties in three states—Georgia, Tennessee, and Illinois—collected the bulk (72 percent) of their tax revenue from this source.[39]

Tobacco and motor fuels Municipalities in six states and the District of Columbia taxed tobacco products in the early 1980s. New York City's cigarette tax accounted for over half of this tax revenue in 1981–82.[40] County governments in five states taxed tobacco products, and Illinois counties accounted for almost two-thirds of this form of revenue.[41] Taxes on various types of motor fuel were levied by municipalities in 13 states and the District of Columbia in the early 1980s. Except for the District of Columbia (which in many ways is more like a state than a local government), Hawaii municipalities led all others in revenue raised from motor fuel taxes (26.0 percent), followed by municipalities in Alabama (22.5 percent).[42] Among the counties in 10 states levying motor fuel taxes, those in Illinois collected over half (52.1 percent) of all revenue from motor fuel taxes, followed by counties in Alabama (13.2 percent) and Nevada (11.8 percent).[43]

Local taxation of alcoholic beverages, cigarettes, and gasoline may cause substantial shifts of purchases out of the taxing jurisdiction, particularly if the locality borders a nontax area. Tax-created price differentials also make organized bootlegging operations profitable, though this is more of an interstate than an interlocal problem.[44] The ease with which cigarettes and alcoholic beverages can be obtained outside a local taxing jurisdiction has no doubt been a factor discouraging some communities from levying these taxes.

Public utilities In the early 1980s local governments in 39 states were deriving revenue from either sales or gross receipts taxes on public utilities (mainly electric, natural gas, and telephone companies). Nationwide, municipalities derived about 3.6 percent of their own-source general revenues from such taxes. From a revenue standpoint, local taxes on public utilities ranked just behind local sales and income taxes and were used by more local governments than either of these two broad-based taxes.[45] Public utility excise taxes tend to be a stable revenue source because consumption of public utility services is relatively stable.

The public utility taxes levied by local governments are no doubt shifted forward to purchasers in the form of higher service prices. Because firms pay this tax as well as individual households, final consumers pay the tax twice, when they purchase utility services and when they buy products and services that require the taxed utility services for their production. Whether the tax has a regressive, proportional, or progressive incidence pattern depends on the relationship between income size and the amount of electricity, natural gas, and telephone service used both directly and indirectly. This same pyramiding phenomenon that complicates the determination of incidence also implies that these taxes create hard-to-trace distortions in relative prices, thereby causing deadweight efficiency losses.

Conclusion

Although the great diversity and variety of the miscellaneous (but by no means minor) revenue sources provide local governments with flexibility in tailoring their local tax structure to local conditions, most of these tax sources are seriously flawed when judged by traditional canons of taxation. For many of these taxes, only their low rates or levels keep them from becoming major problems. At the same time, where local governments use a large number of small taxes, a nuisance is created for taxpayers and the local government incurs higher administrative costs. One might be tempted to conclude that local miscellaneous tax sources constitute a "ragbag" mess. However, there would undoubtedly be considerable resistance to almost any method of replacing the revenues that would be lost if these taxes were abolished wholesale. In contrast, local property, income, and general sales taxes would suffer politically from greater visibility. Moreover, if the proposal to eliminate the deductibility of these latter taxes on federal tax returns is implemented, any such replacement would have yet another hurdle to surmount. The ragbag is therefore likely to be around for years to come.

Summary

Both local general sales and income taxes are important and stable revenue sources for many local governments. While the operation of each of these taxes has posed problems, they both score higher when judged by widely accepted canons of taxation than most other narrow-based, specialized taxes that local governments levy. There appears to be a modest trend toward greater use of sales and income taxes relative to these other types of taxes.

1 The reasons for the shift in reliance from property taxes to charges and miscellaneous sources, including the role of the tax and spending limitation movement of the mid-to-late 1970s, are discussed below. That the tax limitation movement appears to have had no effect on the use of other nonproperty taxes is probably an invalid inference attributable to the level of aggregation of data. Stephen Gold's review of studies to determine the effects of local tax and spending limits reports that in some localities where limits were quite constraining, increases did occur in reliance on other, nonproperty taxes. See Stephen D. Gold, "Results of Local Spending and Revenue Limitations," in *Perspectives on Local Public Finance and Public Policy,* ed. John M. Quigley (Greenwich, Conn.: JAI Press, 1983), pp. 109–50.

2 Changes in detail are constantly occurring in the more than 82,600 local governments. For current information on the revenue sources covered in this chapter, see Commerce Clearing House, *State Tax Reports* (Chicago, Ill., updated monthly).

3 In the five year period from 1971–72 to 1976–77, the number of special districts increased by almost 9 percent. The rapid rise in the number of special districts over the 1972–82 period is described in U.S. Department of Commerce, Bureau of the Census, *1982 Census of Governments,* vol. 4, *Governmental Finances,* no. 5, *Compendium of Governmental Finances* (Washington, D.C.: GPO, 1984), p. x. While this rapid growth of special districts has apparently not been studied systematically, it may be speculated that part of the growth is stimulated by an effort to skirt the debt, tax, and spending limitations imposed on general purpose local government units. See Advisory Commission on Intergovernmental Relations, *State and Local Roles in the Federal System,* A–88 (Washington, D.C.: GPO, 1982), pp. 253–56.

4 The most important references for the discussion of local tax rates and the operating and administrative details of local sales taxes are John F. Due and John L. Mikesell, *Sales Taxation: State and Local Structure and Administration* (Baltimore: Johns Hopkins Univ. Press, 1983); Advisory Commission on Intergovernmental Relations, *Significant Features of Fiscal Federalism: 1982–83 Edition,* M–137 (Washington, D.C.: GPO, 1984); and U.S. Department of Commerce, Bureau of the Census, *1982 Census of Governments,* vol. 4, *Governmental Finances,* nos. 1–5.

5 Advisory Commission on Intergovernmental Relations, *Significant Features of Fiscal Federalism: 1976–77 Edition,* vol. 2, *Revenue and Debt,* M–110 (Washington, D.C.: GPO, 1977), Table 139, p. 254.

6 See Due and Mikesell, *Sales Taxation,* pp. 66–69.

7 The 1986 tax reform proposal eliminated the deductibility of state and local sales taxes. There are good arguments in favor of this reform, but regarding deductibility, it would put sales taxes on the same foot-

ing as a wide array of other local "nuisance" taxes (to be discussed later in the third major section of this chapter). This would remove one of the advantages of using local sales, income, and property taxes, rather than such nuisance taxes, to finance local governments.

8 See Richard A. Musgrave and Peggy B. Musgrave, *Public Finance in Theory and Practice*, 4th ed. (New York: McGraw-Hill, 1984), p. 437.

9 See Due and Mikesell, *Sales Taxation*, Chapter 8, for a discussion of sales tax auditing procedures and experience.

10 Charles M. Tiebout, "A Pure Theory of Local Expenditure," *Journal of Political Economy* 64 (October 1956): 416–24.

11 See Due and Mikesell, *Sales Taxation*, pp. 291–93. Also see John W. Lynch, "Local vs. State Administration of Local-Option Nonproperty Taxes," in *Proceedings of the Sixteenth Annual Conference of the National Tax Association* (1967), pp. 489–504. California's dismal experience with local administration is described in *Let's Make Sense Out of Local Sales Taxes* (San Francisco: California Realtors Association, 1955); and California Senate Interim Committee on State and Local Taxation, *State and Local Sales and Use Taxes in California* (Sacramento: State of California, 1953).

12 For a more extensive treatment of these problems as experienced in California, see Ronald B. Welch, "Two and a Half Years of Progress Toward Integration," *Proceedings of the National Tax Association for 1958*, pp. 128–39.

13 See Due and Mikesell, *Sales Taxation*, p. 324.

14 See J. C. Yokum, *Retailers' Costs of Sales Tax Collections in Ohio* (Columbus: Bureau of Business Research, Ohio State Univ., 1961).

15 See Robert P. Inman, "Fiscal Performance of Local Governments: An Interpretive Review," in *Current Issues in Urban Economics*, ed. Peter Mieszkowski and Mahlon Straszheim (Baltimore: Johns Hopkins Univ. Press, 1979), pp. 285–92.

16 Harry E. McAllister, "The Border Tax Problem in Washington," *National Tax Journal* 14 (December 1961): 374.

17 William Hamovitch, "Effects of Increases in Sales Tax Rates on Taxable Sales in New York City," in *Financing Government in New York City: Report to the Temporary Commission on City Finances* (New York: Graduate School of Public Administration, New York Univ., 1966), pp. 619–34.

18 Harry Levin, "An Analysis of the Economic Effects of the New York City Sales Tax," in *Financing Government in New York City*, pp. 635–91.

19 John L. Mikesell, "Central Cities and Sales Tax Rate Differentials: The Border City Problem," *National Tax Journal* 23 (June 1970): 206–13.

20 The information in the next two paragraphs is taken from New York, State Department of Taxation and Finance, Office of Public Relations, "New York/New Jersey Agreement to Combat Cross-Border Sales Tax Evasion," *News Release*, Release No. 29, 6 June 1985, Albany, New York.

21 Advisory Commission on Intergovernmental Relations, *Significant Features of Fiscal Federalism: 1982–83 Edition*, M–137 (Washington, D.C.: GPO, 1984), p. 90.

22 *Final Report of the Pennsylvania Tax Commission* (Harrisburg, Pa.: Commonwealth of Pennsylvania, March 1981), p. 32.

23 Charleston, South Carolina, adopted an income tax in the early nineteenth century but abandoned it. New York City enacted a local income tax in 1934, but repealed the ordinance in 1935 before any collections were made.

24 In 1981–82, $5 billion of the $6 billion of local income tax revenues came from taxing individuals; $1 billion was derived from local income taxes on corporations. See U.S. Department of Commerce, Bureau of the Census, *1982 Census of Governments*, vol. 4, *Governmental Finances*, no. 5, *Compendium of Governmental Finances* (Washington, D.C.: GPO, 1984), p. 4.

25 Beginning in 1977, any increases in the rate above 4 and 5/16 percent have applied in full only to Philadelphia residents; nonresidents experience a rate increase equal to 75 percent of the increase for residents.

26 William B. Neenan, *Political Economy of Urban Areas* (Chicago: Markham Publishing Co., 1972), pp. 291–92.

27 Advisory Commission on Intergovernmental Relations, *1970 Cumulative ACIR State Legislative Program* (Washington, D.C.: GPO, 1969), subject code 33-22-00, p. 1.

28 A useful guide for local government administration is Commonwealth of Pennsylvania, Department of Community Affairs, *The Administration of the Local Earned Income Tax* (Harrisburg, Pa.: Commonwealth of Pennsylvania, 1971).

29 A study of large cities levying the tax concluded that the local income tax has been used more as a substitute for property tax increases than as a way to fund higher levels of spending than would otherwise have occurred. See Elizabeth Deran, "Tax Structure in Cities Using the Income Tax," *National Tax Journal* 21 (June 1968): 152. See also a study of the degree of reliance on different taxes by Pennsylvania school districts and municipalities that reaches the conclusion that local income taxes and real estate taxes were substituted for each other almost dollar for dollar: James D. Rodgers, *Report of the Task Force on Local Non-Real Estate Taxation to the Pennsylvania Tax Commission* (Harrisburg, Pa.: Commonwealth of Pennsylvania, 1981), pp. 50–51.

30 A review of these techniques may be found in Federation of Tax Administrators, *Revenue Estimating: A Study of Techniques for Estimating Tax Revenues* (Chicago: Federation of Tax Administrators, 1956). Also see this edition, Chapter 5.

31 Neenan, *Political Economy*, pp. 322–23.

32 Collection costs associated with employer withholding of wages and salaries have been estimated to be about 0.6 percent of revenues, whereas administration costs of nonwithheld returns reporting business and professional incomes have been estimated to be almost 8 percent of revenues. See Larry Elison, *The Finances of Metropolitan Areas* (Ann Arbor: Univ. of Michigan, 1964), p. 91.

33 Neenan, *Political Economy*, pp. 147–50.

34 See John F. Due, "Studies of State-Local Tax Influences on the Location of Industry," *National Tax Journal* 14 (June 1961): 163–73; Melvin and Ann White, "A Personal Income Tax for New York: Equity and Economic Effects," in *Financing Government in New York City*, pp. 449–91; and Roger W. Schmenner, *City Taxes and the Location of Industry* (Ph.D. diss., Yale Univ., 1973).

35 The Twenty-fourth Amendment to the U.S. Constitution outlawed the use of poll taxes in federal elections, and in 1966 the U.S. Supreme Court declared state poll taxes unconstitutional for any government election. See Bernard P. Herber, *Modern Public Fi-*

nance: The Study of Public Sector Economics, rev. ed. (Homewood, Ill.: Richard D. Irwin, 1971), p. 255.

36 School District of Pittsburgh v. Electric Welding Co., 142 A.2d 433, 186 Pa. Super. 243 (1958).

37 For a compilation of real estate transfer tax provisions in 10 states and the District of Columbia, see Advisory Commission on Intergovernmental Relations, *Significant Features of Fiscal Federalism: 1976–77 Edition,* vol. 2, *Revenue and Debt,* M–110 (Washington, D.C.: GPO, 1977), Table 95, pp. 170–71.

38 U.S. Department of Commerce, Bureau of the Census, *1982 Census of Governments,* vol. 4, *Governmental Finances,* no. 4, *Finances of Municipal and Township Governments* (Washington, D.C.: GPO, 1984), Table 3.

39 U.S. Department of Commerce, Bureau of the Census, *1982 Census of Governments,* vol. 4, *Governmental Finances,* no. 3, *Finances of County Governments* (Washington, D.C.: GPO, 1984), Table 3.

40 U.S. Department of Commerce, Bureau of the Census, *1982 Census of Governments,* vol. 4, *Governmental Finances,* no. 4, *Finances of Municipal and Township Governments,* Table 3.

41 U.S. Department of Commerce, Bureau of the Census, *1982 Census of Governments,* vol. 4, *Governmental Finances,* no. 3, *Finances of County Governments,* Table 3.

42 U.S. Department of Commerce, Bureau of the Census, *1982 Census of Governments,* vol. 4, *Governmental Finances,* no. 4, *Finances of Municipal and Township Governments,* Table 3.

43 U.S. Department of Commerce, Bureau of the Census, *1982 Census of Governments,* vol. 4, *Governmental Finances,* no. 3, *Finances of County Governments,* Table 3.

44 See Advisory Commission on Intergovernmental Relations, *Cigarette Tax Evasion: A Second Look,* A–100 (Washington, D.C.: GPO, 1985).

45 U.S. Department of Commerce, Bureau of the Census, *1982 Census of Governments,* vol. 4, *Governmental Finances,* no. 4, *Finances of Municipal and Township Governments,* Table 3; and U.S. Department of Commerce, Bureau of the Census, *1982 Census of Governments,* vol. 4, *Governmental Finances,* no. 3, *Finances of County Governments,* Table 3.

User charges and special districts

In response to federal spending cutbacks and the tax limitation movement, user charges have become a major source of local government revenue. User charges and fees rose from 38.0 percent of local revenues in 1972–73 to 40.5 percent in 1976–77 and 47.0 percent in 1981–82, a trend that can be expected to continue into the 1990s. The economic philosophy that resists increases in broad-based taxes does not seem to be opposed to taxes based on the benefits-received principle—that those who use a public service should pay at least part of the costs.

As defined by the U.S. Bureau of the Census, charges are composed of current (user) charges, utility revenue, and liquor store revenue. Current charges are those "amounts received from the public for performance of specific services benefiting the persons charged and from sales of commodities and services. Current charges include fees, tolls, tuition, and other reimbursements for current services. . . ."[1]

User charges function very much like prices charged for privately produced goods. They represent payment for services that would not be provided to the individual if the charge were not paid. For example, an individual may be excluded from playing on a municipal golf course if the required fee is not paid. Individuals or firms, however, do not always have the opportunity to decline the service—refuse collection for example—and thus avoid paying the charge. Other user charges, such as those for electricity and water supply, may vary with the amount of the service used, and the consumer can avoid some (or all) of the charge by reducing consumption.

Practice varies among governments, but usually one of the following two user charge systems is employed: (1) a marginal-cost, multipart charge system that takes into account the varying costs of production and distribution, or (2) an average-cost system that charges the same price per unit regardless of the volume of service consumed or the location of its demand.

This chapter reviews current practice in the employment of user charges and fees by local government and the range of services for which charges are levied. It describes how pricing principles are used in the design of user charge systems to reflect variation in costs and demand, and it discusses such practical considerations as administrative simplicity and citizen acceptance. Next, the chapter describes the structure of charges for individual services such as water supply, sewerage, and refuse collection. This section also reviews fiscal impact fees, an emerging source of revenue levied on new development to recover its attendant off-site public facility capital costs. The effects of user charges are then compared with the effects of the property tax regarding the location of development, the level of service demanded, and the distribution of the financial burden on income groups. Finally, the chapter takes a look at the heavy reliance of special districts on user charges and how this reliance affects provisions of services.

User charges: types and uses

Figure 11–1 shows the variety and extent of user charges and fees. Local governments impose charges not only for such common services as transit, water, and sewerage, but also to cover the expenses of such special services as police protection and crowd control at private events. Typically, the expenses for these services are charged to the sponsor. Fees are also charged for administrative paperwork that primarily benefits individuals (e.g., permits for development and filing fees for tract maps), for licenses to cover the additional expenses to the local government for private activities, such as carnivals, and for overseeing private enterprise. In some cases, license fees are the way a local government shares the profits of a private business (e.g., a taxi service). The fees then are similar to sales or gross receipts taxes.

The degree to which fees and charges are intended to cover the costs of supplying a good or service will vary among services. Those considered to be an ordinary function of local government are not likely to be financed by user fees. Educational services, for example, are provided free by local governments, whereas airport services are subject to user charges. These charges are generally designed to cover all the costs of producing the service. However, there are also services for which the charges do not cover full costs, such as parks and recreation, highways, and sanitation.

Some charges serve as a revenue source or as a method of allocating a service among users without consideration of costs. For example, the relationship between parking fees on city streets and current outlays for the service is minimal. The fees serve mainly as a revenue source and an allocation device.

Table 11–1, which shows revenues from charges as a percentage of outlays for selected services, provides some insight into the potential for increasing revenues from this source. Charges for sanitation still are not very common among local governments, but charges for sewerage have grown significantly since 1977. The highway revenues shown in Table 11–1 are derived primarily from toll bridges, although some toll roads are also included. Given the continuing pressure from federal clean air legislation, it is possible that someday local highway user charges may be instituted in an attempt to curtail traffic and thus reduce automobile pollution in major cities. On the other hand, the use of charges for hospitals, parks, and recreation facilities is not likely to increase substantially.

The extent of user charge growth in comparison with that of other sources of revenue is shown in Table 11–2. Whereas some of the growth in utility charges can be attributed to increased energy costs over the period, the overall rise in current charges and utility revenues is at least partially due to reduced reliance on the property tax. As Table 11–2 shows, property tax revenues have grown more slowly than other major sources of local revenue. In constant dollars, property tax revenues have declined, whereas revenues from charges and sales tax have grown rapidly.

Table 11–1 Charge revenue as a percentage of expenditures.

Service	1976–77 (%)	1981–82 (%)
Parking	128.8	109.9
Water terminals	127.5	94.6
Air transportation	96.9	88.0
Sewerage	37.7	51.8
Hospitals	34.0	36.7
Parks and recreation	15.6	17.0
Highways	17.6	15.9
Sanitation	10.3	15.7

Source: U.S. Bureau of the Census, *City Government Finances in 1981–82* (Washington, D.C.: GPO, 1983), Table 7; U.S. Bureau of the Census, *City Government Finances in 1976–77* (Washington, D.C.: GPO, 1979), Table 8.

Figure 11–1 Types of local government fees, charges, and licenses by service areas.

Police protection
Special patrol service fees
Parking fees and charges
Fees for fingerprints, copies
Payments for extra police services at stadiums, theaters, circuses

Transportation
Subway and bus fares
Bridge tolls
Landing and departure fees
Hangar rentals
Concession rentals
Parking meter receipts

Health and hospitals
Inoculation charges
X-ray charges
Hospital charges, including per diem rates
Ambulance charges
Concession rentals

Education
Charges for books
Charges for gymnasium uniforms
Concession rentals

Recreation
Green fees
Parking charges
Concession rentals
Admission fees or charges
Permit charges for tennis courts, etc.
Charges for specific recreation services
Picnic stove fees
Stadium gate tickets
Stadium club fees
Park development charges

Sanitation
Domestic and commercial trash collection fees
Industrial waste charges

Sewerage
Sewerage system fees

Other public utility operations
Water meter permits
Water services charges
Electricity rates
Telephone booth rentals

Housing, neighborhood and commercial development
Street tree fees
Tract map filing fees
Street lighting installations
Convention center revenues

Commodity sales
Salvage materials
Sales of maps
Sales of codes

Licenses and fees
Advertising vehicles
Amusements (ferris wheels, etc.)
Billiard and pool halls
Bowling alleys
Circus and carnivals
Coal dealers
Commercial combustion
Dances
Dog tags
Duplicate dog tags
Electrician—first class
Electrician—second class
Film storage
Foot peddlers
Hucksters and itinerant peddlers
Heating equipment contractors
Hotels
Junk dealers
Loading zone permits
Lumber dealers
Pawnbrokers
Plumbers—first class
Plumbers—second class
Pest eradicators
Poultry dealers
Produce dealer—itinerant
Pushcarts
Rooming houses
Secondhand dealers
Sign inspection
Solicitation
Shooting gallery
Taxis
Taxi transfer licenses
Taxi drivers
Theaters
Trees—Christmas
Vending—coin
Vault cleaners
Sound truck
Refuse hauler
Landfill
Sightseeing bus
Wrecking license

Source: Selma J. Mushkin and Charles L. Vehorn, "User Fees and Charges," *Governmental Finance*, November 1977, p. 48.

Local government reliance on charges varies among jurisdictions. Table 11–3 shows that special districts depend most on such charges, whereas school districts depend least. Generally, special districts provide utility services, and charges to finance these services are readily acceptable. Educational services, on the other hand, have traditionally been largely provided free of direct charges. Counties and municipalities are general-purpose governments that provide both types of services; thus, their relative reliance on charge revenues lies between that of special districts and school districts.

Table 11–2 Selected city government revenue: 1972–73 to 1981–82 ($ in millions).

	Fiscal years				
Source of revenue	72–73	76–77	79–80	80–81	81–82
Charges (total)	$11,316	$17,766	$25,594	$29,611	$32,850
Current charges	4,533	6,872	9,875	11,200	12,445
Utility revenue	6,619	10,682	15,472	18,140	20,128
Liquor store revenue	164	212	247	271	277
Taxes (total from own sources)	18,477	26,067	31,256	34,104	37,077
Property taxes	11,879	15,653	16,859	18,278	19,502
Sales and gross receipts	3,567	5,805	8,208	8,956	10,195

	Percentage change, selected years			
	Current dollars	Constant (1972) dollars		
Source of revenue	73–82 (%)	73–77 (%)	77–82 (%)	73–82 (%)
Charges (total)	190.3	13.7	17.1	40.0
Current charges	174.5	9.7	16.5	32.4
Utility revenue	204.1	16.8	17.9	46.7
Liquor store revenue	68.9	−5.9	−6.8	−18.4
Taxes (total from own sources)	100.7	2.1	−4.1	−3.2
Property taxes	64.2	−4.6	−13.9	−20.8
Sales and gross receipts	185.8	17.8	12.7	37.8

Source: Derived from U.S. Bureau of the Census, *City Government Finances in 1976–77* (Washington, D.C.: GPO, 1979), Table 1; and U.S. Bureau of the Census, *City Government Finances in 1981–82* (Washington, D.C.: GPO, 1983), Table I.

Table 11–3 Percentage of revenues from various sources for local governments, 1981–82.

Source of revenue	All local governments	Counties	Municipalities	Townships	Special districts	School districts
Intergovernmental revenue	37.0	40.9	27.4	28.5	26.1	54.0
Tax revenue	33.1	33.6	32.1	52.4	9.6	36.7
Charges and miscellaneous general revenue	19.0	22.6	19.7	13.3	39.7	8.9

Source: Derived from U.S. Bureau of the Census, *Governmental Finances in 1981–82* (Washington, D.C.: GPO, 1983), Table 23.

User charge design

User charges and fees have substantial theoretical and practical advantages over taxes as a source of financing certain activities. They promote efficiency by functioning similarly to a pricing system. That is, they ration supply by allocating service to those who demand it most. The flow of user charge revenues signals the need for increasing the supply of a service and furnishes the funds to do it. However, for user charges to achieve their allocation goals, they must be carefully designed.

Principles

Pricing principles in the private economy are relevant to developing a user charge system for publicly provided services. The price of a soda, for example, reflects the cost of producing the soda and transporting it from the site of production to the place of purchase. Increases in these costs correspond to increases in the output of soda. Firms usually find it most profitable to charge a price that includes the marginal costs of production and distribution. Thus, for example, the price charged for a soda will be higher in an area to which the cost of transportation is higher.

Pricing also depends on demand. A consumer's willingness to pay for a soda depends on the satisfaction he or she expects to receive from drinking it. In general, the soda will be purchased if the consumer expects to enjoy it more than he or she would enjoy another product that costs the same amount of money. More sodas will be demanded if the satisfaction with the product increases—on hot days, for example. More sodas may also be demanded if the price goes down. The relationship between the cost of supplying sodas at the given level of output and the demand for soda by all consumers determines the price. In equilibrium, the price paid by the consumers covers the cost to the producers to supply the sodas.

Like prices, user charges should reflect the cost of providing additional units of the publicly provided good. This cost often varies by location. For example, it is more costly to collect refuse in low-density areas that are far away from a landfill site than to collect refuse in high-density areas nearer the landfill. The user charge should be higher for those in the low-density area. User charges also can allocate demand to those users who value the good or service most highly—those who are willing to pay the "price." For example, if a higher toll is charged at peak times for the use of a bridge, those who most value this service would pay the charge; others could defer their use of the bridge to times when the toll was lower.

Costs If user charges are to reflect the costs of providing service, the variables affecting costs are important. They include the interrelationship of output, distribution, customer location, and density of development at that location. In the case of a typical utility—water supply, for example—water is obtained and treated at one location. The cost of producing potable water at this location depends on how much water is to be supplied to the community. Larger volumes of water require larger facilities, more operating materials, and more labor. Thus, there is a positive relationship between long-run costs of the volume of water to be processed and that to be delivered. However, the total long-run cost, relative to increases in output, may not always increase; it may decline or remain constant. Long-run marginal cost has been shown to decline for movements from small to medium-sized water treatment plants but remain constant or even increase as large-capacity water treatment plants are constructed.[2]

Once a treatment plant is constructed, a different set of cost relationships may be in effect. Many costs, such as the building, the land, and large equipment, are fixed during the construction of the plant and do not change with the level of usage. Other costs, primarily short-run operating costs, vary with the volume of water produced each day. The change in these costs may be calculated as the volume of water treated in an existing plant is increased. These costs are termed short-run because they reflect the fact that a plant has already been constructed and can be expanded only with a significant delay in time for planning and construction. These short-run marginal costs of treatment (i.e., the incremental cost of treating one more gallon of water at a given level of operation) generally remain constant (or increase only slightly) in the range of the designed capacity of a plant. However, if the designed capacity is significantly exceeded, marginal costs may rise appreciably.

Whereas the relationship between output and short- and long-run cost is generally quite clear, the relationship of the location of the customer and the density of development at that location to the long-run cost of serving the individual needs to be examined more closely.

Density of development Several studies over the past 20 years have explored the effects of development patterns on the cost of service,[3] with primary emphasis on density. These studies show that the long-run cost of service declines per household as density of development (number of households per acre) increases. Again, the water supply system illustrates this concept. Water pipe is laid down the center of a street and individual service lines extend from the water main to each building. Higher density means more dwelling units per mile of water main as well as reduced cost and connections. Furthermore, the cost of laying a water main increases only in proportion to its diameter, but the volume of water a main can carry increases more than proportionally, according to its square. This means that the average cost per unit of water carried is less in a large-sized main.

Estimates of the relationship between long-run cost of service and density of development are presented in Table 11–4. They indicate that variations in cost of service among densities and types of development can be substantial. A low density single-family housing area is five times as expensive to serve as high-rise apartments, the cost falling from $3,311 per household per year for one dwelling unit per acre to $655 per household per year for 60 dwelling units per acre. The relationship between density and costs is less pronounced for water supply and sewerage. Table 11–4 also shows significant variations in operating (short-run) and capital costs.

Location Another component of the distribution cost of supplying services is customer location at the point of usage relative to the production site. In water supply, for example, the site of production is usually near a major water course. In order to supply water to households or businesses located at some distance from the treatment plant, water mains are laid from the plant to each location. Clearly, the costs will increase with the distance between the plant and the customer. Estimates of this cost of distance for various services are provided in Table 11–5.

Many services are provided at more than one site in a metropolitan area to economize on the cost of transportation and distribution of the service. For example, police and fire stations are located in several neighborhoods. There is, however, a limit to the potential for cost saving. Too many production sites can lead to higher output costs. Increasing the number of water treatment plants, for example, rather than increasing distribution from one plant, usually results in higher costs. Nevertheless, for each public service there will be a different

Table 11–4 The cost of providing public services by property type and density.

Cost	Single-family homes (1,000 units)			
	1 unit/acre	2 units/acre	3 units/acre	5 units/acre
Capital cost				
Police	$ 113,852	$ 111,752	$ 109,652	$ 105,452
Fire	119,918	108,368	96,818	73,718
Sanitation	29,220	27,620	25,220	23,140
Schools	5,353,582	5,353,582	5,353,582	5,353,582
Water supply	7,529,720	3,833,744	2,563,857	1,739,362
Storm drainage	4,835,868	2,420,383	1,595,857	1,068,046
Sanitary sewerage	2,963,624	1,586,257	1,121,045	813,398
Total capital cost	20,945,784	13,441,706	10,865,360	9,176,693
Yearly capital cost	1,828,203	1,167,283	939,488	788,740
Operating cost				
Police	69,817	66,267	62,717	55,617
Fire	135,711	116,011	96,311	56,911
Sanitation	35,287	33,142	30,315	27,780
Schools	1,168,258	1,168,258	1,168,258	1,168,258
Water supply	31,821	31,821	31,821	31,821
Storm drainage	—	—	—	—
Sanitary sewerage	41,289	34,401	32,133	30,604
Yearly operating cost	1,483,183	1,449,900	1,421,555	1,370,991
Total annual cost per dwelling unit	3,311	2,617	2,361	2,160

Cost	Multifamily homes (1,000 units)				
		Walk-up apartments		High-rise apartments	
	Townhouses, 10 units/acre	15 units/acre	30 units/acre	30 units/acre	60 units/acre
Capital cost					
Police	$ 104,852	$ 104,252	$ 103,652	$ 103,652	$ 103,052
Fire	52,974	52,974	52,974	52,974	65,474
Sanitation	21,244	18,140	17,380	15,796	14,820
Schools	4,538,155	4,538,155	4,538,155	1,646,167	1,646,167
Water supply	1,163,154	855,900	485,304	566,792	334,777
Storm drainage	710,649	462,420	231,274	284,552	117,684
Sanitary sewerage	594,021	438,451	354,678	345,062	274,509
Total capital cost	7,185,049	6,470,292	5,886,917	3,027,495	2,556,483
Yearly capital cost	617,607	555,001	494,079	264,018	222,446
Operating cost					
Police	52,067	49,700	46,150	46,150	42,600
Fire	41,589	41,589	41,589	54,722	54,722
Sanitation	25,469	21,686	20,760	18,850	17,640
Schools	988,526	988,526	988,526	269,598	269,598
Water supply	30,103	30,103	30,103	25,538	25,538
Storm drainage	—	—	—	—	—
Sanitary sewerage	28,022	27,250	26,679	22,825	22,476
Yearly operating cost	1,165,776	1,158,854	1,152,807	437,683	432,574
Total annual cost per dwelling unit	1,783	1,714	1,647	702	655

Source: Paul B. Downing and Richard D. Gustely, "The Public Service Costs of Alternative Development Patterns: A Review of the Evidence," in Paul B. Downing, ed., *Local Service Pricing Policies and Their Effect on Urban Spacial Structure* (Vancouver, B.C.: Univ. of British Columbia Press, 1977). Table 8.

Table 11–5 Annual cost of providing public services per mile distant from public facility site.

Service	Capital or operating costs per mile ($)
Police	438[a]
Fire	216[a]
Sanitation	3,360[b]
Schools	19,845[b]
Water supply	21,560[b]
Storm drainage	6,187[c]
Sanitary sewers	12,179[c]
Total cost	68,498

Source: Paul B. Downing and Richard D. Gustely, "The Public Service Costs of Alternative Development Patterns: A Review of the Evidence," in Paul B. Downing, ed. *Local Service Pricing Policies and Their Effect on Urban Spacial Structure* (Vancouver, B.C.: Univ. of British Columbia Press, 1977). Table 9.

[a] Includes only operating costs.

[b] Includes both capital and operating costs.

[c] Includes only capital costs.

combination of production sites and distribution costs, which minimize the total costs incurred in supplying services.

Demand variation Once decisions have been made on the location and the output capacity of the production facilities and the capacity and location of distribution facilities, the demand for the service becomes important. At some point at or beyond the designed capacity of the facility, the short-run marginal costs of serving additional users increase sharply. If the demand for the service varies significantly over time, the facility may periodically face a capacity constraint, commonly called *peak load*. If the facility is financed through general revenues or if the same low average-cost price is charged at all times, the result may be overuse of the facility. At peak load, the incremental cost of serving one more user or one more unit of use far exceeds the average charge paid by the consumer. Overuse implies that the average user subsidizes the peak load user. Overuse also results in increased social or congestion costs; in water supply, pressure is lost; in the supply of electricity, brownouts occur; in highways or travel, delays and traffic jams arise. As the quality of service declines, social and private costs (e.g., lost time and equipment failure) rise. If at peak demand periods, however, consumers are charged a higher rate reflecting the true cost of peak output, then overuse and its attendant costs might be eliminated or at least sharply reduced.

Components

Designing the ideal user charge system requires consideration of the following three major components:

1. *The short-run cost of current output*. Generally, a single charge per unit that varies directly with the quantity consumed will be sufficient. When there are significant peak load demands, this quantity charge should be considerably higher. The time-variable/peak-load volume charge reflects the costs of servicing various residents.
2. *The difference between the quantity charge and the full cost of production when the peak charge does not recover the full capital costs.*

This capacity charge reflects the outlay for the fixed costs of the service (i.e., depreciation and financing of the plant). It may be allocated on the basis of each customer's potential use of the designed capacity. Where fixed costs are not very high, the charge need not be levied.

3. *The long-run cost of serving residents at each location.* This location charge reflects distance and density. It can be paid monthly or as a connection charge or special assessment when the area is served initially.

The end product is a combination of charges that are higher for those who demand more service, for residents who live in areas that are particularly expensive to serve (for reasons of distance and/or density), and for those who use the service during peak periods. Because this pricing system embodies the costs of service, the charges provide residents with proper price signals. Moreover, the adequacy of revenues generated by properly constructed charges provides the local government managers with information on the desirability of increasing the levels of service. Furthermore, developers and prospective new residents can decide whether the value of developing a new area is greater than the cost of providing the required public services. The managers of the public facility can observe the quantity demanded during peak times at the peak load prices. If the total revenues generated will cover the total cost of expansion, it may be worthwhile to expand the facility. A well-designed system of charges can improve the provision of public services by allocating the available supply to those who value it most and by providing accurate information on the desirability of expanding service.

Adding to the complexity of developing this ideal user charge system are a number of practical considerations.

Administrative costs Administrative costs include costs for collecting data on individual consumption of public services, calculating the costs of serving each resident at that volume of use, and billing for and collecting the user charge. These administrative costs might be relatively large for some services. While it is relatively easy and inexpensive to install a water meter, for example, it is quite difficult and expensive to monitor the volume and noxiousness of sewage in the treatment system. Administrative costs for calculating individual usage directly may be so high in some cases that indirect methods should be used instead. For example, volume charges for sewer service can be based on the volume of water consumed. Such indirect measurements can retain the advantages of the volume charge without the disadvantages of administrative costs. Nevertheless, there is a quality problem with indirect measurement. Household sewage, for example, may not be as difficult or as costly to treat as industrial waste; consequently, measuring the volume of water used to indicate the volume of sewage can be misleading and information on the quality of the sewage may be needed.

For many public services, the rate of use among residents (and thus the cost of service per resident) is relatively constant. If the administrative costs of employing variable charges based on volume are higher than the additional revenues collected, variable charges would be uneconomical. Similarly, when variations in cost of serving residents at different locations are small, the extra administrative costs of instituting a variance in the charge system may outweigh any gains in efficiency. Finally, billing costs in a user charge system may be substantial. It is possible that costs would be high enough to prohibit a periodic billing system. But in this age of inexpensive computers a municipality that prepares periodic bills for other services may add the cost of processing another item at a minimum of expense.

Consumer acceptance A second practical consideration is consumers' attitudes toward the user charge system. When the benefits of the public service are easily identified—consumption of water, use of public golf courses, tennis courts, and bridges, for example—user charges are readily understood and accepted by most citizens. However, charges that cannot be related to use so easily (e.g., impact fees charged on development to help finance low-income housing in other parts of a city) will encounter resistance. Furthermore, consumers faced with a user charge system may consider the federal income tax effect. Whereas local taxes are deductible from taxable income, user charges are not. This means that a dollar paid in user charges is more costly to the local resident than a dollar paid in property taxes. (The difference between the two costs will depend on the individual's marginal income-tax rate.) Thus, extensive use of charges can make local government services more expensive to residents. This phenomenon will be most significant for high-income residents and for high-income communities.

Cost of services In general, user charges should reflect the full costs of service, including operation, maintenance, and capital costs for production and distribution. These costs may not be easy to calculate, however, because municipal accounting systems are not necessarily designed for this purpose and the current value or the cost of past capital investment may not be available (most often the case with long-lived assets such as water mains). This can lead to undercharging and a more rapid expansion of service than is economically justifiable. Furthermore, with the user charge below the full cost of providing the service and the demand for and consumption of the service relatively high, the total costs for everyone involved may increase.

There are, however, particular public goods or services—merit goods—for which it is considered counterproductive to charge the full cost of production. Consumption of these goods provides long-run benefits to society as a whole. Recreation, for example, improves health and reduces social unrest, and education improves productivity and enhances the atmosphere of the community. (Precisely which public services are to be included in the category of merit goods is still debatable). Nevertheless, in most jurisdictions some user charges are reduced or eliminated and the more affluent provide some subsidy to enable lower-income individuals to consume these types of goods and services.

User charges for individual services

The production, distribution, and administration costs vary among publicly supplied services, and charges should vary accordingly. This section outlines user charge systems for several services.[4] These systems attempt to incorporate both the theoretically ideal and the practical realities of local government finance.

Water supply

The water supply of a local government closely approximates a privately produced good. In fact, many communities are served by privately owned and operated water utilities. The major arguments for a public system (or a controlled utility) are efficiency, safety, and certainty of supply. Since output of water for a given area (i.e., obtaining it from a source and treating it so that it is fit for human consumption) is subject to decreasing costs as output increases, water is a natural candidate for monopoly; output is most often centered with one supplier, particularly when the source of supply is a river or lake.

The water charge system suggested here consists of a flat amount per gallon consumed plus a fixed distribution charge based on service area, capacity to use the system, and front footage. It covers the cost of service and all expected maintenance costs. Although water pricing policies vary substantially among jurisdictions, the most prevalent system calls for a *declining block rate* volume charge (i.e., a charge that is lower per unit as more water is used) and, perhaps, a front foot charge. The former has been justified with the argument that the average cost per unit of water produced and delivered declines as the volume produced increases. However, an analysis suggests that this may not be the case and that a flat volume rate per unit should be charged instead. Even so, delivering large volumes of water does reduce pipe, meter, and administrative costs, and these savings should be reflected in a proportionately lower capacity charge for large-volume users, unless usage is erratic. However, declining block rates with minimal charges *below* the cost of producing water will encourage waste.

The three major variables affecting distribution costs are:

1. The distance from the source of supply or central distribution site (e.g., treatment plant)
2. The density of customers in an area
3. The capacity of service for each customer (usually measured in terms of the size of the lateral pipe from the water main).

It is not practical to calculate the cost of serving individual customers. Instead, service areas can be delineated so that each is relatively homogeneous in terms of distance and density. An estimate of the marginal cost of distribution to each area may be made and the cost allocated to each customer within the area in proportion to expected consumption. A second part of the distribution charge would be based on the number of feet of street frontage occupied by each customer. The cost of distributing water increases as the number of feet of pipe between customers increases. A front foot charge based on this cost would be levied on each customer. In those few cases where the capacity to receive water is particularly large, a higher charge per unit or an additional capacity charge may be levied. Such a charge would be most significant for large-volume industrial users in outlying areas whose pattern of use may be highly volatile.

While front foot charges are designed to cover the costs of distribution, they reflect only the density portion of distribution costs, not the distance portion. Some local governments, such as Fairfax County, Virginia, have recognized this problem and have adjusted charges for new connections to include at least some of the distance costs. But even these charges include only the capital costs of distribution. Maintenance costs are not included nor are the capacity costs of the treatment facility.

Generally, physical data on which charges are based will not change too rapidly. Therefore, the administrative costs of calculating and applying such charges should not be excessive. With the quantity of water demanded by most residential and probably most commercial users so small relative to total output, the short-run marginal costs of output can be treated as constant, and a flat rate per unit of water consumed can be charged to all classes of consumers.

The most efficient way to measure usage is to meter all connections and bill users periodically. This process is not too expensive and failure to adhere to it will increase waste in water consumption. Theoretically, a peak charge in addition to the average rate should be placed on peak period users, as marginal costs do increase. However, the extra costs involved in metering peak period use may prohibit levying these charges on all but a few large users. In this case, in addition to the variable output charge, the average consumer should pay a capacity charge to help cover the fixed costs of the treatment plant.[5]

Finally, total charges can be billed monthly or bimonthly. An alternative billing method is to levy the distribution charge (but not the user charge) as a lump sum or special assessment at the time of development. The lump-sum charge has the minor advantage of reducing the complexity of the water billing procedure. On the other hand, having the distribution charge appear explicitly on the monthly bill acts as a continual reminder of the cost of location choice made by the consumer. Without further study it is impossible to say whether this advantage offsets the additional administrative costs.

In current practice the structure of the water charge system is not closely related to the cost of service. Users in outlying areas that are expensive to serve are relatively undercharged, whereas users in areas that are less expensive to serve are overcharged. The volume charge, excluding high-volume users, usually exceeds the marginal cost of service. These deficiencies in the pricing system lead to uneconomical growth and demand and costly operation of many local government water systems.

Sanitary sewerage

The general cost characteristics of the sanitary sewerage system are similar to those of the water supply system. The average costs of collection and transmission increase with a greater distance between sewage production and disposal sites. The costs decrease with increases in the density of the population to be served, because a large system decreases the per capita costs. While there are economies of scale in treating sewage, it appears that they are exhausted in systems that serve 100,000 people.[6] For populations of this size or larger, costs are relatively constant for any given percentage of removal of pollutants.

The marginal cost of treating sewage is determined by both the strength (or pollution potential) and the volume of the sewage. For domestic and commercial customers, strength is relatively constant and need not be included as a variable in determining charges. For these users, the volume of sewage is the variable on which to base the output price. Because it is relatively expensive to build meters to measure sewage flows from individual households, a measurement of water consumption might be better. Domestic and ordinary commercial water consumption, exclusive of lawn sprinkling, should reflect a very close approximation of the quantity of sewage discharged. This volume can be estimated by metering water consumption during the winter months. The average of the water meter may be used to determine a monthly charge for the entire year.

For industrial customers the strength of the sewage may be an important variable. To reduce costs, pretreatment of the sewage should be required to bring it down to the average domestic strength. Another alternative is to impose a strength surcharge on the regular volume charge. There also may be significant differences between metered water consumption and sewage flow for large industrial users. Sewage meters, although they are expensive, may be justified in this case. (It should be noted that the federal Water Pollution Control Act requires major industries connected to municipal sewage systems to pay a user charge that covers all costs, including a strength surcharge on the volume of sewage discharged.)

Sewage collection and transmission charges should be calculated in a way similar to that used for water charges. Service areas should be defined, and a charge established for front footage. A capacity charge also should be made on the basis of water meter or water pipe size. The consumption potential of water is a good indicator of the demand for extra sewer capacity. The current practice in charging for sewage sanitation is somewhat more varied than that for water supply. Sewer user charges may simply be a percentage of the water bill. The costs of supplying water, even with a well-designed water user charge, do not necessarily vary with service characteristics in the same way that the cost of sewer service may vary.

Another common system is a flat monthly charge that is equal to the average cost of serving all residents. In this case, high-cost users (in terms of volume and location) are undercharged. As with the water charge, the marginal cost for more use of the service is zero, which leads to demands for excessive and costly service. A third charge system closely reflects the optimal user charge structure. A flat rate is charged per unit of water consumed since this approximates the load placed on the sewerage facilities. This charge may be adjusted for summer lawn watering. A front foot sewer line charge may be employed in conjunction with any of these systems.

Stormwater sewerage

Stormwater will either percolate into the ground or flow across the surface to a water body (e.g., lake or stream). Urban development tends to increase surface runoff because buildings, roads, and parking lots are impervious to water. Storm sewerage costs increase with lower density of development and with a greater area of paved development. While stormwater sewerage costs vary with distance, they differ from sanitary sewerage costs because the collected stormwater runoff is released untreated into nearby surface water bodies rather than routed to the treatment plant.

In practice, user charges for storm sewers, if they exist at all, consist only of service area and front foot charges. Because there is no treatment, no output charge is needed.[7] Note, however, that the service areas will differ from those for sanitary sewers, as the location of stormwater outfalls is likely to differ from the location of treatment plants. The charge for service area would be apportioned among land users on the basis of the surface area of each individual site and the percentage of that area covered by impervious materials. The charge system would be improved if the potential for generating runoff through development of impervious areas were recognized. Furthermore, distance to a viable outfall site should be reflected in the charge. Omission of these two factors can lead to high cost of service and undesirable locations for development.

Refuse collection

Refuse (solid waste) collection, like water supply, closely approximates a private service. Disposal, collection, and transmission costs vary with the volume of refuse collected and the distance and density involved.[8] These costs may include environmental damages because disposal sites can contribute to surface and groundwater pollution.

Individual consumers' variations in volume have only minor effects on cost, but variations in expected volume among residential consumers, and certainly between residential and commercial consumers, can be substantial. Consequently, one part of the charge for each group should reflect a capacity charge of a flat price per unit of refuse multiplied by average volume of refuse. For areas with more than 500 residents, there appears to be a relatively constant return to scale in collection and transmission costs per mile. Disposal costs for a sanitary landfill would probably be subject to decreasing costs for a larger population, but because there is no hard evidence on these costs, it seems that for a population beyond 100,000 the economies of scale are exhausted as well.

Cost-of-service characteristics indicate that a two-part charge system would be an optimal method of allocating costs. First, there should be a disposal charge per unit based on actual volume. Second, there should be a charge for collection and transmission based on the varying costs of serving each collection route. This second charge would, therefore, be higher for areas more distant from the disposal site and less densely developed. In contrast to this system, current practice is often a flat fee independent of volume or location.

There are, however, some practical problems in implementing such a charge system for refuse collection, beginning with measuring volume. A seemingly easy method is to count the number of full or partially full 30-gallon (or some other standard size) trash cans collected from each resident. This measure, however, creates a problem of definition: How tightly packed may a "full" trash can be? Further disadvantages are the time the collector would spend to record the number of cans collected from each site, the probability of errors, and the increased likelihood of consumer complaints. Thus, an approximation of the volume charge should be considered. The best collection system for single-family residences may be to collect no more than a certain number of cans per collection day and to charge a flat volume charge. More cans may be collected, but only at an additional charge and with a prior agreement. Special collection charges may be justified for multifamily residential complexes. It takes less time to collect a number of cans at one location than to collect the same number at different locations; therefore, the collection charge per can should be less for apartments. Multifamily residences and commercial consumers who use special containers and sophisticated handling equipment, such as Dempster Dumpsters, could be charged a lower collection charge per unit.

Highways and bridges

The costs of providing a road or bridge are different from those for other public services. A road or bridge is designed to carry a specific volume of traffic at a specific speed and during a specific time period. If the volume of traffic is below the design capacity, there is no problem of congestion, and the cost of accommodating one more car is minimal. These costs include wear and tear on the road and increased risk of accidents. When traffic exceeds the design capacity, however, congestion results, speed and traffic slow, and travelers suffer delays.

To ensure that those using the road or bridge during high demand or peak traffic times consider the costs they impose on other drivers, a user charge may be imposed during peak traffic periods. In practice, there are two options. One is to operate toll booths with a higher toll during such peak periods as the morning and evening rush hours. The other is to charge no toll during off-peak hours and to operate the booths only during peak traffic hours.[9] The peak load method is seldom used, however. Generally, the toll remains constant at all times of the day, and in many cases discount coupons or tokens are sold to frequent users of the facility. The bargain price implicit in the flat rate discount structure may not accurately reflect the demand for and the value of expanding the facility. This discount may even encourage traffic at peak times rather than discourage it. A peak load charge, on the other hand, would encourage the use of car pools and public transportation. Furthermore, a peak pricing system may give a better reading of total demand for the transportation system as a whole.

Public transit systems

Transit systems also have limited capacity and wide variations in peak and off-peak demands, which implies that the cost of service during peak periods is high. During off-peak periods the incremental costs are much lower, but they are not zero because the transit system uses fuel and drivers as well as equipment. Operating costs are also affected by length of trip, suggesting a charge based on distance traveled on the system. This charge should be higher during peak periods.

The prices employed for most public transit systems, like those for highways and bridges, fail to reflect this cost structure adequately. Typically, the same price is charged during peak and off-peak periods. If persons who use the service during peak periods are sold passes at a discount, peak period prices are actually reduced. Therefore, excess demand during peak hours does not necessarily reflect a true willingness to pay for increased service. On the other hand, the absence of tolls for cars during peak periods would reduce the peak demand for public transit facilities. The mix of incorrect prices provides the policymaker with false information about the level of demand for both systems.

Because the cost of service increases with distance traveled, it would seem appropriate to charge more for longer rides. Several transit services use a practical system of zone fares. The user pays an initial charge, plus zone charges for each boundary crossed. In the absence of a zone charge system, long-distance riders are undercharged and generally overutilize the transit system.

Parks and recreation

The cost characteristics of park and recreation facilities are largely similar to those of highways or bridges. Once a facility is built, the cost of having one more user is essentially zero—at low levels of use. At high levels, however, crowding reduces everyone's enjoyment. Tennis courts are a good example. In low-use periods, courts are always available, but at high-use times, the courts are filled. A court use charge levied during high-use periods would ensure that the courts are employed in an optimal manner. Those who value the use of the courts during high-use time can play (by paying for the service), and those who can rearrange their time can play at an off-peak time and avoid the charge.

Many park and recreation facilities use a system that charges only during peak demand periods. Public golf courses, for example, commonly charge a higher price on weekends. Even when charges are lowered for low-income groups, such as senior citizens, these lower prices are generally offered during off-peak weekday hours. Finally, these special rates reflect the community's assessment that recreation is a merit good.

Development charges and fiscal impact fees

Development charges are another way of pricing public services. The local government charges a land developer a fee that reflects the full capital costs of development to the municipality. Development charges are negotiated between the local government and the developer. They often take the form of in-kind provision of public goods, such as park and school facilities constructed by the developer.

These arrangements reduce local government service costs, but they may also raise the cost of houses in the development. After all, for the developer to make a profit, the development charge will have to be passed on to the consumer. Ultimately, if the price of the house (which includes the cost of building and the cost of public services) is greater than the value of the house to potential buyers, development will be discouraged. In the long run, these charges eliminate the development of uneconomical areas.

The *fiscal impact fee* is an increasingly popular form of development charge. It is a one-time charge intended as payment for the cost of off-site public facilities needed to accommodate the increase in demand generated by the new development. Again, the water system provides a good example. When a large residential subdivision increases the demand for water treatment and distribution, the capital costs of meeting this increase can be calculated. These costs include the portion of treatment plant capacity used by residents of the new subdivision and a pro rata share of the capital cost of the water mains used to bring the water to the subdivision. Collecting a one-time impact fee to cover capital costs and imposing a user charge to cover variable costs thereafter would come close to the theoretical ideal.

In practice, however, impact fees seldom operate in this ideal fashion but are subject to compromise. Usually, they cover far less than the full capital costs attributable to new developments. Often, impact fees are negotiated between the developer and the jurisdiction. Sometimes the developer may donate land for recreational use, for example, instead of paying a fee.

There is little hard data on the use of fiscal impact fees. In three separate survey studies, Paul Downing and James Frank have developed basic data on the use of fiscal impact fees for recreation, sewers, and fire protection.[10] They found 219 recreational impact fees, 190 sewer impact fees, and 21 fire impact fees in the United States at the time of their studies. The largest number of jurisdictions charging impact fees is found in California, perhaps a result of Proposition 13. Florida is another frequent user of impact fees. Other states with substantial use include Oregon, Washington, Texas, Colorado, Minnesota, New York, and Pennsylvania. Fee levels vary from a few dollars to as much as $1,800 per single-family dwelling unit for recreation, $6,200 for sewer, and $600 for fire. The national averages are $377 for recreation, $689 for sewers, and $183 for fire service. Once impact fees are adopted, jurisdictions often employ them for more than one service. Fee revenues are usually segregated from the general fund and are spent mostly for land, capital improvements, and equipment.

There are substantial political advantages to impact fees. The fees are paid by developers rather than by current residents, allowing the government to maintain lower property taxes and user charges. For example, suppose public facility expansion were financed by property taxes. Both existing residents and new residents would pay. Consequently, existing residents would be partially subsidizing new development. If the existing residents do not perceive expansion as valuable, they will resist it. Under an impact fee system, the developer pays the incremental capital costs (which are presumably included in house prices) and there is no additional burden on existing residents. However, developers have resisted paying the sometimes substantial fees. The response has been a compromise, with the developers being charged only a portion of full costs and existing residents subsidizing the balance. To ensure proper appropriation of benefits, courts have required the separation of impact fee revenues. In the absence of court challenges, impact fee revenues have been used to supply facilities to existing (nonpaying) residents as well.

Impact fees are viewed favorably by most local government managers because the funds are available when they are needed. It is not necessary to float bonds or seek authority to raise taxes. Furthermore, the funds are judicially constrained for use in building capital facilities, reducing the risk that funds may be diverted during the annual budget deliberations. Other services for which fiscal impact fees have been adopted include roads, schools, drainage, water, police, solid waste, and libraries. Obviously, any service that requires the expenditure of funds for capital facilities and equipment is a candidate for such fees. It does appear that their use is spreading, especially in the rapidly growing sections of the country.

Comparison of revenue systems

It is important for local government finance managers to understand and consider the effects of various revenue systems on distribution of costs and on individual decisions. Useful for financial planning is a comparison of user charges with the property tax, the other principal source of local government revenue. At issue are three major questions:

1. The effects on land development
2. The effects on demand for publicly provided services
3. The effects on different income groups.

Effects on development

The amount charged for publicly provided services and to whom—developer, future homeowner, or current resident—influences the timing and intensity of development.[11] As noted above, a developer considering investment in a project will estimate the cost to construct or improve houses, office buildings, or other structures as well as development fees, and the price purchasers would be willing to pay for the land and improvements. If the final price will be high relative to demand, the developer may not proceed. The net price to the developer may be the same whether the developer or homeowner pays the fee, unless the local government levies an average-cost user charge on both new and present residents.

Marginal-cost user charges vary among areas served by the local government depending on the difficulty and cost of bringing services to the locality. In areas where charges would be higher, land is less likely to be developed. In lower cost-of-service areas, on the other hand, a marginal-cost user charge will not reduce potential development as much, an advantage for local government because it allows a more efficient service mix.

However, if an average-cost user charge is employed, high-cost areas will pay somewhat less for public services than the full costs. The average cost for the entire city will be below the cost of serving new high-cost areas. These lower average-cost user charges will increase the probability that high-cost areas will be developed. The average-cost user charge in low-cost areas, on the other hand, will be greater than the cost of service, thereby decreasing the potential price of houses and inhibiting development.

The location effects of the general property tax lie somewhere in between those of the two user charge systems. Under an average-cost user charge system, property values will be relatively higher in high cost-of-service areas and lower in low cost-of-service areas than they would be under a marginal-cost user charge system, although this relationship is not perfect.[12] Thus the property tax, based on property values, will reflect in part the undercharging or overcharging inherent in average-cost systems. Many other factors cause variations in the value of property, but it is sufficient to note that a property tax helps offset the inaccuracies of an average-cost user charge. The more closely the user charge reflects differences in the marginal cost of serving different areas, the less it will affect relative property values. It is probably impossible to design a user charge system that captures all differences in the marginal cost of service, but the resultant errors will be reflected in property values. It is advantageous, therefore, to combine a practical marginal-cost user charge with a property tax, thereby encouraging economically efficient development.

As much as development is encouraged, it must also be controlled. An average-cost user charge may promote growth at the expense of the existing population, if the cost of serving the new resident is higher than the average cost of serving current residents. Although the new developments may raise total costs incrementally, the new residents will pay only average costs. Because this is less than the full cost of the services extended to them, new residents are essentially subsidized by the current users, a subsidy that stimulates demand for new developments. A properly designed marginal-cost system would not provide this stimulus because all new residents would pay for the additional incremental costs of the public services. On the other hand, where the marginal cost of serving new residents is below the average cost of serving existing residents, an average-cost user charge would inhibit the growth of the area.

The property tax method of financing public services has an intermediate effect. It stimulates growth less than an average-cost user charge, but it still provides some subsidy from existing residents to new residents whenever the cost to serve new residents is higher than that for existing residents.

Effects on demand

The different methods of financing public services also affect the demand for service. The volume charge of a marginal-cost user charge system reflects the variable cost of increasing output, and residents decide how much to consume based on this cost. An average-cost user charge, however, will not be equal to the short-run marginal cost of increasing output. The charge may be higher or lower than the marginal costs. Therefore, the resident, in adjusting consumption to price, may over- or underconsume the service. For example, in the case of water supply, low-volume users often are charged more than the actual costs they impose on the system; this usually inhibits water consumption.

Financing public services through the property tax implies that the cost to the consumer for the use of additional units is zero. Since this is seldom the case, the property tax stimulates overconsumption of the service and increases the cost of local government—which partially explains the movement toward expenditure control in California and elsewhere.

Lump-sum methods of financing services and average-cost user charges also lead to excessive demand during peak demand periods. A marginal-cost user charge that is higher during peak demand periods would help reduce use of the facility during peak periods and spread it more evenly throughout the day. Peak load charges seem appropriate for such services as urban bridges and highways, public transportation, and recreation facilities.

Effects on different income groups

Local government managers often express concern for the effects of alternative financing systems on people in various income classes. In general, it is presumed that lower-income people should pay less for public services because their ability to pay is less. But how is that amount to be determined? The most common method is to calculate the payment as a percentage of the person's income. A system that calls for a higher percentage of income as income increases is *progressive,* and a system that calls for a higher percentage of income from lower-income people is *regressive*.

Both average- and marginal-cost user charge systems are relatively more regressive than the property tax.[13] However, marginal-cost charges are much less regressive than average-cost charges. When an average-cost user charge is employed, low-income people generally pay more than it actually costs to serve them; in effect, low-income residents subsidize high-income residents. This subsidy does not occur under a marginal-cost user charge system, because high-income people tend to live in large homes located in more distant and less dense areas. Thus their cost of services is higher and they pay higher marginal-cost user charges.

Special districts

The final section of this chapter deals with special districts because of their heavy reliance on user charges to finance services. The Census Bureau defines special districts as limited-purpose governmental units that exist as separate corporate entities and, theoretically, have fiscal and administrative independence from general-purpose governments. Fiscal independence suggests that a special district may determine its budget without review by other local officials or governments, levy taxes for its own support, collect charges for its services, and issue debt without review by another local government.[14] Administrative independence, according to the Census Bureau, means that a public agency such as a special district has a popularly elected governing body that represents two or more state or local governments and performs functions that are essentially different from those of its creating governments.[15] Due to the uniqueness of school districts, this discussion concerns only non-school districts.

Many special districts are, by law, subordinate to a parent governmental unit (or units). These dependent special districts generally have one or more of the following characteristics:

1. The agency officers are appointed by the chief executive and/or governing body of the parent government(s).
2. The agency controls facilities that supplement or take the place of facilities ordinarily provided by the creating government(s).
3. The agency properties and responsibilities revert to the creating government after the agency's debt has been repaid.
4. The agency plans must be approved by the creating government(s).
5. The parent government(s) specifies the type and location of facilities that the agency is to construct and maintain.[16]

The range of services provided by special districts includes water supply, sewerage, refuse, fire protection, housing and urban renewal, and drainage and flood control. The types and numbers of special districts are listed in Table 11–6. The Census Bureau groups special districts into single- and multiple-function categories. As Table 11–6 indicates, nearly all types of districts increased substantially in number between 1962 and 1982. Aside from the "other" category, the greatest growth was in sewer and water supply districts (693.5 percent), natural resources and water supply (203.6 percent), and housing and urban renewal (200.0 percent). Fire protection districts were the most numerous in each year reported.

Fiscal characteristics

Most special districts in metropolitan areas have the right to levy user charges, and they often have significant property taxing powers as well. The property tax is the only form of general tax levied by special districts. Reliance on the

Table 11–6 Number of special districts, selected years, by function.

Function	No. of special districts					% change,
	1962	1967	1972	1977	1982	1962–1982
Single-function districts						
Cemeteries	1,283	1,397	1,496	1,615	1,577	22.9
School buildings	915	956	1,085	1,020	960	4.9
Fire protection	3,229	3,665	3,872	4,187	4,560	41.2
Highways	786	774	698	652	598	−23.9
Health	231	234	257	350	451	95.2
Hospitals	418	537	655	715	775	85.4
Housing and urban renewal	1,099	1,565	2,270	2,408	3,296	200.0
Libraries	349	410	498	586	638	82.8
Drainage and flood control	2,740	2,855	2,869	2,936	2,705	−1.3
Irrigation and soil and water conservation	3,245	3,475	3,530	3,365	3,238	−0.2
Other natural resources	309	209	231	294	298	−3.5
Parks and recreation	488	613	749	829	924	89.3
Sewers	937	1,233	1,406	1,610	1,631	74.1
Water supply	1,502	2,140	2,323	2,480	2,637	75.6
Electric power, gas supply, and transit	116	126	155	224	317	173.3
Other	488	622	889	971	661	35.4
Multiple-function districts						
Sewer and water supply	138	298	629	1,065	1,095	693.5
Natural resources and water supply	56	45	67	71	170	203.6
Other	120	110	207	584	1,332	1,010.1

Source: U.S. Department of Commerce, Bureau of the Census, 1982 Census of Governments, vol. 1, *Governmental Organization*, part 1, *Governmental Organization* (Washington, D.C.: GPO, 1984), Table 9.

property tax may exceed 80.0 percent in such categories as fire protection, health services, and libraries. On the other hand, special districts that provide utility services such as sewerage, water, and electricity rely on charges and use little or no property tax revenue. On average, special districts account for only 1.9 percent of the local government general taxes in the United States, and in no state did special districts raise as much as 9.0 percent of the local taxes.[17]

One of the features that distinguishes special districts from other governmental entities is their heavy use of pricing mechanisms (e.g., user fees, charges, and special assessments). In 1981–82, 39.7 percent of all special district receipts were derived from charges, compared with 19.7 percent for municipalities, 22.6 percent for counties, 13.3 percent for townships, and 8.9 percent for school districts (see Table 11–3). Special districts employ user fees to such an extent because they are a potentially effective means of ensuring a more efficient allocation of public resources.

The special assessment is a financial instrument often employed by special districts. It is levied on property owners for such public works as pavement improvement, drainage, parking facilities, and other capital improvements. Because these public works often enhance the value of nearby land, it is deemed logical to charge part or all of the cost of the works to the landowners. Special assessments are very similar to user fees, in both rationale and economic effects.[18] This lump-sum charge reflects at least part of the location-dependent costs of service; this being the case, the special assessment is roughly equivalent to the present value of future marginal-cost user charges.

In addition to charges and taxes, many special districts receive considerable financial aid from federal, state, and other local sources. Table 11–7 outlines the revenue sources, including intergovernmental revenues, for special districts. In fact, the growth in aid monies has been greater than the growth in revenues from charges.

Table 11–7 Revenue sources for special districts (amounts in $ millions).

					% change		
Revenue source	1966–67	1971–72	1976–77	1981–82	66–67 to 71–72	71–72 to 76–77	76–77 to 81–82
Total revenue	3,778	6,821	14,408	30,961	80.6	111.2	114.9
Taxes	589	968	1,718	2,846	64.4	77.5	65.6
Intergovernmental aid	635	1,550	4,332	8,271	144.1	179.6	90.9
Charges and miscellaneous	1,513	2,672	5,301	12,687	76.6	98.4	139.3

Source: U.S. Department of Commerce, Bureau of the Census, 1982 Census of Governments, vol. 4, *Governmental Finances*, part 1, *Governmental Finances* (Washington, D.C.: GPO, 1982), Table 48.

Administrative control

Special districts are governed by elected or appointed boards that are responsible for such activities as the day-to-day administration of district affairs and the employment of the administrative staff. Board members often rely heavily on professional consultants and appointed committees for decision making on many issues. It is also common for districts to employ a full-time, salaried administrative officer who is responsible for carrying out the policies formulated by the board.

Special districts may be created or dissolved through a number of procedures, including petitions, public hearings, state actions, referenda, and court actions. Petitions and public hearings are the most common. Following numerous public

Table 11–8 Number of special districts (inside and outside SMSAs) in states enacting legislation to control special districts, selected years.

State	1962	1967	% change, 1962–67	1972	% change, 1967–72	1977	% change, 1972–77	1982	% change, 1977–82
California	1,962	2,168	10.5	2,223	2.5	2,227	0.2	2,506	12.5
Nevada	85	89	4.7	134	50.6	132	−1.5	134	1.5
New Mexico	102	97	−5.0	99	2.1	100	1.0	101	1.0
Oregon	727	800	10.0	826	3.1	797	−3.5	825	3.5
Washington	867	937	8.1	1,021	9.0	1,060	3.8	1,130	6.6

Source: U.S. Department of Commerce, Bureau of the Census, Census of Governments, 1962, 1967, 1972, 1977, and 1982.

reports that urged the regulation of special district growth, five states enacted legislation creating "boundary commissions" to control the creation, consolidation, annexation, and dissolution of special districts on a statewide or countywide basis. Table 11–8 shows the states that have enacted this legislation as well as the effects of the legislation on the growth of special districts. Each "boundary commission state" appears to have been successful in curtailing district growth.

Proliferation and efficiency

The number of special districts in the United States has grown steadily over the past several decades, more than doubling between 1952 and 1982 (see Table 11–9). This growth seems contrary to the reform tradition of political science that views centralization as the most logical form of local government. A fragmented local government environment (i.e., one comprising many units of government, including special districts) is considered ineffective, uncoordinated, and unresponsive. A considerable number of private and public organizations have promoted the reform tradition, including the Advisory Commission on Intergovernmental Relations (ACIR), the National Municipal League, and the Committee for Economic Development, which once advocated an 80 percent reduction in the number of governmental units in metropolitan areas in the United States.[19]

On the subject of municipal water supply, ACIR said: "A small number of community water utilities is preferable to a multiplicity of uncoordinated systems . . . . A large number of relatively small water companies or municipal departments is often the result of a lack of coordinated policy for community water resources."[20] ACIR suggests that districts can "inhibit efforts of district consolidation or annexation that would provide more effective and more effi-

Table 11–9 Number of special districts in the United States, 1952–1982.

Year	Number of special districts	% increase from preceding reported year
1952	12,339	—
1962	18,322	48.5
1967	21,264	16.1
1972	23,885	12.3
1977	25,962	8.7
1982	28,588	10.1

Source: Based on data from various volumes of U.S. Department of Commerce, Bureau of the Census, Census of Governments.

cient service to the whole area."[21] In evaluating the overall efficiency of special districts in providing municipal services, ACIR concluded that:

1. Districts frequently provide uneconomical services.
2. Districts distort the political process by competing for scarce public resources.
3. Districts, because of multiplicity, prevent citizens from understanding them and hence controlling them, the result being unresponsive government.
4. Districts increase the costs of government within an area.[22]

Nevertheless, the conclusion that special districts are inherently inefficient (when compared with more centrally supplied services) must be accepted with caution. One California study evaluated the economic performance of 153 sewage plants. Some of the plants were operated by municipalities and others by districts. The special districts were found to be as efficient as general-purpose units of government in the provision of sewage disposal.[23] The nature of the sewage industry itself implies that special districts can be a mechanism for providing efficient service. For example, because many sewage treatment districts operate with economies of scale, smaller communities that desire sewage treatment services often construct their own collection systems and contract with a sewage district for treatment.[24] In this way, small jurisdictions can control their own collection system and realize economies of scale in treatment costs.[25]

That special districts can provide services efficiently stems also from their ability to finance capital expansion. The Metropolitan Water District of Southern California, for example, was formed by a number of municipalities and districts in order to generate necessary funds for investing in facilities to transport water from the Colorado River to the Los Angeles Basin.[26] The economic advantage of this particular institution was cited in 1973 when it was determined that "no single agency could have undertaken such activities without serious diseconomies."[27]

Special districts can also be conducive to efficient consumption, by providing a mechanism through which diverse collective demands for local public goods and services can be met. A community may consist of five distinct neighborhoods, each one characterized by homogeneous preferences for local public services. Under a consolidated local government organization, it is unlikely that the quantities and qualities of the public services provided will match the divergent preferences of each neighborhood.[28] Some individuals will have more public goods and services than they feel necessary at the current tax prices; others will want more goods and services but will be unable to obtain them, irrespective of the tax price.

The ability to create or dissolve special districts permits individuals in such a community to create "collective consumption units." These units can provide services that more closely match the preferences of each neighborhood. The desire of comparatively small communities to take such initiatives was particularly evident with the popularity of "neighborhood governments" during the 1960s and 1970s.[29]

Special districts can also operate within more logical geographical boundaries than can general-purpose units of government. A flood control district that intersects several local governmental boundaries, but serves all the residents of a particular floodplain, may be more desirable than flood control services limited to areas within legally specified political boundaries.

Studies of the effects of special district growth on service costs found that the effective restriction of special district growth by several states led to substantial increases in both local government per capita expenditures and tax shares.[30] These increases were found to be significantly greater than per capita tax and expenditure growth in a number of states where the growth rate of special districts was the greatest.

Another study looked at the effects of special district growth restrictions on the cost of providing water supply, sewage disposal, and fire protection (services most frequently provided by special districts). In a number of states that restricted special district growth there were substantial increases in both current operating costs and combined current capital costs. ACIR itself recognizes "significant diseconomies of scale" in cities of over 250,000 population.[31]

In Sweden the number of local government units was decreased by approximately 80 percent (which is, coincidentally, identical to the consolidation proposal put forth by the Committee for Economic Development in 1966) and the following changes were noted:

1. Voter participation in local elections declined appreciably as the local units increased in size.
2. Citizen participation in joining voluntary civic and service organizations declined appreciably as the local units increased in size.
3. As local units became larger, local elected officials differed more markedly from their constituents in such characteristics as income level, social status, and level of education.
4. The resistance of local elected officials to spending programs decreased as the size of the local unit increased.
5. Local elected officials in larger units of local government tended to "follow the dictates of their conscience" rather than the demands of their constituents, probably due to lack of contact with and concern for constituent preferences.[32]

Further research on citizen attitudes toward local government produced the following results:

1. The popularity of special district government and its change from serving predominantly rural areas toward providing urban services indicate the preference of communities for services tailored to their needs.[33]
2. Nationwide, movements for more centralized local governmental organization are rejected by voters nearly three times as often as they are passed.[34]
3. A nationwide Harris survey clearly demonstrated that citizen confidence and satisfaction with local government increases as the size of the governmental unit decreases.[35]

These arguments imply that the efficient size and number of special districts depend on many factors, differing from district to district. A general decline in number is not necessarily good, and decisions on their expansion or contraction should be made on a case-by-case basis.

Summary

The trend toward increased reliance on user charges as a source of local government revenues is expected to continue. In the case of utility type services, the move away from the property tax and toward the user charge is well under way. Reliance on user charges to finance other public services is less extensive, but growing steadily. Employment of user charges is far greater in special districts than in any other form of local government; however, even in special districts, the level of user charge revenue varies significantly among the types of services provided and among the states using the charge.

When correctly designed, the user charge has several potential advantages over the property tax as a source of local revenue. Charges based on the cost of providing public services allow consumer-taxpayers to evaluate the cost of service against the level of service provided. In many cases the charges will allocate use of the publicly provided good to those who value it most. Payment of the charge indicates the need to expand supply of the service and also provides the revenue to finance the expansion.

The primary disadvantages of the user charge are its regressive nature and its administrative costs. A marginal-cost user charge is regressive when compared with the property tax; however, it is decidedly less regressive than a poorly designed average-cost user charge. Nevertheless, the cost of administering a marginal-cost user charge may be substantial because it is not likely that the property tax will be completely eliminated. There will probably be no significant savings in the administration of thc property tax when more reliance is placed on user charges.

As a means of supplying public services, special districts can combine improved efficiency in production with improved measurement of demand. On the other hand, special districts can be wasteful and unresponsive to the needs and wants of citizens. Nevertheless, user charges, as levied by special districts or other governmental units, can play an important role in the future of local government finance. The trend is clearly positive, and it is growing as citizen concern for the property tax rises.

1 U.S. Department of Commerce, Bureau of the Census, 1967 Census of Governments, *Historical Statistics on Governmental Finance and Employment* (Washington, D.C.: GPO, 1970), p. 135.

2 See Jack Hirshleifer, James C. DeHaven, and Jerome W. Milliman, *Water Supply* (Chicago: Univ. of Chicago Press, 1960).

3 See, for example, Walter Isard and Robert Coughlin, *Municipal Costs and Revenues* (Wellesley, Mass.: Chandler-Davis, 1957); Paul B. Downing, *The Economics of Urban Sewage Disposal* (New York: Praeger Publishers, 1969); Real Estate Research Corporation, *The Costs of Sprawl*, report prepared for the Council on Environmental Quality, Department of Housing and Urban Development, and the U.S. Environmental Protection Agency (Washington, D.C.: GPO, 1974).

4 See Paul B. Downing, "Policy Perspectives on User Charges and Urban Spacial Structure," in *Local Service Pricing Policies and Their Effect on Urban Spacial Structure*, ed. Paul B. Downing (Vancouver: Univ. of British Columbia Press, 1977). The reader might find helpful the discussions by various authors in Selma J. Mushkin, ed., *Public Prices for Public Products* (Washington, D.C.: Urban Institute, 1972).

5 Some cities purposely do not charge high-volume industrial users for the full cost of water and electricity in an attempt to attract more industry to the area.

6 See Downing, *The Economics of Urban Sewage Disposal*.

7 If an effluent fee were charged for stormwater release, then an output charge, and perhaps some treatment, would be appropriate.

8 Paul B. Downing, "Cost and Demand for a Municipal Service" (Unpublished paper, October 1974).

9 Tolls are desirable only if the benefits from controlling use exceed the cost of establishing and operating the system of toll collection.

10 See Paul Downing and James Frank, "Recreation Impact Fees," *National Tax Journal* 36 (December 1983): 477–90; J. Frank, E. Lines, and P. Downing, *Community Experience with Fire Impact Fees* and *Community Experience with Sewer Impact Fees*, Policy Sciences Program (Florida State Univ., 1985).

11 The effects of charges on development are explored by various authors in Downing, ed., *Local Service Pricing Policies and Their Effect on Urban Spacial Structure*.

12 Paul B. Downing, "User Charges and the Development of Urban Land," *National Tax Journal* 26 (December 1973): 631–37.

13 This has been shown in Paul B. Downing, "The Distributional Effect of User Charges" (Unpublished paper, October 1974).

14 U.S. Department of Commerce, Bureau of the Census, 1972 Census of Governments, *Governmental Units in 1972* (Washington, D.C.: GPO, 1975).

15 The special district is one of the two forms of organization most commonly used in lieu of direct municipal provision of services, the other being the municipally owned utility. There is often confusion in terminology between these two organizational forms and *public authorities*, a term that encompasses both.

16 U.S. Department of Commerce, Bureau of the Census, 1967 Census of Governments, vol. 1, p. 13.

17 Derived from U.S. Bureau of the Census, *Governmental Finances in 1981–82* (Washington, D.C.: GPO, 1982).

18 For a more complete discussion, see Richard M. Bird, *Charging for Public Services: A New Look at an Old Idea* (Toronto: Canadian Tax Foundation, 1976), pp. 105–13.

19 Committee for Economic Development, *Modernizing Local Government* (New York, 1966).

20 Advisory Commission on Intergovernmental Relations, *The Problem of Special Districts in American Government: A Commission Report* (Washington, D.C.: GPO, 1964), pp. 74–75.

21 Ibid.

22 Ibid., pp. 74–75.

23 G. Krohm, *The Production Efficiency of Single vs. General Purpose Government: Findings of the Organizational Structure of Local Government and Cost Effectiveness* (Sacramento, Calif.: Office of Planning and Research, 1973).

24 See Assembly Interim Committee on Municipal and County Government, *Special Districts in the State of California: Problems in General and the Consolidation of Sewer and Fire District Acts, 1957–59* (Sacra-

mento, Calif.: State Printing Office, 1959), vol. 6, no. 12.

25 Downing, *The Economics of Urban Sewage Disposal.*

26 San Diego Water Authority, *Report to the California Council on Intergovernmental Relations,* 1973.

27 Ibid.

28 With a constitutionally imposed majority rule, the level of public goods output will most likely correspond to the preferences of the median voter.

29 See Howard W. Hallman, *Neighborhood Government in a Metropolitan Setting* (Beverly Hills, Calif.: Sage Publications, 1974).

30 See Thomas J. DiLorenzo, "The Expenditure Effects of Restricting Competition in Local Public Service Industries: The Case of Special Districts," *Public Choice* 37 (Winter 1981): 569–78; and Stephen L. Mehay, "The Effect of Governmental Structure on Special District Expenditures," *Public Choice* 44 (Winter 1984): 339–48. On the general effects of competition among local governments on the cost of providing local public services, see Thomas J. DiLorenzo, "Economic Competition and Political Competition: An Empirical Note," *Public Choice* 40 (Summer 1983): 203–9; and Richard E. Wagner and Warren Weber, "Competition, Monopoly and the Organization of Government in Metropolitan Areas," *Journal of Law and Economics* 18 (December 1975): 661–84.

31 Advisory Commission on Intergovernmental Relations, *Size Can Make A Difference: A Closer Look,* ACIR Bulletin no. 70–8 (Washington, D.C.: GPO, 1970), p. 2.

32 Jorgen Westerstahl, "Decision-Making Systems" (Paper delivered at the 1973 Annual Meeting of the American Political Science Association).

33 California Local Government Reform Task Force, *Special District Report* (February 1974).

34 "New County, U.S.A.," Report, City-County Consolidation Seminar, The American County, February 1972, p. 10.

35 U.S. Congress, Senate, Committee on Government Operations, Subcommittee on Intergovernmental Relations, *Confidence and Concern: Citizens View Americans and Government,* vols. 1 and 2 (Washington, D.C.: GPO, 1973).

Part four: Financial management

12 Debt management

The sale of bonds is not an everyday occurrence, even for the largest government units. Consequently, finance officers tend to be relatively unfamiliar with the design and sale of long-term debt issues. If this function is managed poorly, however, the city or county that issues the bonds is likely to pay substantially higher interest costs than necessary. This chapter provides the chief administrative officer and the local government finance officer with an overall understanding of capital financing, the types of debt issues available, the unique characteristics of municipal bonds, the factors that determine the credit quality of bonds, the ways municipal bonds are sold, the nature of the bond market, and attempts to broaden this market.

State and local governments raise funds to finance their expenditures principally by taxation, by grants-in-aid from other governmental units, by incurring short-term debt, and by selling bonds. The method or combination of methods selected depends on a number of factors, including the purpose and magnitude of the expenditure, the timing of the benefits that will result from the expenditure, population and income trends, the political environment, and legal constraints.

Principles of capital financing

Expenditures of state and local governments are generally classified as either *current* or *capital,* depending primarily on whether the goods and services purchased are consumed in less or more than one year. Purchases of services and short-life goods are generally classified as current or operating expenses, and purchases of longer-life goods as capital expenditures. Most state and local governments are prohibited by law from financing current expenditures through long-term debt instruments and thereby deferring payment until long after the expenditures have been made and the benefits have been received. They may, however, finance capital expenditures in this way.

Selecting a financing strategy

Public capital expenditures typically include the construction of schools, highways, utility plants, airports, housing, and office buildings. The timing of the outlays for such projects cannot be synchronized with the timing of the benefits received from them; the expenditures are made over a short period of time, whereas the goods are consumed and the benefits received over a longer period. Who then should pay for these projects? Should it be the residents of the community at the time the expenditure is made, the residents of the community at the time the benefits are received, or only those (whether residents or not) who use and benefit directly from the services provided?

The first strategy represents *pay-as-you-acquire* (or *pay-as-you-go)* financing, while the second and third represent *pay-as-you-use* financing. A number of arguments are made for and against each strategy. In favor of pay-as-you acquire is the argument that the choice to spend—made by current residents—should not be imposed on future residents who have had no say in the decision. Other arguments contend that the expenditure will not restrict future borrowing for other projects, and that the interest cost of future borrowing will not be increased by an increase in the amount of debt outstanding. Proponents of *pay-as-you-use* argue that the payment of the cost (the amortization of the bonds) *can* be synchronized with the enjoyment of the benefits, and that as the number of beneficiaries using the facility increases (creating a broader tax base), the cost per capita decreases.

Except for small capital projects, governmental units generally find that the arguments for pay-as-you-use tend to outweigh those for pay-as-you-acquire. Pay-as-you-acquire involves up-front payment, which is usually too much of a burden in the case of large capital projects. Thus, local governments prefer to finance these projects through long-term debt, thereby deferring the payment and spreading it over time.

Planning a bond issue

What happens once a local government has decided to finance a project through long-term debt? First, the chief administrative officer and finance officer must

---

Services provided by municipal bond counsel

Determines whether the legal authority for the issuance of the bonds is consistent with constitutional requirements and limitations.

Ensures that the statutory or charter authority for the issuance of the bonds is consistent with constitutional requirements and limitations.

Prepares the legal documents for the issuance of the bonds, including the legal instruments necessary to authorize the issuance of the bonds and to describe the bonds and their security.

Ensures that the bonds are within the applicable debt limitations.

Ensures that any applicable tax limitation as to rate or amount is observed.

Ensures that any required elections regarding the bonds are called and held in conformity with law.

Reviews the official statement to make certain that the legal information is correct and that no material information has been omitted.

Examines the proceedings of the authorizing body providing for the sale of the bonds to ensure that the bonds will be sold legally.

Ensures that a competitive sale is advertised properly or that an underwriter in a negotiated sale is selected properly.

Determines whether the bid accepted is legally acceptable in a competitive sale.

Answers inquiries from rating services, investors, underwriter's trustees, paying agents and others prior to the delivery of the bonds.

Prepares an unqualified opinion as to the tax-exempt status of bonds.

Source: Adapted from Center for Capital Market Research, *Planning, Designing, and Selling General Obligation Bonds in Oregon: A Guide to Local Issuers* (Eugene, Oregon: Univ. of Oregon, 1978), pp. 2–4.

Services provided by financial advisor

Surveys issuer's debt structure and financial resources to determine borrowing capacity for current and future capital financing requirements.

Gathers all pertinent financial statistics and economic data, such as debt requirement schedule, tax rates, and overlapping debt that would affect or reflect on the issuer's ability and willingness to repay its general obligation bonds.

Determines appropriate user charges and estimates revenue flows for projects to be financed by revenue bonds.

Advises on the time and method of marketing terms of bond issue (including maturity schedule), interest payment dates, and call features.

Prepares, in cooperation with bond counsel, an official statement, notice of sale, and bid form and distributes them to all prospective underwriters and investors.

Evaluates the benefits of obtaining one or more credit ratings and contacts the rating services to ensure that they have all the information and data required to evaluate properly the issuer's credit worthiness.

Is present when sealed bids are opened and stands ready to advise on acceptability of bids.

Helps coordinate the printing, signing, and delivery of the bonds.

Reviews bidding procedures for competitive sales and the securing of an appropriate underwriter for negotiated sales.

Source: Adapted from Center for Capital Market Research, *Planning, Designing, and Selling General Obligation Bonds in Oregon: A Guide to Local Issuers* (Eugene, Oregon: Univ. of Oregon, 1978), pp. 7–9.

ascertain that the government has statutory permission to borrow for the intended purpose: Before floating a bond issue, the government must obtain a legal opinion that the borrowing may be undertaken and that the interest is exempt from federal income taxes, if the bonds are to find buyers in the tax-exempt market. To obtain opinions on these questions, the local government should contact an independent municipal bond counsel and should seek the advice of a financial advisor if needed. While the use of a financial advisor is discretionary, no bond issue should be marketed without the advice of independent counsel.

Next, or simultaneously, the local government must determine the precise cost of the project to be financed. Underestimating may be expensive because the sale of supplementary bonds later may be more difficult and costly. For large projects, this step often requires the assistance of cost engineers.

On the basis of this information, the local government will determine the type and amount of bonds to be issued, decide the time period over which the bonds will mature, and announce its intention to sell or "float" the bonds, which are then sold by bid to an underwriter who in turn markets them to individual or corporate investors.

Once the bond issue has been floated, the local government is responsible for paying periodic interest (called the *coupon amount*) and for repaying the principle (the *maturing amount*) of the bonds. Together, these are called the *debt service*. These and other terms found throughout this chapter can be found in the sidebar, "Debt management terminology."

Debt management terminology

Bond bank A state agency that assists local issuers with the sale of debt. Generally, the bond bank sells its own bonds and uses the proceeds to purchase the debt of cities or counties in the state.

Callable bonds Bonds that may be repurchased at the option of the issuer after a stipulated deferment period (the call date) and before maturity at no more than a stipulated price (the call price). If the called bonds are repurchased with the proceeds of other newly sold bonds, generally at a lower interest cost, the bonds are said to be refunded.

Coupon amount The stipulated dollar interest amount to be paid periodically, generally semiannually, per $1,000 face (par) value bond.

Debt service payments The sum of all the interest payments in a period plus the dollar amounts of any bonds scheduled to mature in the period.

Fixed rate bond Bond on which the coupon interest rate is fixed at the time the bond is sold.

Floating (variable) rate bond Bond on which the coupon interest rate changes over the life of the bond issue, generally in line with changes in market rates. See also *Fixed rate bond*.

Industrial development bonds Bonds sold by a special government industrial district to finance plant and equipment for a private enterprise within its jurisdiction. The plant and equipment are leased to the enterprise and the debt service payments are financed by these proceeds.

Market discount The difference by which the maturity or amortized value of the bond exceeds the market price after the bond has been issued. It is caused by a rise in the market interest rate occurring after the issuance of the bond. For secondary buyers, this discount is generally treated for tax purposes as a capital gain realized at the time of maturity.

Types of debt

The method by which funds are to be raised to pay the debt service affects the type of bonds to be issued. Debt service payments may be financed by the taxpayers in the community as a whole, by the specific users of the services generated by the subject, or by both.

General obligation bonds

When the benefits of the services generated by a project accrue in significant amounts to direct users as well as to those members of the community who do not use the services directly, the project is termed a public good. Examples of public goods are law enforcement, fire protection, schooling, and public health facilities. Because the benefits of public goods are enjoyed by almost all members of the community, the cost of the capital facilities for these activities should be borne by the community as a whole. This can be achieved by the sale of general obligation (GO) bonds whose payments are financed by all taxpayers of the issuing government.

GO bonds are secured unconditionally by the full faith, credit, and taxing powers of the issuing government. If the taxes levied initially are insufficient to meet the debt service payments in any period, the issuer is legally obligated to raise the tax rate or broaden the tax base to obtain the necessary funds. Some

Maturing amount The dollar principal or face (par) value of the bonds that is promised to be repaid at each maturity.

Maturity date (maturity) The date at which the issuer is obligated to repay the principal amount of the bond to the bondholder.

Original issue discount (OID) The amount by which the face or maturity value of the bond exceeds the flotation price at the time of issue. The amortization of this discount is treated as interest income for tax purposes.

Par value The bond principal payable at maturity.

Pollution control bonds Bonds sold by a special government pollution control district to finance the installation of pollution control equipment in a private enterprise within its jurisdiction. The equipment is leased to the private enterprise and the debt service payments are financed by these proceeds.

Prospectus A printed summary issued in conjunction with a public offering of securities. The prospectus contains information regarding the purchase.

Put bond A bond in which the bondholder has the right to sell (put) the bond back to the issuer or a third party at a fixed exercise or strike price. For example, a bond may be puttable every year at par. In this case the bondholder can, if he or she chooses, sell the bonds to the issuer at a price of 100 percent of face value at the end of each year.

Sinking fund A fund established by bond issuers and increased through time for the purpose of either retiring some of the outstanding bonds before their maturity or reducing the risk of default.

Spread The difference between the underwriter's bid on a bond issue and the resale price; includes bid preparation expenses, selling commissions, underwriter's fee, management fee, and profit.

other bonds, however, are secured by designated special taxes and only by general taxes if the special taxes are insufficient. These bonds also are considered general obligation bonds. Although the issuers of general obligation bonds are legally obligated to raise tax revenues to meet shortfalls in scheduled debt service payments, they may sometimes find that obtaining increased revenues is economically impossible or rejected by the electorate. If the scheduled debt service payments are not made in full, the bonds go into default.

Revenue bonds

If the benefits of a project accrue almost entirely to a specific group of readily identifiable purchasers, the project is more a private or merit good than a public good. Examples of such goods include municipally owned electric and water systems, athletic stadiums, auditoriums, and limited access highways and bridges. For the sake of equity, the costs of these projects should be borne primarily by the users. Such projects are best financed by revenue bonds whose debt service payments are to be met by charges placed exclusively on users of the publicly provided services. These charges are referred to as user chargers and may include service charges, tolls, special taxes, admission fees, leases, and rents.

If revenues from user charges are insufficient to meet the debt service payments, the issuer generally is not legally obligated to levy taxes to avoid default. Revenue bonds do not require voter approval and are generally easier to plan than GO bonds. However, they generally carry a higher interest rate because they are not secured by the full faith and credit of the issuer. They also require careful estimates of the user charges to be applied and the revenues to be derived.

Revenue bonds are similar to bonds issued by private enterprises. Some revenue bonds, however, are hybrids, secured first by user charges and, if these are insufficient, backed by the full faith, credit, and taxing powers of the issuing unit or some other governmental unit. These bonds are referred to as indirect general obligation bonds.

Selecting the bond

The type of bond the issuer uses depends on a number of factors:

1. The direct and indirect beneficiaries of the project
2. The time pattern of the stream of benefits generated by the project
3. The legal authority of the municipality to issue general obligation bonds
4. The probability of voter approval of these bonds
5. The legal ability to raise general taxes
6. The revenues that may be raised by alternative types of user charges
7. The cost-effectiveness of user charges (the relation of revenues collected through user charges to the cost of collection)
8. The projected need to finance other projects of equal or higher priority by general obligation bonds and the effect of this issue on the interest cost of those bonds
9. The interest costs of each type of bond.

Furthermore, the dividing line between public and private goods is often unclear: Many public goods such as schools provide greater benefits to some members of the community than to others, and many private goods such as newspapers and airline transportation provide some benefits to nonpurchasers. Thus, it is not always clear what type of bond will finance a particular project most equitably and efficiently.

Political and legal considerations also may affect the decision of what kind of bond to issue. For example, in most states general obligation bonds have to be approved by the voters, and revenue bonds do not. Therefore, projects that may not have a sufficiently large political appeal may be financed by revenue bonds even though principally they may be public goods. Revenue bonds also are exempt from most of the debt ceilings applicable to general obligation bonds. As a result, revenue bonds may be favored if the issuer is close to the debt ceiling or expects to issue large amounts of general obligation bonds in the future to finance projects with a higher priority.

On the other hand, some projects for which revenue bond financing appears most appropriate, because the primary beneficiaries are readily identifiable, may not generate sufficient revenues to meet the debt service payments with reasonable user charges. Such projects may include municipal performing arts centers and sports arenas. These projects can be financed only by general obligation bonds, by the lease-back bonds of a joint powers authority, or by a nonprofit corporation. In a more general context, GO bonds may be preferred because the more secure backing and smaller risk of default permit them to be sold at lower interest costs than comparable revenue bonds. Clearly, the decision to finance a particular project by general obligation or by revenue bonds is complex and involves careful analysis of economic, financial, legal, and political considerations.

Trends in municipal debt

The use of debt by state and local governments has increased rapidly since World War II. As shown in Table 12–1, $102.5 billion of new long-term debt was sold in 1984, more than twice the amount sold in 1980 and almost 28 times the amount issued in 1950. Sales of new general obligation bonds increased from $14 billion in 1980 to $26 billion in 1984, and sales of new revenue bonds increased from $34 billion to $76 billion in the same period. The rise in revenue issues resulted primarily from the increased use of industrial development bonds, particularly for housing and power. In 1984, in order to curb the use of certain types of industrial development bonds, Congress enacted caps on the volume that can be sold in each state in each year. Industrial revenue bonds and other bonds with substantial private use aspects were further restricted in 1986.

Table 12–1 Trend in amounts of municipal debt sold, 1950–1984 ($ billions).

Year	Long-term debt: General obligation bonds	Long-term debt: Revenue bonds	Total	Short-term debt
1950	3.1	0.6	3.7	1.6
1955	4.3	1.7	6.0	2.6
1960	5.2	2.1	7.3	4.0
1965	7.8	3.5	11.3	6.5
1970	12.1	6.1	18.2	17.9
1975	16.1	14.5	30.6	29.0
1980	14.1	34.3	48.4	27.7
1981	12.4	35.3	47.7	37.4
1982	21.0	57.3	78.3	44.7
1983	21.5	64.3	85.7	36.8
1884	26.4	76.1	102.5	30.5

Source: Board of Governors of the Federal Reserve System, *Federal Reserve Bulletin* (Washington, D.C., monthly), various issues; and Securities Data Corporation, *Municipal Bond Data Tape*.

The use of short-term debt also increased sharply in the early 1980s. During the early 1970s, New York City was the largest user of the short-term market in municipals, accounting for about one-fourth of the total note market by 1975. After the New York debt crisis in 1975, however, the city's use of notes and, consequently, the total volume of notes issued fell off. In the early 1980s, however, the volume of note issues rose sharply again, primarily the result of the exceptionally high interest rates in the market at the time. Many issuers financed their needs with short-term notes hoping that interest rates would eventually decline and that they would be able to refinance later when the long-term interest rate had fallen.

The amount of debt issued in revenue bonds has increased much faster in dollar value than has the amount in general obligation bonds. In 1950, revenue bonds accounted for less than 20 percent of all long-term municipal bonds sold. By 1970 this percentage had increased to 34 percent and by 1984 to almost 75 percent. The increased sale of revenue bonds may be attributed to four primary factors:

1. A growing tendency of state and local governments to use debt to finance facilities that traditionally have not been considered to be pure public goods
2. Political pressures that have made it more difficult to obtain a favorable vote to issue general obligation bonds
3. Legal restrictions on general tax increases

4. Periodic declines in interest rates that have encouraged advance refunding of outstanding issues (primarily revenue issues), which originally sold at higher interest rates.

Table 12–2 shows how municipal bonds have been employed. Between 1968 and 1984 the proportion of bonds sold to finance schools and water and sewer facilities declined sharply, whereas the proportion for gas and electric, hospitals, and pollution control increased sharply. These changes reflect the extensive use of revenue bond financing for projects that readily lend themselves to user charges. The increase in bonds to finance pollution control projects has offset almost all of the decline in industrial development bonds. Both are generally financed by revenue bonds.[1]

Table 12–2 Municipal bond sales by purpose.

	1968		1984	
Purpose	$ (billions)	% of total	$ (billions)	% of total
Total	16.4	100.0	101.8	100.0
Schools	4.7	28.6	9.7	9.5
Water and sewer	1.9	11.6	5.9	5.9
Highway and bridge	1.6	9.8	8.8	8.6
Gas and electric	—	—	11.3	11.1
Hospital	—	—	10.2	10.0
Industrial aid	1.6	9.8	4.5	4.4
Pollution control	—	—	14.6	14.3
Public housing	0.7	4.2	20.5	20.1
Other	5.9	36.0	16.3	16.1

Source: *The Bond Buyer 1985 Municipal Statbook* (New York, N.Y.: Bond Buyer, 1986), p. 10
Note: Dashes indicate negligible amounts.

Unique aspects of municipal bonds

Municipal bonds are different from bonds sold by other issuers because the income received by investors from coupon payments and amortization of original issue discounts on municipal bonds is free from most taxing authorities. States may, however, tax the coupon interest on bonds issued by other states and sometimes even their own. In addition, income earned by the appreciation in the price of municipal bonds that arises from the amortization of market discounts (and is caused by increases in interest rates after the bonds were issued) is generally taxable, but at the lower capital gains rate.

Federal tax exemption of the coupon interest and original issue discount significantly affects the market for municipal bonds. Investors usually are concerned with after-tax income. The higher an investor's marginal income tax bracket, the greater the value of the tax exemption and the greater the attractiveness of municipal bonds, even those with a relatively low interest rate. For example, to a private investor who is in a marginal tax bracket of 25 percent, an 8 percent Treasury bond trading at par value and a hypothetical 6 percent municipal bond also trading at par value would both yield the same 6 percent after-tax return. If the private investor were in the 50 percent marginal tax bracket, the 6 percent municipal bond would yield the same after-tax return as a hypothetical 12 percent Treasury bond.

Institutional investors also are subject to different marginal income tax rates. The net income of commercial banks and casualty and property insurance companies is subject to the full corporate tax rate of 46 percent above $100,000.

The net income of pension funds and life insurance companies, however, is untaxed or taxed at considerably lower rates.

Thus, the demand for municipal bonds is restricted to wealthy individuals, commercial banks, and casualty and property insurance companies. At year-end 1983, commercial banks held 34 percent of all long-term municipal securities outstanding, individuals (including trusts) held 41 percent, and casualty and property insurance companies held 21 percent. Thus, these three groups accounted for 96 percent of all holdings of municipal securities.

Not only is the tax-free municipal bond market narrower than the market for most other securities, but it is also more volatile. The pattern of municipal bond sales runs contrary to the cyclical pattern of demand for business loans from banks. The latter picks up when the economy is strong and falls off when the economy contracts. Given this cycle (and given that municipal bonds generally are viewed as less profitable than business loans), commercial bank demand for municipal securities is strong during and immediately after recessions and weak during periods of economic boom. This is particularly true in the market for short-term municipals.

Maturity structure

After a governmental unit selects the appropriate type of bond, a proper maturity structure must be designed. This structure depends on whether the issue is a revenue or GO bond. For revenue bonds, the estimated annual revenues should cover the debt service payments by some accepted multiple called the coverage ratio. This ratio should be checked against those prevailing for similar projects in other jurisdictions. Thus, if the average coverage ratio is 150 percent and the net revenues are $15 million, the debt service payments in any year should total only two-thirds of the net revenues estimated for that year, or $10 million. The longest maturity should not exceed the estimated usable life of the project or the last year for which significant net revenues are estimated.

In contrast, the maturity and debt service structure of new general obligation bonds depends on the estimated annual overall tax revenues of the issuer and the maturity and debt service structure of all current outstanding general obligation bonds. Tax revenue must finance the debt service payments of all GO bonds. Thus, the scheduled debt service payments for all GO bonds should never be greater than the projected current revenues of the issuer in any year, less the estimated other current expenditures in that year. (The projection may include reasonable increases in tax rates.) The greater the debt service payments on current outstanding bonds in any one year relative to the estimated tax revenues less other current expenditures, the smaller should be the amount of new bonds scheduled to mature in that year. To keep debt service payments relatively stable from year to year, new maturities should be structured based on the pattern of the maturities of the outstanding bonds. The maximum length of time to maturity of general obligation bonds generally is prescribed by state statute.

Unlike most federal government or corporation bond issues, new municipal bonds are usually sold in serial form. Serial bonds are a package of individual bonds with more than one term to maturity. Typically, a municipal serial bond issue has maturities ranging from 1 year to more than 20 years. The dollar par (face) value of each maturity may be the same or it may vary. The underwriter who purchases the bonds for resale to investors breaks out the serial package and resells the bonds individually. Because the bond issue matures over time rather than all at once, the serial form often relieves the issuer of the need to establish a sinking fund. General obligation bond issues are usually entirely in serial form. Revenue issues are either entirely in serial form or in serial form up to a date followed by one or more larger "term" bonds, which mature on single dates some years after the last serial maturity. The balloon payment term bonds generally are subject to mandatory call in equal amounts in each year between the maturity of the term bond and the last preceding maturity. This effectively transforms them into serial bonds. As will be discussed later in this chapter, the serial nature of new municipal bonds has complicated the process by which issuers competitively sell new bonds at the lowest possible interest cost.

Call provisions

A call provision permits the issuer to repurchase the bonds before maturity at a predetermined maximum price. Thus, for the purchaser, bonds with call provisions have more than one possible maturity date. Call provisions provide flexibility to the issuer because (1) the bonds can be refinanced if at some time in the future interest rates should decline; (2) bonds can be retired ahead of schedule if funds become available; and (3) bonds with covenants that overly restrict the freedom of the issues can be retired.

Of these reasons, the first is the most common for exercising the call provision on municipal bonds. The second is less important for municipal bonds because municipalities may invest funds to a limited extent in taxable securities, which have higher yields than the cost of borrowing by tax-exempt securities, without paying income taxes on those earnings. The third reason generally applies only to revenue bonds.

Once bonds are issued, their prices vary inversely with the market interest rate. The call provision permits the issuer to repurchase the bonds at a price below their market value and to refinance them at a lower rate if interest rates should decline. This of course benefits the issuer at the expense of the buyer. To compensate for the potential loss in market value or interest income, investors will require for callable bonds a higher initial interest rate than for non-callable bonds. This higher interest rate is referred to as the *call yield premium*. The price at which the bonds may be repurchased is termed the *call price* and is set somewhat above par. The difference between the call price of a bond and its par value is referred to as the *call price premium*. The magnitude of the call yield premium on a particular issue varies with the characteristics of the bond issue and the state of the market at the time the issue is sold initially.

Typically, call provisions also provide for a period of time during which the bonds may not be called. This period is termed the *call protection* or *deferment* period. In general, the call yield premium will be greater with higher current interest rates, lower call price premiums, and shorter deferment periods.

Issuers must weigh the potential benefits of a call provision against the initial higher interest costs. As a compromise, issuers frequently choose call provisions that are economical to exercise only when interest rates decline significantly. This generally has little effect on the initial interest cost of the issue. Also, the initial interest rate may not be much affected if the issue carries a call price well above par value and has a deferment period of at least 10 years. (This, of course, implies that the call provisions will be applicable only to bonds in the serial package that have a minimum of 10 years to maturity.)

Most municipal bonds currently issued are callable. Call provisions have increased with interest rates since World War II.

Put provisions

A put provision permits the bondholder to sell (put) the bonds to the issuer at a predetermined price (called the *exercise* or *strike* price), which is generally set at the par value of the bond. Put options on municipal bonds are a relatively recent innovation. The first puttable bonds were sold in 1980 and have become quite popular. The puts can often be exercised annually, but the put period can be as short as one day. That is, the bondholder can oblige the issuer to purchase the bonds at the put price on any day. The put is valuable to the bondholder when interest rates rise above the fixed coupon on the bond and the bond price declines below par, or when the bondholder faces immediate liquidity needs on a floating or variable rate bond.

The put provision makes it easier for the locality to sell bonds during a period of potentially rising rates and lowers the initial interest rate that the issue must carry, but it also has some disadvantages. The issuing locality, for example, cannot count on a stable interest rate over the life of the issue but must be prepared to pay higher rates to meet the market if necessary. This makes capital project planning more difficult.

In order to provide the funds to purchase bonds when they are put to it, the issuer will acquire a letter of credit from a bank guaranteeing that the bank will purchase (and usually remarket) the bonds at the higher prevailing rate. Because the bonds are puttable on short notice, they are priced as short-term rather than long-term instruments.

Advance refunding

As noted, most callable bond issues have a deferment period that must elapse before the call provision is exercised. However, should interest rates drop sharply after the date of sale, but before the end of the deferment period, the issuer may sell new bonds at the lower rates. The proceeds of this issue then are placed in an escrow account and invested in interest-bearing securities, most often those of the U.S. Treasury. The outstanding bonds are either retired at the first call date (a *crossover refunding*) or legally annulled (a *defeasance refunding*). Unlike a regular refunding, at which time the refunded bonds are retired immediately, an advance refunding simultaneously will have old and new refunding bonds outstanding, thereby increasing the total volume of municipal debt. The net debt of the municipality, however, remains about the same if the amount of assets invested in the bond escrow account is factored out.

The profitability of advance refunding depends not only on the steepness of the decline in interest rates, but also on the amount of profit the Treasury permits between the tax-exempt borrowing rate and the rate earned on the investment of the escrow funds in taxable securities. Until 1978, the profits realized from selling and buying the same thing (arbitrage) were sufficiently high to encourage the use of advance refunding even when the present value of the saving, derived from the fall in the market interest rates, was not very great. The concern for both the proper use of the tax exemption privilege and the increases in interest rates caused by sharp increases in the volume of outstanding municipal securities led the Treasury to minimize the profits that could be obtained from arbitrage. As a result, the volume of advance refunding slowed significantly. In 1985, however, proposals to eliminate advance refunding again led to a surge in this type of issuance.

Credit analysis

Credit analysis is primarily concerned with evaluating credit risk. What is the probability of an issuer's partial or full default? The increased quantity of state and local debt in both absolute and per capita terms has caused credit analysis to be an increasingly important subject for both issuers and investors. The borrower also is concerned with credit risk rating because investors impose higher interest rates on higher risk issues to compensate for greater possible default losses.

Table 12–3 shows that the total outstanding long-term and short-term debt of state and local government has risen steadily over the years. In 1984 it stood at

Table 12-3 Debt service estimates of state and local governments, selected years, 1966–1984.

Item	1966	1969	1973	1978	1982	1984
Debt ($ billions)						
Long-term outstanding	101.0	123.5	172.6	269.0	380.3	485.1
Long-term retired	5.6	6.5	9.0	16.7	21.0	33.9
Short-term outstanding	6.1	10.1	15.9	11.4	19.0	20.0
Interest	3.3	4.4	7.8	14.0	24.1	28.7
Revenue[a] ($ billions)	75.0	101.3	159.5	263.6	399.5	483.2
Debt service[b] (as % of revenue)	20.0	20.7	20.5	16.0	16.1	17.1
Personal income[c] ($ billions)	532.1	683.7	935.4	1,518.4	2,405.6	2,734.1
Debt outstanding[d] (as % of personal income)	20.1	19.5	20.2	18.6	16.6	18.5
Debt per capita ($)	547	661	898	1,286	1,763	2,139

Source: U.S. Department of Commerce, Bureau of the Census, *Governmental Finances* (Washington, D.C.: GPO, years as indicated): in 1965–66, in 1968–69, and in 1972–73, pp. 18, 28, and 52 in each; in 1978, pp. 16, 30, 95; in 1982, pp. 18, 31, 96; in 1983–84, pp. 4, 21, 40; (* combines local and state).

[a]General revenue of state and local governments from own sources plus utility revenue.

[b]Long-term debt retired, short-term debt outstanding, and interest on debt.

[c]U.S. total, for calendar years 1965, 1968, 1977, and 1981, respectively.

[d]Long- and short-term debt outstanding.

approximately $505 billion, or $2,139 per capita—a substantial increase from $107 billion, or $547 per capita, in 1966. This is not as alarming as it appears, however, since the debt outstanding as a percentage of personal income has actually declined from 20.1 percent in 1966 to only 18.5 percent in 1984. Moreover, the ratio of debt service charges to the total revenue of state and local governments has also declined over the same period. Nevertheless, the credit quality of state and local debt varies widely and investors face a small but real risk of default in these securities.

Defaults occur when the terms of the bond contract are breached. The contract itself is called the *bond indenture*. The failure to make the promised coupon and principal payments on time and in the full amount represents a default and usually leads to litigation by the bondholders. The indenture may contain other terms such as periodic payments to a sinking fund, the upkeep of capital projects, or the maintenance of an interest payment reserve which also must be met to avoid default. Failure to meet these requirements, which do not involve cash payments to the bondholders, are called technical defaults and often can be resolved without litigation.

Because the purpose of credit analysis is to assess the financial state of the issuer now and in the future, the financial analyst should use a well-maintained set of financial (revenue, expenditure, and statement of debt) reports. Usually this means using externally (independently) audited statements for the credit analysis. Poorly prepared and reported information indicates a higher credit risk to most analysts because the underlying status of the issuer cannot be determined. Even worse, poorly prepared financial reports usually indicate that the government's financial managers themselves do not understand the importance of proper fiscal control.

Analysis for general obligation bond issues

The exact nature of the credit analysis differs by both the entity and the type of debt. Because general obligation bonds are secured by the full faith, credit, and taxing powers of the issuer, general obligation bond issuers and investors focus their financial analysis on the level and stability of tax revenues. For most local governments, available tax income includes some combination of income, sales, and property taxes. Credit quality depends on the ability of the tax base to generate the required debt service payments and to finance regular current expenditures. This ability depends on economic, financial, and debt factors.

Economic factors Important economic factors include the level and growth of aggregate and per capita income; the trend of population growth; the diversity of the income base; the age distribution of the population; the diversity of industry, employment, and the tax base; the economic soundness of the largest taxpayers; the sensitivity of the tax base to economic fluctuations; the age and condition of the housing stock; and the level of building activity.

Financial factors Financial factors considered in a credit analysis include the composition of the issuer's budget; the sources of revenue; the total debt outstanding; the ability of estimated tax and other receipts to cover interest payments (the coverage ratio); the ability of revenues to meet non-interest current expenditures; budget stability and trends; the quality of financial reporting, auditing, and control systems; and any funded or unfunded pension requirements.

Debt factors The overall net debt outstanding by an issuer is usually analyzed on a per capita basis. The net debt of an issuer includes all long-term debt but deducts any sinking funds or other funds dedicated to the repayment of bonds. The net debt also includes the overlapping debt in a jurisdiction. The overlapping debt of an issuer is the debt burden of other political entities supported by taxes levied in the issuer's jurisdiction.

Although there is no absolute rule about the amount of debt a local issuer can carry, some guidelines appear in the accompanying sidebar, "Checklist: Indicators of Fiscal Health." Tables 12–4 and 12–5 show the median, low, and high net debt per capita for cities and counties for 1985. If the amount of debt greatly exceeds the median value, the debt burden of the city or county bears closer examination. Some issuers can sustain a relatively heavy debt burden, but others cannot.

Table 12–4 Net debt per capita of cities, by population, 1985.

Population	Direct net debt (median)	Overall net debt		
		Low	Median	High
Under 10,000	$792	$151	$1,064	$15,907
10,000 to 24,999	533	134	713	5,843
25,000 to 49,999	384	10	689	4,135
50,000 to 99,999	369	59	658	3,199
100,000 to 199,999	362	85	554	5,211
200,000 to 299,999	539	291	706	1,206
300,000 to 499,999	406	215	718	1,659
500,000 and over	559	271	857	2,001

Source: *1985 Medians, Selected Indicators of Municipal Performance, City and County Debt Medians* (New York, N.Y.: Moody's Municipal Department, 1986), p. 8.

Table 12–5 Net debt per capita of counties, by population, 1985.

Population	Direct net debt (median)	Overall net debt		
		Low	Median	High
Under 100,000	$196	$ 96	$ 488	$156,271
100,000 to 249,999	96	150	580	1,379
250,000 to 999,999	158	275	607	2,071
1,000,000 and ovor	139	168	1,049	1,981

Source: *1985 Medians, Selected Indicators of Municipal Performance, City and County Debt Medians* (New York, N.Y.: Moody's Municipal Department, 1986), p. 8.

Other measures of debt burden include the ratio of debt outstanding to total household and business income in the issuer's jurisdiction; the ratio of debt outstanding to the market value of taxable property; the debt service payments as a percentage of estimated tax revenues; the unused debt margins; and the history of voter approval of tax increases and bond issuance.

Checklist: Indicators of fiscal health Credit industry benchmarks and warning signals for assessing overall net debt, liquidity, short-term debt, and debt service on net direct debt are as follows:

Overall net debt

Overall net debt exceeding 10 percent of assessed valuation

Overall net debt exceeding $1,200 per capita

An increase of 20 percent over the previous year in overall net debt as a percentage of market valuation

Overall net debt as a percentage of market valuation increasing 50 percent over the figure for four years earlier

Overall net debt per capita exceeding 15 percent of per capita personal income

Net direct debt exceeding 90 percent of the amount authorized by state law.

Liquidity

A liquidity ratio of less than one to one (a current account deficit) is considered a negative factor, but it would be mitigated by a prior trend of three or more years showing that the ratio will exceed one to one in the coming year. A less than one-to-one ratio for more than three years is considered a decidedly negative factor.

Short-term debt

Short-term debt outstanding at the end of the year exceeding 5 percent of operating revenues (including tax anticipation notes but excluding bond anticipation notes).

A two-year trend of increasing short-term debt outstanding at the end of the fiscal year (including tax anticipation notes).

Debt service

Debt service on net direct debt exceeding 20 percent of operating revenues is considered a potential problem.

Ten percent is considered acceptable.

Source: Sanford M. Groves and Maureen Godsey Valente, *Evaluating Financial Condition: A Handbook for Local Government* (Washington, D.C.: International City Management Association, 1986), pp. 73, 77, 81, 83.

Analysis for revenue bond issues

While the purposes of credit analysis are the same for both revenue and general obligation issues, the methods of analysis are substantially different. In analyzing credit for a revenue bond, the soundness of the tax base is not ordinarily at issue. Instead, because the debt service will be repaid from revenue generated by the project for which the bond was issued, the nature and revenue potential of the project are the focus of the analysis.

Revenue bond issues are generally grouped in broad classes: water and sewer, resource recovery, housing, health care, power, college and university, and industrial development. In some cases, the local governmental agency may have the choice of issuing revenue bonds or general obligation bonds to finance a project. Most revenue bonds, however, are issued by agencies that are not empowered to float general obligation bonds. Revenue bonds can generally be said to entail project, management, and structuring risk.

Project risk Project risk relates to the profitability and stability of the proposed facility. With electric power bonds, for example, the fortunes of major customers can be an important determinant of the municipal power company's ability to meet debt service requirements. Even if the agency's product is in great demand, competition can make the bonds risky. Although public-sector projects are not usually subject to the same level of competition as private-sector projects, the competitive factor is often very important. A hospital, for example, may have a low market share because of competing health care facilities in its target market. The project risk of a bond issue is usually addressed in a *feasibility study* prepared by one or more consultants. They may be engineers, accountants, or other specialists, depending on the problem at hand. A summary of the consulting study is often included in the prospectus as a *feasibility report*.

Management risk The performance of managers of a revenue project more immediately affects the credit worthiness of revenue bonds than it does the credit worthiness of GO bonds, where it usually plays a minor role. Consequently, managers should expect their performance to be closely scrutinized. For example, investors may deem important whether a housing program will be administered by political appointees or housing professionals. Or, in hospital finance, credit analysts may investigate such details as the training and experience of the doctors.

Structuring risk Finally, the legal structure of the issue is an important credit variable in revenue bond analysis. It determines the source of debt service, third-party guarantees, and bondholder priority, that is, the priority in which bondholders would be paid in the event of default. Whereas project risk governs the underlying cash flow risk of the project, structuring risk governs the dollar value and maturity of bonds, both of which have been based on specific assumptions about cash flow. For example, the bond should include contingencies in the event that construction of a new plant financed by proceeds of the bond issue is delayed. The structure of an issue also governs what if any type of insurance exists against insufficient revenues to meet the debt service payments in full and on time. The mortgages in some single-family housing programs may be insured by the Federal Housing Administration (FHA) for the full amount of the loans, whereas those insured by private mortgage insurance (PMI) programs may have lesser guarantees.

The priority of bondholders as to their legal right to cash flows can affect the credit of a bond, even if all the debt service comes from the same project. All bondholders of a particular issue may not be equal. Again housing bonds are a good example, for in some issues one maturity is senior to others with respect to cash flows arising from mortgage prepayments. This added cash flow reduces the default risk of these bonds relative to the rest of the issue.

The rating agencies

Evaluating credit quality has become increasingly difficult and costly as the complexity of bond issues has increased. The financial, demographic, and other data required to evaluate fully the credit of a tax-exempt issue are seldom readily available to investors. State and local governments are not generally subject to the disclosure requirements imposed on private companies by federal securities laws. Even when available, the data are not always presented in a usable format. Indeed, until the New York City crisis in the mid-1970s, state and local governments, including the largest, rarely issued prospectuses longer than two pages to potential bidders. More detailed information has since been provided.

Because the overall dollar cost of obtaining and analyzing the appropriate information is fixed and, therefore, independent of the amount a purchaser wishes to invest, the cost of credit evaluation per dollar of investment declines as the number of bonds purchased increases. Credit evaluation, then, is most costly for small investors, who purchase only a few bonds. As a result, these investors will require higher interest rates as compensation either for the high costs of conducting a credit investigation or for the greater uncertainty that arises from not conducting one.

The market for bond issues is thus narrowed to those large investors and financial institutions that incur lower relative costs of credit evaluation by spreading the fixed costs over a larger number of bonds. The interest rates paid in this narrow market are higher than in a broader market. To broaden the bond market to include smaller investors and thereby lower their interest rates, state and local government bond issuers may request an independent third party to evaluate the credit worthiness of their bonds and to make this information available to all investors free of charge. The issuer pays the rating agency for the analysis, whose cost will vary. For general obligation bonds, cost depends on population size. For revenue bonds, cost depends on the complexity of the evaluation. Such an expenditure is worthwhile for the issuer if the interest cost savings from increased demand for the bonds exceeds the cost of obtaining the rating. The ratings are reviewed annually by the agency at no additional charge.

The two major municipal bond credit rating agencies are Moody's and Standard & Poor's. Their evaluations are summarized in a letter credit rating and the two agencies use similar rating symbols (see Table 12–6).

Because credit evaluation is to some extent subjective, however, and because different analysts may look at different data or assign different weight to the same data, the rating agencies do not necessarily give the same credit ratings to the same bond issues.

As shown in Table 12–7, the higher the credit rating, the lower the interest rate—not just because of the rating, but because of the underlying credit quality of the issue. That is, ratings provide little new information about credit quality; rather, they primarily transmit the information to a larger population. However, because about 90 percent of publicly underwritten municipal bond issues of $5 million or more are currently rated by one or more rating agencies, it appears that issuers believe that the benefits of the reduction in interest rates generally exceed the cost of the rating. Unrated bonds, on average, trade at the same interest rate as Baa rated bonds, although there is a wide variation.

As Table 12–8 shows, the most frequent bond rating is A. Very few issues receive ratings below Baas. If an issuer expects a rating below investment grade, it will usually not seek a rating. Notes are also rated. Table 12–9 gives the

Table 12–6 Moody's and Standard & Poor's credit ratings for municipal bonds.

Rating		
Moody's[1]	Standard & Poor's[2]	Description
Aaa	AAA	Best quality, extremely strong capacity to pay principal and interest
Aa	AA	High quality, very strong capacity to pay principal and interest
A-1 A	A	Upper medium quality, strong capacity to pay principal and interest
Baa-1 Baa	BBB	Medium grade quality, adequate capacity to pay principal and interest
Ba and lower	BB and lower	Speculative quality, low capacity to pay principal and interest

1 Strongest bonds in A and Baa groups are designated as A-1 and Baa-1, respectively.

2 Plus (+) and minus (−) signs may be added to show relative standing within major rating categories.

Table 12–7 Interest rates on long-term municipal bonds with different credit ratings, October 1984.

Moody's rating	%
Aaa	9.72
Aa	10.10
A	10.28
Baa	10.52
Average	10.13

Source: Moody's Investors Service, *Moody's Municipal and Government Manual* (New York, 1985), p. a10.

Table 12–8 Moody's municipal bond ratings.

	All issues		General obligations	
Rating	No.	%	No.	%
Aaa	482	2.71	130	1.17
Aa1	189	1.06	120	1.08
Aa	1,774	10.00	1,115	10.00
A-1	2,836	15.99	1,891	16.98
A	6,916	39.00	4,530	40.65
Baa-1	2,405	13.56	1,738	15.60
Baa	2,320	13.08	1,546	13.87
Lower than Baa	815	4.60	73	0.65
Total	17,737	100.00	11,143	100.00

Source: *Distribution of Moody's Municipal Bond and Note Ratings* (New York, N.Y.: Moody's Investors Service, 1985).

Table 12–9 Moody's municipal note ratings.

Rating	Description
MIG = Moody's Investment Grade	
MIG1	Best quality
MIG2	High quality
MIG3	Favorable quality
MIG4	Adequate quality

Source: *Fundamentals of Municipal Bonds* (New York, N.Y.: Public Securities Association, 1982), p. 44.

Table 12–10 Moody's municipal note ratings, 1984.

Rating	All issues		General obligations	
	No.	%	No.	%
MIG1	1,556	73.74	1,014	75.33
MIG2	486	23.04	280	20.80
MIG3	60	2.84	46	3.42
MIG4	8	0.38	6	0.45
Total	2,110	100.00	1,346	100.00

Source: *Distribution of Moody's Municipal Bond and Note Ratings* (New York, N.Y.: Moody's Investors Service, 1985).

Moody's rating scale. As Table 12–10 shows, most notes are rated MIG1, the highest rating.

Credit ratings are used by large as well as small investors. Some, such as commercial banks, are restricted by law or by regulations from purchasing lower ("noninvestment") quality securities, often considered those rated Ba or below. Large investors often use the ratings as a yardstick against which to compare their own in-house evaluations. In cases of major discrepancies, they will reevaluate their internal analyses. Some financial institutions, particularly those that underwrite or trade municipal bonds, will make their own evaluations available to their customers.

Municipal bond insurance

A number of private insurance firms will insure municipal bonds so that in the event of a default by the issuer the insurance company pays all coupon and maturity amounts to the investors.[2] The cost of the insurance is charged to the issuer and varies from 0.5 percent to 3.0 percent of the amount of the original principal and interest, both of which depend on the insurance company's evaluation of the risk of default. The insurance decreases the investors' losses in case of default and reduces the interest rate required on the bonds. Standard & Poor's and Moody's give most insured bonds a AAA rating. Whether an issuer should obtain insurance depends on the cost of the insurance relative to the issuer's estimation of the savings to be gained by the reduction in the interest payments over the life of the bond issue.

Official statement and disclosure

About one month before the scheduled sale of the bonds, the issuer should publish a preliminary official statement or prospectus describing the provisions

Bond insurance Insurance against the issuer's ability to repay its debt. Two types of bond insurance exist—*default insurance* and *interest cost insurance.* In default insurance, the most common type, an insurance company guarantees the full and timely payment of the coupon and maturing amount on a bond to the investor in the event that an issuer is unable to pay. In interest cost insurance, a policy is sold to the issuer of a bond by a financial institution guaranteeing that the issuer will pay no more than a maximum rate of interest on a variable rate issue. If the interest rate payable rises above the limit in the policy, the financial institution pays the amount in excess of the guaranteed rate.

of the bond issue and providing information that will permit investors to price the bonds properly. Once the bonds are sold to the winning underwriter, a final official statement is prepared that includes the details of the issue and the coupon rates. Unlike the statements of private issuers, the official statements of state and local governments need not comply with the regulations of the Securities and Exchange Commission (SEC) or any other federal agency.[3]

Prior to 1974, the contents of official statements varied greatly, particularly for general obligation bonds. The statements ranged from one mimeographed sheet—even for large issues—to highly professional booklets of detailed information. Most statements, however, compared poorly with the prospectuses prepared by private issuers.

In 1975, the near default of both the New York State Urban Development Corporation and New York City and the threatened default of a number of other older East Coast cities focused attention on municipal bonds. It was believed that the general lack of relevant information and, in some instances, the inclusion of misleading information in official statements (intentionally and unintentionally) contributed to keeping the true financial condition of issuers hidden from the public and investors. In response to the paucity of information, a number of bills were introduced in Congress to establish minimum standards for official statements and to have bond issuance supervised by a federal agency. Although none of the bills was enacted, issuers did become more aware of the importance of proper disclosure and of the potential for legal liability in cases of inaccurate or omitted information. In addition, a number of states adopted legislation stipulating minimum disclosure requirements. In Oregon, for example, a statute stipulates the following requirements for general obligation issues:

1. The issuer shall prepare and make available upon request to bidders and investors a preliminary official statement that includes the following:
   a. Past and current financing and estimated future financing of the issuer
   b. Brief description of the financial administration and organization of the issuer
   c. Brief description of the economic and social characteristics of the issuer which will permit bidders and investors to appraise the issuer's ability to assume and service adequately the debt obligation
   d. Any other information the issuer may provide or which the Oregon Municipal Debt Advisory Commission may require by rule.
2. The preliminary official statement described in subsection (1) of this section shall be available not later than the date of first publication of the notice of bond sale.
3. The preliminary official statement shall contain the best available information which shall be accurate to the best knowledge of the issuer. However, any errors or omissions in the preliminary official statement shall not affect the validity of the bond issue.[4]

The Oregon Municipal Debt Advisory Commission also has prepared detailed guidelines for official statements for issuers of different sizes.

In 1976, the Government Finance Officers Association (GFOA) (then the Municipal Finance Officers Association) published *Disclosure Guidelines for Offerings of Securities by State and Local Governments*. This publication was followed in 1978 by *Guidelines for the Use by State and Local Governments in the Preparation of Yearly Information Statements and Other Current Information*. Developed by issuers, underwriters, and bond counsels, the GFOA guidelines, which have been widely accepted among issuers, stress the need for issuers not only to prepare a complete and accurate official statement, but to make it available early enough for potential underwriters and investors to study and analyze the contents, that is some 20 to 30 days before the date of sale. This availability of complete and timely information should broaden the market and lower the effective interest cost to the issuer. Finally, the GFOA guidelines have reduced the pressures for federal government supervision.

Two surveys shed light on the types of data underwriters and investors consider most useful in evaluating the credit quality of general obligation bonds. In Table 12–11, the items that the GFOA guidelines recommend for disclosure are ranked according to the importance assigned to them by 25 major underwriters. Similarly, Table 12–12 shows the importance of information about the issue

Table 12–11 MFOA disclosure items ranked in importance by underwriters.

Rank	Disclosure item	Average[a]
1	Financing current obligations with long-term debt	3.88
2	Repayment of long-term debt by issuing additional obligations	3.87
3	Receipts used to repay debt	3.84
4	Accounting practices and deviations	3.80
5–6	Fund trends and changes	3.72
5–6	Retirement plan funding	3.72
7–8	Comparison of operations	3.64
7–8	Changes in tax assessments and collections	3.64
9	Audit reports	3.60
10	Cash flows	3.59
11	Taxation procedures	3.52
12	Budgetary practices	3.50
13	Assessed value of taxable property	3.48
14	Ten largest taxpayers	3.44
15	Emergency funds	3.29
16	Financial statements	3.17

Source: Robert W. Ingram, "A Review of the MFOA Disclosure Guidelines. *Governmental Finance* 7, no. 2 (May 1978): 38.
[a] Maximum score is 4.0.

Table 12–12 Disclosure information ranked in importance by large commercial banks.

Rank	Information item	Average[a]	Standard deviation
1	Total debt outstanding	3.833	0.377
2	Debt to actual value ratio	3.745	0.488
3	Overlapping debt outstanding	3.638	0.529
4	Debt per capita	3.630	0.532
5	Tax collection history	3.625	0.570
6	Changes in financial position	3.596	0.614
7–8	Population trends, income, etc.	3.563	0.542
7–8	Actual value of property in tax jurisdiction	3.563	0.649
9	Operating revenues	3.479	0.618
10	Assessed valuation	3.447	0.746
11	Tax rate limits	3.435	0.620
12	Operating expenditures	3.417	0.679
13	Debt to assessed value ratio	3.386	0.895
14	Accounting policies used	3.277	0.772
15	Principal taxpayers	3.250	0.601
16	Portion of tax rates applicable to debt	3.213	0.690
17	Tax rate history	3.087	0.661
18	Sinking funds applicable to outstanding debt	3.021	0.737
19	Bond rating	2.958	0.771
20	Current assets and liabilities	2.957	0.806
21	Fixed assets	2.333	0.853

Source: Arthur S. Boyett and Gary A. Giroux, "The Relevance of Municipal Financial Reporting to Municipal Security Decisions," *Governmental Finance* 7, no. 2 (May 1978): 30.
[a] Maximum score is 4.0.

and the issuer according to the weight assigned to each by 45 large commercial banks serving as underwriters and investors. Both surveys indicate that factors such as total debt outstanding, debt per capita, and sources of revenue to repay the debt are viewed as the most important information items for analyzing the credit quality of an issue.

As local government financial control systems have been improved, greater emphasis has been placed on gathering, compiling, reporting, and verifying financial data. The increased emphasis on complete and timely disclosure has had an unexpected, but beneficial, side effect. Many issuers had discovered that the information they had been receiving on their own financial position was incomplete and, on occasion, inaccurate, thereby making it difficult to arrive at the best financial decisions or to undertake corrective action in time to prevent more serious difficulties. Now, however, it is much less likely that financial difficulties experienced by issuers will again catch the public, the investors, and the issuers themselves unaware.

Sale of bonds

Municipal bonds are sold by issuers to investors through underwriters. Underwriters, individually for smaller issues or as part of a syndicate for larger issues, buy the entire bond issue (generally in serial form) from the issuer and resell the individual bonds to investors. Thus, underwriters assume the burden of distributing the bonds. If they miscalculate, they risk having to sell the bonds at a price below the purchase price and thereby incurring a loss.

Notice of sale

The notice of sale is the issuer's official notice announcing the intention to sell a bond issue by competitive sale (see next section). The notice of sale provides summary information about the issue, describes the method by which the bonds will be awarded to the winner, and solicits bids. At a minimum, the notice of sale should include:

1. The total par amount
2. The par amounts in each maturity
3. The maturity dates
4. The call provisions, if any
5. The maximum interest cost permitted
6. The minimum dollar bid permitted
7. The time, date, and place where the bids will be accepted
8. The basis on which the issue will be awarded
9. The constraints placed on the bid
10. The size of the good faith check, if required
11. The name of the bond counsel
12. The name of the person who may be contacted for additional information.

The notice of sale should be advertised early and widely to attract the largest number of bidders. Often, advertising requirements are mandated by state law. Advertisement in local and major state newspapers may be sufficient for smaller issues. Larger issues, or those that have regional or larger visibility, should also be advertised in the *Daily Bond Buyer,* a widely recognized publication concerned primarily with the municipal bond industry. The complete notice or a summary of sale should appear at least once in these newspapers 20 to 30 days before the scheduled sale. Studies show that the larger the number of competitive bidders on an issue, the lower the interest cost.[5]

Publicity is only one factor affecting the number of bids received on a competitively sold issue. On the average, the number of bids also increases with the quality of the credit, the degree of stability in the financial markets, and, to some extent, the dollar amount of the issue. Beyond a certain par size, the number of bids declines as underwriters join progressively larger syndicates to finance and market the issue. Thus, both very small and very large municipal bond issues tend to receive fewer bids than do comparable medium-size issues.

Method of sale

Issuers may sell the bond issue to underwriters by competitive (public) sale or by negotiation. In a competitive sale, the issuer announces the particulars of the issue, details the basis on which the bonds will be awarded to a bidder, and solicits bids. In a negotiated sale, the issuer chooses an underwriter (or, for large issues, a syndicate of underwriters) in advance of the sale date, and the price and other particulars of the issue are negotiated between the two parties.

Frequently, the method of sale is stipulated by state statute. Most states require that general obligation bonds be awarded by competitive sale. Revenue bonds usually may be sold by either method. Because of the sharp increase in revenue bond issues in recent years, the proportion of bonds sold by negotiation has increased from 25 percent in 1973, to more than 86 percent of the dollar value of municipal bonds in 1984. Except for small issues, on which bids may be received from private parties, underwriters are either commercial banks or investment banks (securities dealers). Investment banks may bid on all types of municipal securities. Commercial banks are restricted by federal law to bidding only on general obligation bonds and on a limited number of revenue bonds, primarily those issued for housing or university purposes.

Role of the underwriter

The role of the underwriter differs greatly in the two sales methods.

Competitive sale In a competitive sale, the underwriter becomes involved only after the notice of sale has been published, generally two to four weeks before the scheduled date of sale. The design of the issue is fully completed at that time and has been prepared without formal assistance from any bidding underwriters. (To avoid conflicts of interest, in those cases where underwriters, acting as consultants, have provided earlier advice to the issuer in the design of the bond issue, the underwriters often exclude themselves from bidding on the issue.)

On the basis of the notice of sale, underwriters decide whether to prepare a bid. Most larger issues are too risky and too costly for a single underwriter to purchase and distribute, so more than one underwriter will join to form a syndicate. One or more of the larger underwriters, or a regional underwriter on a smaller issue, serves as manager of the syndicate and assumes the major responsibility for preparing the bid. The decision of an underwriter or underwriting syndicate to prepare a bid on an issue is based on the financial conditions in the market, the kind of reception the issue receives from traditional bond buyers, and the past bond experience of the same issuer. Some underwriters bid on bonds of particular issuers for many years and develop files both on the issuer's credit quality and on the customers who prefer these bonds. This kind of preliminary analysis is important because the unusually large number of issues and issuers makes the municipal bond market more segmented than most other securities markets. In 1984, more than 7,000 new bond issues were marketed, most of them sold by different issuers.

If an underwriter decides to prepare a bid, additional work is required to determine the yields each maturity needs to attract investors, to find potential investors, and to prepare a bid that will have a chance of winning the bond issue and yielding a profit when the bonds are reoffered for sale. If the underwriter misgauges the market and prepares a bid based on an expectation to resell the bonds at yields that turn out to be too low, the bond prices will have to be lowered. This would reduce and possibly eliminate the underwriter's expected profit. Underwriters plan to resell the bonds within a few days of the sale, although physical delivery of the bonds by the municipal issuer generally occurs 30 to 60 days after the date of sale. Because payment to the issuer occurs only on delivery of the bonds, underwriters rarely have funds tied up in the issue prior to delivery—except for a small "good faith" check on deposit with the issuer. However, the costs involved in searching the market and preparing the bid are recovered only if the underwriter wins the bids with a spread that is large enough to recover costs and profits when the bonds are resold. Losing underwriters must charge these costs to profits on the issues for which they are the winning bidder. The risk of not recovering preparation costs restricts the effort underwriters put into a competitive bid preparation.

Negotiated sale In a negotiated sale, the underwriter enters the process at a much earlier stage. Once the decision has been made to sell a new bond issue by negotiation, the issuer contacts one or more underwriters to acquaint them with the particulars of the issue and to solicit information on the approximate interest costs, the spread (profit) the underwriter intends to charge, and the services the underwriter will perform. Often issuers first contact the underwriters used in previous sales and with whose services they have been satisfied. The underwriter selected will usually help the issuer design the issue in terms of maturity dates, maturity amounts, and call provision; prepare the official statement; obtain a credit rating; select the appropriate time to market the issue; meet with major potential investors; and comply with the legal requirements.

Because they are involved at this early stage, underwriters can engage in a longer and more intensive search for investors in bonds sold by negotiation than for those sold competitively. This search also may disclose that the issue could be sold at a lower interest cost—if it were redesigned to meet the demands of an investor who wishes to buy a larger amount of bonds with a maturity different from that planned or who wants a particular coupon rate. The issue can be modified to meet these demands before the sale. Unlike a competitive sale date, a negotiated underwriting date can be easily changed. Thus, if the underwriter believes that the market is particularly unsettled or that an unusually large number of similar bond issues are scheduled to be sold on the same day, the sale date can be adjusted. This increased flexibility can reduce interest costs somewhat.

The type of bond sale that is best for the issuer depends on the particular characteristics of the issuer and the issue. Studies have shown that, on the average, bond issues sold by competitive bid have lower interest costs to the issuer than comparable bonds sold by negotiation—even after adjustment for the additional services provided. But wide differences exist. The interest cost savings on competitive sales are usually largest for well-known, high-credit-quality issues; they become smaller as the credit quality of the issuer decreases, and turn negative for low credit quality issues of little-known issuers. For the last group, interest costs appear lower, on average, on negotiated sales. Because of these differences, each finance officer should carefully determine which method is best, basing the opinion on credit quality, national or regional visibility, size of issue, frequency with which issues have been marketed, any special complicating features of the issue, and conditions in the securities market at the time. Because underwriters perform greater services in negotiated sales at no apparent "out-of-pocket" cost, some finance officers may elect to use this easier method without sufficient cost-benefit analysis.

Basis of award

Bids received in competitive sales are awarded according to the criteria specified in the official notice of sale. Generally, the issue is awarded to the bidder asking the lowest interest rate, although on occasion it may go to the highest bidder on the price of the bonds. The coupon rates on the maturities in a serial issue are determined by the bidders. Although the lowest interest cost criterion appears straightforward, this section will show that historically the method by which it has been used in the sale of municipal serial bonds to underwriters has often resulted in the acceptance of an interest cost bid that is higher than necessary to the issuer.

In the market, bonds are traded or priced on the basis of their yield to maturity or, more technically, the internal rate of return. The internal rate of return is calculated by discounting the contractual stream of future coupon payments and the final payment at maturity to the current price. The price of the bond is thus the present value of all future payments. Because more interest income is foregone, the concept of present value places a lower value on each dollar for every future year in which it is paid. If the market interest rate is 10 percent, the present value of one dollar paid 1 year from now is 90.9 cents; paid 2 years from now, 82.6 cents; and paid 10 years from now, 38.6 cents. The higher the market interest rate, the lower the present value of a given future payment.

Prior to the introduction of computers, calculating the yield to maturity on a bond was time consuming. Most participants in the bond market relied on prepared, precomputed bond tables so that given the coupon rate, the par value, the number of years to maturity, and the market price, the yield to maturity could be determined. Conversely, given the going market yield, the market price could be determined. Computing the overall yield to maturity for an issue of serial bonds is much more complex and time consuming than for individual bonds, and for these bonds bond tables are not practical. As a result, yield to maturity has not been a feasible criterion by which to award the underwriting of serial municipal bonds. Thus a simplified interest rate concept—net interest cost (NIC)—has come into use. As shown in the formula below, NIC is calculated by taking the total coupon interest payments scheduled over the life of all bonds in the serial issue, plus any discount below the par value of the issue that the underwriter bids (or minus any premium bid over par), divided by the sum of the product of the par values of each bond and the number of years to its maturity. The last term is referred to as the *number of bond year dollars*. In equation form,

$$\text{NIC} = \frac{\text{Total coupon interest payment} + \text{bid discount (or} - \text{bid premium)}}{\text{Number of bond year dollars.}}$$

NIC is quick and easy to compute. Table 12–13 shows an NIC computation for a three-year serial issue with a par value of $3,000. One thousand dollars is scheduled to mature each year. Coupons are assumed to be paid annually, rather than semiannually. The underwriter places 5 percent coupon rates on each maturity and bids par value for the bonds. The NIC is 5 percent.

When used to award municipal bonds to a bidder, however, NIC has two serious drawbacks. Unlike the yield to maturity, NIC is not based on present value. Ten dollars in coupon interest payments in the first year is valued the same as five dollars paid in the first and second years, and the same as one dollar paid in each of the first 10 years. In all three instances, coupon interest payments total 10 dollars. If these were bids, all three alternatives would have equal NICs. The taxpayers, however, would benefit if they paid the 10 dollars in 1-dollar annual installments, rather than as a lump sum in the first year, because they would pay less in present value terms. As a result, ranking bids by NIC may

Table 12–13 Computation of net interest cost (NIC).

Number of years to maturity (A)	Total par value ($) (B)	Coupon rate (%) (C)	Bond year dollars (A × B) (D)	Coupon payments (C × D) ($) (E)
1	1,000	5	1,000	50
2	1,000	5	2,000	100
3	1,000	5	3,000	150
Total	3,000		6,000	300

Bid discount = 0

$$NIC = \frac{\text{Total coupon payments + bid discount}}{\text{Total bond year dollars}}$$

$$= \frac{\text{Column (E) + 0}}{\text{Column (D)}} = \frac{300 + 0}{6{,}000} = .05$$

$$= 5\%$$

not be the same as ranking by an interest computation employing present value, the latter giving a more accurate measure of the cost of funds to the community.

The yield to maturity for a serial issue is referred to as *true interest cost* (TIC) or the Canadian method. TIC is the weighted average of the yields to maturity of the individual bonds in a serial package with an adjustment for the underwriter's spread.

The NICs and TICs of the bids received may be compared. If the accepted low NIC bid is not also the TIC bid, the issuer is not obtaining a true lowest cost bid. Although legally it may be a correct bid, economically it is not. Accepting such a bid implies that the present value of the coupon interest payments scheduled to be made over the life of the bonds is higher than on another bid.

The second major drawback to the NIC method is that it affects the way bidders construct their bids, causing them to prepare higher interest cost bids. Underwriters are middlemen who buy an entire serial bond issue as a package and sell the individual bonds separately. In order to prepare bids, underwriters first estimate the lowest yields to maturity (*reoffering yields*) that will still enable them to resell the individual bonds to investors. Then they establish the underwriting spread needed to cover preparation and marketing costs and provide a net profit. They place coupon rates on the individual bonds in a pattern that will produce the lowest possible NIC consistent with reselling the bonds at the estimated reoffering yields. If the computations are correct, the underwriter will obtain aggregate revenues (*production*) from the sale equal to the price bid on the issue plus the desired spread. Because the NIC formula does not value dollars paid early any higher than those paid later, it is possible for the underwriter to reduce the NIC of the bid for a given TIC by placing high coupons on the early bonds in the serial issue and low coupons on the later bonds.

The relationship between net interest cost and true interest cost as the coupons are changed is presented in Table 12–14 for the hypothetical three-year serial bond issue described in Table 12–13. These examples assume that TIC is computed on the basis of annual compounding and neglect the underwriter's spread. In the first column, the coupons on the bonds are such that the NIC is always $300, or 5.0 percent. Thus, if NIC were used to award the issue, the issuer would view all these bids as identical. In Bid A, all three bonds have 5.0 percent coupons. Both the NIC and TIC of this bid are 5.0 percent. Bid B is "frontloaded" so that it has a 30.0 percent coupon on the first maturity and 0.0 percent coupons on the other two. Because market yields on these maturities are not likely to follow the same pattern as the coupons, the underwriter would reoffer the first bond to investors at a premium considerably above par value and reoffer the last two bonds at large discounts below par value. These premiums and discounts are between the investor and the underwriter and differ from those between the underwriter and the issuer, which directly affect the NIC or TIC.

Table 12–14 Comparisons of hypothetical bids with net interest cost (NIC) and true interest cost (TIC) constant.

Bid and years to maturity[a]	Coupon rate, NIC, TIC (%)	Annual debt service ($)	Bid and years to maturity[a]	Coupon rate, NIC, TIC (%)	Annual debt service ($)
NIC constant[b]			**TIC constant**		
Bid A			Bid G		
1 year	5.00	1,150.00	1 year	5.00	1,150.00
2 years	5.00	1,100.00	2 years	5.00	1,100.00
3 years	5.00	1,050.00	3 years	5.00	1,050.00
Total	—	3,300.00	Total	—	3,300.00
NIC	5.00	—	NIC	5.00	—
TIC[c]	5.00	—	TIC[c]	5.00	—
Bid B			Bid H		
1 year	30.00	1,300.00	1 year	29.05	1,290.50
2 years	0.00	1,000.00	2 years	0.00	1,000.00
3 years	0.00	1,000.00	3 years	0.00	1,000.00
Total	—	3,300.00	Total	—	3,290.50
NIC	5.00	—	NIC	4.84	—
TIC[c]	5.17	—	TIC[c]	5.00	—
Bid C			Bid I		
1 year	12.00	1,190.00	1 year	11.75	1,187.50
2 years	3.00	1,070.00	2 years	3.00	1,070.00
3 years	4.00	1,040.00	3 years	4.00	1,040.00
Total	—	3,300.00	Total	—	3,297.50
NIC	5.00	—	NIC	4.96	—
TIC[c]	5.04	—	TIC[c]	5.00	—
Bid D			Bid J		
1 year	6.50	1,160.00	1 year	6.45	1,159.50
2 years	5.00	1,095.00	2 years	5.00	1,095.00
3 years	4.50	1,045.00	3 years	4.50	1,045.00
Total	—	3,300.00	Total	—	3,299.50
NIC	5.00	—	NIC	4.98	—
TIC[c]	5.01	—	TIC[c]	5.00	—
Bid E			Bid K		
1 year	2.00	1,130.00	1 year	2.00	1,130.50
2 years	5.00	1,110.00	2 years	5.00	1,110.50
3 years	6.00	1,060.00	3 years	6.05	1,060.50
Total	—	3,300.00	Total	—	3,301.50
NIC	5.00	—	NIC	5.02	—
TIC[c]	4.98	—	TIC[c]	5.00	—
Bid F			Bid L		
1 year	0.00	1,100.00	1 year	0.00	1,101.50
2 years	0.00	1,100.00	2 years	0.00	1,101.50
3 years	10.00	1,100.00	3 years	10.15	1,101.50
Total	—	3,300.00	Total	—	3,304.50
NIC	5.00	—	NIC	5.08	—
TIC[c]	4.92	—	TIC[c]	5.00	—

Source: Center for Capital Market Research, *Improving Bidding Rules to Reduce Interest Costs in the Competitive Sale of Municipal Bonds* (Eugene: College of Business Administration, University of Oregon, 1977).

Note: Dash (—) indicates not applicable.

[a] All bids in this table are predicated on the par amount of $1,000 for each of the years to maturity, totaling $3,000.

[b] The amount bid in each case equals total par value ($3,000).

[c] Interest is compounded annually.

All of the $300 interest payments are made in the first year. The NIC remains at 5.0 percent but the TIC increases to 5.17 percent. Bids C through F frontload progressively less. Bid F is the ultimate in "backloading" because interest is paid only on the three-year bonds. Its coupon is 10.0 percent, and the one- and two-year bonds have 0.0 percent coupons. Thus, $100 is paid in each of the three years the bond issue is outstanding. Again the NIC is unchanged at 5.0 percent, but, because the payments are made later, the TIC declines to 4.92 percent.

It follows that for a given TIC, the NIC will decrease as the frontloading of the coupons increases, and the issuer should make distinctions among these bids. Underwriters can lower the NIC bid on an issue for a TIC that is determined by reoffering yields. An example of this is shown in the second column of Table 12–14 for the same three-year serial bond issue. This time, the TIC is constant at 5.0 percent and the coupons on the individual bonds change from extreme frontloading in Bid H to extreme backloading in Bid L. The corresponding NICs increase from 4.84 percent to 5.08 percent.

When a bond issue is frontloaded, coupon rates of the early bonds will generally be greater than their reoffering yields. These bonds will be resold by the underwriter to investors at a premium above their par values. Conversely, coupon rates of the later bonds will be less than their reoffering yields and will be resold at a discount below their par values.

It is likely that premium and discount bonds will have to be sold at higher "penalty" yields than bonds with coupons close to their reoffering yields (which will be priced at or near par value). The penalty yield is best illustrated with discount bonds. As discussed earlier, income from coupon payments on municipal bonds is exempt from federal income taxes. However, profits realized from increases between the buying price and the price at sale of municipal securities are subject to capital gains taxes. Low coupon bonds sold at initial discounts are subject to a federal capital gains tax on the difference between the original selling price and the maturity par value. They are no longer completely tax-exempt. Investors will purchase these bonds only if they receive yields higher than those on comparable par or completely tax-exempt bonds to compensate for the present value of the capital gains tax at maturity.

Very high coupon bonds that force the bond to be sold at a price of 108 or higher also trade at higher yields than comparable par bonds. Investors require penalty yields on these bonds to compensate for the higher risk and for the cost of having to reinvest the coupon payments at favorable interest rates. The higher penalty yields on either discount or premium bonds reduce the revenues of the underwriters on the resale of the bond issue to investors. To generate enough revenues to pay the issuer the price bid on the overall issue (par value plus a bid premium or minus a bid discount), the underwriter will increase the coupons on some bonds. This raises the NIC on the issue, but by less than the frontloading initially decreased the NIC. Thus the discounts and premiums charged investors by the underwriter indirectly affect the NIC and TIC of a bid.

Because TIC is an average of the yields on the individual bonds, the existence of penalty yields increases the TIC of an issue, even if the coupon structure is designed to lower NIC. The higher yields demanded by investors on the discount and premium bonds created by the underwriters are "passed through" to the issuer in terms of higher TICs. Moreover, because all bidders under NIC are confronted with the same incentives, all bids on an issue may have some penalty yields. Thus, even the low TIC bid received under NIC bidding is likely to be higher than the low TIC bid that may have been received had the issuer used a different award criterion. The source of the higher interest costs is the bidding rules used by the issuer (these rules stipulate NIC), not by the underwriter. The latter only attempts to win the bid and realize a profit within the rules established by the issuer.

If individual bonds need to be reoffered at penalty yields to lower NIC and win the bid, they will be created by the underwriter. The existence and costs of penalty yields when bonds are awarded by NIC can be seen clearly from an issue sold by the state of Minnesota in 1972. While not representative, this issue is useful for purposes of illustration. The issue had a par value of $25 million maturing in equal amounts over 20 years. Seven bids were received. The coupons and reoffering yields of the winning low NIC bidder are shown in Table 12–15. Also shown are the coupons and reoffering yields of the low TIC bidder and estimates of the reoffering yields at which the bonds could have been sold successfully had the coupon rates been at or near their par values. These yields are estimated from the market yields on comparable bonds on the same date.

Table 12–15 Coupon rates and reoffering yields of winning and low TIC bidders and estimated efficient reoffering yields on sample bond issue.[a]

	Winning bidder (low NIC)		Low TIC bidder		Estimated efficient reoffering yield
Years to maturity	Coupon rate	Reoffering yield (%)	Coupon rate	Reoffering yield (%)	
1	50.0	3.65	10.0	3.10	3.10
2	50.0	3.75	10.0	3.40	3.35
3	50.0	4.00	10.0	3.70	3.55
4	50.0	4.20	10.0	3.85	3.75
5	10.0	4.10	10.0	4.00	3.95
6	10.0	4.25	10.0	4.15	4.10
7	5.0	4.25	10.0	4.30	4.20
8	5.0	4.35	4.7	4.30	4.30
9	4.75	4.45	4.7	4.35	4.35
10	4.75	4.55	4.7	4.45	4.45
11	4.75	4.65	4.7	4.55	4.55
12	4.75	4.75	4.7	4.65	4.65
13	5.0	4.85	4.8	4.75	4.75
14	0.1	6.30[b]	4.8	4.85	4.85
15	0.1	6.30[b]	5.0	4.90	4.90
16	0.1	6.30[b]	5.0	4.95	4.95
17	0.1	6.30[b]	5.0	5.00	5.00
18	0.1	6.30[b]	5.0	5.00	5.00
19	0.1	6.30[b]	0.1	6.70	5.05
20	0.1	6.30[b]	0.1	6.70	5.05
NIC (%)		4.58		4.66	—[c]
TIC (%)		5.51		4.90	4.75

[a] State of Minnesota bond issue sold 26 September 1972.
[b] Estimated from price data in financial press.
[c] Not applicable.

On a TIC basis, the low NIC bid was the highest of the seven bids submitted. The low TIC bid was the fourth lowest NIC bid. The penalty yields associated with the 50 percent coupons on the first four maturities relative to the 10 percent coupons of the low TIC bids range from 30 to 55 basis points (one-hundredth of a percentage point). But even the 10 percent coupons would have caused the bonds to sell at premiums priced to require penalty yields. Note how much higher were the reoffering yields on the 10 percent coupon bonds than were the estimated yields on the par bonds of the maturity.

The effect of large discounts below par on reoffering yields is also evident. Reoffering yields jump by 145 basis points from 4.85 percent to 6.30 percent on the winning bid when the coupon declines from 5.0 percent to 0.1 percent between the thirteenth and fourteenth maturities. The penalty yields on these bonds is in excess of one percentage point. Note that even the low bid from the

TIC criterion placed 0.1 percent coupons on the last two maturities so that these bonds also sold at penalty yields. However, if a more efficient award criterion, say TIC, had been specified from the inception, then all the bids would have been lower. At any rate, the combined present value cost of the selection of the "wrong bid," which resulted in penalty reoffering yields, was estimated to be about $1.25 million higher than necessary in interest payments over the life of the bonds. This amount would not have been expended had more efficient bidding procedures been used.

Many issuers and underwriters have been aware of the potential for excessive interest costs when using NIC. To minimize the effects, constraints are often placed on the value of the coupons to be used by bidders. But often these constraints are not as efficient as possible and, on occasion, none are imposed. The Minnesota sale, for example, specified no coupon constraints whatsoever. A survey of municipal bonds sold in 1972 and 1973 (conducted by the Center for Capital Market Research at the University of Oregon) indicated that the excess cost paid over the life of the bonds sold competitively by NIC was between $20 million and $40 million in each of these years. This was only a fraction of one percent of the par value of all bonds sold competitively, but it is a large dollar amount that could be avoided at virtually no cost to the issuer.

Bidding procedures that would avoid these excess interest costs have been developed by the Center for Capital Market Research at the University of Oregon.[6] The Center recommends that all but the smallest issuers use TIC criteria to award their bonds. The widespread use of computers and readily available TIC computer programs no longer make the computation of TIC difficult or time consuming. Because almost all underwriters have now had experience with TIC bidding, the number of bids received should not decline.

Nevertheless, some issuers are required by law to use NIC, and other issuers may feel that the issue size is so small that all the bidders may not have TIC capability. For them, the Center recommends limiting the range of values of the coupons that underwriters may place on the individual bonds; thus, no coupon on a bond could be smaller than that on the preceding maturity. This constraint is termed nondescending order (NDO) and reduces the probability that individual bonds will be reoffered at large discounts or premiums that require costly penalty yields. Because each bond issue is different, however, it is important for finance officers to select the constraints that are most appropriate for their particular use.

Finally, award conditions are improving. In 1978, the last year surveyed, about 40 percent of the dollar volume of all bonds sold competitively was awarded on the basis of *efficient* bidding criteria. This increase from approximately 5 percent in 1972 resulted in significant cost savings to issuers.

Broadening the market

As discussed earlier, the tax-exemption feature effectively narrows the market for municipal securities to investors in high marginal federal income tax brackets (e.g., wealthy individuals, commercial banks, and property and casualty insurance companies), thereby excluding such important investors as endowment funds, foundations, and pension funds. This relatively narrow market may also cause interest rates on municipal securities to be higher after tax adjustments than need be. In addition, the cyclical instability of bank demand for municipal securities has made interest rates on municipal bonds more volatile than on most other securities. The U.S. Treasury and Congress have proposed several options and legislative initiatives to rectify inequities and inefficiencies in the current tax-exempt municipal bond market.

Treasury proposal

For some time, the Treasury has contended that the current form of tax exemption provides an inefficient and costly subsidy to state and local government issuers. It is inefficient because the interest cost savings to issuers is less than the income tax loss to the Treasury. High quality, long-term municipal bonds sell at almost 75 percent of the interest rate on Treasury securities with the same maturity. The cost savings to the tax-exempt issuer, then, is about 25 percent. However, many municipal bonds are purchased by investors whose marginal tax brackets are substantially higher than 25 percent. The loss to the Treasury caused by the reduction of income tax revenues from these investors is greater than the 25 percent interest savings to the local issuers. For example, if the average purchaser of municipal bonds were in the 50 percent federal income-tax bracket, the interest rate to municipal issuers would have to be 50 percent of the interest rate on comparable Treasury securities in order for the gain to the issuer to be equal to the loss to the Treasury.

To increase the efficiency of the subsidy, the Treasury has long proposed a *taxable bond option* (TBO) for issuers. Under this proposal, issuers could sell taxable municipal bonds instead of tax-exempt bonds. This would, of course, increase the interest cost of the bonds. The Treasury, however, would make a direct payment to the issuer to compensate for the higher cost. The Treasury also would collect the full tax revenues from investors. The desirability of the TBO to state and local governments will depend on how much of the interest cost is compensated by the Treasury. The larger the ratio of payment, the more attractive the program. Additionally, notes the Treasury, issuers would benefit from the lower and more stable interest costs to be created by the higher pretax interest rates. With the new rates making municipal bonds attractive to individual and institutional investors in lower marginal tax brackets (e.g., moderate-income households, endowment funds, pension funds, and life insurance companies), the demand for securities will be opened up to a larger number and wider range of investors. Moreover, when commercial banks reduce their demand for municipal securities, these new investors are likely to increase their demand to absorb at least part of the shortfall.

In spite of its intellectual appeal, however, a taxable bond option proposal has not been enacted by Congress, for two major reasons: (1) state and local governments have not found the proposed Treasury payment sufficient to offset the higher taxable interest costs, even though the proposals have called for payments ranging from 30 percent to 40 percent of the market interest rate; and (2) state and local governments are fearful of allowing intervention by the Treasury in their debt-management decisions.

Current legislative initiatives

Another continuing complaint of the Treasury has focused on excessive use of bonds sold for "private use" by for-profit firms and not-for-profit entities. According to the Treasury, some issuers of tax-exempt securities have been netting revenues by investing some of the proceeds from the sale of tax-exempt securities in taxable obligations. Although the Treasury has rules severely restricting this type of arbitrage, it is still possible for an issuer to derive some revenue during a "temporary period" until the bond proceeds are expended on the designated project.

These objections to the use of the tax-exempt bond market have led to a number of new proposals and federal legislative initiatives restricting the volume and type of tax-exempt municipal bonds. Whether any final legislation will emerge is highly uncertain. Nevertheless, the federal government over a number of years has attempted to restrain the volume and types of municipal bonds and that effort can be expected to continue.

Summary

This chapter reviewed the process by which state and local governments finance their capital expenditures through the sale of bonds. Because the municipal bond market is changing rapidly (like most other sectors of the financial marketplace), the finance officer must keep abreast of recent developments and must master the techniques of bond financing. Such knowledge can save the issuing governmental unit considerable amounts in lower interest costs and more favorable terms. This chapter has discussed these changes, analyzed the reasons for them, and provided the fundamentals that permit a finance officer to sell bonds at the lowest cost.

1 Good reviews of trends in municipal debt financing appear in John E. Petersen and Wesley C. Hough, *Creative Capital Financing for State and Local Governments* (Washington, D.C.: Municipal Finance Officers Association, 1983); and John E. Petersen, "Recent Developments in Tax-Exempt Bond Markets," *Working Paper* (Washington, D.C.: Government Finance Officers Association, April 1985).

2 The major firms offering municipal bond insurance are American Municipal Bond Association Corp. (AMBAC), Municipal Bond Insurance Association (MBIA), Financial Guarantee Insurance Company (FGIC), Bond Insurance Guarantee, Inc. (BIGI), Industrial Development Bond Insurance (IDBI), and Health Industry Benefit, Inc. (HIBI).

3 The Municipal Securities Rule-Making Commission was organized in 1975 as an independent, self-regulatory agency to supervise and monitor the activities of firms and individuals engaged in the trading of municipal securities for the protection of investors. It cannot, however, require the issuers to furnish information to investors or underwriters, as does the SEC for private issuers.

4 Oregon Revised Statute 287.018.

5 See, for example, Michael H. Hopewell and George G. Kaufman, "Costs to Municipalities of Selling Bonds by NIC," *National Tax Journal* (December 1974): 531–41.

6 Center for Capital Market Research, *Improving Bidding Rules to Reduce Interest Costs in the Competitive Sale of Municipal Bonds: A Handbook for Municipal Finance Officers* (Eugene: Univ. of Oregon, 1977).

Public pension fund administration

Administration of state and local government employee pension plan programs has become an area of growing concern. These plans cover about 15 million people (either as current employees or beneficiaries) and their potential financial effect on the future budgets of local governments is not yet fully comprehended. The following questions arise: Will pension benefits promised to employees today be adequate in the future? Are the programs being managed in the most secure, efficient, and economical manner? And—most crucial of all—will benefits promised today be affordable by the contributing governments tomorrow?

The long overlooked financial effect of public pensions will remain at the forefront of public financial administration because pensions affect so many people and involve so much money. By the mid-1980s, almost all of the 13 million state and local government employees were covered by some form of pension plan and a growing army of retirees and survivors depended on benefit payments for all or part of their livelihood.

It is estimated that state and local governments pay nearly $25 billion a year in contributions, accounting for about eight cents out of every tax dollar collected. In addition, employees belonging to contributory plans pay an average of 4 percent of their wages to help finance their retirement plans. Despite this high rate of contribution, managers of public pension systems need to be ever mindful of the problem of accumulating sufficient resources to meet future obligations. As the growth in public-sector employment levels off, the number of beneficiaries and the amount of benefit payments will increase relative to current public payroll and tax collections. Unless enough money is set aside today, or the terms and conditions of pensions can be modified, the public sector will increasingly feel the burden of meeting underfunded pension obligations. This sobering prospect has undoubtedly increased the emphasis placed on the management of state and local retirement programs.

The problem of unfunded pension liabilities and the financial burdens they will create for the future has been the subject of much study. Whereas the weakness of many plans led to a rude awakening in the 1970s, more recent trends in pension finances—high investment earnings, lower inflation rates, and a tightening of benefits—have shown favorable improvement. Nevertheless, much depends on the continuation of relatively high real interest rates. The financial soundness of most pension plans and the real worth of the benefits to be paid rest on the ability of the funds to continue to earn good returns on their investments and stay ahead of rises in the cost of living. Failure to do so will mean either a reduction in the real worth of benefits, increased contributions to meet retirement goals, or some combination of the two.

The mounting costs of pensions have been caused in part by a lack of policy concerning their design, financing, and administration. As this chapter will show, if pension practices are not reformed, the problem will become even more difficult in time, because pension obligations by their very nature can leave a legacy of financial and administrative burdens.

Another realm of concern dealt with in this chapter is the great economic power of pension funds as investors. Pension fund investments have diversified, the types of investment have expanded, and legal impediments have been relaxed. The wise pension fund manager will seek the advice of professionals, so as to best handle the funds in his or her control. Finally, as retirement systems have rapidly accumulated assets amounting to over $350 billion, many observers have urged that their investment policies be directed toward socially useful objectives. Adding such responsibilities to the primary objective (or, some would contend, the sole objective) of financing and protecting worker benefits has presented new and difficult challenges to legislators and pension fund managers.

The universe of public pensions

A special census by the Pension Task Force of the U.S. House of Representatives in 1975 counted nearly 5,800 separate public employee retirement systems, covering more than 12.5 million employees.[1] It should be noted that the study included in its definition of a pension plan any arrangement that provided postretirement income (e.g., deferred compensation plans and life insurance contracts), whether administered by a governmental entity or the private sector.

However, for purposes of local government financial management, the definitions used by the U.S. Bureau of the Census and the corresponding numbers may be useful. The Census Bureau excludes the following from its count of public retirement systems: (1) those that forward contributions to private insurance companies as premiums paid for the purchase of annuity policies, (2) those that make direct payments of benefits from annual appropriations of general funds, and (3) those that have members who belong to the Teacher's Insurance and Annuity Association (TIAA) without any state or local supplemental coverage. As a result, only systems administered by a sponsoring state or local government are contained in the census number.[2] The 1982 Census of Governments reported 2,559 systems with a combined membership of 11.6 million employees and almost 3 million current beneficiaries.[3]

Membership at state and local levels

Retirement systems for state and local governments are administered at both the state and local levels. As shown in Table 13–1, 87 percent of the covered employees belong to state-administered systems, which also account for 79 percent of the financial assets. Local governments account for 93 percent of the total number of systems but only 13 percent of the employee membership. The Pension Task Force study estimated, however, that approximately 70 percent of the members of the state-administered system are local government employees.

Table 13–1 Key measures of state and local retirement systems, 1982.

Classification	No. of systems	Total membership (millions)	Beneficiaries (millions)	Receipts ($ billions)	Payments ($ billions)	Assets ($ billions)
Total	2,559	11.61	2.90	48.96	18.27	245.25
State	190	10.14	2.26	37.94	13.47	193.30
Local	2,369	1.47	0.64	11.02	4.80	51.95

Source: U.S. Bureau of the Census, 1982 Census of Governments, *Employee-Retirement Systems of State and Local Governments*, vol. 6, no. 1. (Washington, D.C.: GPO, 1983).

Table 13–2 indicates the growth in the coverage of employees by pension plans from 1950 through 1982. During this period the ratio of active pension plan members to full-time equivalent employees increased from 68 percent to an estimated 93 percent. In view of the wide coverage that already exists and the slowing of growth in government employment, it is unlikely that active membership in plans will grow very rapidly in the future. The number of beneficiaries will continue to grow, however, as the membership matures.

At the local level, 82 percent of all systems are administered by municipalities; 8 percent by townships; 7 percent by counties; and the remainder by school districts and special districts. Membership in county government systems tends to be considerably larger on average (2,200 members) than membership in city government systems (425 members).[4]

Most of the employees belong to a relatively small number of the plans. Of the 2,559 plans, 116 have a membership of approximately 10.6 million, or 92 percent of total members. Thus, there are only approximately 979,000 members for the remaining 2,143 plans, of which nearly 1,700 have fewer than 100 members—only 0.4 percent of total members. These very small systems predominate at the local level.[5]

The contrasts in the number of systems among the individual states are great, ranging from 1 plan to cover all state and local employees in the state of Hawaii to 437 plans in the state of Pennsylvania—according to the Census Bureau—and this number is apparently understated.[6] The sizes of plans vary widely as well, particularly when the very largest systems are considered. Two statewide systems—one in California and one in New York—include more than 500,000 members each, and the largest five systems include 20 percent of all state and local employees who belong to retirement systems.[7]

This tendency to concentrate membership in the largest systems has increased: The portion of employees covered by systems in excess of 100,000 members grew from 50 to 63 percent from 1972 to 1982. The trend toward this type of employee concentration has many advantages in terms of administering and rationalizing plans, especially among potentially competing jurisdictions and groups of employees. On the other hand, greater concentration can lead to political problems and can diminish the power of individual employing governments to control their personnel policies and pension costs.[8]

Table 13–2 State and local pension membership and full-time employment, 1950–1982.

Year	No. of full-time government employees (millions) (A)	Active pension members	
		No. (millions)	% of (A)
1950	3.8	2.6	68.4
1960	5.5	4.5	81.8
1970	8.5	7.3	85.9
1977	10.6	9.7	91.5
1982	10.9	10.1	92.7

Sources: U.S. Congress, House, Committee on Education and Labor, *Task Force Report on Public Employee Retirement Systems* (Washington, D.C.: GPO, 1978), p. 174. For 1977 data, U.S. Bureau of the Census, *Public Employment in 1978* (Washington, D.C.: GPO, 1979), p. 9; U.S. Bureau of the Census, 1977 Census of Governments, *Employee-Retirement Systems of State and Local Governments*, vol. 6, no. 1 (Washington, D.C.: GPO, 1978), p. 11. For 1982 data, U.S. Bureau of the Census, *Public Employment in 1982* (Washington, D.C.: GPO, 1983); and U.S. Bureau of the Census, 1982 Census of Governments, *Employee-Retirement Systems of State and Local Governments*, vol. 6, no. 1 (Washington, D.C.: GPO, 1983), p. v.

Coverage by class of employee

Most jurisdictions have separate plans for different categories of employees. As Table 13–3 shows, general public employee coverage systems represent only 21.6 percent of all plans, but include 63.5 percent of covered employees. Frequently fire and police employees belong to separate small, locally administered retirement systems that often feature plans with relatively liberal age and service requirements and superior benefits. Teachers and other school employees are usually covered by plans administered at the state level. Legislators and judges tend to belong to special plans that appear relatively preferential in benefits, with short service requirements and rapid vesting. The extent to which these separate systems recognize the peculiarities of uncertain and difficult jobs or simply represent a convenient way of increasing compensation levels beyond the public's view is a matter of occasional debate.

Table 13–3 Classes of employees covered by state and local retirement plans, 1982.

Employee class	% of retirement plans			% of retirement plan members		
	Total	State	Local	Total	State	Local
Total	100.0	100.0	100.0	100.0	100.0	100.0
General	21.6	32.6	20.7	63.5	63.6	62.9
Education	2.2	18.9	0.9	30.1	32.9	10.7
Police	31.4	10.5	33.1	1.0	0.4	5.4
Fire	26.4	4.2	28.2	0.8	0.4	3.7
Police and fire	8.1	3.7	8.5	1.1	0.7	4.0
Other	10.3	30.0	8.7	3.6	2.1	13.3

Source: U.S. Bureau of the Census, 1982 Census of Governments, *Employee-Retirement Systems of State and Local Governments*, vol. 6, no. 1 (Washington, D.C.: GPO, 1983), p. 12.

Financial flows and assets

Table 13–4 provides an overview of the financial operations of state and local retirement systems. Retirement funds are financed from three sources—government employer contributions, employee contributions, and investment earnings. In contrast with business programs, state and local retirement plans rely heavily on employee contributions; such plans are called contributory plans. The importance of these current contributions relative to fund earnings is diminishing, however. Between 1977 and 1982, investment earnings rose from 31 to 39 percent of all receipts, a dramatic sign of the growing maturity of the funds and the high rates of return available on investments.

Another indicator of the growing maturity of public pension systems is the growth of payments to retiring employees and to survivors and disabled beneficiaries. Payments almost doubled during this period, from $9.8 billion in 1977 to $18.3 billion in 1982. Although payments in 1982 amounted to only 7.5 percent of system assets, their annual rate of growth (16.9 percent) was slightly greater than the growth rate of assets (16.5 percent) between 1977 and 1982. Barring a resurgence of rapid growth in public-sector employment, benefits paid out should continue to grow in relative importance. They may be offset by a continuation of good investment earnings, but long-term projections are difficult to make. If benefit payments accelerate and investment earnings decrease, employer and employee contributions may need to be increased in order to prevent the level of assets (and future earnings) from eroding.

Not shown in Table 13–4 is the present value of future benefits that will need to be paid and their relationship to existing assets and contributions. The adequacy of assets to offset forecasted future benefits and the ability of current contribution rates to accumulate needed reserves are the major factor in deter-

Table 13–4 Financial data on state and local employee retirement systems, 1967–1982.

Classification	1967	1977	1982
Receipts ($ billion)	6.58	25.35	48.96
Annual growth rate (%)	—	14.50	12.70
Government contributions ($ billion)	3.05	12.40	21.81
Annual growth rate (%)	—	15.00	8.90
% of receipts	46.40	48.80	44.50
% of tax collections	4.00	7.00	8.20
% of payroll	6.90	9.90	11.47
Employee contributions ($ billion)	1.96	5.23	8.12
Annual growth rate (%)	—	10.30	11.40
% of receipts	29.80	20.60	16.60
Investment earnings ($ billion)	1.56	7.44	19.03
Annual growth rate (%)	—	17.30	18.00
% of receipts	23.80	30.60	38.90
Payments ($ billion)	2.68	9.77	18.27
Annual growth rate (%)	—	13.80	16.90
% of receipts	40.80	38.50	37.32
% of assets	6.80	7.90	7.45
Financial assets ($ billion)	39.26	123.48	245.25
Annual growth rate (%)	—	12.10	16.50

Sources: U.S. Bureau of the Census, 1967 Census of Governments, *Employee-Retirement Systems of State and Local Governments* (Washington, D.C.: GPO, 1968); U.S. Bureau of the Census, 1977 Census of Governments, *Employee-Retirement Systems of State and Local Governments,* vol. 6, no. 1 (Washington, D.C.: GPO, 1978); and U.S. Bureau of the Census, 1982 Census of Governments, *Employee-Retirement Systems of State and Local Governments,* vol. 6, no. 1 (Washington, D.C.: GPO, 1983). Data on state and local tax collections and payroll were obtained from U.S. Bureau of the Census, *Governmental Finances in 1981–82* (Washington, D.C.: GPO, 1983), p. 7.

Notes: Dash (—) indicates not applicable. Annual growth rate refers to 1967–1977, 1981–1982.

mining the financial viability of pension funds and their long-term costs to government.

Most public pension plans provide defined benefits, usually set by some formula based on years of service and level of salary toward the end of the employment period. The government is committed to this level of benefits regardless of whether the assets contributed to the pension fund can support it. However, a few employees are enrolled in pension programs that have *defined contributions,* where the participant's benefits are based on the amount contributed by the employer and any income earned from these contributions. As of the late 1970s, only about 2 percent of all public employees were covered by defined contribution plans, and some 16 percent were covered by combination plans that had both defined benefit and defined contribution elements.[9]

There may be some movement toward plans with defined contributions and variable benefits. One advantage of a defined contribution plan is that the government's liabilities are clearly delineated. In a defined benefit plan, if the level of contributions turns out to be inadequate to cover the promised benefits, the sponsors of the plan find themselves in a situation where they must either raise emergency funds or renege on their promises. This cannot occur in a defined contribution plan. Nor can a defined contribution plan be used as a political device to pledge a high level of benefits to be borne by future residents of the community.

Defined contribution plans also present certain advantages to the employee, although these are not always obvious at first glance. Retirement benefits can be made adequate by making the contribution level sufficient, that is, by funding them fully as the liabilities are incurred. The funds can be invested in a balanced portfolio so that the safety of a recipient's pension does not depend solely on the fiscal safety and probity of the sponsor. Moreover, since the benefits are fully funded at the start, there need be no delay in vesting the employee, and there is no difficulty in making the already contributed sum portable.

Table 13–4 also presents a different perspective on the financing of public pension systems, reflecting their importance in the overall government budget. In 1967 government contributions to pension systems represented less than 7.0 percent of payroll costs and 4.0 percent of tax collections. By 1982 the respective figures were 11.5 percent of payroll and 8.2 percent of taxes. It should be borne in mind that approximately three-quarters of state and local government employees belong to plans that also include Social Security coverage, the contribution rates of which are not included in the above figures. Social Security rates have climbed to 7.05 percent of the $39,600 maximum taxable wage base in 1984, substantially increasing the overall retirement-related costs of government employers and employees.

History and legal setting

Public pensions arose earlier than those in the private sector, with the establishment by cities of limited benefit programs for fire fighters, police officers, and teachers in the late nineteenth century. The number of plans accelerated rapidly in the 1930s and 1940s, particularly during the period when public servants were not eligible for Social Security coverage. Approximately one-half of the largest state and local systems were founded between 1931 and 1950. The smaller local plans were late bloomers, two-thirds founded after 1950.[10]

The evolution of plans over a long period—moving ahead in different states at different times under different pressures—has resulted in a heterogeneous mixture of administrative structures, benefit provisions, and funding techniques. Generally, changes have occurred without benefit of consistent policy or legal framework at either the state or the local level. As a result, attempts to rationalize or restructure public employee retirement plans are frequently bogged down in a maze of legal (and moral) conflicts.

Most states share few public pension plan attributes. Often provisions of great substantive importance (benefit levels, contribution formulas, eligibility, funding requirements, and allowable investments) are tucked away in nooks and crannies of various state statutes and shaped by various judicial interpretations. Home rule cities may establish their own systems as they please, or those cities subject to "bracket laws" (specialized legislation that pertains to only one or a few jurisdictions) may be hemmed into antiquated and conflicting requirements. Frequently, common law interpretations of particular issues are relied on in the absence of specific action by a legislative body.

This patchwork of laws can lead to uncertainty and confusion for the employee and the employer. For example, some states have constitutional provisions that treat public employee pension rights once they are conferred, as a fundamental matter of contract that cannot be impaired except through amendment. Other states view such rights as basic statements of policy with no contractual element. Still others view the public servant's pension as tantamount to a gratuity, giving the employee little comfort in terms of the security of the plan's provisions.[11]

Because of the technical complexity and long-range cost effects of laws governing pension provisions and their financing, state and local legislative bodies carry a heavy burden in assessing the implications of pension-related decisions and the condition of retirement funds. In an effort to develop expertise in these matters, many states have created permanent legislative bodies to screen bills and recommend reform measures. Others have attempted, with varying degrees of success, to provide for formal state supervision of local government pension systems. According to recommendations of the Advisory Commission on Intergovernmental Relations (ACIR), such regulatory entities should have the power to provide technical assistance, maintain information, and review and comment on proposed changes in state and local retirement systems.[12]

Public retirement system organization

Establishing retirement policies, administering contributions and benefits, and managing investments are all part of a pension program. But, as so often in state and local government, form does not necessarily follow function in a consistent fashion. The relationships among the various functions of a pension plan's operation are so varied that they defy easy generalization. Although each public employee retirement plan was at one time or another established primarily to provide postretirement payments to employees, the details of a particular plan's relationship to the contributing government, to employees, and to a host of public and private entities that may also be involved in the pension process are subject to great variation.

Structure

The prototypical state or local retirement system is a special trust fund created under the laws of the state or municipality to provide government employees with pensions and other employment-related benefits. Usually, such laws (be they generic or specific) provide that administration of the system shall be the responsibility of a retirement board, a board of trustees, or a particular department or office in the government sponsoring the system. Within the statutory framework, however, the responsibilities and details of practice can vary greatly from one jurisdiction to another.

The statutes themselves differ a great deal as well. Some spell out the operations in detail, while others let the retirement board or responsible department work out the particulars through bylaws and regulations. Some legislative bodies retain close control over the plan's administrative budget through an appropriation process and may see fit to delegate investment and other administrative functions to government departments and offices that are independent of the retirement board.

Retirement boards may be granted either broadly or narrowly defined power and may be either aggressive or passive in setting policy. In some large systems, these boards make legislative recommendations, set investment policy, establish rules of benefit entitlement, review and approve the budget, and hire inside staff and outside consultants to carry on daily operations. (Since it typically has many other things to worry about and has no profound knowledge of finance, the retirement board often delegates authority for making investments.[13]) At the other extreme, retirement boards may be left with relatively little to do, mainly reviewing disability and retirement claims.

In terms of structure, responsibility, and independence of the retirement fund's operation from the sponsoring or contributing governmental unit or units, three broad categories may be identified. In the most prevalent structure or model, the retirement board itself retains the ultimate authority to make operating decisions, either for its direct exercise or for delegation to staff or private agents acting on its behalf.

In a second model, a separate retirement board exists, but some aspects of the system's operation may be entirely beyond the board's control. For example, the investment function may be assigned to a governmental official (such as a comptroller, treasurer, or finance officer) or it may be the responsibility of a separate investment board that invests the pension fund's money along with monies of other state or municipal agencies.[14]

In a third variant, the governing body itself sets policy, and city departments or public officials carry out the administrative duties. Here, the administration of the retirement plan is part of the government's internal activity and no separate board exists to oversee those activities. In this third model, frequently found in smaller systems, an outside private trustee (such as a bank or insurance company) often is delegated the responsibility to execute investment policy. Not infrequently, other services relating to the payment of pension benefits may be assumed by a private trustee for the plan.

According to a survey in the *Pension Task Force Report,* about 68 percent of all systems (88 percent of those with more than 1,000 members) operated under the general supervision of a separate retirement board. In only 54 percent of all plans (about 65 percent of the large ones) did the board have ultimate responsibility for all aspects of policy and administration, including investments. In the other cases, the retirement board shared its responsibility either with a separate investment board or with some official of the governmental body.[15]

Multi-employer systems, in which several local governments (and, perhaps, state agencies) join together in sponsoring and financing the plan, are usually set up under an umbrella of special state authority, and the contributing governments share in the policymaking through representation on a board of trustees. Members of such boards are statutorily defined, appointed, or elected in such a way as to represent the various types of government and, not infrequently, active employees and retirees who are members of the system.[16]

Retirement board membership

Retirement boards usually consist of seven or more members, specified under enabling legislation. Generally, they serve *ex officio*—officials appointed by the chief executive or controlling legislative body, representatives of nongovernmental interests, or representatives elected by plan members. At least 80 percent of retirement boards have elected or appointed officials serving on them; 70 percent have employee representatives (usually elected by members of the system); and 40 percent have members from the public at large.[17]

Professional knowledge of pensions, personnel policies, or finance is not a prerequisite for serving on the board. As a result, most boards—and probably most elected officials who find themselves responsible for retirement system administration—must rely heavily on inside administrators and outside advisors to help set policy and carry on day-to-day operations.

Pension administration

Day-to-day administration of a retirement plan may be lodged in several different places and entail a variety of duties.

Role of the administrator Large systems with broad powers usually have a full-time plan administrator to provide leadership, deal with professional services and the public, and oversee the activities of a staff. In smaller systems, city clerks, finance officers, town managers, and police and fire chiefs may find themselves serving as part-time pension plan administrators and investment officers. In many cases all or a major part of those responsibilities may be carried out by consultants and insurance companies.

Generally speaking, the plan's chief administrative officer should operate under a statement of policy that sets forth his or her responsibilities and authority. These may include overseeing compliance with the laws that control the plan, hiring staff, maintaining records and executing transactions, keeping the retirement board informed, and carrying out policy directives.[18]

A major part of the administrator's job involves dealing with the various technical consultants used to support pension activities. Particularly important to most funds are actuaries, investment advisors, and accountants, whose specialized services either are not affordable on a full-time basis or are of greatest value when rendered on an independent basis.

Accounting and financial reporting The duties of investment advisors and actuaries will be discussed later, but at this juncture it is important to emphasize the need for a strong accounting and reporting system as part of sound pension administration. The accounting and financial reporting practices of public pension systems have been the subject of considerable concern because of a lack of both widely followed standards and timely and useful disclosure. Several organizations in both the private and public sectors are examining how pension accounting and reporting practices can be improved. A stimulus to these efforts is provided by the recurring proposal that federal standards regarding plan disclosures—akin to those enacted for the private sector under the Employee Retirement Income Security Act of 1973 (ERISA)—be enacted for the state and local sectors.[19]

The Public Employee Pension Plan Reporting and Accountability Act of 1984 (PEPPRA) exemplifies efforts to extend federal reporting and fiduciary standards to public systems. If passed, PEPPRA would require public systems to prepare an annual report containing financial and actuarial statements. It would also require systems to prepare "summary plan descriptions" every 10 years and carry out an actuarial valuation of the plan every 3 years. However, the act permits state governors to exempt plans from the reporting and disclosure requirements if the governor certifies that the state law is substantially equivalent to the act, that the state can administer the law, and that the state will collect the required reports.[20]

In addition, PEPPRA would preempt state and local fiduciary requirements and establish federal fiduciary standards for the plans. Investments would be placed under the prudent investor rule, requiring that fiduciaries use the same "care, skill, prudence, and diligence" that a knowledgeable investor would use in the conduct of his or her own affairs.[21] Under PEPPRA, fiduciaries who invest imprudently would be personally liable for whatever losses result and subject to whatever remedial relief a court may consider appropriate.

Benefits design and adequacy

The primary purpose of a pension plan is to provide compensation to employees after they stop working. This is normally done through payment of an annuity in the form of monthly benefit payments. The payments begin when the employee leaves the labor force, usually when the employee goes into normal retirement after having completed a certain number of years of service and having reached a specified age. In state and local plans, the prevailing requirements for retirement are that employees attain an age of between 62 and 65 and that they serve for at least 5 to 10 years. However, as the following sections will show, a substantial variety of factors and formulas are used to calculate the level of benefits, altering both eligibility for retirement and the size of the benefit payments. Only after the characteristics of a particular plan are examined can the adequacy of the pension be determined.

Benefit calculations

In defined benefit plans, which cover approximately 85 percent of all state and local employees, retirement benefits are defined by a formula that takes into consideration an employee's salary and years of service. (In defined contribution plans, there is no benefit formula, aside from basic eligibility rules, since the employer is obligated only to contribute to the plan, and the level of benefits will depend on the life annuity generated by the amount contributed and the investment performance of the fund during the years of contribution and retirement.) Benefit formulas are grouped into two classes: flat benefits and unit benefits. Flat benefits are paid out as either a fixed dollar sum or as a percentage of a salary base. Years of service do not enter into the calculation. Flat benefit plans are of diminishing importance in the state and local sectors and are usually found in small local plans, such as fire and police pension plans.

Unit benefits are tied to length of service, and the employee accumulates units of benefit credit for each year of employment. Two factors of particular importance in the unit benefit calculation are the percentage of service credit used in the formula and the compensation base. The units of service are typically expressed as a percentage of the employee's compensation. Take, for example, an employee who has attained retirement age and has worked for 30 years. If a 2 percent unit credit is used, the monthly benefit payment would be 60 percent of the employee's base monthly compensation as calculated at the time of retirement.

The compensation base involves two subsidiary components: (1) the definition of employee compensation and (2) the time period over which it is measured. Most retirement plans use the employee's base pay as the compensation figure for calculating the pension, but a large number also include overtime pay, sick pay, and longevity pay. Clearly, the more income elements that are added into the base compensation, the larger will be the monthly benefit payments for any given percentage calculation of unit service.

Regarding the time period of compensation, the majority of state and local workers are members of plans that take the average compensation for the last three to five years. However, a large percentage of plans are based on one year or less (either the last year of employment or the year of highest salary), and many local fire and police systems base retirement benefits on pay received during the *last day* of employment.[22] When a very short time interval (such as the last day of employment) is used for the formula and the compensation base is expanded to include overtime and other pay, there is the possibility of abuse. Retiring workers may be given last minute promotions or opportunities to work excessive overtime to enlarge their compensation base and thus increase monthly retirement benefits.

Most employee retirement plans include benefits other than those associated with normal retirement, including disability benefits, death benefits, and survivor benefits. By far the most controversial—and in many ways, the most difficult—benefits to administer are those related to disability. Again, local systems, especially those for fire and police, have been subject to abuses in this area. The Public Pension Task Force reported that 23 percent of police and fire retirees nationally are disability retirees, but the ratio varies among plans from less than 10 to over 80 percent. The report continues:

> A large share of such variations which cannot be attributed to different definitions, environment, etc. result in varying degrees in what might be described as administrative largess. Administrative laxity in the disability area has forced at least one plan in the past into court appointed receivership. Small plans can be particularly vulnerable to abuse in this area.[23]

Cost of living adjustments

The need to keep pension benefits in line with the cost of living has understandably received increasing attention. In an inflationary environment, retirees' benefits can be quickly eroded as the rise in consumer prices lowers the real purchasing power of the monthly retirement check. Most state and local employees are covered by plans that make some sort of adjustment in an effort to keep pace with inflation, although few attempt to fully match rising prices.

Cost of living adjustments can take several forms. For some plans *ad hoc* adjustments are legislated from time to time, as the legislative body controlling benefits sees fit. Other plans have formal requirements that benefits be increased at a constant percentage over time or have benefits geared in some way to increases in the consumer price index. In most cases, however, the percentage increase in any given year is limited. A fairly large number of plans also gear benefits to the level of investment earnings (those in excess of the actuarial assumed rate of earnings, for example).[24]

The importance of cost of living adjustments to the preservation of purchasing power and benefits is illustrated in Table 13–5. At a 6 percent rate of inflation, roughly the average rate for the 1970s, a fixed dollar pension benefit would have only 75 percent of its original purchasing power at the end of 5 years and only 31 percent in 20 years—in the absence of adjustment for increasing prices. Of course, cost of living adjustments represent only one way to protect purchasing power. When benefits are tied to salary level at the time of retirement, the initial benefit will be consistent with the cost of living. And when part of the pension funds are in a variable annuity, where benefits rely in part on investment earnings, benefits will keep pace with inflation, if investment earnings do so. Unfortunately, however, this is not always the case.

Table 13–5 Purchasing power of a fixed dollar amount of benefit after periods of time under various rates of price inflation as a percentage of original (first year) purchasing power.

Time period (years)	Annual rate of inflation (%)			
	0	4	6	8
5	100	82	75	68
10	100	68	56	46
20	100	46	31	21
30	100	31	17	10

Source: Howard E. Winklevoss and Dan M. McGill, *Public Pension Plans* (Homewood, Ill.: Dow Jones-Irwin, 1979), p. 140.

Cost of living adjustments can be prohibitively expensive, and many such provisions carry a cap. For example, the annual cost of a typical plan, when compared with a plan in which benefits are not tied to cost of living, and when approved as a percentage of payroll, may be 140 percent greater if the rate of inflation is 4 percent and 170 percent greater if it is assumed to be 6 percent.[25]

Early retirement

Most retirement plans permit employees to retire with reduced benefits before the normal retirement age. Early retirement eligibility is expressed in terms of age and service (i.e., age 55 with at least 20 years of service). The cost of early retirement can be considerable, not only because benefits need to be paid out over a longer period of time, but also because the income from the assets that would otherwise have been set aside is reduced and has less time to accumulate.

Not infrequently, benefits under early retirement are reduced by some rule of thumb that permits the retiree to receive a percentage of the benefit that would have been paid at normal retirement (a typical discount is to reduce benefits by one-half of one percent for each month before the normal retirement age). However, such rough guides usually result in understating the true cost of providing early retirement to the employer. Thus, early benefits should be actuarially computed so that their total cost over the expected benefit period will be equal to the cost of providing the unreduced benefit at the normal age.

Early retirement may not be simply a nice "fringe." It may also help encourage employees to leave service when their skills are no longer needed or they are not capable of doing the required work. But, unless the reduction in benefits is actuarially computed, the plan may end up heavily subsidizing early retirements.

Income replacement levels

The ultimate objective of retirement benefits should be to give the retiree a level of income sufficient to maintain a reasonable postretirement standard of living. Unfortunately, state and local retirement plans seldom design the benefit package scientifically to accomplish this objective. On the contrary, the package of retirement benefits has tended to grow in a crazy-quilt fashion, with various employee groups alternately trying to get ahead of or catch up with one another.

Given that pension adequacy can be described as a relationship between an employee's income at the time of retirement and the benefits received thereafter, determining this relationship calls for complex calculations involving the retiree's changing circumstances and need for discretionary income. For example, a retired person no longer pays Social Security taxes (and usually receives Social Security benefits), has a different tax status, has completed his or her savings program, and no longer has work-related expenses. Of course, he or she may have offsetting costs in medical and other expenses associated with old age. By and large, however, the expenses of maintaining a given standard of living are less upon retirement. Therefore, the amount of replacement income needed to gain equivalency can be considerably less than the gross income the worker was receiving prior to retirement.[26]

The benefit income needed to provide an equivalent standard of living is computed by taking the preretirement gross income and subtracting federal, state, and local taxes; Social Security taxes; employee contributions to the pension plan (were they made); and certain work-related expenses and personal savings. It is important to note that some employees will receive Social Security benefits in addition to their retirement income from the pension plan.

The results of one study of benefit levels needed to meet a standard of living equivalency are considered in Table 13–6. As the table shows, the factors that consumed income prior to retirement but not after represent an increasing percentage of income as income rises. Replacement income (under the assumed conditions) is calculated to range from 45 to 73 percent for workers covered by Social Security and from 50 to 80 percent for workers not covered by Social Security. Replacement incomes are somewhat lower for covered workers because their contributions to the Social Security system have further reduced their take-home pay.

In the case of employees covered by Social Security, these calculations of gross income replacement needs give only part of the picture; the anticipated Social Security payments also need to be taken into account when determining the net income needs to meet a replacement target. Such calculations are complicated in individual cases, depending on the beneficiary's marital status, earnings history, and various tax exposures. Nonetheless, under appropriate assumptions, general patterns of income replacement represented by Social Security payments and the remaining amounts needed from other sources of income (on an after-tax basis) can be calculated. As Table 13–7 shows, Social Security as a percentage of gross income at retirement drops from 51 to 16 percent over the income range. Because the replacement levels needed to achieve standard of living equivalency also drop as income grows, the remaining amount of net income needed, when expressed as a percentage of gross income, does not vary too greatly; it ranges from 22 to 29 percent, being somewhat higher for the lower and higher income brackets. The results presented in Table

Table 13–6 Standard of living equivalency: retirement incomes needed at various levels of gross earnings at retirement.

Gross earnings at retirement ($) (A)	Retirement income needed for equivalence ($) (B)	Ratio of (B) to (A) (%)
Employees not covered by Social Security		
7,500	5,982	79.8
10,000	7,688	76.9
15,000	9,941	66.3
20,000	11,378	56.9
30,000	13,735	53.1
40,000	19,885	49.7
Employees covered by Social Security		
7,500	5,483	73.1
10,000	7,023	70.2
15,000	8,944	59.6
20,000	10,048	50.2
30,000	13,945	46.5
40,000	17,910	44.8

Source: Howard E. Winklevoss and Dan M. McGill, *Public Pension Plans* (Homewood, Ill.: Dow Jones-Irwin, 1979), pp. 30, 32. For a discussion of how standard of living equivalency is determined and for other assumptions, see Winklevoss and McGill, *Public Pension Plans,* Chapter 2.

13–7 illustrate the importance of taking Social Security benefits into account when designing benefit programs.

Using somewhat different definitions of replacement income, the Pension Fund Task Force study found that as of the mid-1970s, state and local pension plans were providing career employees (i.e., those having 30 years or more of service and retiring at age 65) with net income replacement ratios of 100 percent on average. Replacement rates were definitely higher, on average, for lower income employees. Those employees who also received Social Security did better, with approximately 75 percent enjoying net income replacement ratios in excess of 100 percent.[27]

Table 13–7 Net retirement income needed at various levels of gross earnings for employees covered by Social Security after adjustment for Social Security benefits.

Gross earnings at retirement ($) (A)	Equivalence level, as % of (A)	Social Security benefits, as % of (A)	Net income needed, as % of (A)
7,500	73.1	50.9	22.2
10,000	70.2	46.2	24.0
15,000	59.6	39.5	20.1
20,000	50.2	31.3	18.9
30,000	46.5	21.4	25.1
40,000	44.8	16.1	28.7

Source: Howard E. Winklevoss and Dan M. McGill, *Public Pension Plans* (Homewood, Ill.: Dow Jones-Irwin, 1979), pp. 30, 32; and estimates by author. Social security benefit payments are calculated at Primary Insurance Amount for a single individual retiring at age 65 who has always been covered by the system and whose earnings grew at a uniform 5 percent from date of employment through date of retirement. Net income needed is calculated on an after-tax basis. Calculations are based on early 1980 estimates. See Winklevoss and McGill, *Public Pension Plans,* Chapter 2, for a discussion of methodology.

A note on Social Security

As the preceding discussion has demonstrated, Social Security benefits have a significant effect on overall postretirement income and the need for a pension to provide benefits to reach a given level of replacement. Furthermore, with employer and employee contribution rates steadily rising, participation in Social Security also represents significant costs for both parties.

Historically, a major deterrent to the growth of public retirement systems was exclusion from Social Security coverage. In the 1950s, a series of amendments made it possible for public employees to join Social Security, and a steadily growing number of plans have elected to do so. In 1982, 75 percent of active plan members belonged to retirement systems where some or all of the active members were covered by Social Security.[28]

Unfortunately, the Social Security benefits received by these participants generally have not been taken into consideration in the design of retirement plans; only about 16 percent of all public employee plans use some formal method of integrating pension and Social Security benefits to arrive at a total retirement income package.[29] Moreover, many of the existing integration methods are out of date and have failed to keep up with the enrichment of Social Security benefits. Generally, lack of integration of benefits has led to relatively high rates of replacement for covered retirees, especially in the lower income brackets.[30]

State and local employees can voluntarily join Social Security. Under Public Law 98-21, however, once state or local employees elect to join, they cannot terminate their participation. Before passage of 98-21 in early 1983, several systems—mainly small ones—withdrew from Social Security in the belief that their contributions could earn more benefits if retained for investment and that many employees (and spouses) would get Social Security benefits anyway.

Congress continues to be concerned about the financial consequences and the equity of having a large segment of the work force outside of the Social Security and Medicare systems. Although state and local employee coverage is not now mandatory, it appears that newly-hired state and local employees will soon be required to be covered by mandatory Medicare coverage. This would mean a required 1.45 percent contribution from payroll by both employers and employees. Requirements to join Social Security may soon follow. These moves would enable Social Security to retain those pension systems that elect coverage and would stabilize work force coverage.

Pension costs and financing techniques

Pension cost determination and financing are difficult and controversial issues to be addressed by the policymakers and managers of retirement systems. State and local governments have been slow to recognize the full, multiyear cost consequences of granting benefit promises, frequently leaving the burden of paying the costs to future generations of taxpayers. To the extent that the taxpayers of the future are unable or unwilling to meet these obligations, the security of the pension promise is in jeopardy.

In passing, it should be noted that the selection of funding techniques is primarily a problem for defined benefit plans, where there is a fixed commitment to pay a certain level of benefits—whether the fund has sufficient assets or not. In the case of a defined contribution plan, the government (once having made its contribution) is free of future liability. Future benefit payments depend on how large a contribution has been made and how well the investments have performed. It is important to remember that the present value of the benefits does not depend on the techniques chosen to finance the plan. The cost of the plan to the community as a whole is the same no matter what financing scheme is adopted.

The great divide in financing defined benefit pensions and determining their costs is between those systems that recognize the cost at the time the liabilities for future benefits are created (when the worker earns an increment of the future benefit payment) and those that recognize the pension benefit only at the time a cash payment is made (when the worker collects the benefit). The former approach, which recognizes accrued liabilities, is called *advance* or *reserve funding*. The latter is called *pay-as-you-go funding*. Because the pay-as-you-go approach does not recognize costs and liabilities when they are being created, governments that use this method do not account for the full costs of the plan at the time they are incurred and liabilities that accumulate are not offset by assets set aside to help pay for future benefits through their principal and earnings.[31]

There are variations on the themes of advanced and pay-as-you-go funding, and the particular financing method employed by a system may be a combination. For example, a technique popular at one time (but little used now) is terminal funding. At the time of retirement a lump sum is set aside for the employee. Together with the investment earnings, this sum provides benefit payments throughout retirement. In this case (unlike with pay-as-you-go) some assets are set aside, but not nearly as early as in advanced funding.

Over the years there has been debate as to the advantages of the two funding methods, but the preponderance of opinion and practice is that employers should set aside funds to match benefits as they accrue.[32] Contributions are to be based on actuarial methods that project the benefit payments that will be required in the future. Survey results suggest that only about 17 percent of all plans (and covered employees) rely on pay-as-you-go financing techniques. However, of the remaining 83 percent, a large proportion—25 percent of the total—employ advanced funding methods that are not actuarially based. Even among those plans that are so based, the underlying contribution schemes are often inadequate to fully recognize costs and to accumulate sufficient assets.[33]

Actuarial funding techniques

Although the objectives of an actuarially funded plan are relatively clear, the application can be complex and require the skills of an actuary. To calculate the present value of an uncertain future outflow of benefit payments, the actuary needs to assume future behavior with regard to salary rates, retirements, deaths, and the rate of earnings from investments. On the basis of probabilities, a stream of future benefit payments is projected and converted into present values. Then a scheme is devised to determine the amount and timing of funds that must be set aside in order to ensure the system's ability to meet future payments.

Although a detailed discussion of actuarial terminology and methodology is beyond the scope of this chapter, some fundamental explanations and illustrations useful in clarifying the concepts are discussed below. Typically, the actuary is concerned with determining two types of costs that need to be funded, normal and supplemental. The "normal" cost is the present value of those obligations incurred as a result of employee services in the current period. In addition, there may be costs resulting from unfunded "past service" or "supplemental" liabilities that also need to be met. This second type of liability can be incurred when a new plan is begun or an existing plan is modified (for which contributions were not received at an earlier date.) Also, changes in actuarial assumptions can change liabilities. These costs must also be amortized over a period of time (typically, 30 or 40 years) if the plan is to be fully funded. Neither normal nor supplemental costs are absolute concepts. Each depends on the particular assumptions and the cost or benefit allocation method being used by the actuary.[34]

Pension costs can be allocated in a variety of ways, but the two major methods are the accrued benefit and the projected benefit methods. In the first case, the normal cost is the value of benefits accruing in the current year, and the actuarial liability is equal to all benefits accrued to date. This method tends to establish low initial costs for young entrants and immature pension funds, because interest has a longer time to accumulate and be reinvested. At the same time, it establishes relatively high costs for older workers and mature plans.[35]

In the projected benefit method, the normal cost is projected to remain constant over an employee's career (usually as a constant percentage of wage), if the given assumptions hold. To project benefits, future salary levels must be assumed. The entry age normal method is where one determines the constant amount (or percentage of payroll) that must be set aside to accumulate the desired amount by retirement.

Pension liability and condition

Because there is no single way to determine the costs or required contribution rates of public pension plans, there is much confusion over liability, unfunded liability, and the general financial condition of the plans. First, both liability and unfunded liability are basically matters of definition and they depend on the actuarial methods used to determine costs (or allocate benefits).[36] Thus, the liability or unfunded liability of a particular fund, given the assets on hand, can vary greatly and can be noncomparable among funds. Whatever definition is being used, it will usually be some ratio of assets to liabilities—the degree of funding—and the trend in that ratio will be more important than the actual dollar amount. In other words, some notion of relative magnitude is needed. Second, as discussed below, whatever the particular methods being employed, the credibility and timeliness of the actuarial assumptions are of utmost importance since they, in fact, determine the final value under all methods.

The popular need for a "hard" number has focused debate on the intuitively appealing—but technically troublesome—concept of unfunded liability as a representation of a "debt" that is not covered by assets. This focus is not entirely misplaced, however. A host of studies attempting to make comparisons as rigorous as possible, given the paucity and noncomparability of data, have shown there to be large unfunded liabilities in state and local pension plans that could imperil the security of promises to plan members or the fiscal condition of the underlying sponsors.

The *Pension Task Force Report* estimated that the unfunded liabilities of state and local retirement systems were between $150 and $175 million in 1975.[37] A more recent study, published in 1983 using 1978 data, roughly confirmed the *Task Force Report* and estimated the projected unfunded liabilities of state and local systems at between $103 and $170 billion.[38]

A detailed study of 70 such plans undertaken by the U.S. General Accounting Office reported that 40 of the plans (57 percent) were not contributing enough to contain the growth in unfunded liabilities, much less amortize them in an orderly fashion.[39] The study found that placing the 70 funds in a funding standard similar to that required of private plans by federal regulation would require an increase of $1.4 billion in annual employer contributions.

Still another examination showed serious underfunding of state and local retirement systems in Pennsylvania. After examining the 1978 funding status of 1,993 public retirement systems, the report concluded that the unfunded liabilities of state and municipal systems ranged from $10,000 to $22,800 per member, and that one large system alone showed projected unfunded liabilities of $2.8 billion.[40] Other studies, however, show that the situation is not, in most cases, desperate, and that progress in funding pensions is being made.[41]

Understandably, the varieties of actuarial methods and associated concepts of liability not only have caused anxiety and confusion among experts and lay people alike but have made analysis of plan condition (and its implications for members and contributors) difficult. Experts, for example, are not agreed on what constitutes a satisfactory level of funding (ratio of assets to liability), but there does appear to be agreement that the ratio should be increasing over time and that assets should be sufficient to cover obligations owed to those already retired. In the absence of uniform definitions and consistent applications, the analyst will need to depend on a *series* of indicators of condition, rather than on a single absolute measure of condition.

Actuarial assumptions

Whatever methods are used to determine and pay for pension costs and liabilities, the underlying actuarial assumptions and their plausibility are extremely important in judging the condition of a pension system. Because of the long time periods involved in actuarial analysis, slight changes in assumptions can cause great variation in projections of liability and required contribution rates (although the effect of a change in any one assumption is not always immediately evident).

Generally, the most important assumptions affecting pension fund condition deal with economic trends, interest rates or earnings (used to discount future benefits to present values), future salary levels (since most plans use a final average salary as the basis for benefits), and rates of inflation (for plans with cost of living escalators built into benefits). Assumptions concerning the characteristics of the population of a particular plan can also be important. For example, high rates of early retirement and disability retirement can have severe consequences if the assumptions used do not reflect actual plan experience. Other assumptions, regarding employee turnover and mortality, for example, appear to be less critical in the determination of pension costs.[42]

In present practice, assumptions are often allowed to go out of date because of infrequent reevaluations. Assumptions also have been allowed to offset one another; for example, a low interest rate may be assumed to adjust for the low assumption (or none at all) regarding future salary increases. Yet it is important that each significant assumption used in actuarial calculations be a realistic and explicit estimate of the plan's future experience. Only an assumption conforming to the "real world" will shed light on the condition of a pension plan.[43]

Investment of pension fund assets

Their meteoric rise in assets has made public pension funds increasingly active and sophisticated investors. The trend in the public sector, as in the private sector, has been toward expanding the types of investment that may be made; investors are diversifying their portfolios into new investment areas spurred by a desire to generate greater earnings on investments as more plans have been created, benefits enriched, and defined benefit packages adopted. Use of new investment media has often required the relaxation of legal impediments that traditionally have limited pension investments to high-grade corporate bonds or to federal or state and local government securities.

Types of investments

A basic cleavage in pension investment policies has typically been the choice between (1) debt instruments, which are fixed-income obligations that return a steady stream of interest payments, barring default, and (2) equity securities, which may or may not pay dividends and whose primary attraction is appreciation in capital value. Within these broad classifications, securities may vary by the nature of the issuer, the maturity of the obligation, or the specifics of the security (such as priority of payments and ability to convert from one form of obligation or ownership to another).

Table 13–8 displays the growth and composition of investment assets by state and local retirement systems. It shows the relative concentration on debt instruments, particularly corporate bonds and U.S. government securities, which together made up 65 percent of the assets at the end of 1984. Another important asset is corporate equity, which has grown since 1960. Corporate stocks and bonds combined represented 58 percent of the total assets in 1984.[44]

Table 13–8 Assets of state and local retirement systems, by type of investment, 1950–1984 ($ billions).

Type of investment	1950	1960	1970	1977	1984
Total[a]	4.9	19.7	60.3	132.5	356.7
Deposits and currency	0.1	0.2	0.6	1.7	12.9
Corporate equities	—[b]	0.6	10.1	30.1	86.6
U.S. governments	2.5	5.9	6.6	16.3	109.5
Short-term	0.1[c]	0.3	0.8		
Long-term	2.4	5.4	4.3	6.8	66.8
Agencies	0.0	0.2	1.5	9.6	42.7
State and local obligations	1.5	4.4	2.0	3.5	1.4
Corporate bonds	0.6	7.1	35.0	72.9	120.8
Mortgages	0.1	1.5	5.9	8.0	15.4

Source: Board of Governors of the Federal Reserve System, *Flow of Funds Accounts 1946–1975* (Washington, D.C., December 1976); *Flow of Funds Accounts 1960–1983* (Washington, D.C., September 1984); and *Flow of Funds Accounts 2nd Quarter 1985* (Washington, D.C., September 1985).

[a] Items may not sum to totals due to rounding.
[b] Less than $50 million.
[c] Estimated on basis of distribution of U.S. government obligations in 1951.

Traditionally, state and local pension assets were invested heavily in the obligations of the federal government or those of their own state or sponsoring local government. The rationale for such investments was conservatism—the federal government's debt represented the greatest security in terms of safety and liquidity, even though it offered a low rate of return. In 1950, as Table 13–9 shows, state and local pension systems held more than one-half of their assets in U.S. securities, most of which were concentrated in long-term obligations. Between 1950 and 1970, however, there was a steady decline in the holding of U.S. government bonds as investments in corporate bonds rose.

Since 1970, however, U.S. government obligations have again become an important investment for public retirement systems, in the form of obligations of

Table 13–9 Percentage composition of state and local retirement system assets, by type of investment, 1950–1984.

Type of investment	1950	1960	1970	1977	1984
Total	100.0	100.0	100.0	100.0	100.0
Deposits and currency	2.0	1.0	1.0	1.3	3.6
Corporate equity	1.5	3.0	16.7	22.7	24.3
U.S. governments	51.0	29.9	10.9	12.3	30.7
Short-term	2.0	1.5	1.3		
Long-term	49.0	27.4	7.1	5.1	18.7
Agencies	0.0	1.0	2.5	7.2	11.9
State and local obligations	30.6	22.3	3.3	2.6	0.4
Corporate bonds	12.2	36.0	58.0	55.0	33.9
Mortgages	2.0	7.6	9.8	6.0	4.5

Source: Board of Governors of the Federal Reserve System, *Flow of Funds Accounts 1946–1975* (Washington, D.C., December 1976); *Flow of Funds Accounts 1960–1983* (Washington, D.C., September 1984); and *Flow of Funds Accounts 2nd Quarter 1985* (Washington, D.C., September 1985).

U.S. agencies. These securities serve two functions: they provide long-term investments of highest quality at good yields, and they provide a source of liquidity, either as short-term notes or as long-term securities with broad markets. Moreover, several of the federal agency securities represent investments that support such socially useful activities as housing, small business, and rural development.

State and local government obligations State and local government obligations constitute a controversial form of investment for state and local pensions. Early on, state and local pensions were heavily invested in such securities. First, these securities were typically one of the few allowable forms of investment for public pension funds, and second, public funds were no doubt used to support local markets for such securities, especially when credit markets were unreceptive.

State and local obligations are not basically an attractive investment for pension funds. Since the pension funds themselves do not pay taxes on their earnings, they receive no benefit from the tax-exempt nature of the interest income paid on state and local securities. When freed from investment constraints, state and local pension plans were more than happy to allow their investments in state and local securities to dwindle through the 1960s and 1970s. As a matter of fact, a heavy investment in a locality's own general obligation bonds might be considered a form of "unfunding," for any shortfall in the ability of the fund to pay benefits is a general obligation of the sponsoring municipality and paying back its own bonds only adds to this obligation.

The New York City financial crisis brought heavy investment of the substantial assets of the New York City Employee Pension Funds in the resulting rescue efforts. However, by 1984 state and local government securities represented less than one-half of 1 percent of public pension investments.

Corporate bonds In the 1950s state and local pensions shifted from government securities to corporate bonds, which rose from 12 percent to nearly 60 percent of total assets between 1950 and 1970. During this period, corporate securities replaced U.S. government and state and local obligations as the major fixed-income asset of pension funds.

Corporate bonds are especially appealing to state and local pensions. By and large, the chosen securities are part of larger listed issues that yield relatively high rates of return (in comparison with government securities). After World War II many of the fears about credit quality in private debt dissolved, and plenty of high grade industrial and utility issues were available. For these securities, there are listed secondary markets in such obligations, thereby easing trading and pricing and making the market value of the securities easy to follow. The extensive use of ratings and the fact that the market is regulated by the Securities and Exchange Commission (SEC) give a certain confidence and reliability to those securities.

Corporate equities State and local pension activity in the fixed-income securities of corporations had only gotten underway when yet another investment frontier presented itself—the common stock. Starting in the 1960s, state and local pensions became major purchasers of corporate equities. Pension fund managers and trustees knew that the entry into common stocks presented new problems and greater uncertainty. Yet the pressures of the times—the need to cope with inflation and to maximize the earnings on assets—dictated that prudent investment in long-term growth potential was needed to offset the lackluster performance of fixed income assets. Contemporary studies in the 1960s indicated that over the long run (1926–60), investments in equities had outperformed all others in terms of total return, and that the returns appeared to be increasing.[45]

The move to common stocks could not be accomplished without a further revamping and liberalization of the many restrictions governing allowable investments for state and local governments. In the early 1960s, most public pensions that did permit equity investments allowed them only up to 10 percent of total assets. Subsequently, investment restrictions on equities were relaxed substantially and, in some cases, totally scrapped.[46]

State and local pension plan entry into the stock market has not been accompanied by speculative excesses. Typically, the systems are partial to widely held blue-chip securities with proven dividend records. The performance of the stock market has been volatile, however. After doubling in value during the 1960s, the market averages slumped badly by the mid-1970s, with erratic stops and starts replacing their once robust growth. The 1980s, however, have shown a renewal of relatively sustained growth. For the year 1985, for example, the Standard & Poor's 500 Index registered a 30 percent rate of total return. Although the funds have been cautious in their commitment, public pension investment in equities continues to grow, representing approximately 24 percent of all assets in 1984.

Real estate Investment in real estate is important for some pension funds, but it has never been a major factor in the aggregate. Real estate investment usually has been in mortgages, although some equity interests have been acquired. As Table 13–9 shows, holdings of mortgages grew slowly to 10 percent of total investments between 1950 and 1970, only to fall back to 4.5 percent in 1984.

Mortgages have not been a favored investment because of their illiquidity and the difficulties of servicing them. In addition, pension managers have been reluctant to be in the position of selecting among mortgage purchases (for fear of showing favoritism) or of having to foreclose on someone's home in the case of default (for obvious public relations reasons). Still, several states and some local systems have made a positive effort to acquire mortgages, usually showing a definite preference for in-state and in-town properties.

More recently, public pension investment in the mortgage market has been given a considerable boost by the creation of several new capital market instruments, either backed directly with government guarantees or representing highly protected pools of conventional mortgages.[47] Special pools have been formed using the mortgages of one state to appeal to those who wish to invest in-state. Interest has not been confined to residential real estate, however. Comparisons among commercial mortgage yields and among equity interests in real estate and yields available on common stocks have shown the real estate market to be a consistent winner in the 1970s and 1980s. Some of the larger systems, in search of new avenues for investment, have begun to explore more sophisticated investments in real estate, often taking positions in syndicates and "selling off" depreciation rights to private investors who can use the shelter.

Investment management

Faced with a broad range of potential investment media and changing markets—not to mention greater exposure to official and public scrutiny—the typical pension system manager has turned increasingly to professional help.[48] Many forms of investment advice are available to the pension administrator or board. For example, a large system may elect to develop its own internal staff capability, not only to manage day-to-day operations and investments but also to serve as advisors to the board of trustees. A second option is for the board to delegate its investment responsibilities to an investment committee, a state investment board, or another governmental entity that has investment capability.

The third and most popular option is for the fund to contract with outside investment professionals to manage and advise on its investment decisions. These professionals may be given broad responsibility and decision-making power, not only over the general composition of the portfolio but in the day-to-day selection and sale of specific securities. Or they may serve as consultants or advisors helping to set policy but having no responsibility for particular investment decisions. Another important advisory role is to monitor the investment performance of the fund. The relationship between private investment advisors and the board of trustees is often controlled by statutes governing the degree to which and to whom the fund may delegate investment responsibilities.

There are typically three types of investment managers and counselors: bank trustees, insurance companies, and independent firms of investment counselors, many of which specialize in retirement system investments. The services rendered can vary greatly within any one of the types. For example, a bank trustee may administer an individual fund established solely for the client, or it may combine the client's investments with those of other investors in a commingled fund. Likewise, insurance companies offer a variety of annuity packages.

Investment restrictions State and local retirement systems, operate in an atmosphere where most of their activities—including pension investments—are subject to direct or indirect state and local legal ordinances and constraints. Legal restrictions on investments fall into two major categories: (1) specific statutory and constitutional restrictions that detail the kinds and composition of investment that pensions can make, and (2) general legal doctrines dealing with the prudence of pension fiduciaries or their agents (i.e., investment counselors). Over the past two decades there has been a move away from "laundry lists" of specific types of investments that pensions can make toward a more expansive notion of discretion found in a broad "prudent man" rule.

Placing the fiduciary responsibilities of managing public pension fund investments under a prudent man rule has helped diminish the detailed constraints often found in state law. But the flexibility actually afforded investment managers depends heavily on how the rule is interpreted in a particular state. The basic rule under state and common law was that a trustee was under a duty in administering a trust to exercise such skill as a man or woman of ordinary prudence would exercise when dealing with his or her own property—with a view toward preservation of the estate and of the amount and regularity of the income to be derived.

Different branches of the prudent man rule have developed in state courts. Some states have adopted "legal lists," which allow only a percentage of the assets to be invested according to the prudent man standard. Such legal lists may apply to fiduciaries in general, including pension fund trustees, and can be just as restrictive—and perhaps even more difficult to interpret—as a legal list drawn specifically with public employee pension systems in mind.[49] The *Pension Task Force Report* criticized the consequences of tight restrictions on investment expenses and portfolio composition (whether created by statute or by policy) noting that "first rate investment management and advice may be foreclosed to the pension plans having such restrictions."[50]

Risk and return measures For the most part, pension funds can be thought of as long-term investors with well-defined inflows and predictable outflows. Their stability and long-term horizons give them a low preference for liquidity and an ability to withstand substantial short-term risk. Given a wise portfolio policy and sufficient diversification, pension funds should be able to weather the storms of short-term market fluctuations and achieve high long-term returns.

But the extrapolations used in planning pension fund investment strategies over such long periods of time necessarily involve uncertainty as to future levels of prices and interest rates. The standard analysis used in assessing risk and return in the pension area has relied heavily on historical trends in the rates of return on broad aggregates of investments. One set of general benchmarks (based on studies of long-term rates of return since 1925) is that common stocks on average have returned a compounded annual rate of 9 percent; long-term corporate bonds, 3.8 percent; long-term U.S. government bonds, 3.3 percent, and U.S. short-term notes, 2.3 percent.[51] Of course, the historically higher rates of return on stocks have not been without risks. Maintaining any portfolio involves risk—the risks of both security price fluctuations and possible default. But the long-term record shows that the biggest risk is the loss of purchasing power caused by inflation. During the 50-year period 1925–75, the annual rate of inflation averaged 2.3 percent. More recently, during the period 1975 through 1984, stocks yielded an annual rate of return of 14.5 percent and long-term corporate bonds, 9.6 percent; the rate of inflation was 7.5 percent.[52]

Pension trustees and managers have the impulse, if not the responsibility, to keep close track of results so as to judge the adequacy and value of investment counsel, to see how well investments are performing in comparison to similarly situated systems, and to see how well they are meeting the system's investment objectives. Many private services produce performance measures, often comparing a particular fund's performance to that of a widely used market index, such as the Standard & Poor's 500 or the Moody's Bond Record. Such comparisons can be troublesome for the unwary, primarily because market indices do not reflect the day-to-day problems of managing a portfolio under a particular set of constraints and investment objectives.[53]

Overall, public pension systems have performed as well as other institutional investors, given their historic propensity to invest more heavily in debt instruments. A study of pension investment behavior showed that once the composition of assets was taken into account, there was little to distinguish public from private pension investment results.[54] In years when the stock market has done well, private pensions have tended to do better than their public-sector counterparts. When the reverse has been true (and especially when bond prices have been rising or stable), public funds have performed relatively better.

Alternative investments

How to invest the enormous assets of state and local pensions has been complicated by the perception that public monies should be put toward substantive accomplishments other than simply producing earnings. Great interest has been raised in using these funds to promote "alternative" or "socially useful" investment, whether it be to benefit certain activities directly, such as supporting local housing or development projects, or to withhold funds from undesirable activities, such as investment in South Africa. Demands for such targeting have strengthened over the past decade and occasionally public pension investment policies that limit investments in the hopes of promoting prudence are being replaced by a newer generation of mandates that seek to promote objectives unrelated to the protection of assets of the maximization of earnings.

Surveys taken in the late 1970s and early 1980s indicate that despite the talk about alternative investing, there has been relatively little action. Most of what has occurred has been confined to investment in securities of U.S. agencies that assisted the mortgage market.[55] For example, a survey of 130 systems (representing about 89 percent of all public pension assets) found that only 19 of them actually targeted any investments to promote what might be viewed as socially responsive activities. Setting aside the special case of New York City, where pension funds were used to assist a local government in financial difficulty, the systems directed only $2.4 billion in assets (less than 2 percent of the total) to targeted uses. Various forms of locally directed housing investments (typically federally-guaranteed) constituted half the targeted amount, with the remainder going to a scattering of programs in the broad area of local economic development and renewal activities. Most funds with any targeting at all have limited such investments to a minor fraction of their portfolios (2 to 5 percent).[56]

Most funds do not have targeted investments for the simple reason that their managers do not believe they can earn equivalent returns at the same level of risk. Without specific legislative direction most investment officers are unwilling (and usually unable) to make concessions to preferred activities. Furthermore, there is always the selection problem: of the many claimants to such assistance, which are to be selected and on what terms and conditions?

More recently, citizens and interest groups have promoted policies of *not* investing in certain securities in protest of social policies. A major example is pressure for the divestment of South Africa–related securities. As of mid-1985, some 10 states and at least 18 major cities had enacted laws or ordinances that would restrict or divest investments by companies doing business in that country.[57] The potential effect on investment practices is considerable since it has been estimated that approximately 20 percent of public fund investment is in 300 corporations that have some significant economic contact with South Africa.[58] Generally, the laws calling for restrictions have permitted some leeway by allowing investment in firms that subscribe to a set of principles regarding nondiscrimination (the Sullivan Principles) and that do not sell strategic products or services to the South African government. Nonetheless, the divestiture movement has picked up considerable momentum and by the mid-1980s had already led to the sale by public pension funds of approximately $600 million in South Africa–related stocks and bonds.[59]

It is appropriate to conclude with the subject of investments that have consequences for activities abroad. Over the years, public pension managers have, with rare exception, kept their investments on American shores, if not necessarily in-state. But in an increasingly worldwide economy, the attraction is strong to further diversify holdings and to examine the opportunities to invest elsewhere. A few public systems have started to invest in the stocks and bonds of foreign corporations and governments. With $350 billion in assets and a desire to spread their investment dollars to hedge against risks, pension funds may find foreign securities markets less distant in the coming years.

1 U.S. Congress, House, Committee on Education and Labor, *Task Force Report on Public Employee Retirement Systems* (Washington, D.C.: GPO, 1978), pp. 51–97 (hereafter cited as *Pension Task Force Report*).
2 For an explanation of the Census definitions, see U.S. Bureau of the Census, 1982 Census of Governments, *Employee-Retirement Systems of State and Local Governments,* vol. 6, no. 1 (Washington, D.C.: GPO, 1983), pp. x–xi.
3 Ibid., p. 3.
4 U.S. Bureau of the Census, *Employee-Retirement Systems,* p. 12.
5 Ibid., p. 12.
6 According to the *Pension Task Force Report,* p. 55 (using different definitions), there were 1,413 plans in Pennsylvania.
7 U.S. Bureau of the Census, *Employee-Retirement Systems,* p. vii.
8 See Thomas P. Bleakney, *Retirement Systems for Public Employees* (Philadelphia: Univ. of Pennsylvania, 1972), pp. 20–23.
9 *Pension Task Force Report,* pp. 53–54.
10 Ibid., pp. 61–62.
11 For a comprehensive treatment of participants' rights, see Robert Kalman and Michael Lieby, *The Public Pension Crisis: Myth, Reality, Reform* (Washington, D.C.: American Federation of State, County, and Municipal Employees, 1972), Chapter 5.
12 Advisory Commission on Intergovernmental Relations, *Information Bulletin: State and Local Government Pension Reforms* (Washington, D.C.: GPO, March 1979).
13 *Pension Task Force Report,* p. 65.
14 See, for example, Comptroller General of the United States, *The Investment Decisionmaking Process in New Jersey Public Employee Retirement Plans* (Washington, D.C.: GPO, 1977), Appendix I.
15 *Pension Task Force Report,* p. 205.
16 Ibid., pp. 205–206.
17 Ibid., p. 207.
18 For a discussion, see Municipal Finance Officers Association, Committee on Public Employee Retirement Administration, *Public Employee Retirement Administration* (Chicago. 1977).
19 An extensive examination of issues surrounding retirement system accounting and reporting. See John E. Petersen, *State and Local Pension Financial Disclosure* (Washington, D.C.: Government Finance Research Center, Municipal Finance Officers Association, 1979).
20 U.S. Congress, House, Committee on Education and Labor, *Section-By-Section Analysis of the Public Em-*

ployee Pension Plan Reporting and Accountability Act of 1984 (Washington, D.C.: Committee on Education and Labor, 1984), pp. 1–3.

21 Ibid., pp. 5–9.

22 According to the *Pension Task Force Report,* p. 112, nearly 33 percent of police and fire plans used final day's rate or final year's pay to calculate pension benefits.

23 Ibid., p. 67.

24 Ibid., p. 168.

25 Howard E. Winklevoss and Dan M. McGill, *Public Pension Plans: Standards of Design, Funding, and Reporting* (Homewood, Ill.: Dow Jones-Irwin, 1979), p. 144.

26 Ibid., see Chapter 2 for a detailed discussion.

27 *Pension Task Force Report,* pp. 124–125.

28 U.S. Bureau of the Census, *Employee-Retirement Systems: 1982,* p. ix.

29 *Pension Task Force Report,* p. 111. By 1980, however, plans began to take a lively interest in integration to control the growth in benefits and costs. See Urban Institute, *The Future of State and Local Pensions: Final Report* (Washington, D.C., 1980), p. 17–16.

30 See Sidney T. Kaufman, "Pension Funding Problems," in *1978 Public Employee Conference Proceedings* (Brookfield, Wisc.: International Foundation of Employee Benefit Plans, 1979), p. 25.

31 The decision to fund pertains only to the employers' share. In contributory plans, the employee's contributions are always set aside in a reserve and credited to his or her account.

32 For more discussion of the debate on advanced versus pay-as-you-go financing, see Robert Tilove, *Public Employee Pension Funds* (New York: Columbia Univ. Press, 1976), pp. 131–41.

33 *Pension Task Force Report,* pp. 150–51.

34 See Winklevoss and McGill, *Public Pension Plans,* Part II, for an extended discussion of pension funding techniques and associated actuarial concepts.

35 Ibid., Chapter 6.

36 For an amusing discussion of the different measures of financial condition depending on what funding program and liability concepts are used, see Gary W. Findlay, "Unfunded—Whatever in Wonderland," *Governmental Finance,* March-June, 1979: 17–27.

37 *Pension Task Force Report,* pp. 163–66.

38 Laurence J. Kotlikoff and Daniel E. Smith, *Pensions in the American Economy* (Chicago: Univ. of Chicago Press, 1983), pp. 397–98.

39 U.S. General Accounting Office, Comptroller of the United States, *Funding of State and Local Pension Plans: A National Problem* (Washington, D.C.: GPO, 1979).

40 International City Management Association, "Reforming Public Pension Plans to Avoid Unfunded Liability," *Management Information Service Report,* May 1983: 13.

41 For a discussion on how the long-term prospects are not so bleak if corrective measures are taken and if economic conditions are more reasonable than in the late 1970s, see Urban Institute, *The Future of State,* Chapters 17–19. Progress is reported at the big city level in Advisory Commission on Intergovernmental Relations, *Bankruptcies, Defaults, and Other Local Government Financial Emergencies* (Washington, D.C.: GPO, 1985), pp. 45–50.

42 For a nonrigorous discussion of the relative importance of actuarial assumptions, see John S. Perreca, "How to Understand Your Actuary—Almost," *Pension World,* October 1979: 35–42. For more rigor, see Howard Winklevoss, *Pension Mathematics* (Philadelphia: Pension Research Council, 1978), Chapter 17.

43 *Pension Task Force Report,* pp. 158–162.

44 For a more complete analysis of state and local pension investment practices, see John E. Petersen, *State and Local Government Pension Fund Investment* (Washington, D.C.: Government Finance Research Center, Municipal Finance Officers Association, 1979).

45 One influential study of the period showed that the average yield on a "buy-and-hold" portfolio made up of all New York Stock Exchange listed stocks for the period 1926–1960 was 9 percent. For bonds, the total return was more on the order of 3 percent for the period. Lawrence Fisher and James Lorie, "Rates of Return on Investment in Common Stock," *Journal of Business,* January 1964: 1–26.

46 *Pension Task Force Report,* p. 132.

47 Ronald Struck, "Mortgage Backed Securities: A Primer," *Pension World,* February 1978: 17–21.

48 Tilove, *Public Employee Pension Funds,* pp. 214–20.

49 James D. Hutchinson, "The Compleat Fiduciary," *Pension World,* April 1978: 53.

50 *Pension Task Force Report,* p. 196.

51 Although many have studied long-term rates of return, a commonly cited study in the area is Roger Ibbotson and Rex Sinquefield, "Stocks, Bonds, Bills, and Inflations: Year-by-Year Historical Returns (1926–1974)," *The Journal of Business,* January 1976: 11–47. The returns include both current payments (interest and dividends) and changes in prices.

52 Updated rates of return are author's estimates based on financial series.

53 See Robert Levy, "Common Sense in Comparative Performance," *Pension World,* April 1978: 8–11.

54 See John E. Petersen, *State and Local Pension Fund Investment Performance* (Washington, D.C.: Municipal Finance Officers Association, 1980); and Urban Institute, *The Future of State,* Chapter 13.

55 John E. Petersen and Catherine Spain, *Alternative Investing by State and Local Pension Funds* (Washington, D.C.: Municipal Finance Officers Association, 1980).

56 Paul Zorn, *Public Pension Investment Targeting: A Survey of Practices* (Washington, D.C.: Government Finance Research Center, 1983), pp. 42–43.

57 "Divestment Policies Protest Apartheid" *City and State* (Chicago: Crane publications), September 1985: 1.

58 "Six Take Action in South Africa," *Pension & Investment Age* (Chicago: Crane Publications), 14 October 1985: 60.

59 "Divestment Policies Protest Apartheid," p. 1.

14 Inventory and cash management

Inventory and cash management may appear diverse, but they have two major elements in common. Both involve trade-offs between different types of costs and both have the same basic analytical structure. Although seemingly humdrum activities, when compared, for example, with the work involved in preparing and floating bond issues, they are not to be dismissed lightly. Financial managers who handle these matters efficiently can save a city or county significant amounts of money, which can then be used to help finance expenditures or to hold taxes in check.

Although the financial manager need not be versed in all the details, computer programs, and mathematics relevant to the field of management science, effective evaluation of policies and recommendations requires at least a general understanding of the problems and possible solutions entailed in inventory and cash management. As this chapter shows, a simple approach to inventory and cash management will sometimes work quite well, for the latest or most sophisticated computer program may end up costing more to install and run than it will actually produce in savings.

Inventory management

An inventory is usually thought of as a stockpile of commodities—paper supplies, books, food, chemicals, or hardware. Yet, cash in the city treasury, the number of machines owned, and the amount of operating space are also types of inventories. The number of people standing in line at a bureau counter or the number of cars waiting to pay a toll may be thought of as negative inventory. In these cases, it is called a queue and may be considered a detriment rather than a store of value.

Inventories of commodities would not be necessary at all if completely reliable suppliers were nearby, if they were willing and able to provide instantaneous delivery, and if no costs were incurred in placing and receiving orders. Since these conditions seldom exist, however, the user does well to hold an optimal inventory which is designed to (1) minimize the total of ordering and holding costs, and (2) control the frequency of stockouts or shortages *relative to ordering and holding costs*.

There are two basic inventory models: the safety stock model and the economic ordering quantity (EOQ) model.[1] The safety stock model deals with the optimal inventory size to minimize the costs of stockouts relative to carrying costs. The economic ordering quantity model determines the optimal inventory size and the frequency of orders. These two models are not competitive but complementary. In fact, various dynamic or tracking models may be used to combine the factors into one model.[2]

Three major categories of costs are basic to the various inventory models:

1. *Ordering costs* include the cost of receiving the item into stock and the clerical and correspondence costs of actually placing the order.
2. *Holding costs* (also called carrying costs) include the costs associated with deterioration, possible obsolescence, storage space, insurance, and

imputed financing costs (i.e., the implicit opportunity cost of funds tied up in the inventory). Generally, the carrying cost is estimated as a percentage of the cost of inventory—perhaps as high as 20 to 30 percent per year if obsolescence and insurance are counted in.

3. *Stockout and shortage costs* are the costs of interruption in output, or the losses to consumers if there is no immediately available supply. It is easy to underestimate these costs since some of them are imputed or implicit. One imputed cost of a stockout includes the resentment that may develop among consumers from an interruption or delay of service. There is an implicit political or social cost to such resentment. Although an exact accurate count is not possible, a rough dollar amount (including an estimation of citizen inconvenience) for the cost of a stockout can be calculated.

The safety stock model

A major concern in inventory management is determining the optimal size of the safety stock—the minimum inventory that will reduce to a reasonable level the probability of shortages. Safety stocks are carried because patterns of supply and demand can be somewhat erratic and independent of one another. Obviously, the greater the synchronization between supply and demand flows, the lesser is the need for safety stocks. When supplies are not available or a shortage of raw materials causes a slowdown or shutdown in operations or in the construction of a capital project, losses and costs rise. Furthermore, there are usually extra costs associated with startups to restore full service. In general, operating costs are usually minimized if stockouts can be avoided by keeping service and supplies at a constant level.

Establishing the safety stock involves a careful analysis of activity patterns—that is, how erratic and how great are the possible surges in demand, how dependable are the suppliers, and how long does it take to receive a new shipment? Then the costs of stockouts have to be estimated. What is the cost in lost citizen service and in shutdowns and startups? The answers to these questions are combined into a stockout cost probability function, developed via computer modeling. This function relates the size of the inventory carried to the probability of stockouts occurring in a given time period, multiplied by the estimated costs of a stockout. Clearly the larger the inventory carried relative to its normal use level, the smaller the probability of stockout losses. A smaller inventory increases the probability of stockouts. The physical size of the inventory can be converted to dollars by multiplying the number of units by the price. The stockout loss function graphed against the amount of inventory carried looks something like Figure 14–1.

The analysis also includes the establishment of a reorder point to replenish the inventory when it reaches a certain level. The reorder point is set by analyzing expected levels of use and allowing for expected delivery time after the order is sent.

From the point of view of avoiding stockouts, a large inventory is desirable, but holding costs—insurance, storage, spoilage and obsolescence, and funds tied up in inventory—increase directly with inventory size. Since holding costs can be converted into percentages that are directly related to the size of the inventory carried, they can be converted into an inventory holding cost function, illustrated in Figure 14–2.

The optimal safety stock level is the point where the total of the probable stockout losses and holding costs is at a minimum. Figure 14–3 illustrates a graphic solution of the problem. The optimal inventory size in the example is shown to be the minimum of total cost, point *E* (optimum safety stock). It should be emphasized that this is not the same as reducing the probability of

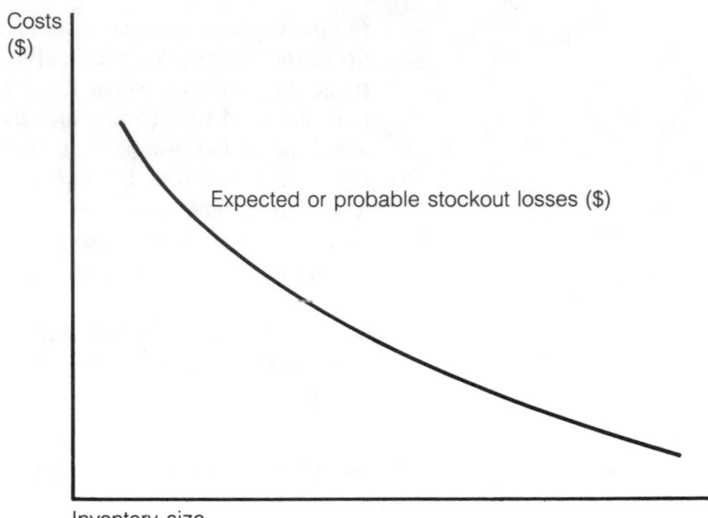

Figure 14–1
Expected stockout losses as a function of inventory size.

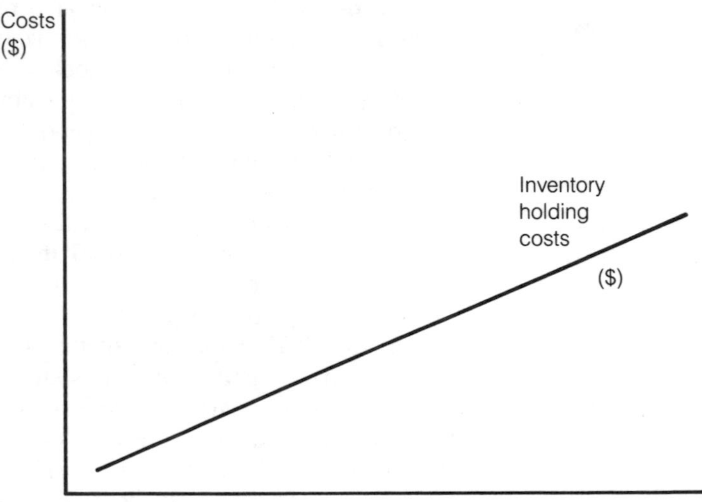

Figure 14–2
Inventory holding costs as a function of inventory size.

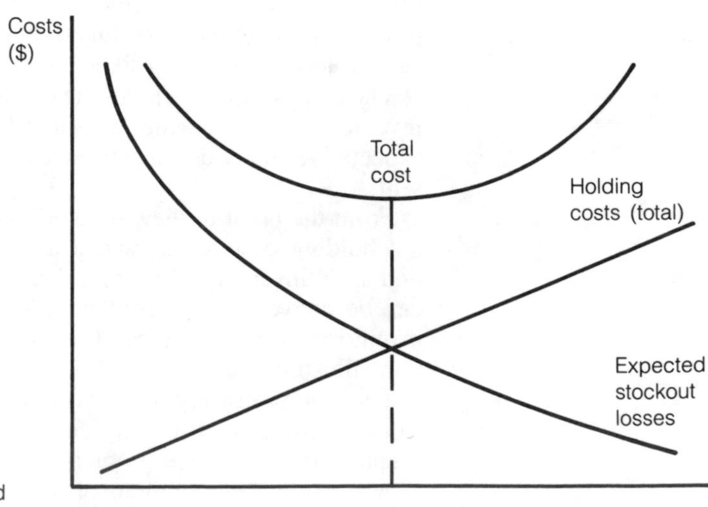

Figure 14–3
Optimal inventory as a function of stockout losses and holding costs.

stockout losses to a minimum. Rather, it is the determination of an acceptable stockout loss level relative to the costs of holding and maintaining inventory.

The solution can also be obtained by marginal analysis. The minimum cost is the point where the first derivative of the holding costs equals the derivative of the stockout loss function, that is, where the marginal costs of the two functions are equal.[3] This would be expressed as:

$$\frac{\partial SO}{\partial X} = \frac{\partial HC}{\partial X}, \quad \text{where} \tag{1}$$

SO = Stockout losses

HC = Holding costs

X = Inventory size.

It might be noted that since the cost of capital is an important part of the holding cost function, a rise in the interest rate would move managers to economize on inventory holdings and run a greater risk of stockout.

This theoretical model underlying inventory policy can be modified, for in practice, smaller cities and counties may find that the costs of operating more complex computer modeling systems may not be worthwhile. Thus, certain rules of thumb have been developed that may approximate the ideal solution. These rules apply to different kinds of activities and are stated as follows: (1) inventories should cover about 15 days' usages; (2) raw material stocks should cover 30 days of normal service; or (3) inventories should be turned over at least four times a year. However, with the availability of small computers, it may pay to move toward the more detailed and sophisticated models.

Since inventories absorb funds (i.e., inventories must be stored and financed), the efficiency with which they are controlled is of considerable interest to the financial manager who wishes to minimize governmental outlays while still providing good service.

The economic ordering quantity model

Once the safety stock level has been established, it is necessary to determine the optimal size and frequency of orders. The economic ordering quantity problem arises because of the ordering costs involved in handling supplies. These costs consist of the clerical and correspondence costs of preparing and placing the order and checking it once it is received. Some part of the ordering costs is the same for any size order, so that if orders are larger, there is a decrease in the amount of ordering costs per *unit* ordered.

If there is an assured supply nearby and/or if usage rates are very stable so that there are no likely stockout losses and thus the required safety stock is zero, the EOQ model solves the whole inventory problem. If not, the EOQ model is generally combined in some manner with the safety stock model.

Solving the EOQ problem involves three variables:

1. Predicted demand or usage for the applicable planning period
2. Holding costs as a percentage of inventory size
3. Ordering or transaction costs.

The idea is to set the size of orders so as to minimize the total of holding and ordering costs for the given period. If, given the rate of usage or demand, smaller orders are placed, the average inventory will be low and holding costs will be held down. On the other hand, a policy of small orders makes it necessary to order more frequently, thereby raising the total ordering costs.

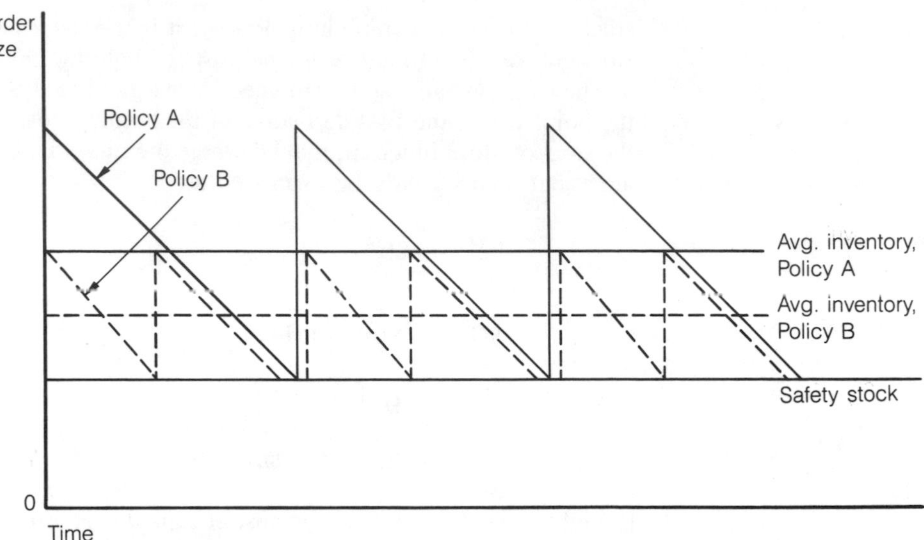

Figure 14–4 Relationship of order size and average inventory size under two inventory policies over time.

In simple situations, the EOQ model is often just superimposed on the safety stock model. Graphically this relation can be depicted as shown in Figure 14–4. The figure shows the relation of order size and average inventory size over time. Under policy A, with larger orders, the average inventory in excess of the safety stock is twice that under policy B; however, in any given time period, there are twice as many orders.

As with determining the safety stock, computers are useful in determining the optimal ordering quantity. The EOQ solution looks something like Figure 14–5. The optimal order size is where the total of ordering costs and holding costs for the period is minimized.

Although the EOQ solution is depicted graphically here in the form of totals, it is clear that the operational solution would be done marginally. The optimal EOQ is the point at which marginal holding costs and marginal ordering costs are equal. For a simple case, the mathematical solution yields the following formula:

$$\text{EOQ} = \sqrt{\frac{2SO}{HU}}, \quad \text{where:} \qquad (2)$$

S = Estimated demand or usage in dollar terms for the period

O = Ordering costs per order

H = Holding costs as a rate for the given period (e.g., 24 percent for a year or 12 percent for six months)

U = Costs per unit.

The formula as given will solve the optimal EOQ in terms of units.[4] If U is dropped out of the equation, EOQ will give the optimal dollar amounts of the order; however, it is useful to have a unit cost when quantity discounts are offered, and when one desires to see the effect on optimal order size as unit costs are varied.

In this analysis, the problem of safety stock and ordering quantity have been treated separately. The average inventory resulting from the economic ordering quantity (one half of the EOQ) has been solved independently and, presumably,

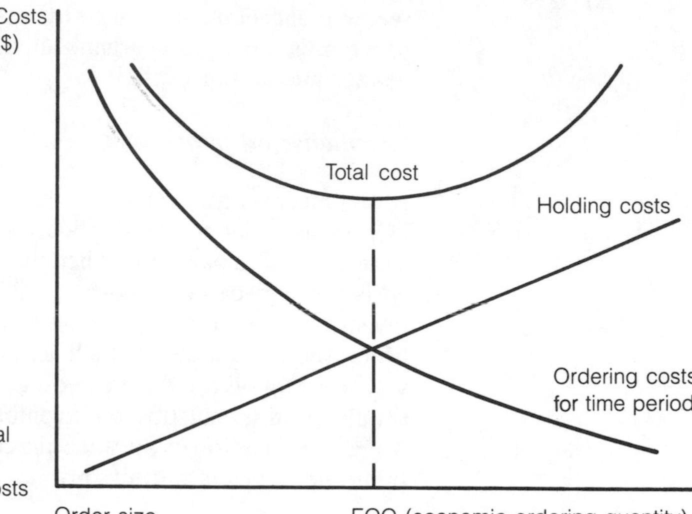

Figure 14–5 Optimal ordering quantity in relation to holding costs and ordering costs.

simply placed on top of the safety stock. In theory at least, the two should be solved simultaneously because a larger EOQ policy results in higher *average* inventories and reduces the probability of being out of stock. Complex computer models can solve the EOQ and safety stock simultaneously, and it is a managerial decision whether the additional precision is worth the extra cost, time, and effort.

In a small city or county where it does not seem efficient to develop a computer program, managers may use simple rules of thumb to determine optimal inventory. It is often worthwhile, however, to prepare a one-time solution by use of more sophisticated methods to ascertain whether the rule of thumb produces a reasonable approximation to the optimal solution.

Whatever inventory system is adopted, it should be audited regularly to see if the program is operating efficiently. If the inventory appears to be excessive, it should be checked to make certain it falls within the established guidelines. Particular attention should be paid to confirm that there is no collusion with suppliers to overbuy particular items.

The financial manager may not have direct responsibility for inventory management; it may rest instead with management science and computer science specialists. As this discussion shows, however, a vital part of inventory holding cost is the cost of the funds absorbed in carrying the inventory. The financial manager should note when *real* interest costs rise and make sure the inventory managers reduce the average inventory accordingly. (Of course, the move may be in the other direction if holding costs drop.)

Implicit stockout approach

Another approach to the safety stock problem avoids the difficulty of making an explicit dollar cost estimate of a stockout. As in the previous models, past operations are studied to determine the probability of a shortage at different levels of inventory. The manager is given an analysis in the form of a choice: either to carry inventory at average holding costs of $100,000 a year, incurring about three stockouts a year, or to raise the inventory size by 10.0 percent, thereby creating carrying costs of approximately $110,000 per year—and so reducing probable stockouts to two per year. If the decision maker takes the second choice, he or she has decided that avoiding all the costs and inconveniences of a probable additional stockout is worth $10,000 a year. Although this seems roundabout, it is nevertheless a perfectly valid approach to solving the program in a nonprofit organization where many of the costs of a stockout are neither precise nor explicit.

Speculative inventories

It is sometimes recommended that inventories should be purchased in advance of need in order to avoid price rises, but this is easier said than done. This strategy yields a gain only when the rise in prices exceeds the inventory carrying costs. Thus if carrying costs are 20.0 percent for the period, the price of the inventory item has to rise by over 20.0 percent to justify carrying excess stock. Moreover interest rates, which are an important part of the holding costs, have a way of rising with the expected rate of inflation. In general, local governments should avoid speculating on inventories, although during periods of uncertainty it may be wise to set advance purchasing contracts with reliable suppliers for future deliveries at definite prices.

Queuing theory

Queuing theory—an offshoot of inventory management theory—deals with negative inventory, the number of people waiting in line to pay an entrance fee or toll or to make a purchase, for example. Typical waiting-line situations occur at ticket booths, cashier windows, golf courses, and ski lifts. Other, less obvious waiting-line situations include prospective patients versus the number of beds in a hospital, processing time versus the number of clerks in an office, and traffic flow versus the width of streets. Negative inventory is considered a detriment rather than a store of value.

Solving waiting-line problems requires the fiscal manager to balance the costs and disutilities of those waiting in line versus the costs of investing in the additional facilities to move the line faster. The municipal executive who states that on the average no citizen will have to wait longer than five minutes for attention has specified a service level policy. Presumably implicit in this policy statement are assumptions about the department's obligations to citizens, notions about courtesy, and knowledge of the costs of maintaining the desired service level. These costs should be carefully analyzed and weighed against the other factors.

Suppose, for example, that the recreation department must decide how many ticket sellers it wishes to have at the municipal swimming pool during the summer. Each seller is to be paid a salary and provided with a changemaking machine, a basic change fund, space, and a counter. The decision makers will have to decide what operating costs and service levels will be acceptable in light of the imputed costs or inconveniences to the patrons waiting in line.

Queuing analysis customarily deals with the probability distributions associated with the rates of arrival of people or items to be processed. The queuing problem is further complicated because the rate of arrivals is usually not constant but instead shows "peaks" and "valleys." Arrivals may be sparse at some times and concentrated at others; there is no way of sorting idle service time. Providing facilities sufficient to cover all the peaks, for example, may require a large investment that will lie idle most of the time. The queue discipline that governs most waiting lines is "first-in, first-out" (FIFO), although sometimes "most vocal" and "VIP" (very important person) prevail. The probable length of the waiting lines and their implicit costs at different levels of service can be compared to the costs of maintaining varying levels of service. The problem is analogous to the safety stock inventory models that weigh the costs of the waiting line (i.e., the stockout costs) against the amount of facilities (i.e., the holding costs). The solution can be obtained by using computer programs.

Summary

A central responsibility of inventory management is determining optimal inventory. This requires a knowledge of the costs of ordering materials, of carrying inventory, and of running short. Both the explicit money costs and the implicit costs of shortages need to be considered. Many factors not easily quantifiable in dollars impinge on inventory decisions. For example, if water main supplies run short, decision makers not only must calculate the costs of having a team of workers standing idle waiting for pipe, meter, and valves to repair the water main, but they also must try to make the more difficult estimate of the cost of the lost good will from the homeowner/citizen/consumer who is impatient and waiting for water. Understanding the logic behind inventory theory can be helpful whether decision makers use computer models or formulate rules of thumb (usually used in smaller jurisdictions).

Cash management

The logic of pairing cash management with inventory in this chapter is that the basic models for managing cash are adaptations of inventory models. In both cases, the manager's challenge lies in maintaining an adequate supply (of inventory or cash) and in reducing transaction costs (of ordering inventory or transferring cash) and opportunity costs (the interest forgone on alternative investments such as marketable securities). This section explores methods for improving the management of cash by investing temporarily idle funds in marketable securities, and thereby obtaining additional revenue. The discussion begins with the basics of cash management, including cash budgeting, and then deals with models useful for determining optimal cash and security positions. The section concludes with guidelines for investing in marketable securities.

Basics of cash management

Three major features of cash management are cash budgeting, cash position, and commercial bank interest and fees. Cash budgeting is the vital initial step in cash management.

Cash budgeting In order to forecast the need for cash balances, the finance officer should prepare a series of periodic cash budgets. Although these budgets can be drawn up for almost any interval, monthly forecasts are the most common.

The cash budget differs from operating and capital budgets in that it is much less detailed. It need only contain aggregates of forecasted cash expenditures and inflows for the period. If proper care has been taken in preparing the operating and capital budgets, if control is exercised over expenditures, and if revenues are stable and relatively predictable, the cash budget is likely to be quite accurate. Because the receipts and expenditures of governments are more predictable than those of business, government cash budgets are generally more accurate than those of business corporations.

Since property tax collections remain a major source of local revenue, the bulk of cash receipts tends to be concentrated in one or two relatively short time periods in the local tax calendar. Other tax receipts may be spread out more evenly over the year. For purposes of cash management, it is important to project when the taxes will actually be collected. In most cases, predictions based upon the analysis of past experience are quite accurate. The cash receipts of municipally operated utilities also must be projected; these receipts may be subject to seasonal fluctuations.

After the timing of projected receipts is forecasted, the finance officer should then forecast cash disbursements. As with cash receipts, general expenses (which include wages and other operating expenses) can be projected with considerable accuracy on the basis of past experience and the adopted budget. The timing of debt servicing (interest and principal repayments) is also quite certain (as it is a contractual obligation).

The forecasts of receipts and disbursements are combined to determine their net effect on the cash position. A sample cash budget for a hypothetical city or county is shown in Figure 14–6. The figures in the bottom row show the forecasted cash position at the end of each month. The cash budget determines the timing and magnitude of projected cash needs and cash surpluses. According to Figure 14–6, the city or county projects an operating cash deficit in January, February, and March; disbursements are expected to exceed receipts during this quarter. The finance officer can plan to meet this deficit either by floating tax anticipation loans or by selling marketable securities purchased during a previous surplus period. In April, the city will receive payment of the semiannual property tax and will thus have surplus funds. The financial officer may either repay the tax anticipation loan or invest any cash in excess of current transaction needs in short-term marketable securities.

Figure 14–6 City/county cash budget for the first six months of 1990 ($000).

Fiscal item	January	February	March	April	May	June
Expected receipts	$ 480	$ 513	$ 718	$3,461	$ 487	$ 496
Expected disbursements	891	902	907	905	1,341	904
Receipts less disbursements	(411)	(389)	(189)	2,556	(854)	(408)
Cash at beginning of month	181	(230)	(619)	(808)	1,748	894
Cumulative cash position at end of month	(230)	(619)	(808)	1,748	894	468

The cash budget is thus used to forecast the cash position of the city or county over a period of time. On the basis of this budget, the finance officer may plan ahead. He or she may invest in marketable securities or repay short-term loans when there are excess funds, and may liquidate securities or borrow on a short-term basis during periods of cash deficit. With proper planning, the efficiency of cash management can be optimized, the net interest earnings on marketable securities maximized, and the interest payments on short-term borrowings minimized. The cash budget is an important tool for achieving these objectives.

Cash position The transaction cash balance—that is, the cash kept on hand by a city or county to cover anticipated short-term needs—should be determined with reference to several factors: the minimum balance required by commercial banks; the cost of bank and market transactions; the consequences of running out of cash; and the difference between current interest rates on transaction balances and those available in the market on short-term securities.

Commercial bank interest and fees Commercial banks provide a wide array of services for which they expect compensation either in the form of an imputed return on the deposits held with them, or in the form of explicit fees. The principal services performed by banks include clearing check deposits, accepting cash deposits, and accounting for checks drawn against the bank account. In most cases, deposit activity in the account is quite straightforward and does not require any special arrangements.

Banks currently pay interest on some portion of the transaction balances on deposit. The interest rate on these deposits is generally set a point or so below the Treasury bill rate. However, the income from the account is offset by the fees charged for servicing the account's activity. Most banks have a schedule of costs on a per item basis for such transactions as processing deposits and paying checks drawn on the account. The account is analyzed each month and the transactions are multiplied by the per-item costs and then totaled. If interest income exceeds the activity costs, the account returns net interest to the depositor. There is a minimum average level of cash balances at which a given account breaks even.

Because banks differ in their interest rates and charges, a city or county would be wise, if possible, to "shop around" and find the bank offering the best net return for the given level of activity. Some local governments periodically place their banking business, like any other purchase, up for competitive bidding. However, various state statutory rules and requirements limit the freedom of the city or county in making depository arrangements. Some require that the city use only banks located in the state or even in the same city, or that deposits be divided proportionately among the local banks. Others may prohibit the local government from carrying its funds in thrift institutions (savings banks and savings and loan associations). Most common are volume restrictions that limit the amounts that can be carried with any single bank. Sometimes the limit is the amount insured by the Federal Deposit Insurance Corporation. More often the limit is determined by a ratio of the deposit to the bank's capital accounts or to the bank's total assets.[5] These various requirements may reduce the flexibility of the city or county in achieving optimal cash management, especially as regards advantages that may be derived from economies of scale in pooling deposits. (Recent experiences of Ohio municipalities suggest that some of the restrictions serve a safety function.)

Bank balances and service charges should be analyzed carefully. If the city's average deposits are in excess of the required offsetting balance, funds may be tied up unnecessarily. However, the problem of determining the economically optimal cash balance must be solved before it can be decided whether excess cash is being carried. It may well be that the local government would do best by maintaining a cash balance in excess of the offsetting amount—if this saves some transaction and supervision costs.

Models for determining cash and security positions

This section discusses models for determining the optimal transaction balance and the excess liquidity balance that may be held in money-market funds or marketable securities. Assume that the local government's holdings of total liquid funds, comprising both cash and marketable securities, has been set. This amount consists of funds appropriated for capital improvements but not yet spent; funds set aside for debt servicing and other special purposes; and funds that have accumulated through the seasonal collections of taxes or through the flotation of tax anticipation loans. Given the total amount of liquid assets, transaction cash, and marketable holdings, the financial manager must decide how much of each to hold.

As with inventory management, the simplest guidelines are "rules of thumb" used by many small local governments. One rule is to hold a certain number of days' expenditures as the transaction balance. For example, the cash balance might be one week's expenditures. If average weekly expenditures are $125,000, this amount would be held in cash at the bank and the residual liquid funds invested in marketable securities. Whenever the cash balance falls below $125,000, securities would be sold to restore the cash balance to that amount. Other rules of thumb based on expenditure patterns can be easily devised. In the case of most local governments, forecasts of cash needs are quite accurate, so the prospect of unexpectedly running out of cash is not very likely.

Rules of thumb may be adequate for smaller local governments where the added effort and expense of administering the more sophisticated models may not be justified. The extra supervisory costs may exceed the possible benefits. The decision whether to use a more complex model often depends on the amount of funds involved and the height of the prevailing interest rates as compared with the extra administrative costs involved.

Analytical models that permit accurate measurement of the optimal cash balance have been developed. The use of the computer has resulted in some fairly complex systems, but the relatively simple models (the EOQ formula and the Miller-Orr model), which are analyzed in the following discussion, are useful for illuminating most of the variables contained in the more complex programs.

The economic ordering quantity (EOQ) formula One common cash model is derived from the economic ordering quantity (EOQ) formula used in inventory management.[6] Here, the carrying cost of holding cash (i.e., the interest differential forgone on the cash balance) is weighed against the estimated fixed cost per transaction of transferring funds from the marketable securities portfolio to transaction holdings. The costs of carrying transaction funds are directly proportional to the average cash balance held (that is, the greater the cash balance maintained, the greater the differential earnings forgone from the investment of these funds in the money market). On the other hand, the total transaction costs vary directly with the number of transactions, and the number of transactions will be lower if a higher average cash balance is maintained. What is involved, therefore, is a trade-off between carrying costs on the one hand and transaction costs on the other.

Figure 14–7 illustrates this trade-off. Assume that the time period measured on the horizontal axis is the interval between property tax payments. And assume that the city or county receives a large amount of cash at the beginning of the period and there are no other receipts during the period; of course, additional cash can be expected to come in at the end of the period. Assume that expenditures are at a steady rate and that total expenditures expected during the period are just equal to the cash receipts. The city or county must decide on the optimal average cash balance. One strategy might be to hold X dollars initially

Figure 14–7 Inventory model applied to cash management.

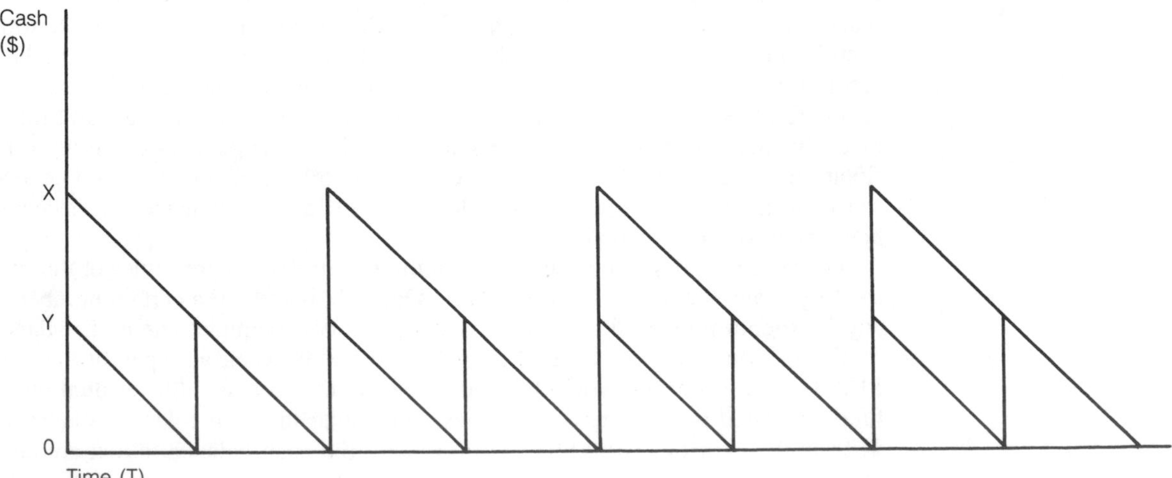

in transaction funds and when this is expended, replenish it by selling X dollars' worth of marketable securities. This transfer of funds would be undertaken whenever cash levels reached zero so there would be four transactions in total, including the original transfer of cash to marketable securities in order to get the cash balance down to X. (Cash receipts would be 4 times X.) The average cash balance is $X/2$ in Figure 14–7. The opportunity cost is simply this average balance times the difference between the rate of interest by the bank and that available on marketable securities (or $X/2$ times i, where i stands for this differential).

Another strategy might be to have maximum cash of the smaller amount, Y, and to transfer Y dollars from marketable securities when the cash balance reaches zero. In this case the number of transactions is eight, twice as many as before, but the average cash balance is less, namely $Y/2$. In order to maintain a lower average cash balance, however, more transactions from marketable securities to cash are required. Thus, on the one hand, a lower cash balance reduces the total earnings forgone on the investment that could otherwise be made (this is equivalent to the carrying cost), but on the other hand it increases the total transfer or transaction costs. The determination of an optimal average cash balance involves a trade-off between these two types of costs, which run in opposite directions. The optimal size cash balance *minimizes* the total of both transaction costs and the opportunity cost of the interest earnings forgone for the period.

The total costs of carrying cash can be expressed in the following equation:

$$P = b\left(\frac{T}{C}\right) + vT + i\left(\frac{C}{2}\right), \quad \text{where:} \qquad (3)$$

P = Total cost of cash management

b = Fixed cost per transaction of transferring funds from marketable securities to cash or vice versa

T = Total amount of cash payments or expenditures over the period involved

C = Size of transfer, which is the maximum amount of cash

v = Variable cost per dollar of funds transferred

i = The excess of the interest rate on marketable securities over the interest rate on transaction balances during the period involved.

In equation (3), b and v reflect the two types of costs—fixed and variable—involved in transferring funds between marketable securities and cash. Included in b, the fixed cost per transaction, are the time it takes the finance officer or other official to place an order with an investment banker, the time the official consumes in recording the transaction, the cost of the secretarial time needed to type the transaction, the time devoted to recording the transaction in the controller's office, and the time needed to record the safekeeping notification. These costs are the same regardless of the size of the transaction and they are incurred each time a transaction takes place. A cost study should be undertaken to determine their approximate magnitude. Since costs vary with office efficiency and wage rates, no one transaction cost figure is appropriate for all local governments. In equation (3), T/C represents the number of transfers during the period, and $b(T/C)$ (transaction costs times the number of transfers) gives the total transactions costs for the period.

The variable costs, v, are made up in large part of brokerage fees, which vary with the volume of dollars transferred and not with the number of individual transactions. In the equation, vT represents total brokerage fees over the period. Since these costs are the same for any number of transfers, they are not a factor in the determination of C (the optimal withdrawal) or $C/2$ (the optimal average balance).

The last term in the equation represents the total earnings forgone during the period by virtue of holding a positive cash balance. (If the cash balance is borrowed from the bank, i represents the interest paid to the lending institution in excess of the amount paid on the city's deposits.) Since $C/2$ represents the average cash balance, the total interest forgone is $C/2$ multiplied by i (the current interest rate advantage on marketable securities). The appropriate base rate interest is the yield on securities which would have to be sold to replenish cash. Generally, this is the rate on short-term market instruments. If C—the initial cash balance and size of transfer—is set at a higher level, the number of transfers between marketable securities and cash—T/C—decreases, so transaction costs also decrease. However, an increase in C results in a greater average cash balance, $C/2$, which in turn results in a higher opportunity cost of interest income forgone. The object is to balance these two costs at the margin so that total costs are minimized.

The equation used to solve for the value of C that results in minimum costs is the well-known economic ordering quantity (EOQ) formula, where C^* is the optimal transfer size and initial cash balance.[7]

$$C^* = \sqrt{\frac{2bT}{i}} \qquad (4)$$

One should note that the size of *average* cash balance, $C^*/2$, varies with the square root of the level of cash payments, T. This implies that as the *level* of total cash expenditures increases, the amount of cash the local government needs to hold increases less than proportionally. In other words, economies of scale are possible in cash management. This argues against the proliferation of special cash funds, for it follows that the combined transactions of two activities can be handled by a smaller balance than the sum of two separate funds. To be sure, the segregation of funds is often required by law. City and county officers should strive to change such laws where possible, since cash management efficiency can be improved if separate accounts can be consolidated. By transacting all banking business through a single account, or through as few as possible, it is possible to release extra funds for portfolio investment.

Along the line of improving cash management, the Advisory Commission on Intergovernmental Relations has suggested the use of zero balance special accounts, where there is only one general account, but where, for control purposes, separate clearing accounts exist for different departments. These clearing accounts are maintained at a zero balance, but the bank will automatically transfer funds from the master account when checks are presented for payment. This gives the financial officer control over the individual accounts. At the same time, by allowing a consolidation of cash, it economizes on the size of the cash balance.[8]

The EOQ formula is used to solve problems like the following.[9] Consider a local government with estimated total cash payments (T) of \$6 million for a three-month period. These payments are expected to remain at a steady rate over the period. The total of explicit and implicit costs per transaction (b) is \$100 and the interest rate advantage on marketable securities (i) is approximately 3.0 percent per annum or 0.75 percent for the quarter. Therefore,

$$C = \sqrt{\frac{2bT}{i}} = \sqrt{\frac{2(100)\ (6{,}000{,}000)}{.0075}} = \$400{,}000 \qquad (5)$$

Thus, the optimal initial cash balance and transfer size is $400,000, and the average cash balance is one-half of $400,000, or $200,000. This means the local government should make 15 transfers from marketable securities to cash for the period (6,000,000 ÷ 400,000).

The optimal number of transactions will be larger if transfer costs are relatively low and interest rates relatively high. On the other hand, the higher the cost per transfer and the lower the interest rate, the higher the optimal average cash balance held over the period and the smaller the number of transfer transactions.

Figure 14–8 illustrates the EOQ formula. The costs of cash management are shown in Example A. Transaction costs are $1,500 (15 transactions at a cost of $100 each), and the cost of interest forgone is $1,500 (the interest rate differential, *i*, times the average balance, $200,000), so total costs are $3,000. The figure shows how these costs vary with initial cash balance and transfer amounts. In Example B, initial cash balance and transfer amounts are $200,000. There are 30 transactions and an average cash balance of $100,000. The higher transaction costs overwhelm the lower interest loss, and total costs rise to $3,750. In Example C, with initial cash balance and transfer size at $500,000, 12 transactions, and an average balance of $250,000, transaction costs are lower, but lost interest earnings rise to offset them, and total costs are $3,075.

Although local government expenditures are usually sufficiently predictable to make the EOQ approach feasible, the flow of cash payments is seldom completely certain. To cover a modest degree of uncertainty, one need only add a precautionary balance so that the transfer from marketable securities to cash is triggered before the cash balance reaches zero. Nevertheless, in general the EOQ model gives the finance officer a fairly good benchmark for judging the optimal cash balance. The model does not have to be used as a precise rule, but it suggests what would be the optimal balance under a given set of assumptions.

The Miller-Orr model For cases in which cash balances fluctuate randomly other models based on control theory are used to determine optimal cash

Figure 14–8 Transaction costs and forgone interest under three sets of assumptions.

Example A		
Initial cash balance		$400,000
Average cash balance		$200,000
Transactions		15
Transaction costs	15 × $100 =	$1,500
Forgone interest	.0075 × $200,000 =	1,500
Total costs		$3,000
Example B		
Initial cash balance		$200,000
Average cash balance		$100,000
Transactions		30
Transaction costs	30 × $100 =	$3,000
Forgone interest	.0075 × $100,000 =	750
Total costs		$3,750
Example C		
Initial cash balance		$500,000
Average cash balance		$250,000
Transactions		12
Transaction costs	12 × $100 =	$1,200
Forgone interest	.0075 × $250,000 =	1,875
Total costs		$3,075

balances. The idea is to set control limits so that when cash reaches an upper limit, it is transferred to marketable securities, and when cash balances touch the lower limit, marketable securities are converted to cash. As long as the cash balance stays between these two limits, no transactions take place.

In the Miller-Orr model, the levels at which the control limits are set depend upon the transaction (or order) costs compared with the opportunity costs of holding transaction balances.[10] As before, assume these two types of costs can be estimated. In essence, the need for cash must be satisfied at the lowest possible total cost. Although there are a number of different applications of control theory, a simple illustration suffices here. The Miller-Orr model specifies two control limits—*h* dollars as an upper bound and zero dollars as a lower bound. This model is illustrated in Figure 14–9. When the cash balance touches the upper bound, *h,* enough marketable securities are purchased to bring the balance down to the bottom range, *z* dollars. When the cash balance touches zero, *z* dollars of marketable securities are sold and the new balance again becomes *z*. If there are possible delays before a transfer can be completed, the minimum bound could be set at some amount higher than zero, and both *h* and *z* would be moved up. The control limits are determined by considering holding and ordering costs and by analyzing the degree of likely fluctuations in cash balances so as to constrain the number of transactions. The greater the likely fluctuations, the wider the setting for the control limits.[11]

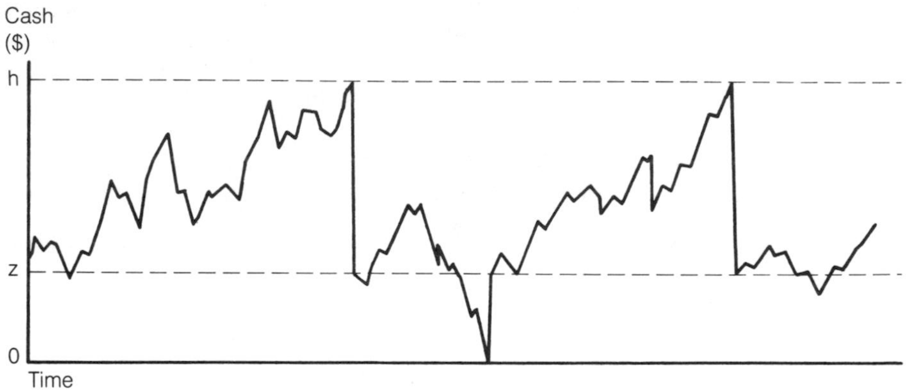

Figure 14–9 Miller-Orr model for cash management using control limits for the purchase and sale of marketable securities.

Summary Since for most local governments cash flow is essentially predictable, the simple EOQ model—which assumes that cash payments and inflows are predictable—may be more useful than the Miller-Orr model—which assumes that inflows and outflows are random. Even for cases of moderate uncertainty, the EOQ model can be modified to incorporate precautionary balances. Because the Miller-Orr model produces considerably higher average cash balances that the EOQ model,[12] when the balances of a local government are higher than even those indicated by the Miller-Orr model (and cash payments are relatively predictable), it is certain that the cash balance is too high.

As with inventory management, although the use of careful analysis employing sophisticated models is worthwhile for larger cities or counties, it may be that the total administrative costs are not worth the extra gains for smaller jurisdictions. Many smaller cities or counties should consider using the computer-directed cash management programs now available at banks and other financial institutions.

Investment in marketable securities

Once a city or county has decided on an optimal cash balance, the rest of its liquid funds may be invested in a portfolio of marketable securities. The choice of securities for the portfolio is a bit limited, since most states restrict the securities in which a local government may invest; nevertheless, some flexibility is still available. The legal list usually permits investment in U.S. Treasury securities, U.S. agency securities, obligations of other municipal governments within the state, and bank certificates of deposit (CDs). This section examines the yield, maturity, safety, and other characteristics of each of these securities and explores why different securities carry different market yields.

Market yields Among the variables that affect market yield are (1) the length of time to maturity, (2) the degree of default risk (3) ease of marketability, and (4) tax status. By analyzing securities on the basis of these variables, the finance officer can assess what must be traded off in order to achieve higher yields. Table 14–1 shows comparative yields for instruments that differ in maturity, default risk, and marketability.[13] In the following discussion, the influence of each of these factors on market interest rates will be examined.

Table 14–1 Comparative yields on various financial instruments, July 1986.

Instrument	Yield (%)
3-month Treasury bill	5.98
3-month commercial paper, through dealers	6.23
6-month certificate of deposit	6.20
Long-term Treasury bond (10 year)	7.39
Long-term corporate bond (highest quality—20 years)	9.10
Long-term tax exempt issues (highest quality)[a]	7.46

Source: *Wall Street Journal,* 31 July 1986.
[a] Bond Buyer Index—Triple A bonds as of 24 July 1986.

Maturity The relationship between yield and maturity can be studied graphically by plotting yield and maturity for securities of the same degree of default risk differing only in length of time to maturity. The yield-maturity relationship is usually presented for default-free Treasury securities. Examples of yield curves (or term structures) are shown in Figures 14–10 and 14–11. Maturity is plotted on the horizontal axis and market yield on the vertical axis; the relationship between market yield and years to maturity is described by the yield curve. Note that in a typical yield curve as of October 1985 (Figure 14–10), the yield curve sloped upward. However, earlier, in March 1980 (Figure 14–11) when inflation peaked, the curve had a strong downward slope.

The direction of the yield curve or term structure generally indicates the market consensus as to the direction of the future level of interest rates. When the market expectations (as to whether the future level of the general interest rate will be upward or downward) are balanced, the curve will slope upward; the short-term rate will be lower than the yields on longer term issues. This is because there is greater potential fluctuation in the price of longer issues if the market interest rate changes; the market generally will accept a lower yield in exchange for greater stability in price. In other words, because some part of the portfolio is designed for turnover or short-term uses, investors want to avoid changes in value at the point of time when liquidity is needed.

Figure 14–10 Market yields as related to years to maturity on U.S. government securities, October 1985.

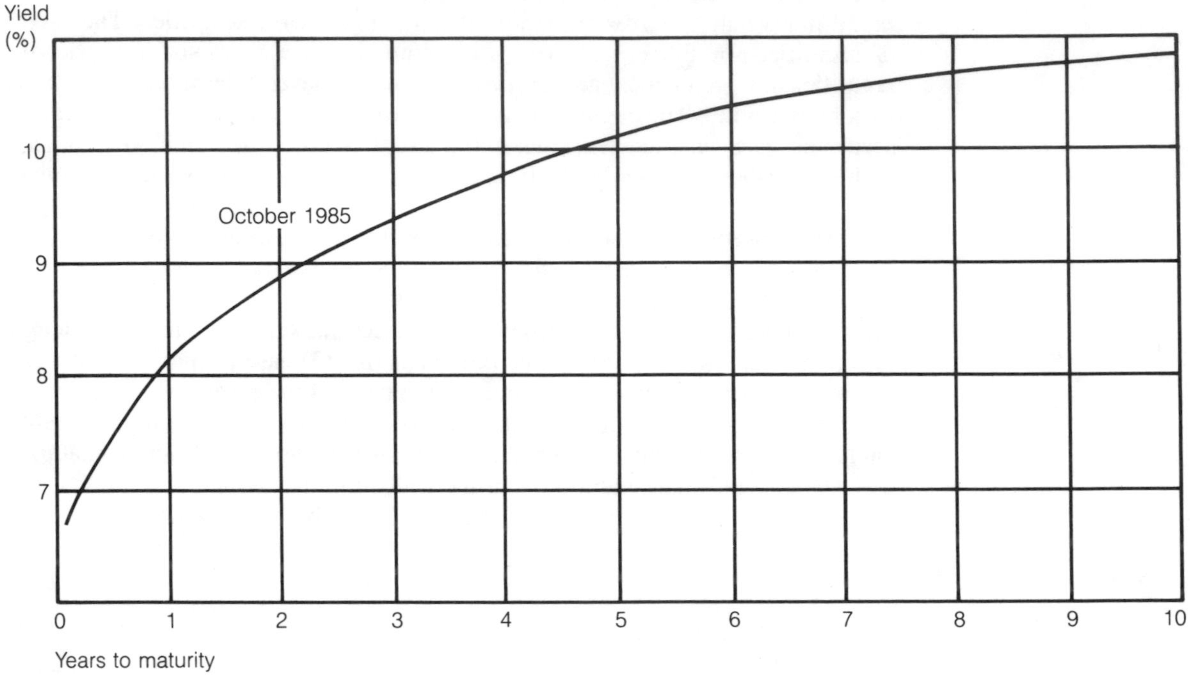

Figure 14–11 Yields as related to years to maturity, U.S. government securities.

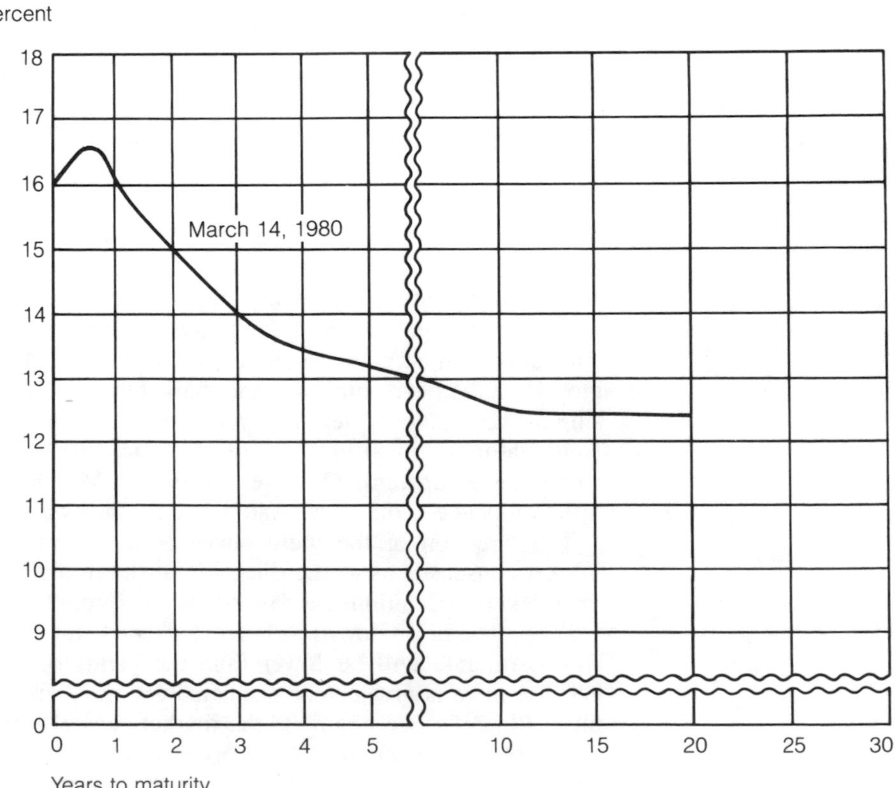

The upward slope of the yield curve will be more pronounced when there is a market expectation that the level of general interest rates is going to rise in the future. Under these conditions, long-term borrowers want to secure funds at the prevailing rates and are willing to contract to pay a somewhat higher rate now because the probability is that borrowing costs will go up still higher in the future. Short-term borrowers pay a lower rate now, but they are likely to have to pay a higher rate when they "roll over" or renew their borrowings in the future. Similarly (but from a contrasting point of view), lenders may decide to forgo the higher longer-term rates and lend short because after they cash in their short-term instruments, there are likely to be higher yields available in the market.

If the market expects a fall in the prevailing interest rates, there will be a reversal in the term structure—a downward sloping yield curve as in Figure 14–11. (The yields on short-term securities in the winter of 1979 and early spring of 1980 were higher than the long terms.) The reasons for this are the reverse of those presented for the pronounced upward sloping yield curve. When a decline in the overall interest rates is anticipated, investors may shift some of their funds to the longer end of the market to lock into the attractive current yields. Some normally long-term borrowers may temporarily pay the higher rates prevailing on the shorter maturities expecting that they will be able to refund at lower rates in the future.

In general, city and county financial managers should not speculate against the yield curve, and they should not invest in longer-term securities when their own obligations are coming due shortly. However, they can put money for sinking fund purposes or future construction into longer-term issues (and obtain higher yields over time) if the maturities of the investments do not extend beyond the date the monies will be needed. The rule is to match the maturities of the portfolio with the due dates of the obligations.

Default risk The second factor making for differences in yield is default risk—the possibility that the borrower will fail to pay principal or interest. Investors demand a risk premium (a higher interest rate) to induce them to invest in securities that are not default-free. All other factors being constant, the greater the possibility (even if small) that the borrower will fail to meet his or her obligations, the greater will be the premium contained in the market yield. Because Treasury securities usually are regarded as default-free, other securities and the yields they offer may be judged in relation to them. The credit worthiness of other obligations frequently is judged on the basis of security ratings provided by Moody's Investors Service and Standard & Poor's, who grade the quality of corporate and municipal securities. By investing in riskier securities, the local government can achieve higher returns, but only with the probability of accepting some default risk.

Marketability Marketability, the third factor accounting for yield differentials, is the ability of the owner of a security to convert the security to cash easily. Marketability has two dimensions—the price and the amount of time required to sell the asset. The two are interrelated in that it is often possible to sell an asset in a short period of time if the seller allows a price concession. For financial instruments, marketability is judged in relation to the ability to execute the sale of a fairly large volume of securities without offering a noticeable price concession. The more marketable the security, the greater the ability of its owner to execute a large transaction near the present quoted price. All other things being equal, the lower the marketability of a security, the greater the yield necessary to attract investors. A yield differential between issues of the same maturity and default risk may be due to differences in their marketability.

Tax status Taxes are the fourth factor affecting observed differences in market yield, the most important being the federal income tax. Because interest income from state and local government securities is tax-exempt, local government securities sell in the market at lower pretax yields than do corporate securities or even Treasury securities of the same maturity. However, because cities do not pay federal taxes on their investment income, a tax exempt feature on their investments is of no use to them. They should not invest in state and local government securities when they can get higher pretax yields on Treasury or other high-grade securities.

Fixed income securities issued when interest rates were lower will sell at a discount below par when the coupon rate they bear falls below the prevailing market yields. Tax status affects the yields on these bonds because, as of this writing, the current interest income is taxed at the ordinary income tax rate whereas capital gains are taxed at the more favorable capital gains rate. Thus, discount bonds bearing low coupon rates may have lower pretax market yields because the eventual recovery of the discount is taxed at the lower capital gains rate. Because a local government's interest income is not taxed, it should take advantage of the higher yields available on high coupon bonds selling at par or above. All other things being the same, local governments should simply invest in securities showing the highest *pretax* return.

Types of marketable securities Among the marketable securities available for local government investment are Treasury securities, agency securities, repurchase agreements, and negotiable certificates of deposit.

Treasury securities U.S. Treasury obligations constitute the largest segment of the fixed-income securities market. Treasury securities are classified as bills, notes, and bonds. Treasury bills, with maturities of 91 days and 182 days, are auctioned weekly by the Treasury, and one-year bills are sold periodically. Treasury bills are sold on a discount basis and are extremely popular as short-term investments. They have a high degree of marketability and are default-free. The market in Treasury bills is very active and transaction costs involved in the purchase of sale of the bills in the secondary market are quite small.

Treasury notes and bonds carry stated interest rates or coupons. Notes are issued for maturities of one to seven years, and bonds are issued for terms of over seven years. However, as notes or bonds approach their due dates, they can be bought on the market to serve the needs of short-term investors. In general, Treasury securities are the safest and most marketable investments; however, except for tax-exempts, they yield the lowest return for a given maturity of all investment instruments.

Agency securities Agency securities, the obligations of various agencies and corporations chartered by the federal government, are guaranteed by the issuer. Principal agencies issuing securities are federal land banks, federal home loan banks, federal intermediate credit banks, the Federal National Mortgage Association ("Fannie Mae"), the Government National Mortgage Association ("Ginnie Mae"), and the banks for cooperatives. These securities are sold in the secondary market through the same dealers who handle Treasury securities. With the increase in the floating supply caused by the sharp increase in agency financing in recent years, marketability has been enhanced considerably. Agency issues are considered highly acceptable by the investment community, and they provide a small yield advantage over Treasury securities of the same maturity. Maturities of these issues range from one month to approximately 15 years. About two-thirds of the securities outstanding mature in less than a year.

Repurchase agreements In an effort to tap new sources of financing, government securities dealers offer repurchase agreements. The repurchase agreement, or "repo" as it is called, provides for the sale of short-term securities by the dealer to the investor with the provision that the dealer will repurchase the securities at a specified price at a specified future date. The investors receive a given yield while they hold the security, essentially the difference between the initial price and the specified repurchase price. The length of the holding period itself is tailored to the needs of the investor. Thus, repurchase agreements can give the local government a great deal of flexibility with respect to maturity. Rates are related to the rates on Treasury bills, the federal fund rate, and loans to government securities dealers by commercial banks.

It would seem that because the collateral involved is a U.S. Treasury security, there would be little risk. However, there have been a significant number of cases where the dealer defaulted on the repurchase agreement and the security backing was never delivered so that the lenders suffered severe losses. It is very important that the dealer have an impeccable credit rating and that the municipal treasurer receive the securities or the deposit before a repo is purchased or sold.

Negotiable certificates of deposit Another short-term investment that may fit the needs of local government portfolios is the negotiable certificate of deposit (CD). A CD is simply the deposit of funds at a commercial bank for a specified period of time and at a specified rate of interest. These short-term investments, which originated in 1961, have become quite popular. Money-market banks quote rates on CDs.

Yields on negotiable CDs tend to be greater than those on Treasury bills of comparable maturity. Original maturities of CDs range from 30 to 360 days. A sizable secondary market has developed for CDs of the large money-market banks. The CDs of smaller banks have limited marketability, so the investor usually must wait until final maturity before funds can be realized. Default risk involves the possibility of bank failure—in most cases a low risk but a risk still greater than that of the other instruments. (The CDs of some savings and loan associations have proven to be quite risky.) Some cities and counties make a practice of investing only in the CDs of local banks doing business within the city. Frequently, the allocation of CDs among banks is determined on the basis of relative deposits or check clearances in the city or county. The idea is to support the local banks that benefit the city or county in a number of ways.

Portfolio of marketable securities The local government investor should choose from the legal list those securities that maximize earnings in keeping with financial needs. Typically, these needs are expressed in terms of maturity—that is, when the funds are likely to be needed—as well as in terms of the requirement of a precautionary balance to meet unexpected cash drains. Although the cash budget is used to determine planned cash needs over the near future, finance officers should also assess the possibility of unexpected cash needs—occasioned by slow revenue receipts, unexpected appropriations, or emergency expenditures. On the basis of these evaluations, the finance officer should come up with a probability distribution of possible cash drains. The costs and embarrassment of a possible shortfall in funds sets the size of the precautionary balance.

Although the securities on the legal list are generally of high quality, the careful financial officer should make sure to limit the risk of default. Tax status is not a direct factor, so the city should simply seek safe securities that provide the greatest pretax return and try to spread maturities so that they coincide with the need for funds. The city or county should arrange to have a steady flow of securities coming due. With proper spacing, a city or county is able to plan for future needs and provide the flexibility to make adjustments with minimum dislocation.

Short-term needs can be satisfied by Treasury bills, repurchase agreements (if handled with care), and certificates of deposit. Treasury notes and bonds and U.S. agency securities can be used for intermediate-term needs. Because of the irregular timing of the issues, it is not always possible to achieve efficient spacing through U.S. agency securities. However, these securities do provide a yield advantage at only a slight sacrifice in marketability.

Generally, some portion of the cash funds of a city or county is unencumbered in that it is not attached to a specific short-term need. Accordingly, the finance officer can invest some of these funds in longer-term Treasury and agency securities. However, when making long-term investments, a most important consideration is the expectation of the future course of interest rates. If a local government invests in long-term securities and if interest rates subsequently rise, the local government will suffer a considerable decline in the market price of its investment. In general, unless the city or county has to eventually meet a long-term obligation of about the same maturity, finance officers should resist the temptation to reach for the higher returns available on long-term securities.

Summary

A well-managed cash flow system will enable the local government to release funds for profitable investment in marketable securities. This part of the chapter has discussed the methods and procedures that can be used in organizing cash flows and positions and has analyzed various aspects of the securities market from a managerial perspective.

Once an optimal cash balance has been determined through the use of various cash management models, any extra municipal treasury funds may be invested in a marketable securities portfolio. The finance officer should be aware of the market yields obtainable on different eligible investments as influenced by maturity, default risk, marketability, and tax status.

1 A very useful inventory analysis is obtainable in "Inventory Management," Chapter 6, Jarl G. Kallberg and Kenneth L. Parkinson, *Current Asset Management: Cash, Credit, and Inventory* (New York: John Wiley & Sons, 1984).

2 If supplies are easily replenished without penalty, then the safety stock can be zero, and the inventory problem is essentially solved by the EOQ model.

3 It may not be correct to speak of two costs in solving for the optimal safety stock. The stockout loss function is really the return from holding an inventory; it is a measure of stockout losses *avoided*. Thus we are really equating the marginal return from the inventory to the marginal costs of carrying the inventory.

4 The number of times orders should be placed during a given period is also solved by the economic ordering quantity—that is, the usage or sales during the period divided by the EOQ gives the number of times orders will be placed.

5 See Advisory Commission on Intergovernmental Relations, *Understanding State and Local Cash Management* (Washington, D.C., May 1977) for a more detailed coverage of these rules.

6 This model was first applied to the problem of cash management by William J. Baumol, "The Transactions Demand for Cash: An Inventory Theoretic Approach," *Quarterly Journal of Economics* 66 (November 1951): 543. It has been further refined and developed by a number of other analysts.

7 For the mathematically oriented reader, we differentiate equation (3), which represents total costs, with respect to C and set the derivative equal to zero obtaining

$$\frac{dP}{dC} = \frac{i}{2} - \frac{bT}{C^2}$$

$$\frac{i}{2} = \frac{bT}{C^2}$$

$$C^2 = \frac{2bT}{i}$$

$$C^* = \sqrt{\frac{2bt}{i}}$$

8 Advisory Commission on Intergovernmental Relations, *Understanding State*, p. 19.

9 See J. Richard Aronsòn and Eli Schwartz, "*Improving Cash Management in Municipal Government,*" *Management Information Service Reports*, International City Management Association, 1, no. LS6 (1969) for additional illustrations. This article builds on a previous article by Aronson, "The Idle Cash

Balances of State and Local Governments: An Economic Problem of National Concern," *Journal of Finance* 23 (June 1968): 499–508.

10 See Merton H. Miller and Daniel Orr, "A Model of the Demand for Money by Firms," *Quarterly Journal of Economics* (August 1966): 413–35.

11 The optimal value of z, the return-to point for security transaction, is

$$z = \sqrt{\frac{3b\sigma^2}{4i}}, \quad \text{where:}$$

b = fixed cost per security transaction

σ^2 = variance of daily net cash flows (measure of dispersion)

i = interest rate per day on marketable securities.

The optimal value of h is simply $3z$. With these control limits set, the model minimizes the total costs (fixed and opportunity) of cash management. Again, the critical assumption is that cash flows are random. The average cash balance cannot be determined exactly in advance, but it is approximately $(z+h)/3$. As experience unfolds, however, it can be calculated easily.

12 Rita M. Maldonado and Lawrence S. Ritter, "Optimal Municipal Cash Management: A Case Study," *Review of Economics and Statistics* 47 (November 1971): 384–88. The authors tested these models on data for the city and county of Honolulu and found that the Miller-Orr model resulted in an average cash balance four times as high as that which resulted from use of the EOQ model.

13 See James C. Van Horne, *The Function and Analysis of Capital Market Rates* (Englewood Cliffs, N.J.: Prentice-Hall, 1970) for an analysis of money-market instruments; and P. Meek, "U.S. Monetary Policy and Financial Markets," Federal Reserve Bank of New York, 1982.

15 Purchasing and risk management

This chapter covers purchasing and risk management. The expertise and insights of the financial manager are needed to manage purchasing, control outlays, and obtain the best value for the funds expended. In addition, careful managerial oversight of risk costs and exposures can balance feasible insurance coverage with a program of risk management to achieve the best protection possible within the limits of the local government budget.

Purchasing

The term "purchasing" or "procurement" is generally used in state and local government to encompass locating, buying, distributing, storing, using, disposing, and paying for goods and services.

The procurement process includes setting standards and specifications, managing inventory, and taking procedural and substantive steps to award orders and contracts. The process summarized in the sidebar "The elements of procurement" begins with the determination of requirements that are based not only on expenditures authorized by the operating budget but also on attempts to forecast both availability and anticipated use of materials and services. The process ends with physical receipt and distribution of goods or completion of contracted services.

The elements of procurement The terms "materials management," "purchasing," and "procurement" are sometimes used interchangeably, but the term "procurement" is the most comprehensive for local government. Its elements include the following:

Requirements determination Standards, specifications, classifications, cataloging, quantitative requirements.

Inventory management Order quantities, stock levels, shelf life, physical inventories, computer models, order points.

Purchasing: preaward Purchase procedures and records, sources of supply, bidding procedures, evaluation of bids, awards of orders and contracts.

Purchasing: postaward Modifications of orders and contracts, receipt and inspection of deliveries, shortages and other discrepancies, payment procedures, audits.

Physical distribution Transportation, receipt, storage, distribution, salvage, disposal.

Source: Abstracted, except for the first paragraph, from Harry Robert Page, *Public Purchasing and Materials Management* (Lexington, Mass.: Lexington Books, D.C. Heath and Company, 1980), pp. 24–26.

In about 33 percent of the cities with populations of over 10,000, purchasing is included within the finance department; in 25 percent of the cities, purchasing is part of a department of administration; 10 percent of the cities have a separate purchasing department; and the remaining 33 percent have other arrangements.[1]

Regardless of organization, however, the finance director is concerned with and involved in purchasing because of the overall budgetary effect of buying goods and services, policy questions on contracting and sources of supply, and opportunities to reduce expenditures through inventory control and timely cash discounting.

Role of the purchasing agent

In organizing and consolidating purchasing requirements, the purchasing agent must use both professional and interpersonal skills to convince the using departments that they are getting good value and service for their budgeted dollars. It is understandable that some departments may want to do their own buying, but the costs of such decentralization may be high—not only in dollars but also in erratic levels of supply, dissatisfied vendors, and items that are over- or underbought at substantially higher costs. The purchasing agent serves other city or county departments by locating reliable sources for both common and specialty items from pencils to police cruisers, facilitating on-schedule delivery of specified quantities, and securing optimal prices through competitive bidding and, where required or permitted, competitive negotiation.

The purchasing agent should be knowledgeable about major sources of supply, reliable vendors, expeditious and economical transport modes, and materials testing. The purchasing agent is the consumer advocate for the employer, and he or she is also an ally of the finance director in searching for the lowest selling price for the required items, in arranging for credit terms in times of slow cash flow, in planning for supply requirements that anticipate shortages and surpluses, in anticipating price increases and decreases, and in developing forms, records, and procedures that facilitate the work of the accounting office.

Purchasing trends

Like other areas of financial management, purchasing changed drastically during the 1970s and early 1980s because of inflation, sharply rising energy costs, budget cutbacks, reduction or elimination of local government services, contracting out of services, and much greater reliance on highly specialized advisory and consulting services. Because of these and other developments, four trends are particularly evident in the procurement field.

Professional management Procurement is increasingly recognized as both a professional activity and a management function. The purchasing agent is at the focal point for central management decisions—especially on sources of supply, finance decisions on short- and long-term costs, and departmental decisions that affect efficiency and effectiveness. The days are gone when the supply clerk might be promoted to do the city's or county's buying. The change began with the formation of the National Institute of Governmental Purchasing (NIGP) in 1944 and continued with the establishment of the NIGP certification program in 1964. Such certification is now available, upon passing examinations and meeting other requirements, for the Certified Public Purchasing Officer (CPPO) and the Professional Public Buyer (PPB).

Cooperative purchasing Cooperative purchasing is not new; it can be traced at least to the 1930s when the Michigan Municipal League bought fire hose for member cities in large quantities at substantial savings. The difference today is that it is much more widespread and has taken three major forms. Some cities and counties piggyback their purchases, especially of heavy equipment, on the buying done by the state highway department and other state government agencies. In some places, a consolidated purchasing agency has been set up by joint action of several local governments. But the method that has caught on most prominently is the joint bid contract; cities, counties, and school districts are starting to see the worth of pooling their efforts as they bid for goods and services.

Diversified purchasing Buying is much more complicated than it used to be, both for individual consumers and for governments. In 1945 you purchased a radio; in 1950 you added a stereo; in 1952 you added a television set. Today, assuming you can afford it, the home audiovisual center includes a tuner, amplifier, speakers, tape deck, TV set, videocassette recorder, and video camera. Similarly, local governments now use computers, police communications systems (and they are systems, not just hardware), and many other forms of technology.

Whereas the communications revolution is well known, not so well known is the extraordinary growth in specialized services, including computer software, data bases, indexing and abstracting services, electronic messages, programmed training courses, financial advisory services, and a range of consulting and advisory services in law, architecture, engineering, management, training, employee relations, internal and external audits, cost allocations, and general management. Many of these services are, at one time or another, procured by local governments.

Legal ramifications Many cities and counties are reviewing their purchasing ordinances in the context of state statutes, federal and state court decisions, and the *Model Procurement Code* of the American Bar Association. The major reason for this is the aggressive enforcement of federal and state antitrust laws. Litigation is likely if a private party suspects anticompetitive actions in licensing, franchising, or contracting. Meticulous standards and procedures are mandatory. (Methods for reducing local government antitrust liability are outlined later in this chapter.)

The balance of this section will cover a few highlights of particular importance to the finance director, the budget officer, and others engaged primarily in financial planning and evaluation: value analysis; legal ramifications of procurement; and the financial implications of short-term versus long-term costs, contracting out, cooperative purchasing, and inventory management.

Value analysis

Value analysis (VA) is an analytical approach to procurement that stresses the functions of systems, products, and services that are being considered for procurement in relation to total cost and requirements for performance, quality, and durability.[2] In its simplest form, VA is applied to a system, product, or service by asking these questions:

1. What is the function of the system, product, or service?
2. What does it do?
3. What does it cost?
4. What are the alternative means of accomplishing the function?
5. How much would each alternative cost?
6. Which alternative is most likely to handle the function at the lowest total cost?

Applications of VA generally fall into three groups: requirements analysis, life-cycle costing, and value incentive contracting.

Requirements analysis concentrates on the functions of the system, product, or service to answer fundamental questions: What is it for? What does it do? What is it supposed to do? Such questions are obvious enough, but they may get overlooked in the minutiae of cost breakdowns, specifications, and the like.

Life-cycle costing—often referred to as total-cost purchasing or least-cost versus low-bid purchasing—is useful in evaluating bids for heavy equipment. In buying heavy equipment, the total cost includes not only the original price but also the maintenance cost (which may be guaranteed by the vendor for a specific number of years) and the repurchase price at the end of a guaranteed period of years. One of the advantages of total-cost purchasing is that suppliers of high quality equipment, whose products provide lower maintenance costs and higher repurchase prices, may submit bids that are highly competitive. If additional cost factors are to be considered in the award of a contract, those factors and how they will be evaluated *must* be clearly spelled out. The local government also *must* award the contract the way it said it would if it is to protect the integrity of the public purchasing process.

Figure 15–1 shows an example of life-cycle costing with three suppliers bidding on a piece of heavy equipment. Total-cost purchasing is sometimes extended to include environmental and other nonmonetary values. An example is the Buy Quiet Program sponsored by the National Institute of Governmental Purchasing. In that program, local governments are encouraged to specify and consider the "value of noise reduction" to the city or county in the evaluation of bids. Factors that make noise reduction valuable include a desire to increase productivity, reduce citizen complaints about noisy equipment, set a good example for the community at large, and minimize disability claims for hearing

Figure 15–1 A decision under total-cost purchasing for equipment.

Supplier	Initial purchase price	Annual guaranteed maintenance cost[a]	Repurchase price at end of contract[a]	Nondiscounted gross cost	Simple average annual cost
A	$23,000	$2,200	$ 1,000	$35,200	$5,867
B	30,000	1,000	10,000	25,000	5,000
C	26,000	2,000	10,000	26,000	5,200

[a]Six years for Supplier A; five years for Suppliers B and C.

The bid specifications are as follows: Supplier A will take care of the machine for six years at a guaranteed maintenance cost of $2,200 per annum and then repurchase the machine at the end of six years for $1,000. Similarly, Supplier B will service and maintain the machine for $1,000 per annum and repurchase the machine for $10,000 at the end of five years. Supplier C charges $2,000 per annum maintenance and will repurchase the machine for $10,000 after five years. Suppose the city uses a 12% overall cost (discount rate) in analyzing such decisions. What is the least-cost purchase? The answer is obtained by comparing the bids on a Uniform Annual Equivalent Cost (UAEC) basis. This involves using interest rate tables to bring each bid to a present value basis and then converting the amount to an annuity for the relevant number of years. This method takes care of the problem when not all the bids run over the same number of years.

Supplier	(1) Purchase price	+	(2) Present value of maintenance costs	−	(3) Present value of repurchase price	=	(4) Present value of bid	(5) Annualized value for appropriate number of years
A	$23,000		$9,045		−$ 507		$31,538[a]	$7,666
B	30,000		3,605		mi 5,674		27,931	7,748
C	26,000		7,210		mi 5,674		27,536	7,639

[a] Six years for Supplier A; five years for Suppliers B and C.

If no other factors enter in, the least expensive total-cost bid is C; this would not have been selected had only the gross costs over the life of the purchase been considered.

loss. Participants also believe that quieter equipment is better engineered, and, as such, is more energy efficient, requires less maintenance, and lasts longer.

Value incentive contracting has been used mostly by the federal government, but it lends itself to occasional application by state and local governments. In this process a value incentive clause (VIC) is included in the bid request form or other solicitation document. The VIC encourages the contractor to propose (in the form and manner specified by the VIC) an alternative approach that will be better and less costly than the specifications require and will not compromise or impair the quality and performance needed for the required function. If the alternative is accepted by the local government, both parties share (in the ratio and manner set forth in the VIC) in the cost savings. It is unlikely that value incentive contracting will become widespread, but it may provide a financial incentive for special applications such as the construction of a new facility.

Legal ramifications

As noted earlier, procurement is one of the areas in which cities and counties are most vulnerable to antitrust litigation. The accompanying sidebar shows that the Local Government Antitrust Act of 1984 has removed the worst threats of

---

Local Government Antitrust Act of 1984 Section 3(a) of the Act establishes an absolute prohibition against the payment of any monetary damages by local governments . . . for any violation of the Sherman Act.

This prohibition will apply to antitrust suits involving challenges to proprietary or commercial actions by a local government as well as governmental actions. While the Act does not prohibit courts from granting injunctions against local governments to halt anticompetitive actions, it does remove the financial incentive to bring antitrust actions against local governments.

Local government officials and employees will be exempt from any monetary damages under the antitrust laws for any action taken in their "official capacity" as officials or employees.

Although the Act improves significantly the municipal or local government antitrust problems, it does not cure them. It does remove the most threatening aspect of such litigation—large money judgments. . . . Antitrust suits will probably continue to be brought against local governments if private parties believe themselves to be significantly harmed by a proposed municipal action, or stand to gain other advantages from litigation.

Source: National Institute of Governmental Purchasing, *NIGP Technical Bulletin,* no. 8–9 (Falls Church, Va., 1984):4.

---

punitive damages, but lawsuits can still be filed by losing vendors on grounds of unfairness or rigged specifications. To minimize such challenges, local governments should observe the following guidelines:

Base procurement decisions on objective criteria that can be justified on a technical basis.

Publicize the availability of procurement policies and criteria before the bidding process starts.

Where appropriate, provide open hearings for major procurement decisions.

Carefully observe fair procedures when making procurement decisions.

Avoid relying on private parties to develop standards, set prices, or establish procurement policy.[3]

Financial implications

The financial implications of procurement permeate almost every aspect of local government, but four are especially relevant for purchasing agents and other financial managers.

Short-term versus long-term costs Purchasing agents should always search for long-term savings. This is seldom a popular approach to procurement, for it is much easier to purchase on the cheap and postpone the catch-up costs to another fiscal year, but the effort should be made to point out the differences in true cost.

Contracting out Service contracts with the private sector are a widely accepted and frequently used alternative service delivery approach. In 1979, one-fourth or more of the cities with populations over 10,000 contracted with private companies for solid waste collection; solid waste disposal; and street repairs, street lighting, and other street-related services.[4] In addition, many cities and counties contract with neighboring local governments and areawide special districts for solid waste disposal, public transportation, airport operation, libraries, public housing, and other services and facilities.

Cooperative purchasing It is time consuming and sometimes costly to get started on cooperative purchasing, but the approach has compelling advantages for smaller cities and counties, including more buying power, better specifications, and better vendor service. In a time of tax limitations and other financial constraints, many local governments have begun serious efforts to cut costs this way. Guidelines for setting up a cooperative purchasing program are available from the National Institute of Governmental Purchasing.[5]

Inventory management The procurement and maintenance of efficient and economical levels of supplies have been covered in Chapter 14. It is enough to emphasize here the importance of ascertaining the true cost of carrying stock versus the cost of the requisition and order process.

Summary

Local government purchasing is becoming more professional, intergovernmental, diversified, and procedural (in the legal sense). While the basic functions—from acquisition to disposition—have not changed, the context today is vastly different from the days when cities and counties (and school districts too) were oblivious to information technology, antitrust laws, and public-private ventures. The purchasing agent of the 1980s must look at true costs and true value as attained through efficient, economical, and fair methods and procedures.

Risk management

In the mid-1980s, local governments began to feel the squeeze of a liability and insurance crisis. Increasingly vulnerable to lawsuits, they found their premiums skyrocketing, their policies canceled, and some coverages unavailable at any price. As a consequence, risk management assumed new importance as local governments sought to avoid or transfer risks, prevent losses, and keep insurance costs under control.

Risk management is a broad field requiring managers to understand the probabilities of losses that can occur from property damage and liability claims, the differences between optimum and maximum insurance coverage, and the costs and benefits of insurance and loss prevention programs. Although cities, counties, and other local governments have carried property, casualty, workers' compensation, and other forms of insurance for many years, the expansion of insurance coverage into the broader field of risk management is a recent development. Since the early 1970s, hundreds of state and local governments have incorporated risk management into their organizations. The Public Risk and Insurance Management Association, organized in 1978 with a handful of members, had 1,085 members by early 1986. The major reasons for this rapid change are better understanding of the true (and increasing) costs of risk, greater appreciation of the need for expertise in this area, awareness of the value of preventive measures to minimize risk, much greater cost consciousness on the part of state and local government managers, a series of federal court decisions that have seriously undermined the doctrine of sovereign immunity, and exposure to lawsuits under the federal civil rights code.[6]

The basic theory of insurance implies that the expected value of the premiums paid will exceed the value of the probable or expected losses. After all, the insurance company must pay its sales personnel, its agents, and its administrative expenses; it must cover losses out of premiums received; and, finally, it is in business to earn a net return on its invested capital. From a purely monetary perspective, therefore, purchasing is a "bad bet" for the policyholder. Nevertheless, there are rational reasons for carrying insurance. By doing so, the policyholder exchanges a certain small current loss (the premium) for an uncertain, but very much larger, possible loss.

Risk management planning

Local governments are subject to four basic kinds of risks that should be isolated, identified, and inventoried to provide the information base for risk management planning.[7] They are (1) real and personal property loss, (2) loss of income or increased costs that result from property loss, (3) personnel loss, and (4) liability. These risks can be identified and classified by reviewing contracts, leases, property inventory records, and other documents; by inspecting buildings and other properties; by locating major areas of potential loss through risk discovery questionnaires; and by diagramming highly programmed operations and activities to locate high risk points.

After the risks have been identified, potential losses should be reviewed and evaluated for potential frequency and severity. Frequency refers to the number of losses; severity refers to the cost or size of losses. The next step is to consider the four basic ways to control risk: avoidance, prevention, assumption, and transfer.

Risk avoidance Obviously, avoiding risk is the best way to handle potential losses. Some risks can be avoided by changing work methods and equipment—installing safety equipment, for example, and making major changes and improvements in solid waste collection methods. A more drastic approach is to stop performing a particular service, activity, or task—for example, by transferring fire protection from an all-volunteer department to another public or private agency.

Risk prevention Risk prevention or loss prevention is best accomplished by safety programs designed to reduce the incidence of accidents and other losses. An effective safety program involves far more than equipment safeguards. It also includes management policies and surveillance, employee training, employee involvement through committees and other means, experience records, and a continuing emphasis on safety.

Specific risk prevention practices include separating the individual responsi-

Risk management policy It may be advisable for the local governing body to adopt a policy statement that clearly assigns authority and responsibility for risk management and recognizes areas of discretion that facilitate placing insurance and taking other measures to control risk. The following paragraphs suggest subjects that could be covered in such a statement.

1. The risk manager shall have responsibility and authority to administer the city's insurance program.

2. Potential catastrophic losses shall be covered by insurance subject to availability at reasonable cost, or by other methods of transfer.

3. The risk manager shall evaluate the city's risk and establish levels of insurance coverage, deductibles, and self-insurance, consistent with General Policy #2.

4. Recognizing that it may be advantageous to the city, the risk manager is to investigate the appropriateness of recommending multiple year contracts with insurance companies and agents.

5. New types of coverage proposed by the risk manager are to be presented to the city council and approved by them before acquisition.

6. Every three years or more often, at the discretion of the city council, the risk manager shall contract with a risk management consulting firm who shall review and evaluate the city's risk management program and make suggestions for improvement.

7. A self-insurance reserve shall be established. The risk manager shall, from this account, fund losses in exposures which are self-insured.

Source: Excerpted, except for the first paragraph, from Phyllis Sherman, *Basic Risk Management Handbook for Local Governments* (Washington, D.C.: Public Risk and Insurance Management Association, 1983), Exhibit 6–1.

bility of reconciling bank statements from the responsibilities of writing checks and making deposits; inventorying equipment, stock items, and other physical assets as part of an annual postaudit; conducting frequent and unannounced safety inspections; enforcing safety rules for hard hats, special shoes, and goggles; reviewing personnel rules for grievance and appeal procedures on safety questions; providing for regular motor vehicle inspections and preventive maintenance; and auditing or validating state-determined experience modification factors for application to workers' compensation insurance coverage.

Risk assumption After taking all feasible steps to eliminate or reduce risk, the next step is to explore methods of risk assumption and transfer. The major methods for full and partial assumption are to charge any loss to the departmental budget (no problem if the loss is small); to have deductibles written into insurance policies; to set up a funded reserve to cover large losses; to assume workers' compensation losses; and to assume physical damage losses to city-owned automobiles and other motor equipment.

Risk transfer The last step in risk control is to transfer risk by hold-harmless agreements, insurance, and insurance pools. Hold-harmless agreements have only limited application, but they can be used in contracts or purchase orders to transfer liability for losses to another organization doing business with the local government. They are worthless, however, unless they are legally enforceable and the contracting person or firm has enough capital, insurance, or other resources to make financial restitution. The other methods of transfer—buying insurance and insurance pools—are covered in subsequent sections of this chapter.

Insurance coverage

There are two main rules of effective insurance management. First, although an organization should be protected against catastrophic losses, it need not insure itself against minor recurrent losses. Second, where the risks are recurrent and financially manageable, self-insurance may be used—that is, the organization itself may assume risks of this kind, covering them with its own funded reserve. For a local government, Nester Roos and Joseph Gerber advise that only potential major losses be covered: "Only those exposures which could financially cripple the city should be insured, making the best use of deductibles and excess coverage as is financially feasible."[8] In bluntest terms, if the municipality gets stuck for a few $500, $1,000, or $5,000 claims, the losses should be taken in stride. This is petty cash—annoying, but of no consequence except for possibly indicating flaws in the prevention program.

Obviously, the guidelines governing appropriate local government coverage are different from those for individual coverage. The major reason is that the municipality has more resources for covering a loss, including federal disaster assistance, federal reserves established for the purpose, the ability to spread losses over a longer period, bond issues, special tax levies, citizen or group donations, and other sources special to each municipality (e.g., pooling risks with other communities).

Moreover, a city or county has a multitude of buildings and cars, not just one or two, so it can count on a reasonably stable statistical dispersion of losses. Thus, for example, if the local government paid no fire insurance premiums on 50 buildings, the amount saved on the annual premiums might pay for a fire loss in any one of them. Similar analysis applies to automobile collision insurance. If the municipality uses 50 cars, it has a risk exposure equivalent to 50 years of driving experience for a single car. If annual premiums are well in excess of the annual expected losses, the locality may not need to carry collision insurance on its vehicles.

Because it can aggregate risks and losses in this way, the local government enjoys a position not available to the individual. The municipality may find that where the losses on single occurrences are relatively small, self-insurance is advantageous. Commercial insurance premiums include a loading charge for the expenses of administration and sales equal to 30 to 40 percent of the total payment. Thus, the municipality may have a lower cost for administration and it does not pay a sales commission on self-insurance.

Several rules of thumb have been developed to help local governments plan cost-effective insurance coverage:

1. Do not insure park shelters, bleachers, swimming pools, small tool sheds, comfort stations, and other such facilities against property damage. Carry property insurance only to cover catastrophic losses.
2. Do not carry collision insurance on automotive equipment.
3. Write insurance contracts that contain higher deductible clauses.

Insurance costs

Local government insurance costs can be reduced by a number of steps, seven of which will be reviewed in this section:

1. Writing fire policies subject to co-insurance clauses (with an agreed-amount endorsement)
2. Using excess coverage insurance

3. Using blanket coverage policies
4. Obtaining bids from competing insurers
5. Writing deductible clauses into policies
6. Creating self-insurance funded reserves
7. Setting up an insurance pool
8. Maintaining effective prevention programs
9. Eliminating duplicate coverage
10. Determining how fire insurance rates on commercial and industrial properties are established[9]
11. Keeping complete loss experience records to help reduce losses and to support arguments for better ratings
12. Working with insurers on property inspections, coverage inventories, and safety programs.

Co-insurance Used in property and casualty insurance, a co-insurance clause requires a specific amount of insurance based on the value of the property insured. For example, a building that has an insurable value of $800,000 might carry a co-insurance clause of 80 percent. This means that the property must be insured at $640,000 (80 percent of $800,000). The trade-offs are reduced premiums in exchange for total coverage up to $640,000, but no coverage beyond that amount. Co-insurance is not the same as a deductible, which applies irrespective of the amount of the loss. Co-insurance must be carried at a specified ratio of the full insurable value of the property. In this example, if the value of the building increases (because of inflation or other reasons) to $1,000,000, and the co-insurance clause is left unchanged, the coverage will still be only $640,000, which amounts to 64 percent rather than 80 percent of the value of the building.

Excess coverage An excess coverage policy is superimposed on a basic policy to cover large but infrequently occurring losses. In the past, excess coverage policies were used mainly in the liability field. Since the mid-1960s, however, such policies have also been used for property. Excess coverage policies can provide a substantial savings in premiums and still offer a significant amount of protection for a catastrophic loss. Realizing the maximum savings from excess coverage, however, requires more than a simple comparison of current premiums on standard full coverage policies with policies that have different excess limits.[10] Writing such policies and comparing costs may be complicated, and insurance experts should be consulted for evaluating the policies.

Blanket insurance Blanket insurance covers a multitude of perils in a single policy, thereby eliminating duplication of coverage and avoiding the cost of holding many separate policies. Blanket policies may be written on particular locations or on all locations collectively. If a blanket policy is carried on all locations, however, there is the chance that a co-insurance deficiency in one building could reduce the total face amount of insurance below the stipulated co-insurance percentage. (See the discussion of co-insurance above.)

Competitive bids Cities and counties can achieve significant savings in premium costs by calling for competitive bids from insurers. Without competitive bidding, some insurers may not bid for city or county policies because they fear favoritism has already directed the contract, and other insurers may exert political pressure on the risk manager. Bidding discourages this activity. Bidding also compels the risk manager to prepare careful specifications and to become more familiar with the hazards that require insurance.

Deductibles A policyholder can save premium costs by accepting larger deductible amounts in policies. In effect, a local government can assume the risk of losses below a certain dollar figure (the deductible). Deductibles should be based on premiums in relation to expected small losses and the financial capacity of the city or county government to carry the costs involved. If possible losses are small and independent—that is, if the losses are not likely to occur in one location or within one type of coverage—the economics favor the deductible clause. The most frequent losses are the smaller ones. Deductibles therefore help the insurance company save money on administrative, processing, and overhead costs while the local government incurs a small dollar loss.

To determine the savings that can be gained by accepting deductibles, the risk manager should consider the size of probable losses and the value of the property being insured. For example, the city or county may realize considerable savings by purchasing a policy with a deductible of $1,000 instead of $100—enough to pay for small losses. Or it may save by forgoing collision insurance on old cars worth less than $2,000. Instead of paying premiums, the local government can assume the risk.

Self-insurance Self-insurance means that the local government assumes a given kind of risk by setting up and maintaining a funded reserve to cover expected losses and by obtaining excess insurance to cover the hazard of large but infrequent losses. Self-insurance is financially hazardous if it is confused with no insurance. In the absence of a funded reserve and an excess coverage policy, the local government does not have self-insurance; it has *no* insurance.

How should a funded reserve be established? W. G. Brockmeier suggests that:

> Reserves may be built up in a number of ways. Where large amounts are involved, it is frequently not feasible to initiate a self-insurance fund by the immediate setting up of full reserves out of available cash. Therefore, in initiating self-insurance, it is often advantageous to begin with a moderate retention of risk and set aside the insurance premiums saved thereby for the creation of the reserve. As the reserve grows, additional exposure can be retained on the same basis and the plan expanded to its full scope over a period of years. On the other hand, if adequate reserves for full-scale operation of the contemplated plan can be set up immediately, the advantages of self-insurance can be more promptly realized.[11]

A funded reserve is similar to a bond sinking fund in several ways. Total size for the fund is decided in advance, and annuity calculations are used to arrive at the annual deposit required to reach the desired fund size. A funded reserve, however, is unlike a bond sinking fund in that the sinking fund must be a set amount whereas the funded reserve, which depends on the value of the underlying properties, may have to grow over time. Under conditions of inflation, a target reserve of $1 million to be created within five years may prove inadequate once it reaches its desired level. If a level payment into the fund suits budget design, the inflation factor can be estimated and subtracted from the interest rates (in the annuity formula). Alternatively, the sinking fund payment may be adjusted each fiscal period to reflect the inflation that has occurred in the preceding period. Once the fund reaches the appropriate size, its interest earnings should be sufficient to provide for a large share of yearly demands on the fund.

There is no single answer to the question of the proper size for a sound self-insurance fund, but knowledge of past experience and of "clustering" of risks is helpful in determining the size of the self-insurance fund. If exposures in property are widely separated, risk is diminished and a smaller fund might suffice. Some sort of fund, however, should be carried to shield the local government from such unusual and difficult-to-insure risks as earthquakes, floods, and environmental impairment.

Insurance pools An increasingly popular approach to restraining the rising costs of risk coverage is the municipal insurance pool. Such pools enable a group of smaller local governments to self-insure (at least for smaller risks) and reduce administrative costs, thus obtaining better terms on broad-based commercial policies. However, it is necessary to make sure that the state laws permit such combinations before a pool can be formed.

Although municipal insurance pools originally concentrated on workers' compensation coverage, many now have broadened to include comprehensive and automotive liability and, in some cases, property insurance. The pools now in existence operate under the following guidelines:

1. The local governments generally pay a premium to the pool in proportion to their budgets, number of employees, payrolls, and other factors.
2. The localities agree to cover small losses on their own, perhaps to a maximum of $1,000 per loss.
3. Losses of up to some amount (e.g., $50,000) will be covered by the pool.
4. The pool will obtain excess risk insurance to cover losses in excess of $50,000, or the localities will each carry their own excess risk insurance.

If the pool initially experiences a surplus in operations, a fund is built up. After the fund reaches a particular amount, the surplus is returned to the participating members. Recognizing the increasing number of risk management pools, the Public Risk and Insurance Management Association established a Pooling Section in 1983 that helps establish new pools and provides an information exchange for section members.

Insurance pools provide significant advantages, including:

More buying power that often produces lower premiums

Broader insurance coverage

Higher loss assumption than any individual local government could assume

Improved risk management services from insurance companies such as safety training, faster claims service, more accurate loss data, and monthly loss reports

More financial resources that may make it possible for the pool to hire a professional risk manager.[12]

Essentially, the pool has the potential to reduce insurance costs because it enables smaller communities that do not have sufficient diversification of risk to self-insure. Moreover, because the pool reduces administrative costs, it enables the combined units to obtain lower rates on the excess risk policies. At any rate, recent experience shows a considerable savings to pool members.[13]

Placing insurance

Once the city or county has decided, at least in a general way, on the type and amounts of its insurance coverage, it needs to place the insurance with one or more carriers. Two ways to place insurance are through competitive bidding and negotiation. A third way, using a local insurance agents association, is not recommended for reasons summarized below.

As suggested earlier, many local governments achieve significant savings in premiums by calling for competitive bids. Bidding discourages local agents from applying political pressure yet provides an equal opportunity for qualified agents to compete for the business. The probable lower costs and higher ethical standards are two compelling reasons for using bidding. Competitive bidding is not always easy, however. Preparing high-quality specifications and prequalifying bidders are time-consuming and difficult tasks that may be costly until the local government has gained experience with the process.[14] Competitive bidding for city or county insurance business works best when financial, loss experience, property inventory, and other records provide trustworthy information of the risk status of the local government. Underwriters also consider the quality of management, commitment to safety and loss control, compliance with insurers' loss control recommendations, and attitudes toward insurance. With such information the underwriter can gain a realistic view of coverage, exposures, and needs. "Insurers want long-term, partnership relations rather than anonymous buyers of a commodity."[15]

Bidding usually should be conducted only once every three to five years for each major classification of insurance. The costs to insurance underwriters for compiling complex bidding information are high, and companies will not undertake such efforts if they might lose the business after one year.

Before the mid-1970s, when local government insurance was modest in coverage and premiums were low, it was a nice gesture to place hometown business with the established hometown network, and the local insurance

---

Avoid exclusionary practices The following practices, whether adopted by regulation or by custom, have the effect of excluding insurance firms or agencies from competing for a municipality's insurance business. As unreasonable restraints on trade, they violate state and federal antitrust laws and must be terminated:

1. Successively awarding insurance coverage to the same firm or agency without affording other firms or agencies the opportunity to compete

2. Splitting the award of insurance coverage among local firms or agencies

3. Awarding the insurance coverage to only local firms or agencies

4. Utilizing competitive bidding but with the restriction that only local firms or agencies be allowed to compete

5. Utilizing an agent of record system but restricting the agent of record to the local firm or agency, which agent retains a percentage of the commission earned on the insurance premium with the remainder of the commission being split on an agreed upon manner among other agencies

6. Awarding the insurance coverage only through local insurance agents' associations or like committees of selected insurance agents

7. Restricting those firms or agencies who can compete for a municipality's insurance coverage to firms or agencies which reside in, maintain offices in, pay taxes in, or maintain some other form of localized contact with the municipality.

Source: Nestor R. Roos and Joseph S. Gerber, *Governmental Risk Management Manual* (Tucson, Ariz.: Risk Management Publishing, 1976 plus supplements), pp. 8–18.

---

agents' association was glad to step in and take care of the problem. But those days are over. The federal antitrust laws clearly state that restricting those who can compete is likely to be illegal. In the accompanying sidebar, Roos and Gerber give unequivocal advice about restricting competition: Don't do it.

All qualified agents and brokers must and should be allowed to compete for the city or county insurance business, but the number of bidders can be kept to a manageable size by prequalification. At the minimum, the local government should publish a newspaper ad (thus providing for public notice) inviting agents and brokers to phone or write for a prequalifying questionnaire. The questionnaire (if carefully drafted) is the major tool in locating those agents and brokers who have good connections with insurance companies interested in and qualified for the local government business.

Because a municipality has large properties, too much risk should not be covered through a single insurance company. A loss that would be catastrophic for a moderate-sized community might also be large enough to exhaust the financial reserves of many moderate-sized insurers. In all cases, before final placement of insurance, it is prudent to analyze the insurance company with respect to assets, reinsurers, kinds of policyholders, and other indicators of financial stability.[16]

It is often advisable to get the help of a risk management consultant to study local needs, recommend coverages, draft insurance specifications, analyze bids, and provide other kinds of technical and professional service throughout the entire process of risk identification, risk evaluation, and subsequent steps. The consultant should of course have no connection with any insurance company, broker, or agent, and must be totally independent to avoid any conflict of interest or any appearance of conflict of interest.

Types of coverage

Local governments need insurance protection against liability, employee dishonesty, workers' compensation claims, and losses for activity interruption.

Liability Many difficult issues arise in the area of liability insurance for accidents caused by municipal employees. Nevertheless, the general precept of carrying insurance for catastrophes while paying insignificant claims out of operating funds is still valid.

The vulnerability of local governments was reinforced by the 1982 U.S. Supreme Court decision, *Community Communications Company, Inc.* v. *City of Boulder,* which opened the door to some 300 lawsuits alleging antitrust violations in the proprietary and commercial activities of local governments. The situation was hastily remedied when Congress passed the Local Government Antitrust Act of 1984 prohibiting the payment of any monetary damages by local governments in cases challenging proprietary or commercial actions by local governments. The law exempts local government officials and employees for actions taken in their "official capacity." This law by no means provides absolute protection against public official or employee liability, but it drastically narrows the grounds for actions involving franchises, city- and county-owned utilities, and related activities.

When deciding on liability coverage, the local government risk manager should begin by studying recent local court cases, with the help of the local government attorney. Together they should review (1) the type of liability claims being made, (2) the frequency of each type of claim, and (3) the level of awards for various cases. It is also important to ascertain whether the municipality has any special immunity from damages arising from wrongs or injuries to others as a result of the activities of its personnel. The extent of this immunity has been the subject of many court cases. Although there used to be considerable immunity against damages arising from "governmental" functions, there is no immunity against general liability for damages arising from "proprietary" functions.

The precedent-setting case of *Russell* v. *Men of Devon* (1788) granted municipalities immunity from liability for the conduct of their employees on the basis "that it is better that an individual should sustain an injury than that the public should suffer an inconvenience." In interpreting this principle, courts have extended immunity from liability to the operations of such government functions as police and fire protection, public health, education, and welfare. It has been withheld, however, from the operations of such proprietary functions as providing water and other utility services and operating swimming pools. In recent years, most states have drastically narrowed immunity; the question of whether a municipality is liable for the torts of its servants (employees) depends on state law.

Recently, there has been a marked trend toward narrowing governmental immunity, both by statute and by court decision. The Insurance Company of North America, commenting on the *Rex peccare non protest* doctrine ("the king can do no wrong"), wrote that sovereign immunity has been partially or totally abolished in more than 40 states, leaving many governmental bodies vulnerable to suits for negligence on the part of their employees. The result has been that cities and other local governments are held liable for a much wider range of activities and services and the line between governmental and proprietary functions is much less clear-cut than it used to be. Thus many cities and other local governments need more liability insurance; managers and finance officers should take even greater care in surveying areas of potential liability to assure that coverage is carried where needed.

The city or county incurs additional liabilities when it commissions independent contractors to construct buildings and roads. The usual comprehensive general liability policy often excludes liability for property damage caused by:

1. Blasting or explosion other than explosion of air or steam vessels, machinery, and power transmitting equipment
2. Collapse of or structural damage to a building or other structure resulting from grading, excavating, pile driving, demolition, and the like
3. Damage to wires, conduits, pipes, mains, sewers, and other subterranean installations where the damage is caused by mechanical equipment while grading, paving, excavating, or drilling.

Presumably, the contractor is the one most responsible for such mishaps; however, because the municipality might be named as a codefendant in such cases, it would be well to carry an umbrella liability policy to help cover the government for damages that are not covered by other policies.

An umbrella policy (the equivalent of the excess coverage policy used in the property field) covers many hazards that may not be mentioned in the regular policies and, in addition, provides much higher maximum coverage. Figure 15–2 shows how umbrella coverage sits on top of other policies to provide additional protection. For claims covered by *both* regular and umbrella policies, the umbrella coverage begins when the other insurance coverage is exhausted. For claims covered *only* by the umbrella policy, the policyholder pays a deductible amount (often around $25,000) before claims are paid. Umbrella policies typically cover general liability, auto liability, personal injury liability, and employers' liability.[17] Because of the volatility of liability insurance, insurers may be reluctant to cover police professional and public officials liability and may have to be pressed to provide such coverage.

Given the tremendous rise in the claims for damages that modern juries are willing to award, umbrella policies are advantageous to municipalities—particularly since damage awards may amount to millions of dollars. Policies with limits of $50,000,000 or more are relatively common.

It is important in drawing up liability policies that the limits chosen apply per occurrence; that there be no aggregate limit during the term of the policy; and that the renewal dates for the umbrella and underlying policies be the same so that both will be in effect should a loss occur. It would be wise to provide for the automatic inclusion of vehicles, streets, buildings, grounds, or other property added or constructed subsequent to the issuance of the liability policy. In this way, absence of explicit notification to the insurer does not interfere with protection. A clause should also be inserted stating that any errors or omissions

Figure 15–2 Umbrella coverage for liability insurance.

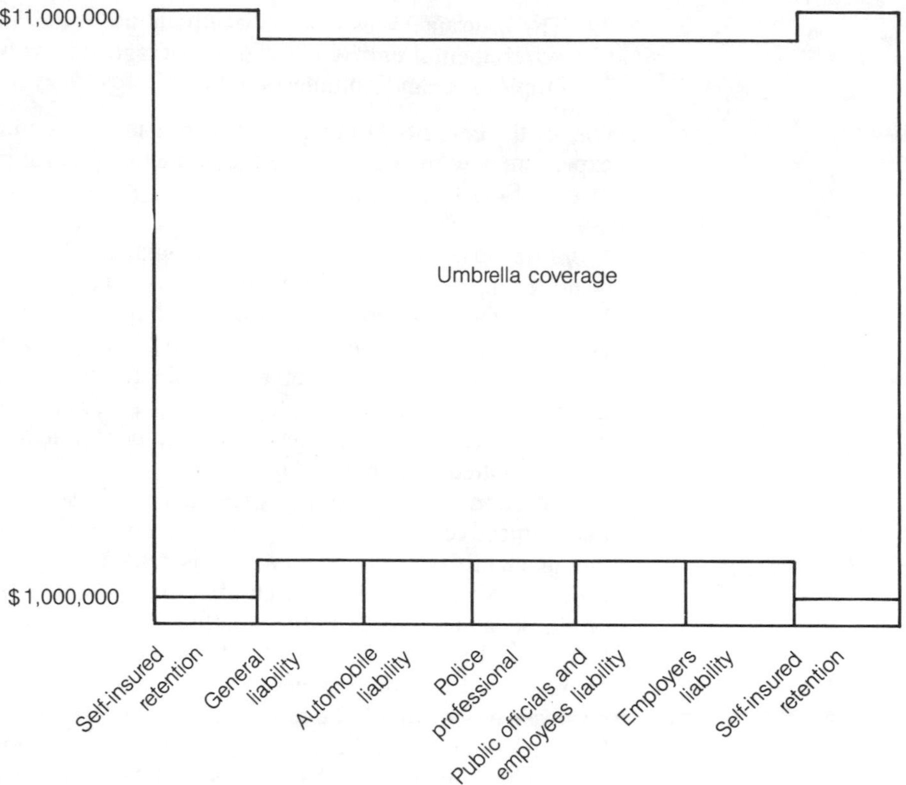

This figure shows how one umbrella policy covers five individual liability insurance policies of $1,000,000 each with umbrella coverage of $10,000,000 on top of the individual policies. Underlying the umbrella policy is a self-insured retention of $25,000. Since umbrella policies vary from company to company, the policy provisions should be checked thoroughly to verify that the scope of the coverage is at least as broad as the underlying policies. In some cases, as this figure shows, the policy terms and conditions of the umbrella provide broader protection than the specific underlying policies.

will not operate to the prejudice of the municipality and that any such property inadvertently omitted or erroneously described shall be included under the policy from its date of inception.

Liability policies should cover not only the municipality but also its appointed officials, agents, employees, and authorized representatives when acting in these capacities for the municipality. Liability policies should rigorously avoid making the local government responsible—via guarantee or warranty—for the information it has provided. This disclaimer does not, however, relieve the local government of the responsibility for maintaining current property inventory records, loss records, loss experience data, accident reports, insurance policy and coverage listings, and related documents. Insurance companies rely on such information to draft complete and accurate proposals.

Federal law and a host of federal court decisions have made liability insurance a complex area. It is important, therefore, in planning liability coverage, to heed these caveats:

1. Federal laws take precedence over state laws. Civil rights laws are a prominent example.
2. State laws may not protect an official or employee outside state boundaries. This is especially important in police work and travel outside the state.

3. The insurance coverage may only apply to the jurisdiction as a governmental entity. If so, the coverage should be extended to officials, employees, and volunteers.

One of the benefits of entering into an insurance contract is that the company's experts review the risks, make recommendations for prevention, and assess the extent of existing hazards.

Employee dishonesty Bonding municipal employees is the customary method of protecting against employee dishonesty. Various types of bonds are available. In the absence of contrary statutory regulations, it is often recommended that the amount of coverage on an individual basis (when a blanket bond is not used) equal the largest amount of negotiable funds (cash, checks, and securities) under the control of the employee at any time. Nevertheless, this coverage can prove inadequate. Many grand thefts are perpetrated over long periods of time, not committed in a single day.

Protection against dishonesty should not rely solely on bonding, however. The main objective should be prevention of embezzlement or other transgressions, and much of the responsibility for this rests on the finance officer. Prevention is based on the development of an effective system of internal control—a system of checks and balances in the handling of assets. For example, the person who acts as cashier should not act also as bookkeeper. Disbursement and receipt forms should be prenumbered and checked. In the case of disbursements, the purchase orders should be reviewed for authorization, the receiving slips should be matched against purchase orders, the invoices should be checked for agreement with both the purchase order and the receiving slip, and all supporting documents should accompany the check so that the local government treasurer can review them before signing the disbursement. Spot checks of inventory, equipment, and properties should be made to ascertain agreement with municipal records, and audits of all offices and procedures should be planned on a frequent but irregular basis. No system is foolproof, but a good system can be a very effective deterrent to theft.

Workers' compensation The local government is liable if any of its employees are injured in the course of work. Thus, several states have imposed statutory obligations to insure such risks. Because workers' compensation claims usually are relatively small or may be spread over time, self-insurance should be encouraged with excess coverage to protect the fund against catastrophe.

Self-insurance for workers' compensation is often appropriate, and it is widespread. Although costs and losses for compensation are more predictable than for other types of coverage, a few guidelines should be followed in deciding whether to self-insure:

1. Analyze loss experience data for the last five years.
2. Obtain good claims handling services, whether internal or external.
3. Conduct regular actuarial analyses to ensure adequacy of the self-insurance fund.
4. Maintain a good safety and loss prevention program.
5. Consider charging back to departmental budgets all, or a portion of, costs involving losses. This is an incentive to encourage better safety and loss control practices.
6. Get excess coverage to protect against very large losses.[18]

Losses for activity interruption Although local governments are not subject to the same business interruption risks as are commercial enterprises, the municipal insurance program should take into account the fact that certain activities yield significant ongoing revenues. A water pumping station may represent a

$200,000 investment but, more important, it may be vital to the income of the entire water system. An airport costing $20,000,000 could conceivably lose gross revenues of $1,000,000 each day that it is closed following a disaster.[19]

The local government should protect itself against interruption of activities by such preventive measures as backup equipment and alternative facilities. It should also consider carrying regular or self-insurance to cover losses when these measures fail. J. D. Todd points out the importance of identifying "those exposures the direct loss of which would not prove too expensive, but which could cause serious repercussions and further losses to the city." Todd's example is the loss of a fire station. This might not in itself be catastrophic, but if the station were the only one in the area, then any fire in town could result in a total loss: "The potential size of ultimate losses resulting from the destruction of a single exposure must be measured to decide on the appropriate means of controlling the losses."[20]

In addition to preparing for potential direct losses to the local government, administrators should consider liability coverage for the contingent losses to the citizens where the contributory negligence of the municipality's operations can be proved.

Summary

Risk management is a broad field, requiring knowledge of both the law and the results of losses occasioned by property damage or liability claims. Good information for municipal departmental experts helps prevent losses, but a balanced insurance program is essential to help restore a municipality to an acceptable state of affairs once a loss does occur. Although the municipality should carry insurance against catastrophic events, self-insurance may be used for minor recurrent risks. A number of guidelines and statistical techniques may be used to ascertain the proper size of the self-insurance fund, and a number of practical steps can be taken to reduce premium costs. Deductibles, blanket insurance, competitive bids, and insurance pools are methods that help cut insurance costs.

The risk manager should note the role of liability insurance under the current broader definitions of government liability. The risk manager is also given the responsibility of protecting against employee dishonesty. Finally, he or she may note the increasing attention being paid to the formation of municipal insurance pools as a method of restraining escalating premium costs.

1 Dan H. Davidson and Solon A. Bennett, "Municipal Purchasing Practices," in *The Municipal Year Book, 1980* (Washington, D.C.: International City Management Association, 1980), pp. 209–11.

2 Most of this section has been abstracted from National Institute of Governmental Purchasing, *Intermediate Public Purchasing and Materials Management* (Falls Church, Va.: 1984).

3 Martin Michaelson and George Mernick, "Antitrust Exposure of Local Governments: A Guide for the Chief Executive," *Management Information Service Report,* International City Management Association, 14, no. 12 (December 1982): 6.

4 Carl F. Valente and Lydia Manchester, "Rethinking Local Services: Examining Alternative Delivery Approaches," *Management Information Service Special Report,* International City Management Association, no. 12 (1984): 1–4.

5 National Institute of Governmental Purchasing, *Background Information and Guidelines for Joint-Bid Cooperative Purchasing* (Falls Church, Va.: 1981).

6 The February and March 1985 issues of *Public Management* provide an overview of the local government insurance market as of early 1985 as well as first-hand reports from 21 cities and counties on the benefits of risk management programs.

7 Some of this discussion of risk management planning is based on Charles K. Coe, *Understanding Risk Management: A Guide for Governments* (Athens: Institute of Government, Univ. of Georgia, 1980).

8 Nester R. Roos and Joseph S. Gerber, "Insurance and Risk Management," *The Municipal Year Book, 1973* (Washington, D.C.: International City Management Association, 1973), p. 113.

9 For a concise description of the fire insurance industry, including methods of setting rates, the application of the grading schedule, and areas of coverage, see Harry C. Bigglestone et al., "Other Organizations and the Fire Service," in *Managing Fire Services,* eds. John L. Bryan and Raymond C. Picard (Washington, D.C.: International City Management Association, 1979), pp. 92–108, 130–32.

10 J. D. Todd, "Management Techniques Applicable to City Insurance Programs," *Municipal Finance* 44 (August 1971):12.

11 W. G. Brockmeier, "Self-insurance vs. Insurance for Large Cities," *Municipal Finance* 44 (August 1971):20.

12 These advantages are abstracted from Alex Brown, "Self-Insurance Pooling Arrives in Colorado," *Colorado Municipalities,* March-April 1982; and Frank E. James, "Insurance Pooling," *Public Management* 67, no. 2 (February 1985):6.

13 New York State Legislature, Assembly Ways and Means Committee, *Municipal Insurance Pools* (Albany, N.Y.: State of New York, January 1980) and *Insurance Decisions: Rising Government Liabilities,* pp. 8–10.

14 Further discussion of both the benefits and the hazards of bidding may be found in Georgia Chapter, Society of Chartered Property and Casualty Underwriters, *Municipal Risk Management* (Cincinnati: National Underwriters Co., 1971), pp. 95–96.

15 Ronald P. Boggs and James A. Swanke, Jr., "Working with an Insurance Market in Turmoil," *Public Management* 67, no. 2 (February 1985): 5.

16 An important source of current information is *Best's Key Rating Guide,* which shows financial and management ratings for all stock companies. The minimum acceptable rating as far as local governments are concerned is A: Class XII.

17 Georgia Chapter, Society of Chartered Property and Casualty Underwriters, *Municipal Risk Management,* p. 107. An informative book that the risk manager should have at hand.

18 Abstracted from Phyllis Sherman, *Basic Risk Management Handbook for Local Governments* (Washington, D.C.: Public Risk and Insurance Management Association, 1983), pp. 50–51.

19 Lost income is a very difficult figure to measure reliably. Not only is income lost from flights that are canceled, but also city businesses may lose customers. Some of the loss undoubtedly is made up by substitute means of transportation.

20 J. D. Todd, *Effective Risk and Insurance Management in Municipal Government* (Austin: Institute of Public Affairs, Univ. of Texas, 1970), p. 61.

16 Unions, wages, and local government finance

Widespread public employee unionization and collective bargaining are among the most significant developments in local government over the past few decades. Whereas only 900,000 workers or 10.8 percent of all public employees were union members in 1960, 5.5 million or 34.9 percent were union members in the early 1980s.[1] Until about 1960, the growth of public-sector employee organizations, although steady, was slow. Because no statute guaranteed public-sector employees the right to bargain collectively, employers were able to resist demands for unionization.

This chapter focuses first on the extent of unionism in local government in the 1980s and the principal labor organizations involved. Next presented is a brief analysis of the legal context of public employee bargaining, with special emphasis on those aspects of bargaining (coverage, scope, and dispute settlement) that most directly affect local government finances. Wages and fringe benefits are then discussed, along with the effects of bargaining on compensation levels and on the municipal budgetary process. The chapter concludes with an analysis of comparable worth ("pay equity"), which promises to be the most important public-sector compensation issue of this decade.

Organizations of public employees

In the early 1980s, total union membership in the United States stood at 19.7 million workers and included approximately 18 percent of the total civilian labor force.[2] These figures reflect a steady decline in private-sector union membership (both in absolute numbers and as a percentage of the total labor force) over the past few decades. In contrast, however, they represent an explosive increase in public-sector union membership (at all levels of government) over roughly the same period. In 1982, almost 50 percent of all full-time *local* government employees were members of labor organizations. This figure is about three times as large as the corresponding percentage for all private-sector employees (see Table 16–1).

In contrast with employee unions in the private sector, public-sector unions are relatively heterogeneous. Some labor organizations are active at only one level of government (local, state, or federal), while others are active at all three levels; some are quite restrictive in their recruiting efforts, seeking to represent public employees in only certain occupations, while others will organize public employees of any type; and some labor organizations actively recruit workers in both the private and the public sectors. Table 16–1 shows that the percentage of organized local government employees varies substantially across functional employment categories, with fire fighters the most highly organized group and hospital employees the least organized.

Traditionally, unions and professional associations have operated with distinct and separate goals, the former more concerned with wages, benefits, and working conditions, and the latter more concerned with professional matters and the quality of services delivered. Today, however, with professional associations

Table 16–1 Percent of full-time employees organized in local government, by function, October 1982.

Local government function	Total full-time employees (000)	Organized full-time employees (000)	Organized employees as % of total
All local governments	7,314	3,579	48.9
Education	3,867	2,214	57.3
Highways	265	95	36.6
Public welfare	199	83	41.7
Hospitals	495	80	16.2
Police protection	513	266	51.9
Fire protection	228	152	66.5
Sanitation (other than sewerage)	108	47	43.8
All other functions	1,639	640	39.1

Source: U.S. Department of Commerce, Bureau of the Census, "Labor-Management Relations in State and Local Governments," *1982 Census of Governments,* vol. 3, *Government Employment* (Washington, D.C.: GPO, 1985).

having become increasingly concerned with the economic well-being of their membership, there is little difference between the two types of organizations.

This section briefly examines some of the major organizations representing significant numbers of local government employees.

AFSCME

The American Federation of State, County, and Municipal Employees (AFSCME) has been one of the most rapidly growing unions of public employees over the past two decades, although much of this growth has been due to AFSCME's absorption of other organizations (e.g., the Civil Service Employees Association in New York in 1978, the Arizona Public Employees Association in 1982, and the Ohio Civil Service Employees Association in 1983).[3] Its membership as of 1984 totaled just over 1 million, about half of whom are employees of local governments. Among its ranks are employees of almost all types (except for fire fighters and teachers) in local and state governments.

Police and fire fighters' organizations

Several organizations represent the majority of organized police officers. The Fraternal Order of Police (FOP) the oldest body, includes supervisors[4] and numbered approximately 170,000 members as of the mid-1980s. Despite the Order's prohibition against strikes, locals have (infrequently) gone on strike.

The International Union of Police Associations (IUPA) broke away from the now defunct International Conference of Police Associations in early 1979 and affiliated with the AFL-CIO. It has suffered a decline in membership in recent years, and as of the mid-1980s numbered approximately 16,000. Like the FOP, the IUPA does not endorse the strike, preferring legislation with binding arbitration. Most of its members are rank-and-file police officers, but the union has also chartered command officer associations.

Although the FOP and IUPA represent the majority of organized police officers, several other organizations (among them AFSCME, the Service Employees International Union [SEIU], and the International Brotherhood of Teamsters, Chauffeurs, Warehousemen, and Helpers of America [IBT] also represent police locals scattered throughout the United States.[5]

The International Association of Fire Fighters (IAFF) is the major organization representing fire fighters. Affiliated with the AFL-CIO, it claims a membership of 163,000, including both uniformed fire fighters and management. It is the only public employee union virtually without substantial competition in its organizational efforts. Like the police organizations, the IAFF has not openly espoused the strike, although this has not deterred some of its locals from striking.

Teachers' organizations

The bulk of the nation's teaching labor force are members of two major organizations, the National Education Association (NEA), which includes over 1,700,000 members, and the American Federation of Teachers (AFT), whose membership numbers approximately 583,000. The NEA is the oldest public-sector labor organization, dating back to the mid-1800s. Historically, the NEA has been concerned exclusively with professional and educational matters, but when faced with growing competition from the AFT in the 1960s, it began to promote collective negotiations among its constituent local associations. Although it is still the largest public-sector organization at any of the three levels of government, the NEA's membership has fallen somewhat over the past several years, reflecting the declining number of elementary and secondary school teachers.

Unlike the NEA, the AFT has managed to maintain its membership during the recent decline in the market for teachers, in part by organizing nurses and allied health care professionals through its Federation of Nurses and Health Professionals affiliate. From time to time in recent years, there have been movements to merge the two national teachers organizations; and, in fact, several local and state AFT and NEA affiliates have combined. However, the AFT's affiliation with the AFL-CIO has proved to be a major obstacle in this regard.

Hospital and health care workers' organizations

As noted earlier, workers in the health care industry are the least organized group of public employees. Only about 16 percent of all full-time workers in local government hospitals are members of labor organizations. Consequently, organized labor has conducted an intensely competitive recruiting drive in the health care industry (both public and private) over the past few years, with a large number of unions actively vying for members.

The American Nurses' Association (ANA) represents about 45,000 public-sector nurses in collective bargaining. Several years ago the ANA, which believes in the rights of supervisors to organize and bargain collectively, rescinded its long-standing no-strike policy. Like the fire fighter and police officer unions, some ANA locals include both supervisors and non-supervisors in the same unit.

The National Union of Hospital and Health Care Employees (NUHHCE), chartered in 1984, is affiliated with the AFL-CIO. The union was formerly a part of "District 1199," a multilocal health-care affiliate of the Retail, Wholesale, and Department Store Union (RWDSU). In 1984, however, after a prolonged political dispute within the RWDSU, all but the New York City local of District 1199 split from the parent body to form the new international health care union. Currently, the NUHHCE and the truncated District 1199 of the RWDSU each represents approximately 75,000 workers in the health care field.

Besides the groups mentioned above, other unions recruiting health care workers include AFSCME, SEIU, and such unlikely organizations as the United Food and Commercial Workers International Union (UFCW), the United Steelworkers of America (USA), the United Automobile Workers of America (UAW), the International Brotherhood of Electrical Workers (IBEW), and the American Federation of Teachers (AFT).

"Mixed" unions

A number of other major organizations that include both public- and private-sector employees in their memberships are the Service Employees International Union (SEIU) and the Teamsters (IBT).

As of the mid-1980s, SEIU membership numbered approximately 850,000 and represented a cross section of building maintenance workers, hospital workers, clerical workers, and various other groups. Approximately half of the SEIU's membership are public employees, the majority of whom work at the local government level (city, county, school district). The SEIU is one of the most rapidly growing U.S. labor organizations, largely as a result of recent mergers with formerly independent public employee organizations in California and several other states.

The Teamsters includes about 115,000 county and municipal employees in its overall membership of nearly 2 million. Most Teamsters' members are recruited from street and sanitation departments, but the union has also organized other groups of public employees, such as police officers, nurses, and clerical personnel. When the Teamsters established its Public Employees Trade Division in 1982, the union voiced a goal of organizing public-sector workers "wherever they are"[6]—the same type of sweeping organizational philosophy expressed by the Teamsters in its private-sector recruiting efforts.

To the list of significant mixed unions should be added the Laborers' International Union of North America (LIU) and the Communications Workers of America (CWA). Both AFL-CIO–affiliated unions represent substantial numbers of local government workers, the former mostly maintenance workers and unskilled construction workers and the latter a wide variety of white collar workers in schools, libraries, hospitals, social service agencies, and other government agencies at both the local and state levels.

It should be noted that the foregoing list of public-sector organizations is far from complete. A considerable number of smaller independent organizations are active in representing local government employees. However, detailed listing of all such groups is not possible since they are exempt from federal regulations that require the reporting of financial reports and other information.

The legal context of public employee bargaining

Government employees were specifically excluded from the 1935 National Labor Relations Act (NLRA) and the 1947 Labor Management Relations Act (LMRA) that bestowed on private-sector employees the right to unionize and bargain collectively. When local government employees did form unions, they had to depend on state or municipal laws, executive orders, or other avenues to protect themselves and legally engage in collective bargaining activities.

In 1959 Wisconsin became the first state to grant collective bargaining rights to local government employees. A surge of legislation in other states soon followed, and by 1985 39 states had laws granting bargaining rights to certain groups of government employees.[7] In several other states, bargaining was authorized by gubernatorial executive orders, state personnel boards, or opinions handed down by attorneys general. As a result, only a handful of states still have no legal or executive basis for authorizing collective bargaining for public employees.

Despite the near universality of legal authorization for collective bargaining, state laws are extremely varied on such issues as coverage, scope of bargaining, and dispute settlement procedures, each of which has significant financial implications. The following sections compare state laws for these three major legislative features.

Coverage and duty to bargain

Some state laws (like those of Michigan and New York) are comprehensive and cover virtually all local public employees, while others restrict coverage to certain groups, such as teachers or fire fighters (e.g., Maryland and Alabama).

The type of negotiations required by the statutes also varies across the states. Some statutes (such as those of Missouri) require only that the public employer "meet and confer" with employees, while most others mandate that "collective bargaining" take place. "Meet and confer" generally means that the public employer agrees only to *discuss* terms and conditions of employment. The agreement reached is written as a memorandum of understanding, rather than as a collective bargaining contract. In most "meet and confer" situations, the employer is not legally bound to negotiate or even to abide by the terms of the agreement. In collective bargaining, on the other hand, the public employer and the public employee representatives are equal parties in negotiations that result in a contract binding on both parties.

Scope of bargaining

As in the private sector, public-sector bargaining topics are classified according to whether they are mandatory, permissible, or illegal. The National Labor Relations Act (NLRA) defines the mandatory scope of bargaining for employees in the private sector as "wages, hours, and other terms and conditions of employment,"[8] but exactly what is mandatory has generated much controversy over the years. As one observer has noted, "mandatory topics[,] . . . those judged to be within the purview of 'wages, hours, and other terms and conditions of employment' . . . [have been] continually stretched to accommodate a wider variety of topics. Students today are astounded to learn that the subject of pensions became a mandatory subject of collective bargaining only after a Supreme Court decision."[9]

Most state laws have borrowed NLRA language in mandating public-sector bargaining over "wages, hours, and other terms and conditions of employment," but these laws also include specific details as to what may or may not be bargained. The Pennsylvania Public Employee Relations Act (Act 195), for example, states that:

> Public employers shall not be required to bargain over matters of inherent managerial policy, which shall include but shall not be limited to such areas of discretion or policy as the functions and programs of the public employer, standards of service, selection and direction of personnel. Public employers, however, shall be required to meet and discuss on policy matters affecting wages, hours and terms and conditions of employment as well as the impact thereon upon request by public employee representatives.[10]

Yet, despite this greater specificity, questions still arise, usually over "other terms and conditions of employment," rather than over wage and hour issues. Consequently, the courts are often called in to determine which subjects are negotiable. As one observer has noted, the result is a "staggering number of scope decisions which appear to be all over the lot. . . . "[11] Certainly from the union's point of view, if the scope of bargaining is too narrow, its potential effect is reduced; and from the perspective of management, if the scope is extremely broad, its operating flexibility may be weakened.

In general, the overall effect of legislation and court decisions has been to limit the scope of public-sector bargaining. There is, however, considerable variation among the states; what may be permissible in one is mandatory in another. For example, although wages are typically the single most important subject of public-sector bargaining, some wage-related issues (such as pensions) are not negotiable in certain states. Instead, they may be decided by legislative bodies. Where such matters are not subject to negotiation, unions frequently resort to lobbying and similar tactics to achieve their goals. Likewise, in the case of hours of work, the scope of collective bargaining is often circumscribed. In education, for instance, most states have set a minimum number of days for instruction, in effect fixing the work year for teachers.[12] Whereas work assignments, transfers, promotions, and layoffs are frequently negotiable issues in private employment, this is less likely to be the case in local government. In some localities, however, certain groups of public employees have been striving to change this and to include staffing requirements and other traditional management prerogatives within the scope of bargaining. In Wisconsin, for example, police officers and fire fighters have succeeded in bringing the personnel practices of police and fire chiefs to the bargaining table.[13]

Interestingly, since some statutes also specify certain subjects as management prerogatives, an "overlap" problem has occasionally arisen where a subject is both a condition of employment and a management prerogative. The best-known example is in teaching, with class size being both a condition of employment and an element of educational policy subject to the determination of management. Teachers in Michigan have successfully bargained for class size limitations, provisions for instruction and curriculum councils, and even student disciplinary procedures.[14]

In a real sense, the statutory and judicial treatment of scope issues is still evolving. In the opinion of one observer, "Decades of controversy have attended the gradual creation of a definition of legal scope in the private sector, and the process is still going on. This process is barely under way in the public sector."[15] Accordingly, it is advisable for public negotiators to try to obtain broad management rights clauses in their collective bargaining contracts.

Strikes and dispute settlement procedures

Until fairly recently, there was a universal ban on striking by state and local government employees. State statutes flatly prohibited strikes and some authorized severe penalties for violators. New York's Taylor Law prescribes forfeiture of tenure and loss of pay for striking government workers. Where no specific statutory mention was made, common law has usually held strikes to be illegal. However, over the past 10 to 15 years, this traditional ban against public-sector strikes has softened somewhat; as of the mid-1980s, 10 states permitted certain groups of public employees to strike.[16]

Although strike authorization laws vary widely across states, common features include the prohibition from striking for public safety employees such as police, fire fighters, and correctional employees, and the requirement that spelled-out dispute resolution procedures be exhausted before employees can legally strike. For example, in Oregon a legal strike cannot occur until both mediation and factfinding procedures have been exhausted and a 30-day period has elapsed after the factfinder's report has been made public.[17]

Despite the potential for permissive strike legislation to increase the level of strike activity by state and local government employees, most states have found that such legislation has made little difference in strike incidence, with the exception of Pennsylvania and Montana where increases in strike activity have occurred after passage of permissive legislation. In fact, since 1979 when the number of state and local government strikers peaked at more than 250,000, the overall level of strike activity by public-sector workers has fallen considerably.

An alternative for resolving public-sector disputes is peaceful impasse resolution procedures such as mediation and factfinding. In mediation, a third party assists management and the union in reaching agreement. Factfinding is more formal, usually used when mediation is unsuccessful. The factfinder is a neutral party who listens to evidence presented by both sides and then makes recommendations for settling the dispute.

A major limitation of both mediation and factfinding is the nonbinding nature of the recommendations, after which the impasse may remain. Consequently, many states (more than 30 as of 1985) provide for binding arbitration as the final step in the impasse resolution process for some or all governmental employees (most often, for police and fire fighters). The two major types of arbitration are "conventional" arbitration, in which the decision-making authority of the arbitrator is unrestricted, and "final offer" arbitration, in which the arbitrator must accept the terms of one of the parties. The major disadvantage of conventional arbitration is its alleged "chilling effect" on negotiations. If each party feels that the arbitrator's decision will only "split the difference" between the labor demand and the management offer, then there is no incentive for either party to compromise. Instead each party will stick to its initial demand (which may be considerably different from what it might ultimately agree to settle for) or even inflate that demand. In contrast, final offer arbitration requires that the arbitrator select the most reasonable terms of one party. Some statutes permit the arbitrator to select these terms item by item, while others require that the most reasonable package be accepted *in toto*. In either variant, the net effect is to encourage both labor and management to formulate more reasonable initial demands and to offer counterproposals in the collective bargaining process.

Unionism and earnings

This section describes how public-sector wage levels are determined, the actual role played by unions, and how fringe benefits fit into the picture. At heart is the controversial issue of whether public-sector employees, as compared with private-sector employees, are overpaid, a conclusion that might be drawn from a cursory look at some of the data and trends.

The ratio of public employee to private employee pay levels has varied substantially over the past few decades. As Table 16–2 shows, from 1955 to 1970 average government employee wages as a percentage of average private-sector employee wages rose from about 91 percent to 102 percent. However, these figures do not necessarily indicate that government employees were formerly underpaid and that by 1970 the situation was reversed. The mix of

Table 16–2 Average annual wages and salaries per full-time equivalent employee, private sector, and state and local governments, 1955–1983.

	Average wages and salaries private sector		Average wages and salaries, state and local government sector		
Year	$	Average annual change[a] (%)	$	Average annual change[a] (%)	% of private sector
1955	3,954	4.3	3,600	4.3	91
1960	4,856	4.2	4,544	4.8	94
1965	5,840	3.8	5,581	4.2	96
1970	7,649	5.6	7,804	6.9	102
1975	10,674	6.9	10,865	6.8	102
1980	15,749	8.1	15,142	6.9	96
1983	19,273	7.0	19,325	8.5	100

Source: U.S. Department of Commerce, Bureau of Economic Analysis, *National Income and Product Accounts of the U.S., 1929–74* (Washington, D.C.: GPO, 1974), and *Survey of Current Business* (various issues, 1975–85).

[a] Average annual rate of change from last listed year.

occupations in the public and private sectors is quite different, and there is no reason to suppose that the "ideal" relative wage ratio ought to equal 1. Rather, the figures simply indicate that wages were rising relatively faster for local and state government employees over the period. The wages and salaries for government employees include both local *and* state employees, although the majority (71 percent in 1983) are in local government.

The rising trend in government worker wages is not surprising. The demand for government services of all kinds—education, health care, public welfare—grew remarkably over this period. Consequently, the demand for public workers to deliver these services also rose. Furthermore, this period of relative wage gains for public employees occurred at precisely the same time that public employee unionism became firmly established among state and local government workers. Since 1975, however, the relative wages of public employees have fallen—along with declining employment and union penetration in the public sector. Moreover, the fiscal difficulties of many municipalities and the growing feeling that public employees may be "overpaid" have put a further damper on the growth of public employee wages. Interestingly, the public-sector/private-sector relative wage ratio appears to be rising again in the mid-1980s, although this may be due in part to the lower private-sector wage growth associated with high levels of unemployment during the period.

Wage determination

Pay policy at the local government level depends on a variety of determining factors: unionism, collective bargaining, minimum wage laws, equal pay legislation and other antidiscrimination statutes, prevailing wage requirements, and merit pay practices. Harry Katz and David Lewin have stated that public pay-setting procedures are probably best viewed as falling within a spectrum bounded by two major idealized types or "models."[18] At one end of the spectrum is the civil service model, in which wages are set at levels prevailing in comparable private-sector jobs. At the other end of the spectrum is the collective bargaining model, whereby labor and management jointly negotiate compensation levels that reflect the relative bargaining power of the two groups.

The civil service model In the civil service model, management has unilateral power to establish pay but ordinarily delegates this authority to an independent commission or agency. Pay is usually determined with reference to comparable jobs in the private sector at the rates prevailing in these jobs. This standard, known as the "prevailing-wage principle," is widely followed by state and local governments when establishing pay-setting procedures. In theory, this practice seems reasonable, for it guarantees (1) equity and (2) efficiency by ensuring through its comparable pay scale that the government employer is able to attract high-quality workers. However, in practice, adherence to the prevailing-wage principle can lead to public-sector pay levels *higher* than those in the private sector.[19]

There are several reasons for this potential upward bias in public-sector pay. First, because procuring wage information from small firms is costly, government employers systematically exclude small firms from their wage surveys. The result is a significant wage bias. It has been estimated that employees in the private sector who work in establishments employing fewer than 250 employees (and who are thus likely to be excluded from salary comparison surveys) are paid approximately 15 to 20 percent less than employees in firms with 1,000 or more employees.[20]

Second, government employers often match private pay levels that have been raised through the exercise of union power and unusual market forces. Yet, they seldom match private pay scales that are unusually low—because of a situation of "monopsony," where one or a few firms employ the bulk of the area's labor force.[21]

Finally, government policy for setting wages for certain "unique" public-sector jobs (jobs with no private-sector equivalents, such as police, fire protection, and sometimes sanitation) also results in an upward bias to public-sector pay. Many municipalities have a system of pay "parity" for these occupations, whereby salaries are tied by some sort of fixed formula.[22] Because of the differences in the attractiveness of the occupations, the parity pay principle has sometimes resulted in overpayment of fire fighters.[23] Clearly, then, the civil service model for determining wages has the *potential* to raise public-sector pay levels above those of the private sector, even in the absence of unionism. This potential, it should be added, seems to be present for all public-sector occupations, except high-level managerial and professional categories.[24]

The collective bargaining model In the collective bargaining model of wage determination, labor and management jointly negotiate compensation levels. Indeed, the concept of bargaining power is one of the major arguments supporting the right of workers to organize and to bargain collectively.[25] A worker facing management alone may be at a substantial disadvantage in negotiating terms of employment, whereas collective negotiation usually results in a more equitable distribution of bargaining power.

Neil Chamberlain has suggested a simple, yet useful, definition of "bargaining power": the ability of one party (e.g., labor) to secure the agreement of another party (e.g., management) on the first party's terms. Labor's ability (or power) to secure an agreement, for example, depends on the costs to management of agreement relative to the costs of disagreement. The costs of agreement include the lost opportunity to obtain a lower wage settlement should management hold out for a longer period of time, while costs of disagreement include those costs incurred by a prolonged strike. Obviously, the higher the ratio of the relative costs of disagreement and agreement to management (or labor), the higher the bargaining power of labor (or management).[26]

If collective bargaining is a viable method of determining wages and other terms of employment for workers in the public sector, then the bargaining power of unions (or of management) must not be "excessive." Most economists would define "excessive" as substantially greater than the norm in the private sector. There, for example, the market restrains and disciplines union wage demands. Were an excessive wage settlement reached, costs would be passed along to the consumer with a resulting decline in quantity demanded. The public sector, however, exhibits much less responsiveness to the market. After all, many of the services performed by public employees are essential and non-substitutable (e.g., police, fire fighting, sanitation). The public usually has neither the desire nor the option to demand fewer such services should they become more expensive as a result of higher wages. Because of low elasticity of demand,[27] some public-sector unions seem to have excessive bargaining power, enabling them to raise wages without fear of job loss, the usual brake on union wage demands in the private sector.[28] According to the Chamberlain bargaining power model, then, many public-sector unions can enhance their bargaining power by making it costly for the public employer to disagree with a given set of demands. These costs may extend beyond the budget, as well. A transport strike, for example, may so inconvenience the local citizenry that enormous political pressure to settle the dispute will be exerted on local officials.

Some economists do note, however, that not all arguments support the notion that the bargaining power of public employee unions is necessarily greater than that of most private-sector unions. Although public employers, as providers of government services, do not face local competition, they are still subject to the "discipline of the budget." In addition, local governments must be concerned with the possible exodus of residents and businesses. Furthermore, unlike private-sector unions, which are generally free to use the strike weapon, public employee unions in the great majority of states are still prohibited from striking for wages.

Effect of unions

As Table 16–3 shows, the effect of unions on wages of local government employees varies by occupation. In the case of teachers, the observed differential has been rather small—5 percent or less. For police officers and fire fighters, the effects have been somewhat greater, perhaps reflecting the bargaining power possessed by these two groups. On the average, however, the findings summarized in the table suggest that public-sector unions have had a positive but limited effect on wages. The estimated relative wage differentials associated with local public employee bargaining are almost never more than 15 percent and usually considerably less. This finding refutes the contention that unionism and collective bargaining have had a substantial effect on the wages of public-sector employees. On the contrary, the effects of unionism on public-sector wages seem to be smaller than those observed for unions in the private sector, where the most reliable evidence suggests that the average union/non-union wage differential is about 15 to 20 percent.

Table 16–3 Wage effects of unions at local government level according to several representative studies.

Occupational group	Time period	Earnings differentials for unionized employees (%)
Fire fighters[a]	1976	0–4
Hospital employees[b]	1977	8–12
Library workers[c]	1977	0
Police, fire fighters, and sanitation workers[d]	1975	7–14
Teachers[e]	1970	0–5
Secretaries[f]	1978	7

[a] Casey Ichniowski, "Economic Effects of the Firefighters' Union," *Industrial and Labor Relations Review* 33 (January 1980): 198–211.
[b] Roger Feldman and Richard Scheffler, "The Union Impact on Hospital Wages and Fringe Benefits," *Industrial and Labor Relations Review,* 35 (January 1982): 190–206.
[c] Ronald Ehrenberg, Daniel Sherman, and Joshua Schwartz, "Unions and Productivity in the Public Sector: The Case of Municipal Libraries," *Industrial and Labor Relations Review,* 36 (January 1983): 199–213.
[d] Richard Victor, "Municipal Unions and Wage Patterns," in Industrial Relations Research Association, *Proceedings of the Thirty-second Annual Meetings* (28–30 December 1979, Atlanta) (Madison, Wisconsin), pp. 294–99.
[e] Robert Thornton, "The Effects of Collective Negotiations on Teachers' Salaries," *Quarterly Review of Economics and Business* 11 (Winter 1971): 37–46.
[f] David Balkin, "The Effect of Unions on the Compensation of Secretaries in Municipal Government," *Journal of Collective Negotiations in the Public Sector,* 13 (1984): 29–37.

Ascertaining whether or not public employees are overpaid has involved comparing public and private compensation levels for similar *jobs* in both sectors, and comparing public and private compensation levels for *workers* of similar characteristics in both sectors. The first approach has been limited because the U.S. Bureau of Labor Statistics (BLS) has only recently begun to collect data on municipal and (comparable) private-sector wage levels, and the BLS sample is rather small, restricted to cities of at least 500,000 population. In 1975 clerical workers in the city governments sampled had a 4 percent average pay advantage over their private industry counterparts. By 1980, however, this advantage disappeared, and municipal clerical workers were paid an average of 2 percent *less* than their private-sector counterparts. A similar turnaround characterized the relative pay performance of skilled maintenance workers. A 7 percent average pay advantage for such municipal workers in 1975 turned into a 3 percent disadvantage by 1980.[29] It is important to note that these averages mask a sizable degree of variation in public/private pay levels across the cities studied, however.

The second approach involves comparing pay levels in both sectors for workers with similar personal characteristics, such as age and education. Sharon Smith's widely cited 1975 findings show that men employed by local governments earned slightly less than their private-sector counterparts, while women earned slightly more. When Smith analyzed new data for 1978, she found that both male and female government employees were at a slight pay disadvantage.[30]

This evidence comparing both public/private jobs and public/private workers supports the conclusion that in general municipal workers are *not* overpaid. Whatever pay advantage some local government workers held over their private-sector counterparts during the early and mid-seventies has apparently disappeared in the more restrictive spending climate of the late seventies and the eighties. That certain occupations and localities overpay their workers is apparently the exception, not the rule.

Fringe benefits

The evidence presented so far has been restricted *only* to wage and salary levels, exclusive of fringe benefits. Fringe benefits include pensions, Social Security, vacations, health benefits, and workers' compensation. Are fringe benefits in the public sector higher than in the private sector? Since 1970 the Labor-Management Relations Service (LMRS) of the National League of Cities has conducted several surveys of benefits paid to municipal employees. The 1982 LMRS survey indicates that cities were indeed spending a higher percentage of pay for fringe benefits than was private industry. For the municipalities studied, fringe benefits comprised 47.5 percent of pay for hours worked in 1979 for police and fire personnel and 43.8 percent for general municipal personnel. The corresponding percentage for all private industry personnel was estimated by the LMRS to be 42.2 percent. Furthermore, the LMRS notes, for employees of municipalities the survey is likely to *underestimate* the true percentages. Because many local government pension plans are inadequately funded, municipalities are reporting pension costs lower than the value of accruing benefits. According to the LMRS survey, the upward adjustment necessary to reflect more accurately the true benefit percentage for municipal workers is from 3 to 6 percent of pay for hours worked.[31]

There is other evidence that public employees enjoy more generous fringe benefits than do private-sector employees. Alicia Munnell and Ann Connolly found that public-sector pension plans are typically more liberal than private-sector plans, even after taking into consideration the employee contributions required by most public plans (and not usually required in private-sector pension plans). Munnell and Connolly also noted that public plans are much more likely to have COLAs (cost-of-living adjustments) and to offer earlier retirement ages than do private plans. Finally, Munnell and Connolly concluded that although *wages* are about equal in both sectors, the generous provisions of public pension plans have resulted in overall superior levels of public-sector compensation. The difference is especially pronounced for uniformed workers (fire and police) at the state and local levels.[32]

One reason for such fringe benefit and compensation differences between the two sectors is that while public-sector wages and salaries are generally set at levels "prevailing" in the private sector, the levels of fringe benefits are not. Local governments (and other governments, as well) would therefore be well advised to apply prevailing standards to the entire compensation package to ensure that their employees are neither underpaid nor overpaid with respect to total compensation. It is important to note that even before widespread unionization, many local governments were relatively generous with fringe benefits.[33] However, higher fringe benefit levels (along with greater job security) were in the past usually considered to be trade-offs for lower pay levels in the public sector—a situation that generally no longer exists today.

Finally, how does unionism affect fringe benefits? Most of the existing studies have estimated the impact of unions only on wages and not on fringe benefits or on total compensation. But a growing body of evidence suggests that private-sector unions have succeeded in raising the level of fringe benefits to a greater extent than they have raised wages,[34] and there are strong *a priori* grounds for supposing that this may also be the case in the public sector. It is easier to mask the real long-run costs of generous fringe benefit settlements at the public-sector bargaining table, particularly in the case of pensions where substantial under-funding may occur. There is also supporting evidence—though limited—that the impact of unions on public-sector fringe benefits may outweigh their impact on wages. One study of fire fighters found that the union/non-union fringe benefit effect was several times as large as the corresponding effect of wages.[35] Similarly, a study of collective bargaining for sanitation workers found a considerably larger union impact on fringe benefits than on wages.[36] It is important to note that not all such studies have reached similar conclusions. Furthermore, although the magnitude of union/non-union relative wage effects in the public sector may understate the effect of unions on total compensation, it is not obvious that it does so by any greater amount than in the private sector.

Collective bargaining and the budget

Although the actual effects of unions on public-sector compensation may not be excessive, it is generally agreed that unions have created additional pressure on local government budgets—both on the budget-making process and on budget size.

When formulating the budget for the forthcoming fiscal year, budget makers should allow sufficient time for the various local departments and agencies to calculate their budgetary requirements, submit them for review, and have them adopted or amended by the governing body. Traditional procedures for and timing of the budget process were originally developed when the public employer exercised sole control over the determination of employee compensation. These traditional practices are not always compatible with the modern restraints imposed by collective bargaining. Budget timetables sometimes break down when collective bargaining continues through the budget finalization date without an agreement. The result, of course, is considerable uncertainty for budget makers, who must await the bargaining outcome before they can determine their final expenditure allocations. In addition, they must often re-order their funding allocations and search for additional revenue sources, or else run the risk of a budget deficit. In short, bargaining is usually associated with a decrease in the public employer's ability to control and manage the budget.

Yet bargaining and budget making are flexible processes, and local governments have availed themselves of a variety of techniques to cope with their diminished control over the budget schedule. Some try to begin the bargaining process as early as nine months before the beginning of the new fiscal year in the hope of reducing the chance that bargaining will continue past the budget finalization date.[37] Indeed, some unions follow the strategy of timing collective bargaining (and perhaps the threat of a strike) to coincide with the budget submission deadline.[38] By exerting union pressure at this time, they try to force the hand of the public employer. Yielding to union demands is the price to be paid for completing the budget according to schedule.

Some local governments have tried to coordinate the collective bargaining schedule and the budget schedule by mandating legislation that ties the bargaining schedule to the fiscal year. For example, a Rhode Island statute requires that organizations of public employees must give written notice requesting collective bargaining at least 120 days before the final date on which the municipality may appropriate funds. According to at least two studies, however, this strategy has not been very successful. Milton Derber found that although two-thirds of the Illinois governmental units that he studied linked their bargaining contract expiration dates to that of the fiscal year, more than half of them failed to reach agreement with the unions before the budget finalization date.[39] In a survey of Iowa municipalities, Richard Kearney reported similar problems in trying to coordinate the budget and bargaining schedules legislatively. Even though the Iowa Public Employee Relations Act sets a deadline of March 15 for the completion of negotiations, nearly 60 percent of the cities analyzed reported at least one existing contract dispute after the deadline.[40]

Other approaches to dealing with the problem of synchronizing the bargaining and budget processes include adopting budgets with *estimates* of wage and salary levels that are still to be negotiated. In his survey of public bargaining practices in Illinois, Derber found this practice to be fairly common.[41] In the event that the estimated wage allowance proves to be too low, however, additional funds may have to be provided. In Derber's survey, such additional funds were normally provided by transfers within or between budget funds, supplemental appropriations, borrowing, or higher taxes.

"Overbudgeting" or "padding" often occurs when future wage settlements are estimated. Funds that can be used to finance a higher-than-anticipated wage settlement are sometimes hidden within various budget categories. However, this practice is marked by disadvantages that limit its usefulness as a management tactic. For example, as Derber notes, many public employers feel that padded items can usually be detected by skillful union negotiators in the budget-search process. In fact, the tactic may even backfire if union negotiators discover the overbudgeted amount and make it a target for additional bargaining demands.[42]

Two other devices that help minimize the extent to which collective bargaining might clash with the budget schedule are the retroactive pay practice and the long-term contract. Retroactive pay allows the terms of the settlement to be backdated to the expiration date of the original contract. Long-term contracts (i.e., contracts of two or three years' duration) are attractive because they reduce the number of opportunities for negotiation impasses to interfere with the budgetary process. Long-term contracts can also save the public employer the additional time and expense of yearly contract negotiations.[43]

Finally, it is important that the public employer have an informed and well-planned negotiation strategy. Such a strategy requires that detailed costing of all union demands be undertaken during negotiations. Careful costing is a *sine qua non* for the public employer in the negotiation process, not only to prevent later budget overruns, but also to inform union negotiators of the true costs to the city or county of a certain proposal.[44] Furthermore, effective negotiations require the public employer to have a positive set of proposals regarding wages, salaries, and fringe benefits. This set of proposals should have as a frame of reference the budget proposed for the coming year and it should be based on such information as changes in the consumer price index, local labor market conditions, and pay levels in other communities. Such a well-planned negotiation strategy will go far to increase the probability of successful negotiations.

Comparable worth

Comparable worth or "pay equity" is a new, significant, and controversial issue that has emerged in the area of public-sector compensation and union-management bargaining. Comparable worth deals with the male-female "pay gap," which, despite nearly two decades of enforcement of civil rights and equal pay laws, has not narrowed. Average annual earnings of women working full time still amount to only about 60 percent of the earnings of full-time employed men. The problem (as both proponents and opponents of comparable worth agree) is *not* primarily one of women receiving lower pay than men in the same jobs—in other words, the problem is not wage discrimination. The Equal Pay Act of 1963 prohibits an employer from paying women less than men for jobs which are the same. Rather, the problem is that employment of women is heavily concentrated in a few occupational categories—secretary, nurse, teacher, for example—that tend to carry with them low pay scales. Comparable worth proponents propose that equal pay be required for jobs that can be shown to be of comparable "worth" or "value" to an employer, even though they are dissimilar. The "worth" or "value" of such jobs is to be determined by a variety of job evaluation techniques.

In 1981 the U.S. Supreme Court opened the door to judicial consideration of sex-based discrimination charges involving inter-occupational wage differences. The case in question—*County of Washington* v. *Gunther* [452 U.S. 161 (1981)]—concerned female prison matrons (guards) who received only 75 percent of male prison guard pay, although a job evaluation had determined that the matrons' jobs were "worth" 95 percent of the male rate. The court did not endorse the comparable worth theory, but it did rule that the county employer had indeed discriminated against the matrons, and it ordered pay remedies. Several other well-publicized court cases (e.g., *AFSCME* v. *State of Washington*) have given further impetus to the comparable worth movement. Furthermore, as of the mid-1980s four states (Washington, Iowa, New Mexico, and Minnesota) and a number of municipalities (e.g., Los Angeles and San Jose) had taken steps to equalize pay levels between predominantly female jobs and comparable male jobs. In addition, a number of other states and municipalities have established task forces to study the possible implementation of comparable worth policies.

On the other hand, during the Reagan administration the federal Equal Employment Opportunity Commission ruled that it will not act on behalf of women who allege discrimination on comparable worth grounds. In addition, many economists have come out strongly against comparable worth pay policies for a variety of reasons:

1. Such policies ignore market demand and supply forces
2. Such policies rely on the process of job evaluation, which at best is inexact and subjective
3. Female job concentration (and, hence, a sizable part of the overall pay gap) is due in large part to the preference of many women for jobs that allow for relatively easy exit from and reentry into the labor force.[45]

Whatever the respective merits of the arguments concerning comparable worth, clearly it constitutes one of the most important compensation issues of the 1980s in the United States. Although not restricted to the public sector, comparable worth is more likely to establish a strong foothold there than in the private sector, at least for the immediate future. This foothold is likely to be established through the collective bargaining process, through legislative action, and through the courts. So far, the comparable worth notion has been pushed principally by AFSCME, the nation's largest union of nonteaching government employees, but several other public-sector unions (e.g., the SEIU and the NEA) have also lent their endorsement.

In light of the growing level of concern over comparable worth, what advice can be given to public-sector employers? For those employers who do *not* currently have job evaluation systems, there is serious disagreement within the legal profession as to whether to initiate such systems. Many legal advisers contend that job evaluation studies should not be undertaken lest employers unwittingly provide potential plaintiffs with ammunition for pay equity suits in the future. Some human resource professionals, on the other hand, have suggested that a carefully crafted pay study can be a useful asset in dealing with comparable worth claims.[46] According to the American Society for Personnel Administration (ASPA), public employers should consider a number of questions in deciding whether a pay study should be undertaken:

1. Is there a need to bring coherence to a wage structure that has developed in an *ad hoc* fashion over the years?
2. Are managers spending a considerable amount of time determining salaries for new positions or adjusting individual wages?
3. Is there a perception among employees that the wage system is haphazard or unfair?
4. Could a job evaluation system be employed to show that some employees' wage demands are inconsistent with the worth of their positions to the organization?

If the answers to these questions are "yes," then ASPA suggests that a pay study is probably appropriate.[47]

Despite the position of some comparable worth advocates that the labor market itself reflects discrimination in pay setting, the courts have generally held that employers do *not* have to ignore the market in setting wage rates. As long as employers can demonstrate that women's access to jobs traditionally held by men is not restricted, market rates generally are a reasonable guideline for pay-setting practices.

Conclusion

This chapter has described the major characteristics of unionism in local government and analyzed the impact of unions on wages and salaries, fringe benefits, and budgets. As the evidence points out, municipal pay levels do not (on average) exceed pay levels for comparable jobs (or comparable workers) in the private sector. However, when fringe benefits are included, the average municipal employee is compensated at a higher rate than is the average private-sector employee. Yet, the principal reason for this "overcompensation" does not appear to be the "excessive" bargaining power of public-sector unions. Indeed, the statistical evidence indicates that the effects of unions on wages in the public sector have been relatively modest. Instead, the reason appears to be the tendency for local governments to follow standards prevailing in the private sector in setting pay levels, but to ignore such standards in deciding fringe benefit levels. In many cases, local government employees enjoy both higher compensation and greater job security. Of course, the job security traditionally associated with public employment is not and never has been absolute for local government employee layoffs do occur. Public employment, however, still appears to be much more "recession-proof" than employment in most industries in the private sector, and a case can be made for public compensation levels to reflect this fact.[48]

The likely spread of pay policies based on comparable worth will no doubt push public-sector compensation to still higher levels and create additional strains on municipal budgets. It is worth noting, however, that if wages are increasingly set automatically according to job evaluation procedures, one of the most important reasons for the existence of unions may disappear. This realization could eventually dampen the desire of unions to adopt comparable worth pay policies. To date, however, this has not happened, as attested by the enthusiasm of AFSCME, SEIU, and several other labor organizations for the "pay equity" movement.

1 Leo Troy and Neil Sheflin, "The Flow and Ebb of U.S. Public Sector Unionism," *Government Union Review,* 2, no. 5 (Spring 1984): 1–2. Public-sector union membership peaked in 1976—numbering more than 6 million—and the numbers have decreased slightly since then.

2 Courtney Gifford, *Directory of U.S. Labor Organizations 1984–85* (Washington, D.C.: Bureau of National Affairs, 1985), p. 2.

3 Troy and Sheflin, "The Flow," p. 34.

4 Hervey Juris and Peter Feuille, *Police Unionism* (Lexington, Mass.: Lexington Books, 1974), p. 11.

5 Ibid., p. 29.

6 Cited in Bureau of National Affairs, *Government Employee Relations Report,* 8 March 1982.

7 In 1985 only the following 11 states had not passed permissive legislation of some type regarding public employee bargaining: Arizona, Arkansas, Colorado, Louisiana, Mississippi, New Mexico, North Carolina, South Carolina, Utah, Virginia, and West Virginia.

8 Title 1, Sec. 8(d) of Labor Management Relations Act, 1947.

9 Walter J. Gershenfeld, "An Introduction to the Scope of Bargaining in the Public Sector," Chapter 1 in Gershenfeld, J. Joseph Loewenberg, Bernard Ingster eds. *Scope of Public-Sector Bargaining* (Lexington, Mass.: Lexington Books, D. C. Heath and Co., 1977), p. 2. The Supreme Court decision alluded to is *Inland Steel Company* v. *United Steelworkers of America,* 336 U.S. 960 (1949).

10 Section 702 of Pennsylvania Act 195 (1970).

11 R. Theodore Clark, Jr., "The Scope of the Duty to Bargain in Public Employment," in Andria S. Knapp, ed., *Labor Relations Law in the Public Sector* (Chicago: American Bar Association, Section of Labor Relations Law, 1977), p. 82.

12 Michael H. Moskow, J. Joseph Loewenberg, and Edward Clifford Koziara, *Collective Bargaining in Public Employment* (New York: Random House, 1970), pp. 241–42.

13 James L. Stern, "The Scope of Bargaining in the Public Sector in Wisconsin," Chapter 9 in Gershenfeld, Loewenberg, Ingster, eds., *Scope of Public-Sector Bargaining,* p. 199.

14 Charles M. Rehmus, "The Scope of Bargaining in the Public Sector in Michigan," Chapter 3 in Gershenfeld, Loewenberg, Ingster, eds., *Scope of Public-Sector Bargaining,* pp. 21–22.

15 B. V. H. Schneider, "Public Sector Labor Legislation—An Evolutionary Analysis," Chapter 6 in Benjamin Aaron, Joseph R. Grodin, and James L. Stern, eds., *Public Sector Bargaining* (Washington, D.C.: Bureau of National Affairs, Industrial Relations Research Association Series, 1979), p. 208.

16 The 10 states and the enactment dates of strike authorization are Alabama (1972), Hawaii (1970), Illinois (1983), Minnesota (1971), Montana (1969), Ohio (1983), Oregon (1983), Pennsylvania (1970), Wisconsin (1978), and Vermont (1973).

17 Robert D. Pursley, "An Analysis of Permissible Strike Authorization among Public Workers," *Journal of Collective Negotiations in the Public Sector,* 13(3) (1984): 266–67.

18 Harry Katz and David Lewin, "Efficiency and Equity Considerations in State and Local Government Wage Determination," *Proceedings of the Thirty-third Annual Meetings of the Industrial Relations Research Association* (Denver, 5–7 September 1980), pp. 90–91.

19 Walter Fogel and David Lewin, "Wage Determination in the Public Sector," *Industrial and Labor Relations Review* 27, no. 3 (April 1974): 411, 413–14.

20 Richard Lester, "Pay Differentials by Size of Establishment," *Industrial Relations* 7, no. 1 (October 1967): 57–67.

21 A situation of employer monopsony (literally, "one buyer") will generally lead to wage levels below those that would exist in a competitive labor market with large numbers of buyers and sellers of labor.

22 Juris and Feuille, *Police Unionism,* pp. 121–22.

23 Fogel and Lewin, "Wage Determination," p. 427.

24 According to Fogel and Lewin "Wage Determination," p. 416, public employees in managerial and professional jobs tend to be more "visible" to a public that is largely skeptical of the value of highly paid employees.

25 For example, according to the Labor Management Relations Act of 1947, the "inequality of bargaining power between employees . . . and certain employers" was held to be one of the justifications for implementing the policies of the Act (Title I, Section 1, of the Labor Management Relations Act, 1947).

26 Neil W. Chamberlain and James W. Kuhn, *Collective Bargaining,* 2d ed. (New York: McGraw-Hill, 1965).

27 The elasticity of demand for labor can be defined as the percent change in quantity demanded given a unit percent change in the wage.

28 There are forces operating in the public sector that *seem* to make the immediate cost of agreement to a union's demands *lower* than might be the case in the private sector. In the case of a multiyear contract or a change in a municipal pension plan, for example, full consequences of the union demands are delayed for several years, or even generations. By that time, political leadership will have changed hands, and the full costs of the agreement will be borne—but by another generation.

29 Felice Porter and Richard L. Keller, "Public and Private Pay Levels: A Comparison in Large Labor Markets," *Monthly Labor Review* 104 (July 1981): 22–26.

30 Sharon P. Smith, "Are State and Local Government Workers Overpaid?" in Werner Z. Hirsch and Anthony M. Rufolo, eds., *The Economics of Municipal Labor Markets* (Los Angeles, Cal.: Institute of Industrial Relations, Univ. of California, 1983).

31 Edward H. Friend and Lorraine A. Lufkin, *Fifth National Survey of Employee Benefits for Full-time Personnel of U.S. Municipalities* (Washington, D.C.: Labor-Management Relations Service of the U.S. Conference of Mayors, 1982), p. 3. The survey reflects data for 1979.

32 Alicia H. Munnell and Ann M. Connolly, "Comparability of Public and Private Compensation: The Issue of Fringe-Benefits," *New England Economic Review,* July/August 1979: 27–45.

33 David T. Stanley, *Managing Local Government under Union Pressure* (Washington, D.C.: Brookings Institution, 1972), p. 83.

34 Richard B. Freeman, "The Effect of Unionism on Fringe Benefits," *Industrial and Labor Relations Review* 34 (July 1981): 489–510.

35 Casey Ichniowski, "Economic Effects of the Firefighters' Union," *Industrial and Labor Relations Review* 33 (January 1980): 198–211.

36 Linda Edwards and Franklin Edwards, "Public Unions, Local Government Structure, and the Compensation of Municipal Sanitation Workers," *Economic Inquiry* 20 (July 1982): 405–25.

37 Alan Edward Bent and T. Zane Reeves, *Collective Bargaining in the Public Sector: Labor-Management*

Relations and Public Policy (Menlo Park, Cal.: Benjamin-Cummings Publishing Co., 1978), p. 19.

38 Stanley, *Managing Local Government*, p. 116.

39 Milton Derber et al., "Bargaining and Budget Making in Illinois Public Institutions" *Industrial and Labor Relations Review* 27, no. 1 (October 1973): 49.

40 Richard C. Kearney, "Monetary Impact of Collective Bargaining," in Jack Rabin et al., *Handbook on Public Personnel Administration and Labor Relations* (New York: Marcel Dekker, 1983), p. 368.

41 Derber et al., "Bargaining and Budget Making," p. 57.

42 Stanley, *Managing Local Government*, p. 119.

43 Joseph Domritz, "Collective Bargaining and Public Administration: The Role of Long-Term Contracts," in *Collective Bargaining and Public Administration* (Chicago: Public Personnel Association, 1971), pp. 16–17.

44 Bent and Reeves, *Collective Bargaining*, p. 135.

45 An article that addresses these economic arguments and criticisms is R. J. Thornton, "The Economic Case Against Comparable Worth," *Journal of Collective Negotiations in the Public Sector* 15(1)(1986): 53–59.

46 "Plan Compensation Studies Carefully Due to Pay Equity Climate, ASPA Says," *Government Employer Relations Report* 23 (20 May 1985): 750.

47 American Society for Personnel Administrators, *Sex and Salary: A Legal and Personnel Analysis of Comparable Worth* (Alexandria, Va.: ASPA Foundation, 1985). The recommendations noted above were excerpted and adapted from the *Government Employee Relations Report* 23 (20 May 1985).

48 See Robert Bednarzik, "The Plunge of Employment During the Recent Recession," *Monthly Labor Review* 98, no. 12 (December 1975): 3–4

17 Capital budgeting

The capital budget indicates the local government's planned outlays on desirable long-term public projects. It analyzes how the city or county plans to finance such projects as roads and bridges, public buildings, utility systems, and recreational and cultural facilities.

This chapter examines the major steps in preparing a capital budget—selecting and evaluating the projects to be undertaken, forecasting the fiscal resources of the community, and projecting the effect of alternative financing methods on the operating budget. The chapter shows in detail how to calculate the net present value or the internal rate of return for projects, how to organize and construct a fiscal resource study based on projected revenues and expenditures, and how to select a financing method for capital needs. The chapter concludes with a brief discussion of pass-through financing, that is, using the credit of the city or county to support projects of nongovernmental organizations.

Selection and evaluation of capital projects

A capital expenditure may be defined as an outlay for the construction or purchase of a facility that is expected to provide services over a considerable period of time, in contrast to a current or operating expenditure, which is for an item or service that is consumed in a short time. Moreover, a capital expenditure usually is relatively large compared with expenditures for items in the operating budget. The definition of a capital expenditure may vary with the size of a community and its budget. In a small locality, expenditures on police patrol cars may be part of the capital budget, whereas in a large city patrol cars may be purchased annually under a regular operating budget appropriation. Even in a large city, however, the operating budget should distinguish between (1) regular operating expenses and (2) recurring expenditures for small capital items. Recurring outlays for such capital items as typewriters should be given special attention even though the appropriation is part of the regular operating budget rather than the capital budget.

In addition to its service as a planning tool, the capital budget has a public relations function. Thus, in many jurisdictions the capital budget will contain maps, attractive sketches, and pictures of proposed capital projects.

Because the capital budget involves relatively large projects meant to serve the city or county for some time, its components should be analyzed carefully. Although requests for capital projects may originate with diverse groups—the operating departments, the administrative officers, the planning commission, or ad hoc committees of interested citizens—the responsibility for analysis and evaluation of capital expenditure requests should be centralized. Decisions on capital projects generally should be given to the planning department or agency under the direction of the chief administrator of the city or county. On the basis of information supplied by economic base studies, land use reports, and population studies, the planning agency—with the direct aid and input of the finance department—should make an economic and financial evaluation of each proposed project, and determine which ones should be included in the capital budget to be submitted to the appropriate local governing body. The priorities, timing, and selection of the projects in the capital improvements program are not the sole responsibility of the finance officer, but the finance department should be instrumental in quantifying the economic desirability of the proposed projects.

Determining worthwhile projects

In theory, determining worthwhile public capital investments is straightforward. A public investment is desirable when the present value of its estimated flow of benefits, discounted at the community's cost of capital, exceed or equals its cost.

Two standard criteria are used for making these determinations: (1) net present value (NPV) and (2) internal rate of return. As shown in the accompanying sidebar, net present value is obtained by subtracting the initial outlays from the gross present value of the benefits, which are calculated by discounting at the community's "interest rate." The stream of net future benefits, which includes all gains to the community, must be quantified: each year's return is discounted to obtain its present value, and the sum of present values is compared with the immediate outlay on the project. If the sum of the present values of the benefits exceeds the outlay, the project should be accepted—if there is no alternative project with a higher NPV.

The internal rate of return (see sidebar) is the rate that brings the present value (PV) of the benefit flow into equality with the initial outlay. If the internal rate of return exceeds the community's interest rate, the project is economically feasible and should be undertaken—if there are no competing alternative projects.

Table 17–1 shows an example of the mechanics of capital project evaluation. The project illustrated would be accepted because at a community cost of capital of 10 percent, the present value of the estimated stream of benefits is $7,156,700—$1,156,700 in excess of the project's cost of $6,000,000. Thus the projected rate of return on the project is higher than the 10 percent discount rate.

Net present value The mathematical formula for obtaining the net present value (NPV) of a project is, generally,

$$\text{NPV} = \text{PV}_{\text{Ben}} - \text{I}$$

$$\text{PV}_{\text{Ben}} = \frac{B_1}{(1 + i)} + \frac{B_2}{(1 + i)^2} + \ldots + \frac{B_n}{(1 + i)^n} + \frac{S_n}{(1 + i)^n}, \text{ where:}$$

B_n = the annual flow of the estimated benefits over n years

S_n = the scrap value or remaining value of the project at the end of its economic life in year n

i = the appropriate discount or interest rate for the community

I = the cost of the project

Internal rate of return The equation for the internal rate of return is formally similar to that for present value:

$$I = \frac{B}{(1 + r)} + \frac{B_1}{(1 + r)^1} + \ldots + \frac{B_n}{(1 + r)^n} + \frac{S_n}{(1 + r)_n}$$

However, in this case, I (the investment cost of the project) is given and the equation must be solved to find r (the rate of return that brings the PV of the benefits equal to the outlay, I. When $r > i$ (the cost of capital), a single project is acceptable. However, if two alternative, substitutable projects differ in the size of the internal rate of return and in the amount of net present value, the one with the higher NPV is preferable.

Quantifying benefits and costs Although simple in theory, public investment decision making is not very easy in practice. For one thing, the benefits of a project are often intangible and difficult to quantify. Their value is often common or social, involving the general welfare of the citizenry and not easily specified in money terms. (Of course, this factor of common value is the very reason that many activities are assigned to the public sector in the first place.) Thus, it is difficult to place a dollar value on many benefits. For example, although a public park provides recreation, fresh air, light to adjoining properties, and beauty to visitors, the monetary value of these benefits is difficult to determine.

Nevertheless, some estimate of the value of benefits can be made by asking certain questions. How much will people pay to use *private* lakes, parks, and preserves? What is the private average outlay for vacations, scenic trips, and outdoor leisure pursuits? What are the outlays for private lawns, landscaping, gardens? Surely a park provides benefits similar in nature to these activities, each of which has a price. Of course, estimating benefits becomes somewhat easier when public services are sold to the public rather than distributed free of charge. By paying for a service, consumers indicate how much they value it. Nevertheless, even under these conditions, some common benefits are not easily captured in the price.

Accounting for the spillover or neighborhood effects of a project is a second difficulty in quantifying benefits. (Some discussion of these matters appears in Chapter 3.) If, for example, the municipality builds a sewage treatment plant, some of the benefits of stream improvement may accrue to other communities in the area. If these external benefits can be measured, should some of their value

Table 17–1 Net present value of capital project.

Year	Investment cost of project	Estimated net annual undiscounted benefits	Discount rate (cost of capital = 10%)	Present value of benefits
			$\frac{1}{(1.10)^n}$	
0	$6,000,000			
1		$1,000,000	.9091	$ 909,100
2		2,500,000	.8264	2,066,000
3		3,000,000	.7513	2,253,900
4		1,500,000	.6830	1,024,500
5		1,000,000	.6209	620,900
6		500,000	.5645	282,300
Total	$6,000,000	$9,500,000		$7,156,700

Net present value = $1,156,700

be included in the accounting? Residents of any given town may obtain the spillover effects from the beneficial activities of other towns. In financially tight times, however, it is difficult to be purely altruistic. Thus, one argument in favor of grants-in-aid from higher levels of government is that the grants compensate the community that undertakes projects whose benefits spill over to citizens of other localities.

Nevertheless, even where a monetary quantification of benefits is difficult to obtain, the analytic techniques described earlier can still be used—albeit in reverse—by posing the following questions: Given the cost of a proposed project and the community's discount rate, what flow of annual benefits would justify the cost of this project? Does this flow of annual benefits, even though not exactly measurable, appear reasonable or attainable? If so, the project is desirable.

Another difficult problem involves estimating the community's cost of capital (or time preference rate), that is, what rate of interest should be used in discounting the stream of benefits from a public project? It might appear that the borrowing rate of the city or county should be appropriate. But, because the interest on municipal debt is exempt from federal income taxation and because payment generally is backed by the taxable wealth of the entire community, the explicit rate on municipal issues is the lowest of all market interest rates. However, this low explicit rate is probably not the true social cost of capital to the community. Because governmental debt is a prior charge on the community's wealth ranking potentially above all other obligations, an increase in debt imposes a "risk charge" on all the income streams or wealth in the community. The burden of this risk charge can raise the cost of capital (i.e., the necessary rate of return) required on all new and renewable capital investments in the area. Decision makers have to account for this additional imputed burden when analyzing the economic desirability of investing in public projects, and they should raise the presumptive discount rate accordingly. An approximation of the true social discount rate might be a rough weighted average of the interest on municipal bonds and the yields on such other claims as bonds, stocks, and mortgages held in the community.[1]

Inflation and real interest rates By their very nature, capital outlays are forward looking. Inflation, therefore, complicates capital planning programs. On the one hand, forecasted inflation raises the expected dollar value of future benefits, apparently increasing the present value of the capital project and leading to a more expansive program. On the other hand, a rise in the expected rate of inflation leads to a rise in the current nominal rate of interest in the money and capital markets. Thus, the rate of interest is highest during an inflationary period. This increase in the discount rate reduces present value of future benefits. Under equilibrium conditions (if all estimations are accurate), these factors cancel out and the real value of any project remains unchanged. Unfortunately, inflation may also weaken the economic fiber of the community and make it difficult to find the resources to support public programs over time.

Conflicting criteria The two standard criteria described earlier, net present value and internal rate of return, will indicate whether a single capital project is acceptable, but the two criteria can give conflicting signals. Under the constraint of a limited budget (when more socially desirable projects pass the economic test than the fixed budget can allow) or when mutually exclusive alternative projects are ranked (only one of which will be selected because they ultimately serve the same function), some projects that show higher rates of return may rank lower in terms of net present value. In this case, selecting the best project is a true economic problem. Projects may receive conflicting rankings because they differ in one or more of the following:

1. Shape of the benefit flow over time
2. Investment size
3. Duration of the benefit flow.

A case where the shape of the benefit flow differs is illustrated in Table 17–2. Project A has a higher internal rate of return than Project B (11.7 percent for A against 10.0 percent for B). But at a cost of capital or discount rate of 6.0 percent, Project B's net present value would be higher than that for A ($113,532 for B against $85,510 for A). As always, where this type of rating conflict appears, the project with the higher internal rate of return has the higher earlier benefit flow; the rival project with the higher net present value has relatively higher benefit flow in later periods. If the choice of projects is made on the basis of the rate of return, earlier benefits will be at the cost of greater returns later on, and this trade-off will be at a higher rate than the community's cost of capital. Thus, the most desirable project is the one with the greatest net value of total benefit flows as determined by the community's time preference or discount rate (i.e., the project selected by the net present value criterion).

Table 17–2
Comparison of projects when shape of cash flow differs.

Project A

Year	Outlay	Benefits	Discount rate (6%)	Present value of benefits
0	$1,000,000			
1		$ 700,000	.9434	$ 660,380
2		200,000	.8900	178,000
3		200,000	.8396	167,920
4		100,000	.7921	79,210
	$1,000,000	$1,200,000		$1,085,510

Project A has a net present value of $85,510. Its internal rate of return is 11.7%.

Project B

Year	Outlay	Benefits	Discount rate (6%)	Present value of benefits
0	$1,000,000			
1		$ 100,000	.9434	$ 94,340
2		200,000	.8900	178,000
3		700,000	.8396	587,720
4		320,000	.7921	253,472
	$1,000,000	$1,320,000		$1,113,532

Project B has a net present value of $113,532. Its internal rate of return is 10.0%.

It should be noted that the net present value depends heavily on the estimate of the appropriate discount rate. At higher discount rates, the advantage of Project B over Project A begins to disappear. At 10 percent Project B just qualifies as feasible with a zero net present value, whereas Project A would still have a positive net present value and would therefore be more desirable. This simply means that in times of high *real* interest rates (i.e., when there is a tight supply of capital), financial managers must try for projects with returns that will come in the near term rather than in the distant future.

A case where the size of two projects differs is illustrated in Table 17–3. Here the smaller project, A, has the greater rate of return, but the larger project, B, has the higher net present value. This means that the $200,000 increment in Project B earns benefits at a rate higher than the community's cost of capital even though there is an "averaging down" of the internal rate. If the bigger project is conceived in two parts, one of which is an incremental increase over the smaller project, it becomes clear that the criterion of net present value gives the correct answer.

Table 17–3
Comparison of projects when size differs.

Project	A	B	Project B – A[a]
Cost	$1,000,000	$1,200,000	$200,000
Present value of benefits at 10.0%	1,500,000	1,770,000	270,000
Internal rate of return	12.50%	12.25%	11.00%
Benefit/cost ratio	1.50X	1.48X	1.35
Net present value	$ 500,000	$ 570,000	$ 70,000

[a] This is the difference between A and B, considered as an independent project that is an incremental increase to A.

A case of differing durations of benefit flows cannot be resolved simply. The problem is that not only may internal rates of return differ, but a net present value of, for example, $100,000 for a stream of benefits lasting five years cannot be directly compared to the net present value of $120,000 for an alternative project that lasts seven years. Actually, what is involved is a comparison of different strategies carried out over time and not merely a comparison of two projects. The comparison of strategies may not be too difficult if it can be assumed that each project can be renewed at the end of its life at the same costs and benefits as the current project. In this case, the net present value of each project can be annualized (reconverted into an equivalent flat annuity over the life of each project). These amounts can be compared directly. Table 17–4 illustrates such a problem. Although the net present value of Project B is larger, the equivalent present value annuity of Project A (at 10 percent) is $18,450 and the equivalent annuity of B is $17,040 per year. Thus a series of A projects is preferable to one of B projects because the former results in a higher stream of net benefits over time.

Table 17–4
Comparison of projects when duration differs (using method of annualization).

Project A

Year	Outlay	Return	Discount rate (10%)	Present valuc
0	$80,000			
1		$ 60,000	.909	$ 54,540
2		50,000	.826	41,300
3		40,000	.751	30,040
	$80,000	$150,000		$125,880

Net present value = $125,880 − 80,000 = $45,880.
Equivalent annuity for three years at 10% = $18,450.

Project B

Year	Outlay	Return	Discount rate (10%)	Present value
0	$170,000			
1		$ 80,000	.909	$ 72,720
2		70,000	.826	57,820
3		60,000	.751	45,060
4		50,000	.683	34,150
5		40,000	.621	24,840
	$170,000	$300,000		$234,590

Net present value = $234,590 − $170,000 = $64,590.
Equivalent annuity for five years at 10% = $17,040.

However, in the case where the future renewal costs and benefits of each project may not be an exact reduplication of the present project, annualization will not work. The solution must be obtained by comparing the net present value of a series of linked, shorter-lived projects to the net present value of an alternative series of longer projects, both ending at a reasonable common time. Thus, if capital Project A lasts four years and rival Project B lasts six years, a comparison of the total net present value of three A-type projects with forecasted costs and benefits renewed at the end of four years and eight years should be made with the total net present value of two linked B-type projects.

Project analysis in practice Present value analysis for capital investment programming appears to be quite complicated, but it is the estimation of benefits and not the actual calculations that is difficult. However, an attempt to make present value analyses of projects is worthwhile even if some of the variables must be best-guess estimates. In any case, the exercise should improve the evaluation of the economic desirability of many capital projects.

Several practical considerations affect the selection of capital projects. The arbitrary constraint of a fixed budget may be irrational and may force decision makers to select less efficient projects or delay the implementation of worthwhile improvements. If economically desirable projects cannot be undertaken because of a limited budget, public officials may attempt to persuade the public to accept a larger one, consistent with existing and future debt obligations. Before pressing this case, of course, the budgeter must be certain that all the costs and benefits have been counted and that the discount rate to be used is not too low. If it is not feasible to accommodate all worthwhile noncompeting projects *in the short term,* the second best solution is to ensure that the projects selected within the budget limit show the highest combined net present value.

One tendency of capital planning that should be avoided is the temptation to place funds in new projects and to delay the repair and renovation of existing facilities. "Cities often defer maintenance and replacement because it is a relatively painless short-run way to reduce expenditures and ease financial strain."[2] Such deferrals, however, can be costly, creating short-term community hazards and costs and leading to larger capital expenditures in the future. Maintenance and repair should not be ignored in the formulation of the capital budget. In many instances, such activities may show the highest net present value of benefits.

Another proviso that should be kept in mind in constructing the capital budget is that the object of the capital planner is to increase the general wealth and welfare of the city and its population, not just to better the position of the public treasury. Only over time will an improvement with diffuse benefits bring about increased revenues. In the meantime, expenditures exert a direct effect on the local budget. Nevertheless, political pressure to concentrate on one-sided counting of explicit costs must not lead the capital planner to ignore the wider social and societal benefits of a project.

Using economic base, land use, and population studies

An effective capital budgeting program rests on a foundation of economic base studies, land use reports and maps, and population and migration studies, which provide underlying information for projecting fiscal resources, measuring need, and indicating the best location for capital projects. Although the local planning commission often conducts such studies, all too often they are forgotten, left to gather dust in a back room.

Economic base studies consist of data (e.g., size, employment, and location) on existing industries. They should include an economic history of the city or county; an analysis of trends in economic development; and forecasts of employment, wages, construction, and the locations of economic activity in the area. Land use studies show population density and contain an inventory of industrial, residential, recreational, commercial, and vacant land. These studies can be used to determine the amount of land available for various sorts of future development. Population and migration studies detail present population characteristics, income, and human resources. They indicate where people currently live and where they are likely to move in the future. Population studies comprise data on age classes so that projections can be made for the size of the future labor force, the demand for schooling, and facilities needed for older people. Capital budget makers should be involved in the design of these studies so that the type of data gathered helps answer specific questions.

On the capital expenditure side of the budget, capital budgeters may want answers to the following types of questions: What industries are developing? What support will these industries need in terms of streets, docks, fire control equipment, or other government facilities? If the migration and land use studies indicate new areas to which the population is moving, what new facilities will be needed in the way of schools, transportation, parks, and recreation? If the city or county wants to discourage this migration (from older to newer parts of the area, for example), what improvements might slow movement from the older areas? The studies may also point out trends in operating expenditures for social services, public safety, and general government programs as the population structure and land use patterns change.

On the forecasted revenue side of the budget, a similar set of questions might be asked: What is the likely growth of various parts of the local economy? Does an analysis of this growth provide enough information to estimate future tax sources? For example, will the value of downtown property decline? Will a decline in the property tax base be offset by growth in the earned income tax? Do the land use and migration studies indicate whether the movement path of the population is toward local vacant land that is likely to be developed and added to the tax base? Can it be assumed that future growth of the property tax base area will be slower or faster than past trends?

Forecasting fiscal resources

Because the capital budget is by its very nature forward-looking, one of its most important components is the forecast of resources and responsibilities over a period of years, which provides the essential fiscal framework for the capital program. Fiscal resources are projected in terms of normally anticipated sources of revenues, normal expenditures, and existing debt service obligations. The financial impact of the desired capital improvements—given their estimated costs, the timing of construction starts and outlays, and the construction funds that may be available as grants from other governmental units—is measured against the forecast of resources. This comparison provides a forecast of the resources available under the existing tax structure and prepares the community for required fiscal changes and adjustments. It also provides a picture of how much of the capital budget can be supported directly out of current revenues, how any necessary bond financing can be serviced, and what tax increase (if any) will be required. Generally, if the fiscal forecast is to be a useful planning tool, it should extend for five or six years.

In order to forecast normal recurring revenues and operating expenditures, their components must be separated into readily definable major categories. The behavior of these categories can be subjected to historical or trend analysis to ascertain past trends, or to one of the more sophisticated forecasting methods described in Chapter 5. In any case, the forecasts should not be made on a purely mechanical basis; the budgeter should interview local government officials to see if any special factors may suggest deviations from past trends and relationships. Some parts of the capital budget itself may influence revenue trends. However, unless there are strong local characteristics that differ from national patterns, the projections should be consistent with the overall trends in local government finance and with the developments in the national economy.

To the extent possible, the forecaster should adjust the revenue and expenditure projections for inflation. In a certain sense, the rate of price increases may already be accounted for insofar as historic trends reflect the rate of past inflation. Moreover, if inflation increases nominal costs and expenditures, it also increases the dollar amount of potential revenues. In general, however, inflation complicates financing local government activities because not all costs and revenues run parallel.

A fiscal forecast is conveniently summarized in a master table that presents projections of the sums of the major revenue sources and the projected major expenditure items. A hypothetical illustration of such a forecast is shown in Table 17–5. (Details on preparing this table follow.) Its major function is to project the differences between total future operating revenues and expenditures so as to give an estimate of *future net available fiscal capacity,* that is, the potential funds that may be used either for direct expenditures on capital items or for service charges on additional debt incurred to finance capital improvements under the existing fiscal structure.

Table 17–5 General fund fiscal projections and the capital budget (in $ thousands).

Category	1987	1988	1989	1990	1991	1992	1993
1 Projected operating revenues	6,000	6,500	7,000	7,300	7,700	8,000	8,400
2 Less projected operating expenditures	5,000	5,800	6,300	6,600	7,000	7,300	7,700
3 Gross cash flow from operations	1,000	700	700	700	700	700	700
4 Debt service on existing obligations (interest plus amortization)	500	500	350	300	250	200	150
5 Gross funds flow after debt service charges	500	200	350	400	450	500	550
6 Less projected recurring capital expenditures	200	300	350	400	450	500	500
7 Net funds[a]	300	(100)	-0-	-0-	-0-	-0-	50
8 Less proposed major capital expenditures	1,000	1,000	1,000	500	500	-0-	-0-
9 Net new financing required[b]	700	1,100	1,000	500	500	-0-	(50)

[a] Parentheses indicate deficit.
[b] Parentheses indicate surplus.

Users of the fiscal forecast section of the capital budget study should note two underlying assumptions. First, no new major operating functions will be undertaken by the local government in the period under review. (Even if this is not the case, the budget can still be useful, because it gives an estimate of future fiscal resources that might be available for any new functions.) Second, the revenue forecasts are based on an analysis of existing taxes and tax rates. This is necessary because the revenue projected by the existing tax structure serves as a base for estimating both the additional revenue that might be obtained by an increase in the existing taxes and the level of activity the local economy can support.

In summary, then, constructing the fiscal forecast necessitates three steps:

1. Analyzing past revenue data and developing a forecast of normal recurring future revenues
2. Analyzing past expenditure data and developing a forecast of normal recurring future expenditures

3. Comparing projected revenues and operating expenses to provide an estimate of the projected fiscal resources of the local government on the basis of its current revenue structure.

The formal capital improvements program is related to the local government's fiscal resources. Usually, additional funds will be necessary to finance the program. If so, the budget maker should present alternative financial plans that indicate the timing and fiscal impact of raising these funds through different possible combinations of debt and tax increases. This step will be discussed in detail later.

Forecasting revenues

Much of the following discussion is based on the trend analysis method of forecasting. (Chapter 5 outlines other forecasting techniques; the planner should use those statistical tools and methods that are best adapted to the problems at hand.) Future revenues may be projected by studying past data on existing revenue sources. Projections should be based on existing tax rates applied to a forecast of the growth of the existing tax base. Existing rates are used because the basic purpose of the fiscal forecast is to generate reasonable estimates of what changes in the rates, if any, will be necessary to support the financing of the planned and desired level of future capital projects.

In analyzing past trends, it is improper simply to chart trends in total revenues. Rather, the analyst must distinguish between the effects of natural economic growth in the tax base and the effects of past legislated or structural changes in the tax system. For example, past increases in revenues could have been caused by a rise in tax rates, a change in assessment levels, or the institution of a new tax. The projection of the overall trend of combined revenues can also be misleading if the returns from individual taxes are growing at different rates. A relatively stable total revenue trend, for example, might be the result of a slow decline in the returns from major tax source A and a concomitant increase in revenue from new tax source B. By breaking out the two taxes historically, analyzing them separately for trends, and then combining the results, the analyst may find that after a brief period of stability, forecasted total revenues should start climbing significantly.

In order to make a useful and consistent analysis of past revenue trends, the following points should be noted:

1. The major revenue sources in past operating budgets should be classified under consistent headings. Sometimes budget classifications change, in which case current classifications should be used and past revenue classifications should be made consistent with them.
2. As a major source of local government revenue, the property tax and its projection are worth some study. In analyzing property tax revenue, the trend in the total levy should not be overemphasized. The growth in the assessment base is the most significant variable in any forecast. Thus, a sudden jump in the assessment base should lead to further questioning. The rise may have resulted from an increase in the assessment ratio (e.g., from 40 percent to 60 percent) rather than from true economic growth. In projecting property tax revenues, the land base study and detailed analysis and knowledge of the local area can prove very useful. Whether any major developments are pending, how much land is still open for development and improvement, and whether any significant amount of property might be taken off the rolls in the future should also be considered.
3. A newly instituted tax requires careful analysis, for its growth rate can be overestimated if the base year revenues do not represent a full fiscal

year. Moreover, the first years after the imposition of the tax may show a rapid rate of growth in revenues; some of this may be caused by improvement in administration as the local government becomes accustomed to the tax. Such growth is not likely to continue indefinitely at the same rate.

4. Finally, when making projections, analysts should modify past trends by any recently observed changes in patterns. Assume, for example, that the observed overall compound rate of growth for a local earned income tax over the last 10 years was 8 percent. However, in earlier years the growth rate was about 7 percent, and this has gradually increased to almost 9 percent per year. The projection rate might best be set at 9 percent per year or even slightly higher.[3]

Forecasting expenditures

Again, as in forecasting revenues, the major emphasis in this section rests on the use of trend analysis. However, the points noted are useful in any case where careful classification and handling of the data may be necessary. Often, the methods cited in Chapter 5 will be superior to the extrapolation of trends in projecting the future. Forecasting expenditures requires that individual outlays be grouped into workable categories, that operating expenditures be separated from recurring capital expenditures (which may be made from the general fund), and that service charges on existing debt be isolated.

Past expenditures are analyzed to determine the trends and relationships of each major component. Where these trends appear consistent with general economic developments, they are used in making forecasts. As in the case of revenue analysis, local government officials should be questioned about significant deviations from past trends to learn whether special factors are likely to affect expenditure patterns in the future.

In making expenditure projections, the analyst must apply informed judgment to the following issues:

1. Budget classifications may have changed in the time period under review. In that case, the existing budgetary classification should be used and past data arranged to conform to current usage.
2. For new government functions, the rate of expenditure growth may be quite high in the early years and then decline after the function has become established. The projections should take these changing rates into consideration and adjust the average historic rate of growth.
3. Totally new functions may have no historic record of past expenditures; consequently, they should be given a separate line in the forecast. The estimate of expenditures on such functions will have to be developed from interviews with relevant officials and must incorporate the reasonable judgment of the analyst. Methods using regression models are often useful in this case. The amounts forecasted and the rate of growth also can be compared with the experience of other similar local governments that have already instituted the function.

The framework of the fiscal resource study

How might the fiscal planning budget be worked out? This section illustrates some of the specific factors that enter into the construction of the fiscal resource study.

Table 17–5 is the key table for projecting the fiscal resources of a hypothetical city for six years. The base year 1987 is the current operating year. Row 1 shows the projected current operating revenues for the next six years. (It does not include any grants from other governments that are to be used for capital improvements.) Row 2 is the projected level of current operating expenditures. Row 3 is the difference between current revenues and expenditures. Rows 4 and 6 show service charges on already existing debt and expenditures for such recurring capital items as police cars, typewriters, and sanitation equipment. These items are subtracted to produce Row 7, the projected annual net cash flow of the municipality. This amount may be used to help finance *new* capital projects and to help cover the service charges on additional debt obligations, which may be floated to finance the capital budget. Row 8 shows the proposed capital expenditures taken from the capital budget itself. Row 9 shows the net new capital funds that will be required to finance the capital budget. It does *not,* however, show the full fiscal impact of the budget over time; doing so would necessitate extrapolating the impact of the bond financing plan on the tax structure of the city. (This is discussed in more detail later in this chapter.)

Supporting data The figures summarized in Table 17–5 are derived from more detailed analyses and forecasts. Tables 17–6 through 17–11 show the data and analysis required to compile Table 17–5.

Table 17–6 Schedule for derivation of projected operating revenues (in $ thousands).

Year	Real estate taxes	Personal property taxes	Fines	User charges	Federal and state grants	Miscel-laneous	Total
1987	4,500	300	100	370	700	30	6,000
1988	4,680	300	100	665	725	30	6,500
1989	4,867	300	100	953	750	30	7,000
1990	5,062	300	100	1,033	775	30	7,300
1991	5,264	300	100	1,206	800	30	7,700
1992	5,475	300	100	1,270	825	30	8,000
1993	5,694	300	100	1,426	850	30	8,400

Table 17–6 shows the main components of the overall projection of revenues on Row 1 of Table 17–5. Each major revenue item is projected separately for each year. For example, Table 17–7 is a breakdown of the major components of the forecast of real estate tax revenues—a major item in most local budgets.

A similar analysis is undertaken for expenditures. Thus Table 17–8 shows the classifications of the major operating expenditures and recurring capital expenditures. Each of these should be forecasted separately to obtain the projection shown in Row 2 of Table 17–5. The recurring capital expenditures may be

Table 17–7 Schedule for derivation of projected real estate taxes.

Year	(A) Assessed value ($000)	(B) Existing millage ($000)	(C) Levy (C = A × B)	(D) Collections ($000)	(E) Collection as percentage of levy (E = D ÷ C)
1987	$230,750	20	$4,615	$4,500	97.5
1988	238,776	20	4,776	4,680	98.0
1989	248,316	20	4,966	4,867	98.0
1990	259,590	20	5,192	5,062	97.5
1991	265,859	20	5,317	5,264	99.0
1992	279,337	20	5,586	5,475	98.0
1993	290,510	20	5,810	5,694	98.0

Table 17–8 Schedule for derivation of projected operating expenditures and recurring capital expenditures (in $ thousands).

	Operating expenditures								
Year	Adminis-trative	Judicial	Correc-tions	Welfare	Health and hospital[a]	Miscel-laneous	Total	Total recurring capital expenditures	Total
1987	1,000	610	550	2,500	90	250	5,000	200	5,200
1988	1,040	634	560	2,750	566	250	5,800	300	6,100
1989	1,082	660	570	3,025	713	250	6,300	350	6,650
1990	1,125	686	580	3,328	731	150	6,600	400	7,000
1991	1,170	714	590	3,660	716	150	7,000	450	7,450
1992	1,217	742	600	4,026	665	50	7,300	500	7,800
1993	1,265	772	600	4,429	584	50	7,700	500	8,200

[a] A new hospital wing will be completed by 1988.

broken down further into the categories shown in Table 17–9. The schedule of existing debt service (see Table 17–10) is relatively easy to obtain, because it is a projection of the already obligated annual interest charges and amortization on the existing debt.

Schedule of capital improvements After the fiscal resource study has been developed, the next phase in the construction of the capital budget entails detailing the costs of the capital projects for the next six years. The projected capital improvements program should be summarized in a table. Although the format can vary, this table should include the following (see Table 17–11).

1. A complete list of major capital improvements
2. Estimates of the total cost of each improvement
3. Outside sources of financing such as state or federal grants and private gifts. (The difference between the total cost of a project and the available grants is the net burden that must be borne by the fiscal capacity of the local government.)

Table 17–9 Schedule for derivation of projected recurring capital expenditures from general fund (in $ thousands).

Year	Administrative	Judicial	Corrections	Welfare	Miscel-laneous	Total
1987	100	10	30	58	2	200
1988	150	10	30	108	2	300
1989	150	10	40	148	2	350
1990	200	10	40	148	2	400
1991	200	10	50	188	2	450
1992	250	10	50	188	2	500
1993	250	10	50	188	2	500

Table 17–10 Schedule for derivation of service charges on existing debt, 6% interest (in $ thousands).

Year	Balance outstanding as of December 31	Debt retirement	Interest	Total debt service
1987	1,876	387	113	500
1988	1,489	411	89	500
1989	1,078	285	65	350
1990	793	252	45	300
1991	541	218	32	250
1992	323	181	19	200
1993	142	142	8	150

Table 17–11 Schedule of capital improvements projects (in $ thousands).

Project	1987	1988	1989	1990	1991	1992	1993
Home for elderly							
Addition and reconstruction	1,500	1,500	1,500	0	0	200	200
Less grants	1,000	1,000	1,000	0	0	200	200
Net cost to city	500	500	500	0	0	0	0
Prison improvements	200	100	100	0	0	0	0
Recreation	0	0	0	300	300	0	0
Street improvements	700	700	700	200	200	0	0
Less grants	400	300	300	0	0	0	0
Net cost to city	300	400	400	200	200	0	0
Total: Projects gross	2,400	2,300	2,300	500	500	200	200
Less total grants	1,400	1,300	1,300	0	0	200	200
Net cost to city	1,000	1,000	1,000	500	500	0	0

4. The scheduling of construction starts and annual expenditures. (In most cases, the expenditures for a project will be spread over a number of years.)

The optimal timing of municipal debt issues is a special problem in finance and depends on the level and trend in interest rates and the spread between municipals and short-term U.S. government bonds. Often there may be some savings if the local unit floats all the bonds immediately and invests the proceeds until they are needed in short-term Treasury issues.

Financing needs On the basis of the fiscal resource study, the analyst can determine the financing needs for the capital improvements program. According to the projections in Table 17–5, the net funds available to support new projects total $300,000 in 1987. It is expected that this will turn into a deficit of $100,000 by 1988. For 1989 through 1992, the plan is for the budget to be in balance. In 1993, a modest surplus of $50,000 is projected.

Assuming the city follows through with its capital program, Row 9 shows the required new financing; starting with $700,000 in 1987, and $1,100,000 in 1988. The requirements of the program taper off to $500,000 in 1990 and 1991. There are no new large projects for 1992, nor any requirements for funds; and 1993 actually projects a surplus of $50,000. The total capital financing required from 1987 through 1992 equals $3,800,000.

Financing concepts

The next step in capital budget preparation is to devise a financial plan and show its effects on the tax structure of the city. The two basic concepts for financing capital programs are *pay-as-you-go (or pay-as-you-acquire)* and *pay-as-you-use*. In practice, many plans incorporate elements of both of these two basic models.

In the 1950s, many writers on local finance were advocating pay-as-you-go capital financing as a way of saving on interest charges. Pay-as-you-go meant that the local government was to allocate a significant portion of operating revenues each year to a capital reserve fund. The monies in this fund were to be used for annual capital improvements or saved until they were sufficient for large projects. In any case, a regular capital allocation would be made from the operating budget to smooth budget allocations for capital expenditures and eliminate the need for bond financing. Because the local government would save the interest charges that would have been incurred on the debt, the absolute amount of payments for any given capital program would cost less over time than if it were financed through the flotation of bonds. Pay-as-you-go carried the cachet of "good planning" and was adopted by many communities.

However, pay-as-you-go financing incurs certain difficulties both in practice and in theory. For pay-as-you-go financing to function well, capital projects must be evenly spaced over time (i.e., large projects must be relatively rare). Yet such an even flow of capital expenditures is likely only in large jurisdictions where projects average out over time, and even here the capital program is likely be be "lumpy," demanding unusually heavy outlays from time to time. Under strict pay-as-you-go financing, some of these projects would have to be delayed until the funds could be accumulated. In the meantime, the community could be denied a very desirable facility, or a vital part of a total system (e.g., a road link or docking facility) would have to be postponed with a resultant loss to the community's economy. Moreover, if public funds are accumulated for future expenditure, the municipality has taken over a savings function for its citizens. The citizens might have more urgent uses for these funds, which might generate higher returns than the interest the government could earn while waiting to build a project.

If the population is relatively mobile, pay-as-you-go financing may not be equitable. For example, some citizens of a given town may contribute heavily to capital improvements, but before they have a chance to enjoy them, may move to a different area and may have to start paying for capital improvements all over again. Conversely, a new resident moving into a community that has completed the bulk of its capital program will enjoy the use of these facilities without having contributed to their financing. Pay-as-you-go financing may also cause problems with intergenerational equity. Older families will be taxed immediately to pay for capital facilities that may last long past their lifetimes, whereas the use and enjoyment of these facilities will accrue to younger people who may have made very little payment on them.

Most of the problems of pay-as-you-go plans can be avoided by the pay-as-you-use method. In its pristine theoretical form, pay-as-you-use financing means that every long-run improvement is financed by serial debt issues with maturities arranged so that the retirement of debt coincides with the depreciation of the project. When the project finally ends, the last dollar of debt is paid off. If a replacement facility is desired, it should be financed by a new bond issue tailored in the same manner. Under pay-as-you-use, each group pays for its own capital improvements. No one is forced to provide free goods for a future generation or to contribute toward facilities for a town in which he or she may not live, nor will new members of the community reap where they have not sown.

It would appear that the weight of the theoretical analysis is in favor of pay-as-you-use financing. Even the major argument for pay-as-you-go financing—the saving on total interest costs over time—is erroneous. It ignores the private time value of money and the fact that the interest borrowing costs of the local government generally are lower than those of the rest of the financial market. In any case, over the years, the increasing constraints on the fiscal resources of local communities have generally forced the abandonment of most pay-as-you-go budgets.[4]

Comparing alternative financing plans

It is generally useful to compare alternative financing plans to show their projected effect on the local millage rate and on the financial position and credit rating of the community. Table 17–12 shows the fiscal effects of three possible financing plans. Plan A, pay-as-you-go, involves complete financing from current revenue; Plan B, pay-as-you-use, rests completely on debt and bond financing; and Plan C is a mixed plan that finances 30 percent of the net new financial requirement with taxation and the remaining 70 percent with debt. Of course, these various plans simply provide a guideline; the program eventually adopted is ultimately the responsibility of the political decision makers.

Plan A: Financing from current revenue (pay-as-you-go) Under Plan A, the local government's net new financing requirements are covered entirely by taxation. In Table 17–12, under Plan A, Row 1 shows the annual amount to be financed. Row 2 shows the amount by which the real estate tax rate (in terms of mills) would have to rise to provide the needed funds. (Taxes other than real

Table 17–12 Effects of alternative capital financing plans on local millage rate (base is 20.0).

Plan A (pay-as-you-go)—current revenue financing	1987	1988	1989	1990	1991	1992	1993
1 Net new financing required for operations and capital budget ($000)	700	1100	1000	500	500	0	(50)
2 Additional mills required (to the nearest tenth)	3.0	4.7	4.0	1.9	1.9	—	—
3 Approximate revenue increase ($000)	692	1122	993	493	505	—	—
4 Total millage	23.0	24.7	24.0	21.9	21.9	20.0	20.0

Plan B (pay-as-you-use)—100% debt financing (bond financing for capital requirements only)	1987	1988	1989	1990	1991	1992	1993
1 New debt required to finance capital budget (nearest $100,000)	700	1100	1000	500	500	—	—
2 Amortization of debt (15 year issues)	47	120	187	220	253	253	253
3 Add interest (6% on outstanding balance)	42	105	158	177	194	178	163
4 Funds needed for service charges on new debt	89	225	345	397	447	431	416
5 Additional mills required	.4	.9	1.4	1.5	1.7	1.6	1.4
6 Approximate revenue increase	92	215	348	389	452	447	407
7 Total millage	20.4	20.9	21.4	21.5	21.7	21.6	21.4

Plan C (combined)—30% current financing and 70% debt financing	1987	1988	1989	1990	1991	1992	1993
1 New debt required (nearest $100,000)	480	770	700	350	350	—	—
2 Amortization of debt (15 year issues)	33	84	131	154	177	177	177
3 Add interest (6% on outstanding balance)	29	74	111	124	136	125	114
4 Funds needed for service charge on new debt	62	158	242	278	313	302	291
5 Other funds required (nondebt)	210	330	300	150	150	—	—
6 Total revenue requirement	272	488	542	428	463	302	291
7 Additional mills required	1.2	2.0	2.2	1.6	1.8	1.1	.1
8 Approximate revenue increase	277	478	546	415	479	307	290
9 Total millage	21.2	22.0	22.2	21.6	21.8	21.1	20.1

estate might be used in the actual financing, but the financial impact is usually quite clear if it is presented in terms of the required rise in the millage.) Row 4 gives the total millage required to carry out both the ordinary operation of the community and the capital program.

When the capital program is lumpy and the municipality's financial needs fluctuate, pay-as-you-go produces a fluctuating tax rate (even though the tax base is relatively stable). These variations in tax rates make the costs of improvements very clear to the citizens of the community and probably induce conservative decisions regarding the desirability of improvements. On the other hand, fluctuating tax rates create uncertainty and may hinder good decision making. Under Plan A the total millage must rise to 24.7 before falling back to the baseline of 20 mills required before the capital improvements plan was put into effect.

Plan B: Debt financing (pay-as-you-use) In Plan B, the community's net new financial requirements are covered by issuing debt. Row 1 under Plan B shows the timing of debt issues to coincide with capital expenditures. Row 2, the debt amortization requirement, must be based on the issue length of serial bonds (normally 15 to 25 years.) Interest payments, calculated at an *average* rate are shown in Row 3. Row 4 (the sum of Rows 2 and 3) presents the total debt service on the new bonds. Generally, under pay-as-you-use programs, the millage rate (or equivalent taxes) would remain relatively constant for the first year or so; afterwards, the increasing service charges on the net debt would necessitate raising the millage rate. Nevertheless, the variations in tax rates induced by this plan are considerably milder than those associated with pay-as-you-go. The use of bond financing allows a much smoother budgetary transition—one of the main advantages of debt financing. Row 7 shows the millage rate rising from the base of 20 mills to 21.7 mills in 1991. Thereafter the millage rate decreases in small annual increments.

Plan C: Combined financing Any number of mixed plans of debt and current tax financing is possible. For purposes of viewing the alternatives, the finance officer should present at least one sample combined plan. Plan C of Table 17–12, for example, combines 70 percent debt and 30 percent current financing through increased taxes. Generally, the tax rate fluctuations in a combined plan are milder than those for pay-as-you-go but more pronounced than those in a pay-as-you-use plan.

Feasibility of debt financing

If bond financing is to be used, the debt-carrying capacity of the community must be analyzed. Tables 17–13 and 17–14 show the basic factors used to measure the projected debt of the capital program against the carrying capacity of the municipality. (See Chapter 12 for additional discussion of these factors.) Column C of Table 17–13 shows the ratio or percentage of outstanding general fund debt to the true (or estimated market) value of taxable property. Column E shows the total of the old and projected new debt. Column F then provides the ratio of total projected debt to the value of the local property tax base. The general rule of thumb for the credit worthiness of local government debt is that it should not exceed a 10 percent ratio of funded debt to true property value. The hypothetical case is well within this rough guideline.

Another measure of debt capacity is the ratio of debt service charges to current revenues. The framework for forecasting this ratio is shown in Table 17–14. Column C gives the ratio of the service charges on the existing general fund debt to projected revenues. Column E shows the total service charges on the combined old and projected new debt. Municipal bond analysts assume that

Table 17–13 Schedule of projected debt and true value of assessments.

Year	(A) Existing debt outstanding as of Dec. 31 ($000)	(B) True value of assessable property ($000)	(C) Debt outstanding as % of true valuation (C = A ÷ B)	(D) Projected new debt as of Dec. 31 ($000)	(E) Projected total debt outstanding ($000) (E = A + D)	(F) Projected debt outstanding as % of true valuation (F = E ÷ B)
1987	1,876	384,583	0.5	700	2,576	0.7
1988	1,489	397,960	0.4	1,753	3,242	0.8
1989	1,078	413,860	0.3	2,633	3,711	0.9
1990	793	432,650	0.2	2,946	3,739	0.9
1991	541	443,098	0.1	3,226	3,767	0.9
1992	323	465,561	0.1	2,973	3,296	0.7
1993	142	484,183	0.0	2,720	2,862	0.6

Note: Column A is from Table 17–10.
Column B is based on Table 17–7, assuming that the ratio of assessed value to market value is approximately 60% in this jurisdiction.
Column D is from Table 17–12, Plan B, assuming that each new debt issue is amortized in equal amounts over 15 years.

Table 17–14 Schedule of debt service and projected revenue under capital budget financing Plan B.

Year	(A) Service on existing debt ($000)	(B) Projected revenue ($000)	(C) Debt service as % of projected revenue (C = A ÷ B)	(D) Debt service, Plan B	(E) Total projected debt service (E = A + D) ($000)	(F) Total projected debt service as % of projected revenue (F = E ÷ B)
1987	500	6,000	8.3	89	589	9.8
1988	500	6,500	7.7	225	725	11.2
1989	350	7,000	5.0	345	695	9.9
1990	300	7,300	4.1	397	697	9.5
1991	250	7,700	3.2	447	697	9.1
1992	200	8,000	2.5	431	631	7.9
1993	150	8,400	1.8	416	566	6.7

Note: Column A is from Table 17–10.
Column B is from Table 17–6.
Column D is from Table 17–12.

a ratio of less than 20 percent of debt service charges to revenues is reasonable. If a debt plan were adopted, it would be important to note whether the peak debt service charges would go past this point. Again, the hypothetical case appears to be prudently managed. Debt service as a percentage of projected revenues is forecasted to peak in 1988 at a level of 11.2 percent and to decline thereafter.

User charges and revenue bonds

In the hypothetical capital budget, the funds to be raised for debt service were to come from general taxation. This is the appropriate source of funds when (1) the benefits of a project accrue to the community as a whole; (2) it is impossible to measure the precise amount of benefits accruing to particular individuals; or (3) it is impossible to exclude anyone from using or enjoying overall services provided. A new city hall would be an example of such a generalized project.

The benefits generated by some kinds of capital investments, however, accrue more directly to individual users; in such cases the government can charge users for these services—for example, admission fees for the use of a swimming pool or toll charges to motorists for crossing a bridge. Revenue bonds with interest and amortization covered by these user charges may be the appropriate method of financing such facilities. Moreover, given the necessity to constrain government expenditures and the frequent resistance to increases in broad-based taxes, it is likely that revenue bonds will be used even more in the future.

If a capital improvement is to be financed fully by revenue bonds, the revenues projected should at least cover the maintenance and operating costs of the facility and the interest and service charges on the bonds. The forecasted revenue should show the ability to cover these costs, probably with some margin of safety.

Sometimes a project provides benefits beyond those the immediate users can be expected to support. For example, a recreational facility in a poor neighborhood may provide benefits to the whole city in excess of the revenues it generates. For a project to be economically feasible and socially worthwhile, the flow of benefits (including those for which there is no charge), discounted at the social cost of capital, should equal or exceed the total outlay on the project. However, to the extent that benefits may accrue to nonusers, the project may be partly financed with general debt, or partially subsidized through a service charge from the general fund.

Although a user charge system can provide the basis for efficient economic decision making, it is often criticized on grounds of equity. User charges generally will weigh more heavily on the budget of a poor person than that of a rich person and can prevent the poor from taking full advantage of available and needed municipal services. Moreover, the services that should be provided by governments are those that are not fully supplied by the private sector; the community may have social reasons to encourage their consumption by people who cannot afford them. It is clear that, by their nature, a significant part of government services must be subsidized by the community as a whole. The challenge of the public official is to find the optimal balance between efficiency in the supply of public services and equity among the citizens.

Tailoring debt to the cost curve

If a project is financed with a serial bond issue, the maturities can be designed so that the total of the service charges on the debt *and the facility maintenance costs* (excluding the variable operating costs) are reasonably flat over the life of the project. This is another application of the general rule that each group of users should pay the same level of capital costs over time.

If the debt service alone is flat, the following problem may occur. Suppose the project under consideration costs $15,000,000 and is estimated to last 15 years with an average interest rate of 5 percent. An approximately flat debt service charge schedule would appear as shown in Table 17–15. Under this scheme, the repayments of principal are higher in later years, but of course interest charges are lower. Thus the total debt service payments are relatively constant for taxpayers each year.

However, the service charges on the debt are not the only capital cost borne by the taxpayers; full costs include maintenance and repair of the facility. Suppose repairs, modifications, and maintenance costs (exclusive of operations) are estimated to be $250,000 in year 1, but will rise at about the rate of $50,000 a year to a total of $950,000 in year 15. In this case, a flat repayment of the principal in the amount of $1,000,000 per year best equalizes total annual capital costs. The capital cost schedule would appear as shown in Table 17–16. Total capital costs, including major repairs and maintenance, are constant. This may be a more equitable method of spreading the financial burden. The early users who have the advantage of using new, efficient equipment and facilities

Table 17–15 Debt service schedule (in $ thousands).

Year	Amortization of principal	Interest	Total debt service
1	700	750	1,450
2	700	715	1,415
3	800	680	1,480
4	800	640	1,440
5	900	600	1,500
6	900	555	1,455
7	900	510	1,410
8	1,000	465	1,465
9	1,100	415	1,515
10	1,100	365	1,465
11	1,100	310	1,410
12	1,200	255	1,455
13	1,300	195	1,495
14	1,300	130	1,430
15	1,300	65	1,365

pay somewhat heavier debt service charges. The later users are compensated for the declining efficiency of the installation with lower debt financing costs.

"Pass-through" financing

In the 1970s and 1980s there has been a spate of what may be called "pass-through" financing bond issues, involving local finance officers and planning personnel in some very sophisticated financial dealings. In a pass-through finance project, the state or local government lends its credit and tax-free status to some other institution or private enterprise without taking responsibility for the final outcome. For example, a nonprofit hospital may wish to finance an expansion of its facilities. The city may float bonds for the necessary amount and turn the funds over to the hospital. The obligation to repay interest and principal rests with the hospital. There may be a reserve fund to help repay the debt; nevertheless, the indenture may clearly state that neither the city nor the state nor any political subdivision is in any way pledged to repay the bonds.

Another type of pass-through bond may involve a leveraged lease for a new building to be constructed in a development area. A private individual or consortium may furnish the initial equity capital; the local government will sell bonds to the bank to cover the mortgage; and the leasor undertakes to pay a rental fee sufficient to cover the mortgage (and thus retire the bonds) and pay a return to the equity investors. The leasor receives the low, tax-free rate on the mortgage; the bank receives tax-free interest; and the equity holders have the tax

Table 17–16 Capital cost schedule (in $ thousands).

Year	Amortization of principal	Interest	Total debt service	Maintenance and repair	Total capital cost
1	1,000	750	1,750	250	2,000
2	1,000	700	1,700	300	2,000
3	1,000	650	1,650	350	2,000
.					
.					
.					
.					
.					
14	1,000	100	1,100	900	2,000
15	1,000	50	1,050	950	2,000

advantages provided by the investment tax credit and accelerated depreciation. The gain to the local government is that by putting this package together, an employer may have been induced to relocate to a redevelopment area.

Subsidized mortgage schemes involve selling tax-free bonds and then lending the money to institutions engaged in financing private housing mortgages (e.g., banks and savings and loan associations). These institutions then re-lend the money to qualified low-income home buyers at a rate lower than a free market would otherwise dictate. In recent years, however, Congress has severely restricted the use of this type of bond.

Although these classes of bonds are not legal obligations of the sponsoring governments, local governments should be extremely cautious about entering into such financing schemes. The security and the probability of the repayment plan should be checked meticulously. Having lent the local government's name to the transaction, municipal officials cannot be sure that the city or county will escape the "moral obligation" to repay in the event that the primary borrowers default on their payments.

Housing finance bonds appear particularly pernicious. They do not raise additional funds from the capital markets; they merely shift funds around. Essentially, they favor one class of borrower over another. If they help one part of the housing market, they hurt another, or they harm some other "worthy" class of borrowers (e.g., the public utilities) by reducing the available credit and raising the interest rates on the issue of regular bonds. As long as tax-free bonds may be used for such purposes as subsidized private mortgages, it is probably competitively advantageous for any single locality to make use of the device. The Tax Reform Act of 1986, however, severely limits the tax-free status of bonds floated for many of these pass-through financing schemes.

Summary: The capital budget and the fiscal plan

Economic and fiscal factors determine a local government's capital budget and fiscal plan. The initial step is to implement rules for selecting capital projects. This involves quantifying benefit flows, applying the concept of present value, and using the correct estimate of the community's discount rate. Only projects with a positive net present value of benefits should be put into the capital improvements program.

The second step is to forecast the fiscal capacity of the local government. Will the predicted growth of local revenues and wealth carry the service charges on the debt incurred to finance the capital improvements? Although measuring fiscal capacity is considered an independent test and, indeed, allows for the use of more objective data than does estimating the benefits involved in the net present value analysis of project selection, the two tests are related: If the project is economically desirable, then in one way or another it should generate sufficient social wealth to finance its carrying costs.

In the case of revenue bonds—which are becoming increasingly prevalent—the projected level of user charges or rents is substituted for the estimate of community benefits. The flow of revenue must cover repair and operating costs and return a sufficient amount to cover the interest charges and the amortization of debt equal to the investment in the project.

The third step is to select a financing method. On the grounds of equity between generations and between in- and out-migrants, long-term debt is the optimal method for financing long-lived local capital projects. The operational counterpart of this concept requires that the debt issue be tailored to the useful life of the project so that bonds are retired at the same rate as the capital is worn out. In short, this means that serial bonds should be used and that the periodic amount of bonds retired should be correlated to the reduction in the economic value of the project over time. (When this is done properly, there is no need for the use of depreciation in a purely governmental accounting system.)

Serial bond financing leads to intergenerational equity because, in each time period, those who receive the benefits pay the equivalent of the user costs. The current generation is not constrained to reduce its income to transfer wealth to the future. This would occur if current taxes were used to pay for the capital improvement. Nor is the reverse true; when serial bond financing is used, the current generation cannot enjoy the present services of capital improvements and leave to future generations the burden of retiring a balloon payment at the end of the asset's life.

The problem of equity between new residents and out-migrants is analogous to that of intergenerational equity. When local debt is properly used, new residents take up the financing burden in their taxes and enjoy the benefits of the community assets; out-migrants have already paid for their share of capital use during their residency.

Finally, the capital improvements program cannot be considered only in financial terms. The objective of the program is to plan for a level of social capital such that the municipality maintains a viable economic base and provides those amenities necessary for the well-being of its citizens. The final test of a successful program is that at the end of the planning horizon, the local government shows a relative improvement in indicators of private wealth, economic activity, health, education, and social contentment.

1 For a more detailed discussion, see Eli Schwartz, "The Cost of Capital and Investment Criteria in the Public Sector," *Journal of Finance* 25 (March 1970): 135–42.

2 Sanford M. Groves, *Evaluating Financial Condition: An Executive Overview for Local Government,* handbook No. 1, in *Evaluating Local Government Financial Condition,* Sanford M. Groves and W. Maureen Godsey, 5 handbooks (Washington, D.C.: International City Management Association, 1980), p. 15.

3 This is based on the following three articles by J. R. Aronson and E. Schwartz: "Forecasting Future Revenues," *Management Information Service Report,* International City Management Association, July 1970; "Forecasting Future Expenses," *Management Information Service Report,* International City Management Association, November 1970; and "Capital Budget Finance," *Management Information Service Report,* International City Management Association, February 1971.

4 J. R. Aronson and John L. Hilley, *Financing State and Local Governments,* 4th ed. (Washington, D.C.: Brookings Institution, 1986), Chapter 9.

Selected bibliography

The following bibliography is selective, including basic and introductory references. Many additional books, periodical articles, and other references are cited in the endnotes to the individual chapters.

1 The finance function in local government

Advisory Commission on Intergovernmental Relations. *Significant Features of Fiscal Federalism, 1984 Edition*. Washington, D.C.: GPO, 1985.

Aronson, J. Richard. *Public Finance*. New York: McGraw-Hill, 1985.

Aronson, J. Richard, and Hilley, John L. *Financing State and Local Governments*. 4th ed. Washington, D.C.: Brookings Institution, 1986.

Bahl, Roy W. *Financing State and Local Government in the 1980s*. New York: Oxford Univ. Press, 1984.

Bradbury, Katharine L.; Downs, Anthony; and Small, Kenneth A. *Urban Decline and the Future of American Cities*. Washington, D.C.: Brookings Institution, 1982.

Burkhead, Jesse, *Government Budgeting*. New York: John Wiley & Sons, 1956.

Crecine, John. *Financing the Metropolis: Public Policy in Urban Economics*. Beverly Hills, Calif.: Sage Publications, 1970.

Harrell, Rhett D. *Banking Relations: A Guide for Government*. Chicago, Ill.: Government Finance Officers Association, 1986.

Hatry, Harry P., and Peterson, George E., eds. *Guides to Managing Urban Capital Series*. 6 vols. Vol. 1, *Guide to Managing Urban Capital: A Summary*. Vol. 2, *Guide to Assessing Capital Stock Condition*. Vol. 3, *Guide to Benchmarks of Urban Capital Condition*. Vol. 4, *Guide to Selecting Maintenance Strategies for Capital Facilities*. Vol. 5, *Guide to Setting Priorities for Capital Investment*. Vol. 6, *Guide to Financing the Capital Budget and Maintenance Plan*. Washington, D.C.: Urban Institute Press, 1984.

Levine, Charles H., ed. *Managing Fiscal Stress*. Chatham, N.J.: Chatham House, 1980.

Levine, Charles H.; Rubin, Irene S.; and Wolohojian, George G. *The Politics of Retrenchment*. Beverly Hills, Calif.: Sage Publications, 1981.

Mendonsa, Arthur A. *Simplified Financial Management in Local Government*. Athens: Institute of Government, Univ. of Georgia, 1969.

Moak, Lennox L., and Hillhouse, Albert M. *Concepts and Practices in Local Government Finance*. Chicago: Municipal Finance Officers Association, 1975.

Wildavsky, Aaron, ed. *The Politics of the Budgetary Process*. 4th ed. Boston: Little, Brown & Co., 1984.

2 The fiscal problems of the fragmented metropolis

Advisory Commission on Intergovernmental Relations. *Bankruptcies, Defaults and Other Local Government Financial Emergencies*. Washington, D.C.: GPO, 1985.

______. *Fiscal Disparities: Central Cities and Suburbs, 1981*. Washington, D.C.: GPO, 1984.

______. *Improving Urban America: A Challenge to Federalism*. M–107. Washington, D.C.: GPO, 1976.

Aronson, J. Richard, and Schwartz, Eli. "Financing Public Goods and the Distribution of Population in a System of Local Governments." *National Tax Journal* 26 (June 1973): 137–60.

Bahl, Roy, ed. *The Fiscal Outlook for Cities*. Syracuse, N.Y.: Syracuse Univ. Press, 1978.

Banfield, Edward. *The Unheavenly City Revisited*. Boston: Little, Brown & Co., 1974.

Bradbury, Katharine L.; Downs, Anthony; and Small, Kenneth A. *Urban Decline and the Future of American Cities*. Washington, D.C.: Brookings Institution, 1982.

Downs, Anthony. *Urban Problems and Prospects*. Chicago: Markham Publishing Co., 1970.

Glazer, Nathan, ed. *Cities in Trouble*. Chicago: Quadrangle Books, 1970.

Goodall, Leonard E., and Sprengel, Donald P. *The American Metropolis*. 2d ed. Columbus, Ohio: Charles E. Merrill Publishing Co., 1976.

Hawley, Amos, and Rock, Vincent, eds. *Metropolitan America*. New York: Halsted Press, 1975.

Hirsch, Werner Z. *The Economics of State and Local Governments*. New York: McGraw-Hill, 1970.

Hirsch, Werner Z., et al. *Fiscal Pressures on the Central City: The Impact of Commuters, Nonwhites, and Overlapping Governments*. New York: Praeger Publishers, 1971.

Meyer, John; Kain, John; and Wohl, Martin. *The Urban Transportation Problem*. Cambridge, Mass.: Harvard Univ. Press, 1965.

Mills, Edwin, and Hamilton, Bruce. *Urban Economics*. 3d ed. Glenview, Ill.: Scott, Foresman, 1984.

Murphy, Thomas P., and Warren, Charles R. *Organizing Public Services in Metropolitan America*. Lexington, Mass.: Lexington Books, 1974.

Netzer, Dick. *Economics and Urban Problems: Diagnoses and Prescriptions*. New York: Basic Books, 1970.

Peterson, Paul E., ed. *The New Urban Reality*. Washington, D.C.: Brookings Institution, 1985.

Thomlinson, Ralph. *Urban Structure: The Social and Spatial Structure of Cities*. New York: Random House, 1969.

3 Fiscal structure in the federal system

Advisory Commission on Intergovernmental Relations. *Block Grants: A Comparative Analysis*. A–60. Washington, D.C.: GPO, 1977.

______. *Block Grants: A Roundtable Discussion*. A–51. Washington, D.C.: GPO, 1976.

______. *Categorical Grants: Their Role and Design*. A–52. Washington, D.C.: GPO, 1978.

______. *Community Development: The Workings of a Federal-Local Block Grant*. A–57. Washington, D.C.: GPO, 1977.

______. *Fiscal Balance in the American Federal System*. 2 vols. Washington, D.C.: GPO, 1967.

______. *Improving Federal Grants Management*. A–53. Washington, D.C.: GPO, 1977.

______. *Safe Streets Reconsidered: The Block Grant Experience—1968–1975*. A–55. Washington, D.C.: GPO, 1977.

______. *Safe Streets Reconsidered: The Block Grant Experience—1968–1975: Part B, Case Studies*. A–55a. Washington, D.C.: GPO, 1977.

______. *The State and Intergovernmental Aids*. A–59. Washington, D.C.: GPO, 1977.

______. *Summary and Concluding Observations*. A–62.Washington, D.C.: GPO, 1978.

Aronson, J. Richard, and Hilley, John L. *Financing State and Local Government*. 4th ed. Washington, D.C.: Brookings Institution, 1986.

Barfield, Claude E. *Rethinking Federalism: Block Grants and Federal, State, and Local Responsibilities*. Washington, D.C.: American Enterprise Institute, 1981.

Break, George F. *Financing Government in a Federal System*. Washington, D.C.: Brookings Institution, 1980.

Cole, Richard L., and Caputo, David A. *Urban Politics and Decentralization: The Case of General Revenue-Sharing*. Lexington, Mass.: Lexington Books, 1974.

Glendening, Parris N., and Reeves, Mavis Mann. *Pragmatic Federalism: An Intergovernmental View of American Government*. Pacific Palisades, Calif.: Palisades Publishers, 1977.

Heller, Walter W. *New Dimensions of Political Economy*. New York: W. W. Norton & Co., 1966.

Oates, Wallace E. *Fiscal Federalism*. New York: Harcourt Brace Jovanovich, 1972.

______. ed, *Financing the New Federalism: Revenue Sharing, Conditional Grants and Taxation*. Baltimore: Johns Hopkins Univ. Press, 1975.

______. ed, *The Political Economy of Fiscal Federalism*. Lexington, Mass.: Lexington Books, 1977.

4 Local government expenditures and revenues

Aaron, Henry. *Who Pays the Property Tax? A New View*. Washington, D.C.: Brookings Institution, 1975.

Advisory Commission on Intergovernmental Relations. *Significant Features of Fiscal Federalism, 1985 Edition*. M–141. Washington, D.C.: GPO, 1986.

______. *1982 Tax Capacity of the Fifty States.* M–142. Washington, D.C.: GPO, 1985.

Aronson, J. Richard, and Hilley, John L. *Financing State and Local Governments.* 4th ed. Washington, D.C.: Brookings Institution, 1986.

Bahl, Roy W. *Financing State and Local Government in the 1980s.* New York: Oxford Univ. Press, 1984.

Baumol, William. "The macroeconomics of Unbalanced Growth: The Anatomy of Urban Crisis." *American Economic Review* 57 (June 1967): 415–26.

Bradford, David F.; Malt, Richard A.; and Oates, Wallace E. "The Rising Cost of Local Public Services: Some Evidence and Reflections." *National Tax Journal* 22 (June 1969): 185–202.

Break, George F. *Financing Government in a Federal System.* Washington, D.C.: Brookings Institution, 1980.

Due, John F., and Mikesell, John L. *Sales Taxation: State and Local Structure and Administration.* Baltimore: Johns Hopkins Univ. Press, 1983.

Ebel, Robert D., and McGuire, Therese J., eds. *Final Report of the Minnesota Tax Study Commission.* Vols. 1 and 2. St. Paul, Minn.: Butterworth Legal Publishers, 1986.

Mikesell, John L. *Fiscal Administration: Analysis and Applications for the Public Sector.* Chicago: Dorsey Press, 1986.

Musgrave, Richard A., and Musgrave, Peggy B. *Public Finance in Theory and Practice.* 4th ed. New York: McGraw-Hill, 1984.

Pechman, Joseph A. *Who Paid the Taxes, 1966–85?* Washington, D.C.: Brookings Institution, 1985.

U.S. Department of Commerce, Bureau of the Census. *Governmental Finances in 1983–4.* GF84, no. 5. Washington, D.C.: GPO, 1985.

Wasylenko, Michael J. "Business Climate, Industry Location and Employment Growth." Paper presented at the Seventy-eighth Annual Conference of the National Tax Association Tax Institute of America, 1985. Denver, Colo.

5 Forecasting local revenues and expenditures

Armstrong, Jon Scott. *Long-Range Forecasting: From Crystal Ball to Computer.* 2d ed. New York: John Wiley & Sons, 1984.

Helmer, Olaf. *The Use of the Delphi Technique—Problems of Educational Innovations.* Santa Monica, Calif.: Rand Corp., 1966.

Kmenta, Jan. *Elements of Econometrics.* New York: Macmillan Co., 1971.

Makridakis, Spyros, and Wheelwright, Steven C. *Forecasting: Methods and Applications.* New York: John Wiley & Sons, 1978.

Pindyck, Robert S., and Rubinfeld, Daniel L. *Econometric Models and Economic Forecasts.* 2d ed. New York: McGraw-Hill, 1981.

Ross, John, and Burkhead, Jesse. *Productivity in the Local Government Sector.* Lexington, Mass.: Lexington Books, 1974.

Schroeder, Larry D.; Sjoquist, David L.; and Stephan, Paula E. *Understanding Regression Analysis. An Introductory Guide.* Beverly Hills, Calif.: Sage Publications, 1986.

Wheelwright, Steven C., and Makridakis, Spyros. *Forecasting Methods for Management.* 2d ed. New York: John Wiley & Sons, 1977.

Wonnacott, Thomas H., and Wonnacott, Ronald J. *Introductory Statistics for Business and Economics.* 3d ed. New York: John Wiley & Sons, 1984.

6 Budgeting

Aronson, J. Richard, and Hilley, John L. *Financing State and Local Governments.* Chapter 10. Washington, D.C.: Brookings Institution, 1986.

Crecine, John P. *Government Problem Solving: A Computer Simulation of Municipal Budgeting.* Chicago: Rand McNally & Co., 1969.

Gramlich, E. M. *Benefit-Cost Analysis of Government Programs.* Englewood Cliffs, N.J.: Prentice-Hall, 1981.

Hay, Leon E. *Accounting for Governmental and Nonprofit Entities.* 7th ed. Homewood, Ill.: Richard D. Irwin, 1985.

Hayes, Frederick O'R., et al. *Linkages: Improving Financial Management in Local Government.* Washington, D.C.: Urban Institute, 1982.

Kerrigan, Harry D. *Fund Accounting.* New York: McGraw-Hill, 1969.

Lee, Robert D., Jr., and Johnson, Ronald W. *Public Budgeting Systems.* 3d ed. Baltimore: University Park Press, 1983.

Lindholm, Richard W., and Wignjowijoto, Hartojo. *Financing and Managing State and Local Government.* Chapters 5–9. Lexington, Mass.: Lexington Books, 1979.

Lyden, Freemont J., and Lindenberg, Marc. *Public Budgeting Theory and Practice.* New York: Longman, 1983.

Lyden, Freemont J., and Miller, Ernest G., eds. *Public Budgeting: Program Planning and Implementation.* 4th ed. Englewood Cliffs, N.J.: Prentice-Hall, 1982.

Lynch, Thomas D. *Public Budgeting in America.* 2d ed. Englewood Cliffs, N.J.: Prentice-Hall, 1985.

Lynn, Edward S., and Freeman, Robert J. *Fund Accounting: Theory and Practice.* 2d ed. Englewood Cliffs, N.J.: Prentice-Hall, 1983.

Mikesell, John L. *Fiscal Administration: Analysis and Application for the Public Sector.* Chicago: Dorsey Press, 1986.

Mishan, E. J. *Cost-Benefit Analysis.* 3d ed. Boston: George Allen & Unwin, 1982.

Moak, Lennox L., and Hillhouse, Albert M. *Concepts and Practices in Local Government Finance.* Chicago: Municipal Finance Officers Association, 1975.

Municipal Finance Officers Association (now Government Finance Officers Association). *Governmental Accounting, Auditing, and Financial Reporting.* Chicago, 1980.

Quade, E. S. *Analysis for Public Decisions.* New York: American Elsevier, 1975.

Simon, Herbert A. *Administrative Behavior: A Study of Decision-Making Processes in Administrative Organizations.* New York: Free Press, 1976.

Wanat, John. *Introduction to Budgeting.* North Scituate, Mass.: Duxbury Press, 1978.

Wildavsky, Aaron. *The Politics of the Budgetary Process.* Boston: Little, Brown & Co., 1964.

7 Financial accounting, reporting, and auditing

American Accounting Association. Committee to Prepare a Statement of Basic Accounting Theory. *A Statement of Basic Accounting Theory.* Evanston, Ill., 1966.

American Institute of Certified Public Accountants. State and Local Government Committee. *Audits of State and Local Governmental Units.* Industry Audit Guide. New York: American Institute of Certified Public Accountants, 1986.

Anthony, Robert N. *Financial Accounting in Nonbusiness Organizations: An Explanatory Study of Conceptual Issues.* Stamford, Conn.: Financial Accounting Standards Board, 1978.

Coopers & Lybrand and the University of Michigan. *Financial Disclosure Practices of the American Cities: A Public Report.* New York: Coopers & Lybrand, 1976.

Davidson, Sidney, et al. *Financial Reporting by State and Local Government Units.* Chicago: Center for Management of Public and Nonprofit Enterprise, Graduate School of Business, Univ. of Chicago, 1977.

Financial Accounting Standards Board. "Objectives of Financial Reporting by Nonbusiness Organizations." In *Statement of Financial Accounting Concepts, No. 4.* Stamford, Conn., 1980.

Freeman, Robert J., and Lynn, Edward S. *Fund Accounting.* Englewood Cliffs, N.J.: Prentice-Hall, 1974.

Hay, Leon E. *Accounting for Governmental and Nonprofit Entities.* Homewood, Ill.: Richard D. Irwin, 1980.

Henke, Emerson O. *Introduction to Nonprofit Organization Accounting.* Boston, Mass.: Kent/Wadsworth, 1979.

Holder, William. *A Study of Selected Concepts for Government Financial Accounting and Reporting.* Chicago: National Council on Governmental Accounting, 1980.

National Council on Governmental Accounting. *Governmental Accounting and Financial Reporting.* Chicago: Municipal Finance Officers Association, 1980.

Petersen, John E., and Watt, Pat. *The Price of Advice: Choosing and Using Financial Advisors.* Chicago, Ill.: Government Finance Officers Association, 1986.

8 Computer applications

American Management Systems, Inc. *Local Government Financial System (LGFS): Summary Of Capabilities.* Arlington, Va., 1984.

Management Science America, Inc. *MSA Software: Information Expert.* Atlanta, Ga., 1985.

———. *MSA Software: Education Expert Series.* Atlanta, Ga., 1985.

———. *MSA Software: Government Customers.* Atlanta, Ga., 1985.

McLeod, Raymond, Jr. *Management Information Systems.* 2d ed. Chicago: Science Research Associates, Inc., 1983.

Peat Marwick. *Governmment Information Management Systems.* New York, 1982.

———. *ONLINE FAMIS: Interactive Processing.* New York, 1982.

Systems & Computer Technology Corp. *Inte-*

grated Financial Information System: For Local Government. Malvern, Pa., 1985.

Weinberg, Steven J. "Why Choose an Accounting Software Package?" *Management Accounting,* February 1980: 44–47.

Wilkinson, Joseph W. *Accounting and Information Systems,* 2d ed. New York: John Wiley & Sons, 1986.

9 The property tax

Aaron, Henry J. *Who Pays the Property Tax?* Washington, D.C.: Brookings Institution, 1975.

Advisory Commission on Intergovernmental Relations. *Financing Schools and Property Tax Relief—A State Responsibility.* A–40. Washington, D.C.: GPO, 1973.

______. *Property Tax Circuit-Breakers: Current Status and Policy Issues.* M–87. Washington, D.C.: GPO, 1975.

Aronson, J. Richard. "Property Tax," Chapter 16. In *Public Finance*. New York: McGraw-Hill, 1985.

Aronson, J. Richard, and Hilley, John L. *Financing State and Local Governments.* 4th ed. Washington, D.C.: Brookings Institution, 1986.

Break, George F., ed. *Metropolitan Financing and Growth Management Policies*. Madison: Univ. of Wisconsin Press, 1978.

Case, Karl E. *Property Taxation: The Need for Reform.* Cambridge, Mass.: Ballinger Publishing Co., 1978.

Church, Albert M., and Gustafson, Robert H. *Statistics and Computers in the Appraisal Process.* Chicago: International Association of Assessing Officers, 1976.

Committee on Fiscal Affairs and Ad Hoc Group on Urban Problems. *Taxes on Immovable Property.* Paris: OECD, 1983.

Gold, Steven D. *Property Tax Relief.* Lexington, Mass.: D.C. Heath, 1979.

Harriss, C. Lowell, ed. *The Property Tax and Local Finance.* Proceedings of the Academy of Political Science, vol. 35, no. 1, 1983.

Holland, Daniel M., ed. *The Assessment of Land Value*. Madison: Univ. of Wisconsin Press, 1970.

International Association of Assessing Officers. *Analyzing Assessment Equity: Techniques for Measuring and Improving the Quality of Property Tax Administration.* Chicago, 1977.

______. *Automated Mass Appraisal of Real Property.* Chicago, 1974.

______. *Improving Real Property Assessment.* Chicago, 1978.

______. *Property Tax Reform: The Role of the Property Tax in the Nation's Revenue System.* Chicago, 1974.

Lindholm, Richard W. *Property Taxation and the Finance of Education.* Madison: Univ. of Wisconsin Press, 1974.

Lindholm, Richard W., ed. *Property Taxation USA.* Madison: Univ. of Wisconsin Press, 1967.

Lynn, Arthur D. *The Property Tax and Its Administration.* Madison: Univ. of Wisconsin Press, 1969.

Netzer, Dick. *Economics of the Property Tax*. Washington, D.C.: Brookings Institution, 1966.

Paul, Diane B. *The Politics of the Property Tax.* Lexington, Mass: Lexington Books, 1975.

Peterson, George E., et al. *Property Taxes, Housing and the Cities*. Lexington, Mass.: Lexington Books. 1973.

Research and Technical Services Department. International Association of Assessing Officers. *Understanding Real Property Assessment: An Executive Summary for Local Government Officials*. Chicago, 1979.

Schroeder, Larry D., and Sjoquist, David L. *The Property Tax and Alternative Local Taxes: An Economic Analysis*. New York: Praeger Publishers, 1975.

10 Sales taxes, income taxes, and other nonproperty tax revenues

Advisory Commission on Intergovernmental Relations. *Local Nonproperty Taxes and the Coordinating Role of the State, A Commission Report.* A–9. Washington, D.C.: GPO, 1961.

______. *Local Revenue Diversification: Income, Sales Taxes and User Charges*. A–47. Washington, D.C.: GPO, 1974.

Commonwealth of Pennsylvania. *Final Report of the Pennsylvania Tax Commission.* Harrisburg, Pa., 1981.

______. Department of Community Affairs. *The Administration of Local Earned Income Tax*. Harrisburg, Pa., 1971.

Due, John F., and Mikesell, John L. *Sales Taxation: State and Local Structure and Administration.* Baltimore: Johns Hopkins Univ. Press, 1983.

Lindholm, Richard W., and Wignjowijoto, Hartojo. *Financing and Managing State and*

Local Government. Chapters 24–28. Lexington, Mass.: Lexington Books, 1979.

Moak, Lennox L., and Cowan, Frank, Jr. *Manual of Suggested Practice for Administration of Local Sales and Use Taxes.* Chicago: Municipal Finance Officers Association, 1961.

Quigley, John M., ed. *Perspectives on Local Public Finance and Public Policy.* Greenwich, Conn.: JAI Press, 1983.

Sigafoos, Robert A. *The Municipal Income Tax: Its History and Problems.* Chicago: Public Administration Service, 1955.

Smith, R. Stafford. *Local Income Taxes: Economic Effects and Equity.* Berkeley: Institute of Governmental Studies, Univ. of California, 1972.

11 User charges and special districts

Advisory Commission on Intergovernmental Relations. *Local Revenue Diversification: Income, Sales Taxes and User Charges.* A–47. Washington, D.C.: GPO, 1974.

______. *Regional Decision Making: New Strategies for Substate Districts.* A–43. Washington, D.C.: GPO, 1973.

Bird, Richard M. *Charging for Public Services: A New Look at an Old Idea.* Toronto: Canadian Tax Foundation, 1976.

Criz, Maurice. *The Role of User Charges and Fees in City Finance.* Management Information Service Reports, vol. 14, no. 6. Washington, D.C.: International City Management Association, 1982.

Downing, Paul B., ed. *Local Service Prices and Their Effect on Urban Spacial Structure.* Vancouver: Univ. of British Columbia Press, 1977.

Downing, Paul B. *User Charges and Service Fees.* Information bulletin of the Management, Finance, and Personnel Task Force of the Urban Consortium, Public Technology, Inc. Washington, D.C.: Department of Housing and Urban Development, Office of Policy Development and Research, 1981.

Fisher, Glenn W. *Financing Local Improvements by Special Assessment.* Chicago: Municipal Finance Officers Association, 1974.

Gitajn, Arthur. *Creating and Financing Public Enterprises.* Washington, D.C.: Government Finance Research Center, 1984.

Goetz, Charles J. "The Revenue Potential of User-Related Charges in State and Local Governments." In *Broad-Based Taxes: New Options and Sources,* ed. Richard A. Musgrave. Baltimore: Johns Hopkins Univ. Press, 1973.

Mushkin, Selma, ed. *Public Prices for Public Products.* Washington, D.C.: Urban Institute, 1972.

Netzer, Dick. *Local Alternatives to the Property Tax: User Charges and Nonproperty Taxes. Working Paper No. 4, Tax Analysis Series. Washington, D.C.: Academy for State and Local Government, 1983.*

Tax Foundation. Special Assessment and Service Charges in Municipal Finance. Government Finance Brief 20. New York: Tax Foundation, 1970.

Turvey, Ralph, ed. *Public Enterprise.* Harmondsworth, Middlesex, England: Penguin Books, 1968.

12 Debt management

Advisory Commission on Intergovernmental Relations. *Understanding the Market for State and Local Debt.* M–104. Washington, D.C.: GPO, 1976.

Calvert, Gordon L., ed. *Fundamentals of Municipal Bonds.* 9th ed. Washington, D.C.: Securities Industry Association, 1972.

Center for Capital Market Research. *Improving Bidding Rules to Reduce Interest Costs in the Competitive Sale of Municipal Bonds.* Eugene: College of Business Administration, Univ. of Oregon, 1977.

______. *Planning, Designing and Selling General Obligation Bonds in Oregon: A Guide to Local Issuers.* Eugene: Univ. of Oregon, 1978.

Davidson, Sidney, et al. *Financial Reporting by State and Local Units.* Chicago: Univ. of Chicago Press, 1977.

Doty, Robert W., and Petersen, John E. "The Federal Securities Laws and Transactions in Municipal Securities." *Northwestern Law Review,* July-August 1976: 283–412.

Fabozzi, Frank J., et al. *The Municipal Bond Handbook.* Vols. 1 and 2. Homewood, Ill.: Dow Jones–Irwin, 1983.

Fabozzi, Frank J., and Pollack, Irving M. *The Handbook of Fixed Income Securities.* Homewood, Ill.: Dow Jones–Irwin, 1983.

Gelfand, David M. *State and Local Government Debt Financing.* 2 vols. Wilmette, Ill.: Callaghan & Co., 1985.

Hopewell, Michael H., and Benson, Earl D. *Alternate Methods of Estimating the Cost of Inefficient Bids on Serial Municipal Bond Issues.* Eugene: College of Business Administration, Univ. of Oregon, 1975.

Kaufman, George G. "The 'Oregon' Bond Project: Review and Evaluation." *Municipal Finance Journal,* Summer 1980: 192–97.

Moak, Lennox L. *Administration of Local Government Debt.* Chicago: Municipal Finance Officers Association, 1970.

Municipal Finance Officers Association. *Disclosure Guidelines for Offerings of Securities by State and Local Governments.* Chicago, 1976.

_____. *Guidelines for Use by State and Local Governments in the Preparation of Yearly Information Statements and Other Current Information.* Chicago, 1978.

_____. *Observations Concerning the Rating of Municipal Bonds and Credits.* Chicago, 1971.

_____. *Procedural Statements in Connection with the Disclosure Guidelines for Offerings of Securities by State and Local Governments and the Guidelines for Use by State and Local Governments in the Preparation of Yearly Information Statements and Other Current Information.* Chicago, 1978.

Mussa, Michael L., and Kormendi, Roger C. *The Taxation of Municipal Bonds.* Washington, D.C.: American Enterprise Institute, 1979.

Rabinowitz, Alan. *Municipal Bond Finance and Administration.* New York: Wiley-Interscience, 1969.

Twentieth Century Fund. *The Rating Game: Report of the Twentieth Century Fund Task Force on Municipal Bond Credit Ratings.* New York, 1974.

13 Public pension fund administration

Advisory Commission on Intergovernmental Relations. *Bankruptcies, Defaults, and Other Local Government Financial Emergencies.* Washington, D.C.: GPO, 1985.

_____. *State and Local Pension Systems, Federal Regulatory Issues.* A–71. Washington, D.C.: GPO, 1980.

Bleakney, Thomas P. *Retirement Systems for Public Employees.* Philadelphia: Univ. of Pennsylvania Press, 1972.

International City Management Association. *Reforming Public Pension Plans to Avoid Unfunded Liability.* Management Information Service Reports, vol. 15, no. 5. Washington, D.C., May 1983.

Kotlikoff, Laurence J., and Smith, Daniel E. *Pensions in the American Economy.* Chicago: Univ. of Chicago Press, 1983.

Municipal Finance Officers Association Committee on Public Employee Retirement Administration. *Public Employee Retirement Administration.* Chicago, 1977.

Munnell, Alicia Haydock, in collaboration with Connolly, Ann M. *Pensions for Public Employees.* Washington, D.C.: National Planning Association, 1979.

Myers, Robert J. *Indexation of Pension and Other Benefits.* Homewood, Ill.: Richard D. Irwin, 1978.

Ott, David J., et al. *State and Local Finances in the Last Half of the Seventies.* Chapters 3 and 4. Washington, D.C.: American Enterprise Institute for Public Policy Research, 1975.

Petersen, John E. *State and Local Pension Fund Investment Performance.* Washington, D.C.: Municipal Finance Officers Association, 1980.

_____. *State and Local Pension Financial Disclosure.* Washington, D.C.: Government Finance Research Center, Municipal Finance Officers Association, 1979.

Tax Foundation. *Employee Pension Systems in State and Local Government.* New York, 1976.

Tilove, Robert. *Public Employee Pension Funds.* New York: Columbia Univ. Press, 1976.

U.S. Congress. House. Committee on Education and Labor. *Section-By-Section Analysis of the Public Employees Pension Plan Reporting and Accountability Act of 1984.* Washington, D.C.: GPO, 1984.

_____. *Task Force Report on Public Employee Retirement Systems.* Washington, D.C.: GPO, 1978.

U.S. General Accounting Office. Comptroller General of the United States. *Funding of State and Local Pension Plans: A National Problem.* Washington, D.C.: GPO, 1979.

Urban Institute. *The Future of State and Local Pensions: Final Report.* Washington, D.C., 1980.

Winklevoss, Howard, and McGill, Dan. *Public Pension Plans.* Homewood, Ill.: Dow Jones–Irwin, 1979.

Zorn, Paul. *Public Pension Investment Targeting: A Survey of Practices.* Washington, D.C.: Government Finance Research Center, 1983.

14 Inventory and cash management

Advisory Commission on Intergovernmental Relations. *Investment of Idle Cash Balances by State and Local Governments: Report A–3.* Washington, D.C.: GPO, 1961.

———. *Investment of Idle Cash Balances by State and Local Governments: Supplemental to Report A–3.* Washington, D.C.: GPO, 1965.

———. *Understanding State and Local Cash Management.* M–112. Washington, D.C.: GPO, 1977.

Aronson, J. Richard. "The Idle Cash Balances of State and Local Governments: An Economic Problem of National Concern," *Journal of Finance* 23 (June 1968):499–508.

Aronson, J. Richard, and Schwartz, Eli. *Improving Cash Management in Municipal Government.* Management Information Service Reports, vol. 1, no. LS–6. Washington, D.C.: International City Managers' Association, 1969.

Baumol, William J. "The Transactions Demand for Cash: An Inventory Theoretic Approach." *Quarterly Journal of Economics* 66 (November 1951).

Deloitte Haskins & Sells Government Services Group. *Implementing Effective Cash Management in Local Government: A Practical Guide.* Chicago: Municipal Finance Officers Association, 1977.

Jones, John A., and Howard, Kenneth S. *Investment of Idle Funds by Local Governments: A Primer.* Chicago: Municipal Finance Officers Association, 1973.

Kallberg, Jarl G., and Parkinson, Kenneth L. *Current Asset Management: Cash, Credit, and Inventory.* New York: John Wiley & Sons, 1984.

League of California Cities. *Treasury Cash Investment Management.* Sacramento, 1972.

Miller, Girard. *Investing Public Funds.* Chicago, Ill.: Government Finance Officers Association, 1986.

Miller, Merton H., and Orr, Daniel. "A Model of the Demand for Money by Firms." *Quarterly Journal of Economics,* August 1966: 413–35.

Monhollon, Jimmie R., and Picou, Glen. *Instruments of the Money Market.* 3d ed. Richmond, Va.: Federal Reserve Bank of Richmond, 1975.

Orgler, Yair. *Cash Management.* Belmont, Calif.: Wadsworth Publishing Co., 1970.

Twentieth Century Fund. *The Rating Game: Report of the Twentieth Century Fund Task Force on Municipal Bond Credit Ratings.* New York, 1974.

Van Horne, James C. *Financial Management and Policy.* 2d ed. Englewood Cliffs, N.J.: Prentice-Hall, 1971.

15 Purchasing and risk management

Braun, J. Peter. *Total-Cost Purchasing.* Management Information Service Reports, vol. 3, no. S–4. Washington, D.C.: International City Management Association, 1971.

Coe, Charles K. *Understanding Risk Management: A Guide for Governments.* Athens: Institute of Government, Univ. of Georgia, 1980.

Davidson, Dan H., and Bennett, Solon A. "Municipal Purchasing Practices." *The Municipal Year Book, 1980.* Washington, D.C.: International City Management Association, 1980, pp. 209–20.

Gipson, Jack P. *The New CGL Policies: A Guide for Public Agencies.* Washington, D.C.: Public Risk and Insurance Management Association, 1986.

Lakefish, Richard. *Purchasing Through Intergovernmental Agreements.* Management Information Service Reports, vol. 3, no. S–6. Washington, D.C.: International City Management Association, 1971.

Municipal Index: The Purchasing Guide for City, Township, County Officials and Consulting Engineers. Atlanta, Ga.: Communication Channels, annual.

National Institute of Governmental Purchasing. *Background Information and Guidelines for Joint-Bid Cooperative Purchasing.* Falls Church, Va., 1981.

Page, Harry Robert. *Public Purchasing and Materials Management.* Lexington, Mass.: Lexington Books, D.C. Heath & Co., 1980.

Public Management 60, nos. 2 and 3 (February and March 1985).

Roos, Nestor R., and Gerber, Joseph S. *Governmental Risk Management Manual.* Tucson, Ariz.: Risk Management Publishing, 1976, plus supplements.

———. *Insurance Risk Management.* Management Information Service Reports, vol. 2, no. LS–6. Washington, D.C.: International City Management Association, 1970.

Sherman, Phyllis. *Basic Risk Management Handbook for Local Governments.* Washington, D.C.: Public Risk and Insurance Management Association, 1983.

Society of Chartered Property and Casualty Underwriters. Georgia Chapter. *Municipal Risk Management.* Cincinnati: National Underwriters Company, 1971.

Valente, Carl F., and Manchester, Lydia. *Rethinking Local Services: Examining Alternative Delivery Approaches.* Management Information Service Special Reports, no. 12.

Washington, D.C.: International City Management Association, 1984.

Valente, Paula R. *Current Approaches to Risk Management: A Directory of Practices.* Management Information Services Special Reports, no. 7. Washington, D.C.: International City Management Association, 1980.

16 Unions, wages, and local government finance

Aaron, Benjamin, et al. *Public Sector Bargaining.* Washington, D.C.: Bureau of National Affairs, 1979.

Baywood Publishing Company. *Journal of Collective Negotiations in the Public Sector,* quarterly.

Bureau of National Affairs. *Government Employee Relations Report.* Washington, D.C., weekly.

Freeman, Richard. "Unionism Comes to the Public Sector." *Journal of Economic Literature* 24, no. 1 (March 1986): 41–86.

Gershenfeld, Walter; Loewenberg, Joseph J.; and Ingster, Bernard. *Scope of Public-Sector Bargaining.* Lexington, Mass.: D.C. Heath & Co., 1977.

Gifford, Courtney D. *Directory of U.S. Labor Organizations, 1984–1985.* Washington, D.C.: Bureau of National Affairs, 1984.

Katz, Harry, and Lewin, David. "Efficiency and Equity Considerations in State and Local Government Wage Determination." *Proceedings of the Thirty-third Annual Meeting of the Industrial Relations Research Association.* Denver, 1980: 90–91.

Levine, Marvin J. *Labor Relations in the Public Sector: Readings, Cases and Experimental Exercises.* 2d ed. Columbus, Ohio: Grid Publishing Co., 1985.

Lewin, David; Feuille, Peter; and Kochan, Thomas. *Public Sector Labor Relations: Analysis and Readings.* 2d ed. Sun Lakes, Ariz.: Thomas Horton & Daughters, 1981.

Rabin, Jack, et al. *Handbook on Public Personnel Administration and Labor Relations.* New York: Marcel Dekker, 1983.

Stanley, David. *Managing Local Government under Union Pressure.* Washington, D.C.: Brookings Institution, 1972.

Stieber, Jack. *Public Employee Unionism.* Washington, D.C.: Brookings Institution, 1973.

Troy, Leo, and Sheflin, Neil. "The Flow and Ebb of U.S. Public Sector Unionism." *Government Union Review* 5, no. 2 (Spring 1984): 1–149.

Wellington, Harry H., and Winter, Ralph K., Jr. *The Unions and the Cities.* Washington, D.C.: Brookings Institution, 1972.

17 Capital budgeting

Aronson, J. Richard. "Cost Benefit Analysis and the Social Cost of Capital." Chapter 8. In *Public Finance.* New York: McGraw-Hill, 1985.

Aronson, J. Richard, and Schwartz, Eli. *Capital Budget Finance.* Management Information Service Reports, vol. 3, no. S–2. Washington, D.C.: International City Management Association, 1971.

Beenhakker, Henri L. *Capital Investment Planning for Management and Engineering.* Rotterdam, The Netherlands: Rotterdam Univ. Press, 1975.

Boness, A. James. *Capital Budgeting: The Public and Private Sectors.* New York: Praeger Publishers, 1972.

Groves, Sanford M., and Valente, Maureen Godsey. *Evaluating Financial Condition: A Handbook for Local Government.* Washington, D.C.: International City Management Association, 1986.

Miller, Girard, comp. *Capital Budgeting: Blueprints for Change.* Chicago: Government Finance Officers Association, 1985.

Moak, Lennox L., and Killian, Kathryn W. *Capital Program and Capital Budget Manual.* Chicago: Municipal Finance Officers Association, 1964.

Steiss, Alan Walter. *Local Government Finance: Capital Facilities Planning and Debt Administration.* Lexington, Mass.: Lexington Books, 1975, 1978.

Wilkes, F. M. *Capital Budgeting Techniques.* 2d ed. New York: Wiley, 1983.

List of contributors

Persons who have contributed to this book are listed below with the editors first and the authors following in alphabetical order. A brief review of experience and training is presented for each author. Because many of the contributors have published extensively, books, monographs, articles, and other publications are omitted.

J. Richard Aronson (Editor and Chapter 17) is the William L. Clayton Professor of Business and Economics at Lehigh University. He is also Director of the Fairchild-Martindale Center for the Study of Private Enterprise. His educational background includes a bachelor's degree from Clark University, a master's from Stanford University, and a doctorate from Clark. He has taught at Worcester Polytechnic Institute and Clark University and has been a Fulbright Scholar at the University of York, England. His professional activities include serving as a commissioner on the Public Employee Retirement Study Commission of the Commonwealth of Pennsylvania.

Eli Schwartz (Editor and Chapters 14 and 17) is Professor of Economics and Finance at Lehigh University and holds the Charles Macfarlane Chair in Theoretical Economics. He has a bachelor's degree from the University of Denver, a master's degree from the University of Connecticut, and a doctorate from Brown University. He has taught at Michigan State University, the London School of Economics, and the Autonomous University of Madrid. He has wide experience as a consultant in the financial and economics fields with a number of private and public organizations.

David S. Arnold (Chapter 15) was on the staff of the International City Management Association from 1949 until his retirement in 1985. He had a variety of responsibilities in research, writing, editing, and publications production. For 24 years he was editor of the ICMA Municipal Management Series. He holds a bachelor's degree from Lafayette College and a master's in public administration from the Maxwell School, Syracuse University.

Roy Bahl (Chapter 4) is Maxwell Professor of Political Economy at the Maxwell School, Syracuse University. Previously he served as Director of the Metropolitan Studies Program, as Economist for the International Monetary Fund, and as Assistant Professor of Economics at West Virginia University. He holds a bachelor's degree from Greenville College, Illinois, and a doctorate in economics from the University of Kentucky. President of the National Tax Association—Tax Institute of America (1985), he has served widely as a consultant to various public and private agencies, including central and local governments in developing countries, as well as the International Monetary Fund, AID, the World Bank, and Standard & Poor's Corporation.

Marvin R. Brams (Chapter 6) is an economist and Associate Professor in the College of Urban Affairs and Public Policy at the University of Delaware. A faculty member of the M.P.A. program, he specializes in public policy analysis, public finance, and financial management. He holds bachelor's and master's degrees in business administration from Northeastern University, a master's degree in counseling from the University of Delaware, and a doctorate in economics from Clark University. He has served as a consultant to federal, state, and local governments and to business firms in the private sector.

Thomas J. DiLorenzo (Chapter 11) is Visiting Professor of American Business at Washington University in St. Louis, on leave from George Mason University. He is an adjunct scholar of the Cato Institute in Washington, D.C. He holds a Ph.D. in economics from Virginia Polytechnic Institute and State University. He is the author of numerous books and articles on labor unions, public choice, urban public finance, and the commercial nonprofit sector of the economy.

Paul B. Downing (Chapter 11) is Professor of Economics and Policy Sciences at Florida

State University. He received a Ph.D. in economics from the University of Wisconsin. He has been employed by various federal agencies and has taught at the University of California at Riverside and the Virginia Polytechnic Institute.

Philip J. Fischer (Chapter 12) is the Director of the Municipal Finance Analysis Group at Citicorp Investment Bank. Previously he taught finance at the State University of New York and was also a financial analyst with Mobil Corporation. He holds a bachelor's degree in Chemical Engineering from Oregon State University, a Juris Doctorate from Loyola School of Law, and an M.B.A. degree and a Ph.D. degree in finance from the University of Oregon.

James A. Hall (Chapter 8) is Associate Professor of Accounting at Lehigh University, where he teaches management information systems, decision support systems, and accounting. He has been a member of the Lehigh faculty for seven years, and he worked with AT&T in computer electronics for seven years. He also has experience as a systems analyst and EDP auditor. He holds a bachelor's degree in accounting and a master's degree in business administration from the University of Tulsa and a doctorate from Oklahoma State University. He is a member of the American Accounting Association and the Institute of Internal Auditors.

William W. Holder (Chapter 7) is Director of the Master of Accounting Program and an Associate Professor of Accounting at the University of Southern California. He holds a bachelor's degree in business administration from Oklahoma State University and both a master's in accountancy and a doctorate in business administration from the University of Oklahoma. He has contributed to several books and research monographs and has published numerous articles in professional and academic journals. He has served as Head of Accounting Services at Oklahoma State University, as a practicing CPA, and as a faculty resident with Peat, Marwick, Mitchell & Company and with Price Waterhouse. He is a member of council of the AICPA and served for four years as a member of the AICPA State and Local Government Committee.

George G. Kaufman (Chapter 12) is the John F. Smith Professor of Finance and Economics at Loyola University of Chicago, where he has been a faculty member since 1981. He previously taught at the University of Oregon, where he was Director of the Center for Capital Market Research, and he was a Senior Economist at the Federal Reserve Bank of Chicago. He holds a bachelor's degree from Oberlin College, a master's degree from the University of Michigan, and a doctorate from the University of Iowa.

Julius Margolis (Chapter 2) is Professor of Economics at the University of California at Irvine. He has been the Director of the Institutes of Public Policy Analysis at Stanford University and the University of Pennsylvania. He has held professorships of economics, planning, business, engineering, and public policy at the University of Chicago, Stanford, the University of California at Berkeley, and the University of Pennsylvania, and he has consulted with federal, state, and local governments. He received a Ph.D. in economics from Harvard University and holds other degrees from the City College of New York and the University of Wisconsin.

Wallace E. Oates (Chapter 3) is Professor of Economics at the University of Maryland. After receiving his Ph.D. in economics from Stanford University in 1965, he joined the faculty at Princeton University, where he was a member of the Princeton Economics Department until 1979. His primary fields of interest are the economics of state and local government and environmental economics. He has served as an advisor to the state governments of New Jersey, New York, and Maryland and to various federal agencies on both fiscal and environmental matters, and he has worked with the Commission of the European Communities on issues concerning the fiscal structure of the EEC.

John E. Petersen (Chapter 13) is Senior Director of the Government Finance Research Center (GFRC) of the Government Finance Officers Association. He also has served as financial advisor to many federal agencies, state governments, and municipalities, including the U.S. Treasury, the U.S. Environmental Protection Agency, the Department of Transportation, and the states of Oregon, Alaska, Tennessee, and New York. In addition, he has undertaken studies for a number of nonprofit and private organizations, including the Twentieth Century Fund, the National Science Foundation, and the Time-Life Corporation. He holds a B.A. in economics from Northwestern University, an M.B.A. from the Wharton School, and a Ph.D. from the University of Pennsylvania.

Arnold H. Raphaelson (Chapter 9) is Professor of Economics at Temple University. His educational background includes a bachelor's degree from Brown University, master's degrees from Columbia and Clark Universities, and a doctorate from Clark University. He has taught at the University of

Maine and has served as both a professional staff member and a consultant to the U.S. Senate Subcommittee on Intergovernmental Relations.

James D. Rodgers (Chapter 10) is Professor of Economics and Head of the Department of Economics at Pennsylvania State University, where he has been a faculty member since 1969. He received a bachelor's degree from East Texas State University and a doctorate in economics from the University of Virginia. He served as research director for the Pennsylvania Tax Commission, 1979–81, in the area of local nonproperty taxation.

Leonard I. Ruchelman (Chapter 1) is Professor of Urban Studies and Chair of the Department of Urban Studies and Public Administration, Old Dominion University. He has worked extensively with local agencies in southeastern Virginia.

Larry D. Schroeder (Chapter 5) is Professor of Public Administration and Economics and Director of the Metropolitan Studies Program at the Maxwell School, Syracuse University. He holds a doctorate in economics from the University of Wisconsin as well as degrees from Central College, Iowa, and Northern Illinois University. His recent research has focused primarily on forecasting government revenues and expenditures and on financial administration in developing countries.

Paul L. Solano (Chapter 6) is a political economist and Associate Professor in the College of Urban Affairs and Public Policy at the University of Delaware. He specializes in public finance and financial management, public policy analysis, and political economy as faculty member of the M.P.A. and Ph.D. programs. He holds a bachelor's degree from Northeastern University and a doctorate from the University of Maryland. He has worked as a budget analyst/planner for county government and as program evaluation analyst for the Agency for International Development, and he has served as a financial consultant for state and local governments.

Robert J. Thornton (Chapter 16) is Professor and Chairman of Economics at Lehigh University. He formerly served as a research assistant with the Brookings Institution. He holds a bachelor's degree from Xavier University and master's and Ph.D. degrees from the University of Illinois. He is currently a member of the editorial board of the *Journal of Collective Negotiations in the Public Sector*.

Illustration credits

Chapter 1 Figure 1–1: U.S. Bureau of the Census, Current Population Reports, Series P–23, no. 130, *Popular Profile of the United States: 1982* (Washington, D.C.: GPO, 1983), p. 10; Figure 1–2: Advisory Commission on Intergovernmental Relations, in *The Municipal Year Book, 1984* (Washington, D.C.: International City Management Association, 1984), p. 74; Figure 1–3: Compiled from data found in U.S. President, *Economic Record of the President* (Washington, D.C.: GPO, 1983), p. 293.

Chapter 7 Figure 7–4: U.S. General Accounting Office, Comptroller General of the United States, *Self-Evaluation Guide for Government Audit Organizations,* Audit Standards Supplement Service, no. 9 (Washington, D.C.: GPO, 1976), summarized in William W. Holder and Raymond J. Clay, "Criteria for Internal Auditing," *Hospital Progress,* January 1979: 52.

Chapter 8 Figures 8–4 and 8–5: Raymond McLeod, Jr., *Management Information Systems,* 2d ed. © 1983, Science Research Associates, Inc., by permission of the publisher.

Chapter 10 Figure 10–1: Department of Finance and Records, City of Duluth, Minnesota; Figure 10–2: Department of Finance, New Orleans, Louisiana.

Chapter 11 Figure 11–1: Selma J. Mushkin and Charles L. Vehorn, "User Fees and Charges," *Governmental Finance,* November 1977: 48.

Chapter 14 Figure 14–9: Merton H. Miller and Daniel Orr, "A Model of the Demand for Money by Firms," *Quarterly Journal of Economics* 80 (August 1966): 420, © 1966, reprinted by permission of John Wiley & Sons, Inc.; Figure 14–10: Adapted from *Wall Street Journal,* 4 October 1985; Figure 14–11: Prepared by Federal Reserve Bank of St. Louis, released 9 May 1980.

Index

Municipal Management Series

Management Policies in Local Government Finance Third Edition

Text type
Times Roman, Helvetica

Composition
Mid Atlantic Photo Composition, Inc.
Baltimore, Maryland

Printing and binding
Kingsport Press
Kingsport, Tennessee

Design
Herbert Slobin